IFIP Advances in Information and Communication Technology 643

Editor-in-Chief

Kai Rannenberg, Goethe University Frankfurt, Germany

Editorial Board Members

IFIP – The International Federation for Information Processing

IFIP was founded in 1960 under the auspices of UNESCO, following the first World Computer Congress held in Paris the previous year. A federation for societies working in information processing, IFIP's aim is two-fold: to support information processing in the countries of its members and to encourage technology transfer to developing nations. As its mission statement clearly states:

> IFIP is the global non-profit federation of societies of ICT professionals that aims at achieving a worldwide professional and socially responsible development and application of information and communication technologies.

IFIP is a non-profit-making organization, run almost solely by 2500 volunteers. It operates through a number of technical committees and working groups, which organize events and publications. IFIP's events range from large international open conferences to working conferences and local seminars.

The flagship event is the IFIP World Computer Congress, at which both invited and contributed papers are presented. Contributed papers are rigorously refereed and the rejection rate is high.

As with the Congress, participation in the open conferences is open to all and papers may be invited or submitted. Again, submitted papers are stringently refereed.

The working conferences are structured differently. They are usually run by a working group and attendance is generally smaller and occasionally by invitation only. Their purpose is to create an atmosphere conducive to innovation and development. Refereeing is also rigorous and papers are subjected to extensive group discussion.

Publications arising from IFIP events vary. The papers presented at the IFIP World Computer Congress and at open conferences are published as conference proceedings, while the results of the working conferences are often published as collections of selected and edited papers.

IFIP distinguishes three types of institutional membership: Country Representative Members, Members at Large, and Associate Members. The type of organization that can apply for membership is a wide variety and includes national or international societies of individual computer scientists/ICT professionals, associations or federations of such societies, government institutions/government related organizations, national or international research institutes or consortia, universities, academies of sciences, companies, national or international associations or federations of companies.

More information about this series at https://link.springer.com/bookseries/6102

Zhongzhi Shi · Jean-Daniel Zucker ·
Bo An (Eds.)

Intelligent Information Processing XI

12th IFIP TC 12 International Conference, IIP 2022
Qingdao, China, May 27–30, 2022
Proceedings

 Springer

Editors
Zhongzhi Shi
Institute of Computing Technology
Chinese Academy of Sciences
Beijing, China

Jean-Daniel Zucker
IRD, Sorbonne University
Bondy, France

Bo An
Nanyang Technological University
Singapore, Singapore

ISSN 1868-4238   ISSN 1868-422X   (electronic)
IFIP Advances in Information and Communication Technology
ISBN 978-3-031-05912-4   ISBN 978-3-031-03948-5   (eBook)
https://doi.org/10.1007/978-3-031-03948-5

This Springer imprint is published by the registered company Springer Nature Switzerland AG
The registered company address is: Gewerbestrasse 11, 6330 Cham, Switzerland

Preface

This volume comprises the proceedings of the 12th IFIP International Conference on Intelligent Information Processing (IIP 2022). As the world proceeds quickly into the Information Age, it encounters both successes and challenges, and it is well recognized that intelligent information processing provides the key to solving many challenges in the Information Age. Intelligent information processing supports the most advanced techniques that are able to change human life and the world. However, the path to success is never a straight one. Every new technology brings with it many challenging problems, and researchers are in great demand to tackle these problems. The IIP conference provides a forum for engineers and scientists in research institutes, universities, and industries to report and discuss their latest research progress in all aspects of intelligent information processing.

We received more than 56 papers for IIP 2022, of which 37 papers were included in the program as regular papers and six as short papers. All papers submitted were reviewed by three reviewers. We are grateful for the dedicated work of both authors and reviewers.

A conference such as this cannot succeed without help from many individuals who contributed their valuable time and expertise. We want to express our sincere gratitude to the Program Committee members and referees, who invested many hours for reviews and deliberations. They provided detailed and constructive review comments that significantly improved the quality of the papers included in these proceedings.

We were very grateful to have the sponsorship of the following organizations: IFIP TC12, the Shandong University of Science and Technology, and the Institute of Computing Technology of the Chinese Academy of Sciences. We specially thank Qingtian Zeng, Yongquan Liang, Shujuan Ji, and Zhongying Zhao for organizing the conference and Peiling Li and Xiaoli Guan for carefully checking the proceedings.

Finally, we hope you find this volume inspiring and informative. We wish that the research results reported in the proceedings will lead to exciting new findings in the years to come.

March 2022

Zhongzhi Shi
Jean-Daniel Zucker
Bo An

Organization

General Chairs

E. Mercier-Laurent, France
M. Li, Canada
Q. Zeng, China

Program Chairs

Z. Shi, China
J. Zucker, France
B. An, Singapore

Local Organization Committee

Yongquan Liang (Chair), China
Shujuan Ji (General Secretary), China
Zhongying Zhao (Vice General Secretary), China

Program Committee

B. An, Singapore
S. Ding, China
Q. Dou, China
E. Ehlers, South Africa
J. Fan, China
O. Hussain, Australia
S. Ji, China
X. Jiang, China
H. Leung, Hong Kong
Y. Liang, China
G. Li, Australia
J. Li, Australia
Z. Li, China
H. Ma, China
W. Mao, China
Z. Meng, China
E. Mercier-Laurent, France
M. Owoc, Poland
V. Palade, UK

A. Rafea, Egypt
Z. Shi, China
ZP. Shi, China
Y. Song, China
L. Su, China
S. Vadera, UK
G. Wang, China
P. Wang, USA
S. Wang, China
Y. Xu, China
Yue Xu, Australia
Q. Zeng, China
B. Zhang, China
J. Zhang, China
P. Zhang, China
S. Zhang, China
Z. Zhang, China
Z. Zhao, China
Y. Zhou, China

Abstracts of Keynotes and Invited Presentations

Machine Learning for Decision Support in Complex Environments

Jie Lu

Australian Artificial Intelligence Institute, University of Technology Sydney, NSW, 2007, Australia

Abstract. The research will present how machine learning can innovatively and effectively learn from data to support data-driven decision-making in uncertain and dynamic situations. A set of new fuzzy transfer learning theories, methodologies and algorithms will be presented that can transfer knowledge learnt in one or more source domains to target domains by building latent space, mapping functions and self-training to overcome tremendous uncertainties in data, learning processes and decision outputs (classification and regression). Another set of concept drift theories, methodologies and algorithms will be discussed about how to handle ever-changing dynamic data stream environments with unpredictable stream pattern drifts by effectively and accurately detecting, understanding, and adapting concept drift in an explanatory way, indicating when, where and how concept drift occurs and reacting accordingly. These new developments enable advanced machine learning and therefore enhance data-driven prediction and decision support systems in uncertain and dynamic real-world environments.

Making Machine Learning Fairer

Xin Yao[1,2]

[1] Research Institute of Trustworthy Autonomous Systems (RITAS), Department of Computer Science and Engineering, Southern University of Science and Technology (SUSTech), Shenzhen, China
[2] CERCIA, School of Computer Science, University of Birmingham, UK
xiny@sustech.edu.cn

Abstract. As the rapid development of artificial intelligence (AI) and its real-world applications in recent years, AI ethics has become increasingly important. It is no longer a nice feature to consider, but a must for both AI research and applications. First, this talk first tries to recall what classical ethics is about from an historical perspective. It tries to understand how technology ethics and AI ethics grow out of the broad ethics field. Specific features of AI ethics will be discussed. Second, a brief review of current research into AI ethics will be given. Key research topics will be extracted from a large number of reports to give a more concrete picture of most important issues covered in AI ethics. Third, we will examine the fairness issue in AI ethics and demonstrate how an algorithmic approach could help machine learning to be fairer. In other words, the results from machine learning will have less biases. Finally, some open research questions will be touched upon. (This talk is partly based on the following paper: Zhang Q., Liu J., Zhang Z., Wen J., Mao B., Yao X. (2021), Fairer Machine Learning Through Multi-objective Evolutionary Learning. In: Farkaš I., Masulli P., Otte S., Wermter S. (eds) Artificial Neural Networks and Machine Learning – ICANN 2021. ICANN 2021. Lecture Notes in Computer Science, vol 12894. Springer, Cham. https://doi.org/10.1007/978-3-030-86380-7_10.).

Multiagent Reinforcement Learning: Models and Modelling

Ho-fung Leung

Department of Computer Science and Engineering and Department of Sociology,
The Chinese University of Hong Kong
lhf@cuhk.edu.hk

Abstract. In this talk we shall present our recent works on multi-agent reinforcement learning. In multi-agent reinforcement learning, agents interact with one another in a multi-agent system. They continuously revise their decision policies by learning from their experiences of interacting with other agents. Generally, a social norm of action will emerge at some point. I shall describe our research results in multi-agent reinforcement learning, and discuss what we can learn from these results. I shall also highlight some theoretical results on mathematical modelling of multi-agent reinforcement learning.

Affective Brain-Computer Interface and Applications

Bao-Liang Lu

Department of Computer Science and Engineering,
Shanghai Jiao Tong University
bllu@sjtu.edu.cn

Abstract. Affective brain-computer interface (aBCI) is a type of human-computer interface that can recognize and/or regulate emotions. In particular, according to whether to regulate emotions, aBCI can be divided into two categories. The first category is emotion recognition BCI, which can recognize emotions based on the brain signals collected by external devices. The second category is emotion recognition and regulation BCI, which can not only recognize emotions but also regulate emotions by stimulating specific brain areas. Currently, most research is focused on emotion recognition BCI. The study on emotion regulation BCI is highly limited. This talk will introduce our recent work on emotion recognition BCI and applications. Specifically, we will introduce a multimodal affective BCI framework of combining EEG signals and eye movement signals, a plug-and-play domain adaptation for cross-subject EEG-based Emotion Recognition, GAN-based methods for EEG data augmentation, and the practical application of aBCI to depression evaluation.

Accurate, Secure and Privacy-Preserving Brain-Computer Interfaces

Dongrui Wu

School of Artificial Intelligence and Automation,
Huazhong University of Science and Technology
drwu@hust.edu.cn

Abstract. Brain-computer interface (BCI) is a direct communication pathway between the brain and an external device. Because of individual differences and non-stationarity of brain signals, a BCI usually needs subject-specific calibration, which is time-consuming and user unfriendly. Sophisticated machine learning approaches can help reduce or even completely eliminate calibrations, improving the utility of BCIs. Recent studies also found that machine learning models in BCIs are vulnerable to adversarial attacks, and brain signals also contain lots of private information, so the security and privacy of BCIs are also important considerations in their commercial applications. This talk will introduce transfer learning approaches for expediting BCI calibration, and its adversarial attack and privacy protection approaches. The ultimate goal is to implement accurate, secure and privacy-preserving BCIs.

General Real-World Decision-Making
by Offline Reinforcement Learning

Yang Yu

National Key Laboratory for Novel Software Technology, Nanjing University
yuy@nju.edu.cn

Abstract. While reinforcement learning (RL) has shown super-human decision-making ability in playing games, the community is expecting RL will be able to solve real-world problems that are out of games. In general, real-world RL was quite difficult to come true. To achieve a good policy, an RL training process commonly explore the environment by thousands of trials and errors, which can incur unbearable cost. An apparent cause of the difficulty is the missing of a cost-free playing ground, i.e., an environment model, for RL training. However, learning an effective environment model from data is inhibited by high compounding error, stated by the *simulation lemma* firstly proved in 2002. Nearly 20 years later, we now have established a new theory with compounding error eliminated. The new theory allows us to learn effective environment models. We show that environment model learning enables truly offline RL, which makes zero trial errors to train a policy. We also show that such offline RL can be applied in a wide range of real-world tasks.

Rethinking the Learning Mechanism of GNN

Chuan Shi

Beijing University of Posts and Telecommunications
shichuan@bupt.edu.cn

Abstract. In recent years, researchers began to study how to apply neural network to graph data, forming a research boom of graph neural network (GNN). Most GNNs are equivalent to a low-pass filter, which aggregates the feature information of neighbor nodes along the network structure, and realizes the effective fusion of network structure and attribute features. Although GNNs have achieved great success in academic research and practical applications, they still leave some open problems on learning mechanisms of GNNs. In this talk, we will rethink some key operations of GNNs and report some recent progress in this field. This talk will focus on, but not limit to, following questions: fusion mechanism of structure and features, uniform message aggregation mechanism, the role of low-pass filtering, and reliable graph structure for GNN. The answers to questions will give the insightful investigation on the learning mechanism of GNNs and guide us design better GNNs.

Rethinking the Learning Mechanism of CNN

Beijing University of Posts and Telecommunications

Abstract.

Contents

Multiagent Systems

Social Computing

Blockchain Technology

Game Theory and Emotion

Pattern Recognition

Image Processing

Applications

Machine Learning

An AdaBoost Based - Deep Stochastic Configuration Network

Chenglong Zhang[1], Shifei Ding[1(✉)], and Ling Ding[2]

[1] School of Computer Science and Technology, China University of Mining and Technology, Xuzhou 221116, China
dingsf@cumt.edu.cn
[2] Xuhai College China University of Mining and Technology, Xuzhou 221008, China

Abstract. Deep stochastic configuration network (DSCN) is an incremental learning method for large-scale data analysis and processing, which has the advantages of lower human intervention, higher learning efficiency and stronger generalization ability. For improving the stability of DSCN, a deep stochastic configuration network based on AdaBoost is proposed, termed as AdaBoost-DSCN. In our proposed model, the AdaBoost learning approach is adopted, the weights of the base models are adjusted adaptively according to the training results, then the base models are combined to generate a stronger model, which is beneficial to reduce the influence of random parameters on network performance of DSCN. Experimental results on complex function approximation problems and large-scale regression datasets show that AdaBoost-DSCN has higher regression accuracy for large-scale data regression analysis compared with DSCN, AdaBoost-SCN, SCN.

Keywords: Deep stochastic configuration network · Ensemble learning · Neural network · AdaBoost

1 Introduction

Stochastic configuration network (SCN) proposed by Wang and Li in 2017, is an incremental model, its nodes in hidden layer can be increased gradually according to the preset conditions [1]. As the parameters of SCN are configured by stochastic configuration (SC) algorithm, and the network structure can be determined by supervision mechanism adaptively, SCN has a series of advantages of less human intervention, faster learning efficiency and better generalization performance. It has been extensively studied and applied in the areas of power big data processing [2], EEG signal analysis [3], fault diagnosis [4], online measurement problems [5, 6], robotic grasping recognition [7] and defect recognition [8].

Since SCN was proposed, it has been favored by domestic and foreign researchers for its lower human intervention, higher learning efficiency and stronger generalization ability [1]. In the aspects of network structure, SCN was expanded into 2-D stochastic configuration network (2DSCN) and deep stochastic configuration network (DSCN) respectively, showing the great potential in the field of image processing [9, 10].

Z. Shi et al. (Eds.): IIP 2022, IFIP AICT 643, pp. 3–14, 2022.
https://doi.org/10.1007/978-3-031-03948-5_1

However, as the training process of SCN mainly depends on the training samples, with the increase of nodes in the hidden layer, it is easy to over-fitting, which reduces the robustness and generalization of the network. Training multiple neural network models using distributed and ensemble learning strategies can improve the accuracy and generalization performance of SCN significantly improved. Negative correlation learning (NCL) and cooperative learning paradigm were applied to calculate the parameters of ensemble models respectively [11, 12]. Parallel stochastic configuration network (PSCN) which used different objective functions to train multiple sub-networks in parallel, and adopts fuzzy evidence theory to fuse the results [13]. Unlike the above model, stochastic configuration network ensembles with selective base models was introduced [14]. Otherwise, ensemble learning methods include Stacking, Bagging and AdaBoost were introduced into SCN for solving different problems [15–17].

DSCN, as the deep structure of SCN, has been proved the performance in image processing and complex function approximation problems [10]. Except for the prediction interval of crude oil carbon residue, DSCN is seldom used in the field of regression [18]. During to the construction process of DSCN, some ensemble method used in SCN are no longer suitable for DSCN, in the first place, we cannot use these methods, including negative correlation learning, cooperative learning paradigm etc. to calculate the output weights of ensemble DSCN model [11, 12, 14]; in the second place, parallel [13], stacking [15], Bagging [16] and AdaBoost [17] were applied to solve different scenarios. AdaBoost method can adjust the weights of base learners according to the training errors of samples and improve the performance of the learners by weighting, which is sensitive to outliers and noise data. It can effectively overcome the over-fitting problem of the DSCN model [19], like the use of AdaBoost in SCN [17], a deep stochastic configuration network based on AdaBoost is proposed, named as AdaBoost-DSCN.

The rest parts of this paper are given as lists: Sect. 2 reviews the framework of deep stochastic configuration network. In Sect. 3, the theory of AdaBoost-DSCN is presented in detail. Section 4 gives some experimental results on complex function approximation problems and large-scale regression datasets. Finally, some conclusions and future works are described in Sect. 5.

2   Revisit of DSCN

Deep stochastic configuration network (DSCN) is the deep version of SCN, unlike other deep neural networks, it can start from one hidden layer with only one node, gradually increase the number of nodes and hidden layers to build the deep structure, in which input weights and biases can be configured through supervision mechanism and the output weights are calculated by using the least square method. As can be seen in Fig. 1, the network structure of DSCN is differs from the structure of other deep models. The number of hidden layers and its nodes are not fixed and it can be increased gradually according to the training errors [10].

The modeling learning process of DSCN is described as lists [10]:

Given a set of training data, $X = \{x_1, x_2, \ldots, x_N\}$ and $Y = \{y_1, y_2, \ldots, y_N\}$ represent the input data and corresponding label. $x_i = \{x_{i,1}, x_{i,2}, \ldots, x_{i,d}\} \in R^d$, d indicates the feature dimension; $y_i = \{y_{i,1}, y_{i,2}, \ldots, y_{i,m}\} \in R^m$, m expresses the label dimension; $i = 1, 2, \ldots, N$, N is the number of training samples.

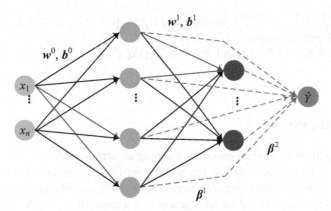

Input layer   Hidden layer 1   Hidden layer 2   Output layer

Fig. 1. The structure of stochastic configuration network [10]

It is supposed that $L_n - 1$ nodes in nth layer of DSCN have been configured, compute the training error vector by using Eq. (1), then judge whether meet the preset conditions $n = n_{max}, L_n = L_{n_{max}}$ or $\|e\|_F^2 \leq \varepsilon$, n_{max} is defined as the maximum number of layers; $L_{n_{max}}$ denotes the maximum number of nodes in nth layer; ε represents the preset error.

$$e_{L_n-1}^n = e_{L_n-1}^n(X^{n-1}) = [e_{L_n-1,1}^n(X^{n-1}), e_{L_n-1,2}^n(X^{n-1}), \ldots, e_{L_n-1,m}^n(X^{n-1})]^T \quad (1)$$

Assign initial input weight $w_{L_n}^n$ and bias $b_{L_n}^n$ of node L_n in nth layer by using to Eq. (2) and Eq. (3):

$$w_{L_n}^n = \lambda \times [2 \times rand(N, T_{max}) - 1] \quad (2)$$

$$b_{L_n}^n = \lambda \times [2 \times rand(1, T_{max}) - 1] \quad (3)$$

where λ represent the scale factor of input weight and bias; T_{max} expresses the maximum number of candidate nodes.

The candidate $w_{L_n}^{n*}$ and $b_{L_n}^{n*}$ with the largest value of $\xi_{L_n}^n = \sum_{j=1}^m \xi_{L_n,j}^n \geq 0$ are determined as the input weight and bias of node L_n:

$$h_{L_n}^n = \phi[(w_{L_n-1}^n)^T X^{n-1} + b_{L_n-1}^n]^T (X^0 = X, X^{n-1} = H_{L_{n-2}}^{n-2}, n \geq 2) \quad (4)$$

$$\xi_{L_n,j}^n = \frac{\left\langle e_{L_n-1,j}^n, h_{L_n}^n \right\rangle^2}{\left\langle h_{L_n}^n, h_{L_n}^n \right\rangle} - (1 - r - \mu_{L_n})\left\langle e_{L_n-1,j}^n, e_{L_n-1,j}^n \right\rangle \quad (5)$$

where $h_{L_n}^n$ is denoted as the output of node L_n; $j = 1, 2, \ldots, m$; $r \in (0,1)$; $\{\mu_{L_n}\}$, in which $\mu_{L_n} \leq 1 - r$ and $\lim_{L_n \to +\infty} \mu_{L_n} = 0$, represents a nonnegative real number sequence.

The output weight matrix β can be evaluated according to Eq. (6):

$$\beta^* = \arg\min_{\beta} \|H\beta - Y\|_F^2 = H^+ Y \quad (6)$$

where $H = [H_{L_1}^1, H_{L_2}^2, \ldots, H_{L_n}^n]$, among them $H_{L_n}^n = [h_1^n, h_2^n, \ldots, h_{L_n}^n]$; H^+ is denoted as the Moore–Penrose inverse of H.

The output $\hat{Y}$ of DSCN is calculated by using Eq. (7):

$$\hat{Y} = H\beta \tag{7}$$

3 AdaBoost-DSCN

AdaBoost [19, 20] is a classical ensemble learning algorithm which is widely used for the ensemble of neural networks. It can avoid over-fitting problem and improve the generalization ability of neural network models for solving classification and regression problems by combining multiple weak learners into a strong learner [21, 22].

In the process of incremental learning modeling of DSCN, the input weights and biases of hidden layer nodes are mainly dependent on the scale factor λ. However, for different large-scale training datasets, the performance of DSCN is easily limited by the setting range of the scale factor λ and affected by the randomness of the allocation of input weights and biases. To improve the stability and avoid over-fitting problem of DSCN, an AdaBoost-based deep stochastic configuration network (AdaBoost-DSCN) is proposed by training multiple DSCN-based learner models. Firstly, through training multiple DSCN-based learner models, iterative training is carried out based on AdaBoost algorithm; Secondly, the weighted majority voting method is adopted to reduce the weights of the training samples with better results and improve the weights of the training samples with poor results; Finally, a strong learner model is obtained by weighted combination according to the training results of each learner.

Therefore, the AdaBoost-DSCN model is described as follows [23, 24]:

Given a set of training data, $X = \{x_1, x_2, \ldots, x_N\}$ indicates the input data, $x_i = \{x_{i,1}, x_{i,2}, \ldots, x_{i,d}\} \in R^d$, d represents the feature dimension; $Y = \{y_1, y_2, \ldots, y_N\}$ is denoted as the corresponding label, $y_i = \{y_{i,1}, y_{i,2}, \ldots, y_{i,m}\} \in R^m$, m is the label dimension; among them $i = 1, 2, \ldots, N$, N is the number of training samples.

Step 1: Initialize the distribution weight of training samples through Eq. (8):

$$\alpha_k = [\alpha_{k,1}, \alpha_{k,2}, \ldots, \alpha_{k,N}], \ \alpha_{k,i} = \frac{1}{N} \tag{8}$$

where $k = 1, 2, \ldots, K$, K is the number of base learners; $i = 1, 2, \ldots, N$, N is the number of training samples.

Step 2: Training the K DSCN-based learners iteratively, and calculate the errors of each sample according to Eq. (9):

$$\sigma_k = f_k - Y \tag{9}$$

where $\sigma_k = [\sigma_{k,1}, \sigma_{k,2}, \ldots, \sigma_{k,N}]$, f_k is the regression results of kth base learner, $k = 1, 2, \ldots, K$.

Step 3: According to the sample errors of Eq. (9), update the distribution weight of training samples by using Eq. (10):

$$\alpha_{k,i} = \begin{cases} \alpha_{k,i} \times c \ if \ |\sigma_{k,i}| > \mu \\ \alpha_{k,i} \ else \end{cases} \tag{10}$$

where c is the control factor of the distribution weight; u is the threshold of sample error which is used for determining the base learner outliers.

Step 4: Calculate the weight of DSCN-based learners according to Eq. (11):

$$\alpha_k = (0.5/e^{s_k}) \Big/ \sum_{k=1}^{K} (0.5/e^{s_k}) \tag{11}$$

where s_k represents the summation of regression errors of training samples, where $s_k = s_k + \alpha_{k,i}$ when $|\sigma_{k,i}| > \mu$.

Step 5: Construct the AdaBoost-DSCN model according to the weights of base learners as Eq. (12):

$$f = \sum_{k=1}^{K} f_k \alpha_k \tag{12}$$

where f is denoted as the output of AdaBoost-DSCN model.

4   Experiments

All the experimental codes of the paper are programed based on MATLAB 2019b, which running on a PC with Intel (R) Core (TM) i7-9750H 2.60 GHz CPU, NVIDIA GPU GTX1650 and 64 GB RAM.

4.1   Benchmark Datasets

To illustrate the performance of AdaBoost-DSCN, two complex function approximation problems (Eqs. (13) and (14)) and four large-scale regression datasets (Table 1) of KEEL (Knowledge Extraction based on Evolutionary Learning, http://www.keel.es/) are selected as benchmark datasets. The descriptions of these benchmark datasets are introduced as lists.

Real-Valued Function $f_1(x)$ [25]:

$$f_1(x) = 0.2e^{-(10x-4)^2} + 0.5e^{-(80x-40)^2} + 0.3e^{-(80x-20)^2} \tag{13}$$

Table 1. The attributes of four large-scale regression datasets.

Datasets	Input features	Instances
MV	10	40768
Compactiv	21	8192
Pole	26	14998
Ailerons	40	13750

The training dataset has 1000 samples while the test dataset is consisted of 300 samples, all the training samples and test samples are uniformly distributed in [0, 1] respectively.

Real-Valued Function $f_2(x)$ [26]:

$$f_2(x) = 0.8e^{-0.2x}\sin(10x) \tag{14}$$

It is the same as $f_1(x)$, the training samples and test samples are generated from a regularly spaced grid over [0, 5], and the training dataset and test dataset are consisted of 1000 and 300 samples respectively.

To reduce the influence of different feature ranges on the model, the input and output vectors of four large-scale regression datasets from KEEL are normalized into [0, 1], in which 75% of the samples are selected as the training dataset randomly while the rest are determined as the test dataset.

4.2 Evaluation Indicator and Parameters Setting

4.2.1 Evaluation Indicator

To verify the regression accuracy of AdaBoost-DSCN, SCN [1], DSCN [10], AdaBoost-SCN [17] are chosen as the compared models, then we run each model 10 times, root mean square error (RMSE) (Eq. (15)) and its standard deviations of all the results are determined for ensuring the fairness of the experiments.

$$\text{RMSE} = \sqrt{\frac{1}{N}\sum_{i=1}^{N}(y_i - \hat{y}_i)^2} \tag{15}$$

where y_i is the actual value of sample i; $\hat{y}_i$ denotes the regression result of sample i; N indicates the number of samples.

4.2.2 Parameters Setting

In the experiments, the parameters of related models are set as follows: all the models adopt the sigmoidal function (Eq. (16)) as activation function, the nodes in the hidden layers of all the models are set as 25, 50 respectively, some other parameters of each model are given especially.

$$S(x) = \frac{1}{1 + e^{-x}} \tag{16}$$

SCN: the rand λ of SCN are chosen from set {0.9, 0.99, 0.9999, 0.99999, 0.999999} and {0.5, 1, 5, 10, 30, 50, 100, 150, 200, 250} adaptively; the maximum number $T_{\max}$ of candidate nodes is set to 200; the tolerance error ε is set as 0.001.

DSCN: the maximum number of layers $n_{\max}$ is set to 2; the r and λ of SCN are chosen from set {0.9, 0.99, 0.999, 0.9999, 0.99999, 0.999999} and {0.5, 1, 5, 10, 30, 50, 100, 150, 200, 250} adaptively; the maximum number $T_{\max}$ of candidate nodes is set to 200; the tolerance error ε is set as 0.001.

The parameters of AdaBoost-SCN and AdaBoost-DSCN are similar as SCN and DSCN respectively, except for the number of base learner K is set to 5, the weight control factor c is set to 1.1, the threshold of sample point error μ is set to 0.001.

4.3   Results and Discussion

The average test results of AdaBoost-DSCN, SCN, DSCN and AdaBoost-SCN on function approximation problems are given in Tables 2 and 3, in which L represents the maximum number of nodes in each hidden layer, DSCN and AdaBoost-DSCN has 2 hidden layers for solving these problems. As can be seen from Table 2, it obviously that AdaBoost-DSCN outperform other models in terms of both average test results on two complex function approximation problems. With the increase of the maximum number of nodes, the test results of DSCN and AdaBoost-DSCN are enhanced greatly, which shows that AdaBoost-DSCN and DSCN have better fitting effect than SCN and AdaBoost-SCN for function approximation problems, the AdaBoost-DSCN and AdaBoost-SCN have higher regression accuracy than DSCN and SCN, verifies the effectiveness of AdaBoost ensemble learning. At the same time, the fitting curves of AdaBoost-DSCN model to function approximation problems are shown in Fig. 2.

Table 2. Performance comparison of four models on $f_1(x)$.

Models	Test results (RMSE)	
	$L = 25$	$L = 50$
SCN	3.8546e−02 ± 3.0835e−03	8.9775e−03 ± 3.4369e−03
DSCN	1.5178e−02 ± 3.1029e−03	4.3556e−04 ± 2.7920e−04
AdaBoost-SCN	3.7056e−02 ± 1.7307e−03	7.6905e−03 ± 1.4554e−03
AdaBoost-DSCN	1.1990e−02 ± 2.1957e−03	1.8511e−04 ± 8.2268e−05

Table 3. Performance comparison of four models on $f_2(x)$.

Models	Test results (RMSE)	
	$L = 25$	$L = 50$
SCN	6.2263e−02 ± 3.2845e−02	1.3861e−03 ± 6.9197e−04
DSCN	6.8888e−03 ± 6.3440e−03	5.2601e−05 ± 3.0592e−05
AdaBoost-SCN	4.2098e−02 ± 1.4116e−02	6.2471e−04 ± 1.3571e−04
AdaBoost-DSCN	2.0983e−03 ± 1.5434e−03	2.5195e−05 ± 4.9656e−06

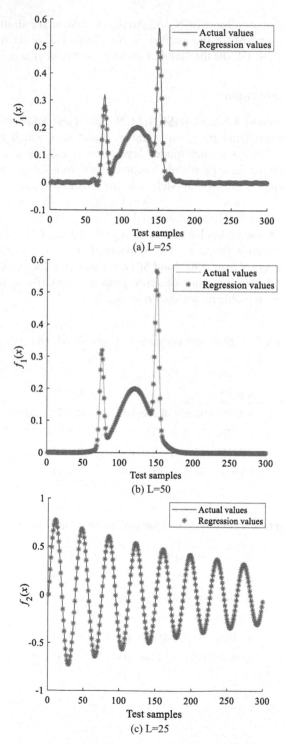

(a) L=25

(b) L=50

(c) L=25

Fig. 2. Fitted curves of AdaBoost-DSCN on function approximation problems

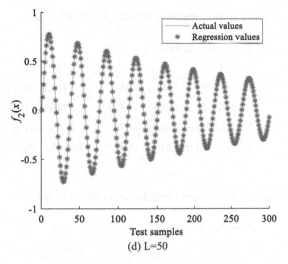

(d) L=50

Fig. 2. continued

Tables 4, 5, 6, and 7 demonstrates the average test results of AdaBoost-DSCN, SCN, DSCN and AdaBoost-SCN on large-scale regression datasets, among them L indicates the maximum number of hidden layer nodes, meanwhile DSCN and AdaBoost-DSCN has 2 hidden layers for solving these problems.

Table 4. Performance comparison of MV dataset.

Models	Test results (RMSE)	
	$L = 25$	$L = 50$
SCN	4.4904e−02 ± 4.7017e−03	2.2737e−02 ± 1.6510e−03
DSCN	3.0270e−02 ± 2.4272e−03	1.5521e−02 ± 1.0531e−03
AdaBoost-SCN	3.6555e−02 ± 1.6602e−03	1.8546e−02 ± 3.5122e−04
AdaBoost-DSCN	**2.3075e−02 ± 1.4101e−03**	**1.2987e−02 ± 2.6917e−04**

Table 5. Performance comparison of Compactiv dataset.

Models	Test results (RMSE)	
	$L = 25$	$L = 50$
SCN	9.3403e−02 ± 6.1868e−03	4.3051e−02 ± 1.5580e−03
DSCN	4.0368e−02 ± 5.0512e−03	2.8340e−02 ± 8.0883e−04
AdaBoost-SCN	7.7458e−02 ± 4.1736e−03	3.3792e−02 ± 1.0012e−03
AdaBoost-DSCN	**3.2994e−02 ± 1.4950e−03**	**2.6748e−02 ± 6.9538e−04**

Table 6. Performance comparison of Pole dataset.

Models	Test results (RMSE)	
	$L = 25$	$L = 50$
SCN	2.8158e−01 ± 7.9057e−03	2.3198e−01 ± 8.0734e−03
DSCN	2.4445e−01 ± 4.2805e−03	2.0740e−01 ± 7.4167e−03
AdaBoost-SCN	2.7025e−01 ± 4.0141e−03	2.2043e−01 ± 1.8525e−03
AdaBoost-DSCN	**2.3317e−01 ± 3.6195e−03**	**1.9688e−01 ± 3.6832e−03**

Table 7. Performance comparison of Elevators dataset.

Models	Test results (RMSE)	
	$L = 25$	$L = 50$
SCN	3.8277e−02 ± 1.2402e−03	3.6015e−02 ± 1.0447e−03
DSCN	3.6754e−02 ± 1.3041e−03	3.9248e−02 ± 5.9949e−03
AdaBoost-SCN	3.7417e−02 ± 1.1559e−03	3.5584e−02 ± 5.1169e−04
AdaBoost-DSCN	3.5959e−02 ± 6.0075e−04	**3.4545e−02 ± 1.1014e−03**

As we can see from Tables 4, 5, 6, and 7, AdaBoost-DSCN model has the smallest test errors on the large-scale regression data set of MV, Compactiv, Pole and Elevators compared with SCN, DSCN and AdaBoost-SCN model. Compared with DSCN and SCN, AdaBoost-DSCN and AdaBoost-SCN can improve the regression accuracy further, which indicates that DSCN has stronger capability of large-scale data regression compared with SCN, and AdaBoost ensemble learning approach can be used for solving the over-fitting problem of DSCN.

In conclusion, with the increase of data dimension and data scale, AdaBoost-based deep stochastic configuration network improves the regression accuracy and stability of DSCN, which is superior to SCN, DSCN and AdaBoost-SCN models.

5   Conclusion

DSCN can allocate weights and biases of nodes and construct deep network structure adaptively through supervision mechanism, which has faster learning efficiency and higher learning accuracy. To avoid over-fitting problem of the DSCN for solving regression problems, AdaBoost ensemble learning strategy is merged into DSCN, then deep stochastic configuration network based on AdaBoost is proposed, termed as AdaBoost-DSCN. Experimental results on the complex function approximation problems and some large-scale regression datasets demonstrate that AdaBoost-DSCN can improve the training accuracy of DSCN and overcome the problems of model instability and over-fitting which caused by random configuration of parameters and strong dependence on training samples. In the future, image classification is one of the important research fields of machine learning, AdaBoost-DSCN will be used to solve this kind of problem to obtain higher classification accuracy.

Acknowledgements. This work is supported by the National Natural Science Foundation of China under Grant No. 61976216 and No. 61672522.

References

1. Wang, D., Li, M.: Stochastic configuration networks: fundamentals and algorithms. IEEE Trans. Cybern. **47**(10), 3466–3479 (2017)
2. Huang, C., Huang, Q., Wang, D.: Stochastic configuration networks based adaptive storage replica management for power big data processing. IEEE Trans. Indust. Inf. **16**(1), 373–383 (2020)
3. Pang, L., Guo, L., Zhang, J.: Subject-specific mental workload classification using EEG and stochastic configuration network (SCN). Biomed. Sign. Process. Contr. **68**, 102711 (2021)
4. Liu, J., Hao, R., Zhang, T.: Vibration fault diagnosis based on stochastic configuration neural networks. Neurocomputing **434**, 98–125 (2021)
5. Wang, W., Wang, D.: Prediction of component concentrations in sodium aluminate liquor using stochastic configuration networks. Neural Comput. Appl. **32**(17), 13625–13638 (2020)
6. Wang, W., Jia, Y., Yu, W.: On-line ammonia nitrogen measurement using generalized additive model and stochastic configuration networks. Measurement **170**, 108743 (2021)
7. Pan, J., Luan, F., Gao, Y.: FPGA-based implementation of stochastic configuration network for robotic grasping recognition. IEEE Access **8**, 139966–139973 (2020)
8. Zhao, J., Hu, T., Zheng, R.: Defect recognition in concrete ultrasonic detection based on wavelet packet transform and stochastic configuration networks. IEEE Access **9**, 9284–9295 (2021)
9. Li, M., Wang, D.: 2-D stochastic configuration networks for image data analytics. IEEE Trans. Cybern. **51**(1), 359–372 (2021)
10. Wang, D., Li, M.: Deep stochastic configuration networks with universal approximation property. In: 2018 International Joint Conference on Neural Networks (IJCNN), pp. 1–8. IEEE, Rio de Janeiro Brazil (2018)
11. Wang, D., Cui, C.: Stochastic configuration networks ensemble with heterogeneous features for large-scale data analytics. Inf. Sci. **417**, 55–71 (2017)
12. Ai, W., Wang, D.: Distributed stochastic configuration networks with cooperative learning paradigm. Inf. Sci. **540**, 1–16 (2020)
13. Zhang, C., Ding, S., Zhang, J.: Parallel stochastic configuration networks for large-scale data regression. Appl. Soft Comput. **103**, 107143 (2021)
14. Huang, C., Li, M., Wang, D.: Stochastic configuration network ensembles with selective base models. Neural Netw. **137**, 106–118 (2021)
15. Pratama, M., Wang, D.: Deep stacked stochastic configuration networks for lifelong learning of non-stationary data streams. Inf. Sci. **495**, 150–174 (2019)
16. Li, K., Wang, W., Wang, Y.: Application of ensemble stochastic configuration network in aquaculture water quality monitoring. Trans. Chin. Soc. Agricult. Eng. (Trans. CSAE) **36**(4), 220–226 (2020)
17. Qu, H., Feng, T., Wang, Y.: AdaBoost SCN algorithm for optics fiber vibration signal recognition. Appl. Opt. **58**(21), 5612–5623 (2019)
18. Lu, J., Ding, J.: Construction of prediction intervals for carbon residual of crude oil based on deep stochastic configuration networks. Inf. Sci. **486**, 119–132 (2019)

19. Hansen, L.K., Salamon, P.: Neural network ensembles. IEEE Trans. Pattern Anal. Mach. Intell. **12**(10), 993–1001 (1990)
20. Freund, Y., Schapire, R.E.: A decision-theoretic generalization of online learning and an application to boosting. J. Comput. Syst. Sci. **55**(1), 119–139 (1997)
21. Opitz, D.W., Maclin, R.F.: An empirical evaluation of bagging and boosting for artificial neural networks. In: Proceedings of International Conference on Neural Networks (ICNN 1997), pp. 1401–1405. IEEE, Houston (1997)
22. Liu, L., Hua, Y., Zhao, Q.: Blind image quality assessment by relative gradient statistics and AdaBoosting neural network. Signal Process. Image Commun. **40**, 1–15 (2016)
23. Luo, Y., Wang, B.: Prediction of negative conversion days of childhood nephrotic syndrome based on PCA and BP-AdaBoost neural network. IEEE Access **7**, 151579–151586 (2019)
24. Li, S., Wang, J., Liu, B.: Prediction of market demand based on AdaBoost_BP neural network. In: 2013 International Conference on Computer Sciences and Applications, pp. 305–308. IEEE, Wuhan (2013)
25. Tyukin, I. Y., Prokhorov, D. V.: Feasibility of random basis function approximators for modeling and control. In: 2009 IEEE Control Applications, (CCA) & Intelligent Control, (ISIC), pp. 1391–1396. IEEE, St. Petersburg (2009)
26. Li, M., Wang, D.: Insights into randomized algorithms for neural networks: practical issues and common pitfalls. Inf. Sci. **382**, 170–178 (2017)

Comparative Study of Chaos-Embedded Particle Swarm Optimization

Dongping Tian[(⊠)], Bingchun Li, Chen Liu, Haiyan Li, and Ling Yuan

School of Computer Science and Technology, Kashi University, Xuefu Avenue,
Kashi City 844006, Xinjiang, China
tdp211@163.com

Abstract. Particle swarm optimization (PSO) is a population-based stochastic search algorithm that has been widely used to solve many real-world problems. However, like other evolutionary algorithms, PSO also suffers from premature convergence and entrapment into local optima when addressing complex multimodal problems. In this paper, we propose a chaos-embedded particle swarm optimization algorithm (CEPSO). In CEPSO, the chaos-based swarm initialization is first applied to yield high-quality initial particles with better stability. Afterwards the chaotic inertia weight and the chaotic sequence based random numbers are introduced into the velocity update scheme for PSO to improve its global and local search capabilities. In addition, two different mutation strategies (chaos and levy) are utilized to enhance the swarm diversity without being trapped in local optima. Finally, the CEPSO proposed in this work is compared with several classical PSOs on a set of well-known benchmark functions. Experimental results show that CEPSO can achieve better performance compared to several other PSO variants in terms of the solution accuracy and convergence rate.

Keywords: Particle swarm optimization · Chaos · Swarm diversity · Inertial weight · Premature convergence · Local optima · Mutation strategy

1 Introduction

Particle swarm optimization (PSO) is a stochastic population-based method motivated by the intelligent collective behaviour of some animals such as flocks of birds and schools of fish [1]. Due to the advantages of PSO include fast convergence toward the global optimum, easy implementation and fewer parameters to adjust. All of these make it as a potential method to solve different optimization problems in a wide variety of applications, such as text mining [2], data clustering [3], image processing [4], optimal scheduling [5] and machine learning [6], etc. Meanwhile, an numerous number of different PSO variants have been proposed by researchers in the literature, and most of them can achieve encouraging results and impressive performance. However, PSO still suffers from the issues of premature convergence and entrapment into local optima like other stochastic search techniques, especially in the context of the complex multimodal

© IFIP International Federation for Information Processing 2022
Published by Springer Nature Switzerland AG 2022
Z. Shi et al. (Eds.): IIP 2022, IFIP AICT 643, pp. 15–29, 2022.
https://doi.org/10.1007/978-3-031-03948-5_2

optimization problems. To tackle the above issues, a huge number of PSOs have been developed to enhance the performance. From the literature, these previous works can be roughly divided into the following categories: (i) swarm initialization. Note that in (i), some PSO variants are initialized with chaos sequence [4, 7], opposition-based learning [2, 8], and some other initialization strategies [9] instead of the purely random mechanism to improve PSO performance. In particular, the chaos based swarm initialization has been extensively studied in our prior works [10, 11] with significantly improved performance. (ii) Parameter selection. The parameters inertia weight [4], acceleration coefficients [10], and random numbers [2] attract much more attention and have become focus of research in the area of PSO in recent years. (iii) Non-parametric update. In this paradigm, there is no need to tune any algorithmic parameters in PSO by removing all the parameters from the standard particle swarm optimization [12, 13]. (iv) Multi-swarm scheme. In (iv), the whole swarm in PSO can be divided into several sub-swarms during the search process so as to explore different sub-regions of the solution space with different search strategies [14, 15]. (v) Hybrid mechanism. As for (v), different evolutionary algorithms (such as genetic algorithm [8], cuckoo search [16], differential evolution [17], simulated annealing [18], artificial bee colony [19], firefly algorithm [20]) and evolutionary operators (like crossover [21], mutation [11]) are integrated together to improve the performance of PSO.

Motivated by the above PSO researches, we put forward a chaos-embedded particle swarm optimization (CEPSO). On the one hand, the chaos-based swarm initialization is applied to yield high-quality initial particles with better stability. On the other hand, the chaotic inertia weight and chaotic sequence based random numbers are introduced into the velocity update scheme for PSO to balance the exploration and exploitation and thus result in a better optimal solution. In addition, two different mutation operators (Gaussian and chaos) are utilized to enhance the swarm diversity and avoid the premature convergence of the CEPSO. Conducted experiments validate that the proposed PSO outperforms several state-of-the-art PSOs regarding their effectiveness and efficiency in the task of numerical function optimization. The rest of this paper is organized as follows. Section 2 introduces the standard PSO. In Sect. 3, the CEPSO is elaborated from three aspects of swarm initialization, parameter selection and mutation strategies adopted in this work, respectively. Experimental results on a set of well-known benchmark functions are reported in Sect. 4. At length, the concluding remarks and future work are provided in Sect. 5.

2 Standard PSO

Particle swarm optimization [1] is a population based meta-heuristic algorithm. The basic principle of PSO mimics the swarm social behaviour such as bird flocking and fish schooling. In PSO, the population is called a swarm and each individual in the swarm is referred as a particle. Each particle in the swarm represents a potential solution to an optimization problem. Specifically, the position of the ith particle can be expressed as a D-dimensional vector $X_i = [x_{i1}, x_{i2}, \ldots, x_{iD}]$ where $x_{ij} \in [x_{min}, x_{max}]$ denotes the position of the jth dimension of the ith particle, and the corresponding velocity can be shown as $V_i = [v_{i1}, v_{i2}, \ldots, v_{iD}]$ where $v_{ij} \in [v_{min}, v_{max}]$ is used to reduce the likelihood of the particles flying out of the search space. The best previous position (the position giving the best fitness value) of the ith particle is denoted by $pbest_i = (pbest_{i1}, pbest_{i2}, \ldots, pbest_{iD})$, while the global best position of the whole swarm found so far is indicated as $gbest$ $= (gbest_1, gbest_2, \ldots, gbest_D)$. To start with, the particles are randomly distributed over the search space with random velocity values. Followed by each particle's velocity is updated using its own previous best experience known as the personal best experience ($pbest$) and the whole swarm's best experience known as the global best experience ($gbest$) until a global optimal solution is found. In PSO, each particle is associated with two properties (velocity vector V and position vector X) and it moves in the search space with a velocity that is dynamically adjusted according to $pbest$ and $gbest$ simultaneously. Mathematically, velocity and position of particles are updated according to the following formula:

$$v_{ij}(t+1) = \omega \times v_{ij}(t) + c_1 \times r1_{ij} \times [pbest_{ij}(t) - x_{ij}(t)] + c_2 \times r2_{ij}$$
$$\times [gbest_j(t) - x_{ij}(t)] \tag{1}$$

$$x_{ij}(t+1) = x_{ij}(t) + v_{ij}(t+1) \tag{2}$$

where ω is the inertia weight used for balancing the global and local search. In general, a large inertia weight facilitates the global exploration while a small inertia weight tends to facilitate the local exploitation. c_1 and c_2 are positive constants and called the acceleration coefficients reflecting the weight of the stochastic acceleration terms that pull each particle toward $pbest_i$ and $gbest$ positions, respectively. $r1_{ij}$ and $r2_{ij}$ denote two random numbers uniformly distributed in the interval [0,1].

Algorithm 1: Pseudocode of the standard PSO algorithm

Input: w_0: inertia weight, c_1, c_2: acceleration factors, N: swarm size,
      D: swarm dimension.
Process:
1.   Randomly initialize the particles of swarm.
2.   **while** *number of iterations* or *the stopping criterion* is not met **do**
3.   Update the inertia weight.
4.   **for** n=1 **to** N **do**
5.   Find $pbest$.
6.   Find $gbest$.
7.   **for** d=1 **to** D **do**
8.   Update velocity of particles by Eq.(1)
9.   Update position of particles by Eq.(2)
10.   **end for**
11.   **end for**
12.   **end while**
Output: $gbest$ particle as the final optimal solution.

---

3 Proposed CEPSO

3.1 Swarm Initialization

Swarm initialization plays a crucial role in any population based evolutionary algorithms as it affects the convergence speed and quality of the final solution. In general, random initialization is the most frequently used method to generate initial swarm in absence of any information about the solution. From the literature, it can be seen that different initialization strategies have been tested with PSO to improve its performance. Particularly, the chaotic sequence rather than random sequence based initialization is a powerful strategy to diversify the particles of swarm and improve the performance of PSO by preventing the premature convergence [7]. Moreover, it is reported that the stability of PSOs and the quality of final solution can also be improved to some extent [4, 10]. Based on this argument, the commonly used logistic map is employed to generate the initial position instead of the uniform position, which can be described as follows:

$$Ch_{i+1} = \mu \times Ch_i \times (1 - Ch_i), i = 0, 1, 2, \cdots \qquad (3)$$

where Ch_i denotes the ith chaotic variable in the interval (0,1), such that the initial Ch_0 $\in$ (0,1) and $Ch_0 \notin$ (0,0.25,0.5,0.75,1). μ is a predetermined constant called bifurcation coefficient. When μ increases from zero, the dynamic system generated by Eq. (3) changes from one fixed-point to two, three,..., and until 2^i. During this process, a large number of multiple periodic components will locate in narrower and narrower intervals of μ as it increases. This phenomenon is obviously free from constraint. But μ has a limit value $\mu_t = 3.569945672$. Note that when μ approaches the μ_t, the period will become infinite or even non-periodic. At this time, the whole system evolves into the chaotic state (behavior). On the other hand, when μ is greater than 4, the whole system becomes unstable. Hence the range [μ_t,4] is considered as the chaotic region of the whole system. Its bifurcation diagram is illustrated in Fig. 1.

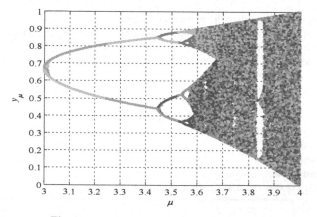

Fig. 1. Bifurcation diagram of logistic map

As described above, the pseudocode of logistic map can be described as below, which is able to generate chaotic sequence and avoid plunging into the small periodic cycles effectively.

Algorithm 2: Pseudocode of logistic map for chaotic sequence

Input: μ: bifurcation coefficient.
Process:
1.   Randomly initialize chaotic variables.
2.   **while** *number of maximal iterations* is not met **do**
3.   **if** chaotic variable plunges into fixed points or small periodic cycles **do**
4.   Implement a very small positive random perturbation.
5.   Map them by Eq.(3).
6.   **else**
7.   Update chaotic variables by Eq.(3) directly.
8.   **end if**
9.   **end while**
Output: the generated chaotic variables.

3.2 Parameter Selection

Proper selection of PSO parameters can significantly affect the performance of particle swarm optimization. It is generally believed that a larger inertia weight facilitates global exploration while a smaller inertia weight tends to facilitate local exploitation to fine-tune the current search space. By changing the inertia weight dynamically, the search capability of PSO can be dynamically adjusted. This is a general statement about the impact of w on PSO's search behavior shared by many other researchers. Based on the nature of ergodicity and non-repetition of the chaos mentioned in Sect. 3.1, the chaotic inertia weight [22] is applied in this work to strike a better balance between the exploration and exploitation, which is defined by adding a chaotic term to the linearly decreasing inertia weight as follows:

$$w(t) = (w_{\max} - w_{\min}) \times \frac{t_{\max} - t}{t_{\max}} + w_{\min} \times ch \tag{4}$$

where $ch \in (0,1)$ is a chaotic number, w_{max} and w_{min} denote the initial value and final value of inertia weight respectively. t is the current iteration of the algorithm and t_{max} is the maximum number of iterations the PSO is allowed to continue.

Note that the random numbers r_1 and r_2 are the key components affecting the convergence behavior of PSO. It is reported that the convergence of PSO is strongly connected to its stochastic nature and PSO uses random sequence for its parameters during a run. In particular, it has been shown that the final optimization results may be very close but not equal when different random sequences are used during the PSO search process [23]. Thus the chaotic sequence generated by Eq. (3) is used to substitute the random numbers r_1 and r_2 in the velocity update equation (the value of Ch varies between 0 and 1) [2].

$$v_{ij}(t+1) = \omega \times v_{ij}(t) + c_1 \times Ch \times [pbest_{ij}(t) - x_{ij}(t)] + c_2 \times (1 - Ch)$$
$$\times [gbest_j(t) - x_{ij}(t)] \tag{5}$$

3.3 Mutation Strategy

Mutation strategy is an important part of evolutionary computation technique, which can effectively prevent the loss of population diversity and allow a greater region of the search space to be covered. Based on this fact, different mutation operators, such as wavelet [4], gaussian [11], cauchy [11] and levy [24], have been widely used in evolutionary computation, especially for PSO to enhance its global search ability. However, these mutation techniques are not suitable for all kinds of problems, that is to say, most of them are problem-oriented. Thus the two most commonly used mutation strategies, gaussian and chaos, are alternately exploited to mutate the *pbest* and *gbest* based on the swarm diversity defined below, which is expected to well guide the search process of the particle swarm.

$$Div(t) = \frac{1}{N} \sum_{i=1}^{N} \sqrt{\sum_{j=1}^{D} (x_{ij}(t) - \overline{x_j(t)})^2} \tag{6}$$

$$\overline{x_j(t)} = \frac{1}{N} \sum_{i=1}^{N} x_{ij}(t) \tag{7}$$

where N is the swarm size, D denotes the space dimension, $x_{ij}(t)$ is the jth value of ith particle in the tth iteration and $\overline{x_j(t)}$ is the average value of the jth dimension over all the particles in the swarm.

So far, the procedure of CEPSO can be succinctly described as follows.

Algorithm 3: Pseudocode of the proposed CEPSO algorithm

Input: $c_1=c_2=2$, $Div(0)=0$, swarm size N, swarm dimension D,
       the threshold of swarm diversity Div_{th}.
Process:
1.   Initialize the particles of swarm by **Algorithm 2**.
2.   **while** *maximum number of iterations ($t≤t_{max}$)* is not met **do**
3.   Calculate w by Eq.(4).
4.   Calculate r_1 and r_2 by Eq.(3).
5.   **for** $n=1$ **to** N **do**
6.   Find *pbest* .
7.   Find *gbest*.
8.   **for** $d=1$ **to** D **do**
9.   Update velocity of the particles by Eq.(5).
10.   Update position of the particles by Eq.(2).
11.   **end for**
12.   **end for**
13.   Calculate $Div(t)$ according to Eq.(6).
14.   **if** $(Div(t) ≤ Div_{th})$ **do**
15.   Update *pbest* and *gbest* by Gaussian mutation.
16.   **else**
17.   Update *pbest* and *gbest* by Chaos mutation.
18.   **end if**
19.   **end while**
Output: *gbest* particle as the final optimal solution.

---

4 Experimental Results and Discussion

To evaluate the performance of the proposed CEPSO, extensive experiments are conducted on a set of well-known benchmark functions consisting of four global optimization problems. Particularly, the performance of PSO with different swarm initialization and different inertia weights are completely compared and investigated respectively. Note that all the test functions are to be minimized, they are numbered f_1–f_4 given in Table 1, including their expression, dimension, allowable search space, global optimum and property, respectively.

Table 1. Dimensions, search ranges, global optimum values and properties of test functions

Test functions	Dimensions (n)	Search range	Global optimum	Properties
Sphere (f_1)	10/30	$[-10,10]^n$	0	Unimodal
Schwefel (f_2)	10/30	$[-100,100]^n$	0	Unimodal
Rastrigin (f_3)	10/30	$[-5.12,5.12]^n$	0	Multimodal
Ackley (f_4)	10/30	$[-32,32]^n$	0	Multimodal

(1) Sphere function

$$\min f_1(x) = \sum_{i=1}^{n} x_i^2$$

where the global optimum $x^* = 0$ and $f(x^*) = 0$ for $-10 \leq x_i \leq 10$.

(2) Schwefel function

$$\min f_2(x) = \sum_{i=1}^{n} |x_i| + \prod_{i=1}^{n} |x_i|$$

where the global optimum $x^* = 0$ and $f(x^*) = 0$ for $-100 \leq x_i \leq 100$.

(3) Rastrigin function

$$\min f_3(x) = \sum_{i=1}^{n} [x_i^2 - 10\cos(2\pi x_i) + 10]$$

where the global optimum $x^* = 0$ and $f(x^*) = 0$ for $-5.12 \leq x_i \leq 5.12$.

(4) Ackley function

$$\min f_4(x) = -20\exp\left(-0.2\sqrt{\frac{1}{n}\sum_{i=1}^{n} x_i^2}\right) - \exp\left(\frac{1}{n}\sum_{i=1}^{n}\cos(2\pi x_i)\right) + 20 + e$$

where the global optimum $x^* = 0$ and $f(x^*) = 0$ for $-32 \leq x_i \leq 32$.

Figure 2 depicts the 2-dimensional graphical shows of the four well-known benchmark functions.

To illustrate the effect of different initialization methods, inertia weights and mutation strategies mentioned above, different combinations of PSO with random/chaos swarm initialization, standard/chaotic parameters, and without/chaos mutation are tested respectively. For readability, note that different PSO paradigms are specified in Table 2 by their acronyms, respectively.

Consider the following given conditions: the swarm size $N = 40$, the standard parameters include $w_{max} = 0.9$, $w_{min} = 0.4$ and the acceleration coefficients $c_1 = c_2 = 2$ for all the related PSO variants. The threshold of the swarm diversity is predetermined $Div_{th} = 2.8e-20$ by trial and error. For each test function, 30 independent runs are performed by each PSO, and each run is with 1000 iterations. The algorithm terminates when it reaches the maximum number of allowed iterations.

From Table 3, it can be clearly observed that CEPSO evidently outperforms other PSO variants on all the four test functions. Taking f_1 and f_2 for example, note that under the same conditions of the swarm initialization and related parameters, the PSOs with mutation strategies markedly surpass those without mutations. This validates the importance of mutation operators to sustain the swarm diversity without being trapped in local optima. In particular, it is worth noting that the performance of PSO with chaos

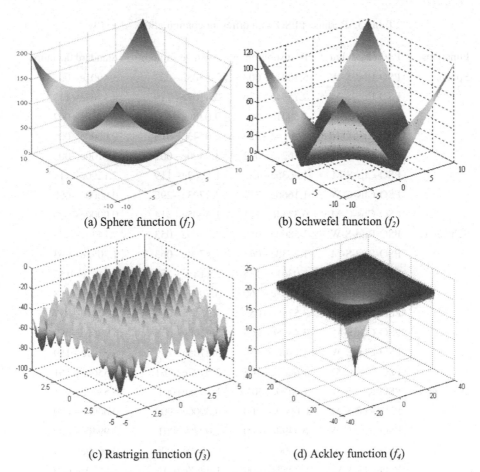

(a) Sphere function (f_1)   (b) Schwefel function (f_2)

(c) Rastrigin function (f_3)   (d) Ackley function (f_4)

Fig. 2. Graphical shows of the benchmark test functions

Table 2. Acronyms of different PSO variants

Initialization	Parameters	Mutation	Acronym
Random	Standard	Without	PSO-Rnd-S-W
		Gaussian/chaos	PSO-Rnd-S-M
	Chaos-based	Without	PSO-Rnd-C-W
		Gaussian/chaos	PSO-Rnd-C-M
Chaos	Standard	Without	PSO-Chs-S-W
		Gaussian/chaos	PSO-Chs-S-M
	Chaos-based	Without	PSO-Chs-C-W
		Gaussian/chaos	PSO-Chs-C-M

Table 3. Results of PSO with different configurations ($d = 10$)

Functions	PSO algorithm	Best solution	Average solution	Standard deviation
Sphere	PSO-Rnd-S-W	5.1001e−003	5.8303e−002	5.1901e−002
	PSO-Rnd-S-M	2.7594e−126	2.4107e−119	4.1704e−119
	PSO-Rnd-C-W	1.3901e−002	9.0386e−002	7.0010e−002
	PSO-Rnd-C-M	8.2914e−320	6.0543e−313	0.0000e−000
	PSO-Chs-S-W	1.1621e−002	3.9400e−002	2.5100e−002
	PSO-Chs-S-M	1.6636e−132	1.5062e−119	2.1290e−119
	PSO-Chs-C-W	1.1666e−315	3.2793e−298	0.0000e−000
	PSO-Chs-C-M	6.3734e−321	1.4005e−314	0.0000e−000
Schwefel	PSO-Rnd-S-W	1.5868e−053	4.7589e−053	2.2430e−053
	PSO-Rnd-S-M	1.2530e−063	1.4764e−063	1.3052e−063
	PSO-Rnd-C-W	2.0361e−155	2.1141e−155	2.1141e−155
	PSO-Rnd-C-M	4.7263e−160	3.7903e−158	5.1224e−158
	PSO-Chs-S-W	3.5786e−057	3.9307e−057	2.7731e−057
	PSO-Chs-S-M	3.4395e−065	3.5180e−058	4.9752e−058
	PSO-Chs-C-W	2.7406e−159	5.2705e−159	5.6281e−159
	PSO-Chs-C-M	1.6481e−165	2.5707e−161	3.5564e−161
Rastrigin	PSO-Rnd-S-W	1.0499e+001	1.1238e+001	6.5312e−001
	PSO-Rnd-S-M	0.0000e−000	0.0000e−000	0.0000e−000
	PSO-Rnd-C-W	6.4490e−000	1.0079e+001	2.9940e−000
	PSO-Rnd-C-M	0.0000e−000	0.0000e−000	0.0000e−000
	PSO-Chs-S-W	9.7562e−000	1.4498e+001	3.2530e−000
	PSO-Chs-S-M	0.0000e−000	0.0000e−000	0.0000e−000
	PSO-Chs-C-W	8.8020e−001	6.2974e−000	3.8701e−000
	PSO-Chs-C-M	0.0000e−000	0.0000e−000	0.0000e−000
Ackley	PSO-Rnd-S-W	8.3506e−016	7.6226e−007	7.9614e−007
	PSO-Rnd-S-M	5.8233e−017	7.5088e−007	5.2016e−006
	PSO-Rnd-C-W	7.6952e−016	6.6319e−007	3.0892e−008
	PSO-Rnd-C-M	5.5511e−017	6.9783e−007	7.6836e−007
	PSO-Chs-S-W	7.6952e−016	7.1015e−007	7.6836e−007
	PSO-Chs-S-M	4.8102e−017	6.8769e−009	7.6836e−008
	PSO-Chs-C-W	5.3357e−016	8.3361e−008	5.4387e−008
	PSO-Chs-C-M	9.2618e−018	5.1679e−010	2.3911e−010

swarm initialization is far superior to those corresponding PSOs with random initialization except for PSO-Chs-S-W and PSO-Rnd-S-W for function f_1, which implies that PSO with the chaos-based initialization can alleviate its inherent defects of low stability. In other words, just as the conclusions drawn in references [4, 7], this fully demonstrates the significance of the high-quality initial particles to the convergent performance of PSO algorithm. In addition, note also that PSO with the chaotic parameters can achieve better performance than those with the standard parameters under the same other experimental conditions. As for the test function f_3, due to it owns a large number of local optima, thus it is difficult to find the global optimization values. However, it is interesting to note that its optimal value can be found based on the PSO-Rnd-S-M, PSO-Rnd-C-M, PSO-Chs-S-M and PSO-Chs-C-M respectively so as to further show the importance of mutation operation. Likewise, CEPSO is able to get better solutions for function f_4 even though it has one narrow global optimum basin and many minor local optima. In sum, the promising results obtained by the CEPSO are largely attributed to the chaos-based swarm initialization, the chaotic inertia weight and chaotic sequence based random numbers as well as two different mutation strategies (chaos and levy), all of these are complementary to each other and the appropriate combination makes them benefit from each other.

To illustrate the particles search process, Fig. 3 depicts the evolution curves of PSO with different configurations for all the four test functions, which clearly shows that PSO-Chs-C-M performs much better than the other PSO variants in almost all cases. To be specific, taking Fig. 3(a) for example, the evolution curve of PSO-Chs-C-M consistently decreases fastly compared to that of PSO-Rnd-S-W, PSO-Rnd-C-W and PSO-Chs-S-W respectively. In contrast, the convergence rates of PSO-Rnd-S-M and PSO-Chs-S-M are not as fast as that of PSO-Chs-C-M, PSO-Chs-C-W and PSO-Rnd-C-M, both of them evolve slowly as the search proceeds but are better than the PSO-Rnd-S-W, PSO-Rnd-C-W and PSO-Chs-S-W respectively. On the other hand, it is interesting to note that PSO-Chs-C-M yields the fastest convergence rate at the early 150 iterations in Fig. 3(c). Compared to PSO-Rnd-S-W, PSO-Rnd-C-W, PSO-Chs-S-W and PSO-Chs-C-W, the other three PSOs with mutation also evolve fast in the early 500 iterations and finally converge to the global optima.

To further validate the effectiveness of the proposed algorithm, CEPSO is compared with the other seven PSO variants in Table 4, including LPSO [25], FIPSO [26], HPSO-TVAC [27], DMSPSO [28], CLPSO [29], LFPSO [30] and OPSO [31]. Note that the dimension of all the functions is set as 30 in this section. The mean best solution (Mean) and standard deviation (Std.) are applied to measure the performance. From the results shown in Table 4, we can see that CEPSO gets rank 1 three times in spite of the rank 3 on function f_4. According to the final rank, it is clearly observed that CEPSO can achieve better performance than the others in terms of the average best solution and standard deviation. To summarize, the encouraging results obtained by the CEPSO are largely ascribed to the chaos-based swarm initialization, chaotic parameters and multi-mutation strategies exploited in this work, respectively.

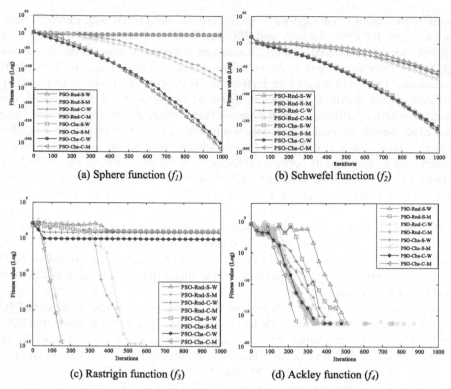

(a) Sphere function (f_1)   (b) Schwefel function (f_2)

(c) Rastrigin function (f_3)   (d) Ackley function (f_4)

Fig. 3. Evolution curves of PSO with different configurations

Table 4. Comparison of CEPSO with other seven PSO variants ($d = 30$)

Func	Item	CLPSO	HPSO-TVAC	FIPSO	LPSO	DMSPSO	LFPSO	OPSO	CEPSO
f_1	Mean	1.58e−12	2.83e−33	2.42e−13	3.34e−14	2.65e−31	4.69e−31	6.45e−18	**8.06e−106**
	Std.	7.70e−13	3.19e−33	1.73e−13	5.39e−14	6.25e−31	2.50e−30	4.64e−18	**3.58e−102**
	Rank	8	2	7	6	3	4	5	1
f_2	Avg.	2.51e−08	9.03e−20	2.76e−08	1.70e−10	1.57e−18	2.64e−17	1.26e−10	**2.62e−49**
	Std.	5.84e−09	9.58e−20	9.04e−09	1.39e−10	3.79e−18	6.92e−17	5.58e−11	**5.11e−50**
	Rank	7	2	8	6	3	4	5	1
f_3	Avg.	9.09e−05	9.43e−00	6.51e+01	3.51e+01	2.72e+01	4.54e−00	6.97e−00	**0**
	Std.	1.25e−04	3.48e−00	1.34e+01	6.89e−00	6.02e−00	1.03e−01	3.07e−00	**0**
	Rank	2	5	8	7	6	3	4	1
f_4	Avg.	3.66e−07	7.29e−14	2.33e−07	8.20e−08	1.84e−14	**1.68e−14**	6.23e−09	6.36e−14
	Std.	7.57e−08	3.00e−14	7.19e−08	6.73e−08	4.35e−15	**4.84e−15**	1.87e−09	8.09e−13
	Rank	8	4	7	6	2	1	5	3
Avg. rank		6.25	3.25	7.50	6.25	3.50	3.00	4.75	1.50
Final rank		6	3	7	6	4	2	5	1

5 Conclusions and Future Work

In this paper, we propose a chaos-embedded particle swarm optimization algorithm (CEPSO). On the one hand, the chaos-based swarm initialization is first used to yield high-quality initial particles with better stability. On the other hand, the chaotic inertia weight and the chaotic sequence based random numbers are introduced into the velocity update scheme for PSO to improve its global and local search ability. In the meanwhile, two different mutation operators (chaos and levy) are used to enhance the swarm diversity and avoid the premature convergence. At length, extensive experiments on a set of well-known benchmark functions demonstrate that CEPSO is much more effective than several other PSOs in dealing with numerical function optimization.

As future work, we plan to compare CEPSO with more state-of-the-art PSO variants in the task of complex multi-optima and multi-objective problems, or even some real-world applications from other fields to further investigate the effectiveness of the CEPSO. More interesting future work is to introduce the other most common chaotic maps, viz. Tent map, Lozi map, Arnold's cat map, Sinai map, Burgers map, Dissipative standard map, Tinkerbell map, Circle map and Sinusoidal map, into the PSO to investigate how to improve its performance without being trapped in local optima. Meanwhile, we also intend to delve deeper into the parallelization of CEPSO for large-scale optimization problems and exploring the use of different chaotic parameters for PSO in different scenarios simultaneously, especially for the adequate parameter tuning in a wide range of problems. Lastly, and arguably most importantly, the qualitative relationships between the chaos-based swarm initialization and the stability of PSO, from the viewpoint of mathematics, will be elaborated and proved comprehensively.

Acknowledgment. This work is fully supported by the Program of the Science and Technology Department of Xinjiang Uygur Autonomous Region (No. 2022D01A16) and the Program of the Applied Technology Research and Development of Kashi Prefecture (No. KS2021026).

References

1. Kennedy, J., Eberhart, R.: Particle swarm optimization In: IEEE Conference on Neural Networks (ICNN 1995), pp. 1942–1948 (1995)
2. Bharti, K., Singh, P.: Opposition chaotic fitness mutation based adaptive inertia weight BPSO for feature selection in text clustering. Appl. Soft Comput. **43**, 20–34 (2016)
3. Chuang, L., Hsiao, C., Yang, C.: Chaotic particle swarm optimization for data clustering. Expert Syst. Appl. **38**(12), 14555–14563 (2011)
4. Tian, D., Shi, Z.: MPSO: Modified particle swarm optimization and its applications. Swarm Evol. Comput. **41**, 49–68 (2018)
5. Petrović, M., Vukovic, N., Mitic, M., et al.: Integration of process planning and scheduling using chaotic particle swarm optimization algorithm. Expert Syst. Appl. **64**, 569–588 (2016)
6. Das, P., Behera, H., Panigrahi, B.: A hybridization of an improved particle swarm optimization and gravitational search algorithm for multi-robot path planning. Swarm Evol. Comput. **28**, 14–28 (2016)
7. Tian, D.: Particle swarm optimization with chaos-based initialization for numerical optimization. Intell. Autom. Soft Comput. **24**(2), 331–342 (2018)

8. Dong, N., Wu, C., Ip, W., et al.: An opposition-based chaotic GA/PSO hybrid algorithm and its application in circle detection. Comput. Math. Appl. **64**, 1886–1902 (2012)
9. Xue, B., Zhang, M., Browne, W.: Particle swarm optimisation for feature selection in classification: novel initialisation and updating mechanisms. Appl. Soft Comput. **18**, 261–276 (2014)
10. Tian, D., Zhao, X., Shi, Z.: Chaotic particle swarm optimization with sigmoid-based acceleration coefficients for numerical function optimization. Swarm Evol. Comput. **51**, 126–145 (2019)
11. Tian, D., Zhao, X., Shi, Z.: DMPSO: Diversity-guided multi-mutation particle swarm optimizer. IEEE Access **7**(1), 124008–124025 (2019)
12. Beheshti, Z., Shamsuddin, S.: Non-parametric particle swarm optimization for global optimization. Appl. Soft Comput. **28**, 345–359 (2015)
13. Liu, Z., Ji, X., Liu, Y.: Hybrid non-parametric particle swarm optimization and its stability analysis. Expert Syst. Appl. **92**, 256–275 (2018)
14. Chen, Y., Li, L., Peng, H., et al.: Dynamic multi-swarm differential learning particle swarm optimizer. Swarm Evol. Comput. **39**, 209–221 (2018)
15. Xia, X., Gui, L., Zhan, Z.: A multi-swarm particle swarm optimization algorithm based on dynamical topology and purposeful detecting. Appl. Soft Comput. **67**, 126–140 (2018)
16. Bouyer, A., Hatamlou, A.: An efficient hybrid clustering method based on improved cuckoo optimization and modified particle swarm optimization algorithms. Appl. Soft Comput. **67**, 172–182 (2018)
17. Mao, B., Xie, Z., Wang, Y., et al.: A hybrid differential evolution and particle swarm optimization algorithm for numerical kinematics solution of remote maintenance manipulators. Fusion Eng. Des. **124**, 587–590 (2017)
18. Javidrad, F., Nazari, M.: A new hybrid particle swarm and simulated annealing stochastic optimization method. Appl. Soft Comput. **60**, 634–654 (2017)
19. Li, Z., Wang, W., Yan, Y., et al.: PS-ABC: A hybrid algorithm based on particle swarm and artificial bee colony for high-dimensional optimization problems. Expert Syst. Appl. **42**(22), 8881–8895 (2015)
20. Aydilek, İ: A hybrid firefly and particle swarm optimization algorithm for computationally expensive numerical problems. Appl. Soft Comput. **66**, 232–249 (2018)
21. Meng, A., Li, Z., Yin, H., et al.: Accelerating particle swarm optimization using crisscross search. Inf. Sci. **329**, 52–72 (2016)
22. Feng, Y., Yao, Y., Wang, A.: Comparing with chaotic inertia weights in particle swarm optimization. In: IEEE Conference on Machine Learning and Cybernetics (ICMLC 2007), pp. 329–333 (2007)
23. Alatas, B., Akin, E., Ozer, A.: Chaos embedded particle swarm optimization algorithms. Chaos Solitons Fractals **40**(4), 1715–1734 (2009)
24. Wang, H., Wang, W., Wu, Z.: Particle swarm optimization with adaptive mutation for multimodal optimization. Appl. Math. Comput. **221**, 296–305 (2013)
25. Kennedy, J., Mendes, R.: Population structure and particle swarm performance. In: IEEE Congress on Evolutionary Computation (CEC 2002), pp. 1671–1676 (2002)
26. Mendes, R., Kennedy, J., Neves, J.: The fully informed particle swarm: simpler, maybe better. IEEE Trans. Evol. Comput. **8**(3), 204–210 (2004)
27. Ratnaweera, A., Halgamuge, S., Watson, H.: Self-organizing hierarchical particle swarm optimizer with time-varying acceleration coefficients. IEEE Trans. Evol. Comput. **8**(3), 240–255 (2004)
28. Liang, J., Suganthan, P.: Dynamic multi-swarm particle swarm optimizer. In: IEEE Conference on Swarm Intelligence Symposium (SIS 2005), pp. 124–129 (2005)

29. Liang, J., Qin, A., Suganthan, P., et al.: Comprehensive learning particle swarm optimizer for global optimization of multimodal functions. IEEE Trans. Evol. Comput. **10**(3), 281–295 (2006)
30. Haklı, H., Uğuz, H.: A novel particle swarm optimization algorithm with Levy flight. Appl. Soft Comput. **23**, 333–345 (2014)
31. Ho, S., Lin, H., Liauh, W., et al.: OPSO: Orthogonal particle swarm optimization and its application to task assignment problems. IEEE Trans. Syst. Man Cybern. A Syst. Hum. **38**(2), 288–298 (2008)

A Novel Feature Selection Algorithm Based on Aquila Optimizer for COVID-19 Classification

Ling Li[1], Jeng-Shyang Pan[1,2], Zhongjie Zhuang[1],
and Shu-Chuan Chu[1,3(✉)]

[1] College of Computer Science and Engineering, Shandong University of Science
and Technology, Qingdao 266590, China
scchu0803@gmail.com
[2] Department of Information Management, Chaoyang University of Technology,
Taichung, Taiwan
[3] College of Science and Engineering, Flinders University, 1284 South Road,
Clovelly Park, SA 5042, Australia

Abstract. To this day, the prevention of coronavirus disease is still an arduous battle. Medical imaging technology has played an important role in the fight against the epidemic. This paper is to perform feature selection on the CT image feature sets used for COVID-19 detection to improve the speed and accuracy of detection. In this work, the population-based intelligent optimization algorithm Aquila optimizer is used for feature selection. This feature selection method uses an S-shaped transfer function to process continuous values and convert them into binary form. And when the performance of the updated solution is not good, a new mutation strategy is proposed to enhance the convergence effect of the solution. Through the verification of two CT image sets, the experimental results show that the use of the S-shaped transfer function and the proposed mutation strategy can effectively improve the effect of feature selection. The prediction accuracy of the features selected by this method on the two open datasets is 99.67% and 99.28%, respectively.

Keywords: COVID-19 · Aquila optimizer · Feature selection · CT image

1 Introduction

Since the discovery of Severe Acute Respiratory Syndrome coronavirus 2 (SARS-CoV-2) in 2019, it has caused an unprecedented situation worldwide. As of December 17, 2021, there have been 271,963,258 confirmed cases of coronavirus disease (COVID-19) worldwide, including 5,331,019 deaths [1]. Thousands of people are infected with this dangerous virus every day. Although many people have been vaccinated, the coronavirus continues to mutate. By December 18th, 2021, a new variety of SARS-CoV-2, Omicron, had been found in 89 countries [2].

© IFIP International Federation for Information Processing 2022
Published by Springer Nature Switzerland AG 2022
Z. Shi et al. (Eds.): IIP 2022, IFIP AICT 643, pp. 30–41, 2022.
https://doi.org/10.1007/978-3-031-03948-5_3

Preventing and diagnosing COVID-19 remains a daunting task. For the diagnosis of coronavirus, Reverse Transcription Polymerase Chain Reaction (RT-PCR) is the preferred method for detecting COVID-19, but false negatives will still occur. People infected with the virus may even need to undergo multiple tests before they can be detected. According to [3], chest X-ray and CT scan images may play an important role in accurately diagnosing this disease. Some radiologists recommend using chest X-ray images to diagnose COVID-19 cases. Although nucleic acid testing has become the benchmark for the diagnosis of coronavirus infections, medical imaging diagnosis continues to play an important role.

Deep learning is considered to be one of the best methods for processing medical images, but the network architecture of deep learning is often more suitable for large data sets. On the other hand, some of the features extracted through deep learning can be too sufficient, with redundant and irrelevant features, which can lead to poor classification accuracy. The purpose of the feature selection is to select the most appropriate portion of the many original features to improve the accuracy of the classification. At the same time, removing irrelevant features can also reduce the dimension of the data and the cost of model training.

Metaheuristic algorithms [4] have shown good performance in many fields [5, 6] and have been widely applied to feature selection problems in recent years [7–11]. Aquila Optimizer (AO) [12] is a newly proposed metaheuristic algorithm for solving continuous optimization problems. AO simulates the four behaviors of Aquila hunting to search for the optimal solution. It has two different exploration strategies and two exploitation strategies, which can efficiently search in space. AO algorithm has been successfully used for feature selection. Abd Elaziz et al. [13] used MoblieNetV3 [14] to extract image features and used AO to perform feature selection on the extracted features. However, this method only uses 0.5 as thresholds to convert continuous values into binary form. Once the solution value is 0, it is easy to fall into the local optimum. Therefore, an improved binary version of the AO algorithm is proposed for feature selection in this paper. And a new mutation strategy is used to speed up the convergence when the update method does not work well. The main work of this paper is listed as follows.

(1) Analyze the change of the solution value in the binary AO algorithm. Before using the update operator, change the 0 of the solution value to -1 to prevent the effect of the update operator from weakening.
(2) An S-shaped transfer function is introduced to convert continuous values into binary form, instead of the previous conversion method of a fixed threshold.
(3) A new mutation strategy is used when the solution performance is not good.

The rest of this paper will be organized as follows: Sect. 2 briefly introduces AO algorithm and the fitness function for feature selection. In Sect. 3, a new binary version AO algorithm is proposed, and a new mutation strategy is proposed. In Sect. 4, the comparative results of the experiments are given, and the results are analyzed. Corresponding conclusions are drawn in Sect. 5.

2   Related Work

2.1   Aquila Optimizer (AO)

AO algorithm is a newly proposed population-based optimization [15–18] method, which is inspired by the prey behavior of Aquila in nature. The mathematical model of AO is as follows.

The first step is the process of expanded exploration, which mathematical formula is as follows.

$$X_i^{t+1} = X_{best} \times (1 - \frac{t}{T}) + X_M^t - X_{best} * rand \tag{1}$$

$$X_M^t = \frac{1}{N} \sum_{i=1}^{N} X_i^t \tag{2}$$

where T represents the total number of iterations, and t represents the current number of iterations. X_{best} is the best solution in the previous t iterations. X_M^t represents the average value of the solutions in the current solution space. The calculation formula is shown in Eq. (2). $rand$ represents a random number between 0 and 1. N is the number of agents in the population.

The second step is narrowed exploration. In this process, levy flight is used to perturb X_{best}. The author of the AO algorithm calls it a contour flight with a short glide attack. This strategy is mathematically formulated as follows.

$$X_i^{t+1} = X_{best} \times Levy(D) + X_R^t + (y - x) * rand \tag{3}$$

where X_R represents a randomly selected agent in the population. D is the dimension space. $Levy(D)$ is calculated using Eqs. (4–5). y and x represent the search of the spiral shape, which are calculated using the Eqs. (6–7).

$$Levy(D) = s \times \frac{\mu \times \sigma}{|v|^{\frac{1}{\beta}}} \tag{4}$$

$$\sigma = \left(\frac{\Gamma(1 + \beta) \times sin(\frac{\pi \beta}{2})}{\Gamma(\frac{1+\beta}{2}) \times \beta \times 2^{\frac{\beta-1}{2}}} \right) \tag{5}$$

where $s = 0.01$ and $\beta = 1.5$. μ and v are random numbers between 0 and 1.

$$y = r \times cos(\theta), \quad x = r \times sin(\theta) \tag{6}$$

$$r = r_1 + U + D_1, \quad \theta = -\omega \times D_1 + \theta_1, \quad \theta_1 = \frac{3 \times \pi}{2} \tag{7}$$

where $U = 0.00565$ and $\omega = 0.005$. r_1 is a random number between 1 and 20. D_1 is an integer that gradually increases from 1 to D.

The third step is extended exploitation. In this process, Aquila uses the selected target area to approach the prey and attack. This method is mathematically shown in Eq. (8).

$$X_i^{t+1} = (X_{best} - X_M^t) \times \alpha - rand \times ((UB - LB) \times rand + LB) \times \delta \tag{8}$$

where α and δ are the adjustment parameters of the exploitation process, which are fixed at 0.1. UB and LB respectively represent the upper and lower bounds of a given problem.

The fourth step is narrowed exploitation. When Aquila approaches its prey, it attacks the target based on its random movement. It is mathematically formulated as follows.

$$X_i^{t+1} = QF \times X_{best} - G_1 \times X_i^t \times rand - G_2 \times Levy(D) + rand \times G_1 \qquad (9)$$

where QF represents the value of the quality function of the t-th iteration, and its definition is shown in Eq. (10).

$$QF = t^{\frac{2 \times rand - 1}{(1-T)^2}} \qquad (10)$$

$$G_1 = 2 \times rand - 1, \quad G_2 = 2 \times (1 - \frac{t}{T}) \qquad (11)$$

where G_1 in Eq. (9) represents various actions of AO during the tracking of the best solution. It is calculated by Eq. (11). G_2 represents a factor decreasing from 2 to 0.

2.2 Fitness Function

For the feature selection problem, the two elements of classification error and the number of selected features are generally considered comprehensively and strive to achieve the goal of fewer features selected and high classification accuracy. In this work, the objective function shown below is used.

$$fitness = \alpha * \gamma_R(D) + \beta * \frac{|S|}{|D|} \qquad (12)$$

where $|S|$ represents the number of features selected, $|D|$ represents the number of features in the original dataset. $\gamma_R(D)$ is the error rate of the classifier. In this work, Support Vector Machine (SVM) [19] is used as the classifier. α and β are weight coefficients, generally speaking, $\alpha = 0.99$, $\beta = 0.01$ [8,20].

3 A New Improved Binary Aquila Optimizer

3.1 Analysis and Advancement for Binary Aquila Optimizer

Abd Elaziz et al. [13] proposed a binary version of the AO algorithm for feature selection. Its method of converting continuous values into binary form is shown in Eq. (13).

$$BX_{ij} = \begin{cases} 1, & X_{ij} > 0.5 \\ 0, & X_{ij} \leq 0.5. \end{cases} \qquad (13)$$

where i is the i-th agent in the population, and j represents the j-th dimension. This method can quickly convert continuous values into binary form, but when

BX_{ij} is 0, the effect of the update method shown in Eqs. (1–11) will be greatly reduced. The two pie charts in Fig. 1 show the changes in subsequent solutions when the solution value is 0 and 1, respectively. It can be found that when $BX_{ij} = 0$, after the subsequent update process, the agent in the population has a probability of more than 87% that it will not change its value, and its value will always be 0. The probability of the agent changing the value is only 12.36%. When $BX_{ij} = 1$, there is a 56.15% probability that the agent will not change its value, and a 43.85% probability that it will change its value.

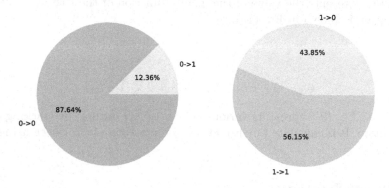

Fig. 1. The probability of change in solution value

In consideration of the above situation, when the position is updated using Eqs. (1–11), the solution value is changed from 0 to -1. And the S-shaped transfer function [20, 21] shown in Eqs. (14–15) is used to convert continuous values into binary form. Figure 2 shows the probability of whether the subsequent solution changes after using the S-shaped transfer function and changing the solution value from 0 to −1. It can be seen that after using these two methods, when $X_{ij} = 0$, the probability of the individual changing the value is increased by 4.06% than before. When $X_{ij} = 1$, the probability of the individual changing the value is 18.12% higher than before.

$$S(x) = \frac{1}{1 + e^{-10(x-0.5)}} \qquad (14)$$

$$X_{ij} = \begin{cases} 1, & S(X_{ij}) \geq rand \\ 0, & S(X_{ij}) < rand \end{cases} \qquad (15)$$

3.2   A New Mutation Strategy for Binary Aquila Optimizer

A new binary mutation strategy to improve the convergence of the algorithm is proposed in this section when the update effect is not good. Figure 3 shows

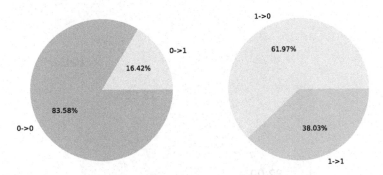

Fig. 2. The probability of the solution value changing after using the method described in Sect. 3.1

the comparison of fitness value between the updated solution and the previous solution during the first 20 iterations. It can be found that 82% of the updated solutions are worse than the previous solution, and only 18% of the solutions have a better effect after the update. In this case, a mutation strategy is proposed. This strategy is used when the updated solution does not converge well. It is mathematically formulated as follows.

$$XA = ((1 - X_{worst}) \cup X_{best}) + X_i^t \tag{16}$$

$$X_{ij}^{t+1} = \begin{cases} 1, & XA_j * 0.5 \geq rand \\ 0, & XA_j * 0.5 < rand \end{cases} \tag{17}$$

where $\cup$ represents the bitwise OR operation, and j represents the jth dimension in a solution. $rand$ is a random number between 0 and 1. X_{worst} is the worst-performing individual in the population. The mutation strategy uses the idea of the opposition-based learning [22] and considers the opposite position of X_{worst}. Since the effect of X_i^t itself is better than that after the update, the position of X_i^t also is considered. Table 1 shows the influence of X_{wost}, X_{best}, and X_i^t on the position of the individual in the next iteration.

4 Experimental Results

4.1 Dataset Description

This section introduces the two datasets used in the work, both of which are CT image sets for COVID-19. The open-source Densnet121 [23] network is used to extract features from images. After extracting image features from each dataset, we keep the same data split, and these split data are fed to the feature selection process. The two CT image sets used are described in detail below. Figure 4(a) and (b) show sample images from Dataset1 and Dataset2, respectively.

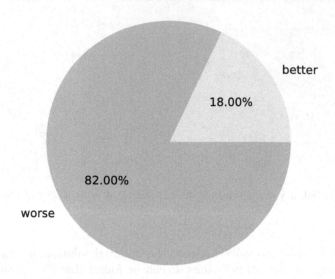

Fig. 3. The result of comparing the updated solution with the previous solution in terms of fitness

Table 1. The influence of X_{worst}, X_{best}, X_i^t on X_i^{t+1}

X_{worst}	X_{best}	$(1 - X_{worst}) \cup X_{best}$	X_i^t	X_i^{t+1}
0	0	1	0	0 or 1
0	1	1	0	0 or 1
1	0	0	0	0
1	1	1	0	0 or 1
0	0	1	1	1
0	1	1	1	1
1	0	0	1	0 or 1
1	1	1	1	1

(1) Dataset1: COVID-CT dataset [24]: The images in this database are collected from hospitalized patients in Sao Paulo, Brazil. It contains 349 CT images of COVID-19 patients and 463 CT images of uninfected persons.

(2) Dataset2: SARS-CoV-2 CT image dataset [25]: This dataset is an open-source dataset, containing 1252 (COVID-19) positive CT images and 1230 CT images of uninfected patients, a total of 2482 CT images. These data are collected from real patients at the Sao Paulo Hospital in Brazil.

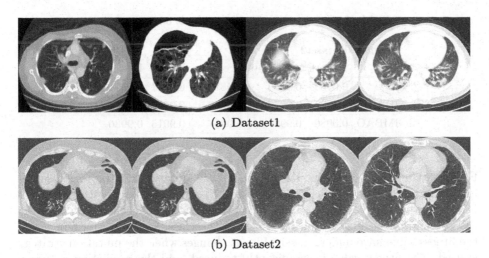

(a) Dataset1

(b) Dataset2

Fig. 4. Sample images taken from two datasets

4.2 Experiments Setting

For the convenience of representation, the AO algorithm using the methods described in Sect. 3.1 is called IBAO. When it adds the mutation strategy described in Sect. 3.2, it is called IMBAO. They perform 90 iterations on each dataset, running 15 times independently. Each population has 40 agents.

4.3 Comparison of the Proposed Algorithms with Existing AO

In this section, the proposed IBAO and IMBAO are compared to the existing AO algorithm [13]. Tables 2 and 3 provide detailed performance metrics of the three feature selection methods applied to COVID-19 prediction on two image sets.

From the comparison result of IBAO and AO in Table 2 that the use of the S-shaped transfer function and the conversion of the solution value from 0 to −1 slightly improve the fitness value. It is worth noting that the smaller the fitness value, the better the feature selection method. It can be seen from Table 3 that IBAO is better than AO in four aspects: Fitness, Accuracy, Precision, and

Table 2. Comparison of three methods on Dataset1

Method	Dataset1				
	Fitness	Accuracy	Precision	Recall	F1-score
AO	0.0369	0.9667	0.9595	0.9726	0.9660
IBAO	0.0336	0.9667	0.9474	0.9863	0.9664
IMBAO	0.0275	0.9733	0.9726	0.9726	0.9726

Table 3. Comparison of three methods on Dataset2

Method	Dataset2				
	Fitness	Accuracy	Precision	Recall	F1-score
AO	0.0184	0.9859	0.9872	0.9831	0.9851
IBAO	0.0129	0.9879	0.9957	0.9788	0.9872
IMBAO	0.0080	0.9939	0.9957	0.9915	0.9936

F1-score. On the two datasets, IMBAO using the mutation strategy has a significant improvement in Fitness, Accuracy, and F1-score compared with IBAO. On Dateset2, the accuracy of the IMBAO method has even reached 0.9939. From the comparison results, it can be seen that the classification performance and the fitness value have undergone significant changes when the mutation strategy is used. The fitness value is significantly reduced, and the prediction accuracy and other performance are significantly improved. The comparison results prove the effectiveness of the proposed methods.

4.4 Comparison of the Proposed Method with Other Optimization Algorithms

In this section, IMBAO is compared with four feature selection methods based on optimization algorithm, namely DA [26], SSA [27], GWO [20] and SMA [7]. Tables 4 and 5 show the comparison results of five feature selection methods on the two datasets.

Table 4. Comparison of five algorithms on Dataset1

Method	Dataset1				
	Fitness	Accuracy	Precision	Recall	F1-score
IMBAO	0.0050	0.9967	1.0000	0.9925	0.9962
DA	0.0277	0.9783	0.9674	0.9851	0.9760
SSA	0.0219	0.9833	0.9778	0.9851	0.9814
GWO	0.0250	0.9817	0.9814	0.9776	0.9795
SMA	0.0302	0.9400	0.9204	0.9478	0.9338

It can be seen from Tables 4 and 5 that the proposed method IMBAO performs best on both datasets. In terms of Fitness, IMBAO is far superior to other methods. On Dataset1, according to Fitness, the rankings are IMBAO, SSA, GWO, DA, SMA. But on Dataset2, the rank according to the Fitness is IMBAO, DA, SSA, SMA, GWO. In terms of Accuracy, IMBAO has the best accuracy, and SMA has the worst accuracy on Dataset1. This is consistent with

Table 5. Comparison of five algorithms on Dataset2

Method	Dataset2				
	Fitness	Accuracy	Precision	Recall	F1-score
IMBAO	0.0092	0.9928	0.9917	0.9947	0.9931
DA	0.0178	0.9883	0.9856	0.9924	0.9890
SSA	0.0183	0.9871	0.9834	0.9924	0.9890
GWO	0.0197	0.9867	0.9819	0.9931	0.9875
SMA	0.0192	0.9839	0.9803	0.9893	0.9848

the situation on Dataset2. In terms of Precision, IMBAO performed the best on the two datasets, and the precision even reached 1.0 on Dataset1. IMBAO is also the best on the two evaluation indicators of Recall and F1-score. The comparison results powerfully illustrate the effectiveness of IMBAO in feature selection.

5 Conclusion

The analysis of medical images plays an important role in the diagnosis and treatment of diseases. Therefore, this paper proposes a feature selection method to improve the effectiveness of using CT images to predict COVID-19. This method uses AO algorithm as the optimizer and finds the best solution from 2^n solutions. S-shaped transfer function and a new mutation strategy proposed are used. And to prevent the effect of the update operator of the algorithm from decreasing, the solution value of 0 is changed to -1. Extensive evaluation experiments are performed on two CT image datasets, and the proposed method is compared with various feature selection methods. Experiments prove that the proposed method not only effectively improves the effect of AO algorithm for feature selection, but also has superior results compared with SMA, SSA, GWO, and other methods.

Acknowledgements. This work is supported by the National Natural Science Foundations of China (No. 61872085).

References

1. From WHO Coronavirus (COVID-19) Dashboard. https://covid19.who.int/
2. From the Report of CBS NEWS. https://www.cbsnews.com/news/omicron-89-countries-cases-doubling-fast-world-health-organization/
3. Singh, D., Kumar, V., Kaur, M., et al.: Classification of COVID-19 patients from chest CT images using multi-objective differential evolution-based convolutional neural networks. Eur. J. Clin. Microbiol. Infect. Dis. **39**(7), 1379–1389 (2020). https://doi.org/10.1007/s10096-020-03901-z

4. Wang, G.G., Tan, Y.: Improving metaheuristic algorithms with information feedback models. IEEE Trans. Cybern. **49**(2), 542–555 (2017). https://doi.org/10.1109/TCYB.2017.2780274

5. Xu, X.W., Pan, T.S., Song, P.C., Hu, C.C., Chu, S.C.: Multi-cluster based equilibrium optimizer algorithm with compact approach for power system network. J. Netw. Intell. **6**(1), 117–142 (2021)

6. Wu, J., Xu, M., Liu, F.F., Huang, M., Ma, L., Lu, Z.M.: Solar wireless sensor network routing algorithm based on multi-objective particle swarm optimization. J. Inf. Hiding Multim. Signal Process. **12**(1), 1–11 (2021)

7. Abdel-Basset, M., Mohamed, R., Chakrabortty, R.K., Ryan, M.J., Mirjalili, S.: An efficient binary slime mould algorithm integrated with a novel attacking-feeding strategy for feature selection. Comput. Indust. Eng. **153**, 107078 (2021). https://doi.org/10.1016/j.cie.2020.107078

8. Hu, P., Pan, J.S., Chu, S.C.: Improved binary grey wolf optimizer and its application for feature selection. Knowl. Based Syst. **195**, 105746 (2020). https://doi.org/10.1016/j.knosys.2020.105746

9. Zhang, Y., Gong, D.W., Gao, X.Z., Tian, T., Sun, X.Y.: Binary differential evolution with self-learning for multi-objective feature selection. Inf. Sci. **507**, 67–85 (2020). https://doi.org/10.1016/j.ins.2019.08.040

10. Pan, J.S., Tian, A.Q., Chu, S.C., Li, J.B.: Improved binary pigeon-inspired optimization and its application for feature selection. Appl. Intell. 1–19 (2021). https://doi.org/10.1007/s10489-021-02302-9

11. Du, Z.-G., Pan, T.-S., Pan, J.-S., Chu, S.-C.: QUasi-Affine TRansformation evolutionary algorithm for feature selection. In: Wu, T.-Y., Ni, S., Chu, S.-C., Chen, C.-H., Favorskaya, M. (eds.) Advances in Smart Vehicular Technology, Transportation, Communication and Applications. SIST, vol. 250, pp. 147–156. Springer, Singapore (2022). https://doi.org/10.1007/978-981-16-4039-1_14

12. Abualigah, L., Yousri, D., Abd Elaziz, M., Ewees, A.A., Al-qaness, M.A., Gandomi, A.H.: Aquila optimizer: a novel meta-heuristic optimization algorithm. Comput. Indust. Eng. **157**, 107250 (2021). https://doi.org/10.1016/j.cie.2021.107250

13. Abd Elaziz, M., Dahou, A., Alsaleh, N.A., Elsheikh, A.H., Saba, A.I., Ahmadein, M.: Boosting covid-19 image classification using Mobilenetv3 and aquila optimizer algorithm. Entropy **23**(11) (2021). https://doi.org/10.3390/e23111383

14. Howard, A., et al.: Searching for Mobilenetv3. In: Proceedings of the IEEE/CVF International Conference on Computer Vision, pp. 1314–1324 (2019)

15. Pan, J.S., Tsai, P.W., Liao, Y.B.: Fish migration optimization based on the fishy biology. In: 2010 Fourth International Conference on Genetic and Evolutionary Computing, pp. 783–786. IEEE (2010)

16. Chu, S.-C., Tsai, P.-W., Pan, J.-S.: Cat swarm optimization. In: Yang, Q., Webb, G. (eds.) PRICAI 2006. LNCS (LNAI), vol. 4099, pp. 854–858. Springer, Heidelberg (2006). https://doi.org/10.1007/978-3-540-36668-3_94

17. Pan, J.S., Song, P.C., Pan, C.A., Abraham, A.: The phasmatodea population evolution algorithm and its application in 5G heterogeneous network downlink power allocation problem. J. Internet Technol. **22**(6), 1199–1213 (2021)

18. Pan, J.-S., Meng, Z., Xu, H., Li, X.: QUasi-Affine TRansformation Evolution (QUATRE) algorithm: a new simple and accurate structure for global optimization. In: Fujita, H., Ali, M., Selamat, A., Sasaki, J., Kurematsu, M. (eds.) IEA/AIE 2016. LNCS (LNAI), vol. 9799, pp. 657–667. Springer, Cham (2016). https://doi.org/10.1007/978-3-319-42007-3_57

19. Cortes, C., Vapnik, V.: Support-vector networks. Mach. Learn. **20**(3), 273–297 (1995). https://doi.org/10.1007/BF00994018

20. Emary, E., Zawbaa, H.M., Hassanien, A.E.: Binary grey wolf optimization approaches for feature selection. Neurocomputing **172**, 371–381 (2016). https://doi.org/10.1016/j.neucom.2015.06.083
21. Li, L., Pan, T.S., Sun, X.X., Chu, S.C., Pan, J.S.: A novel binary slime mould algorithm with au strategy for cognitive radio spectrum allocation. Int. J. Comput. Intell. Syst. **14**(1), 1–18 (2021). https://doi.org/10.1007/s44196-021-00005-0
22. Tizhoosh, H.R.: Opposition-based learning: a new scheme for machine intelligence. In: International Conference on Computational Intelligence for Modelling, Control and Automation and International Conference on Intelligent Agents, Web Technologies and Internet Commerce (CIMCA-IAWTIC 2006), vol. 1, pp. 695–701. IEEE (2005). https://doi.org/10.1109/CIMCA.2005.1631345
23. Maftouni, M., Law, A.C.C., Shen, B., Grado, Z.J.K., Zhou, Y., Yazdi, N.A.: A robust ensemble-deep learning model for COVID-19 diagnosis based on an integrated CT scan images database. In: Proceedings of the IIE Annual Conference, pp. 632–637. Institute of Industrial and Systems Engineers (IISE) (2021)
24. Yang, X., He, X., Zhao, J., Zhang, Y., Zhang, S., Xie, P.: COVID-CT-dataset: a CT scan dataset about COVID-19 (2020)
25. Angelov, P., Almeida Soares, E.: SARS-CoV-2 CT-scan dataset: a large dataset of real patients CT scans for SARS-CoV-2 identification. MedRxiv (2020). https://www.kaggle.com/plameneduardo/sarscov2-ctscan-dataset
26. Sen, S., Saha, S., Chatterjee, S., Mirjalili, S., Sarkar, R.: A bi-stage feature selection approach for COVID-19 prediction using chest CT images. Appl. Intell. 1–16 (2021). https://doi.org/10.1007/s10489-021-02292-8
27. Faris, H., et al.: An efficient binary salp swarm algorithm with crossover scheme for feature selection problems. Knowl. Based Syst. **154**, 43–67 (2018). https://doi.org/10.1016/j.knosys.2018.05.009

Inductive Light Graph Convolution Network for Text Classification Based on Word-Label Graph

Jinze Shi[1], Xiaoming Wu[1(✉)], Xiangzhi Liu[1], Wenpeng Lu[2], and Shu Li[1]

[1] Shandong Computer Science Center (National Supercomputer Center in Jinan),
Qilu University of Technology (Shandong Academy of Sciences),
Jinan, Shandong, China
wuxm@sdas.org, liuxzh@sdas.org
[2] Qilu University of Technology (Shandong Academy of Sciences),
Jinan, Shandong, China
lwp@qlu.edu.cn

Abstract. Nowadays, Graph Convolution Networks (GCNs) have flourished in the field of text classification, such as Text Graph Convolution Network (TextGCN). But good performance of those methods is based on building a graph whose nodes consist of an entire corpus, making their models transductive. Meanwhile rich label information has not been utilized in the graph structure. In this paper, we propose a new model named Inductive Light Graph Convolution Networks (ILGCN) with a new construction of graph. This approach uses labels and words to build the graph which removes the dependence between an individual text and entire corpus, and let ILGCN inductive. Besides, we simplify the model structure and only remain the neighborhood aggregation, which is the most important part of GCNs. Experiments on multiple benchmark show that our model outperforms existing state-of-the-art models on several text classification datasets.

Keywords: Text classification · Graph convolution networks · Word-label graph · Inductive light graph convolution network

1 Introduction

Text classification is one of the classic problems of Natural Language Processing (NLP), and there are many applications including but not limited to SPAM detection [1], Computational phenotyping [2], and so on. The most critical intermediate step is the text representation learning. Traditional methods of text representation are mostly hand-made, such as Term Frequency - Inverse Document Frequency (TF-IDF) [3], bag-of-words [4] and n-grams [5]. With the development of deep learning methods, models such as convolutional neural networks (CNN) [6] and recurrent neural networks (RNN) [7,8] have been applied to the text representation learning and achieved remarkable results. In recent years,

© IFIP International Federation for Information Processing 2022
Published by Springer Nature Switzerland AG 2022
Z. Shi et al. (Eds.): IIP 2022, IFIP AICT 643, pp. 42–55, 2022.
https://doi.org/10.1007/978-3-031-03948-5_4

GNN has been gradually explored by researchers due to its effectiveness in capturing global and associated data structure [9–11], and has been applied in the field of text classification [12–15] and achieved state-of-the-art results in several text classification datasets. However, many GNN-based models are transductive. They use an entire corpus to construct a graph, including unlabeled texts that need to be predicted and causing the following practical problems:

1. Transductive model is not conducive to large-scale text classification and time-demanding application. Because the model should be retrained again at each time a new text coming in, due to using the whole corpus as nodes.
2. It's not conducive to online test, since the graph structure and model parameters depend on the complete corpus including all the texts whether its labeled or not, and it cannot be modified after training.
3. Rich label information is not utilized in the graph structure, but only used as targets of training.

To solve the above drawbacks, we proposed a new graph neural network for text classification in this paper, called Inductive LightGCN and a new way to construct graph using labels and nodes. Instead of building the whole corpus as a graph, we use words of all texts and corresponding labels to build a graph, making the model inductive and utilizing information carried by labels. Meanwhile, this graph significantly reduces the memory requirements of the graph. Inspired by LightGCN [16], we simplified the original GCN model structure by eliminating nonlinear functions and weight matrices within the layers. Through the empirical assessment on three text classification benchmark datasets, our ILGCN demonstrated comparable results to state-of-the-art models: TextGCN [13], Simplifying Graph Convolutional Networks (SGC) [14] and Simple Spectral Graph Convolution (SSGC) [15], even achieved the SOTA results in two datasets.

To summarize, this work makes the following main contributions:

- We prove that the feature transformation and nonlinear activation impose negative effects on TextGCN.
- We propose a inductive model, ILGCN, which is largely simplified and based on a new construction of graph.
- Our model achieves state-of-the-art results in several text classification datasets and rationality of ILGCN is shown by means of in-depth analyses.

2   Preliminaries

We will introduce TextGCN. Then the ablation experiments, which prove the problems of nonlinear activation and feature transformation in TextGCN, are performed, which will prove the rationality of combining LightGCN's ideas into ours model.

Table 1. Performance of TextGCN and its variants.

	Accuracy	
	Ohsumed	R52
TextGCN	0.685	0.940
TextGCN-n	0.686	0.945
TextGCN-f	0.680	0.934
TextGCN-fn	0.680	0.934
TextGCN-fn-l2	0.685	0.940

2.1 TextGCN Brief

In the first step, TextGCN [13] simply sets feature matrix $X = I$ as an identity matrix, initialize the input variable to a simple identity matrix. Using the Pointwise Mutual Information (PMI) which consisted of word occurrence in texts, as text-word edges and word co-occurrence in the whole corpus as the edge weights between words. Using TF-IDF of the words in the texts as the weight between the words and the texts. The definition of elements in the adjacency matrix:

$$A_{ij} = \begin{cases} \text{PMI}(i,j) & \text{i, j are words, PMI } (i,j) > 0 \\ \text{TF-IDF}_{ij} & \text{i is text, j is word} \\ 1 & i = j \\ 0 & \text{otherwise} \end{cases} \tag{1}$$

The PMI value of a word pair i, j is defined as:

$$\text{PMI}(i,j) = log\frac{p(i,j)}{p(i)p(j)} \tag{2}$$

$$p(i,j) = \frac{\#W(i,j)}{\#W} \tag{3}$$

$$p(i) = \frac{\#W(i)}{\#W} \tag{4}$$

where $\#W(i)$ is the number of sliding windows in which word i appears; $\#W(i,j)$ is the number of pair i,j appear in the same window; and $\#W$ is the total number of sliding windows in the whole corpus. TextGCN uses a simple two layers GCN model and is defined as:

$$Y = \text{softmax}(\tilde{A}\text{ReLU}(\tilde{A}XW_0)W_1) \tag{5}$$

where $\tilde{A} = D^{-\frac{1}{2}}AD^{-\frac{1}{2}}$ is the normalized symmetric adjacency matrix; $W_0 \in \mathbb{R}^{(n+m) \times d_0}$ and $W_1 \in \mathbb{R}^{d_1 \times d_0}$ respectively denote the trainable feature matrix of two layers; ReLU$(\cdot)$ is the nonlinear activation; and softmax$(\cdot)$ is the classifier function. The model structure of TextGCN completely follows GCN [9], including nonlinear activation function and feature transformation matrix.

2.2 Empirical Explorations on TextGCN

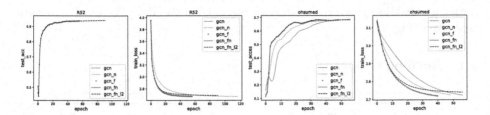

Fig. 1. Training curves (training loss and testing accuracy) of TextGCN and its four simplified variants.

We conduct ablation studies on TextGCN to test the effectiveness of nonlinear activation and feature transformation. By using data and evaluation protocol same as TextGCN. We implement four variants of TextGCN:

- TextGCN-n, which removes the nonlinear activation.
- TextGCN-f, which removes the first layer's feature transformation W_0
- TextGCN-fn, which removes W_0 and he nonlinear activation.
- TextGCN-fn-l2, which removes the nonlinear activation and W_0, but L_2 regularization for W_1 is also added.

Results are shown in Table 1. As can be seen that when nonlinear is removed (i.e., TextGCN-n), the performance on two different datasets is improved. When the feature transformation of the first layer is removed (i.e., TextGCN-f, TextGCN-fn), the performance decreased compared with the original model on the two datasets, but better than the model with L_2 regularization(i.e., TextGCN-fn-l2). Based on these observations, we can draw the following conclusions:

1. Adding nonlinear activation in TextGCN have negative effects, because TextGCN-n has improved the effect in two corpora.
2. Removing W_0 in TextGCN reduces the effect compared with TextGCN. In this case, whether nonlinear activation was removed or not has no significant effect on the results.
3. After removing the W_0, and adding the regularization of the second layer W_1, effect of TextGCN-fn has been improved, indicating that the reason of the lower performance of TextGCN-fn is the overfitting of W_1 to the training set, so removing feature transformation is feasible.

We plot the changes of training loss and testing accuracy as Fig. 1 for deep insights. And the empirical experiments show that TextGCN's nonlinear activation and feature transformation will increase the difficulty of training, and it is necessary to suppress the overfitting of feature transformation to the training set by dropout or L_2 regularization, otherwise the performance will become worse. Based on the above viewpoints, we propose the ILGCN.

3   Method

In this section we will describe our method in detail. First, describing how to construct a text-label graph for a whole corpus. Then the ILGCN model structure is showed (Fig. 2).

3.1   Building Graph

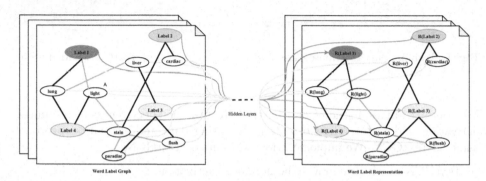

Fig. 2. Schematic layout of graph convolution part of ILGCN. Including 4 label nodes and some word nodes. Black bold edges are word-label edges and gray edges are word-word edges. $R(x)$ means the representation (embedding) of x. Different labels are filled with different colors. (Color figure online)

We normally define an undirected graph as $G = (V, E, A)$, nodes $W = [w_1, ..., w_m]$ and label nodes $L = [l_1, ..., l_n]$, which together constitute the node set $V = [v_1, ..., v_{m+n}]$. Each node v_i corresponds to a d-dimensional feature vector $x_i \in \mathbb{R}^d$ and $X \in \mathbb{R}^{(m+n) \times d}$, which represents feature matrix of all nodes. We set $X = I$, which is the same as TextGCN. And $A \in \mathbb{R}^{(n+m) \times (n+m)}$ is the symmetric adjacency matrix where A_{ij} represents the weight of edges between node v_i and v_j. We set $A_{ij} = 0$ if there is no edge between v_i and v_j; edge weight between two word nodes w_i and w_j is calculated by Point-wise Mutual Information (PMI); the edge weight between a word node w_i and a label node l_j is obtained by TF-IDF of the word in the label, in which term frequency is the number of times the word appears in the label, inverse label frequency is logarithmically scaled inverse fraction of the number of labels that contain the word. Finally, the weight between node i and node j is defined as:

$$A_{ij} = \begin{cases} \text{PMI}(i, j) & i, j \text{ are words, PMI}(i, j) > 0 \\ \text{TF-IDF}_{ij} & i \text{ is a label, } j \text{ is a word} \\ 0 & \text{otherwise} \end{cases} \quad (6)$$

The PMI value of a word pair i, j is the same as (2), (3), (4). The difference of A between ILGCN and TextGCN is that if we don't set $A_{ij} = 0$ not 1 when $i = j$, because with I as X, adding a node self-connection is equal to the weighted sum of the embeddings propagated at each layer of ILGCN. This is similar to LightGCN.

Compared with the previous methods for constructing the graph, our method can effectively reduce the number of nodes in the graph, especially when the size of the corpus is very large. This means that the word-label graph will consume less memory. Moreover, because the graph does not use the texts, it is more friendly to the new test data. Because the graph is only related to the words contained in the datasets, the model becomes a decoupled model.

3.2 ILGCN

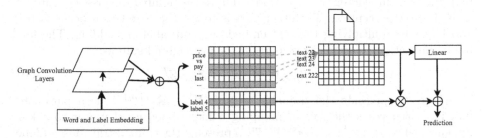

Fig. 3. Overall layout of ILGCN. The black bold arrows are representations of information transfer. The blue dashed lines represent the constructing process of text embeddings. (Color figure online)

After the construction of the graph is completed, the adjacency matrix A and the feature matrix X are taken as the input of the ILGCN model. In our proposed model, feature transformations W_0 and W_1 in the graph convolution part of TextGCN are abandoned as well as the activation function, and we only remain the adjacency matrix and trainable embedding matrix. The convolutional layer of ILGCN is defined as:

$$Z_i = \tilde{A} Z_{i-1} \tag{7}$$

where Z_i represents the embedding of the nodes trained at layer i. $\tilde{A}$ is defined in the same way as formula (5). $\tilde{A}$ restricts the growth of embedding and gathers information from different neighbor nodes to the central node with different weights. It should be noted that the $\tilde{A}$ here does not be added self-connection, so we adopt the weighted sum which plays the same role. Through weighted sum, ILGCN fuses the embedding representation extracted by graph convolution structure at each layer to represent the embedding of the trained words and the labels in the end. The formula is as follows:

$$Z = \sum_{l=0}^{L} \alpha_i Z_i \tag{8}$$

where Z_i represents the embedding matrix of the i-th layer, X is used as the initialization feature matrix of Z_0; α_i represents the weighting coefficient; L represents the total number of layers of the graph convolution model. Since different convolution layers extract different information and can reduce oversmoothing, we decided to use layer combination to get the final representations.

We can get text embeddings through multiplying trained word embeddings with $D \in \mathbb{R}^{t \times (n+m)}$ matrix without combine the texts in the graph. D represents text vector of unclassified texts; t represents the number of unclassified texts. The value of text i and word j in the matrix D is calculated by the ratio of number of word j in the text i and total number of words in the text i. We need to note that the pair of label and text is set as 0 and get the text embeddings as:

$$Z_{text} = DZ \tag{9}$$

Finally, the prediction part of the model is composed of two parts. One is to map the text embedding of $n + m$ dimension to the number of classes C through a single-layer perceptron. The other part is to get the correlation between text and labels by multiplying the text embedding and label embedding. The final model prediction consists of two parts through weighted sum as:

$$Y = \beta Z_{text} W + (1 - \beta) Z_{text} Z_{labels}^T \tag{10}$$

where β represents the trainable weight; $W \in \mathbb{R}^{(n+m) \times C}$ is a parameter matrix, which plays the role of mapping a high-dimensional vector to a low-dimensional vector; $Z_{labels}^T \in \mathbb{R}^{C \times (n+m)}$ represents the trained transpose of label embedding part of Z. The goal of training is to minimize the cross entropy loss between ground truths label and predicted labels:

$$Loss = - \sum_{d \in Y_D} \sum_{c=1}^{C} Y_{dc} (\beta \ln Z_{dc}^{linear} + (1 - \beta) \ln Z_{dc}^{label}) \tag{11}$$

where Y_D is the set of text indices that have labels; C is the dimension of the output features, which is equal to the number of classes; Y is the label indicator matrix; $Z^{linear} = Z_{text} W$ and Z_{labels} represents the prediction results of the two parts that make up the prediction results respectively. The overall ILGCN model is schematically illustrated in Fig. 3 (Table 2).

4   Experiment

4.1   Setting

4.1.1   Datasets

Table 2. Statistics of the datasets.

#Corpus	#Texts	#Train	#Test	#Word	#Nodes	#Classes	#Average length
R8	7674	5485	2189	7688	7696	8	65.72
R52	9100	6532	2568	8892	8944	52	69.82
Ohsumed	7400	3357	4043	14157	14180	23	135.82
MR	10662	5331	5331	18764	18766	2	20.39

For experiments, we utilize four widely used datasets including Ohsumed, R52 and R8 of Reuters 21578 and Movie Review (MR).

- R8 and R52[1] are two subsets of Reuters 21578 database. The R8 dataset has 8 different classifications and contains 7674 texts, including 5485 training texts and 2189 test texts. R52 has 52 different classifications, with a total of 9100 texts, which are divided into 6532 training texts and 2568 test texts. The data distributions of these two data sets are uneven.
- Ohsumed[2] is obtained from Medline Database, containing 7400 texts in 23 classifications, which are split into 3357 training texts and 4043 test texts.
- MR[3] is a binary corpus of film reviews, with a total of 10,662 film reviews as text data, divided equally into 5,331 text data in each of the two categories as what Tang, Qu, and Mei do.

In order to ensure the consistency of the experimental results, we used the same preprocess method as what TextGCN do for the four datasets. We first preprocessed all the datasets by cleaning and tokenizing texts as [6]. We then removed stop words defined in NLTK6 and low frequency words appearing less than 5 times for R8, R52 and Ohsumed.

4.1.2 Baselines

For baselines, we compared our proposed approach with the following three state-of-the-art models: TextGCN, SGC and SSGC. And the results of these baseline models are obtained directly from TextGCN [13], SGC [14], SSGC [15].

- TextGCN. Proposed by Yao et al. 2019, a graph-based text classification model, performing graph convolutions on a single large graph for whole corpus.
- SGC. Defined by Wu et al. 2019, a graph-based model, reducing the excess complexity through successively removing nonlinearities and collapsing weight matrices between consecutive layers.
- SSGC. Proposed by Zhu et al. 2021, a variant of GCN which uses a modified Markov Diffusion Kernel.

4.1.3 Hyperparameter Details

The layer combination coefficient $\hat{I}\pm_i$ is uniformly set as $1/(L+1)$ where K is number of layers. After testing K from 1 to 5, we choose K equal to 2 for 2-layer ILGCN and 4 for 3-layer ILGCN. $\hat{I}^2$ is initialized to 0.5 and can not be trained. Dropout ratio is set as 0.5 and Dropout layer is applied before the dense layer, because feature transformation is not used in the graph convolution layer, so it is not necessary to add dropout to control its overfitting. We used the Adam optimizer [18] and set the learning rate to 0.002 for MR and 0.02 for others, and randomly selected 10% of the training set as validation. As designed in TextGCN, we stop training if the validation loss value is less than the average value of the past ten epochs or reaches 200 epochs.

---

[1] https://www.cs.umb.edu/smimarog/textmining/datasets/.
[2] http://disi.unitn.it/moschitti/corpora.htm.
[3] https://github.com/mnqu/PTE/tree/master/data/mr.

4.2   Performance Comparison with Different Layers

Table 3. The comparison of accuracy between ILGCNs at different layers.

Layer	R8	R52	Ohsumed	MR
1 layers	96.7 ± 0.2	94.1 ± 0.2	63.2 ± 0.8	73.1 ± 3.5
2 layers	97.5 ± 0.1	94.1 ± 0.1	66.1 ± 0.6	77.4 ± 0.1
3 layers	97.5 ± 0.1	94.4 ± 0.1	66.3 ± 0.2	77.3 ± 0.3
4 layers	97.4 ± 0.1	94.3 ± 0.2	–	–

We study the influence of models with different layers and record the accuracy of ILGCN on all four datasets, so as to study the performance of ILGCN against oversmoothing. Due to hardware limitations, the results of the 4 layers model are only tested and compared on two datasets–R8 and R52. The experimental results are shown in Table 3.

We can see that the results of the 1-layer ILGCN are generally bad, with 1 to 3% lower accuracy compared to 2-layer ILGCN. Main reason is only using one layer ILGCN to aggregate node information is not enough. The word could not gather other words' information through the label connected directly, and label information is difficult to get information for two-hops through the adjacent words. Through the results of the three layers and four layers ILGCN, we can clearly see that increasing the number of layers does not have a significant impact on the results, indicating that ILGCN has a very strong ability to resist oversmoothing. But through the four-layer ILGCN, we can see a slight decrease of accuracy in the results. The intuitive explanation is that the two-layer model is enough to aggregate all the required information, while more layers would learn a lot of redundant and useless knowledge, which leads to a decrease in the accuracy of the model.

4.3   Experimental Results

Table 4. The comparison of results between ILGCN and the state-of-the-art models.

Model	R8	R52	Ohsumed	MR
TextGCN	97.0 ± 0.2	93.8 ± 0.2	68.2 ± 0.4	76.3 ± 0.3
SGC	97.2 ± 0.1	94.0 ± 0.2	**68.5 ± 0.3**	75.9 ± 0.3
SSGC	97.4 ± 0.1	**94.5 ± 0.2**	**68.5 ± 0.1**	76.7 ± 0.0
ILGCN	**97.5 + 0.1**	94.4 ± 0.1	66.3 ± 0.2	**77.4 ± 0.1**

Table 4 shows the experimental results of using identity matrix as input for our model compared with other models. We can see that our model outperforms SGC, TextGCN and SSGC on multiple datasets, which is showing the competitiveness of ILGCN in text corpora. It can be seen from Table 4, compared with other models, our model performs better in R8, R52 and MR datasets, but has some shortcomings in ohsumed. We believe that main reason our model can perform better than TextGCN in some datasets is that TextGCN contains some unnecessary linear or nonlinear transformations, which increase the training complexity of the model. Therefore, our model achieves better performance than TextGCN by removing some nonlinear activation and feature transformations. The key difference between our model and SGC or SSGC is the use of word-label graph which helps us to obtain additional information and accomplishes more accurate predictions. By analyzing the accuracy and F1-score of the model in the different categories of the ohsumed dataset, we believe that the main reason for the poor performance of ILGCN in the ohsumed data set is that there is considerable overlap between the words contained in the different categories.

4.4   Memory Consumption

As shown in the Table 5, our model has a significant advantage over TextGCN in memory consumption.

As discussed in Subsect. 3.1, we do not use texts as our nodes which constructing our graph, instead use the label. And in general, the number of labels is much smaller than the number of the texts. So comparing with TextGCN, which including all texts as its nodes, ours not only reduces a lot of memory consumption, but also solves the problems of transductive of using the entire corpus. The more texts in the corpus, the better our method can reflect the optimization in memory consumption.

Table 5. Comparison of memory consuming.

Datasets	R8	R52	Ohsumed	MR
TextGCN	1800M	2470M	3545M	6606M
Ours	452M	610M	1534M	2687M

4.5   Ablation Study

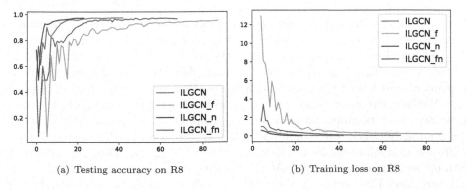

(a) Testing accuracy on R8   (b) Training loss on R8

Fig. 4. Training curves (training loss and testing accuracy) of ILGCN and its three variants.

We perform ablation studies on R8 dataset to further analyze the effectiveness of removing feature transformation and nonlinear activation in ILGCN. Table 6 shows the results and Fig. 4 shows the training curves of ILGCN and its three variants. Since loss values fluctuates sharply in some models at the beginning, we set learning rate of ILGCN-f as 0.07 and others as 0.02, then keep other hyper-parameters same. Figure 4 shows the results after the fourth epoch.

In ILGCN-f, we add a feature transformation matrix at second layer. As shown in Table 6, ILGCN-f performs much worse than ILGCN, which demonstrates the effectiveness of removing it. In our opinion, the main reason is that feature transformation matrix increases the difficulty of training process.

Table 6. Performance of ILGCN and its variants on R8.

Mode	ILGCN	ILGCN-f	ILGCN-n	ILGCN-fn
Accuracy	97.5 + 0.1	96.2 ± 0.4	97.2 ± 0.1	96.8 ± 0.2

In ILGCN-n, we add a nonlinear activation function at first layer which imposes negative effect compared with ILGCN. Adding nonlinear activation, such as ReLU, make embedding matrix unnecessarily sparser and imposes negative effect to ILGCN though training speed is much faster because of simpler embedding matrix.

In ILGCN-fn, we add both nonlinear activation and feature transformation at first layer and second layer separately. It's performance is better than ILGCN-f but worse than ILGCN-n. We believe nonlinear activation decreases the training difficulty which still higher than ILGCN-n due to feature transformation.

Therefore, it's effective to remove feature transformation and nonlinear activation.

5   Related Work

5.1   GNN

Bruna et al. [19] firstly proposed graph convolutional network on the frequency domain, which can apply the model to graphs. Then, M. Henaff et al. [20] and M. Defferrard et al. [12] further refined the model. The former extends model to large-scale, high-dimensional tasks and simplifies the formulas and the latter designs a local filter to extract local features. Finally, with the help of Kipf [9] and Welling, the most famous model of graph convolution network, is finally proposed. And its simple intuitive idea has inspired many spatial GCNs, including Neural Networks for Graph (NN4G) [21] with sum as the clustering idea; Diffusion-Convolutional Neural Networks (DCNN) [22], DCRNN [23] and Graph Sample and Aggregate (GraphSAGE) [11] with mean as the clustering idea, and Mixture Model Networks (MoNet) [24]; Graph Attention Network (GAT) [10] and Graph Isomorphism Network (GIN) [25] use weighted sum as the clustering idea. The first industrial recommendation system based on GCN [9]; Chen et al. [26] further studies the oversmoothing problem of GCN; Ma et al. [27] and Wang et al. [28] propose Disentangled Graph Collaborative Filtering (DGCF) and Neural Graph Collaborative Filtering (NGCF) that let multiple dimensions partitioned artificially into a few parts that are as orthogonal as possible to extract information.

5.2 Text Classification

Text classification is a classic problem in NLP. Traditional machine learning methods solve text classification relying on feature extraction, such as TF-IDF (Term Frequency-Inverse Document Frequency) [3], N-gram [5] and Bag-of-Words [5]. Then combines extracted features with machine learning methods such as support vector machine [29], Naive Bayes [30], K-NearestNeighbor (KNN) [31] and other methods to complete classification. With the development of deep learning, Yoon Kim proposes TextCNN [6] which solves NLP problem using CNN firstly; then Long Short-Term Memory Network (LSTM) model [7,8] has been designed and applied to NLP issues; more recently, Transformer [32] and Bidirectional Encoder Representations from Transformers (BERT) [33], have further enhanced the effectiveness of text classification. With the development of GNN, some graph-based classification models are gradually emerging [10,11]. Yao et al. [13] proposes Text-GCN and achieved state-of-the-art results on several mainstream datasets. Subsequently, the SGC [14], which removes the nonlinear activation and simplify the feature transformation matrix, is proposed to take text classification as a downstream task and achieved good results; SSGC [15], a variant of GCN which uses a modified Markov Diffusion Kernel, also achieves the state-of-the-art results on several text classification datasets.

6   Conclusion

In this paper, we proved the redundant part of TextGCN and propose a new text classification model named ILGCN, which simplifies the graph structure and only remain the most important part–neighbor aggregation– to get a better performance. We construct a word-label graph which makes model inductive and let model can leverage neglected information of labels. Experiments show that our model is competitive in many mainstream datasets with many state-of-the-art models.

Acknowledgment. This work is supported by National Key Research and Development Project (2018YFE0119700), Key Research and Development Project of Shandong Province (2019JZZY010132, 2019-0101), the Natural Foundation of Shandong Province (ZR2018MF003), Plan of Youth Innovation Team Development of colleges and universities in Shandong Province (SD2019-161).

References

1. Jindal, N., Liu, B.: Review spam detection. In: Proceedings of the 16th International Conference on World Wide Web (2007)
2. Zeng, Z., Deng, Yu., Li, X., Naumann, T., Luo, Y.: Natural language processing for EHR-based computational phenotyping. IEEE/ACM Trans. Comput. Biol. Bioinf. **16**(1), 139–153 (2019)
3. Joachims, T.: A probabilistic analysis of the Rocchio algorithm with TFIDF for text categorization. Department of Computer Science, Carnegie-Mellon University, Pittsburgh, PA (1996)
4. Zhang, Y., Jin, R., Zhou, Z.-H.: Understanding bag-of-words model: a statistical framework. Int. J. Mach. Learn. Cybern. **1**(1–4), 43–52 (2010)
5. Wang, S.I., Manning, C.D.: Baselines and bigrams: simple, good sentiment and topic classification. In: Proceedings of the 50th Annual Meeting of the Association for Computational Linguistics (Volume 2: Short Papers) (2012)
6. Kim, Y.: Convolutional neural networks for sentence classification. Eprint arXiv (2014)
7. Kalchbrenner, N., Grefenstette, E., Blunsom, P.: A convolutional neural network for modelling sentences. arXiv preprint arXiv:1404.2188 (2014)
8. Gehring, J., et al.: Convolutional sequence to sequence learning. In: International Conference on Machine Learning (PMLR) (2017)
9. Kipf, T.N., Welling, M.: Semi-supervised classification with graph convolutional networks. arXiv preprint arXiv:1609.02907 (2016)
10. Veličković, P., et al.: Graph attention networks. arXiv preprint arXiv:1710.10903 (2017)
11. Hamilton, W.L., Ying, R., Leskovec, J.: Inductive representation learning on large graphs. arXiv preprint arXiv:1706.02216 (2017)
12. Defferrard, M., Bresson, X., Vandergheynst, P.: Convolutional neural networks on graphs with fast localized spectral filtering. arXiv preprint arXiv:1606.09375 (2016)
13. Yao, L., Mao, C., Luo, Y.: Graph convolutional networks for text classification. Proc. AAAI Conf. Artif. Intell. **33**, 7370–7377 (2019)
14. Wu, F., et al.: Simplifying graph convolutional networks. In: International Conference on Machine Learning (PMLR) (2019)
15. Zhu, H., Koniusz, P.: Simple spectral graph convolution. In: International Conference on Learning Representations (2021)
16. He, X., et al.: LightGCN: simplifying and powering graph convolution network for recommendation. In: Proceedings of the 43rd International ACM SIGIR Conference on Research and Development in Information Retrieval (2020)
17. Wang, X., et al.: Neural graph collaborative filtering. In: Proceedings of the 42nd International ACM SIGIR Conference on Research and Development in Information Retrieval (2019)
18. Kingma, D.P., Ba, J.: Adam: a method for stochastic optimization. arXiv preprint arXiv:1412.6980 (2014)
19. Bruna, J., et al.: Spectral networks and locally connected networks on graphs. arXiv preprint arXiv:1312.6203 (2013)
20. Henaff, M., Bruna, J., LeCun, Y.: Deep convolutional networks on graph-structured data. arXiv preprint arXiv:1506.05163 (2015)
21. Micheli, A.: Neural network for graphs: a contextual constructive approach. IEEE Trans. Neural Netw. **20**(3), 498–511 (2009)

22. Atwood, J., Towsley, D.: Diffusion-convolutional neural networks. In: Advances in Neural Information Processing Systems (2016)
23. Li, Y., et al.: Diffusion convolutional recurrent neural network: data-driven traffic forecasting. arXiv preprint arXiv:1707.01926 (2017)
24. Monti, F., et al.: Geometric deep learning on graphs and manifolds using mixture model CNNs. In: Proceedings of the IEEE Conference on Computer Vision and Pattern Recognition (2017)
25. Xu, K., et al.: How powerful are graph neural networks? arXiv preprint arXiv:1810.00826 (2018)
26. Chen, D., Lin, Y., Li, W., Li, P., Zhou, J., Sun, X.: Measuring and relieving the over-smoothing problem for graph neural networks from the topological view. Proc. AAAI Conf. Artif. Intell. **34**(04), 3438–3445 (2020)
27. Ma, J., et al.: Disentangled graph convolutional networks. In: International Conference on Machine Learning (PMLR) (2019)
28. Wang, X., et al.: Disentangled graph collaborative filtering. In: Proceedings of the 43rd International ACM SIGIR Conference on Research and Development in Information Retrieval (2020)
29. Burges, C.J.C.: A tutorial on support vector machines for pattern recognition. Data Min. Knowl. Disc. **2**(2), 121–167 (1998)
30. Leung, K.M.: Naive Bayesian classifier, pp. 123–156. Polytechnic University Department of Computer Science/Finance and Risk Engineering (2007)
31. Cover, T., Hart, P.: Nearest neighbor pattern classification. IEEE Trans. Inf. Theor. **13**(1), 21–27 (1967)
32. Vaswani, A., et al.: Attention is all you need. arXiv preprint arXiv:1706.03762 (2017)
33. Devlin, J., et al.: Bert: pre-training of deep bidirectional transformers for language understanding. arXiv preprint arXiv:1810.04805 (2018)

Sparse Subspace Clustering Based on Adaptive Parameter Training

Kexuan Zhu[ID] and Min Li[✉]

School of Information Engineering, Nanchang Institute of Technology, No. 289 Tianxiang Road, Nanchang, Jiangxi, People's Republic of China
`liminghuadi@hotmail.com`

Abstract. There are many researches on sparse subspace clustering, but there are few related studies on its parameter optimization. In this paper, we propose an adaptive training parameter method to improve the manual selection process of convex optimization regularization parameters and improve the accuracy of subspace clustering. Experiments were carried out on multiple datasets, and the clustering accuracy is improved. The results prove that the improved parameter training process can improve the clustering accuracy of subspace clustering.

Keywords: Adaptive parameter training · Spectral clustering · Sparse subspace clustering · Curve fitting

1 Introduction

Cluster analysis belongs to the category of data mining and refers to the process of dividing a given physical or abstract object into classes composed of similar individuals. Traditional clustering methods can be roughly divided into division method, hierarchical method, grid-based method, density-based method, model-based method. The advantage of these clustering methods is that they can successfully cluster low-dimensional data [1]. However, with the development of computer technology and the improvement of people's ability to obtain data, the scale of the acquired data is larger and the data structure is more complicated. Such as images, texts, web documents, and gene expression data, their dimensionality often reaches hundreds or thousands of dimensions, or even higher. To solve the problem of clustering data in high-dimensional spaces, R. Agrawal proposed the Subspaces Clustering algorithm [2].

The subspace clustering algorithm has attracted much attention since it was proposed. Subspace clustering solves the problem of poor performance of traditional clustering algorithms on high-dimensional datasets. However, it is not practical to represent complex high-dimensional data only utilizing a single subspace, so scholars consider using multiple subspaces to solve this problem. How to better divide the subspace is the focus of subspace clustering research. After continuous improvement and experiments, the subspace clustering algorithm has been widely used in clustering problems of high-dimensional data in various fields [3].

© IFIP International Federation for Information Processing 2022
Published by Springer Nature Switzerland AG 2022
Z. Shi et al. (Eds.): IIP 2022, IFIP AICT 643, pp. 56–64, 2022.
https://doi.org/10.1007/978-3-031-03948-5_5

Elhamifar and Vidal et al. proposed the Sparse Subspace Clustering algorithm (SSC) in 2009 [4]. The algorithm constructs an affinity matrix through self-representation between data and uses spectral clustering to obtain clustering results. To improve the performance of sparse subspace clustering, the following aspects are worth studying.

1. The design of regularization [5, 6] makes the generated affinity matrix more conducive to the clustering process.
2. Robustness research [7, 8], to obtain a good clustering effect under various noise interference.
3. Exploration in application [9, 10].

In-depth optimization studies have been carried out in these aspects, and significant results have been achieved.

This paper aims to improve the clustering accuracy of the original sparse subspace. In this study, we improve the training process of regression parameters in the algorithm to obtain a better coefficient matrix, to have better clustering results. The results of experiments indicate that sparse subspace clustering based on adaptive parameter training proposed by us can improve clustering accuracy.

2 Sparse Subspace Clustering

The idea of the Sparse Subspace Clustering (SSC) algorithm is that the point x_i is represented by a linear combination of other data points in the subspace. A sparse coefficient matrix is obtained by imposing constraints. The obtained coefficient matrix is input into the spectral clustering to obtain the clustering results. If we superimpose all data points in the same subspace to the column of the data matrix X, SSC can be expressed as a linear equation $X = XC$, where C is a self-expression coefficient matrix.

Under the assumption that the subspaces are independent of each other, we can find the optimal structure of the coefficient matrix C by minimizing some norms of C. That is, solving:

$$\min_{c} \frac{1}{2}\|X - XC\|_2^2 + \lambda\|C\|_1, s.t.diag(C) = 0 \qquad (1)$$

The first term of the formula ensures the minimum error between the data represented by the coefficient matrix and the original data. The second term of the formula aims to solve the sparse form of the coefficient matrix C. SSC needs to constrain the number of zero elements in C to be much greater than the number of non-zero elements, that is, constrain $min\|C\|_0$. But the problem here is non-convex. The l_0-norm constraint is replaced by the convex approximation problem $min\|C\|_1$. The third term of the formula restricts the diagonal elements of C to 0 to avoid self-representation. The obtained coefficient matrix is processed to obtain the similarity matrix. Process the obtained coefficient matrix to obtain the similarity matrix:

$$W = |C| + |C|^T \qquad (2)$$

Then the graph is constructed with the similarity matrix W, and the spectral clustering method is used for clustering. Let the Laplacian matrix of data X is:

$$L_C = Diag(W*1) - W \tag{3}$$

According to graph theory, the Laplacian matrix of the graph is obtained by subtracting the weight matrix from the corresponding degree matrix. Similarly, the similarity matrix W is used as the weight matrix when the original data is constructed as a graph. 1 is the column vector of all 1, then $Diag(W*1)$ is the degree matrix of the graph.

The constructed Laplacian matrix is standardized by $D^{-1/2}LD^{-1/2}$ and the eigenvectors corresponding to the smallest k eigenvalues of the standardized L_C are calculated. The k eigenvectors are formed into an eigen matrix f, and then k-means clustering is performed on each row of the eigen matrix. The sparse subspace clustering process is as follows (Fig. 1):

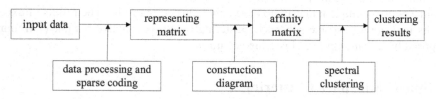

Fig. 1. Flow chart of SSC model

3 Sparse Subspace Clustering Based on Adaptive Parameter Training

3.1 Algorithmic Ideas

The sparse subspace clustering algorithm uses Lasso regression to train the coefficient matrix. The algorithm requires repeated experiments to train the regression parameters λ which is quite cumbersome. A large number of results of experiments show that the value of λ will affect the clustering results. To solve this problem, we propose an adaptive parameter training method, which avoids the process of selecting parameters manually. Concretely as the following optimization model:

$$\min_c \tfrac{1}{2}\|X - XC\|_2^2 + \lambda\|C\|_1, s.t.diag(C) = 0, \lambda \propto f(\|C\|_1), \lambda > 0 \tag{4}$$

λ is used to constrain the two properties of the coefficient matrix. On the one hand, it constrains the sparseness of the coefficient matrix, on the other hand, it ensures that the matrix has a good representation ability [11].

If the number of subspaces k and the dimension d are known, Soltanolkotabi et al. in 2014 revealed the phenomenon found in the parameter training process: the l_1-norm of C_j will swing up and down according to a certain trend, changing the value of λ will cause the fluctuation of the l_1-norm of C_j to change.In the problem of motion segmentation, this trend is described by $1/\sqrt{d}$ [12]. Inspired by this when facing the data of unknown subspace dimensions, the method of curve fitting is used to describe the l_1-norm of the coefficient matrix by us. Then the regular parameter is written $\lambda \propto f(C_1)$.

The training model is updated to:

$$\min_c \frac{1}{2}\|X - XC\|_2^2 + \lambda_0\|C\|_1 + \lambda_i\|C\|_1$$

$$s.t.diag(C) = 0, \lambda_i \propto f(\|C\|_1), \lambda_i > 0, \quad i = 1, 2, \ldots n \tag{5}$$

According to the sparsity constraint of the original algorithm, the initial training sparse matrix regular parameter is 0.001 [4]. Since repeated constraints and training will cause the performance of the coefficient matrix to deteriorate, the optimization model is modified as:

$$\min_c \frac{1}{2}\|X - XC\|_2^2 + \lambda_0\|C\|_1 + \lambda_i\|B\|_1$$

$$s.t.diag(C) = 0, \lambda_i \propto f(\|B\|_1), \lambda > 0, C = B, XB = X, i = 1, 2, \ldots n \tag{6}$$

To retain the coefficient matrix with global sparsity and local performance, we take the coefficient matrix:

$$D = (C + B)/2 \tag{7}$$

Then the alternating minimization method is used to solve the model.

3.2 Model Training Process

Model Updating
To facilitate the optimization process:

$$\min_c \frac{1}{2}\|X - XC\|_2^2 + \lambda_0\|C\|_1 + f(\|B\|_1)\|B\|_1 \tag{8}$$

1. Update **C**

Fixed B, solve C^{t+1} corresponding subproblems:

$$C^{t+1} = arg \min \frac{1}{2}\|X - XC\|_2^2 + \lambda_0\|C\|_1 \tag{9}$$

Derivation is equal to 0, then C^{t+1} is:

$$C^{t+1} = E - \lambda_0 (X)^{-1} \left(X^{-1} \right)^T \tag{10}$$

2. Update **B**

Fixed **C** to solve the corresponding problem B^{t+1}:

$$B^{t+1} = arg\ min f(\|B\|_1) \|B\|_1 \tag{11}$$

Let the above derivation:

$$f'(B)B + f(B) = 0 \tag{12}$$

Since the two-step operation is used in this paper, **C** and **B** are updated successively. And **C = B** before updating **B**, so replace the fitting variable with the updated C^{t+1} to get:

$$f'(C)B + f(C) = 0 \tag{13}$$

Then B^{t+1} is:

$$B^{t+1} = -\frac{f(C)}{f'(C) + \varepsilon} \tag{14}$$

Where ε is an arbitrary integer, avoiding the zero-dividing operation.

Model Processes and Algorithms

The original SSC clustering process is improved by the above model as shown in Fig. 2:

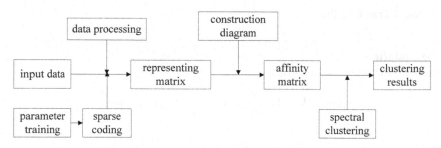

Fig. 2. Flow chart of parameter training SSC model

The model training algorithm is as follows:

Algorithm 1: APSSC
Input: $D \times N \in R^n$ data matrix **X**   Step 1 Data preprocessing and outlier deletion;   Step 2.1 Solves the optimal **C** matrix and train the fitting coefficient;   Step 2.2 Obtains $f(\|C\|_1)$, as the constraint parameter of solving **B** matrix, solving coefficient matrix **B**;   Step 3 Uses Equation (2) to construct the similarity matrix **W**;   Step 4 Solves the corresponding Laplacian matrix for spectral clustering;   **Output**: Clustering results.

4 Experimental Results and Analysis

To evaluate the performance of our algorithm, we have conducted extensive experiments on two kinds of standard datasets: low-dimensional UCI datasets and face image datasets (Extended Yale B). We chose both the classical algorithms and the latest proposed algorithms for comparison, such as Sparse Subspace Clustering (SSC) [4], k-means algorithm, spectral clustering algorithm (SC), random sparse subspace clustering (S^3COMP-C) [13], and sparse subspace clustering based on orthogonal matching pursuit (SSCOMP) [14]. For most of the algorithms mentioned above, the code is released by the authors based on the Matlab platform. For a fair comparison, all algorithms are run with the suitable parameter setting.

We use the clustering error to measure the performance of algorithms. The subspace clustering error is defined as the ratio of the misclassified data to the total number of data, with a value range of [0, 1]. The larger the error rate is, the worse the clustering effect is.

$$error\ rate - \frac{error}{n} \tag{15}$$

This paper evaluates clustering performance by accuracy, which is defined as:

$$accuracy = 1 - error\ rate \tag{16}$$

4.1 Low-Dimensional Data Clustering

This part of the experiment was carried out on the commonly used UCI data set. The purpose is to prove the effectiveness of the proposed algorithm for low-dimensional data clustering. The proposed spectral clustering algorithm obtains the value of clustering parameter k through training optimization. Table 1 shows the clustering accuracy of the corresponding optimal k value.

As can be seen from Table 1, APSSC achieves better clustering results in all data sets. Especially for data sets of Iris, Wine, Air, APSSC is significantly better than SSC. This proves that the improved method is feasible.

Table 1. Accuracy of the improved method and original algorithm in UCI datasets

Data	SSC	APSSC
Iris (k = 3)	0.51	**0.83**
Vote (k = 2)	0.5	**0.61**
Wine (k = 3)	0.56	**0.80**
WBC (k = 2)	0.66	**0.70**
Ionosphere (k = 2)	0.51	**0.63**
Diabetes (k = 2)	0.54	**0.66**
Air (k = 3)	0.41	**0.78**

The SSC algorithm has obvious advantages in high-dimensional data, it performs poorly on low-dimensional datasets. Compared with the SSC algorithm, APSSC has significantly improved clustering accuracy on low-dimensional datasets. This proves that our method improves the limitation of the SSC in the low-dimensional data clustering tasks to a certain extent.

4.2 High-Dimensional Data Clustering

The extended Yale B datasets used in this experiment have a total of 38 people, each with 29 photos. The integrated datasets have a dimension of 32,256 dimensions, with a total of 1 102 data. To reduce the complexity of the experiment, the number of categories $l \in \{2, 3, 4, 5, 6, 7\}$ is used for the significance experiment by us. The results are shown in Table 2:

Table 2. Accuracy of improved algorithm and other algorithms in extended Yale-B

Method	2	3	4	5	6	7
SSC	0.9593	0.9521	0.7155	0.8345	0.8103	0.8291
K-means	0.54	0.481	0.301	0.2933	0.2318	0.2245
SSCOMP	0.929	0.8878	0.8385	0.7991	0.7659	0.7432
S^3COMP-C	0.9593	0.937	0.918	0.899	0.8744	0.8496
SC	0.55	0.362	0.297	0.2534	0.223	0.201
APSSC	**0.99**	**0.965**	**0.94**	**0.9124**	**0.881**	**0.8567**

Compared with other algorithms, APSSC significantly improves the clustering accuracy. The experimental results also show that the adaptive parameter training method reduces the complicated parameter selection process on the one hand, and improves the clustering accuracy of the algorithm on the other hand.

5   Summary and Outlook

This study focuses on improving the accuracy of the sparse subspace clustering algorithm. To obtain the coefficient matrix with good representation ability by considering both the global structure and local sparsity of the data, the sparse coding process of the training matrix is optimized. Experimental results prove that the proposed curve fitting norm matrix parameter method proposed in this paper can improve the clustering accuracy.

For the problem of model optimization, the swarm intelligence algorithm has been developed quite maturely. Combining the good optimization ability of swarm intelligence with sparse subspace clustering algorithm parameter training may be able to obtain better results. This is the direction of the author's next effort.

Acknowledgments. Research on this work was partially supported by grants from and National Nature Science Foundation of China (No. 62166028).

References

1. Dong, W.: Research of Sparse Subspace Clustering. Jiangnan University (2019). https://doi.org/10.27169/d.cnki.gwqgu.2019.000010
2. Agrawal, R., Gehrke, J., Gunopulos, D., Raghavan, P.: Automatic subspace clustering of high dimensional data for data mining applications. ACM SIGMOD Rec. **27**(2), 94–105 (1998). https://doi.org/10.1145/276305.276314
3. Hong, W., Wright, J., Huang, K., Ma, Y.: Multi-scale hybrid linear models for lossy image representation. IEEE Trans. Image Process. **15**(12), 3655–3671 (2006). https://doi.org/10.1109/TIP.2006.882016
4. Elhamifar, E., Vidal, R.: Sparse subspace clustering. In: 2009 IEEE Conference on Computer Vision and Pattern Recognition, pp. 2790–2797 (2009). https://doi.org/10.1109/CVPR.2009.5206547
5. Elhamifar, E., Vidal, R.: Clustering disjoint subspaces via sparse representation. In: Proceedings of the 2010 International Conference on Acoustics, Speech, and Signal Processing (ICASSP), Dallas, pp. 1926–1929. IEEE (2010). https://doi.org/10.1109/ICASSP.2010.5495317
6. Liu, G.C., Yan, S.C.: Latent low-rank representation for subspace segmentation and feature extraction. In: Proceedings of the 2011 IEEE International Conference on Computer Vision (ICCV), Barcelona, pp. 1615–1622. IEEE (2011). https://doi.org/10.1109/ICCV.2011.6126422
7. Wu, F., Yuan, P., Shi, G., Li, X., Dong, W., Wu, J.: Robust subspace clustering network with dual-domain regularization. Pattern Recogn. Lett. **149**, 44–50 (2021). https://doi.org/10.1016/j.patrec.2021.06.009
8. Guo, L., Zhang, X., Liu, Z., Xue, X., Wang, Q., Zheng, S.: Robust subspace clustering based on automatic weighted multiple kernel learning. Inf. Sci. **573**, 453–474 (2021). https://doi.org/10.1016/J.INS.2021.05.070
9. Ma, L., Wang, C., Xiao, B., Zhou, W.: Sparse representation for face recognition based on discriminative low-rank dictionary learning. In: 2012 IEEE Conference on Computer Vision and Pattern Recognition, pp. 2586–2593 (2012). https://doi.org/10.1109/CVPR.2012.6247977

10. Tron, R., Vidal, R.: A benchmark for the comparison of 3-d motion segmentation algorithms. In: Proceedings of the 2007 IEEE Computer Society Conference on Computer Vision and Pattern Recognition (CVPR), pp. 1–8. IEEE, Minneapolis (2007). https://doi.org/10.1109/CVPR.2007.382974
11. Wang, W., Li, X., Feng, X., Wang, S.: A survey on sparse subspace clustering. IEEE J. Autom. Sin. **41**(8), 1373–1384 (2015). https://doi.org/10.16383/j.aas.2015.c140891
12. Soltanolkotabi, M., Elhamifar, E., Candès, E.J.: Robust subspace clustering. Ann. Statist. **42**(2), 669–699 (2014). https://doi.org/10.1214/13-AOS1199
13. Li, C.G., You, C., Vidal, R.: Structured sparse subspace clustering: a joint affinity learning and subspace clustering framework. IEEE Trans Image Process **26**(6), 2988–3001 (2017). https://doi.org/10.1109/TIP.2017.2691557
14. You, C., Robinson, D., Vidal, R.: Scalable sparse subspace clustering by orthogonal matching pursuit. In: Proceedings of the IEEE Conference on Computer Vision and Pattern Recognition, pp. 3918–3927 (2016). https://doi.org/10.1109/CVPR.2016.425

A Hybrid Multi-objective Optimization Algorithm with Improved Neighborhood Rough Sets for Feature Selection

Tao Li[1,2,3]($\boxtimes$) , Jiucheng Xu[1,2,3] , Meng Yuan[1] , and Zhigang Gao[1]

[1] College of Computer and Information Engineering, Henan Normal University,
Xinxiang 453007, China
litao@htu.edu.cn

[2] Key Laboratory of Artificial Intelligence and Personalized Learning in Education,
Xinxiang, Henan, China

[3] Engineering Laboratory of Intelligence Business & Internet of Things,
Xinxiang, Henan, China

Abstract. Feature selection is an effective method for dimensionality reduction in machine learning and data mining. However, it is challenging to select the optimal feature subset with smaller size and higher classification accuracy from high-dimensional data. In this paper, a new approach for feature selection using multi-objective optimization algorithm with improved neighborhood rough sets is proposed. Firstly, the improved neighborhood positive region considering the classification information in the boundary domain is presented to measure the importance of feature more accurately. Then, two optimization objectives are designed to evaluate the quality of the candidate feature subsets. The non-dominated sorting operator and the crowding distance operator are employed to obtain the optimal solution sets. Finally, we utilize the feature kernel to study the relationship between the solutions in the same Pareto front. The performance of the proposed algorithm is examined on ten benchmark data sets and the results are compared with state-of-the-art algorithms to verify the validity. Experimental results show that the proposed algorithm can obtain the high-quality tradeoff between feature subset size and classification accuracy.

Keywords: Feature selection · Neighborhood rough set ·
Multi-objective optimization

Supported by the National Natural Science Foundation of China under Grant 61976082, the Key Scientific Research Project of Henan Provincial Higher Education under Grant 22B520013 and the Doctoral Scientific Research Foundation of Henan Normal University under Grant 20210248.

© IFIP International Federation for Information Processing 2022
Published by Springer Nature Switzerland AG 2022
Z. Shi et al. (Eds.): IIP 2022, IFIP AICT 643, pp. 65–79, 2022.
https://doi.org/10.1007/978-3-031-03948-5_6

1   Introduction

In the are of big data, redundant features and irrelevant features in high dimensional data may lead to the curse of dimensionality, which presents a challenge for machine learning and data ming [1]. Dimensionality reduction technology can address the issues powerfully. It mainly consists of feature selection (FS) method and feature extraction (FE) method [2]. Although FE can reduce the dimensionality, it may produce new features. While FS can obtain a feature subset that maintains the physical meanings of original features. More importantly, it can enhance the performance of the training model. So, we focus mainly on feature selection in this paper.

In recent years, many researchers have studied extensively the feature selection methods based on evolutionary algorithms (EAs) [3–5]. From the perspective of optimizing the number of objectives, evolutionary algorithm is divided into single objective optimization and multi-objective optimization. Most feature selection methods based on single-objective evolutionary algorithms aim to maximize the classification accuracy or minimize the number of features. While feature selection based on multi-objective evolutionary algorithms have attracted much attention by researchers. But most of them only integrate two objectives or more into a single objective without considering the relationship between objectives. For example, Consider the relationship between feature number and classification accuracy, Jimnez F. et al. [6] proposed a feature selection methodology composed by the application of the multi-objective evolutionary algorithm for online sales forecasting. Wang Z. [7] presented a multi-objective evolutionary algorithm with class-dependent redundancy for feature selection based on a relevance measure and new redundancy measure. It is generally known that multi-objective optimization problems are expert in solving conflicts between objectives. Some papers apply non-dominated relationship to tackle the conflicts between classification performance and the size of feature subset. For instance, Xue B. et al. [8] presented the study on multi-objective particle swarm optimization for feature selection and generates a Pareto front of non-dominated solutions (feature subsets). For tackling the feature selection problem with unreliable data, Zhang Y. et al. [9] proposed an effective multi-objective feature selection algorithm based on bare-bones particle swarm optimization, where the reliability and the classification accuracy are taken as the two objectives. Xu H. [10] proposed a duplication analysis-based EA (DAEA) for multiobjective feature selection, and obtained the good classification and generalization results.

Although many EAs have been successfully applied to feature selection problem, there are still two issues that need further study. Firstly, the information contained in the classification boundary region is not been considered. It is clear that the redundant features and relevant features can convert to each other. This phenomenon directly affects the fault tolerance of classification systems. So, we should take the boundary information into account to enhance the relationships between the condition features and decision features so as to further improve the performance of EAs. Secondly, most EAs only present the solutions without relationship between different solutions is analyzed. Many solutions can be obtained by multi-objective evolution algorithm, but it is still a thorny issue to select the most reasonable solution from solution sets. Therefore, we need to further study the relationship between the solutions in the same Pareto front.

Motivated by the above two main issues, we present a hybrid multi-objective optimization algorithm with improved neighborhood rough sets for feature selection. The performance of proposed method is examined on ten publicly available data sets and twelve algorithms to verify the effectiveness. The remaining part of the paper is organized as follow: Sect. 2 provides the related work. In Sect. 3, the proposed algorithm is presented. Section 4 gives the experimental design and result analysis. Finally, the conclusion and the future research direction are presented in Sect. 5.

2 Related Work

2.1 Neighborhood Rough Set

Feature selection based on neighborhood rough set is to find a minimal feature subset with the same distinguishing ability as all features. While the ability to distinguish is measured by the size of positive region. In other words, we tend to find the lager positive region in which the significant features are essential for classification. Suppose the universal $U = \{x_1, x_2, \cdots, x_{|U|}\}$, attribute set $A = \{a_1, a_2, \cdots, a_{|A|}\}$, $A = C \cup D$ and $C \cap D = \varnothing$, where C is the condition attributes and D is the decision attributes, the value domain $V = V_C \cup V_D$, V_C and V_D is the value of the C and D, information function $F : U \times A \to V$, then $S = (U, A, V, F)$ is denoted as an information system.

Definition 1. Information system $S = (U, A, V, F)$, for $\forall B \subseteq A$, the undistinguishable relation of B on the domain U is defined as

$$IND(B) = \{(x, y) \in U \times U | f(x, a) = f(y, a), \forall a \in B\} \tag{1}$$

The partition of the universal U denoted as $U/IND(B) = \{[x]_B | x \in U\}$, where $[x]_B$ represents the equivalent class of any object x in U under attribute set B. Here the $[x]_B = \{y \in U | (x, y) \in IND(B)\}$ is called knowledge granularity.

Definition 2. Suppose a neighborhood decision system $NDS = \{U, A, V, F, \varepsilon\}$, $A = C \cup D$ and $\forall B \subseteq C$, for $\forall x_i \in U$, the neighborhood of the x_i is $\varepsilon(x_i) = \{x | \triangle(x, x_i) \leq \varepsilon, x \in U\}$. The decision attribute D divides U into N equivalent classes $\{X_1, X_2, \cdots, X_N\}$. So the neighborhood negative region and positive region of decision D with respect to B are respectively denoted as

$$\overline{N_B}X = \bigcup_{i=1}^{N}\{x_i | \varepsilon_B(x_i) \cap X \neq \varnothing, x_i \in U\} \tag{2}$$

$$\underline{N_B}X = \bigcup_{i=1}^{N}\{x_i | \varepsilon_B(x_i) \subseteq X, x_i \in U\} \tag{3}$$

It is clear that the boundary region $BN_B(X) = \overline{N_B}X - \underline{N_B}X$. The importance of attributes is measured by $|\underline{N_B}X|/|U|$, where the $|\underline{N_B}X|$ is the number of sample contained by X within a certain neighborhood and the $|U|$ is the size of sample space. Hence, we can see that the hidden information in the boundary area is not considered when calculating the importance of attributes.

2.2   Multi-objective Optimization

Considering the global optimization ability, the multi-objective evolutionary algorithm based on population search is suitable for solving the feature selection problem [11]. In the process of feature selection, the candidate feature subset usually contains relevant and redundant features, and the redundant features should be removed to reduce the size of the feature subset, so the size of feature subset and the classification performance are considered as two optimization objectives. In order to judge the pros and cons of the solution of different objectives, the definition of the Pareto-dominance and the Pareto front are described [12,13].

Definition 3. Suppose objective vector $y = (f_1(x), f_2(x), \cdots, f_n(x))$, where solution vector $x = (x_1, x_2, \cdots, x_m)$. The Ψ is the solution space, for $\forall a \in \Psi$, $\forall b \in \Psi$, if $\forall i \in 1, 2, \cdots, n$ makes $f_i(a) \leq f_i(b)$ and $\exists j \in 1, 2, \cdots, n$ makes $f_j(a) < f_j(b)$, then it is called a dominates b and denoted as $a \Rightarrow b$.

Definition 4. For decision variables $x \in R^m$, if it does not exist $c \in R^m$ makes $c \Rightarrow x$, then x denote as the Pareto optimal solution and T^* is the Pareto optimum solutions set, so we defined the Pareto front (PF) as:

$$PF = \{F(x) = (f_1(x), f_2(x), \cdots, f_n(x)) | x \in T^*\} \tag{4}$$

3   Proposed Multi-objective Optimization Algorithm with Improved Neighborhood Rough Sets

3.1   Improved Neighborhood Rough Sets

Here, the neighborhood rough set is adopted to construct granular models for feature selection. The neighborhood rough set theory holds that the more detailed description of attributes, the higher the division between samples. But there are still two defects: first, the sample in the positive region is calculated without considering the information in the boundary area, which leads to the lack of hidden classification information. Second, there are still redundant attributes in condition attributes, and it is disadvantageous for obtaining low-dimensional feature subset. In order to solve the issues, a new neighborhood positive region computing method is proposed in this paper.

Definition 5. Given neighborhood decision system $NDS = \{U, A, V, F, \varepsilon\}$, $A = C \cup D$, C is the condition attribute and D is the decision attribute. The decision attribute D divides U into K equivalent classes $X_1, X_2, \cdots, X_K$, and the conditional attribute C divided U into $\{C_1, C_2, \cdots, C_n\}$ based on the neighborhood. Then the new neighborhood positive region and the dependence degree of decision attributes on conditional attributes are respectively defined as

$$LN_CX = \bigcup_{i=1}^{N}\{x_i | argmax(\varepsilon_C(x_i) \cap X), x_i \in U\} \tag{5}$$

$$\varphi_C(D) = |LN_CX|/|U| \tag{6}$$

The value of $\varphi_C(D)$ represents the rate of the sample being divided in the positive region. The greater value of the $\varphi_C(D)$ indicates that the partition under the attributes (feature subsets) can obtain stronger classification ability. While the smaller value of the $\varphi_C(D)$, the lower classification ability under the attributes.

Theorem 1. $NDS = \{U, A, V, F, \varepsilon\}$, the $\triangle$ is the measure function on U, if A_1, $A_2 \subseteq C$ and $A_1 \subseteq A_2$, then $\forall X \subseteq U$, $LN_{A_1}X \subseteq LN_{A_2}X$.

Proof. Suppose $x_i \in U$ and $A_1 \subseteq A_2$, if $x_i \in \varepsilon_{A_2}$ we can get that $x_i \in \varepsilon_{A_1}$ according to $\triangle_{A_1}(x_1, x) \leq \triangle_{A_2}(x_1, x)$. So we have $\varepsilon_{A_1}(x) \supseteq \varepsilon_{A_2}(x)$. Given $\varepsilon_{A_1}(x) \subseteq LN_{A_1}X$, where X is the samples of a decision class and it is easy to obtain $\varepsilon_{A_2}(x) \subseteq LN_{A_2}X$. While there may exists x_i that makes $\varepsilon_{A_1}(x) \nsubseteq LN_{A_1}X$ and $\varepsilon_{A_2}(x) \subseteq LN_{A_2}X$, so we get $LN_{A_1}X \subseteq LN_{A_2}X$.

Inference 1. If $A_1 \subseteq A_2 \subseteq A_3 \subseteq \cdots \subseteq C$, then it can get $\varphi_{A_1}(D) \leq \varphi_{A_2}(D) \leq \varphi_{A_3}(D) \leq \cdots \leq \varphi_C(D)$.

The inference 1 shows that the more the selected attributes, the more accurate the description of the sample. In other words, the sample in the different classes will have a greater difference with more features, which helps to distinguish the samples. But the attribute subset often have irrelevant attributes and redundant attributes that may increase the complexity of classification models. Therefore, it is necessary to reduce the size of subset of candidate features.

Definition 6. $NDS = \{U, A, V, F, \varepsilon\}$, $A = C \cup D$ and $E \subseteq C$, If E meets the two conditions simultaneously : 1) $\varphi_E(D) = \varphi_C(D)$; 2) $\forall a \in E$, $\varphi_E(D) > \varphi_{E-\{a\}}(D)$, then we call attribute subset E is a relative reduction of C.

Definition 6 explains that the attribute subset after reduction maintains the core attributes of knowledge system. This helps to establish an efficient classification model, because it removes the irrelevant features and redundant features.

3.2 Design of Two Objective Functions

As mentioned above, the combination of different features directly affects classification performance. That is to say, when the important features are deleted, it deteriorates the classification performance. While adding the important features it can improve the classification performance. Obviously, there is a conflict between the number of important features and the classification performance. It is worth noting that the measurement of the importance of features has been calculated by Eq. (6). In order to evaluate each candidate feature subset better, objective functions F_1 and F_2 are designed. Among them, F_1 is the feature selection rate and it is used to evaluate the size of feature subset on different scale data sets. while F_2 is the classification error rate. Therefore, the two objective functions are respectively defined as

$$F_1 = SR = |N_s|/|N_f| \tag{7}$$

$$F_2 = Err = \frac{FP + FN}{FP + FN + TP + TN} \tag{8}$$

In Eq. (7), the $|N_s|$ and the $|N_f|$ stand for the number of selected features and original features, respectively. While in Eq. (8), the FP, FN, TP and TN denote false positives, false negatives, true positives and true negatives, respectively.

3.3   Feature Kernel Set for Pareto Front

To further study the relationship between the solutions in the same Pareto front, the intersection of feature subsets in the Pareto front solution set is calculated. The purpose of this process is to obtain the key features shared by different candidate feature subsets, which are the essential features in the non-dominated solutions. Suppose $S = \{S_1, S_2, \cdots, S_n\}$ is the feature subsets in the PF respects to F_1 and F_2, where n is the number of solutions. Then, the feature kernel set (FKS) can be defined as $FKS = \bigcap_{i=1}^{n} S_i$.

3.4   Complete Procedure of the Proposed MOINR

In this chapter, a new approach to feature selection using multi-objective optimization algorithm with improved neighborhood rough sets is presented. The proposed algorithm is illustrated in Algorithm 1. The code of lines 5–10 explain the feature importance calculated by the new dependence degree of decision attributes on conditional attributes. The lines 18–19 describe the measure value of each candidate solution on two objective functions. While the lines 21 is to calculate the non-dominant solutions and constructing non-dominant Front. In addition, the individual crossover operator, individual mutation operator and population update operator are listed in lines 23–26.

Assuming that the number of objective functions is N_o and the size of population is N_p. At the same time, the number of the initial feature and the selected feature are recorded as N_f and N_s, respectively. It is easy to know that the time complexity of NSO is $O(N_o \times N_p^2)$, and the time complexity of $ICDO$ is $O(N_o \times N_p \times logN_p)$, while the time complexity of computing neighborhood positive domains is $O(N_f \times N_s^2 \times N_p \times logN_p)$. In this case, the time complexity of $MONPR$ is calculated as $O(T \times (N_f \times N_s^2 \times N_p \times logN_p + N_o \times N_p^2 + N_o \times N_p \times logN_p))$. According the asymptotic time complexity theory, the time complexity of $MONPR$ is reduce to $O(T \times N_s^3 \times N_p \times logN_p)$ at least.

4 Experimental Design and Result Analysis

4.1 Data Sets and Parameter Setup

The simulations are conducted on Core(TM) i5-4440, 3.10 GHz CPU, 8 GB RAM and the proposed algorithm are implemented in MATLAB R2014a and WEKA

Algorithm 1. Multi-objective Optimization Algorithm with Improved Neighborhood Rough Sets (MOINR)

Input: $Data = (x_1, x_2, \cdots, x_N, y)$, the number of iteration T, the population size N_p and feature importance lower limit λ, neighborhood value ε.
Output: Pareto solution sets
1: Initialization population individual.
2: $CS = \oslash, t = 0$ //Initialization candidate subset and iteration number
3: **while** the t meet maximum iteration T
4: **for** $i =1$ to N_p **do**
5:    $F_{set}(i) = Data(pop_{index}(i) == 1)$ // Select the features of the index value equal to 1
6:    **for** $j =1$ to $|F_{set}|$ **do**
7:       $A_j \in F_{set} - CS$
8:       $\underline{LN_{A_j \cup CS}}X = \bigcup\limits_{k=1}^{N} \{x_k | argmax(\varepsilon_{A_j \cup CS}(x_k) \cap X), x_k \in U\}$
9:       $\varphi_{A_j \cup CS}(D) = |\underline{LN_{A_j \cup CS}X}|/|U|$
10:       $INV(A_j) = \varphi_{\overline{A_j \cup CS}}(D) - \varphi_{A_j}(D)$
11:    **end for**
12:    **if** $INV(A_j, CS) < \lambda$ **then**
13:       $CS = CS \cup A_j$
14:       **goto** 6
15:    **else**
16:       $OFS(i) = CS$
17:    **end if**
18:    $indiv_1 = F1(OFS)$ //Calculating objective functions F1.
19:    $indiv_2 = F2(OFS)$ //Calculating objective functions F2.
20: **end for**
21: $PF = NSO(pop)$ // Measure the non-dominating relationship of each individual.
22: $pop_{distance} = ICDO(pop, front)$ // Calculating the distance between individuals in the front
23: $Chrom(pop_c) = Chrom(pop)$ // Individual crossover operation.
24: $Chrom(pop_m) = Chrom(pop_c)$ // Individual mutation operation.
25: $Pop = pop \cup pop_m$ // Merge the father population and offspring population.
26: $Pop = newsort(Pop)$ //Form new population with the same size.
27: $Front = update(front)$
28: $t = t + 1$
29: **end While**

3.8.0 software. Table 1 shows that the ten data sets are adopted for testing the proposed algorithm, and these data sets are available from the University of California Irvine (UCI).

In order to verify the credibility and stability of the experimental results, the process of randomly selection is repeated ten independent times for obtaining the statistically meaningful experimental results and the artificial neural network is adopted as a classifier. In the process of iteration, the crossover operator and mutation operator are used for produce new population. The crossover factor $CF = 0.8$ and mutation factor are $MF = 0.1$. In order to ensure that each feature is selected with the same probability, the length of the P_1 is equal to the dimension of the original dataset. While the population size $P_n{=}20$ and the number of iteration $T{=}100$. In the process of calculating the importance of features, the neighborhood value ε is fixed to 0.9 and the threshold of feature importance λ is set as 0.01.

Table 1. Experimental data sets description

No.	Data sets	No. of features	No. of instances	No. of classes
1	Wine	13	178	3
2	Vehicle	18	846	4
3	Lymph	18	148	4
4	WDBC	30	569	2
5	Ionophere	34	351	2
6	SPECTE	44	80	2
7	Sonar	60	208	2
8	Synthetic	60	600	6
9	Hill-valley	100	606	2
10	Musk	166	476	2

In Table 2, FKS and FS respectively represent the feature kernel set and the best feature subset in Pareto front obtained by MOINR . While the ACC is the classification accuracy of FS. It can be seen that the number of feature contained by FKS is not more than 5 on eight data sets. When the FKS is combined with other features, it can significantly enhance classification ability of the algorithm. For example, when the KFS of Wine data set combined with the 10th and 11th features, its classification accuracy can reach to 97.58%. For WDBC data set, 98.73% of the classification accuracy was obtained when the 18th and 29th features are added to the corresponding KF. Therefore, the space of features combination is reduced by the obtained FKS. More importantly, it is helpful to select smaller subset with higher classification accuracy.

4.2 Performance Comparison Between MOINR and Other Algorithms

In order to verify the effectiveness and advantages of the proposed algorithm, the performance of the MOINR is evaluated by comparing with three groups representative methods. 1) Classical filter algorithms: ReliefF [14], mRMR [15], FSIG [16] and SBMLR [17]. 2) Single objective wrapper algorithms: BGAFS [18], MDEFS [19], BPSO [20] and BACO [21]. 3) Multi-objective wrapper algorithms: MPPSO [22], MOEA/D [23], FWSP [24] and NSGAII [12] MORS.

Table 2. The best classification accuracy by feature kernel sets in MOINR

Dataset	Indicator	ID of Features
Wine	FKS	1,12,13
	FS	1,10,11,12,13
	ACC	**97.58%**
Vehicle	FKS	1,10
	FS	1,7,10,13,14
	ACC	**72.22%**
Lymph	FKS	2,13,18
	FS	2,7,9,13,15,18
	ACC	**88.31%**
WDBC	FKS	1,16,22,25
	FS	1,16,18,22,25,29
	ACC	**98.73%**
Ionophere	FKS	10,17
	FS	3,4,9,10,17
	ACC	**91.83%**
SPECTE	FKS	19,40
	FS	4,17,18,19,21,22,25,26,27,29,30,33,36,38,39,40,42
	ACC	**80.31%**
Sonar	FKS	11,36,47
	FS	11,22,36,47
	ACC	**83.99%**
Synthetic	FKS	40,43,56
	FS	19,27,35,40,43,46,57
	ACC	**95.33%**
Hill-valley	FKS	1,4,23,59,69,70,75,82,98
	FS	1,4,16,19,23,24,43,45,47,51,56,59,69,70,75,76,82,98
	ACC	**76.11%**
Musk	FKS	9,10,28,44,49,53,56,71,72,79,83,99,107,132,135,138,147,152,161
	FS	9,10,17,20,28,44,46,49,53,56,64,66,71,72,77,78,79,82,83,85,87,90, 94,95,99,105,107,111,117,120,125,131,132,135,138,147,149,152,156,161
	ACC	**81.19%**

In this paper, the classification accuracy (ACC) and selection rate (SR) are taken as two indicators to evaluate the performance of the proposed algorithm. In order to show the improvement of classification performance after reduction, we also present the results using the original data set (OD). In the tables, the W/L/T represents the number of wins/loss/ties for MOINR in comparison with the other algorithms on the ten data sets. The BAVE and BSTD represent the average and standard deviation of the all data sets for each algorithm, respectively. While the AVE and STD show the average and standard deviation of the ACC and SR for each data set in ten runs, respectively. In addition, we rank the algorithms according to the BAVE and the values are shown in the parentheses. The maximum ACC and minimum SR are highlighted in bold for each data set. Besides, the T-test is utilized to test the significance of the proposed algorithm.

4.2.1 Comparison with Classical Filter Algorithms

Tables 3 and 4 show the average classification accuracy and average feature selection rate. In the tables, four representative classical filter algorithms are compared with the proposed algorithm. 1) ReliefF is a filtering algorithm based on sample learning that can select the appropriate feature according the threshold of feature importance. 2) mRMR is developed based on the redundancy of features and the correlation between features and labels, which used mutual information as the feature selection criterion. 3) FSIG is an effective feature selection method based on information gain, whose selection criterion is the contribution of the feature to the classification system. 4) SBMLR is a sparse multinomial logistic regression method that can obtain the most informative features.

Table 3. Average ACC to MOINR and the comparison with four classical filter algorithms in ten runs

Dataset	OD		MOINR		ReliefF		mRMR		FSIG		SBMLR	
	AVE(%)	STD(%)	AVE(%)	STD(%)	AVE(%)	STD(%)	AVE(%)	STD(%)	AVE(%)	STD(%)	AVE(%)	STD(%)
Wine	96.63	0.00	**94.36**	7.43	87.36	12.38	91.64	7.13	92.42	6.65	91.50	5.27
Vehicle	44.80	0.00	**72.22**	8.78	41.91	3.64	42.59	1.38	41.42	1.46	45.57	4.28
Lymph	82.43	0.00	**86.62**	4.90	79.28	3.88	78.68	5.79	77.55	4.39	75.08	3.14
WDBC	89.86	0.00	**98.51**	0.68	92.37	2.01	88.99	2.81	91.06	1.56	85.14	1.54
Ionophere	82.34	0.00	**92.60**	3.27	87.48	4.53	89.03	2.77	86.56	2.06	80.77	6.87
SPECTE	76.25	0.00	**80.31**	8.34	79.43	1.92	77.25	2.42	81.08	2.26	74.25	10.02
Sonar	67.79	0.00	**86.45**	2.45	69.64	2.48	69.04	2.73	68.40	2.88	72.48	4.00
Synthetic	94.67	0.00	**95.45**	2.00	53.33	1.91	74.48	5.36	75.67	4.90	86.16	8.88
Hill-valley	51.98	0.00	**81.05**	0.66	56.27	8.00	51.82	0.50	51.67	0.43	52.06	0.12
Musk	75.21	0.00	**93.06**	2.36	67.06	5.05	57.21	2.59	67.97	5.00	69.90	2.46
W/L/T	10/0/0		0/0/10		10/0/0		10/0/0		10/0/0		10/0/0	
T-test	0.0074		–		0.0038		0.0028		0.0029		0.0005	

Table 4. Average SR to MOINR and the comparison with four classical filter algorithms in ten runs

Dataset	OD		MOINR		ReliefF		mRMR		FSIG		SBMLR	
	AVE(%)	STD(%)	AVE(%)	STD(%)	AVE(%)	STD(%)	AVE(%)	STD(%)	AVE(%)	STD(%)	AVE(%)	STD(%)
Wine	100	0.00	**32.05**	17.82	36.92	14.39	38.46	19.86	36.92	14.39	34.62	18.84
Vehicle	100	0.00	**27.68**	15.21	27.78	15.21	27.78	14.34	27.78	15.21	27.78	15.21
Lymph	100	0.00	**26.36**	23.75	27.78	15.21	27.78	14.34	27.78	15.21	27.78	15.21
WDBC	100	0.00	29.52	10.44	26.67	14.91	18.33	10.09	26.67	14.91	**5.00**	2.40
Ionophere	100	0.00	23.95	15.23	26.47	14.85	16.18	8.90	26.47	14.85	**7.35**	4.00
SPECTE	100	0.00	36.11	16.67	26.14	14.76	12.50	6.88	18.18	10.16	**6.80**	3.50
Sonar	100	0.00	20.00	2.64	17.50	9.86	9.17	5.05	13.33	7.45	**7.50**	4.10
Synthetic	100	0.00	29.00	9.47	17.50	9.86	**8.33**	4.30	13.33	7.45	13.33	7.50
Hill-valley	100	0.00	32.43	5.90	10.50	5.92	**3.00**	1.41	8.00	4.47	3.50	0.71
Musk	100	0.00	27.11	2.92	48.19	2.69	**3.01**	1.56	4.82	2.69	3.31	1.82
W/L/T	10/0/0		0/0/10		4/6/0		3/7/0		4/6/0		3/7/0	
T-test	0.0000		–		0.6151		0.0128		0.0451		0.0045	

The results of Table 3 indicate that the MOINR can obtain the highest classification accuracy in ten runs. The reason is that the four comparison algorithms belong to the filter type, and the evaluation of feature importance only according to the relationship between the features and the classification labels. While in the proposed algorithm, the relationship among features and the relationship between features and classification labels are considered simultaneously to measure the quality of the feature subset. Therefore, the proposed MOINR can improve the classification accuracy. From Table 4, it seems that the MOINR algorithm is not outstanding in the feature selection rate, which may be caused by the larger threshold of feature importance.

4.2.2   Comparison with Single Objective Wrapper Algorithms

It is meaningful to compare the proposed algorithm with the single objective wrapper algorithm, because the multi-objective method can better explain how to find the best compromise solutions. Hence, four single objective algorithms are employed in this paper. The BGAFS and the MDEFS are binary genetic algorithm and binary differential evolution algorithm, respectively. The objective functions of the BGAFS and MDEFS are the ratio of within-class distance and between-class distance. The smaller the ratio, and the better the quality of the selected feature subset. While the BPSO and the BACO are the binary particle swarm optimization algorithm and binary ant colony optimization algorithm, respectively. The objective functions of BPSO and BACO are the classification accuracy of the selected feature subset on the training model.

Table 5. Average ACC to MOINR and the comparison with four single objective wrapper algorithms in ten runs.

Dataset	OD		MOINR		BGAFS		BPSO		MDEFS		BACO	
	AVE(%)	STD(%)	AVE(%)	STD(%)	AVE(%)	STD(%)	AVE(%)	STD(%)	AVE(%)	STD(%)	AVE(%)	STD(%)
Wine	96.63	0	94.36	7.43	94.94	1.38	**98.25**	1.16	96.07	1.21	97.33	1.65
Vehicle	44.80	0	**72.22**	8.78	48.88	0.92	52.29	3.81	48.88	0.92	49.75	4.89
Lymph	82.43	0	**86.62**	4.90	82.43	0.00	50.35	5.68	82.43	0.00	89.42	1.86
WDBC	89.86	0	**98.51**	0.68	92.75	1.57	98.49	0.48	90.76	1.49	98.40	0.30
Ionophere	82.34	0	92.60	3.27	89.60	38.24	**93.55**	0.38	83.83	14.30	94.85	0.40
SPECTE	76.25	0	**80.31**	8.34	78.75	3.06	69.65	2.93	76.56	3.59	59.67	5.70
Sonar	67.79	0	86.45	2.45	67.55	3.65	88.55	1.44	63.58	7.19	**89.34**	0.70
Synthetic	94.67	0	**95.45**	2.00	77.67	0.00	75.02	5.42	77.67	0.00	71.73	3.50
Hill-valley	51.98	0	**81.05**	0.66	51.94	0.07	78.81	0.74	51.90	0.10	78.10	0.50
Musk	75.21	0	**93.06**	2.36	70.94	0.60	87.73	1.20	75.84	0.00	86.97	0.90
W/L/T	10/0/0		0/0/10		10/0/0		7/3/0		9/1/0		6/4/0	
T-test	0.0074		–		0.0052		0.0613		0.0025		0.1015	

Table 5 reveals the average classification accuracy of comparative approaches in ten runs. We can see that the proposed algorithm can get the highest average classification accuracy on seven data sets. In most cases, the proposed algoorithm also has a significant advantage over BGAFS, MDEFS, BPSO and BACO. This is because the multi-objective algorithm can select the Pareto solution sets instead of the single solution obtained by the single objective algorithm. It helps us to find more reasonable and comprehensive feature subsets. In addition, Table 6 reflects the average feature selection rate obtained by MOINR against other four single algorithms. It can be observed that the MOINR has gained the minimum average feature selection rate on half of the data sets.

Table 6. Average SR to MOINR and the comparison with four single objective wrapper algorithms in ten runs.

Dataset	OD		MOINR		BGAFS		BPSO		MDEFS		BACO	
	AVE(%)	STD(%)	AVE(%)	STD(%)	AVE(%)	STD(%)	AVE(%)	STD(%)	AVE(%)	STD(%)	AVE(%)	STD(%)
Wine	100	0	**32.05**	17.82	40.38	3.85	46.15	0.00	96.15	4.44	42.30	9.93
Vehicle	100	0	27.68	15.21	38.89	0.00	**26.39**	5.32	38.89	0.00	30.55	7.17
Lymph	100	0	**26.36**	23.75	38.89	0.00	27.78	5.56	38.89	0.00	30.55	7.17
WDBC	100	0	**29.52**	10.44	42.50	1.67	31.33	4.30	31.67	1.92	18.33	4.30
Ionophere	100	0	**23.95**	15.23	38.24	0.00	26.18	3.80	24.26	6.52	16.18	3.80
SPECTE	100	0	36.11	16.67	41.48	3.40	13.43	2.82	27.84	7.04	**12.50**	2.94
Sonar	100	0	20.00	2.64	39.58	1.60	29.17	2.15	25.00	2.36	**9.17**	2.15
Synthetic	100	0	29.00	9.47	**23.33**	0.00	29.17	2.15	24.33	0.00	29.17	2.15
Hill-valley	100	0	32.43	5.90	37.00	0.00	26.75	2.20	31.00	1.41	**5.50**	1.30
Musk	100	0	**27.11**	2.92	40.96	1.59	28.16	0.57	27.71	0.00	33.31	0.78
W/L/T	10/0/0		0/0/10		9/1/0		8/2/0		7/3/0		5/5/0	
T-test	0.0000		–		0.0016		0.9924		0.2439		0.1895	

4.2.3 Comparison with Multi-objective Wrapper Algorithm Results

In order to further verify the competitiveness of the proposed algorithm, the advanced multi-objective wrapper algorithms are compared and analyzed, such as MPPSO, MOEA/D, FWSP and NSGAII. As it can be seen in the tables, the MPPSO is the multi-population based particle swarm optimization, which adopts average classification accuracies and the number of features as two optimization objectives. The MOEA/D is multi-objective evolutionary algorithm based decomposition, which also can obtain the better trade-off among the objective functions. And the NSGAII is a fast and elitist multi-objective genetic algorithm, which adopts the non-dominated sorting to analyze the relationship between different objective function solutions.

Table 7. Average ACC to MOINR and the comparison with four multi-objective wrapper algorithms in ten runs.

Dataset	OD		MOINR		MPPSO		MOEA/D		FWSP		NSGAII	
	AVE(%)	STD(%)	AVE(%)	STD(%)	AVE(%)	STD(%)	AVE(%)	STD(%)	AVE(%)	STD(%)	AVE(%)	STD(%)
Wine	96.63	0	94.36	7.43	89.15	7.96	**96.07**	9.21	94.94	6.32	83.86	8.92
Vehicle	44.80	0	**72.22**	8.78	47.13	9.48	68.50	10.44	64.80	12.78	43.67	9.36
Lymph	82.43	0	**86.62**	4.90	85.67	6.86	84.43	5.93	81.75	5.04	84.99	7.08
WDBC	89.86	0	**98.51**	0.68	97.48	2.26	96.32	7.55	94.23	10.21	95.15	8.89
Ionophere	82.34	0	92.60	3.27	**95.10**	1.33	86.50	8.82	84.33	8.82	94.74	7.19
SPECTE	76.25	0	**80.31**	8.34	62.03	7.85	74.54	5.63	79.74	8.09	72.93	6.23
Sonar	67.79	0	86.45	2.45	**91.14**	1.96	79.32	4.19	80.01	36.67	83.17	5.33
Synthetic	94.67	0	95.45	2.00	66.96	6.10	95.80	3.13	**97.00**	3.33	81.47	6.21
Hill-valley	51.98	0	**81.05**	0.66	77.09	2.39	71.67	6.76	79.68	5.42	69.04	8.84
Musk	75.21	0	**93.06**	2.36	85.80	1.13	85.43	24.10	90.92	8.61	84.27	4.26
W/L/T	10/0/0		0/0/10		8/2/0		8/2/0		9/1/0		10/0/0	
T-Test	0.0074		–		0.0498		0.0050		0.0135		0.0105	

In Table 7, we can find that MOINR can effectively reduce the average classification rate on the Vehicle, Lymph, WDBC, SPECTF, Hill-valley and Musk

Table 8. Average SR to MOINR and the comparison with four multi-objective wrapper algorithms in ten runs.

Dataset	OD		MOINR		MPPSO		MOEA/D		FWSP		NSGAII	
	AVE(%)	STD(%)	AVE(%)	STD(%)	AVE(%)	STD(%)	AVE(%)	STD(%)	AVE(%)	STD(%)	AVE(%)	STD(%)
Wine	100	0	**32.05**	17.82	43.08	24.68	37.25	13.67	40.82	14.29	47.69	14.79
Vehicle	100	0	**27.68**	15.21	45.37	25.60	38.46	44.44	31.53	17.14	35.81	19.07
Lymph	100	0	26.36	23.75	**25.00**	22.54	37.58	18.93	28.45	12.32	41.67	20.50
WDBC	100	0	**29.52**	10.44	19.63	12.30	30.17	9.35	31.74	12.96	20.83	11.23
Ionophere	100	0	**23.95**	15.23	34.41	18.91	27.91	12.47	26.16	8.82	31.99	9.61
SPECTE	100	0	36.11	16.67	24.30	11.22	**34.82**	11.75	40.27	15.06	40.96	12.85
Sonar	100	0	**20.00**	2.64	28.83	10.25	21.67	5.33	24.62	6.11	23.51	6.92
Synthetic	100	0	29.00	9.47	31.50	11.49	28.38	7.19	**28.34**	8.56	30.17	11.23
Hill-valley	100	0	32.43	5.90	37.55	12.13	35.74	9.52	35.18	10.11	**23.71**	12.31
Musk	100	0	**27.11**	2.92	34.16	5.37	30.22	7.39	31.41	6.83	32.87	6.59
W/L/T	10/0/0		0/0/10		8/2/0		8/2/0		9/1/0		8/2/0	
T-test	0.0000		–		0.2130		0.0209		0.0015		0.123	

data sets. From Table 8, it is observed that the smallest average feature selection rate achieved by MOINR on six datasets.

Furthermore, the significant test on classification accuracy and selection rate are presented in the paper. Obviously, the values of T-test are below 0.05 for most cases in the tables. It shows that the improvement of the proposed algorithm in classification accuracy and feature selection rate is notable. Thus, the proposed multi-objective optimization algorithm with improved neighborhood rough sets can accurately depict the uncertainty of samples in classification boundaries. More importantly, the MOINR can achieve the better compromise solutions.

5 Conclusion and Future Work

In this paper, a hybrid multi-objective optimization algorithm with improved neighborhood rough sets is proposed to solve the feature selection problem. The neighborhood positive region calculation method is improved to describe the discriminability of samples more accurately. Then the improved neighborhood rough model is used to select the important features. At the stage of evolutionary computation, the classification error rate and feature selection rate two objectives are designed to evaluate the candidate feature subset. Besides, the scale of feature subset is reduced and classification accuracy is improved by the feature kernel set. Therefore, the proposed algorithm can select the optimal feature subset with smaller size and higher classification accuracy.

Although multi-objective optimization algorithm can effectively handle feature selection problem, it is not excellent in terms of time cost. In the future works, we will focus on the study of faster non-dominated sorting methods and multi-objective optimization algorithms for more than two optimization objectives to deal with high-dimensional data sets.

References

1. Guyon, I., Elisseeff, A.: An introduction to variable feature selection. J. Mach. Learn. Res. **3**, 1157–1182 (2003)
2. Chandrashekar, G., Sahin, F.: A survey on feature selection methods. Pergamon Press, Inc. (2014)
3. Faris, H., et al.: An efficient binary salp swarm algorithm with crossover scheme for feature selection problems. Knowl. Based Syst. **154**, 43–67 (2018)
4. Mukhopadhyay, A., Maulik, U., Bandyopadhyay, S., Coello, C.A.C.: Survey of multiobjective evolutionary algorithms for data mining: Part II. IEEE Trans. Comput. **18**(1), 20–35 (2014)
5. Das, A.K., Das, S., Ghosh, A.: Ensemble feature selection using bi-objective genetic algorithm. Knowl. Based Syst. **123**, 116–127 (2017)
6. Jimnez, F., Snchez, G., Garca, J.M., Miralles, L., Miralles, L.: Multi-objective evolutionary feature selection for online sales forecasting. Neurocomputing 234(C), 75–92 (2016)
7. Wang, Z., Li, M., Li, J.: A multi-objective evolutionary algorithm for feature selection based on mutual information with a new redundancy measure. Inf. Sci. **307**, 73–88 (2015)

8. Xue, B., Zhang, M., Browne, W.N.: Particle swarm optimization for feature selection in classification: A multi-objective approach. IEEE Trans. Cybern. **43**(6), 1656–1671 (2013)
9. Zhang, Y., Gong, D.W., Zhang, W.Q.: Feature selection of unreliable data using an improved multi-objective PSO algorithm. Neurocomputing 171(C), 1281–1290 (2015)
10. Xu, H., Xue, B., Zhang, M.: A duplication analysis-based evolutionary algorithm for biobjective feature selection. IEEE Trans. Evolution. Comput. **25**(2), 205–218 (2021)
11. Jin, X., Bo, T., He, H., Hong, M.: Semisupervised feature selection based on relevance and redundancy criteria. IEEE Trans. Neural Netw. Learn. Syst. **28**(9), 1974–1984 (2017)
12. Deb, K., Pratap, A., Agarwal, S., Meyarivan, T.: A fast and elitist multiobjective genetic algorithm: NSGA-II. IEEE Trans. Evol. Comput. **6**(2), 182–197 (2002)
13. Zhu, Y., Liang, J., Chen, J., Ming, Z.: An improved NSGA-III algorithm for feature selection used in intrusion detection. Knowl. Based Syst. **116**, 74–85 (2017)
14. Robnik, Ikonja, M., Kononenko, I.: Theoretical and empirical analysis of relieff and rrelieff. Mach. Learn. 53(1–2), 23–69 (2003)
15. Peng, H., Long, F., Ding, C.: Feature selection based on mutual information: criteria of max-dependency, max-relevance, and min-redundancy. IEEE Trans. Pattern Anal. Mach. Intell. **27**(8), 1226–1238 (2005)
16. Cover, T.M., Thomas, J.A.: Elements of Information Theory. Wiley, Tsinghua University Press (1991)
17. Scholkopf, B., Platt, J., Hofmann, T.: Sparse multinomial logistic regression via Bayesian l1 regularisation. In: International Conference on Neural Information Processing Systems, pp. 209–216 (2006)
18. Dong, H., Li, T., Ding, R., Sun, J.: A novel hybrid genetic algorithm with granular information for feature selection and optimization. Appl. Soft. Comput. **65**, 33–46 (2018)
19. Ot, A., Ttn, B., Sm, C.: A novel wrapper-based feature subset selection method using modified binary differential evolution algorithm. Inf. Sci. **565**, 278–305 (2021)
20. Yang, C.S., Chuang, L.Y., Ke, C.H., Yang, C.H.: Boolean binary particle swarm optimization for feature selection. Evol. Comput. 2093–2098 (2008)
21. Tabakhi, S., Moradi, P., Akhlaghian, F.: An unsupervised feature selection algorithm based on ant colony optimization. Eng. Appl. Artif. Intel **32**(6), 112–123 (2014)
22. Kl, F., Kaya, Y., Yildirim, S.: A novel multi population based particle swarm optimization for feature selection. Knowl. Based Syst **219**(4), 1–14 (2021)
23. Zhang, Q., Liu, W., Li, H.: The performance of a new version of moea/d on cec09 unconstrained mop test instances. In: IEEE Congress on Evolutionary Computation (CEC 2009), pp. 203–208 (2009)
24. Das, A., Das, S.: Feature weighting and selection with a pareto-optimal trade-off between relevancy and redundancy. Pattern Recogn. Lett. **88**, 12–19 (2017)

Augmenting Convolution Neural Networks by Utilizing Attention Mechanism for Knowledge Tracing

Meng Zhang[1], Liang Chang[1,2], Tieyuan Liu[1,2(✉)], and Chen Wei[1]

[1] Guilin University of Electronic Technology, Guilin 541004, China
lty205@guet.edu.cn
[2] Guangxi Key Laboratory of Trusted Software, Guilin 541004, China

Abstract. The devastating, ongoing Covid-19 epidemic has led to many students resorting to online education. In order to better guarantee the quality, online education faces severe challenges. There is an important part of online education referred to as Knowledge Tracing (KT). The objective of KT is to estimate students' learning performance using a series of questions. It has garnered widespread attention ever since it was proposed. Recently, an increasing number of research efforts have concentrated on deep learning (DL)-based KT attributing to the huge success over traditional Bayesian-based KT methods. Most existing DL-based KT methods utilize Recurrent Neural Network and its variants, i.e. Long Short-Term Memory (LSTM), Gated Recurrent Unit (GRU) etc. Recurrent neural networks are good at modeling local features, but underperforms at long sequence modeling, so the attention mechanism is introduced to make up for this shortcoming. In this paper, we introduce a DL-based KT model referred to as Convolutional Attention Knowledge Tracing (CAKT) utilizing attention mechanism to augment Convolutional Neural Network (CNN) in order to enhance the ability of modeling longer range dependencies.

Keywords: Student performance prediction (SPP) · Knowledge Tracing (KT) · Convolutional Neural Network (CNN) · Attention mechanism (AM)

1 Introduction

With the continuous development of society, education issues are becoming more and more important, and the issue of teaching students according to their aptitude is particularly important. How to provide different students with training programs that suit their abilities, so that different students can better develop their own potential, is an important issue facing current education. And with the spread of the new coronavirus, more and more students cannot go back to school to study, and there is an urgent need for an online learning system to plan feasible learning plans for students. Therefore, with the continuous development of deep learning, one of the successful tasks of various neural networks is knowledge tracking (KT) [1]. The goal of knowledge tracking is to analyze

© IFIP International Federation for Information Processing 2022
Published by Springer Nature Switzerland AG 2022
Z. Shi et al. (Eds.): IIP 2022, IFIP AICT 643, pp. 80–86, 2022.
https://doi.org/10.1007/978-3-031-03948-5_7

and evaluate students' knowledge status in the process of students' learning, so as to predict students' performance in the next time series and give appropriate suggestions [2].

Therefore, we can know that knowledge tracking plays an important role in the online education system. According to recent researches, many scholars have proposed different methods to solve this problem, including Bayesian Knowledge Tracing (BKT) [1], Deep Knowledge Tracing (DKT) [3], Dynamic Key-Value Memory Networks (DKVMN) [4], Convolutional Knowledge Tracing (CKT) [5], these excellent methods use different models to track the knowledge level of students, by modeling students' practice sequences and other information, although each model has obtained relatively good results, but different models have some potential problems that are not well resolved.

Models utilized in most of these methods are either RNNs or CNNs. CNNs behave well in modeling local features. However, CNNs are inadequate to perform good at long term sequence modeling. Therefore, it is a natural idea to combine a mechanism which models long term sequences well. One of the mechanisms that is fit for this requirement is attention mechanism [6]. In this case, we attempt to combine CNN with attention mechanism. To the best of our knowledge, this is the first paper utilizing attention mechanism with CNN in knowledge tracing area. The model is referred to as Convolutional Attention Knowledge Tracing (CAKT), which handles both short and long student learning sequences better.

2 Related Works

2.1 Deep Learning-Based Knowledge Tracing

The introduction of deep learning into the field of knowledge tracking is an important turning point. The DKT model [1] proposed in 2015 has received a lot of attention from researchers once it was proposed, and it has improved the accuracy of model prediction to a new level. It analyzes the accuracy of the model through the area under the curve (AUC). After a lot of experiments, it has been proved that its accuracy is much better than the traditional knowledge tracking model.

2.2 Convolutional Neural Network

CNNs have provided a successful example employed in many areas such as computer vision, natural language processing, etc. [8, 9]. In 2020, Convolutional Knowledge Tracing (CKT) models individualization of students in a more precise way and shows notable results demonstrating the effectiveness of CKT.

2.3 Attention Mechanism

RNN has the problem of long-term dependence, which makes it unable to better perceive the connection between long-sequence information, and the long-term dependence makes DKT unable to utilize the long-sequence input. The attention mechanism allows to model the dependencies of input and output sequences regardless of their length in the sequence, and is more suitable for modeling long-distance dependencies. Attention mechanism has proved to be effective in various fields because of its strong modeling ability [10, 11]. Recently, a self-attentive model [12] called SAKT (Self-Attentive Knowledge Tracing) has been introduced in KT. SAKT simply utilizes transformer architecture to solve long term modeling problems.

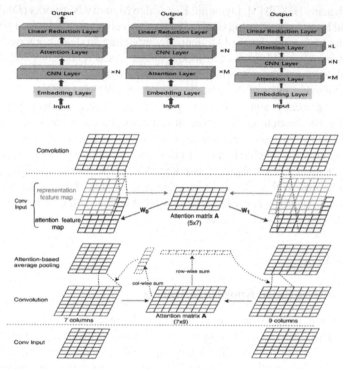

Fig. 1. The architectures of CAKT model.

3   Model Architecture

3.1   Problem Definition

The knowledge tracing task can be described as a supervised learning task, through the interaction sequence in the process of students doing questions, this sequence contains the questions and other information of the students. where the parameter n is the total number of student interactions in this training, $X = (x_0, x_1, \ldots x_{n-1}, x_n)$, where n is the total number of the student's interactions' times, the task of knowledge tracing is to predict the performance of the student's next interaction x_{n+1}. When interactions are considered as the form of question-answer [12], $X_t = \{q_t, a_t\}$, where q_t is the question that the student attempts at time step t and a_t indicates the correctness of the student's answer, $a_t \in \{0, 1\}$ where 1 indicates a correct answer whilst 0 stands for a wrong one.

3.2 CAKT

The architecture of CAKT model is shown in Fig. 1, containing an Embedding Layer, several Convolutional Layers, an Attention Layer, and a Linear Dimension Reduction Layer. The design of the model utilized for both Embedding Layer and Convolutional Layer is similar to that proposed by CKT.

We follow the architecture of attention mechanism in [13], but we slightly modify the architecture in order to fit our task.

$$\text{score}_i = h_{attn}^T \, \sigma \, (W_{attn} \, V_i + b_{attn}) \tag{1}$$

$$\alpha_i = \frac{\exp(\text{score}_i)}{\sum_{i=1}^{n} \exp(\text{score}_i)} \tag{2}$$

$$Output_{sum} = \sum_{i=1}^{n} \alpha_i V_i \tag{3}$$

where W_{attn} is the attention weight parameter matrix, V_i is the output of the convolutional layer, h_{atten}^T is the parameter. Attention bias parameter is b_{attn}, and is element-wise multiplication, σ stands for tanh function. αi is the attention score of V_i. We get the attention output Output sum in formula (3).

In order to reduce the dimension, we add a linear layer at the end of the attention layer. The computation of linear layer is written below:

$$y_t = W_{oy} \, Output_{sum} + b_y \tag{4}$$

In order to reduce the dimension, we add a linear layer at the end of the attention layer. The computation of linear layer is written below:

$$L = \sum_{t=1}^{N} (a_t \log y_t + (1 - a_t) \log(1 - y_t)) \tag{5}$$

The goal of model training is to minimize the similarity of students learning sequence predictions. The parameters are learned by minimizing the cross entropy loss between p_t and r_t.

$$\gamma = -\sum_t (r_t \log(p_t + (1 - r_t) \log(1 - p_t)) \tag{6}$$

4 Experiments

4.1 Datasets Description

We use two open-source public datasets and conduct extensive experiments to verify the excellent effect of the CAKT model. The information contained in the two datasets is shown in Table 1 with the information concerning the datasets shown below:

ASSISTments2009: This dataset was gathered by the ASSISTments online tutoring platform during the school year from 2009 to 2010.

ASSISTments2015: The ASSISTments online tutoring platform collected this dataset in 2015, covering response records of students.

Table 1. Statistics of all datasets

Datasets	Statistics		
	Students	Concepts	Records
ASSIST2009	4417	124	328 K
ASSIST2015	19,840	100	683 K
STATICS	333	1223	189 K
Sythetic	4000	50	200 K
ASSISTChall	1709	102	943 K

4.2 Comparison Methods

We compared CAKT with several classic methods including DKT, DKVMN and CKT. The details of the comparison methods include the following:

DKT utilizes RNN for modeling students' learning performance, we chose LSTM for our implementation because of its stronger modeling capability.

DKVMN Through the dynamic and static network, the knowledge level of students is continuously updated in the process of student training.

CKT models individualization in the student learning process by applying CNNs.

Experimental code We obtained the source code of the DKVMN model and CKT model released by the original author from the open source website, and combined our ideas to better carry out experiments. The original implementation of DKT was programmed by Lua, instead, we used Python to re-implement the DKT model.

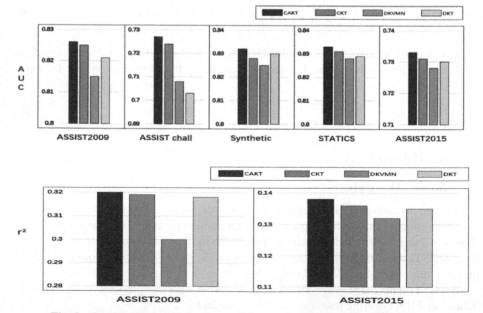

Fig. 2. Results of our model and comparison methods experimented in datasets.

4.3 Experimental Setup

For our experiment, all of the proposed models including data preprocessing, model training and evaluating are implemented by Python, using the deep learning framework Tensorflow on a Linux server with a six-core 2.5 GHz Intel Xeon E5-2678 CPU and an NVIDIA GeForce RTX 2080Ti GPU. At each stage of the model, we tune the parameters by randomly initializing the weights and biases of each layer from a Gaussian distribution with zero mean and standard deviation. The size of the amount of data put into the model for each batch is 50. The epoch number is set to 100. To avoid phenomena such as overfitting, we set the dropout parameter of the model to 0.2, the learning rate to 0.03, and the decay every 10 steps to 0.2.

4.4 Conclusions

In order to better judge the performance of CAKT, we adopt the mainstream judgment criteria to analyze the performance of the model. We chose two classic indicators including Area Under Curve (AUC) and coefficient of determination (r^2).

The judgment standard of the experiment is that the higher the index parameters of the model, the higher the prediction accuracy of the model and the better performance. The experimental results of the model can be seen intuitively in the bar graph in Fig. 2. From the comparison of the bar graphs, we can intuitively feel that all the indicators of the CAKT model have improved the performance of the previous models. CAKT obtains a test AUC of 82.6% whilst the highest comparison method, namely, CKT gets 82.4%. The prediction results effectively demonstrate the capabilities of our proposed model.

References

1. Corbett, A.T., Anderson, J.R.: Knowledge tracing: modeling the acquisition of procedural knowledge. User Model. User-Adap. Inter. **4**, 253–278 (1994)
2. Nagatani, K., Zhang, Q., Sato, M., Chen, Y.Y., Chen, F., Ohkuma, T.: Augmenting knowledge tracing by considering forgetting behavior. In: Proceedings of the 28th International Conference on World Wide Web, pp. 3101–3107, April 2019
3. Piech, C., et al.: Deep knowledge tracing. In: Proceedings of the 28th International Conference on Neural Information Processing Systems, pp. 505–513, December 2015
4. Zhang, J., Shi, X., King, I., Yeung, D.Y.: Dynamic key-value memory networks for knowledge tracing. In: Proceedings of the 26th International Conference on World Wide Web, pp. 765–774, April 2017
5. Shen, S., et al.: Convolutional knowledge tracing: modeling individualization in student learning process. In: Proceedings of the ACM SIGIR Conference on Research and Development in Information Retrieval, pp. 1857–1860, July 2020. https://doi.org/10.1145/3397271.3401288
6. Vaswani, A., et al.: Attention is all you need. In: Proceedings of the 31st International Conference on Neural Information Processing Systems, pp. 6000–6010, December 2017
7. Bello, I., Zoph, B., Le, Q., Vaswani, A., Shlens, J.: Attention augmented convolutional networks. In: 2019 IEEE/CVF International Conference on Computer Vision (ICCV), October 2019. https://doi.org/10.1109/ICCV.2009.00338

8. Krizhevshy, A., Sutskever, I., Hinton, G.E.: ImageNet classification with deep convolutional neural networks. Commun. ACM **60**(6), 84–90 (2017). https://doi.org/10.1145/3065386
9. Kim, Y.: Convolutional neural networks for sentence classification. In: Proceedings of the 2014 Conference on Empirical Methods in Natural Language Processing (EMNLP 2014), pp. 1746–1751, October 2014. https://doi.org/10.3115/v1/D14-1181
10. Chorowski, J., Bahdanau, D., Serdyuk, D., Cho, K., Bengio, Y.: Attention-based models for speech recognition. In: Proceedings of the 28th International Conference on Neural Information Processing Systems, pp. 577–585, December 2015
11. Luong, T., Pham, H., Maning, C.D.: Effective approaches to attention-based neural machine translation. In: Proceedings of the 2015 Conference on Empirical Methods in Natural Language Processing (EMNLP 2015), pp. 1412–1421, September 2015. https://doi.org/10.18653/v1/D15-1166
12. Pandey, S., Karypis, G.: A self-attentive model for knowledge tracing. arXiv preprint arXiv: 1907.06837 (2019)
13. Feng, W., Tang, J., Liu, T.X., Zhang, S., Guan, J.: Understanding dropouts in MOOCs. In: Proceedings of the 33rd AAAI Conference on Artificial Intelligence, vol. 33(01), pp. 517–524 (2019). https://doi.org/10.1609/aaai.v33i01.3301517

Data Mining

Data Mining

Interactive Mining of User-Preferred Co-location Patterns Based on SVM

Yuxiang Zhang[2], Xuguang Bao[1,2], Liang Chang[1,2(✉)], and Tianlong Gu[1,3]

[1] Guangxi Key Laboratory of Trusted Software, Guilin 541004, China
[2] Guilin University of Electronic Technology, Guilin 541004, China
changl@guet.edu.cn
[3] Jinan University, Guangzhou 510632, China

Abstract. Co-location pattern mining plays an important role in spatial data mining. With the rapid growth of spatial datasets, the usefulness of co-location patterns is strongly limited by the huge amount of the discovered patterns. To overcome this drawback, several statistics-based methods have been proposed to reduce the number of discovered co-location patterns. However, these methods cannot guarantee that their mined patterns are really user-preferred. Therefore, it is crucial to help users discover the co-location patterns they preferred through effective interactions. This paper proposes a newly interactive approach based on SVM, in order to discover user-preferred co-location patterns. First, we presented an originally interactive framework to help the user discover his/her preferred co-location patterns. Then, we designed a filtering algorithm with a small part of patterns as the training set of the SVM model for the provision of each interactive process, by which a high efficiency could be achieved by the optimization of the SVM model. Finally, the system was verified on both the real data sets and the synthetic data sets, accompanying with the 80% prediction accuracy.

Keywords: Spatial data mining · Interesting co-location patterns · Machine learning · Support vector machines · Interactive system

1 Introduction

Spatial co-location pattern mining is an important task in spatial data mining. A spatial co-location pattern represents a subset of spatial features whose instances are frequently located in spatial neighborhoods [1]. Co-location patterns can support decision making in various domains. For example, government agencies collect co-location patterns that residents are interested in to plan reasonable bus routes. Other application domains include biology, air pollution and earth science [2].

There exists a common problem in spatial co-location patterns mining, that is, only a small part of user-preferred patterns can be found by traditional mining methods. In general, the participation index (PI) value proposed by Shekhar and Huang [3] is used to measure the interest level of a co-location pattern [4], i.e., Given a user-specified prevalence threshold min_prev, for a co-location pattern c, if $PI(c) \geq$ min_prev holds, c

© IFIP International Federation for Information Processing 2022
Published by Springer Nature Switzerland AG 2022
Z. Shi et al. (Eds.): IIP 2022, IFIP AICT 643, pp. 89–100, 2022.
https://doi.org/10.1007/978-3-031-03948-5_8

is considered prevalent (interesting). However, the PI value is an objective measurement and satisfies the anti-monotonicity (i.e., $PI(c) \geq PI(c')$ if $c \subseteq c'$), if a co-location is prevalent, all its subsets are also prevalent. Thus, growing the size of spatial datasets, common frameworks generate numerous prevalent co-location patterns, amongst them only a small fraction might be user-preferred. Thus, several condensed representations of prevalent co-locations are proposed in the related literature including maximal co-location [5], closed co-location patterns [6], and super participation index closed co-location patterns [7].

However, it is found that the co-location patterns with a high PI value are often common senses, e.g. {hospital, pharmacy}. Hence, they may be redundant to one user yet the above-mentioned condensed representations are unable to filter them out. Users assess whether they prefer a co-location pattern according to their subjective judgments. Therefore, the mining methods should be based on solid interactivity with the user to discover user-preferred co-location patterns. Motivated by the interactive mining methods in transactional data mining, several methods of user-preferred co-location patterns mining based on probability [8] and ontologies [9] are proposed. Although these interactive methods can discover co-location patterns that users are really interested in, they still have some shortcomings. The probabilistic method only concerns with the composition of co-location patterns, similar combinations of co-location patterns will be judged as user-preferred patterns. The ontology-based method only concerns the semantics of co-location patterns. It is assumed that if a co-location pattern is user-preferred, other co-location patterns with similar semantics are also user-preferred.

In order to overcome the above shortcomings and improve the accuracy of co-location patterns mining. In this paper, an interactive mining method based on support vector machine (IMMBS) is proposed to discover user-preferred co-location patterns. Our goal is to help a particular user interactively discover interesting co-location patterns according to his/her real interest. Instead of requiring the user to explicitly express his/her real interesting co-location patterns, we alleviate the user's burden by only asking him/her to choose a small set of sample co-location patterns according to his/her interest for several rounds.

SVM is a supervised machine learning algorithm in the field of machine learning, it is mainly used for classification problems and has been successfully applied in text classification [10], biological information [11], image recognition [12], etc. As a standard classification tool, SVM does not need to rely on all the data, that it, only a part of support vector is used to make hyperplane decisions. In IMMBS, we train the SVM model with a small subject of co-location patterns and the SVM model learns combinations of different features. Therefore, the shortcomings of the composition or semantics of the co-location patterns are solved.

Figure 1 shows the description of IMMBS. It is similar to the process of traditional interactive co-location patterns mining, which requires a set of prevalent co-locations as the input. In each interaction, the filtering algorithm selects several (e.g., 10–30) co-location patterns from candidate set to present to the user. The user then indicates his/her preference on each provided co-location pattern, and these labelled co-location patterns are inputted into the SVM model as the training set. Next, the SVM model learns from the training set and predicts the candidate set. IMMBS outputs the prediction results of each co-location pattern in the candidate set and the distance from each pattern to the hyperplane, and updates the training set. The interaction process continues for several rounds until no further changes are made in forecast results, or the user stops the process.

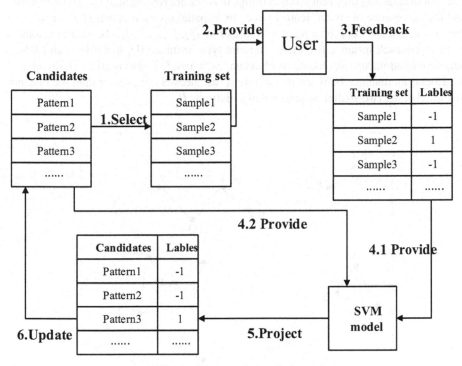

Fig. 1. Framework description.

In summary, this paper makes the following three contributions for interactive co-location pattern mining.

1) A novel interactive mining framework is designed to enable users to discover their preferred co-location patterns. This framework avoids using the objective PI value as a threshold, and assists different users in effectively discovering the patterns they are really interested in.
2) We propose a method to calculate the similarity between different co-location patterns based on the features of the pattern, and design a filtering algorithm based on this similarity and the support vectors of different co-location patterns.
3) The SVM model is optimized to assist IMMBS to achieve higher accuracy through fewer interactions, thus reducing the pressure of user selection.

2 Related Work and Problem Statement

2.1 Prevalent Co-location Patterns

In a spatial database, different kinds of things in space are represented by spatial features, and the occurrence of spatial features once in a spatial position is called an instance of this spatial feature. Let F be a set of n features $F = \{f_1, f_2, ..., f_n\}$, S be a set of instances of F, where each instance is a tuple <feature type, instance ID, location>, and R be a neighbor relationship over locations of instances, where R is symmetric and reflexive. If the Euclidean distance between two different instances is not greater than the distance threshold d, the two spatial instances will satisfy the R.

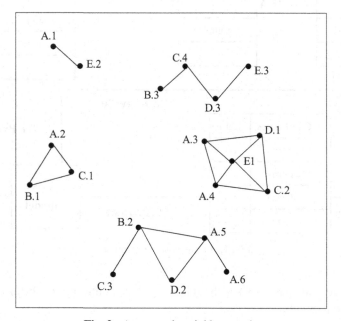

Fig. 2. An example neighbor graph.

A co-location pattern c is composed of a set of spatial features (i.e., c is a subset of F). The number of features in c is called the size of c. If any instance set satisfies the relationship R with other instances in the instance set, then a clique is formed by the instances in the instance set. A row instance I of a co-location c is a set of instances in S. The set of all row instances of c is called table instance of c. If the Participation index (PI) of a co-location pattern c is no less than a given prevalence threshold min_prev (i.e. $PI(c) \geq min\_prev$), then c is defined as a prevalent co-location pattern.

Figure 2 shows an example of spatial instance distribution. It contains 5 features (A, B, C, D, E), where $A.1$ is represented as the first instance of A. This space contains 5 instances of A, 3 instances of B, 4 instances of C, 3 instances of D, and 3 instances of E. The connection lines indicate that two spatial instances meet the neighbor relationship. For example, $A.1$ and $E.2$ are mutual neighbors. $\{A.2, B.1, C.1\}$ is formed into a clique, and it is a row instance of a 3-size co-location pattern $\{A, B, C\}$. Since, the table instance of the co-location pattern $\{A, B, C\}$ is namely $\{\{A.2, B.1, C.1\}\}$ for the reason that there are no other instances that contain the features A, B, and C. If $PI(\{A, B, C\}) \geq$ min_prev, $\{A, B, C\}$ will be defined as a prevalent co-location pattern.

Huang et al. previously reported that a join-based algorithm discovery prevalent co-location patterns [4]. However, this algorithm is inefficient when processing dense spatial databases. Yoo and Shekhar proposed the partial-join approach [13] and join-less approach [14], which solved the efficiency disadvantage of the join-based approach by constructing a neighboring list through the materialization of the whole spatial data.

2.2 Interaction with Users in Pattern Mining

In transactional data mining, many interactive systems have been proposed. The common ideas are as follows: given a set of candidate patterns, the system selects several sample patterns for the user, then requires the user to express his/her preferences on the sample patterns. Finally, the personalization model is utilized to estimate the user's prior knowledge. This system outputs all user's preferred patterns through multiple interactions. However, spatial data is much more complex than transactional data, which leads to the fact that interactive mining methods in transactional data cannot be applied to spatial data mining.

In co-location patterns mining, several interactive systems have been proposed to discover user-preferred co-location patterns. Bao et al. [15] proposed an interactive ontology-based method, where ontologies were used to select the sample patterns and update the candidates. Wang et al. [8] presented an interactive probabilistic postmining method to discover user-preferred co-location patterns by iteratively obtaining user feedback and probabilistically refining preferred patterns. However, two similar co-location patterns are outputting the same result using these two methods. The user's preferences are subjective, so that small differences make the user give different choices in practical cases. Therefore, in this paper, we present a novel filtering algorithm and an interactive system, which are more adaptable than the existing methods, to assist the user in discovering his/her preferred co-location patterns through an interactive process.

2.3 Problem Statement

The problem of post-mining preferred spatial co-location patterns through interactive feedback can be stated as follows. Given a set of prevalent co-location patterns, the system outputs the ideal user-preferred co-location patterns according to the user's feedback, and at the same time minimize the user's efforts in providing feedback.

Considering the uncertainties of the user's ideal preference, in this paper we design a novel filtering to learn the prior knowledge of the user and use the SVM model to predict the user-preferred co-location patterns. The basic idea of this method is: given a set F of prevalent co-location patterns, there exists a set F_l of ideal preference co-location patterns in F for a user. Actually, the system does not know which pattern belong to F_l in the interactive process. The pattern in F_l is selected by the filtering algorithm as much as possible. Then the user labels the selected patterns and put them into the SVM model for training. According to the output data of the SVM model, the patterns in F is selected again by the system. The resultant output set would finally be close to the user's ideal preference result set after repeated interactions.

3 Algorithm

3.1 Similarity Calculation of Co-location Patterns

In traditional transactional data mining, Jaccard index is widely adopted to measure the distance between two item-sets. However, this index cannot be used to calculate the similarity between two co-location patterns in co-location data mining because there exist no conceptions of transactions in spatial data. Thus, we calculate the similarity between co-location patterns based on the characteristics of different co-location patterns, and the similarity measure is defined as follows:

$$similarity(c_1, c_2) = \frac{|T(c_1) \cap T(c_2)|}{|T(c_1) \cup T(c_2)|} \tag{1}$$

Where c_1 and c_2 are two different co-location patterns, $T(c_1)$ is the features contained in c_1. A larger value of $similarity(c_1, c_2)$ demonstrates the similarity of the two co-locations, i.e., c_1 and c_2.

For example, let $c_1 = \{A, B, C, D, E\}$, $c_2 = \{B, D, F, G\}$, $T(c_1) \cap T(c_2) = \{B, D\}$, $T(c_1) \cup T(c_2) = \{A, B, C, D, E, F, G\}$, so $similarity(c_1, c_2) = 2/7$.

3.2 SVM Model

The co-location patterns marked by the user are used as the training set of SVM model. Assuming a training set S = $[(x_1, y_1), (x_2, y_2), ...,(x_n, y_n)]$, where $x_i = (x_{i1}, x_{i2}, ..., x_{im})$ represents a vector of input; y_i denotes the corresponding output vector; n means the sample number; m denotes the number of input vector dimension.

The distance from each pattern to the hyperplane is an important measure in the filtering algorithm. This distance is calculated by the SVM model in each prediction process. The equation dividing the hyperplane is expressed as $\omega^T x + b = 0$, where the direction of the hyperplane is determined by the normal vector ω and b is the displacement term which determines the distance between the hyperplane and the origin. The distance from each pattern to the hyperplane is denoted as d.

$$d = \frac{|\omega \cdot x + b|}{||\omega||} \tag{2}$$

The SVM performance and overfitting phenomena are affected by kernel function selection and hyperparameter optimization [16]. Thus, accuracy is evaluated in each training step, so if all parameter combinations have been examined, then the best kernel parameter will be used to build the SVM. Finally, the classification accuracy of the obtained SVM will be evaluated.

The specific process of the SVM model is shown in Algorithm 1, where *kernels* contain kernel functions such as *liner, rbf*. The prediction score of each kernel function is calculated, and the maximal one is selected as the kernel function of the training model. Then the candidate set is predicted. Finally, the distance from each pattern to the hyperplane and the prediction result is the output.

Algorithm 1 SVM model

Input:
  CS: A set of candidates.
  TS: A set of training samples.
Output:
  $Result$: The label of each pattern in the candidate set, distance_set.
Variables:
  $kernels$: the set of kernel functions.
Method:
  1) **For Each** $kernel$ in $kernels$ **Do**
  2)   score_list.add(svc($kernel,TS$));
  3) train_model(max_sore_list,TS);
  4) predict_model(CS);
  5) cal_distance();
  6) **Return** $Result$;

Assume that there are n labeled patterns in the training set, SVM model training typically needs $O(n^2)$ calculation.

3.3 Filtering Algorithm

A good selecting method contributes to the improvement of interaction efficiency. To enable users to obtain co-location patterns with different features more efficiently, the patterns outputted by the SVM model near the hyperplane (i.e., the predicted ambiguous patterns) are also given to users for re-label. Therefore, we design a new filtering algorithm based on the similarity calculation method of transactional data and the distance from each co-location pattern output from the SVM model to the hyperplane. The idea is as follows:

1) The proportion of different quantitative feature patterns in the candidate sets is calculated and divided into several small candidate sets according to the number of features.
2) The filtering algorithm selects a pattern with the maximum PI value into the training sets.
3) The union operation is performed for each feature of the training set.
4) Calculate the similarity between the candidate set and the union generated in the previous step.
5) The similarity of each pattern in the candidate set is added to the distance from each pattern to the hyperplane output by the SVM model, and the value is denoted as *sum*

In each small candidate set generated in step 1, the algorithm could choose the pattern corresponding to the minimum sum value and put it into the training set. Algorithm 2 shows the pseudocode of the filtering algorithm. It contains three parts: 1) calculating the proportions of the patterns of different sizes (lines 1 and 2); 2) adding the filter parameters (similarity and distance) for each pattern (lines 5–7); 3) filtering by proportion (lines 8 and 9). The computational complexity of the three parts is O(|CS|), O(|CS|), and O(|sizes|). Note that TS is empty in the initial and the pattern with the maximum PI is put into TS. DIS is the distance output by the SVM model. If the system interacts with the user for the first time, the DIS will be empty and only the similarity will be calculated.

Algorithm 2 Filtering Algorithm

Input:
  CS: A set of candidates.
  TS: A set of training samples.
  DIS: A set of each pattern to hyperplane.
Output:
  TS
Variables:
  pattern: The co-location pattern in the candidate set.
  sizes: The proportion of different quantitative feature patterns.
  u: The union of all features in the training set.
  sum: The sum of similarity and distance of each pattern.
Method:
  1) **For Each** *pattern* in *CS* **Do**
  2)   sizes = cal_size();
  3) **If** *TS* == NULL **Then**
  4)   *TS*.Add(max_PI(*CS*));
  5) *u* = union(*TS*);
  6) **For Each** *pattern* in *CS* **Do**
  7)   sim_list.Add(cal_similarity(*pattern*,*u*));
  8) *sum* = sim_list + *DIS*;
  9) **For Each** *size* in *sizes* **Do**
  10)   *TS*.Add(min_sim_list(*size*));
  11) **return** *TS*;

---

4   Evaluation of the Experiment

In this chapter, we used both real data sets and synthetic data sets to verify the accuracy of the IMMBS and the effectiveness of the algorithm.

4.1   Experimental Analysis of Real Data

Experimental analysis of the real dataset was mainly used to verify the accuracy of IMMBS. The real dataset was a spatial POI dataset of urban elements in Beijing, which contained 16 spatial features. The number of spatial instances was 90 000 and the spatial range was 18 km × 18 km. We mined 960 prevalent co-location patterns by setting the minimum prevalence threshold as 0.4 and setting the distance threshold as 80 m.

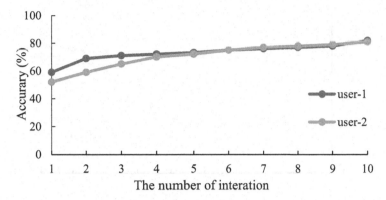

Fig. 3. Forecast results of different users.

The effectiveness of IMMBS for users with different prior knowledge was proved more intuitively. We simulated two different user preferences as the standard set user-1 and user-2 to verify the accuracy of IMMBS. The measurement formula of accuracy in the experiment is Accuracy $= (M \cap N)/(M \cup N)$, M is expressed as a standard set (user-1 or user-2), N is expressed as the result set output by IMMBS.

Figure 3 shows the accuracy of IMMBS under different users. In the previous few interactions, the prediction accuracy of the two users was different. This was because the screened co-location patterns in the previous few times were rarely interesting to user-2. IMMBS's prediction accuracy for the two users tended to be the same after seven interactions. Thus, the prediction result showed that IMMBS was effective in predicting according to the preferences of different users.

The accuracy comparison between IMMBS and other interactive methods was exhibited in Fig. 4. F-1 was the accuracy rate of the interactive probabilistic post-mining method [8] under the same conditions and F-2 was the accuracy rate of the interactive mining method based on ontology [17] under the same conditions. The accuracy rate of IMMBS was higher than that of F-1 and F-2 under the same number of interactions. Thus, the prediction result showed that IMMBS was effective in predicting according to the preferences of different users.

4.2 Experimental Analysis of Synthetic Data

Evaluations based on the synthetic datasets illustrated the effectiveness of IMMBS on the dataset of different sizes and the effectiveness of the filtering algorithm.

Figure 5 showed the accuracy of 10 interactions using IMMBS in datasets of different sizes. S-1, S-2, S-3 was the accuracy rate with different capacity of input dataset, corresponding to 15000, 25000 and 35000 respectively. The results verify that IMMBS is effective on the dataset of different sizes.

The accuracy of IMMBS interacting was shown with the same user under the two algorithms (Fig. 6). The novel filtering algorithm was confirmed to be effective for IMMBS, by comparing a random algorithm. Obviously, the novel filtering algorithm was superior in the improvement of interaction efficiency and prediction accuracy of IMMBS.

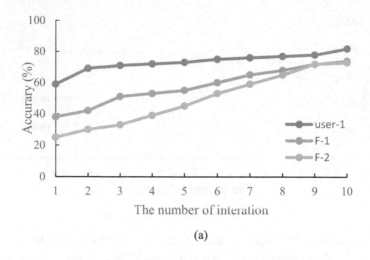

(a)

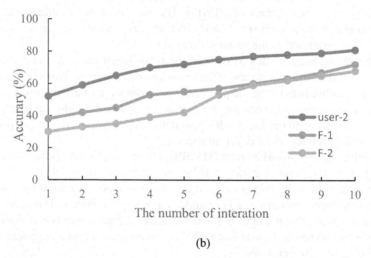

(b)

Fig. 4. (a) Comparison result of user-1, (b) Comparison result of user-2.

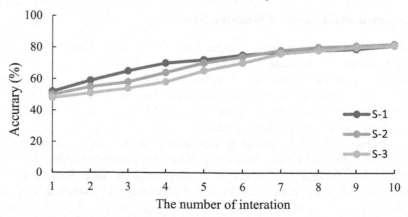

Fig. 5. Forecast results for different data set sizes.

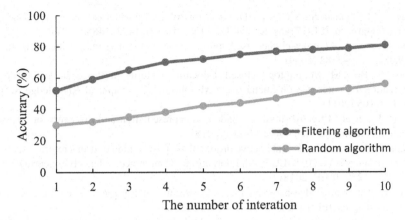

Fig. 6. Forecast results of different filtering algorithms.

5 Conclusions

In traditional co-location patterns mining approaches, the measurement was objective and users passively accept the results. In this paper, we designed a system IMMBS to find interesting patterns by interacting with users. Different from traditional mining methods, IMMBS with the SVM model was applied to predict the candidate sets by acquiring the user's prior knowledge. A filtering algorithm was designed to select the training sets for reducing the number of interactions and improving the efficiency of IMMBS.

We will apply new machine learning methods to interactive spatial co-location patterns mining in the following study. A new filter algorithm not only assists users to filter most of the co-location patterns, but also keeps the representative co-location patterns.

Acknowledgements. This work was supported in part by grants (No. U1811264, No. U1711263, No. 61966009, No. 62006057, 61762027) from the National Natural Science Foundation of China, in part by grants (No. 2018GXNSFDA281045, No. 2019GXNSFBA245059) from the Natural Science Foundation of Guangxi Province, and in parts by grants (No. AD19245011) from the Key Research and Development Program of Guangxi Province.

References

1. Verhein, F., Al-Naymat, G.: Fast mining of complex spatial co-location patterns using GLIMIT. In: Seventh IEEE International Conference on Data Mining Workshops (ICDMW 2007), pp. 679–684. IEEE (2007)
2. Anderson, J.M., et al.: Simulations of VLBI observations of a geodetic satellite providing co-location in space. J. Geodesy **92**(9), 1023–1046 (2018). https://doi.org/10.1007/s00190-018-1115-5
3. Shekhar, S., Huang, Y.: Discovering spatial co-location patterns: A summary of results. In: Jensen, C.S., Schneider, M., Seeger, B., Tsotras, V.J. (eds.) SSTD 2001. LNCS, vol. 2121, pp. 236–256. Springer, Heidelberg (2001). https://doi.org/10.1007/3-540-47724-1_13

4. Huang, Y., Shekhar, S., Xiong, H.: Discovering colocation patterns from spatial data sets: a general approach. IEEE Trans. Knowl. Data Eng. **16**(12), 1472–1485 (2004)
5. Wang, L., et al.: An order-clique-based approach for mining maximal co-locations. Inf. Sci. **179**(19), 3370–3382 (2009)
6. Yoo, J.S., Bow, M.: Mining top-k closed co-location patterns. In: Proceedings of 2011 IEEE International Conference on Spatial Data Mining and Geographical Knowledge Services, pp. 100–105 (2011)
7. Wang, L., et al.: Effective lossless condensed representation and discovery of spatial co-location patterns. Inf. Sci. **436**, 197–213 (2018)
8. Wang, L., Bao, X., Cao, L.: Interactive probabilistic post-mining of user-preferred spatial co-location patterns. In: 2018 IEEE 34th International Conference on Data Engineering (ICDE), pp. 1256–1259. IEEE (2018)
9. Bao, X., et al.: Knowledge-based interactive postmining of user-preferred co-location patterns using ontologies. IEEE Trans. Cybern. 1–14 (2021)
10. Haddoud, M., Mokhtari, A., Lecroq, T., Abdeddaïm, S.: Combining supervised term-weighting metrics for SVM text classification with extended term representation. Knowl. Inf. Syst. **49**(3), 909–931 (2016). https://doi.org/10.1007/s10115-016-0924-1
11. Bertoni, A., Folgieri, R., Valentini, G.: Bio-molecular cancer prediction with random subspace ensembles of support vector machines. Neurocomputing **63**, 535–539 (2005)
12. Inglada, J.: Automatic recognition of man-made objects in high resolution optical remote sensing images by SVM classification of geometric image features. ISPRS J. Photogrammetry Remote Sens. **62**, 236–248 (2007)
13. Yoo, J.S., Shekhar, S., Smith, J., Kumquat, J.P.: A partial join approach for mining co-location patterns. In: Proceedings of ACM IWGIS, pp. 241–249 (2004)
14. Yoo, J.S., Shekhar, S.: A joinless approach for mining spatial colocation patterns. IEEE Trans. Knowl. Data Eng. **18**(10), 1323–1337 (2006)
15. Bao, X., Wang, L.: Discovering interesting co-location patterns interactively using ontologies. In: Bao, Z., Trajcevski, G., Chang, L., Hua, W. (eds.) DASFAA 2017. LNCS, vol. 10179, pp. 75–89. Springer, Cham (2017). https://doi.org/10.1007/978-3-319-55705-2_6
16. Yang, K., et al.: Towards factorized SVM with Gaussian Kernels over normalized data. In: 2020 IEEE 36th International Conference on Data Engineering (ICDE). IEEE (2020)
17. Bao, X., Wang, L., Xiao, Q.: OICPM: an interactive system to find interesting co-location patterns using ontologies. In: Chen, L., Jensen, C.S., Shahabi, C., Yang, X., Lian, X. (eds.) APWeb-WAIM 2017. LNCS, vol. 10367, pp. 329–332. Springer, Cham (2017). https://doi.org/10.1007/978-3-319-63564-4_29

Classification Between Rumors and Explanations of Rumors Based on Common and Difference Subsequences of Sentences

Xiaoping Sun[1(✉)], Junsheng Zhang[2], and Yufei Sang[3]

[1] Key Lab of Intelligent Information Processing, Institute of Computing Technology, Chinese Academy of Sciences, Beijing, China
sunxiaoping@ict.ac.cn
[2] Institute of Scientific and Technical Information of China, Beijing, China
zhangjs@istic.ac.cn
[3] School of Economics, Capital University of Economics and Business, Beijing, China

Abstract. Preventing explosion of rumors on the Internet asks for a quick automatic detection mechanism that can detect rumors according to the given true information. Previous automatic rumors detection models are mainly built by training a supervised classification model on a labeled dataset containing rumor samples and true information samples. However, in many real cases, there is only one short piece of available true information sample given by an authority in form of an explanation or a correction of a rumor. The explanation sample is often short and very similar to rumor samples, making it difficult to train a discriminative classifier to check whether a piece of information is a rumor or an explanation of rumors. It is necessary to build a model to detect whether a short text is a rumor text or an explanation of rumors, which can be used to as evidences for detecting and refuting rumors. In this paper, we presented a sentence preprocessing method that extracts the leftmost longest common sequence to obtain the common and difference subsequences between the rumor text and its explanation text to compose samples and train a supervised model for classification between rumors and explanation of rumors. Experiments show the effectiveness of the proposed method.

Keywords: Rumors · Explanation of rumors · Classification · Sentence subsequence

1 Introduction

With the boom of the mobile Internet and social media, rumor spreading has caused huge impact on social development, especially during the pandemic of Covid-19 since 2019 [1]. Rumors can be quickly spread on the Internet in form of short texts through social media platforms like Weibo or Twitter [2]. For example, during the pandemic of COVID-19, there are lots of rumors on that drinking much more tea or vinegar can

© IFIP International Federation for Information Processing 2022
Published by Springer Nature Switzerland AG 2022
Z. Shi et al. (Eds.): IIP 2022, IFIP AICT 643, pp. 101–113, 2022.
https://doi.org/10.1007/978-3-031-03948-5_9

protect people from infection. To prevent rumors from being spread on the Internet, automatic rumor detection techniques becomes necessary tools [3, 4]. Supervised automatic rumor detection models mainly treat the problem as a binary classification problem over a training sample set consisting of positive and negative sample cases [5]. There lacks interpretation in such supervised models. Evidence aware models leverage clues extracted from positive or negative samples to give evidences on the prediction results [6]. However, training samples of rumors are often imbalanced, especially in COVID-19 rumor detection tasks. There is still a challenge in finding positive samples because most posted information are rumors and there is often only one or few piece of information published by an authority as an explanation of rumors. Detecting whether a text is a rumor or an explanation of a rumor can help make a more explainable rumor classification model. This issue has not been fully recognized in the misinformation detection research. Moreover, the text of an explanation information is often very similar to texts of those widely disseminated rumors, which makes it difficult to discriminate a rumor text from an explanation text of the rumor by a classification model trained over imbalanced data sample set. To address this problem, we present a data preprocessing method that extracts common and difference subsequence between a rumor text and its corresponding explanation text to compose a rumor sample and its explanation sample for training a supervised model. Using common and difference subsequences as the training samples can make the sample features more discriminative and thus can be used to build more accurate classification model for predicting rumor text and their explanation text. We collected a set of samples of COVID-19 rumors, where each sample has a rumor text, a refutation text and an explanation text given by a medical authority. Experiments show that using the common and difference subsequences of text samples to train a supervised model can improve the accuracy of classification on rumors and explanation of rumors.

2   Related Work

Automatic misinformation detection models can be categorized into two classes, content-based methods [7] and network-based methods [3, 8]. In content-based methods, detecting misinformation is modeled as a binary classification problem. A classifier is trained on a given sample set consisting of true information samples and misinformation samples. SVM and deep learning models have been investigated for this task. The core challenge in content-based methods is the feature selection of misinformation sample data sets [9]. Many language features have been investigated for building misinformation classifier [10, 11]. In network-based methods, features of propagation network of misinformation on the Internet are leveraged to detect the misinformation event [12, 13].

The difficulties of misinformation detection lie mainly in that misinformation propagation are often event related [5, 14]. Texts are often short and samples are often imbalanced because in the beginning stage of the propagation of an event, most available samples are misinformation samples and there is even no positive information available. Moreover, explanation, refutation and correct information are published by authorities. So the number of positive information samples is often extremely small at the beginning stage of an event, which makes it difficult to obtain a balanced training sample set. For example, in an authority site where refutation on COVID-19 rumors are published, each statement about a rumor has one explanation and one conclusion description, but there are already hundreds or thousands of rumors on the social networks [15]. Those official explanation or conclusion can be used to detect misinformation but there is still few work on leveraging this information due to that the official explanation text is often quite similar to rumor text, which makes it difficult to train a supervised model for detecting whether a text is a rumor, or is an explanation of a rumor. Evidence-aware misinformation prediction has been studied [1, 6, 16]. However, most works need an enough number of positive samples to train a model and give clues on a prediction that why a text is misinformation or not. It is necessary to investigate how to leverage the explanation text of rumors to detect misinformation. Moreover, explanation texts given by an authority to clarify rumors can be used as explanation of classification results on rumors. The first step is to make a classification between a piece of rumor and an explanation of rumors. Automatic detection of explanation texts of rumors can help find the explanations for rumors.

3 Model

Given a set of short texts consisting of samples of pairs of rumors and their corresponding explanations, the task is to build a predictor to judge whether one given input sample text is a rumor or an explanation of a rumor. To discriminate a rumor from its explanation, a solution is to train a supervised classification model on a training set consisting of two sets of samples: one sample set contains rumor texts, and another contains explanation texts. Then we use the sample set to train a classifier that predicts a sample's type. Since the texts of explanation are often very similar to the rumor texts, we proposed to use sentence difference of samples texts as the texts of samples to build a classifier.

The main idea is that the difference between a rumor text and its explanation text is more representative than the original texts of the rumor and its explanation. It is because that a pair of rumor and explanation often shares too many words, and the difference between a rumor and its explanation often contains those common words among samples, which can be ignored in training a model. We leverage the difference part between sentences to train a classifier for classifying samples into two classes: a rumor or an explanation of a rumor.

Figure 1 depicts the whole framework of training a classification model from samples of rumor texts and explanation texts. The first part is the training sample preprocessing module that extracts difference and common subsequences from rumor texts and their corresponding explanation texts. Specifically, the difference subsequences can be obtained from the results of common subsequences. Then, the original sample texts are transformed into a set of subsequences of common parts and difference part of the original texts of samples. Those subsequences of texts are concatenated to form a new text string for each sample. Finally, those newly composed samples are used as the training samples to train a supervised classification model.

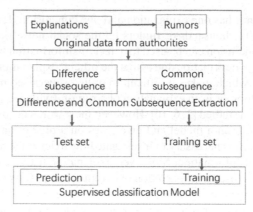

Fig. 1. Framework of processing explanations and rumors for training supervised classification models.

3.1 Data Samples

To ease discussion, we use the following symbols to represent samples. Given a rumor sample data set M, each sample t in M contains four items:

(1) $t.T$: the sentence text of a rumor t;

(2) $t.L$: a label indicating if the rumor $t.T$ is a piece of rumor, true information or unknown information;

(3) $t.E$: the explanation text to show why the rumor is labeled as $t.L$.

(4) $t.F$: the conclusion text on the rumor label, i.e., giving the final judgement based on the explanation.

This kind of samples can be collected from those official rumor information management websites, where each sample consists of an explanation of refutation on one rumor. We will use this sample data set to train a predicator for text classification between rumor and explanation, or conclusion of a rumor based on sentence subsequences.

Table 1 shows three examples of samples. Each row represents one sample, consisting of a sample label, sample sentence texts, an explanation and a conclusion. There are three different labeled samples. For example, the first row is labeled as a rumor, saying that "*people do not need wearing mask after vaccination*". The explanation is given on why this argument is false and the conclusion is given by a famous doctor who is an authoritative professor in COVID-19 medication. From this example, one can see that the three text components of the first sample case are quite different in syntax level. The explanation text is much longer than the rumor text and contain words from the original rumor's text, while the conclusion text is totally different from the rumor text. The explanation of row 1 shares words "*vaccination*" and "*protection*" with the rumor text, so this common part can be deemed as the core content related to both the rumor and the explanation of the rumor. If these two words are treated as features, then the explanation text could be also classified as a rumor text. To reduce this ambiguity in training samples, we assume that the difference part between rumor text and explanation texts are more discriminative features. For example, in row 1, the difference part between the explanation and the rumor text is about why one should pay attention to the protection even after vaccination.

Table 1. Examples of sample sets

t	t.L(Label)	t.T(Text)	t.E(Explanation)	t.F(Conclusion)
1	RUMOR	We do not need wearing a mask for protection after vaccination.	China's vaccine is mainly whole virus inactivated vaccine. Its safety is very good. If its effect is evaluated, the antibody appears after the first dose, which is about 60% and 70%. 14 days after the second dose, its antibody level can reach nearly 90%. There is no antibody until at least two to three weeks after the vaccination. There is still a risk of infection between the vaccination and the production of the antibody, and personal protection should also be paid attention to.	Zhong Nanshan denied it.
2	TRUE	The dog in the infected person's home is weakly positive	A news report confirmed that a pet dog was tested weakly positive for the virus test, according to the Hongkong Wenhui network. Hongkong food and health secretary Chen Zhaoshi stressed on 28, there is no evidence that dogs will spread COVID-19 to humans. She called on pet owners to pay attention to personal protection. Chen Zhaoshi said that the dog would receive medical supervision from the veterinarian and take samples for testing. It would not be returned until the test results were negative.	Chen Zhaoshi, director of the Hongkong food and food administration, stressed that although there was a weak positive finding, there was no evidence that dogs would transmit COVID-19 to humans.
3	UNKNOWN	The virus will stay in the throat for 4 days. Can it be remedied?	There is a rumor that "COVID-19 has to stay in the throat for 4 days before reaching the lung. At this point, the patient will begin to have symptoms of cough and sore throat. But if you drink a lot of water and gargle with warm water, salt or vinegar, you can eliminate the virus." There is still no positive or negative evidence show that the virus will stay in the throat for 4 or more days. In addition, brine, vinegar and water did not kill COVID-19.	There is no research data to support this statement.

The second row in Table 1 is a sample of true information saying that a virus test on a pet dog of a patient shows a positive result. It is true according to the official report. The explanation and the conclusion both repeat the details of the official report. There are many common parts in the rumor, explanation and conclusion text. When removing those common part from the explanation text, the difference part is the official confirmation that can be used as features to determine the text type.

The third row in Table 1 contains an unknown sample case which means that it is still unclear that whether the text is a rumor or not. Similarly, the difference part can be used to distinguish the conclusion text from the original rumor text. However, the explanation text contains a subsequence string that repeats the original rumor text, makes it difficult to obtain a discriminative feature for classifying the rumor text and the explanation text for this sample case. When removing those common parts, it can be more distinguishable as an explanation sample. Thus, the observation on the sample texts shows that both the common parts and the difference parts between texts can play important roles in making discriminative features for training a supervised classification model that can be used to distinguish the explanation of rumors from rumors.

3.2 Sentence Subsequence Preprocessing

To extract common and difference part from sample texts in the training set M, sentence text S of a rumor or an explanation is firstly represented as an n-gram character sequence

$S = \{S_1, S_2,...., S_n\}$, where S_i is a ith n-gram character in S. n-gram is a widely used text feature model that takes every n consecutive words from a text sequence as one keyword unit. In processing Chinese texts, an n-gram unit consists of n consecutive characters from the text. In this work, we use the uni-gram model as the basic unit for representing rumor texts because the word segmentation problem can be skipped when using uni-gram to represent Chinese text sentences. Thus, each uni-gram of a sentence is treated as a character.

A subsequence s of k characters in S is a character sequence $s = \{S_j, S_{j+1},..., S_{j+k}\}$ for $1 \leq j \leq n - k$. Two subsequences of characters are equal if each corresponding character is the same.

Two types of subsequences are defined for two sentence sequences of characters. A common subsequence contains characters shared by two sequences while a difference subsequence records the different part between two sentence sequences.

Definition 1 (Common subsequence). Given two sentence character sequences S and T, the common part between two sentence character sequences is a set of subsequences, denoted as $C(S, T) = \{s_1, s_2,..., s_m\}$, where s_i is a subsequence in both S and T. That is, $C(S, T)$ contains sub-characters that are shared by two sentences S and T.

Definition 2 (Difference subsequence). The difference between S and T contains s of characters that are obtained by excluding their common part from S, denoted as $D(S, T) = S - C(S, T)$. Similarly, the difference between T and S is defined as $D(T, S) = T - C(S, T)$. So the difference between two sentence character sequences is not symmetric.

Both the common part and difference part between two text character sequences can be used as features to train a supervised classification model. Thus, we need to extract common sequences and difference sequences for two text character sequences. Note that the difference subsequence in Definition 2 is defined based on the common subsequence in Definition 1. Thus, to obtain the difference between two sentences S and T, we first compute the common part shared by S and T and then the difference part can be obtained from the common part.

The common subsequence is obtained by the algorithm *computecomm* in Fig. 2. In the algorithm, line 4 to 19 is the loop to traverse each character of S to find if there is any common character in T. During the loop, if there is a common character from S for current character of T, then it will be added to the current common subsequence list (*subc1* in line 6 of *computecomm*) until it encounters a different character of T. Then current common subsequence is recorded and is initialized for the next possible common subsequence. It can be shown that the algorithm *computecomm* can find leftmost longest common subsequences of S and T in at most $O(N_1 * N_2)$ time, where N_1 and N_2 is the length of S and T.

Definition 3. The leftmost longest common subsequence of S in T is a character sequence $l_1 = \{S_{i+0}, S_{i+1},..., S_{i+k}\}$ in S s.t. that there is a subsequence $l_2 = \{T_j, T_{j+1},..., T_{j+k}\}$ in T with $S_i = T_j$, $S_{i+1} = T_{j+1},...,$ and $S_{i+k} = T_{j+k}$, but there is no such subsequence of $l_1 = \{T_{p+0}, T_{p+1},..., T_{p+n}\} = \{S_{i+0}, S_{i+1},..., S_{i+n}\}$ with $p < j$ and $n \leq k$.

That is, we only locate the first occurrence of a common subsequence of S in T. For example, let $S = $ "*the covid-19 syndrome include cough, chill and muscle pain*" and T

```
ALGORITHM:computecomm
INPUT:   S: Sentence character sequence
         T: Sentence character sequence
OUTPUT subsame: list of common sub-sequence of S and T
         allc: string of common sequence part
 1  n1 = len(S);n2 = len(T)
 2  i = 0,j = 0
 3  subc1 = [];subsame = []
 4  while(i<n1):
 5      if (S[i] == T[j]):
 6          subc1.append(i #find the start of common part
 7          i = i + 1;j = j + 1
 8          if j>=n2:
 9              j = 0
10          continue
11      else:
12          if len(subc1)>0 #record the common part
13              subsame.append(subc1)
14              subc1 = []
15              j = 0
16          else:
17              j = j + 1
18          if j>=n2:
19              i = i + 1;j = 0
20  if len(subc1) > 0:
21      subsame.append(subc1);subc1 = []
22  subsamestr = [];allc = ''
23  for s in subsame:
24      st = ''
25      cstart = s[0]
26      cend = len(s)
27      for c in s:
28          st = st + c1[c]
29      subsamestr.append([st,cstart,cend])
30      if len(st)>0:
31          allc = allc +segword(st) + ' '
32  return subsamestr, allc
```

Fig. 2. Algorithm for finding the common part from sentence character sequence S and T.

= "*cough, chill are common syndrome. cough, chill and muscle pain are also reported widely*". Here, "*cough, chill*" is a common subsequence for S and T, but "*cough, chill and muscle pain*" is also a common subsequence for S and T. In this example, "*cough, chill*" is the leftmost longest common subsequence while "*cough, chill and muscle pain*" is not because when matching "*cough, chill and muscle pain*" of S in T, "*cough, chill*" is already matched before. Thus, "*cough, chill and muscle pain*" will not be extracted as a longer common subsequence. We do not use the longest common subsequence because that the longest common sequence will overlap those shorter common subsequences. The leftmost longest common subsequence is the first occurrence of a common sequence. Using the leftmost longest common subsequence can avoid those shorter common subsequences being overlapped.

Theorem 1. All leftmost longest common subsequences of S in T can be obtained by the algorithm *computecomm* with time complexity of $O(N_1 * N_2)$.

Proof. Assume there is such a common subsequence $l_1 = \{S_i, S_{i+1},..., S_{i+k}\}$ starting at S_i in S, with corresponding subsequence $l_2 = \{T_j, T_{j+1},..., T_{j+k}\}$ in T. That is, S_{i-1} is different from T_{j-1}. Since the algorithm *computecomm* iterates every character of S

started at line 4, it must meet the character S_{i-1} and thus, any previous subsequences will be recorded and a new subsequence will be started by line 12–15 where iteration in T is restarted from the beginning by line 15. Thus, the next loop will check S_i by starting from the very beginning part of T to find the common character for S_i. If there is a character $T_p = S_i$, then, it will be recorded into the common subsequence, denoted as *subc1* in line 6 of the algorithm *computecomm*, until meeting a different character, then the recorded subsequence *subc1* is a common subsequence within l_1 and l_2 and is the left most common subsequence of S in T. If it is not the left most, there must be another subsequence l_3 starting before *subc1*. But it is impossible, because the checking point starts at the beginning item of T for l_1, l_3 cannot be missed by *subc1*. Thus, *subc1* must be a left-most common subsequence of S in T. The whole scanning procedure in T for each character of S is at most one time. So the time complexity of the algorithm *computecomm* is $O(N_1*N_2)$. □

After obtaining common parts of S and T, we remove those common subsequences from S to obtain the difference part between S and T. Figure 3 depicts the procedure *computediff* that leverages the algorithm *computecomm* in Fig. 2 to get the difference subsequences. Note that during the procedure of locating the common subsequences in the algorithm *computecomm* in Fig. 2, the starting and ending position of a common subsequence is also recorded in line 29. We can use the position information to remove common parts from sentence character sequence S for obtaining the difference between S and T. In *computediff*, first, *computecomm* procedure is called to obtain the common subsequence list that contains all the matched leftmost common subsequence. Then, *computediff* iterates each character of S in line 4. Within each loop of a character of S, there is another loop for each common subsequence, where if current character of S is within a common sequence, then skip this character and record the difference subsequence that has been located and go for the next character (line 11 to line 14). If current character of S does not exist in any common subsequence, then put it into the current difference subsequence and go to the next character at line 16 and line 17.

The loop from line 4 to line 17 in the algorithm *computediff* also takes $O(N_1 * N_2)$ because it has one loop for each character of S and within each loop there is one scan for all the common subsequence that has at most N_2 items.

```
ALGORITHM: computediff(S, T)
INPUT:        S: Sentence character sequence
              T: Sentence character sequence
OUTPUT:       difflist: difference part of S and T
              allc: string of difference sub sequence

 1  n1 = len(S);n2 = len(T)
 2  i = 0; l2 = len(T); diff = [];difflist=[];
 3  commlist, comstr = compuecomm(S,T)
 4  while(i<n1):
 5      iinsame = False
 6      for c in commlist:
 7          if i>=c[1] and i <c[1]+c[2]:
 8              iinsame = True
 9              break
10      if iinsame:
11          if len(diff)>0:
12              difflist.append(diff)
13              diff = []
14          i = i + 1
15      else:
16          diff.append(c1[i])
17          i = i + 1
18  if len(diff)>0:
19      difflist.append(diff)
20  allc = "
21  for sc in difflist:
22      if len(sc)>0:
23          allc = allc + " ".join(sc) +" "
27  return difflist,allc.strip()
```

Fig. 3. ALOGRITHM *computediff* for finding the difference part from sentence character sequence S and T.

3.3 Training a Supervised Classification Model by Subsequences of Sample Sentences

We use common and difference parts of sentence of sample texts to build a new sample set from the original sample set M for training a supervised classification model. Specifically, for each sample case t in M, we use the difference and common parts between rumor text $t.T$, rumor explanation $t.E$ and rumor conclusion $t.F$ to compose the samples to train a classification model for determining three classes: *rumor*, *explanation*, and *conclusion* class.

That is, for each sample t with $t.T$ as a *rumor* sample, $t.E$ as an *explanation* sample and $t.F$ as a *conclusion*, we apply the common subsequence extractor $C(S,T)$ and difference subsequence extractor $D(S, T)$ to compose three new sample texts from the original texts of $t.T$, $t.E$ and $t.F$, which are used as three new sample texts, represented by $t'.T$, $t'.E$ and $t'.F$ for three classes: *rumor*, *explanation*, and *conclusion* respectively. After processing all samples of M, we build a new sample set M_e and we can train a supervised model P_e over M_e to classify a text into three classes: *rumor*, *explanation*, and *conclusion*.

For each training sample t in M, we consider three different strategies for transforming t into t'. In the follow three strategies, the *explanation* sample is obtained by the difference between the original rumor text and the original explanation, and the *conclusion* sample is obtained by the difference between the original rumor text and the original explanation text. The difference is how to compose a rumor sample text:

Case (1): $t'.T = t.T$, $t'.E = D(t.E, t.T)$, and $t'.F = D(t.F, t.T)$. The original rumor text is kept as a new sample of *rumor* class;

Case (2): $t'.T = C(t.T, t.E)$, $t'.E = D(t.E, t.T)$, and $t'.F = D(t.F, t.T)$. The *rumor* sample text is the common part between the original rumor text and the original explanation;

Case (3): $t'.T = C(t.T, t.E) \cup C(t.T, t.F)$, $t'.E = D(t.E, t.T)$, and $t'.F = D(t.F, t.T)$. The *rumor* sample text combines the common part between the original rumor and the original explanation and the common part between the original rumor text and the original conclusion text.

The rational is that the shared common part of the rumor and its explanation is the core text of the rumor. The difference between the rumor text and the explanation text is the representative part of explanation. The conclusion text is also represented by the difference parts between the original rumor and its conclusion text.

After processing the original training data sample set M, we can obtain a new training sample set M_e consisting samples for *rumor*, *explanation* and *conclusion* class. Then, we can used M_e to train a supervised classification model like SVM model or Bayesian model.

4 Experiments

To evaluate the proposed method, we collect a set of officially published COVID-19 rumor refutation information data set consisting of 134 rumors and their corresponding explanation texts and conclusion texts. Then we apply the preprocessing in Sect. 3.3 to build three new different training sample text sets with different configurations using sentence common parts and sentence difference operators. For comparison, a simple sample set without using the preprocessing method is built where the original texts of rumor, explanation and conclusion of a sample are directly used as three new samples for class *rumor*, *explanation* and *conclusion* (*Original* in the Table 2).

Three types of classification models are evaluated on the training sample sets, naive Bayesian model (NB1 and NB2), SVM model (SVC1, SVC2 and SCVRBF) and kNN model (KNN_5_distance and KNN_5_uniform, using two different distance model in KNN). Table 2 shows the accuracy of the models obtained by training on the original sample data sets and three data sets consisting of sentence difference and common parts. It can be seen that training on the sample data set obtained by configuration defined in Case (1), (2) and (3) can help models achieve improvements on the prediction quality. Moreover, the training sample set obtained by using configuration in Case (3) can achieve the best overall performance (the best average scores shown in Tables 2 and 3). In Case (3) configuration, the rumor sample text combines all the common subsequences obtained with the explanation text and the conclusion text. It can help reserve more information of rumor samples. Table 3 shows the models' performance on three classes. In most tests, the improvement is obvious when using the common parts and difference part as sample texts to train supervised classification models compared with the models trained on the original sample texts.

Table 2. Accuracy of models training on different sample sets

Model	Original	Case (1)	Case (2)	Case (3)
NB1	0.843	0.891	0.891	0.891
NB2	0.333	0.333	0.333	0.333
SVC1	0.925	0.963	0.965	0.968
SVC2	0.928	0.965	0.965	0.965
SVCRBF	0.866	0.878	0.893	0.888
KNN_5_distance	0.836	0.930	0.923	0.928
KNN_5_uniform	0.746	0.881	0.883	0.888
Average score	0.783	0.834	0.836	**0.837**

Table 3. F-score of performances on three classes by models training on different sample sets.

Performance on classes	Original	Case (1)	Case (2)	Case (3)
NB1-Rumor	0.861	0.889	0.889	0.889
NB2-Rumor	0.500	0.000	0.000	0.000
SVC1-Rumor	0.949	0.985	0.985	0.989
SVC2-Rumor	0.949	0.985	0.985	0.985
SVCRBF-Rumor	0.913	0.907	0.933	0.924
KNN_5_distacne-Rumor	0.847	0.950	0.942	0.946
KNN_5_uniform-Rumor	0.736	0.908	0.917	0.920
NB1-Explanation	0.820	0.865	0.862	0.867
NB2-Explanation	0.000	0.500	0.500	0.500
SVC1-Explanation	0.933	0.957	0.964	0.964
SVC2-Explanation	0.935	0.960	0.964	0.964
SVCRBF-Explanation	0.867	0.847	0.864	0.858
KNN_5_distacne-Explanation	0.804	0.906	0.899	0.906
KNN_5_uniform-Explanation	0.706	0.843	0.846	0.851
NB1-Conclusion	0.857	0.924	0.928	0.921
NB2-Conclusion	0.000	0.000	0.000	0.000
SVC1-Conclusion	0.891	0.946	0.947	0.950
SVC2-Conclusion	0.897	0.951	0.947	0.947
SVCRBF-Conclusion	0.807	0.889	0.889	0.889
KNN_5_distacne-Conclusion	0.859	0.936	0.929	0.933
KNN_5_uniform-Conclusion	0.808	0.893	0.889	0.897
Average scores	0.759	0.811	0.813	**0.814**

5 Conclusion

In this paper, we proposed a method to extract common and difference subsequences of sentence texts as samples to train supervised classification models to classify samples into rumor, explanation and conclusion class. The leftmost longest common subsequence is extracted as the common part from two sample sentence texts. Difference part between two sample texts is obtained by removing common subsequences from the origin sentence. Common and difference subsequences are combined in different ways to compose samples of rumor, explanation and conclusion classes. Experiments shows that when using the difference subsequence between rumor and explanation texts as the explanation samples, using the difference subsequence between rumor and conclusion texts as the conclusion samples, and combining common subsequences obtained from both explanation and conclusion texts as the rumor samples, the model achieves the best overall performance of classification accuracy compared with models trained on the original sample texts. The subsequences of sample sentences can be further investigated to reflect richer features of samples for training supervised models.

Acknowledgement. This work was partially supported by the Joint Project of CAS and Austria on ADaptive and Autonomous Data Performance Connectivity and Decentralized Transport Decision-Making Network (ADAPT, No. 881703) and the Innovation Funding Project "Internet Fake News Detection Method Research" (No. MS2021-05) granted by Institute of Scientific and Technical Information of China.

References

1. Martinez Monterrubio, S.M., Noain-Sánchez, A., Verdú Pérez, E., González Crespo, R.: Coronavirus fake news detection via MedOSINT check in health care official bulletins with CBR explanation: the way to find the real information source through OSINT, the verifier tool for official journals. Inf. Sci. **574**(1), 210–237 (2021)
2. Zubiaga, A., Aker, A., Bontcheva, K., Liakata, M., Procter, R.: Detection and resolution of rumours in social media: a survey. ACM Comput. Surv. **51**(2), 1–36 (2019)
3. Sharma, K., Qian, F., Jiang, H., Ruchansky, N., Zhang, M., Liu, Y.: Combating fake news: a survey on identification and mitigation techniques. ACM Trans. Intell. Syst. Technol. **10**(3), 1–42 (2019)
4. Harper, L., et al.: The battle between fake news and science. J. Pediatr. Urol. **16**(1), 114–115 (2020)
5. Bondielli, A., Marcelloni, F.: A survey on fake news and rumour detection techniques. Inf. Sci. **497**, 38–55 (2019)
6. Popat, K., Mukherjee, S., Strötgen, J., Weikum, G.: Where the truth lies: explaining the credibility of emerging claims on the web and social media. In: Proceedings of the Proceedings of the 26th International Conference on World Wide Web Companion (Perth, Australia, 2017), pp. 1003–1012. International World Wide Web Conferences Steering Committee (2017)
7. Pan, J.Z., Pavlova, S., Li, C., Li, N., Li, Y., Liu, J.: Content based fake news detection using knowledge graphs. In: The Semantic Web – ISWC 2018. ISWC 2018. LNCS, vol. 11136. Springer, Cham (2018). https://doi.org/10.1007/978-3-030-00671-6_39
8. Zhou, X., Zafarani, R.: Network-based fake news detection: a pattern-driven approach. SIGKDD Explor. Newsl. **21**(2), 48–60 (2019)

9. Thorne, J., Vlachos, A., Christodoulopoulos, C., Mittal, A.: FEVER: a large-scale dataset for Fact Extraction and VERification. In: Proceedings of the North American Chapter of the Association for Computational Linguistics, 16 April 2018, pp. 809–819. Association for Computational Linguistics (2018)
10. Volkova, S., Shaffer, K., Jang, J.Y., Hodas, N.: Separating facts from fiction: linguistic models to classify suspicious and trusted news posts on Twitter, pp. 647–653. Association for Computational Linguistics, Vancouver, Canada (2017)
11. Wadden, D., et al.: Fact or fiction: verifying scientific claims. In: Proceedings of the Empirical Methods in Natural Language Processing, 30 April 2020, pp. 7534–7550. Association for Computational Linguistics (2020)
12. Wu, K., Yang, S., Zhu, K.Q.: False rumors detection on Sina Weibo by propagation structures. In: Proceedings of the International Conference on Data Engineering, 13 April 2015, pp. 651–662 (2015)
13. Tschiatschek, S., Singla, A., Rodriguez, M.G., Merchant, A., Krause, A.: Fake news detection in social networks via crowd signals. In: Proceedings of the Web Conference, 23 April 2018, pp. 517–524, Republic and Canton of Geneva, CHE (2018)
14. Lazer, D.M.J., et al.: The science of fake news. Science 359(6380), 1094–1096 (2018)
15. Grimes, D.R.: Health disinformation & social media: The crucial role of information hygiene in mitigating conspiracy theory and infodemics. EMBO Rep. 21(11), e51819 (2020)
16. Samadi, M., Talukdar, P., Veloso, M., Blum, M.: ClaimEval: integrated and flexible framework for claim evaluation using credibility of sources. In: Proceedings of the Thirtieth AAAI Conference on Artificial Intelligence, pp. 222–228. AAAI Press, Phoenix, Arizona (2016)

Double-Channel Multi-layer Information Fusion for Text Matching

Guoxi Zhang[1,2], Yongquan Dong[1,2(✉)], and Huafeng Chen[1,2]

[1] School of Computer Science and Technology, Jiangsu Normal University,
No. 101 Shanghai Road, Tongshan District, Xuzhou 221006, Jiangsu, China
tomdyq@163.com
[2] Xuzhou Engineering Research Center of Cloud Computing,
No. 101 Shanghai Road, Tongshan District, Xuzhou 221006, Jiangsu, China

Abstract. Text matching is one of the fundamental tasks in natural language processing. Most of the existing models focus only on encoding the text itself but ignore other semantic information which may further improve matching accuracy. In this paper, we propose a novel model for text matching with double-channel multi-layer information fusion. It treats text and part-of-speech information of words in a sentence as double-channel information which is fused by multi-layer interactions. Meanwhile, our model uses a Siamese network structure to learn common and unique features of two sentences, which can improve its ability to learn the relationship between two sentences while reducing the parameter size and complexity. Experimental results on SNLI dataset show that our model can achieve better performance than baseline methods.

Keywords: Text matching · Neural network · Information fusion · Siamese net

1 Introduction

With the continuous development of the Internet, big data and artificial intelligence, modern lifestyles are gradually becoming intelligent and automated. Accurate and rapid matching of semantic similarity between two texts has a profound impact on intelligent search, intelligent marking, intelligent translation and other applications [4]. Currently, text matching research has been applied to many fields, such as information retrieval, interpretation recognition and automatic question-answering tasks. The research on text matching has important theoretical significance and practical value for the further development of these fields [6].

Most traditional matching models focus only on the encoding of the text itself, but it is difficult for these approaches to take into account both local and global information. The models that can be achieved are generally large in scale, with high training consumption, and the original semantic information is lost after encoding. Therefore, how to represent text more effectively and make it more suitable for text matching is a key problem to be solved. In this paper,

© IFIP International Federation for Information Processing 2022
Published by Springer Nature Switzerland AG 2022
Z. Shi et al. (Eds.): IIP 2022, IFIP AICT 643, pp. 114–123, 2022.
https://doi.org/10.1007/978-3-031-03948-5_10

we embed the part-of-speech tag vector similarly, so that our model can obtain more input to improve the matching accuracy. At the same time, we explore and propose a new information fusion method due to the different semantic relations between the part-of-speech and the words themselves. Afterwards, we perform a series of tests to compare the accuracy of our model with that of the baseline model.

2 Related Works

For text matching problem, deep learning models are one of the mainstream solutions, which can be divided into representation-based matching models and interaction-based matching models.

The representation-based matching models learn the representation of sentences A and B separately and then obtain the matching by defining the matching function, such as vector dot product, Euclidean distance, etc. The whole representation learning framework is a double tower structure, which means two sentences are processed individually. A classical representation-based matching model generally has three layers, respectively, input layer, representation layer and matching layer.

Typical representation-based matching models are as follows:

- DSSM [5] is a DNN-based model. The model uses word-hashing for encoding the two sentences at the input layer, and word-bag at the representation layer. Then the matching layer is used to calculate the vector distance between the two sentences, and finally obtain the matching score. The significance of this model lies in the three-layer paradigm of input-representation-matching.
- ARC-I [3] uses convolution and pooling as the representation layer based on DSSM to capture word order information in the sentence. Therefore, the representations can capture the word order information better than DSSM. However, the pooling is carried out in the local window, so the global information cannot be obtained to some extent.
- CNN-DSSM [9] adds word-trigrams in the input layer to extract the local information of word order, compared with DSSM. The convolution of the representation layer adopts the method of TextCNN to capture the context information of sentences A and B through the convolutional sliding window of $n = 3$. The maximum pooling can obtain the maximum value of each feature map extracted by the convolution, thus capturing the global context information to a certain extent. Compared with ARC-I, this model can maximize the pooling operation of the whole sentence in each feature map and obtain the global relationship.

Compared with the representation-based matching models, the interaction-based matching models do not directly learn the representation of sentences A and B. Instead, it first interacts the two sentences, then extracts the features through the interactive matching information, and finally learns the extracted matching information with various network structures through integration to get the final matching score. The matching process of this model can be roughly divided into two steps: interaction and aggregation. The biggest difference between an interaction-based model and a representation-based model is that sentences A and B interact ahead of time, so most of the work of the model focuses on how to design the interaction between sentences A and B.

Typical interaction-based matching models are as follows:

- ARC-II [3] extracts the word vectors obtained by the convolution of N-gram in sentences A and B, and carried out element-wise calculation to obtain a matching matrix. Compared with ARC-I, it uses the matching matrix of sentences A and B text at the beginning, and obtains the interaction information of both in advance. It has a better ability to capture the information matching, and the convolution and pooling process retain the order information.
- ESIM [2] is an enhanced version of LSTM. It achieves better results through detailed sequential network design and considering both local inference and global inference. Two kinds of LSTM are used to extract and encode the vectors a into weighted vectors a' in the local inference. After that, it performs element-wise multiplication and subtraction with the original vector, and 4 groups of vectors are concatenated into one group with shape $(a', a, a' - a, a' \otimes a)$, which is equivalent to enrich the extracted information.
- BiMPM [10] regards two sentences as a bilateral relationship with consideration of the relationship both from A to B and from B to A of two sentences in the matching process. Therefore, four different attention methods are used to reflect the multi-perspective thought. However, the network structure is complex and has a lot of computation, which is slow for large-scale text matching computation.

3   Model

In this section, we present Double-Channel Multi-layer Information Fusion Model, i.e. DMIF for text matching.

The input of our model is a batch of tuples (w_a, w_b, l), where w_a and w_b denote sequences of words in two sentences, and l denotes the true matching label of two sentences. The goal of our model is to predict sentence-pairs' relation and divide them into certain classes.

As our model needs to get part-of-speech information, the dataset needs to be preprocessed. Specifically, it takes out the corresponding part-of-speech tags of each word in w_a and w_b, and combines them with original data. The combined data structure is of the shape $(w_a, w_b, pos_a, pos_b, l)$. Besides, there are usually numerous unknown words in the test set, so we generate the sub-word of the unknown words through N-gram, and try to embed the known words in the sub-words and average them, which can reduce the number of unknown words and further improve the matching performance.

3.1 Framework

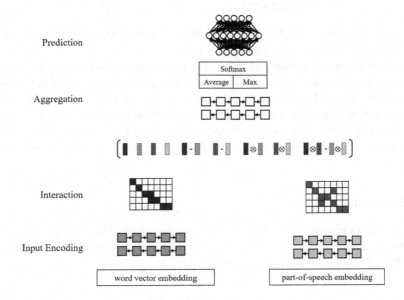

Fig. 1. Framework of Double-Channel Multi-layer Information Fusion Model

Figure 1 is an overview of our model framework. It is an interaction-based model. Specifically, it can be divided into four layers from bottom to top: input encoding layer, interaction layer, aggregation layer and prediction layer. We will introduce our model more detailedly in the next subsections.

3.2 Input Encoding

Word-Vector Encoding. We encode words in the sentences as vectors by GloVe embedding [8]. Then, we use bidirectional LSTM (BiLSTM) as the fundamental block of our model to represent each word in the input sequences.

$$\hat{a}_i^w = \textbf{BiLSTM}(w_a, i), \forall i \in [1, \ldots, l_a],$$
$$\hat{b}_i^w = \textbf{BiLSTM}(w_b, i), \forall i \in [1, \ldots, l_b]. \tag{1}$$

where $\hat{a}_i^w$ is the i-th word's hidden state over the input sequence w_a generated by BiLSTM. $\hat{b}_i^w$ is generated similarly. l_a and l_b are lengths of the two sentences, similarly hereinafter.

Part-of-Speech-Vector Encoding. Our model encodes the part-of-speech tag of each word in the two input sequences by a similar method with word-vector encoding, and the results are also involved in the subsequent processing together with the word-vector encoding.

$$\hat{a}_i^p = \mathbf{BiLSTM}(pos_a, i), \forall i \in [1, \dots, l_a],$$
$$\hat{b}_i^p = \mathbf{BiLSTM}(pos_b, i), \forall i \in [1, \dots, l_b]. \tag{2}$$

where $\hat{a}_i^p$ is the i-th word's hidden state over the input sequence pos_a generated by BiLSTM. $\hat{b}_i^p$ is generated similarly as well.

Since the semantic features of word vectors and part-of-speech tags are often different, it is not possible to construct a single-pipeline network. Therefore, we decided to set two different input coding layers, and the two coding layers have similar structures. In order to capture the similarities between the two sentences and reduce the size of our model, we use Siamese structure to process the input data, which means the network shares parameter values when processing both sequences.

3.3   Interaction

In the interaction layer, in order to enhance the information, we use the attention mechanism used in the ESIM model [2], which balances attention on the bidirectional sequential encoding of the input.

Word Interaction. In particular, we use Eq. (3) to compute the similarity of the implicit state tuples $(\hat{a}^w, \hat{b}^w)$ and $(\hat{a}^p, \hat{b}^p)$ between two sentences to calculate the concern weight.

$$e_{ij}^w = (\hat{a}_i^w)^T \hat{b}_j^w$$
$$e_{ij}^p = (\hat{a}_i^p)^T \hat{b}_j^p \tag{3}$$

where e_{ij}^w and e_{ij}^p are attention weights to reflect the similarity of hidden state tuple $(\hat{a}_i^w, \hat{b}_j^w)$ and $(\hat{a}_i^p, \hat{b}_j^p)$, respectively.

Sequence Interaction. Word interaction is determined by the previously calculated attention weight e_{ij}, which is used to obtain a local correlation between two sentences. For the hidden state of the word in one sentence, that is, $\hat{a}_i$, which has encoded the word itself and its context, e_{ij} is used to identify and combine the relevant semantics in another sentence, as shown in Eqs. (4) and (5).

$$\tilde{a}_i = \sum_{j=1}^{l_b} \frac{\exp\left(e_{ij}^w\right)}{\sum_{k=1}^{l_b} \exp\left(e_{ik}^w\right)} \hat{b}_j^w, \forall i \in [1, \dots l_a]$$

$$\tilde{b}_j = \sum_{i=1}^{l_a} \frac{\exp\left(e_{ij}^w\right)}{\sum_{k=1}^{l_a} \exp\left(e_{kj}^w\right)} \hat{a}_i^w, \forall j \in [1, \dots l_b] \tag{4}$$

$$\tilde{a}_i^p = \sum_{j=1}^{l_b} \frac{\exp\left(e_{ij}^p\right)}{\sum_{k=1}^{l_b} \exp\left(e_{ik}^p\right)} \hat{b}_j^p, \forall i \in [1, \ldots l_a]$$

$$\tilde{b}_j^p = \sum_{i=1}^{l_a} \frac{\exp\left(e_{ij}^p\right)}{\sum_{k=1}^{l_a} \exp\left(e_{kj}^p\right)} \hat{a}_i^p, \forall j \in [1, \ldots l_b]$$

$$(5)$$

We expect that such an operation will help improve the information on local and sequential interactions between elements in a tuple to capture the relationship between two sentences better. To make our model further enhance the interaction information collected above, we use difference and element-wise products in series with the pre-interacted and post-interacted vectors $\hat{a}^w$ and $\tilde{a}^w$ or $\hat{b}^w$ and $\tilde{b}^w$ respectively, to enhance the interaction information. We deal with part-of-speech tag features, $\hat{a}^p$ and $\tilde{a}^p$ or $\hat{b}^p$ and $\tilde{b}^p$, in similar way, as shown in Eq. (6).

$$m_a = [\tilde{a}^w, \hat{a}^w, \tilde{a}^p, \hat{a}^p, \tilde{a}^w - \hat{a}^w, \tilde{a}^p - \hat{a}^p, \tilde{a}^w \otimes \hat{a}^w, \tilde{a}^p \otimes \hat{a}^p, \tilde{a}^w \otimes \tilde{a}^p - \hat{a}^w \otimes \hat{a}^p]$$

$$m_b = \left[\tilde{b}^w, \hat{b}^w, \tilde{b}^p, \hat{b}^p, \tilde{b}^w - \hat{b}^w, \tilde{b}^p - \hat{b}^p, \tilde{b}^w \otimes \hat{b}^w, \tilde{b}^p \otimes \hat{b}^p, \tilde{b}^w \otimes \tilde{b}^p - \hat{b}^w \otimes \hat{b}^p\right]$$

$$(6)$$

3.4 Aggregation

In order to determine the overall relationship between the two sentences, we use the aggregation layer to combine the interaction information of the two sentences enhanced by the aforementioned processing. We use BiLSTM to perform the aggregation in sequence according to Eq. (7).

$$\tilde{m}_{a,i} = \textbf{BiLSTM}\left(m_a, i\right), \forall i \in [1, \ldots l_a]$$

$$\tilde{m}_{b,i} = \textbf{BiLSTM}\left(m_b, i\right), \forall i \in [1, \ldots l_b]$$

$$(7)$$

The aggregation layer converts the resulting vector obtained above into a fixed-length vector by using Eqs. (8) and (9) to calculate the average and maximum pooling. All these vectors are then concatenated to form the final fixed length vector, which is fed into the final classifier to determine the overall relationship between the two sentences.

$$\tilde{m}_{a,\text{ave}} = \frac{1}{l_a} \sum_{i=1}^{l_a} \tilde{m}_{a,i}, \tilde{m}_{a,\text{max}} = \max_{i=1}^{l_a} \tilde{m}_{a,i}$$

$$(8)$$

$$\tilde{m}_{b,\text{ave}} = \frac{1}{l_b} \sum_{j=1}^{l_b} \tilde{m}_{b,j}, \tilde{m}_{b,\text{max}} = \max_{j=1}^{l_b} l_b \tilde{m}_{b,i}$$

$$(9)$$

$$v = [\tilde{m}_{a,\text{ave}}; \tilde{m}_{a,\text{max}}; \tilde{m}_{b,\text{ave}}; \tilde{m}_{b,\text{max}}]$$

$$(10)$$

3.5   Prediction

The prediction layer is to evaluate the label probability distribution of the two sentences. After the representation of the two sentences is obtained, the label probability distribution of the two sentences can be obtained through the multi-layer perception (MLP) classifier, and set the network size according to the actual situation, as an example shown in the following Table 1, where the class corresponding to the maximum probability is the prediction result generated by DMIF.

Table 1. An example of MLP structure

Layer	Output dimension(s)
Fully-connected 1	600
Fully-connected 2	150
Fully-connected 3	3

4   Experimental Setup

4.1   Datasets

The **SNLI corpus** [1] is a corpus composed of 570K manually annotated English sentence pairs, which is balanced by annotated implication, contradiction and neutral classification, and supports natural language reasoning tasks. This is a benchmark dataset that is widely used to evaluate textual representational systems, especially those induced by representational learning methods. Here, we will use this data set to train the model and compare it with the original model.

4.2   Training Hyperparameters

To compare the accuracy between our model and the baseline model, we set the same hyperparameters as that in ESIM [2] model. In the experiments, we use Adam method for optimization. The first and second value of momentum are set to 0.9 and 0.999. The initial learning rate is set to 0.0004. When training, data loader pushes a batch of data with 32 groups of sentences. The hidden layers' dimension are set to 300. The optimal accuracy of 3 Bernoulli tests with 5 epochs of training each time will be used as the basis for evaluating the accuracy of the model.

5   Results and Discussion

5.1   Experimental Results

We use SNLI data set to train and test the model, and use ESIM as baseline. As ESIM uses non-public pre-training data, there are objective differences in training environment. Therefore, we use the model reproduced by ourselves to set the same hyperparameters for testing under the same hardware environment. The experimental results are shown in the Table 2. Although there is a certain gap between the accuracy of our model and the model reported in the paper [2], our model performs better than the re-implement model with 1% relative accuracy improved. Therefore, we believe that our model has better performance under the same conditions. At the same time, it can be found that our model adds a relatively independent channel to input part of speech information, while the model size does not increase exponentially. Therefore, it can be considered that our model does optimize the parameter size to some extent.

Table 2. Accuracies of different models on SNLI.

Model	Num_of_params ($\times 10^7$)	Train acc. (%)	Test acc. (%)
600D ESIM [2] (re-implement)	2.84	93.64	85.43
Siamese ESIM [7] (re-implement)	2.06	95.29	85.91
DMIF	2.92	95.20	**86.34**

5.2 Analysis and Discussion

Compared with the baseline model, we apply more than one method to improve the performance of text-matching mission. To confirm that the optimized model does have a performance improvement effect, we performed ablation tests on the model using a control variable method. The results are shown in the Table 3.

Table 3. Ablation tests on SNLI dataset.

Model	Test Acc.
ESIM	85.43
ESIM+Siamese network	85.73
ESIM+POS embedding	85.68
DMIF	**86.34**

We also try to add some layers with higher complexity at the prediction layer, but we find that the accuracy did not improve with the increase of model parameters. Specifically, the experimental results are shown in the Table 4 below.

Table 4. More complex models' test on SNLI datasets

Model	Num_of_params($\times 10^7$)	Test Acc.
Baseline	2.84	85.43
DMIF	2.92	**86.34**
DMIF+resnet34	3.78	85.03
DMIF+resnet50	7.24	84.48

6   Conclusions and Future Work

Compared with the baseline model, the model proposed in this paper can obtain more input information by inputting part-of-speech tag sequence, reduce the number of parameters to be trained by using Siamese structure, and adjust the information aggregation method. Experimental results show that our model performs better in the task of text matching.

In the future, we plan to put prior knowledge or statistical features into the model inputs and propose better feature construction strategies to improve the accuracy of the model. In addition, we will also try to improve the traditional model by strengthening the interaction between layers and across layers with the expectation of reducing the loss of the model as it propagates forward.

Acknowledgements. This work is supported by the National Natural Science Foundation of China (No. 61872168) and Graduate Research and Practice Innovation Program of Jiangsu Normal University (No. 2021XKT1380).

References

1. Bowman, S.R., Angeli, G., Potts, C., Manning, C.D.: A large annotated corpus for learning natural language inference. In: Proceedings of the 2015 Conference on Empirical Methods in Natural Language Processing (EMNLP). Association for Computational Linguistics (2015)
2. Chen, Q., Zhu, X., Ling, Z.H., Wei, S., Jiang, H., Inkpen, D.: Enhanced LSTM for natural language inference. In: Proceedings of the 55th Annual Meeting of the Association for Computational Linguistics, vol. 1, Long Papers, pp. 1657–1668 (2017)
3. Hu, B., Lu, Z., Li, H., Chen, Q.: Convolutional neural network architectures for matching natural language sentences. In: Advances in Neural Information Processing Systems, pp. 2042–2050 (2014)
4. Hu, W., Dang, A., Tan, Y.: A survey of state-of-the-art short text matching algorithms. In: Tan, Y., Shi, Y. (eds.) Data Mining and Big Data, pp. 211–219. Springer Singapore, Singapore (2019)
5. Huang, P.S., He, X., Gao, J., Deng, L., Acero, A., Heck, L.: Learning deep structured semantic models for web search using clickthrough data. In: Proceedings of the 22nd ACM International Conference on Information & Knowledge Management, pp. 2333–2338 (2013)

6. Huang, Z., Cao, L.: Deep learning for text matching: a survey. In: 2021 5th Annual International Conference on Data Science and Business Analytics (ICDSBA), pp. 66–70. IEEE (2021)
7. Liu, Y., et al.: An enhanced ESIM model for sentence pair matching with self-attention. In: CCKS Tasks, pp. 52–62 (2018)
8. Pennington, J., Socher, R., Manning, C.D.: GloVe: global vectors for word representation. In: Proceedings of the 2014 Conference on Empirical Methods in Natural Language Processing (EMNLP), pp. 1532–1543 (2014)
9. Shen, Y., He, X., Gao, J., Deng, L., Mesnil, G.: A latent semantic model with convolutional-pooling structure for information retrieval. In: Proceedings of the 23rd ACM International Conference on Conference on Information and Knowledge Management, pp. 101–110 (2014)
10. Wang, Z., Hamza, W., Florian, R.: Bilateral multi-perspective matching for natural language sentences. In: Proceedings of the 26th International Joint Conference on Artificial Intelligence, pp. 4144–4150 (2017)

Augmenting Context Representation with Triggers Knowledge for Relation Extraction

En Li[1], Shumin Shi[1,2(✉)], Zhikun Yang[1], and He Yan Huang[1,2]

[1] School of Computer Science and Technology, Beijing Institute of Technology,
Beijing, China
{3220190822,bjssm,3120191065,hhy63}@bit.edu.cn
[2] Beijing Engineering Research Center of High Volume Language Information
Processing and Cloud Computing Applications, Beijing, China

Abstract. Relation Extraction (RE) requires the model to classify the correct relation from a set of relation candidates given the corresponding sentence and two entities. Recent work mainly studies how to utilize more data or incorporate extra context information especially with Pre-trained Language Models (PLMs). However, these models still face with the challenges of avoiding being affected by irrelevant or misleading words. In this paper, we propose a novel model to help alleviate such deficiency. Specifically, our model automatically mines the triggers of the sentence iteratively with the sentence itself from the previous iteration, and augment the semantics of the context representation from BERT with both entity pair and triggers skillfully. We conduct extensive experiments to evaluate the proposed model and effectively obtain empirical improvement in TACRED.

Keywords: Triggers representation · Knowledge augment · Context aware · Relation extraction

1 Introduction

Relation Extraction (RE) aims to extract the organized relational knowledge in the shape of "knowledge graphs" from unstructured text [4]. For example, given the sentence "The *kitchen* is the last renovated part of the *house*" and a pair of nominals *kitchen* and *house*, the main goal of RE is to classify relation "*part_of*" from the context between these entity pair. It is the most powerful support for many downstream applications like graph completion, question answering, web search, information retrieval, path inference and logical rule reasoning [17].

Recently, self-attention such as Transformer [15] has also been explored for RE and has shown unexpectedly high performance. One popular paradigm of applying Transformer for RE is to leverage a single pre-trained language model which is pre-trained on large-scale unsupervised corpus, and fine-tune it on the

© IFIP International Federation for Information Processing 2022
Published by Springer Nature Switzerland AG 2022
Z. Shi et al. (Eds.): IIP 2022, IFIP AICT 643, pp. 124–135, 2022.
https://doi.org/10.1007/978-3-031-03948-5_11

specific task [7]. The other popular use case is to leverage the relational facts from knowledge graphs to guide relation selection.

Usually, models based on Transformer locate the target entity pair by replacing them with special tokens or inserting typed markers and incorporate the corresponding feature transferred by Transformer to fit RE task. It seems like the researchers have formed a consensus that fusing the entity information is enough for identifying the correct relationship between the entity pair. However, these models fail to make correct extractions which are easy for human to understand, considerably hinder the performance of these fine-tuned models. In addition, utilizing existing relational facts is indeed a potential way towards more powerful RE models, but it has improved frustratingly slowly [16].

In this paper, we hope to alleviate this above problems by mining triggers of the sentence with the fine-tuned model from the previous iteration to make further use of training corpus. In other words, we introduce an auxiliary task that allows the model to score all tokens, augmenting context representation with real keywords which we define as triggers knowledge for RE and discard irrelevant tokens automatically.

The idea behind the auxiliary task is simple, we change the original sentence S into S_1 by randomly masking some tokens $(t_{m1}, t_{m2}, ... , t_{mn})$ and generate the labels y and y_1 with the same fine-tuned models. If the labels y and y_1 are different, we set the score of masked tokens $(t_{m1}, t_{m2}, ... , t_{mn})$ as 1 which means these tokens act as an import role in the current model. We repeat the same operation to predict each token an accurate score in the preprocessing step. We also locate the positions of the target entity pair to prevent them from being masked and finally concatenate these encodings including trigger, entity pair as well as the sentence encoding (embedding of the special first token in the setting of BERT [3]) as the input to a multi-layer neural network for classification.

We believe if the model can score the tokens correctly, its decision surface will be more robust about irrelevant or misleading words and encode more information about the keywords to obtain the better capability of classification. Hence, compared with previous models, our model can alleviate the wrong label problem by highlighting important tokens and do not need additional data.

In summary, the contributions can be summarized as follows: 1) We introduce a fresh perspective to mine the triggers of the sentence by exploring the fine-tuned model from the last iteration. 2) We instantiate the above model as an augment layer on the top of the pre-trained model. This allows the model to augment context representation with the knowledge of keywords and entity pair to combine their benefits. 3) Extensive experiments on TACRED [24] show that the proposed framework outperforms the previous methods, achieving the empirical results.

2   Related Work

The pioneering works on supervised RE research employed a hand-built pattern approach, designing specific features [1] or kernel functions [2] to extract corresponding semantic relation between the entity pair in the text [6]. However, these methods are very time-consuming, human-intensive and quickly replaced.

Later inspired by the success of deep learning models in other NLP tasks, the deep learning-based RE has been extensively studied, which improves the performance significantly and promote the follow-up research greatly. Studies in deep learning mainly focus on designing complex matching networks to model the relationship among text, entities and relations. [21] creatively come up with the concept of position embedding to specify the relative distances between words and entities and apply it to an end-to-end convolutional neural network (CNN), which shows promising results. To better handle long-distance dependency and time sequence between entity pair, [22] combine the concept of recurrent neural networks (RNN) for RE, which perform a max-pooling operation to effectively model feature extraction for prediction. [9] further use the weight of attention mechanism to aggregate global relational information. In order to consider the dependencies between entities, [23] adopt graph neural networks (GNN) over dependency trees to build entity graphs and identify the correct relations by inference models.

As compared to deep learning, RE is greatly enhanced by Pre-trained Language Models (PLMs), which benefits from bidirectional Transformer layers [15] and are pre-trained on large-scale unsupervised corpus [12]. Recent work on RE can be roughly divided into two categories. One focuses on fine-tuning pretrained language models on text with linked entities using relation-oriented objectives. [13] simply replace the entity mentions with special masks before feeding the text to BERT for fine-tuning, providing strong baseline for future research. [19] further incorporate entity-level information into the pretrained language model by insert special tokens before and after the target entities. [14] explore whether two relation instances share the same entities by proposing a matching-the-blanks objective and achieve new state-of-the-arts. The other line of work mainly studies injecting external context information into pre-trained language models. Methods of such, including Know-BERT [11] and ERNIE [25], align entities to their corresponding entities in KGs by encoding the graph structure and take the informative entity embeddings as input to the Transformer. Similarly, to improve the description accuracy of relation vectors, K-Adapter [18] injects factual and linguistic knowledge by introducing a plug-in neural adaptor. LUKE [20] further extends the pre-training objective of masked language modeling to entities and proposes an entity-aware self-attention mechanism.

3   Approach

In this section, we first formally introduce the problem of Relation Extraction and the input format. Then we present an overview of the proposed model and present each module in detail.

3.1 Problem Define

For supervised Relation Extraction, the input is a sentence S consisting of n tokens t_1, t_2,...,t_n, an entity e_1 with the span (i, j) and another entity e_2 with the span (p, q). The task is, for the target entity pair, to predict a correct relation from candidates. Usually let R denote a set of pre-defined relation labels (including $no\_relation$). Then the output of the task is a structured triples $Y_r = \{(e_1, e_2, r) : e_1, e_2 \in S, r \in R\}$.

3.2 Input Format

To make the model better capture the dependencies between the subject and object, we insert the special markers at the beginning and end of the entities. Specifically, we define special makers as $ and # and insert them before and after the subject and object, therefore modifying the input text to the format of "The $ kitchen $ is the last renovated part of the # house #".

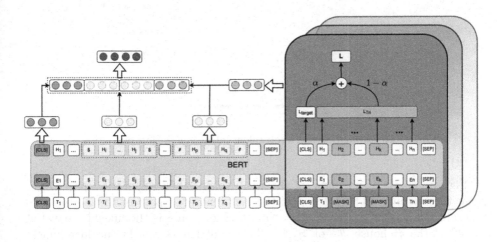

Fig. 1. Our model architecture

3.3 Model Architecture

As shown in Fig. 1, our approach consists of a triggers generation task and a relation classification task. The former first takes the input sentence and generate a batch of masked sentences by randomly masking certain tokens, trying to score all the tokens to distinguish the real keywords and irrelevant words by a loss function $\mathcal{L}$. To be specific, if the predictions of the augmented sentence and original sentence are consistent, these masked tokens will be de-emphasized for achieving better result or they will be considered as keywords in inference step. The later task mainly captures both the semantics of the sentence and the triggers mined in the former task to better fit the classification task.

Definition of the Triggers Generation Task. The triggers generation step in training phase is described as follows. Given a sentence S with special markers, we construct a batch of masked sentences $(S'_1, S'_2, ..., S'_n)$ and predict the relation of all sentences with the same model. If the predicted labels are same, the masked tokens will be set to be 0. Otherwise, we will set the corresponding important tokens to be 1 as they have much impact on target task. Besides, to get rid of noises and make the label prediction more accurate, we abandon the training data that the predicted label of original sentence is wrong. To speed up the time of the preprocessing, we generate augmented sentences incrementally with a generation ratio β and larger means generate more sentences each epoch. Then we set the score for each token according to whether the label is same with the original sentence. The amount of masked tokens is controlled by a proportional parameter, which is related to the length of original sentence and set to 0.3 empirically.

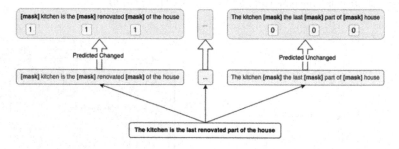

Fig. 2. An example of the weak token labels generation procedure

Figure 2 shows an example of the weak token labels generation procedure, given the sentence "The *kitchen* is the last renovated part of the *house*", we generate the masked sentence $S'_1 =$ "[mask] \$ kitchen \$ is the [mask] renovated [mask] of the # house #" or $S'_2 =$ "The \$ kitchen \$ [mask] the last [mask] part of [mask] # house #". S'_1 does not change the prediction label, so the masked tokens are labeled by 0, that is, $Y_1 = (\_; 0; \_; 0; \_; 0; \_)$, where "$\_$" does not contribute to the loss function. On the other hand, S'_2 flips the original prediction of S, so we have $Y_2 = (1; \_; 1; \_; 1; \_; 1)$. After getting the binary output vector, we fine-tune the triggers generation task with cross-entropy loss to pick out real triggers:

$$\mathcal{L}_{TRI} = -\sum_i l_{TRI}(y_i, y_i^t) \qquad (1)$$

$$y_i^t = \sigma(w_{TRI}^i M(t_i)) \qquad (2)$$

Where $M(t_i)$ denotes the model from the previous epoch, w_{TRI} is the fully connected layer of the i-th token for triggers generation task, σ is a softmax operation, y_i denotes the weak label of token t_i.

Co-training Framework. One straight-forward way to make full use of the triggers is training the target task with triggers generation task jointly. Intuitively, if some keywords highlight the essence of the sentence exists in training data, we can readjust the weight of the tokens according to their relative importance to the target task and guide the model to capture more important information. Then we jointly optimize the two objectives in the training stage, the overall loss can be defined as a linear combination of two parts:

$$\mathcal{L} = \alpha \mathcal{L}_{target} + (1 - \alpha)\mathcal{L}_{TRI} \tag{3}$$

$$\mathcal{L}_{target} = \sum_{i=1} l_{target}(y_i, y_i^s) \tag{4}$$

where l_{target} is the loss function of the target task; y_i and y_i^s denote the actual label of sentence s_i and the predicted label for the target task respectively; $\mathcal{L}_{target}$ denotes the loss function of the target task while $\mathcal{L}_{TRI}$ represents the triggers generation task; α is a linear combination ratio which controls the relative importance of two losses.

After assigning the corresponding weight to each word, we will extract the words that help improve the target prediction and combine with the original model. Specifically, given a sentence S with entity e_1 and e_2, suppose its final hidden state output from BERT module is H. Then H_i to H_j are the final hidden state vectors from BERT for entity e_1, and H_p to H_q are the final hidden state vectors from BERT for entity e_2. We can get a vector representation for each of the two target entities by applying the average operation to corresponding vectors. Then each of the two vectors are fed into a feedforward network after an activation operation (i.e. $tanh$), and the outputs for e_1 and e_2 are H_1' and H_2' respectively:

$$H_1' = W_1 \left[tanh \left(\frac{1}{j - i + 1} \sum_{t=i}^{j} H_t \right) \right] + b_1 \tag{5}$$

$$H_2' = W_2 \left[tanh \left(\frac{1}{q - p + 1} \sum_{t=p}^{q} H_t \right) \right] + b_2 \tag{6}$$

To obtain a vector H_0' as the representation of the aggregate sequence, we do the same thing as before for the hidden state of first special token $[CLS]$:

$$H_0' = W_0 \left(tanh \left(H_0 \right) \right) + b_0 \tag{7}$$

To further leverage the information of the triggers, we apply a weighted sum of the reweighted tokens to get a single vector representation following with a $tanh$ activation operation and a fully connected layer.

$$H_t' = W_t \left[tanh \left(\frac{1}{k} \left(y_1^t * H_{t1} + ... + y_k^t * H_{tk} \right) \right) \right] + b_t \tag{8}$$

Where k means a total of k trigger tokens in this sentence mined and y_k^t represents the corresponding score reweighted for each token.

We concatenate H_0', H_1', H_2', H_t' following a fully connected layer and a softmax layer, which can be expressed as following:

$$h = W_3 \left[concat \left(H_0'.H_1'.H_2'.H_t' \right) \right] + b_3 \tag{9}$$

$$p = softmax \left(h \right) \tag{10}$$

Matrices W_0, W_1, W_2, W_t have the same dimensions, i.e. $W_0 \in R^{d \times d}, W_1 \in R^{d \times d}, W_2 \in R^{d \times d}$ and $W_3 \in R^{L \times 4d}$, where d is the hidden state size from BERT and L is the number of relation types; p is the probability output; b_0, b_1, b_2, b_3, b_t are bias vector and we apply dropout before each fully connected layer during training.

4   Experiement

4.1   Dataset and Evaluation Metric

We evaluate the framework on TACRED [24] dataset in our experiments. TACRED was originally produced by human annotations with 106,264 examples built over English newswire and web text used in the TAC KBP English slot filling evaluations during the period 2009–2014. The dataset contains 41 semantic relation types and one artificial relation type *no_relation*, which means that the relation does not belong to any of the 41 relation types. Besides, we evaluate Precision (P), Recall (R), and F1 scores following official suggestions in [24].

4.2   Implementation Details

In our experiments, we use the uncased basic model for the pre-train BERT model and tune all hyper-parameters based on F1 score on development set. We trained our model with 5 epochs and set learning rate as 2e-5. To accelerate the training speed, the maximum sequence length is set to 128 in our experiments and the extra length will be cut in each batch. Besides, we add dropout before each encoder layer and BertAdam optimizer is used. Further, we employ rigorous experiments to find the optimal hyper-parameters: loss combination ratio $\alpha \in \{0.7, 0.9\}$ and data generation ratio $\beta \in \{0.6, 1.0, 2.0\}$.

4.3   Compared Methods

We compare out method against results by multiple classic methods recently published:

- **PA-LSTM** [24] creatively combines the bi-directional LSTM [5] with position-aware attention to encode the text into an embedding, which is then fed into a softmax layer to predict the relation.

- **C-GCN** [23] proposes an extension of graph convolutional network which pools information over arbitrary dependency structures and apply a novel pruning strategy to the input trees by keeping words immediately around the shortest path [10] between the two entities to obtain the representation of entities.
- **BERT-BASE** [13] is the first to successfully apply BERT in relation extraction. They concatenate the embedding of the BERT with position embedding and the final prediction is based on the concatenation of the final hidden state in each direction from the BiLSTM, fed through an MLP.
- **BERT-EM** [14] explores variants of architectures for extracting representations from deep Transformers network and present a pre-trained training objective of matching the blanks. In our experiment, we reimplement it without the pre-trained task.
- **R-BERT** [19] is a model that locate the target entities and transfer the information through the pre-trained architecture following incorporate the corresponding encoding of the two entities into the pretrained language model for relation classification.
- **SpanBERT** [8] extends BERT by introducing a training objective of span prediction and replacing the entity pair by their NER tags, achieving improved performance on RE.

4.4 Result and Analyse

Table 1. Experimental results on TACRED

Model	TACRED		
	Prec.	*Rec.*	$F1$
sequence-based models			
PA-LSTM	67.7	63.2	65.4
C-GCN	69.9	63.3	66.4
Transformer-based models			
BERT$_{BASE}$	73.3	63.1	67.8
BERT$_{EM}$	69.4	66.8	67.9
R-BERT	71.9	62.5	67.3
SpanBERT	70.2	66.3	68.2
Our model	**71.3**	**65.4**	**68.7**

Table 1 shows the experimental results of different models on TACRED. All experiments are based on the publicly available implementation of base version of $BERT_{BASE}$ as the encoder, and we rerun their officially released code using the recommended hyper-parameters in their papers. There is no doubt that

Transformer-based models surpasses all sequence-based models, so we mainly compare our model with some classical Transformer-based models. Besides, we want to demonstrate the specific contributions by the components besides the pre-trained BERT component. For this purpose, we compare our model with $BERT_{BASE}$, $BERT_{EM}$ and R-$BERT$ respectively. As we can see, our model gets much improvement compared to $BERT_{BASE}$ and $BERT_{EM}$, which demonstrates the strong empirical results based on the proposed approach cause these two other models merely use the context representation enhanced by BERT for relational classification. We infer that it is because the representation of the $[CLS]$ is just a general sentence representation rather than a maximum adaptation to relation extraction. It also can be observed that our model achieves 1.4 F1 absolute points better than R-$BERT$, indicating that score generation can promote the accuracy of the model not rely solely on the augment of the entity pair. Besides, we compare our own model with the latest pre-trained language model $SpanBERT$ and achieve comparable results, which will be the direction of our future research.

Table 2. Results with different settings on TACRED

Settings	TACRED		
	Prec.	*Rec.*	*F*1
DEFAULT	**71.3**	**65.4**	**68.7**
w/o triggers knowledge	70.0	65.0	67.4
w/o separate tokens	72.3	60.7	66.0
w/o entities	67.1	61.8	64.3

4.5 Triggers Knowledge Study

In this part, we first analyze the method of incorporating triggers knowledge and then we detect the effectiveness of different label generation ratio.

For triggers knowledge, we create three more different settings as Table 2. "w/o triggers knowledge" means we don't perform treatment on data features in preprocessing step. The second configuration is to discard the special separate tokens (i.e. '$' and '#') but keep the average pooling of entities representation. "w/o entities" just takes the hidden vector output of the "[CLS]" for classification. From the ablation study, we get the observation that when one component is discarded, the performance will decline with varying degrees. Without triggers knowledge, the performance drops sharply which demonstrates the triggers knowledge incorporated is useful for this task. Special separate tokens are also important, we infer that an early fusion of separate tokens can further improve performance cause they transfer the location information of entities into the model. Of the methods, "w/o entities" has the worst performs, with its almost 4.4 F1 points worse than our model, which means entity information makes important contributions to our approach.

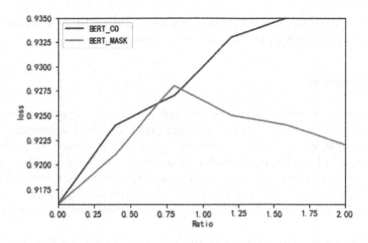

Fig. 3. Experiments on different generation ratio

For label generation ratio, we conduct experiments under different generation ratio β as Fig. 3. The larger β means each epoch more masked sentences are generated as training samples. $BERT_{MASK}$ means just carry out the token score generation study for BERT model but don't augment the sentence vector with keywords. In the beginning, the two models continue to improve with more masked sentences generated. However, the performance of $BERT_{MASK}$ degrades dramatically after β is greater than 0.8. One possible reason is that identifying relevant words and merging the reweighted tokens directly will influence the robustness of our model, resulting in sufficient learning on pre-trained knowledge.

4.6 Training Cost Comparison

One possible questioned shortcoming of our method is the extra training cost of the token score generation. To further evaluate the extra cost, we conduct extended experiments on loss value of specific time scaled. The detailed results on three different models are presented in Table 3. Note that our method contains more parameters, so it converges slower at the beginning. However, our model starts to achieve a lower loss than other models in later iterations since it can provide complementary information for BERT. Besides, as shown in Fig. 3,

Table 3. Experiments on loss value of specific time scaled

Time/min	20	40	60	80
$BERT_{BASE}$	0.588	0.113	0.016	0.015
R-BERT	0.633	0.105	0.014	0.011
Our model	**0.701**	**0.128**	**0.012**	**0.008**

compared with the total training time, this cost is completely acceptable since the final performance gain justifies the extra training cost.

5 Conclusion

In this paper, we present a simple but effective approach to incorporate triggers knowledge for Relation Extraction. Triggers generation task automatically produces token-level attention labels and picks out real keywords by probing the fine-tuned model from the previous iteration. We further integrate the semantics of entity pair and triggers knowledge to augment the sentence representation. We conduct experiments on the TACRED benchmark dataset and achieve competitive results. In future work, we will extend to span-level keywords augmentation.

Acknowledgement. The authors wish to thank the reviewers for their helpful comments and suggestions. This work was also supported by the National Key Research & Development Program (Grant No. 2018YFC0831700) and National Natural Science Foundation of China (Grant No. 61671064, No. 61732005).

References

1. Alicante, A., Corazza, A.: Barrier features for classification of semantic relations. In: Proceedings of the International Conference Recent Advances in Natural Language Processing 2011, pp. 509–514 (2011)
2. Bunescu, R., Mooney, R.: A shortest path dependency Kernel for relation extraction. In: Proceedings of Human Language Technology Conference and Conference on Empirical Methods in Natural Language Processing, pp. 724–731 (2005)
3. Devlin, J., Chang, M.W., Lee, K., Toutanova, K.: BERT: pre-training of deep bidirectional transformers for language understanding. arXiv preprint arXiv:1810.04805 (2018)
4. Han, X., et al.: More data, more relations, more context and more openness: a review and outlook for relation extraction. arXiv preprint arXiv:2004.03186 (2020)
5. Hochreiter, S., Schmidhuber, J.: Long short-term memory. Neural Comput. **9**(8), 1735–1780 (1997)
6. Huffman, S.B.: Learning information extraction patterns from examples. In: Wermter, S., Riloff, E., Scheler, G. (eds.) IJCAI 1995. LNCS, vol. 1040, pp. 246–260. Springer, Heidelberg (1996). https://doi.org/10.1007/3-540-60925-3_51
7. Jiang, H., et al.: Relation extraction using supervision from topic knowledge of relation labels. In: IJCAI, pp. 5024–5030 (2019)
8. Joshi, M., Chen, D., Liu, Y., Weld, D.S., Zettlemoyer, L., Levy, O.: SpanBERT: improving pre-training by representing and predicting spans. Trans. Assoc. Comput. Linguist. **8**, 64–77 (2020)
9. Lin, Y., Shen, S., Liu, Z., Luan, H., Sun, M.: Neural relation extraction with selective attention over instances. In: Proceedings of the 54th Annual Meeting of the Association for Computational Linguistics, vol. 1, Long Papers, pp. 2124–2133 (2016)
10. Liu, Y., Wei, F., Li, S., Ji, H., Zhou, M., Wang, H.: A dependency-based neural network for relation classification. arXiv preprint arXiv:1507.04646 (2015)

11. Peters, M.E., et al.: Knowledge enhanced contextual word representations. arXiv preprint arXiv:1909.04164 (2019)
12. Sarzynska-Wawer, J., et al.: Detecting formal thought disorder by deep contextualized word representations. Psychiatry Res. **304**, 114135 (2021)
13. Shi, P., Lin, J.: Simple BERT models for relation extraction and semantic role labeling. arXiv preprint arXiv:1904.05255 (2019)
14. Soares, L.B., FitzGerald, N., Ling, J., Kwiatkowski, T.: Matching the blanks: distributional similarity for relation learning. arXiv preprint arXiv:1906.03158 (2019)
15. Vaswani, A., et al.: Attention is all you need. In: Advances in Neural Information Processing Systems, pp. 5998–6008 (2017)
16. Verga, P., Belanger, D., Strubell, E., Roth, B., McCallum, A.: Multilingual relation extraction using compositional universal schema. arXiv preprint arXiv:1511.06396 (2015)
17. Wang, H., Lu, G., Yin, J., Qin, K.: Relation extraction: a brief survey on deep neural network based methods. In: 2021 The 4th International Conference on Software Engineering and Information Management, pp. 220–228 (2021)
18. Wang, R., et al.: K-adapter: infusing knowledge into pre-trained models with adapters. arXiv preprint arXiv:2002.01808 (2020)
19. Wu, S., He, Y.: Enriching pre-trained language model with entity information for relation classification. In: Proceedings of the 28th ACM International Conference on Information and Knowledge Management, pp. 2361–2364 (2019)
20. Yamada, I., Asai, A., Shindo, H., Takeda, H., Matsumoto, Y.: LUKE: deep contextualized entity representations with entity-aware self-attention. arXiv preprint arXiv:2010.01057 (2020)
21. Zeng, D., Liu, K., Lai, S., Zhou, G., Zhao, J.: Relation classification via convolutional deep neural network. In: Proceedings of COLING 2014, the 25th International Conference on Computational Linguistics: Technical Papers, pp. 2335–2344 (2014)
22. Zhang, D., Wang, D.: Relation classification via recurrent neural network. arXiv preprint arXiv:1508.01006 (2015)
23. Zhang, Y., Qi, P., Manning, C.D.: Graph convolution over pruned dependency trees improves relation extraction. arXiv preprint arXiv:1809.10185 (2018)
24. Zhang, Y., Zhong, V., Chen, D., Angeli, G., Manning, C.D.: Position-aware attention and supervised data improve slot filling. In: Proceedings of the 2017 Conference on Empirical Methods in Natural Language Processing, pp. 35–45 (2017)
25. Zhang, Z., Han, X., Liu, Z., Jiang, X., Sun, M., Liu, Q.: ERNIE: enhanced language representation with informative entities. arXiv preprint arXiv:1905.07129 (2019)

Does Large Pretrained Dataset Always Help? On the Effect of Dataset Size on Big Transfer Model

Xue Li[1], Kai Jiang[1], Qiang Duan[1], Rui Li[1], Yang Tian[1], Qibin Chen[1], Xiangyu Zhu[1], Yongfei Jia[2], and Hui Zhang[1(✉)]

[1] Inspur Academy of Science and Technology, Shandong, China
zhanghui@inspur.com
[2] Qilu University of Technology (Shandong Academy of Sciences), Shandong, China

Abstract. Transfer learning often refers to an approach concerning machine learning in which the programmers relocate an initially developed model as the starting point for a model on a consequent task. It is evident that deep neural networks entail massive datasets to build and train feasible models. To gain massive and qualified datasets, nonetheless, seems expensive and time-consuming. This paper firstly examines the scale of a dataset so as to train an effective model as well as pertinent reactions corresponding to partial changes made to the scale of the dataset. In the practical experiments via training deep neural networks, we simplify hyperparameter tuning via transfer of pre-trained representations, hence promoting sample efficiency. To verify the usefulness of pre-trained models in datasets of different sizes, we have done relevant experiments on two benchmark datasets, cifar10 and cifar100. The results demonstrate that the larger the size of the pre-trained model, the better the fine-tuning effect of the network. With detailed analysis of primary elements contributing to high transfer performance, we aim to utilize pre-trained models with more efficient performance on dataset named as ImageNet-21k to benefit the computer vision research, in contrast to traditional models pre-trained on the smaller dataset, ILSVRC-2012.

Keywords: EfficientNet · Group normalization · MixUp · Residual networks · Transfer learning · Weight standardization

1 Introduction

As the data volume grows rapidly, it is common to build the deep learning model in a fast and convenient way. However, due to the insufficiency of labelled data, it is time-consuming to collect labelled data and build a deep neutral network from the scratch. Thus, it is necessary to make effective use of the model and the data with labels [17]. Given the considerable consumption of compute and time

---

X. Li, K. Jiang and Q. Duan—Equal contribution.

© IFIP International Federation for Information Processing 2022
Published by Springer Nature Switzerland AG 2022
Z. Shi et al. (Eds.): IIP 2022, IFIP AICT 643, pp. 136–147, 2022.
https://doi.org/10.1007/978-3-031-03948-5_12

required to develop neural network models pertinent to those problems, it is a popular approach in deep learning to harness pre-trained models as the starting point on computer vision tasks. With a vast and generic dataset established, less compute and fewer data points will give an edge to initializing subsequent tasks through the imported weights from pre-trained dataset [10].

Employing pre-trained weights and large models is becoming a substantial approach for image classification tasks, which generally considers ImageNet as the training dataset [11]. Scholars like Yosinski et al. simply utilized the ImageNet dataset [19]. Nevertheless, primary differences are manifested between natural image classification and the target tasks in terms of task specifications, features, and sizes, the effects of transfer deserve further study [14]. It can be intriguing to scrutinize whether the traits of transfer learning differ when employing a dataset from a distinctive domain. Our research starts with drawing upon pre-trained model for transfer learning to explore impacts on dataset scale, hence examining the interaction between sizes of architecture and data as well as training hyperparameters. With such a mechanism, residual neutral networks with 50 layers will be pre-trained on a larger dataset ImageNet-21k including images of 14M and a smaller dataset ILSVRC-2012 containing images of 1.3M.

Recent progress in deep learning has been largely attributed to the scale and diversity of data gathered in recent years. Thanks to data augmentation, we are able to considerably multiply the data diversity to enlarge the scale of models for training, acquiring proliferated new data. When it comes to train neural networks of massive size, we usually employ strategies including flipping, padding, and cropping. However, it ought to be noticed that massive deep neural networks tend to reveal unexpected conditions, sometimes negative, in spite of its large size and presumed powerfulness. For instance, they can store and react to some opposite cases. In order to mitigate the negative effects, a brief learning mechanism named MixUp [21] was put forward. This tool regularizes the neural network to sustain reaction of linear correlations amid training cases. It is indicated that MixUp greatly enhances the effectiveness of generalization concerning cutting-edge frameworks of neural network via a series of tests on UCI datasets, CIFAR-10 [21], as well as ImageNet-2012 [2]. In addition to its powerfulness on generalization, deep learning can be more stable and faster by batch normalization [7] which standardizes the inputs to a layer for every sub-batch through re-entering and re-scaling. As a milestone work in deep learning, it is conducive to speeding up the process of training and convergence and preventing the overfitting problem as well. Subsequently, encouraged by the development of batch normalization, layer normalization [1], instance normalization [6], and group normalization [18] emerged one after another, which promotes the development of deep learning in multiple dimensions.

Being an integral part of the computer vision including video surveillance and image retrieval, object detection serves to concisely identify the location and category of a particular object in targeted images or even videos. There are basically two approaches for object detection, that is, one-stage and two-stage (one-stage network is represented by Yolo [12] and two-stage network is

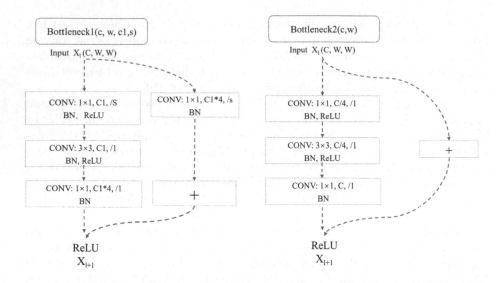

Fig. 1. Bottleneck architectures

represented by Faster-RCNN [13]). In fact, dramatic progress can be witnessed in object detection algorithm in terms of feature extraction, image expression, classification, and recognition via models of feature extraction and transfer learning capabilities of deep convolutional neural networks. In future studies, we intend to achieve the goals of object detection and semantic segmentation by drawing upon the Big Transfer Model constructed below.

2   Approach

The generalizability of features has been examined in several studies, with a success of transfer learning testified. It should be noticeable that fine-tuning serves as a regular scheme for transfer learning. In the wake of re-examining the standards of residual network and fine-tuning the model on assigned objects, our model with larger dataset via diversifying the size of pertinent datasets works better than previous ones.

2.1   A Parsimonious Model - ResNet 50

Breakthrough regarding image classification can be made due to deep convolutional neural networks. Propelled by an increasing importance of depth, the problem of network degradation arises. To grapple with this tricky problem, He K. et al. [3] proposed a solution in which residual network is established by constructing residual blocks consisting of shortcut connection x and residual function $F(x)$. A residual block can be expressed as: $x_L = x_l + \sum_{i=l}^{L-1} F(x_i, W_i)$. The structure of ResNet is shown in Fig. 1 and Fig. 3.

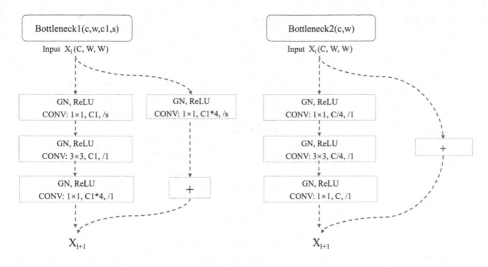

Fig. 2. The modified residual network

After analyzing the propagation formulation of the deep residual module and processing a series of ablation experiments, the modified residual networks [4] put forward, rendering the model training more effective and the ability of generalization stronger. The primary components of ResNet-V2 in our paper are shown in Fig. 2.

2.2 The Big Transfer Model

The idea of Big Transfer (BiT) [8] offers a generic method consisting of minimal tactics yet acquiring satisfactory results on more tasks. There are two steps in the construction of BiT: Upstream and Downstream. To be specific, Upstream is the process of pre-training while Downstream refers to the process of fine-tuning. The scale of the Upstream in pre-training model is reflected in the size of each training dataset, instead of the size of the model. According to the size of each dataset, three pre-training models (BiT-S, BiT-M, and BiT-L) corresponding to 5 different architectures (ResNet-50, ResNet-101, ResNet-50x3, ResNet-101x3, and ResNet-152x4) are designed, which matches the datasets of ILSVRC-2012 (1.3 m), ImageNet-21k (14 m), and JFT (300 m) respectively. After training the Upstream network, what we need to do is to transfer to Downstream tasks. Kolesnikov A. et al. [8] use a heuristic method called BiT-HyperRule to select and adjust several important hyperparameters - training schedule length, data resolution as well as whether to use MixUp regularization. Since this method is generic, each BiT model only requires one-time pre-training, hence the following tasks of fine-tuning to downstream becoming easier. It should be noticed that BiT in this study wins over the traditional ILSVRC-2012 pre-training via training on the public ImageNet-21k.

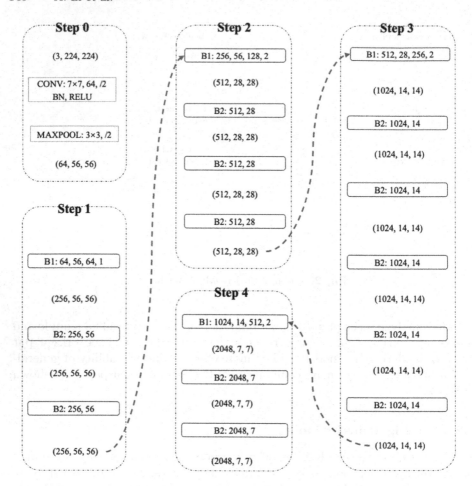

Fig. 3. The ResNet-50 model

2.3   Data Augmentation - MixUp

To multiply the amount of data, we resort to the technique of data augmentation, assuming that $batch_{x1}$ is one of batch sample while $batch_{y1}$ is the label corresponding with it. In this vein, $batch_{x2}$ is the other batch sample while $batch_{y1}$ is the label corresponded with it. Moreover, $\lambda \in [0, 1]$ and the hyperparameter α determines degree of interpolation. With the relevant variables clarified, the algorithm is presented below,

$$\lambda \sim Beta(\alpha, \alpha), \; for \; \alpha \in (0, \infty)$$

$$mixed_{batch_x} = \lambda \times batch_{x1} + (1 - \lambda) \times batch_{x2}$$

$$mixed_{batch_y} = \lambda \times batch_{y1} + (1 - \lambda) \times batch_{y2}$$

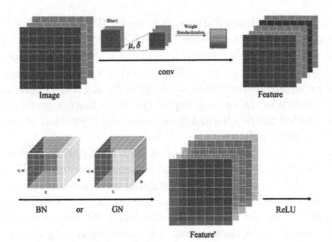

Fig. 4. Weight Standardization: normalize convolution kernels; Normalization Approach: the left part in light blue represents Batch Norm, and the right part in light blue indicates Group Norm. (Color figure online)

2.4   Group Normalization with Weight Standardization

On the basis of unfixed dimension of batch, batch normalization may vary in effect. For instance, it differs in training and test. Typically, we will move average in the training set to pre-calculate the mean and variance. In the test, these values will not be calculated thereafter, put in use directly. Nevertheless, when the distribution of training and test vary, the pre-calculated parameters on the training set cannot represent the testing data, hence resulting in inconsistency. Through separating the channels into different groups, group normalization computes the variance and mean to standardize the data in every group. The accuracy of computation by group normalization is steady within a considerable batch scales owing to its immunization of batch sizes.

The formulas shown below belong to the conventional normalization operation. Above all, it sets $i = (i_N, i_C, i_H, i_W)$, so x_i refers to a point at a specified position in the feature map.

$$\mu_i = \frac{1}{m} \sum_{k \in S_i} x_k \tag{1}$$

$$\sigma_i = \sqrt{\frac{1}{m} \sum_{k \in S_i} (x_k - \mu_i)^2 + \epsilon} \tag{2}$$

$$\widehat{x_l} = \frac{1}{\sigma_i} (x_i - \mu_i) \tag{3}$$

$$y_i = \gamma \hat{x}_i + \beta_i \tag{4}$$

It can be observed that the distinction between BN and GN lies in the range of S_i in formula 1 and 2. To be specific, S_i in BN is $S_i = \{k \mid k_c = i_c\}$, S_i in GN is $S_i = \{k \mid k_N = i_N, [\frac{k_C}{C/G}] = [\frac{i_C}{C/G}]\}$, in which $k_N = i_N$ makes the calculation on the same graphs' feature map. As G means that C is divided into G groups, G serves as a hyperparameter which is set to 32 by default. Therefore, the idea of GN is to normalize in the same group of the same feature map. Now that the group is only divided in the channel dimension, the operation of normalization is independent of the batch size.

In the three-dimensional cube in Fig. 4, façade C and N represent channel and batch size respectively while the third dimension represents H and W. The dimension size is H * W, which can be elongated into one dimension, so that the whole can be represented by three-dimensional graphics. It can be seen that the calculation of BN is related to the batch size (the light blue area is the part for calculating the mean and variance) while the calculation of GN is not related to the batch size. To avoid the dependence on batch size and realize the mini-batch size, a method called Weight Standardization was proposed directly deal with the weight of convolution kernel. In this sense, there lies pertinent flexibility that the developers can optimize the performance on mini-batch size training with a combination of GN and WS.

3   Experiments and Results

In Sect. 3, we provide an outline of our experiment regarding two upstream models taking backbone as ResNet 50-V2 pre-training on ImageNet21K and ILSVRC-2012. Subsequently, we evaluate their performance on downstream task by referring to CIFAR-10 and CIFAR-100.

3.1   Data Description

The labeled subsets CIFAR-10 and CIFAR-100 are collected by Vinod Nair et al., extracted from tiny images dataset of 80M [9]. Basically, the CIFAR-10 dataset contains 60000 color images in resolution of 32×32 in 10 classes, with each class including 6000 images. Akin to the CIFAR-10, this dataset possesses 100 classes, each with 600 images (500 training images and 100 testing images per class). With 100 classes in the CIFAR-100 integrated into 20 superclasses, each of its image is labeled "fine" (certain class to which it should be categorized) and "coarse" (certain superclass to which it should be categorized).

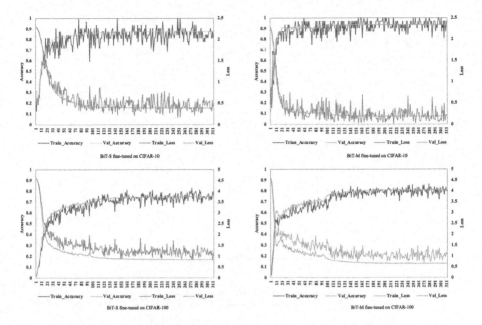

Fig. 5. Results with Bit-S and Bit-M

3.2   Details About Hyperparameters in Upstream and Downstream

Resembling separate units of nervous system, upstream part in deep learning is engaged in pre-training while downstream is used for fine-tuning to a specific task. With regard to the upstream section where this study draws upon the warm-up method to render the learning rate climb to $0.03 \times \frac{batchsize}{256}$ and the weight decay of the optimizer be 0.0001, we seek reference from procedures taken by Kolesnikov, A. et al. [8] who drew upon unified hyperparameters: SGD with momentum of 0.9, initial learning rate of 0.03, batch size of 4096, and the size of input data being 224 × 224. With 90 epochs trained by BiT-S and BiT-M, the learning rate was divided by 10 in the 30th, 60th, and 80th generations.

After training the upstream part, we need to fine-tune it into the downstream task. To perform pertinent functions Kolesnikov, A. et al. proposed a heuristic approach named BiT-Hyperrule. The SGD with momentum was set to 0.9, learning rate to 0.003, and batch size to 512. It entails selecting and adjusting several critical hyperparameters containing schedule length in which the small tasks (less than 20k) were trained with 500 steps while the medium tasks (ranging from 20K to 500K) with 10K steps, images' resolution as well as necessity of using MixUp data augmentation in which the α is set to 0.1. In particular, the procedures of images' resolution are akin to the standard process of handling data, that is, resizing, cropping, and flipping. To be specific, the target image can be rectified into a square, randomly cropped out of a smaller one, and finally flipped in horizontal at random during the training period, which differs from the fixed size reshaped during the testing period.

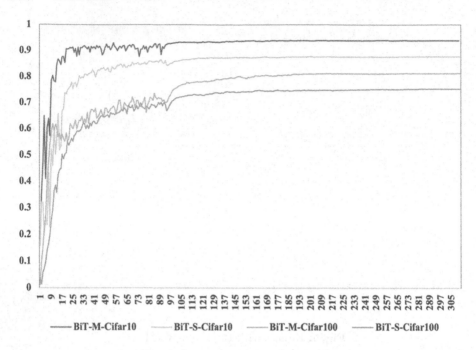

Fig. 6. Improvement in test accuracy

3.3   Results

BiT-M represents model pre-trained on ImageNet-21k and BiT-S means model pre-trained on ILSVRC-2012. The dataset pretrained on BiT-M is 10 times bigger than BiT-S. In the fine-tune task, we obtain the accuracy of 93.9% and 87.7% on CIFAR-10 and the accuracy of 81.3% and 75.3% on CIFAR-100 after running fine-tuning of the model BiT-M and BiT-S. The details are presented in Fig. 6. As seen from this figure, the performance of the model is logarithmically refined along with the rise in the number of pre-training data.

It can be seen from Fig. 5 that the visual representations of BiT-M have been significantly refined with a training on ImageNet-21k, satisfactory accuracy can be obtained with large-scale pre-training models even when the sample data per category is small. However, in our practice, we show that the accuracy is related to the class of the dataset, and when the class is very different from the dataset of the pretrained model and the samples are small, the training with the pretrained model is not only low in accuracy but also time-consuming.

3.4   Compared with the EfficientNet Model

To validate the learning ability in the Big Transfer Model, we compare those experimental results mentioned above with the EfficientNet [15] model in Sect. 4. Typically, if the model is designed to be too wide [20], deep [3], or with high resolution [5], it will soon be saturated, and the efficiency will be deteriorated despite being useful at the beginning. To address such an issue, we employ the EfficientNet where these features are scaled in a more organized way. The NAS (neural network search) is used to find a better backbone, that is, EfficientNet-b0. By scaling the width, depth, and resolution of the B0 model at the same time, they gain the EfficientNet b1–b7.

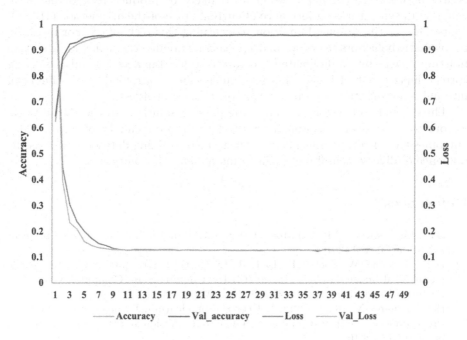

Fig. 7. EfficientNet on CIFAR-100

As we can see from Fig. 7, the test accuracy is about 95% on CIFAR-10, which is very similar to the BiT-M fine-tuned on CIFAR-10, but it converges faster in 50 epochs. Thus, it testifies that the BiT model has better transfer learning ability and the EfficientNet model has stronger convergence ability.

4   Discussions and Future Work

The smaller datasets of computer vision like ILSVRC-2012 which contains images of 1.28M tend to produce proper outcome when following traditional training steps. Due to the advancement in computing techs, such standard procedures enable datasets of larger size such as ImageNet-21k which includes images of 14.2M to be processed. Nonetheless, it is deficient of existing mechanisms for training datasets of larger scale. To address this issue, on the one hand, we scrutinized Big Transfer model with architecture ResNet-50 V2 on various datasets, and on the other hand, we propose a few fundamental principles for handling larger datasets so as to increase the image's classification accuracy. The results acquired in this research verify the weight of dataset scale concerning visual representations. In this sense, it will provide a deep insight for those who have access to either large or small computational resources.

As a novel discipline, there are still quite an amount of work in both theoretical and practical aspects of deep learning [22]. With the application of deep neural networks to computer vision, it is likely to produce results that rival against or even surpass performance of current state-of-the-art methods [16]. Of course, there still lie some limitations concerning this technology. For instance, problematic behaviors can occur in deep learning architectures, including sorting blurring images into a designated category of typical images and misclassifying correct images out of minor changes, which can be ascribed to the limits of internal representations and misreading of image semantics.

Thus, instead of seeking for all-encompassing solutions in the future work, we ought to conduct a thorough study of the reproducibility of cutting-edge outcomes and of correlations between the scale of training dataset as well as the influence of diverse neural models in terms of generalizability.

References

1. Ba, J.L., Kiros, J.R., Hinton, G.E.: Layer normalization. arXiv preprint arXiv:1607.06450 (2016)
2. Deng, J., Dong, W., Socher, R., Li, L.-J., Li, K., Fei-Fei, L.: ImageNet: a large-scale hierarchical image database. In: 2009 IEEE Conference on Computer Vision and Pattern Recognition, pp. 248–255. IEEE (2009)
3. He, K., Zhang, X., Ren, S., Sun, J.: Deep residual learning for image recognition. In: Proceedings of the IEEE Conference on Computer Vision and Pattern Recognition, pp. 770–778 (2016)
4. He, K., Zhang, X., Ren, S., Sun, J.: Identity mappings in deep residual networks. In: Leibe, B., Matas, J., Sebe, N., Welling, M. (eds.) ECCV 2016. LNCS, vol. 9908, pp. 630–645. Springer, Cham (2016). https://doi.org/10.1007/978-3-319-46493-0_38
5. He, Y., Lin, J., Liu, Z., Wang, H., Li, L.-J., Han, S.: AMC: AutoML for model compression and acceleration on mobile devices. In: Proceedings of the European Conference on Computer Vision (ECCV), pp. 784–800 (2018)
6. Huang, X., Belongie, S.: Arbitrary style transfer in real-time with adaptive instance normalization. In: Proceedings of the IEEE International Conference on Computer Vision, pp. 1501–1510 (2017)
7. Ioffe, S., Szegedy, C.: Batch normalization: accelerating deep network training by reducing internal covariate shift. In: International Conference on Machine Learning, pp. 448–456. PMLR (2015)
8. Kolesnikov, A., et al.: Big Transfer (BiT): general visual representation learning. In: Vedaldi, A., Bischof, H., Brox, T., Frahm, J.-M. (eds.) ECCV 2020. LNCS, vol. 12350, pp. 491–507. Springer, Cham (2020). https://doi.org/10.1007/978-3-030-58558-7_29
9. Krizhevsky, A., Hinton, G., et al.: Learning multiple layers of features from tiny images (2009)
10. Pan, S.J., Yang, Q.: A survey on transfer learning. IEEE Trans. Knowl. Data Eng. **22**(10), 1345–1359 (2009)

11. Raghu, M., Zhang, C., Kleinberg, J., Bengio, S.: Transfusion: understanding transfer learning for medical imaging. arXiv preprint arXiv:1902.07208 (2019)
12. Redmon, J., Divvala, S., Girshick, R., Farhadi, A.: You only look once: unified, real-time object detection. In: Proceedings of the IEEE Conference on Computer Vision and Pattern Recognition, pp. 779–788 (2016)
13. Ren, S., He, K., Girshick, R., Sun, J.: Faster R-CNN: towards real-time object detection with region proposal networks. In: Advances in Neural Information Processing, vol. 28, pp. 91–99 (2015)
14. Soekhoe, D., van der Putten, P., Plaat, A.: On the impact of data set size in transfer learning using deep neural networks. In: Boström, H., Knobbe, A., Soares, C., Papapetrou, P. (eds.) IDA 2016. LNCS, vol. 9897, pp. 50–60. Springer, Cham (2016). https://doi.org/10.1007/978-3-319-46349-0_5
15. Tan, M., Le, Q.: EfficientNet: rethinking model scaling for convolutional neural networks. In: International Conference on Machine Learning, pp. 6105–6114. PMLR (2019)
16. Voulodimos, A., Doulamis, N., Doulamis, A., Protopapadakis, E.: Deep learning for computer vision: a brief review. Comput. Intell. Neurosci. **2018** (2018)
17. Weiss, K., Khoshgoftaar, T.M., Wang, D.D.: A survey of transfer learning. J. Big Data **3**(1), 1–40 (2016). https://doi.org/10.1186/s40537-016-0043-6
18. Wu, Y., He, K.: Group normalization. In: Proceedings of the European Conference on Computer Vision (ECCV), pp. 3–19 (2018)
19. Yosinski, J., Clune, J., Bengio, Y., Lipson, H.: How transferable are features in deep neural networks? arXiv preprint arXiv:1411.1792 (2014)
20. Zagoruyko, S., Komodakis, N.: Wide residual networks. arXiv preprint arXiv:1605.07146 (2016)
21. Zhang, H., Cisse, M., Dauphin, Y.N., Lopez-Paz, D.: mixup: beyond empirical risk minimization. arXiv preprint arXiv:1710.09412 (2017)
22. Zhao, Z.-Q., Zheng, P., Xu, S.-T., Wu, X.: Object detection with deep learning: a review. IEEE Trans. Neural Netw. Learn. Syst. **30**(11), 3212–3232 (2019)

Using Multi-level Attention Based on Concept Embedding Enrichen Short Text to Classification

Ben You, XiaoHong Li$^{(\boxtimes)}$, QiXuan Peng, and RuiHong Li

College of Computer Science and Engineering, Northwest Normal University, Lanzhou, China
xiaohongli@nwnu.edu.cn

Abstract. Aiming at the defects of short text, which lack context information and weak ability to describe topic, this paper proposes an attention network based solution for enriching topic information of short text, which can leverage both text information and concept embedding to represent short text. Specifically, short text encoder is used to enhance the representation of short texts in the semantic space. The concept encoder obtains the distribution representation of the concept through the attention network composed of *C-ST* attention and *C-CS* attention. Finally, Concatenating outputs from the two encoders creates a longer target representation of short text. Experimental results on two benchmark datasets show that our model achieves inspiring performance and outperforms baseline methods significantly.

Keywords: Short text representation · Knowledge base · Conceptualization · BERT · Attention mechanism

1 Introduction

The task of categorizing short texts is one of the important methods for a wide range of applications, including web search, news classification. Short texts lack enough contextual information, which poses a great challenge for short text classification. An essential intermediate step for text classification is text representation. According to the different ways of leveraging external sources, previous text representation methods can be divided into two categories: explicit representation and implicit representation [1].

For explicit approaches, a short text is represented as a sparse vector by labeling, POS tagging, and syntactic parsing. Researchers develop effective features from many aspects, such as knowledge base. Although explicit models are easily understandable by humans, it is difficult for the models to capture deep semantic information from the contexts. Besides, they also suffer from the data sparsity problem.

In terms of implicit representation, a short text is usually mapped to an implicit space and represented as a dense vector [2] which is called embedding. Encoder-decoder framework is also frequently adopted to capture the semantics of texts [3]. An implicit representation model can capture rich information from context and facilitate text understanding with the help of deep neural networks. However, implicit representation model ignores semantic relations such as *isA* and *isPropertyOf* that exist in knowledge bases.

Such information is helpful for understanding short texts, especially when dealing with previously unseen words.

It is ineffective to use either explicit or implicit representations independently for short text representation or classification. Previous work combined the two and used a rich knowledge base to enrich the prior knowledge of short texts by conceptualizing [4]. However, there are still two major problems. First, when conceptualizing the short text, improper concepts are easily introduced due to the ambiguity of entities or the noise in knowledge bases. For example, *"Steve Jobs established Apple"*, the conceptual *fruit* and *company* of *Apple* were extracted, but obviously *fruit* is not an appropriate concept which is caused by the ambiguity of *Apple*. Second, it is necessary to consider the relative importance of the concepts. For the same example, we extract the concepts *individual* and *entrepreneur* of *Steve Jobs* from the knowledge base. Despite the fact that they are both correct concepts, *entrepreneur* is more specific than *individual*.

In this work, we proposes an attention network based solution for enriching topic information of short text, which can leverage both concept embedding and text information to represent short text. Specifically, short text encoder is used to enhance the representation of short texts in the semantic space. The concept encoder obtains the distribution representation of the concept through the attention network composed of two-level attentions. Finally, Concatenating output from the two encoders creates a longer target representation of short text.

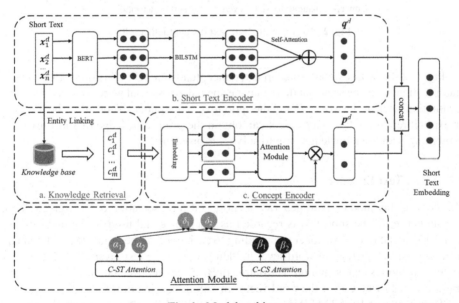

Fig. 1. Model architecture

2 Proposed Model

The overall architecture of our model (MACE) is shown in Fig. 1, which can be divided into three parts: concepts extraction, short text encoder and concept encoder.

We are given a set of documents D with a set of document labels Y where each document $d \in D$ is composed of multiple words $W^d = \{w_0^d, w_1^d, ..., w_n^d\}$. The input of our model is a short text d, where w_i^d represents i-th word in the short text d.

2.1 Concepts Extraction

The task of this module is to extract relevant conceptual knowledge from the external knowledge base. We use the *IsA* relationship to define the relationship between entities and concepts. Specifically, given a short text d, the goal is to find a concept set $C^d = \{c_1^d, c_2^d, ..., c_m^d\}$ related to the entities in the short text, where c_i^d is one of the concepts. First, entity linking technology is needed to identify entities in short text. Then for each entity, it needs to be conceptualized and its conceptual information is obtained from the external knowledge base. We utilize the existing entity-concept knowledge base (Microsoft Concept Graph) [5] to obtain conceptual information. It is a huge entity-concept knowledge base and has excavated *IsA* data from billions of web pages, with tens of millions of entities and millions of concepts, which is of great help to the understanding of short texts.

Short text: no <u>tsunami</u> but <u>**FIFA**</u>' s corruption storm rages on

Concepts: [natural disaster] [event]   [sport organization]

Fig. 2. Example of short text conceptualization.

Figure 2 shows an example of short text conceptualization. For this short text of sport classification, it can be seen that there may be specialized special words in a certain field or situation, such as the word *FIFA* in the sport text. It does not exist in either the implicit or explicit representation. Our model can obtain the prior knowledge of short texts by combining with the knowledge base to solve this problem.

2.2 Short Text Encoder

The goal of this module is to generate a short text representation q for a given short text sequence d. The short text is regarded as a sentence and used as the input of the BERT [6], and the word vector corresponding to each word of the sentence is calculated. Here we use the average of word-level hidden states in the last layer of BERT as the abstract semantics representation. The output of BERT is a representation of the sequence $(x_1^d, x_2^d, ..., x_n^d)$ where x_i^d is the word vector in 768-dimension of w_i^d.

Then a layer of BiLSTM [7] is used on top of BERT. BiLSTM includes both forward and backward networks, which solves the problem of traditional LSTM model that cannot be processed due to serialization. Let the number of hidden units of each unidirectional LSMT be u. We denote the short text representation sequence as $H = (h_1^d, h_2^d, ..., h_n^d)$ where $h_i^d \in \mathbb{R}^{2u}$ is the vector representation for word w_i^d after BERT and BiLSTM.

After that, the self-attention mechanism is adopted to solve the problem of vanishing gradient of BiLSTM. We use the scaled dot-product attention mechanism [3], which distinguishes the importance of different features, ignores unimportant features, and focuses attention on important features. Finally, the module obtains word vector $h_i^* \in \mathbb{R}^{2u}$ corresponding to word w_i^d.

2.3 Concept Encoder

Given a concept representation set T^d of size m denoted as $\{t_1^d, t_2^d, ..., t_m^d\}$, where t_i^d is the i-th concept vector, the goal of this module is to generate vector representation p for T^d.

In order to reduce the ambiguity of entities or the noise of external knowledge and the bad influence on incorrect concepts, we adopt the *Concept towards Short Text* (*C-ST*) attention [8] which is used to measure semantic similarity between the i-th concept and the short text q. C-ST attention is given by the following formula:

$$\alpha_i = softmax(w_1^T \tanh(W_1 \times concat[t_i^d; q^d] + b_1)) \tag{1}$$

Here α_i represents the attention weight of the i-th concept to the short text. A larger α_i means that the i-th concept is more similar to the short text in semantics. $W_1 \in \mathbb{R}^{d_a \times (2u+d)}$ is the parameter matrix and $w_1 = \mathbb{R}^{d_a}$ is the parameter vector where d_a is a hyperparameter, and b_1 is the bias. It should be noted that an entity may correspond to more than one concept. Therefore, for multiple concepts, we set the hyperparameter K as the maximum number of concepts that an entity can obtain.

In addition, based on consideration of the relative importance of concepts, *Concept towards Concept Set* (*C-CS*) is defined to measure the importance of each concept c_i^d:

$$\beta_i = softmax(w_2^T \tanh(W_2 t_i^d + b_2)) \tag{2}$$

Here β_i denotes the attention weight from the i-th concept to the entire concept set C_i^d. $W_2 \in \mathbb{R}^{d_b \times d}$ is a weight matrix and $w_2 \in \mathbb{R}^{d_b}$ is a weight vector where d_b is a hyperparameter, and b_2 is the bias.

The final attention weight of each concept is obtained by combining α_i and β_i with:

$$\delta_i = softmax(\gamma \alpha_i + (1 - \gamma)\beta_i) \tag{3}$$

Here δ_i represents the final attention weight from the i-th concept towards the short text, and $\gamma \in [0, 1]$ is the hyperparameter that manually adjusts the importance of α_i and β_i.

In the end, the final attention weight is used to calculate the weighted sum of the concept vector to obtain the semantic vector which represents the concepts:

$$p^d = \sum_{i=1}^n \delta_i^d t_i^d \tag{4}$$

After obtaining the semantic concept representation, we combine it with short text representation by concatenating them. Then we apply an output layer on the join vector to convert the output numbers into probabilities for classification.

3 Experiments

In this section, we conduct extensive experiments to evaluate our method.

3.1 Dataset

We use two benchmark short text classification datasets for evaluation. TagMyNews [9], a news dataset, and Snippets [10], contains Google search snippets. The details about such corpora are shown in Table 1.

Table 1. Details of the experimental datasets.

	Classes	Docs	Avg len per doc
TagMyNews	7	32,567	8
Snippets	8	12,332	17

In experiment, each dataset is randomly split into 80% for training and 20% for testing. 20% of the randomly selected training examples are used to development set.

3.2 Compared Methods

We compared our proposed method with the following methods. two feature-based methods, two deep learning methods and BERT.

SVM + BOW and SVM with unigram characteristics [11]. SVM + LDA, which is characterized by LDA [12]. Bidirectional long short-term memory (BiLSTM) with attention mechanism (AttBiLSTM) [13]. Convolutional neural network (CNN) [14]. BERT (bert-base-uncased) with fine-tuning and BERT without fine-tuning.

3.3 Evaluation Results and Analysis

For the parameters of all the compared models, we performed grid-search on their appropriate ranges. Glove [15] is used for concept embeddings with the number of concepts at $K = 5$. Only the final two layers of BERT and our model are fine-tuned and the maximum input length is 512. We adopt the standard cross-entropy loss function and Adam algorithm with learning rate $2e-4$ to train our model. The epoch of each dataset is 15 and the batch size is 128.

To evaluate the performance, we adopted two popular metrics: accuracy and F1 score, which are widely used to evaluate the performance of classification.

Text Classification Performance. In the first set of experiments, we compare the classification performance of our method against all the compared methods on the two datasets. As shown in Table 2.

The proposed method achieves the best results on both datasets. Because our model considers the knowledge base and attention. On both datasets, the SVM model (SVM

+ LDA) that uses topic information produces better results than the model that does not use topic features (SVM + BOW). This observation shows that the topic representation captured at the corpus level helps to alleviate the data sparseness problem in short text classification [16]. The neural models based on CNN or AttBILSTM produce better results than traditional methods show the effectiveness of representation learning in neural networks for short texts.

Compared with traditional methods and deep learning methods, the pre-training model BERT is better than the previous two. BERT with fine-tuning is more effective than it without fine-tuning proves that fine-tuning can be used to adapt to specific tasks. Although the effect of the latter is worse (BERT (wo/fine-tuing)), it still performs better than traditional methods, which shows the strong effect of BERT.

Table 2. Reslults of compared models on different datasets.

	TagMyNews		Snippets	
	Accuracy	F1	Accuracy	F1
SVM + BOW	0.259	0.058	0.210	0.080
SVM + LDA	0.616	0.593	0.689	0.694
CNN	0.843	0.843	0.944	0.944
Attn + BILSTM	0.820	0.821	0.944	0.943
BERT (wo/fine-tuning)	0.700	0.700	0.762	0.754
BERT (fine-tuning)	0.890	0.876	0.965	0.954
MACE	**0.908**	**0.894**	**0.977**	**0.971**

Effects of Hyperparameters. We further analyze the impact of the two main hyperparameters in our model, i.e., the number of concepts K and the value of γ.

We conducted experiments on the impact of the number of concepts K corresponding to an entity in a short text on classification performance. The classification accuracy with the number of concepts on the test sets are shown in Fig. 3. We can clearly see that achieves the highest accuracy with K = 5. When K = 0, no conceptual information is used, and the effect of using the BERT model alone is not as good as the model of using conceptual knowledge. It shows that a reasonable number of concepts will enable the model to achieve the best results on different datasets. However, an excessive number of concepts will result in a decrease in accuracy. The possible reason is that the increase in the number of concepts will confuse the semantics of short texts.

To verify the effectiveness of the two attention mechanisms, we studied the influence of the parameter γ that adjusts the two attention weights on the results. Manually adjusting the parameter γ from 0 to 1 and the step size is 0.25. The experimental results are shown in Table 3. It can be seen from Table 3 that when $\gamma = 0.50$, the model effect achieves the best effect on both datasets. When the parameter γ is set to 0 or 1, the effects are both worse on two data sets.

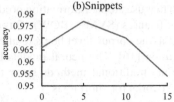

Fig. 3. Influence of different K on accuracy.

Table 3. The effect of different γ on the accuracy.

	TagMyNews	Snippets
$\gamma = 0$	0.891	0.953
$\gamma = 0.25$	0.903	0.970
$\gamma = 0.50$	**0.908**	**0.978**
$\gamma = 0.75$	0.900	0.954
$\gamma = 1.00$	0.883	0.960

4   Conclusion

In this paper, we propose an attention network which can leverage both text information and concept embedding to represent short text. First of all, short text encoder is used to enhance the representation of short texts in the semantic space. In addition, concept encoder obtains the distributed representation of the concept through the two attention networks. Finally, Concatenating outputs from the two encoders creates a final target representation of short text. On two short text classification datasets, the results show that our proposed model outperforms traditional methods, deep learning methods and original BERT.

Acknowledgements. This work was supported in part by National Natural Science Foundation of China (No. 61762078, 61967013), University Innovation and entrepreneurship Fund Project (2020B-089), Supported by science and technology program of Province (20JR5RA518), Natural Science Foundation of Province (20JR10RA076).

References

1. Wang, Z., Wang, H.: Understanding short texts. In: The Association for Computational Linguistics (Tutorial), Stroudsburg, Pennsylvania. ACL (2016)
2. Bengio, Y., Ducharme, R., Vincent, P., Janvin, C.: A neural probabilistic language model. J. Mach. Learn. Res. **3**, 1137–1155 (2003)
3. Vaswani, A., et al: Attention is all you need. In: Advances in Neural Information Processing Systems 30: Annual Conference on Neural Information Processing Systems, La Jolla, CA, pp. 5998–6008. NIPS (2017)

4. Wang, J., Wang, Z., Zhang, D., Yan, J.: Combining knowledge with deep convolutional neural networks for short text classification. In: 26th International Joint Conference on Artificial Intelligence, pp. 2915–2921. IJCAI.org, USA (2017). https://doi.org/10.24963/ijcai.2017/406
5. Wang, Z., Wang, H., Wen, J., Xiao, Y.: An inference approach to basic level of categorization. In: Proceedings of the 24th ACM International Conference on Information and Knowledge Management, pp. 653–662. ACM, New York (2015). https://doi.org/10.1145/2806416.280 6533
6. Devlin, J., Chang, M., Lee, K., Toutanova, K.: BERT: pre-training of deep bidirectional transformers for language understanding. In: Proceedings of the 2019 Conference of the North American Chapter of the Association for Computational Linguistics: Human Language Technologies, Stroudsburg, Pennsylvania, pp. 4171–4186. ACL (2019). https://doi.org/10. 18653/v1/n19-1423
7. Zhang, S., Zheng, D., Hu, X., Yang, M.: Bidirectional long short-term memory networks for relation classification. In: Proceedings of the 29th Pacific Asia Conference on Language, Information and Computation, Stroudsburg, Pennsylvania. ACL (2015)
8. Chen, J., Hu, Y., Liu, J., Xiao, Y., Jiang, H.: Deep short text classification with knowledge powered attention. In: The Thirty-Third AAAI Conference on Artificial Intelligence, pp. 6252–6259. AAAI Press, Palo Alto (2019). https://doi.org/10.1609/aaai.v33i01.33016252
9. Vitale, D., Ferragina, P., Scaiella, U.: Classification of short texts by deploying topical annotations. In: Baeza-Yates, R., et al. (eds.) ECIR 2012. LNCS, vol. 7224, pp. 376–387. Springer, Heidelberg (2012). https://doi.org/10.1007/978-3-642-28997-2_32
10. Xuan, H.P., Nguyen, M.L., Horiguchi, S.: Learning to classify short and sparse text & web with hidden topics from large-scale data collections. In: 17th International Conference on World Wide Web, pp. 91–100. ACM, New York (2008). https://doi.org/10.1145/1367497. 1367510
11. Wang, S., Manning, C.: Baselines and bigrams: simple, good sentiment and topic classification. In: 50th Annual Meeting of the Association for Computational Linguistics, Stroudsburg, pp. 90–94. ACL (2012)
12. Blei, D., Ng, A., Jordan, M.: Latent Dirichlet allocation. J. Mach. Learn. Res. **3**, 993–1022 (2003)
13. Zhang, D., Wang, D.: Relation classification via recurrent neural network. CoPR arXiv:1508. 01006 (2015)
14. Kim, Y.: Convolutional neural networks for sentence classification. In: Proceedings of the 2014 Conference on Empirical Methods in Natural Language Processing, Stroudsburg, Pennsylvania, pp. 1746–1751. ACL (2014). https://doi.org/10.3115/v1/d14-1181
15. Pennington, J., Socher, R., Manning, C.: GloVe: global vectors for word representation. In: Proceedings of the 2014 Conference on Empirical Methods in Natural Language Processing, Stroudsburg, Pennsylvania, pp 1532–1543. ACL (2014). https://doi.org/10.3115/v1/d14-1162
16. Zeng, J., Li, J., Song, Y., Gao, C., Lyu, M., King, I.: Topic memory networks for short text classification. In: Proceedings of the 2018 Conference on Empirical Methods in Natural Language Processing, Stroudsburg, Pennsylvania, pp. 3120–3131. ACL (2018). https://doi. org/10.18653/v1/d18-1351

Multiagent Systems

Pre-loaded Deep-Q Learning

Tristan Falck and Elize Ehlers[(✉)]

Kingsway Campus, University of Johannesburg,
Auckland Park, Johannesburg 2092, South Africa
emehlers@uj.ac.za

Abstract. This paper explores the potentiality of pre-loading deep-Q learning agents' replay memory buffers with experiences generated by preceding agents, so as to bolster their initial performance. The research illustrates that this pre-loading of previously generated experience replays does indeed improve the initial performance of new agents, provided that an appropriate degree of ostensibly undesirable activity was expressed in the preceding agent's behaviour.

Keywords: Reinforcement learning · Q-learning · Deep-Q learning · Experience replay · Neural networks

1 Introduction

Deep-Q learning, first implemented by Deepmind Technologies in 2013 [5], served as the first major reconciliation between reinforcement learning and deep learning. Broadly speaking, deep-Q learning entails that an agent receives reward or penalty signals according to its performance within an environment - neural network technologies which control the agent use these signals to learn the behaviour which maximises the expected rewards [5].

Since its introduction, deep-Q learning has come to include techniques aimed at stabilizing the training of the constituent neural network. Among the first was allowing the agent in question an experience replay memory buffer [5,9]; this circular buffer allows the agent to sample from previous experiences within its environment when learning, which diversifies and decorrelates its training data [5,9].

This paper explores another potential use of the experience replay memory, specifically how it can be used to bolster the initial performance of a totally untrained agent through sharing the memories of a preceding agent. Section 2 of the paper explores the provenance of Q-learning, neural networks and deep-Q learning, respectively. Section 3 explores the agent- and environment-designs used for the experiments, as well as the nature of the experiments themselves. Section 4 illustrates the results of pre-loading the memory buffers of deep-Q learning agents, and Sect. 5 provides an interpretation thereof.

© IFIP International Federation for Information Processing 2022
Published by Springer Nature Switzerland AG 2022
Z. Shi et al. (Eds.): IIP 2022, IFIP AICT 643, pp. 159–172, 2022.
https://doi.org/10.1007/978-3-031-03948-5_14

2 Background

2.1 Q-Learning

Foundations. Provided that an agent's environment is stochastic and constituted by Markovian transitions[1] and additive rewards, the environment is considered a *Markov Decision Process* (MDP) problem [7]. Among the most fundamental tools in solving MDPs, which could also be considered the most popular equation in the field of reinforcement learning, is the *Bellman equation* [7] described by Eq. 1.

$$U(s) = max_a \sum_{s'} P(s'|s,a)[R(s,a,s') + \gamma U(s')] \tag{1}$$

The Bellman equation defines a harmony between the state-utilities of an MDP. Specifically, for a state s the utility $U(s)$ is defined as the expected value of the reward $R(s,a,s')$ for the transition between s and the next state s' summed with the product between the utility of the next state $U(s')$ and a discount factor γ, provided that the agent chooses optimal actions. In this way, the Bellman equation recursively defines the utility of a state in terms of the utility of the best following state.

The Bellman equation was intended for MDPs, which are inherently stochastic [7]. The equation may, however, also model deterministic environments. In deterministic contexts, the transition to a state s' from s given an action a is fixed, thus removing the need to account for expected values. Hence, the equation simplifies to the representation shown by Eq. 2. Given that this research deals in deterministic problems, the deterministic representation of the Bellman equation is used moving forward.

$$U(s) = max_a[R(s,a,s') + \gamma U(s')] \tag{2}$$

Despite its usefulness, the Bellman equation defines the utility of a state in terms of the corresponding optimal action available to the agent. The equation does not, therefore, account for ostensibly suboptimal actions. We can recover more specific information through a *Q-function* $Q(s,a)$ which returns the expected utility of taking an action a within state s [7]. We can thus redefine the deterministic Bellman equation so as to replace the utility function with the Q-function as follows.

$$Q(s,a) = R(s,a,s') + \gamma max_{a'}[Q(s',a')] \tag{3}$$

Equation 3's representation of the Q-function is either recovered (if possible) or approximated in the process of *Q-learning* [7], wherein an agent uses the maximal Q-values across encountered states to define an optimal policy.

---

[1] A transition between a state s and s' is *Markovian* provided that it is dependent only on s, and not preceding states [7].

Temporal Difference Q-Learning. Temporal difference Q-learning entails recovering the Q-function through value iteration; this could be thought of as the quintessential implementation of Q-learning. For each transition, the *temporal difference* (TD) described by Eq. 4 is used to update the preceding Q-value as described by Eq. 5 [7]. In this context, α is known as the *learning rate* [7].

$$TD = R(s, a, s') + \gamma max_{a'}[Q(s', a')] - Q(s, a) \tag{4}$$

$$Q(s, a) \leftarrow Q(s, a) - \alpha \cdot TD \tag{5}$$

Assuming that ϵ-greedy exploration (see Algorithm 2) is used, we may describe the full temporal difference Q-learning algorithm as follows. We assume that an epsilon value of $\epsilon \in [0, 1]$ is chosen and that $A(s)$ represents the set of actions available to the agent for the state s.

Algorithm 1. Temporal Difference Q-learning

1: **while** s is not terminal **do**
2:     $a \leftarrow \epsilon\text{-greedy}(s)$
3:     $Q(s, a) \leftarrow Q(s, a) - \alpha \cdot [R(s, a, s') + \gamma max_{a'}[Q(s', a')] - Q(s, a)]$
4: **end while**

Algorithm 2. ϵ-greedy Exploration Strategy

1: Randomly generate $r \in [0, 1]$
2: **if** $r > \epsilon$ **then**
3:     $a \leftarrow argmax_a Q(s, a)$
4: **else**
5:     $a \leftarrow$ random value from $A(s)$
6: **end if**

Temporal difference Q-learning recovers a tabular approximation of the Q-function known as a Q-table, which is to say that a table mapping a state s to the corresponding Q-values $\{Q(s, a) \mid a \in A(s)\}$ for each state in the environment must be maintained. In this regard, temporal difference Q-learning can be thought of as approximating the agent function rather than the agent program. Herein lies one of the key weaknesses of temporal difference Q-learning: the space-complexity of the Q-table grows linearly with the number of states in the environment. For state-spaces consisting of more than 10^6 states [7], this approach converges far too slowly assuming it does not become entirely intractable. Additionally, temporal difference Q-learning does not allow for generalization across similar states [5]. These shortcomings of temporal difference Q-learning serve as the impetus for more sophisticated means of approximating the Q-function, such as deep-Q learning.

2.2 Neural Networks

Foundations. The history of neural networks can be traced back to linear regression, one of the simplest machine learning algorithms. The first step came in evolving the concept of linear regression into perceptron learning - this was achieved through passing the output of the linear regression model through a threshold function, which would output one if the threshold was surpassed and zero otherwise [7]. Perceptron learning was capable of solving problems of binary classification, provided that the data were linearly separable [7].

The next evolution came in composing perceptrons into layered architectures, where adjacent layers of perceptrons were connected through weighted edges. This structure, known as a multilayer perceptron, allowed the inputs of later perceptrons to be the weighted summations - with the addition of a bias variable - of previous perceptrons' outputs [6]. A multilayer perceptron is a type of neural network; a neural network describes a network of units or neurons each equipped with some activation function through which the unit's input is passed, and so multilayer perceptrons can be viewed as neural networks possessing threshold activation functions. Despite the apparent simplicity of a perceptron unit, multilayer perceptrons are capable of realizing $NAND$ gates [6], and can therefore perform any realizable computation if made large enough.

Traditional perceptron learning came to evolve into logistic regression, which saw the perceptron's hard threshold function replaced with the smoother sigmoid function. Unlike perceptron learning, logistic regression could facilitate the gradient descent optimization algorithm since the sigmoid function is differentiable [7]. In the same manner, and with the same impetus, multilayer perceptrons evolved into more contemporary neural networks. The threshold activation functions within the network's units were replaced with sigmoid activation functions, allowing the neural network to exhibit the complex computational power of the multilayer perceptron while also facilitating gradient descent. Key to implementing gradient descent within neural networks, however, was the back-propagation algorithm developed by Hinton et al. in 1986 [8], which yields the requisite partial derivatives for gradient descent.

Today, the study of neural networks continues to elucidate their potential: techniques on regularization and new activation functions such as ReLu allow for the creation of deeper neural networks [6], and more specific architectures are illustrating their capabilities, such as with convolutional neural networks within the field of computer vision [7].

Functionality and Algorithms. Provided that a neural network has at least two layers, with the first of which possessing a nonlinear activation function, it will conform to the universal approximation theorem [7], which is to say that it may approximate any continuous function to an arbitrary degree of accuracy. This property lends neural networks the flexibility to solve both classification- and regression-based problems of numerous kinds.

The inference and training of a feedforward[2] neural network are performed by forward-propagation and back-propagation, respectively. For a layer l in the network, we define σ^l as its activation function, w^l as its weight matrix, b^l as its bias vector and a^l as its output vector. Forward-propagation, through which the network process input data into a prediction, is described by Algorithm 3.

Algorithm 3. Forward-propagation for input x

1: $a^{l_{input}} \leftarrow x$
2: **for** $l \leftarrow 1, l_{output}$ **do**
3:     $a^l \leftarrow \sigma^l(a^{l-1} \cdot w^l + b^l)$
4: **end for**
5: **return** $a^{l_{output}}$

Neural networks train through optimization algorithms such as stochastic gradient descent or the more recent Adam optimization. Requisite to the more popular optimization techniques is the back-propagation algorithm; this provides the partial derivatives of the loss function with respect to all the weight- and bias-variables within the network [8]. We define L as the loss function and δ^l as the error of a layer[3] l. We further define w^l_δ and b^l_δ as summing the partial derivatives of the loss w.r.t the weights and biases - respectively - for layer l across multiple training examples. The back-propagation algorithm is detailed by Algorithm 4, assuming that an input x has been forward-propagated [6].

Algorithm 4. Back-propagation for input x

1: $\delta^{l_{output}} \leftarrow \nabla_a L \odot a'$
2: **for** $l \leftarrow l_{output} - 1, 1$ **do**
3:     $\delta^l \leftarrow ((w^{l+1})^T \cdot \delta^{l+1}) \odot a'$
4: **end for**
5: $w^l_\delta \leftarrow w^l_\delta + \delta^l \cdot a^{l-1}$
6: $b^l_\delta \leftarrow b^l_\delta + \delta^l$

As mentioned, back-propagation is requisite to many of the optimization algorithms used in training neural networks. This project, however, will make use of stochastic gradient descent (SGD), specifically. Lastly, we define the learning rate of the neural network as η [6] in order for the training of a neural network to be described by Algorithm 5.

---

[2] A neural network containing only forward-connections [7].
[3] This error is technically defined as a vector of the derivatives of the loss function w.r.t the layer's weighted summation which is passed through the activation [6].

Algorithm 5. Neural network training with SGD

1: **for** $batch \leftarrow batches$ **do**
2:     **for** $x \leftarrow batch$ **do**
3:         Forward-propagate x ▷ See Algorithm 3
4:         Back-propagate   ▷ See Algorithm 4
5:     **end for**
6:     **for** $l \leftarrow 1, layers$ **do**
7:         $w^l \leftarrow w^l - \frac{\eta}{length(batch)} w^l_\delta$
8:         $b^l \leftarrow b^l - \frac{\eta}{length(batch)} b^l_\delta$
9:     **end for**
10: **end for**

2.3 Deep-Q Learning

Foundations. Given its intractability for large state-spaces and inability to generalize, temporal difference Q-learning is very seldomly implemented for realistic applications; other means of approximating the Q-function are necessary. Any number of machine learning algorithms may be used to approximate the Q-function (such as linear models, which have been used for this purpose before [5]). Neural networks, however, are especially good candidates given their conformation to the universal function approximation theorem. That is, the complexity and dimensionality of the Q-function do not serve as obstacles to the neural network approximating it.

Mnih et al., 2013 patented the so-called *deep-Q learning* algorithm in their paper *Playing Atari with Deep Reinforcement Learning* [5], which entailed that the Q-function approximation was facilitated by a convolutional neural network. The algorithm was trained to play seven distinct Atari games given only raw pixel data from the games as input. At the time, this deep-Q learning system outperformed all previous machine learning approaches for six of the Atari games, and surpassed expert human-level play for three of them [5].

Experience Replay Memory. As originally highlighted in the paper which introduced deep-Q learning, a key obstacle faced by the learning algorithm is the stability of the contained neural network's training. Most deep learning architectures require that their training data is *independent and identically distributed* (i.i.d.) [5,7,9]. This property certainly does not hold for unaltered Q-learning data; not only is $Q(s, a)$ dependent on $Q(s', a')$ for transitionally adjacent states s and s', the former is defined explicitly in terms of the latter (see Eq. 3). This strong correlation throughout the Q-values necessitates mechanisms through which the data can be made to be i.i.d.

The first mechanism used to combat dependency within Q-learning data was the inclusion of an *experience replay memory buffer*, the notion of which was first introduced by Long-ji Lin in 1992 [4]. The experience replay is a circular $LIFO^4$ data buffer which tracks (s, a, r, s') tuples, the entries of which correspond

---

[4] Last-in first-out.

to a state, action taken, reward received and resultant state, respectively [4]. For each of the deep-Q learning agent's training steps, the agent will randomly sample multiple 'experience' tuples from its replay memory and use those as its training data. This inclusion of an experience replay memory redistributes and thus diversifies the data recovered from the agent's environment, making it an invaluable tool for stabilizing deep-Q learning.

The ability of an agent to encode past experiences into its training also entails a less obvious utility: the experience replay makes the agent more robust against catastrophic forgetting [7].

Target Network. Unlike with supervised applications of neural networks, deep-Q learning is not provided with a stationary ground-truth for its training; rather, the deep-Q system backpropagates an error it itself generates through the Bellman equation [5]. The target of a deep-Q network - therefore - is intrinsically non-stationary. While this variation within the target cannot be circumvented, it can be mitigated through the use of a *target network*. The target network within a deep-Q learning system is a copy of the primary network which is only synchronised therewith at certain intervals - this more stable network is delegated the task of generating the truth-values to be used in for training.

Contemporary Deep-Q Learning. Following its advent, deep-Q learning has come to include numerous techniques aimed at improving its stability and policy generation. Shaul et al., 2016 improved the foundational experience replay through prioritized sampling [9,10]; that is, the likelihood of an experience being sampled therefrom was made proportional to that experience's significance. It was demonstrated that deep-Q learning agents which made use of prioritized experience replays outperformed those without in 41 of the 49 Atari games used for assessment [10].

Another advance within the field was that of double deep-Q learning, which adjusted the loss calculation of the constituent neural network so as to combat overestimation bias [3,9]. Dueling deep-Q learning - on the other hand - cleaved the agent's neural network into two streams following the initial layers, and each stream was delegated the task of regressing segments of a decomposed Q-function [9,12]. This allowed for the lose inference of a state's value without the need for coupling it with some specific action [9,12].

3   Implementation

3.1   Environment: The *Snake* Game

This research aims to assess the potentiality of pre-training deep-Q learning agents with the experience replay memories of preceding agents, thus allowing the new agents some degree of competence prior to any interfacing with their environments. Consequent experiments therefore require an environment into which deep-Q learning agents may be deployed for training and assessment.

Candidate environments for such reinforcement-learning systems vary greatly in nature, ranging from turn-based board games to the Atari games used by Deepmind's original implementation of the deep-Q learning algorithm [5,7]. Generally speaking, the most popular environments used are simple in nature - such as the pole-balancing problem [7] or the multi-armed bandit problem.

This research makes use of the *Snake* game as the agents' environment. The game was chosen as it is simplistic and its rules easily understood, but - given that the enponymous snake's tail increases in length as it performs well within the game - the difficulty of the game scales roughly with the agent's performance. For an illustration of the game, please see Fig. 1.

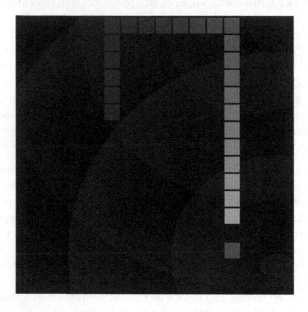

Fig. 1. A cropped screenshot from the program illustrating the *Snake* game being played by a well-trained agent.

Rules of the *Snake* Game. The rules of *Snake* vary across implementations, however this research makes use of the following rule-set:

– The snake (agent) may move up, down, left or right at any given frame (that is, the snake may move backwards into its tail at any moment, differentiating the game from its regular human-playable implementation).
– The snake may not collide with a wall or its tail, as doing so will reset the game and the current score.
– Upon finding the 'food' object within the game, the score will increment, the snake's tail will grow by a single unit and a new 'food' object will be initialized randomly within the map.

Reward Structure. In order to facilitate reinforcement learning within the system's agents, reward- and punishment-signals must be recovered from the environment according to their actions [5,7]. These rewards - as is the case with most reinforcement learning implementations - are scalar in nature, and are for this research expressed as integer values. Numerous potential reward structures exist, however this research made use of an adapted version of that proposed by Hennie de Harder, 2020 [2] in her own application of deep reinforcement learning to the game of Snake. Specifically, the actions and corresponding rewards are detailed in Table 1.

Table 1. Table detailing the rewards and punishments (right) corresponding to given actions (left).

Snake moves closer to food	$R = 1$
Snake moves further from food	$R = -2$
Snake retrieves food	$R = 10$
Snake collides with wall or tail	$R = -100$

3.2   Agents

Neural Networks and Q-Networks. The system's agents themselves are deep-Q learning agents, which is to say that a given agent achieves function-approximation Q-learning through neural network technologies and an experience replay memory buffer [5,7]. Unlike the original deep-Q learning algorithm - which made use of convolutional neural networks to facilitate the learning - this research saw the implementation of feedforward artificial neural networks. A neural network framework was created and assessed in a general context prior to its deployment within the deep-Q learning system; specifically, a neural network was created using the framework and assessed on the MNIST dataset of handwritten digits, upon which it achieved an accuracy of roughly 95% accuracy. The framework was also successfully evaluated on a series of regression-based tasks, given that deep-Q learning ultimately entails that the networks regress Q-values.

For the implementation used within this research, neural networks used by the system were wrapped into new Q-network objects, simplifying communication between the neural network and its containing agent.

State Structure and the Experience Replay Buffer. At each frame of the game's operation, the agent recovers a binary string constituting the state-structure is recovered from the environment. Each bit within the state-structure binary string - which was proposed by Hennie de Harder, 2020 [2] - represents some component of the game's current properties relative to the agent, and the input layers of neural networks are designed so as to directly receive the string as input. The exact nature of the state-structure binary string - along with the resultant actions of the agent - is illustrated by Fig. 2.

At any given frame, the immediate state-structure information is unlikely to be passed directly into the deep-Q learning agent's neural network, as it is initially saved into the experience-replay memory buffer. Given that this implementation sees the experience replay implemented as a circular buffer, the new binary string will replace the oldest in the replay. At each frame of the game's operation, a random sample is drawn from the replay to generate a training dataset for the main neural network controlling the agent. For this implementation, the experience replay buffer was made to hold 25000 experience entries, and each random training sample would consist of 100 experiences.

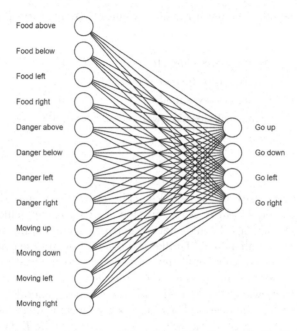

Fig. 2. The state-structure binary string proposed by Hennie de Harder, 2020 [2], along with the actions to which the regressed Q-values of the illustrated neural network map (for simplicity, hidden layers have been omitted the diagram).

Exploration Strategy: The Epsilon-Greedy Algorithm. As can often be the case with reinforcement learning problems [7], the exploration/exploitation dilemma arises in the context of deep-Q learning. Modern strategies aimed at handling the dilemma can entail the tempering of exploration according to time such as with simulated annealing [7], or the dilemma could be handled probabilistically through - for example - the *softmax* function [11]. This probabilistic approach by way of *softmax* is especially desirable for Q-learning, since the magnitude of regressed Q-values is generally proportional to the agent's confidence within that action.

The attractiveness of more sophisticated exploration strategies notwithstanding, this research makes use of the ϵ-greedy strategy (see Algorithm 2) - which entails the hard-coding of an ϵ-value to weight exploration and exploitation. This decision was made as the degree of exploration had a significant effect on the results of the research, and was thus subjected to manual engineering.

3.3 Pre-loading Experience Replays

In order to evaluate the potentiality of pre-loading new agents with preceding agents' replay memory buffers, the buffers themselves were implemented as serializable objects. Upon the instantiation of a new agent, the program allows for it to be fitted with a preceding agent's replay memory buffer which had been written to disk. For each of the experiments performed, a pre-trained agent was made to act within the environment until its replay memory buffer had been fully populated, after which the replay was written to disk.

The new agents, in possession of the pre-loaded replays, were made to sample from the replays and train for each of the entries within the replay (that is, 25000 training cycles) prior to their true deployment into the game. Upon their true deployment, the agents' neural networks were given deterministic control over the snake ($\epsilon = 0$). Three primary experiments were performed within this research, each of which adjusted the agent's behaviour through tuning the ϵ-value (and - in turn - also adjusted its experience replay buffer). Each of the neural networks within the tested agents were constituted by a 12-neuron input layer, two 8-neuron hidden layers and a 4-neuron output layer.

Experiments

- $\epsilon = 0.0$: The preceding agent's primary neural network was given deterministic control of the snake without any exploration.
- $\epsilon = 0.4$: 40% of the agent's actions were random, with the remaining 60% of the actions being controlled by the primary neural network within the system.
- $\epsilon = 1.0$: The snake behaved entirely randomly with no input from the primary neural network.

3.4 Technical Details of Implementation

The neural network and Q-network frameworks used within the system were created using the Java programming language, inclusive of the linear-algebra- and calculus-based functionality constituent to their operation. The *Snake* game and illustrations of both the neural network and the agent's performance were created through the JavaFX platform. In order to record results, the Python scripting language along with the *Matplotlib* library were used.

4   Results

The research successfully proved that pre-loading a deep-Q learning agent's replay memory buffer does indeed bolster its initial performance upon deployment. Figure 3 compares the initial performances of two agents, with one in possession of a pre-loaded replay; the average reward is observably higher across the activity period for the agent with the pre-loaded replay.

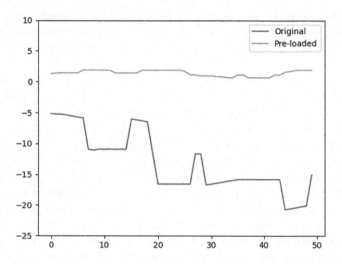

Fig. 3. A comparison between the performance of a regular deep-Q learning agent over its initial 10,000 frames of activity and that of one equipped with a pre-loaded replay memory buffer ($\epsilon = 0.4$), with the ϵ-values of each agent having been set to 0.0.

Unexpectedly, the success of pre-loading an agent's replay memory buffer was heavily dependent on the value of ϵ in the ϵ-greedy exploration strategy. Notably, the new agent's initial performance seemed to scale with the degree of randomness present within the activity of the preceding agent. Figure 4 compares the initial performances of three agents possessing pre-loaded memory buffers, and illustrates that the more stochasticity was in the preceding agent's activity (and thus its replay), the better the new agent performed.

5   Analysis and Critique

Interpretation of Effect of ϵ on New Agent Performance. The effect of ϵ on the performances of agents possessing pre-loaded replay memory buffers was unexpected, though not inexplicable: an initial observation within the field of reinforcement learning is that pure master-generated data is not enough, and agents need to know what the 'wrong' answers are as well as what the 'right' answers are [7].

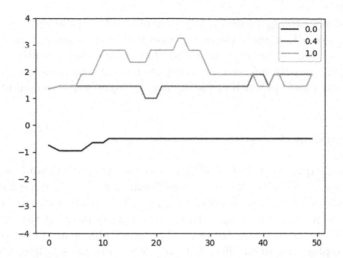

Fig. 4. The initial performances of three agents each in possession of pre-loaded replay memories. The experience-replay memories were generated by agents with $\epsilon = 0.0$, $\epsilon = 0.4$ and $\epsilon = 1.0$, respectively. The performance of each agent was measured over its initial 10,000 frames, with the ϵ-values of each agent having been set to 0.0.

Ultimately, the new agent performed best when its preceding agent behaved entirely randomly ($\epsilon = 1.0$). On the other hand, the new agent performed poorly if the preceding, well-trained agent was given deterministic control of the snake ($\epsilon = 0.0$). When considering how the deep-Q agents regress Q-values, this makes some intuitive sense. At any given time, the agent should regress at most two positive Q-values and at least two negative values for the current state (there are always at least two undesirable actions within the game). The deterministic agent's replay buffer includes very few mistakes, and so the new agent is less likely to be capable of regressing the negative Q-values. When the preceding agent behaves randomly, however, the new agent is transitively exposed to negative reward signals, thus learning to regress negative Q-values for undesirable actions.

Despite its success, it is hypothesised that pre-loading an entirely random replay memory buffer is better due to the nature of the *Snake* game - at any given moment, at least a quarter of the actions available to the agent are desirable. In a more complex context where such desirable actions are less common, lower ϵ-values, and thus lower degrees of randomness from the preceding agents, is expected to outperform entirely random replay memory buffers.

Future Work. A sensible next step in exploring pre-loaded replay memory buffers is to do so in more complex environments - those where the proportion of desirable actions is far exceeded by that of undesirable actions. A replay memory buffer encodes no assumptions as to its own generation, and so the exact nature of the replays to be pre-loaded could be augmented in two ways. Firstly, multiple replay buffers from different agents could be concatenated into a single, massively pre-aggregated replay memory buffer, upon which a new agent could train. Secondly, some of the experiences within the resultant massive replay could be generated by humans; provided that an adequate number of negative experiences (those with negative rewards) are present within the massive replay, the experiences aimed at teaching the agents the 'right' answers could be human-generated.

6 Conclusion

This research explored deep-Q learning and its provenance, and assessed the potentiality of pre-loading a new deep-Q learning agent's experience replay memory buffer with that of a previous agent. Neural network and Q-network frameworks were created, along with the toy environment of the *Snake* game within which agents could be assessed. The research illustrated that pre-loading experience replay memory buffers within new agents does bolster their initial performance upon their deployment. Given that such agents generally require adequate exposure to negative reward signals, the pre-loading of memory replays only illustrated desirable results provided that there was an adequate degree of randomness within the preceding agent's behaviour.

References

1. Dittrich, M.-A., Fohlmeister, S.: A deep q-learning-based optimization of the inventory control in a linear process chain. Prod. Eng. Res. Devel. **15**(1), 35–43 (2020). https://doi.org/10.1007/s11740-020-01000-8
2. de Harder, H.: Snake played by a deep reinforcement learning agent. Towards Data Science (2020). https://towardsdatascience.com/snake-played-by-a-deep-reinforcement-learning-agent-53f2c4331d36. Accessed 2 Nov 2021
3. van Hassalt, H., Guez, A., Silver, D.: Deep Reinforcement Learning with Double Q-learning (2015)
4. Lin, L.: Reinforcement Learning for Robots Using Neural Networks. Carnegie Mellon University, Pittsburgh (1992)
5. Mnih, V., et al.: Playing Atari with deep reinforcement learning (2013)
6. Nielsen, M.: Neural Networks and Deep Learning. Determination Press (2015)
7. Russell, S., Norvig, P.: Artificial Intelligence: A Modern Approach, 4th edn. Pearson, Upper Saddle River (2020)
8. Rumelhart, D., Hinton, G., Williams, R.: Learning representations by back-propagating errors. Nature **323**(6088), 533–536 (1986)
9. Sanghi, N.: Deep Reinforcement Learning with Python, 1st edn. Apress, Bangalore (2020)
10. Schaul, T., Quan, J., Antonoglou, I., Silver, D.: Prioritized experience replay. In: ICLR 2016 (2016)
11. Tokic, M., Palm, G.: Value-difference based exploration: adaptive control between epsilon-greedy and softmax. In: Bach, J., Edelkamp, S. (eds.) KI 2011. LNCS (LNAI), vol. 7006, pp. 335–346. Springer, Heidelberg (2011). https://doi.org/10.1007/978-3-642-24455-1_33
12. Wang, Z., Schaul, T., Hessel, M., van Hasselt, H., Lanctot, M., de Freitas, N.: Dueling network architectures for deep reinforcement learning (2016)

Resource Scheduling for Human-Machine Collaboration in Multiagent Systems

Yifeng Zhou[✉], Kai Di, Zichen Dong, and Yichuan Jiang

School of Computer Science and Engineering, Southeast University,
Nanjing 211189, China
yfzhou@seu.edu.cn

Abstract. To solve the human-machine resource scheduling problem in multiagent systems, we represent the complex constraints among subtasks by a directed graph and model the transmission effect of uncertainty of task execution in the modeling of human-machine collaboration. We prove that the human-machine resource scheduling problem is NP-hard and propose a heuristic scheduling algorithm to solve the problem. The algorithm determines the task priority based on cumulative delay risk estimation and time period division, so as to produce the resource scheduling scheme. Through experiments employing PSPLIB dataset, we validate the performance of the proposed heuristic algorithm by comparing with an optimal solution and the algorithm allocating resources based on the waiting time of tasks.

Keywords: Multiagent system · Resource scheduling · Human-machine collaboration

1 Introduction

Resource scheduling is one of the key problems of agent collaboration in multi-agent systems [3,6]. It mainly focuses on how to effectively schedule resources to maximize the utilization of resources, so as to improve the task completion rate and optimize the system utility [5]. In the human-machine collaboration scenario, i.e., the set of agents is composed of resources of human and machine, there are complex constraints among subtasks of a task, and it is difficult to estimate the execution time when human resources execute the task; these problems bring challenges to the resource scheduling in human-machine collaboration in multiagent systems [13,14].

Previous related work pays little attention to the transmission effect of uncertainty when there are complex constraints among subtasks on task execution in human-machine collaboration scenarios in multi-agent systems [2–4,8,9,12,13]. To solve the problem, we represent the complex constraint relationship between subtasks by a directed graph and model the transmission effect of uncertainty of task execution in the modeling of human-machine cooperative resource scheduling problem in this paper. We further prove that the problem is NP-hard, and

© IFIP International Federation for Information Processing 2022
Published by Springer Nature Switzerland AG 2022
Z. Shi et al. (Eds.): IIP 2022, IFIP AICT 643, pp. 173–184, 2022.
https://doi.org/10.1007/978-3-031-03948-5_15

propose a heuristic scheduling algorithm that determines the task priority based on the cumulative delay risk estimation and time period division of tasks and then generates the resource scheduling scheme.

Through experiments employing PSPLIB dataset [1], we validate the performance of the proposed heuristic algorithm from four aspects: the task completion rate, the algorithm running time, the average waiting time, and the resource utilization rate.

2   Related Work

2.1   Resource-Constrained Project Scheduling

The resource-constrained project scheduling problem (RCPSP) [4], which is one of the most important problems in operations research and management science, focuses on the allocation of tasks with the goal of minimizing the execution time of the task set under the dependency constraints of tasks and resources. Tirkolaee et al. [12] consider a nonlinear programming modeling of a multi-objective multi-modal RCPSP and propose the efficient Pareto-based metaheuristics to solve the problem, which can maximize the net present value and minimize the completion time. Lin et al. [9] formalize the multi-skill resource-constrained project scheduling problem (MS-RCPSP) considering the resources like manpower or multipurpose machine, and introduce a genetic programming hyper-heuristic algorithm to address the problem, aiming at minimizing the makespan of the project. Although these works perform well in the scheduling problem with task constraints, the impact of involvement of human resources on task execution, e.g., the uncertainty of task execution, has not been fully considered in these works.

2.2   Task Allocation for Human-Machine Collaboration

Task allocation in multiagent systems often focuses on designing efficient task allocation algorithms to optimize the utility of agent collaboration. Wu et al. [13] use Markov decision process (MDP) to study how machine performance affects the human-machine trust and formalize the optimization problem considering the effect of human-machine trust where an optimal task allocation policy is proposed to minimize the average cost of tasks. Cai et al. [3] model the relationship of human-machine detection success rate in a human-machine collaborative task, and propose a linear program-based efficient near-optimal solution, which can significantly improve the task performance. Compared with these works, this paper pays more attention to the complex constraints of tasks and the transmission effect of uncertainty of task execution in resource scheduling for human-machine collaboration.

3   Problem Formulation

In this section, the human-machine resource scheduling problem in multiagent systems is formally defined.

Resource Model for Human-Machine Collaboration: The resources in the human-machine collaboration in multiagent systems can be broadly classified into two categories $R = R_h \cup R_c$, i.e., the human and machine resources, where each type of resources in R can be represented by R_i.

Task Model for Human-Machine Collaboration: The human-machine collaboration task generally consists of multiple segments, each requiring different types of human and machine resources. Each task in the task set T can be represented by a tuple, $T_i = \{V_i, E_i, A_i, W_i, D_i, R_i\}, i \in \{1, ..., |T|\}$. V_i and E_i denotes the set of vertices and edges of subtasks of task T_i; and all subtasks form a directed graph $G = <V, E>, \bigcup_{i=1}^{|T|} V_i = V, \bigcup_{i=1}^{|T|} E_i = E$. A_i and D_i denote the arrival time and deadline of task T_i. $W_i = \{w_{i1}, ..., w_{ij}\}, j \in \{1, ..., |T_i|\}, w_{ij} \in \mathbb{R}^+$ denotes the execution time matrix of subtasks v_{ij}. $R_i = \{r_{i1}, ..., r_{ij}\}, j \in \{1, ..., |T_i|\}$ denotes the matrix of resource types required by the subtask v_{ij}.

Assuming that the execution time of v_{ij}, w_{ij}, obeys the Gaussian distribution of $X \sim N(\mu, \sigma^2)$. The larger σ will lead to the higher uncertainty of completion time and the higher risk of postponement. Thus, the execution time of v_{ij} is estimated as

$$\widetilde{w}_{ij} = \mu(w_{ij}) + \eta * \sigma(w_{ij}) \tag{1}$$

where η is a constant in $[0, 3]$ (when $\eta = 3$, it can be approximated as an upper bound for the estimation).

Optimization Objective: The task T_i is completed if all its subtasks v_{ij} are completed before the deadline D_i. The allocation scheduling policy can be denoted by $\Pi<v_{ij}, r_{ij}, t_{ij}>$, which means the resource r_{ij} in R is allocated to v_{ij} at time t_{ij}. Thus for any task T_i, its gain can be expressed as

$$U_i = \begin{cases} 1, \forall t_{ij} + \widetilde{w}_{ij} \leq D_i \\ 0, \exists t_{ij} + \widetilde{w}_{ij} > D_i \end{cases}, v_{ij} \in T_i \tag{2}$$

The final completion time of the task T_i is represented by τ_i. Then by adjusting the allocation scheduling policy, the total benefit that can be obtained is expressed as

$$U = \sum_{i \in T} I(D_i - \tau_i) \tag{3}$$

where $I(\cdot)$ is the indicator function that takes the value of 1 when the variable is greater than or equal to 0, and 0 otherwise

Human-Machine Resource Scheduling Problem (HMRSP): Given a set of tasks T, a set of resources R, design an allocation strategy $\Pi<v, r, t>$ that maximizes the number of tasks to be completed by the deadline. For each $v_{ij} \in V$, at any moment $t \in [0, \tau_i]$, the binary decision variable x_{ijt}^k indicates whether v_{ij} starts to occupy resources R_k at t; and for each task T_i, the continuous decision variable $\tau_i \in \mathbb{N}$ indicates the final completion time of task T_i. The human-machine resource scheduling problem (HMRSP) can be modeled as:

$$\max \frac{1}{|T|} \sum_{i=1}^{|T|} I\left(D_i - \tau_i\right) \tag{4}$$

$$\text{s.t.} \quad \sum_{t=0}^{\tau_i} \sum_{k=1}^{|R|} x_{ijt}^k t \geq A_i, v_{ij} \in V \tag{5}$$

$$\sum_{t=0}^{\tau_i} \sum_{k=1}^{|R|} x_{ijt}^k (t + \widetilde{w}_{ij}) \leq \tau_i, v_{ij} \in V, \tau_i \in \mathbb{N} \tag{6}$$

$$\sum_{t=0}^{\tau_i} \sum_{k=1}^{|R|} x_{ijt}^k = 1, v_{ij} \in V \tag{7}$$

$$\sum_{t=0}^{\tau_i} x_{ijt}^{r_{ij}} = 1, v_{ij} \in V \tag{8}$$

$$\sum_{t=0}^{\tau_i} \sum_{h=1}^{|R|} x_{ijt}^h (t + \widetilde{w}_{ij}) \leq \sum_{t=0}^{\tau_i} \sum_{h=1}^{|R|} x_{ikt}^h t \tag{9}$$

$$v_{ij}, v_{ik} \in V, \ j \neq k, (j,k) \in E_i \tag{10}$$

$$\sum_{i=1}^{|T|} \sum_{j=1}^{|V_i|} \sum_{t=\max\left(0,t'-w_{ij}+1\right)}^{t'} x_{ijt}^k \leq N_k \tag{11}$$

$$N_k = |R_k|, t' \in \{0, \ldots, \tau_i\} \tag{12}$$

$$x_{ijt}^k \in \{0,1\}, v_{ij} \in V, R_k \in R, t \in \{0, \ldots, \tau_i\} \tag{13}$$

Theorem 1. *The HMRSP problem is NP-hard when $|R| \geq 3$.*

Proof. First, the HMRSP problem is NP, since it is easy to construct a task assignment and scheduling scheme and then verify the maximum completion time of its tasks in polynomial time; and then the NP-hardness of the problem can be proved via reducing to the Subset Product Problem (SP) [7]. The SP problem can be described in the following form: given a set $A = \{1, 2, \ldots, v\}$ and $a_i \in \mathbb{N}^+, i \in A$, does there exist a subset $A' \subseteq A$ such that $\prod_{i \in A'} a_i = \prod_{i \in A \setminus A'} a_i = \sqrt{\prod_{i \in A} a_i} \equiv B$?

To demonstrate SP $\leq_p$ HMRSP, an instance of HMRSP is constructed. Let $N = v + 3, M = 3, \alpha_{i1} = \alpha_i, \alpha_{i2} = \beta_i, \alpha_{i3} = \gamma_i$, all elements in the instance can be presented as follows: $\alpha_i = 0, \quad \beta_i = \alpha_i - 1, \quad \gamma_i = 0; \alpha_{v+1} = 0, \quad \beta_{v+1} = 1, \quad \gamma_{v+1} = B + 1; \alpha_{v+2} = 2B + 1, \quad \beta_{v+2} = \frac{1}{B+1}, \quad \gamma_{v+2} = \frac{B^2+2B+1}{B+2}; \alpha_{v+3} = \frac{B^2+2B+1}{B+1}, \quad \beta_{v+3} = \frac{1}{B^2+3B+2}, \quad \gamma_{v+3} = 0; D = B^2 + 3B + 3, \quad t_0 = 1/2$.

Clearly, the above construction can be done in polynomial time.

- If for an instance of SP, I_{SP}, there exists a subset A' satisfying $\prod_{i \in A'} a_i = \prod_{i \in A \setminus A'} a_i = \sqrt{\prod_{i \in A} a_i}$ then for instances of the HMRSP problem, there exists a scheduling q satisfying $\tau_i \leq D$. Given a solution of I_{SP} to the task $v+1, v+2, v+3$ build a scheduler in the order of q'. The task completion time τ_i

is denoted as B^2+3B+3, leaving two gaps for resource 2: the first is to reserve B workload at moment 1 and the second at moment $B+2$ The second is to set aside a gap of length B^2+2B, the workload is $B+2$. Scheduling tasks with index $i \in A'$ that fill the first time gap (e.g. after task $v+1$), and the remaining tasks fill the second gap (after tas $v+2$ after the task). (The total load of the first task subset is then $t \prod_{i \in A'} (1 + \beta_i) = 1 \prod_{i \in A'} a_i = B$. The total load of the second task subset is $t \prod_{i \in A \setminus A'} (1 + \beta_i) = (B+2) \prod_{i \in A \setminus A'} a_i = B^2+2B$).

 – If there exists a completion time for an instance of HMRSP $\tau_i \leq D = B^2 + 3B + 3$ of the scheduling q then for instances I_{SP} there exists a subset $A' \subseteq A$ satisfying $\prod_{i \in A'} a_i = \prod_{i \in A \setminus A'} a_i = \sqrt{\prod_{i \in A} a_i} = B$. It is easy to verify that if such a scheduling q exists, then it must contain a sequence of tasks in the order $v + 1, v + 2, v + 3$ sequence (any other sequence consisting of three tasks $\tau_i > D$). As mentioned above, this scheduling plan leaves two gaps for resource 2. Therefore, the set of tasks A must be arranged in the gaps. Then we can have that there must exist a subset $A' \subseteq A$ satisfying $\prod_{i \in A'} (1 + \beta_i) \leq B, (B+2) \prod_{i \in A \setminus A'} (1 + \beta_i) \leq B^2 + 2B$, i.e., $\prod_{i \in A'} (1 + \beta_i) \leq B, \prod_{i \in A \setminus A'} (1 + \beta_i) \leq B$. Since $\prod_{i \in A'} (1 + \beta_i) = \prod_{i \in A} a_i = B^2$, it can be concluded that $\prod_{i \in A'} (1 + \beta_i) = \prod_{i \in A'} a_i = B, \prod_{i \in A \setminus A'} (1 + \beta_i) = \prod_{i \in A \setminus A'} a_i = B$.

4   Algorithm Design

4.1   Heuristic Scheduling Algorithm for Human-Machine Collaboration

We prove the HMRSP problem is NP-hard in Sect. 3 and thus an optimal solution cannot be obtained in polynomial time. In the scheduling process, the priority of tasks determines the order of tasks to obtain resources, which is the key factor affecting the completion rate of tasks. Hence, we consider determining the priority of executable tasks by calculating the cumulative delay risk and dividing the execution time through task topology.

On the one hand, this paper considers a measure of precursor task execution uncertainty in the task priority calculation. Considering that the cumulative delay risk is a common metric in project scheduling robustness studies [10], the subtask v_{mn}'s risk weight is defined as

$$\delta_{mn} = \frac{\sigma(w_{mn})}{\sum_{v_{ij} \in V_i} \sigma(w_{ij})} \quad (14)$$

Since the delay in the completion of any precursor task will directly affect the actual start time and completion time of the current task, i.e., the delay risk of the current task will increase due to any precursor task delay. Thus, the cumulative delay risk of v_{mn} is:

$$\varphi_{mn} = \delta_{mn} + max\{\delta_{mi}, (i,n) \in E_m, v_{mi}, v_{mn} \in V_m\} \quad (15)$$

The cumulative delay risk value reflects the extent that the task could be affected by the uncertainty of task execution time; and it has a cumulative feature in the task topology.

On the other hand, since tasks have corresponding deadlines, it is necessary to specify the amount of execution time that can be set for each subtask, i.e., the total execution time needs to be divided according to the task topology. In this paper, we consider the division in proportion to the delayable time. Since the critical path affects the specific execution time of the task, and the deadline is a constraint on all the subtasks, the partial critical path (PCP) division method [2] is employed in this paper. Algorithm 1 is the recursive process of solving partial critical paths.

Algorithm 1: *PartialCriticalPath(PCP)*

    Input: Task set T, node v_{ij}
    Output: Partial set of critical paths
 1 **Initialize:** $p \leftarrow v_{ij}$, $v' \leftarrow v_{ij}$, v' marked as assigned
 2 **while** v' *exits unassigned predecessor node* v_p, **do**
 3     $p \leftarrow v_p + p$
 4   v_p marked as assigned
 5     $v' \leftarrow v' \cup v_p$
 6 $P \leftarrow P + p$
 7 $v' \leftarrow v' \cup p$'s end node
 8 **while** $v' \,! = null$ **do**
 9   **foreach** $v_p \in pred\left(v'\right)$ *in* G **do**
10   **if** v_p *unassigned* **then**
11             $P' \leftarrow PartialCriticalPath(T', v_{ij})$
12             $P \leftarrow P \cup P'$
13     $v' \leftarrow \mathrm{pred}\left(v'\right)$ in p
14 **return** P

After obtaining partial critical paths, the total execution time is then needed to be divided. For the topology G composed of a set of subtasks, we firstly need to calculate the earliest start time, the latest start time, and the earliest completion time for v_{ij}.

v_{ij}'s Earliest Start Time is calculated as

$$T_{ij}^{\mathrm{ES}} = \begin{cases} A_i, & pred\left(v_{ij}\right) = \varnothing \\ \max_{v_{ip} \in pred(v_{ij})} \left\{T_{ip}^{\mathrm{ES}} + \widetilde{w}_{ip}\right\}, & o.w. \end{cases}, v_{ij} \in V \tag{16}$$

v_{ij}'s Earliest Completion Time (ECT) is calculated as

$$T_{ij}^{\mathrm{EC}} = T_{ij}^{\mathrm{ES}} + \widetilde{w}_{ij}, v_{ij} \in V \tag{17}$$

v_{ij}'s Latest Completion Time (LCT) is calculated as

$$T_{ij}^{LC} = \begin{cases} D_i, & succ(v_{ij}) = \varnothing \\ \min_{v_{iq} \in succ(v_{ij})} \left\{ T_{iq}^{LC} - \widetilde{w}_{iq} \right\}, & o.w. \end{cases}, v_{ij} \in V \qquad (18)$$

Then, the total execution time is divided by the task topology diagram structure according to the set of obtained partial critical paths (as shown in Algorithm 2). Then the deadline for v_{ij} is calculated as

$$d_{ij} = T_{i1}^{ES} + \frac{T_{ij}^{EC} - T_{i1}^{ES}}{T_{ik}^{EC} - T_{i1}^{ES}} \times (T_{ik}^{LC} - T_{i1}^{ES}), v_{ij} \in V \qquad (19)$$

Algorithm 2 focuses on the division of the total execution time for the nodes on the derived partial critical path.

Algorithm 2: *TaskProcessing*

Input: Task set T_i

Output: Executable tasks set T_i^e, blocking tasks set T_i^b

1 **Initialize:** $T_i^e \leftarrow \varnothing$

2 **foreach** $v_{ij} \in V_i$ **do**

3 $\quad$ Calculate the earliest start time T_{ij}^{ES} according to equation (16)

4 $\quad$ Calculate the earliest completion time T_{ij}^{EC} according to equation (17)

5 $\quad$ Calculate the latest completion time T_{ij}^{LC} according to equation (18)

6 $P \leftarrow PCP(T_i, v_{i\ exit})$

7 **foreach** $p \in P$ **do**

8 $\quad$ **foreach** $v_{ij} \in p$ **do**

9 $\quad\quad$ Calculate subtask v_{ij}'s deadline d_{ij} according to equation (19)

10 $T_i^e \leftarrow v_{ij}, \forall v_{ij} \in V_i, pred(v_{ij}) = \varnothing$

11 $T_i^b \leftarrow T_i - T_i^e$

12 **return** T_i^e, T_i^b

Through Algorithm 2, the execution time of the task can be divided to each subtask by considering partial critical path division method. However, it ignores the cumulative impact of the precursor tasks which may cause uncertain execution time; and the partial critical path division process leads to the fragmentation of the inherent backward and forward dependencies in the task topology graph. Thus we consider the following three aspects: the cumulative delay risk, the deadline, and the successor tasks of the task for the specific resource allocation. The task priority can be defined as:

$$p_{ij} = \alpha\varphi_{ij} + \beta d_{ij} + \gamma N_{ij} \qquad (20)$$

where N_{ij} denotes the number of successor waiting vertices in the task topology, and $\alpha \in (0,1], \beta \in [-1,0), \gamma \in (0,1]$ is the weight factor. By combining the factors of the cumulative delay risk, the deadline and the number of successor tasks, the comprehensive index to measure the resource allocation priority of each task can reflect the impact of precursor task execution uncertainty impact, the deadline urgency and the inherent topological properties of successor tasks.

Algorithm 3 starts with a priority calculation for each executable task (line 2), followed by dynamic maintenance through the priority queue. It takes out the task with the highest priority at the top of the priority queue each time for resource allocation and assigns the task with the lowest expected completion time among all resources (lines 5–7), and then generates a scheduling scheme and updating the resource occupation time (lines 8–9) and finally update the priority queue (line 10).

Algorithm 3: *Heuristic*

Input: Executable tasks set T^e, blocking tasks sets T^b, resources set R
Output: Distribution schemet $\Pi<v, r, t>$

1 **Initialize:** set resource availability time T_R to 0; $\Pi \leftarrow \varnothing$
2 Calculate the priority for each p_{ij} according to (20)
3 $P \leftarrow \text{PCP}(T_i, v_{i\ \text{exit}})$
4 Add $v_{ij} \in T^e$ to the priority queue in ascending order of priority $\text{PQ}<p_{ij}, v_{ij}>$
5 **while** *PQ is not empty* **do**
6 $\quad$ $v_{ij} \leftarrow \text{PQ.peek}$
7 $\quad$ PQ delete v_{ij}
8 $\quad$ $r_{\min} \leftarrow \text{argmin}_{h \in R_{r_{ij}}} T_{R_h}$
9 $\quad$ $\Pi \leftarrow \Pi + <v_{ij}, r_{\min}, T_{R_h}>$
10 $\quad$ $T_{R_h} \leftarrow T_{R_h} + w_{ij}$
11 $\quad$ Move successor task of T^b of v_{ij} that can perform the assignment to T^e and add it to the PQ
12 **return** Π

---

5   Experimental Validation

5.1   Experimental Settings

The data used in the experiments are obtained from the PSPLIB dataset [1], which originated from the resource-constrained project scheduling problem [4, 9,12]. The experiments are solved by CPLEX for integer programming. The subtask dependencies in the experiments are generated through the network complexity parameters [11]. Each task consists of an average of eight subtasks with backward and forward dependencies, and the mean execution time obeys a normal distribution and the standard deviation being a multiple of the mean in the interval [0.1, 0.6]. The deadline of the task is the minimum completion time calculated by PSPLIB based on the average execution time of the task multiplied by a factor with an offset of 40 units of time. Each subtask is set to occupy one unit of resource. The experimental performance of the algorithm are tested in four aspects: the task completion rate, the running time of the algorithm, the average waiting time of the tasks, and the resource utilization rate; and there are two methods for comparison: 1) OPT, the optimal solution (solved by CPLEX), and 2) WT, which allocates resources based on the waiting time of tasks [5,6]. The heuristic scheduling algorithm proposed in this paper is denoted by HC.

5.2   Experimental Results

To validate the performance of the proposed HC algorithm, the task completion rate is tested. Figure 1 presents the results of task completion rate obtained by HC, OPT and WT.

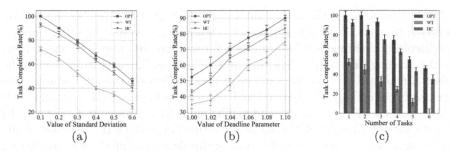

Fig. 1. Experimental results of task completion rate employing HC, OPT and WT algorithms.

From the results, OPT and HC perform much better than WT, and the performance of HC is close to the optimal solution. From Fig. 1(a) and 1(c), with the increase of the standard deviation of task execution time and the number of tasks, the task completion rate of different algorithms are decreasing. The potential reason is that the actual execution time of tasks fluctuates more and the delay risk of each task keeps increasing, thus leading to an increase in the cumulative delay risk of tasks and a decreasing task completion rate with a higher total number of tasks; with the number of tasks increases, the number of tasks waiting for the same resource increases, leading to an increased probability of tasks being delayed and a decreasing task completion rate. From Fig. 1(b), with the increase of task deadline, the task completion rate of different algorithms increase. The potential reason is that with the task deadline increases, the execution time for each subtask increase, the time available to deal with task delay increases, thus more tasks can be completed before the deadline, and the task completion rate keeps increasing.

In order to investigate the key features of the proposed HC algorithm, the algorithm runtime, the average waiting time and the resource utilization are also tested; Fig. 2 presents the experimental results.

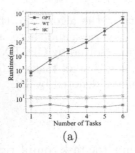 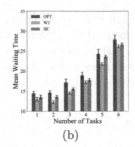 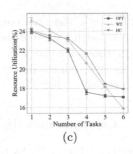

(a)   (b)   (c)

Fig. 2. Experimental results of the algorithm runtime, the average waiting time and the resource utilization

Figure 2(a) presents the tests results of the impact of the number of tasks on algorithm runtime. With the increase of the number of tasks, the OPT running time increases continuously and is much larger than HC and WT algorithms; and the running time of HC algorithm and WT algorithm are within 10 ms. The potential reason is that as the number of tasks increases, the OPT state space increases exponentially; the HC and WT algorithms have much lower time complexity, thus the efficiency of HC and WT is much higher than OPT. Figure 2(b) presents the tests results of the average waiting time. With the increase of the number of tasks, the average waiting time of the algorithms all show an increasing trend, and the average waiting time of OPT is larger than that of HC algorithm, while the average waiting time of HC algorithm is close to that of WT algorithm. The potential reason is that as the number of tasks increases, the number of tasks waiting for the same resource increases with the same amount of resources, thus leading to the increase of the average task waiting time; the WT algorithm gives priority to assign tasks with longer waiting time, the HC algorithm takes into account the cumulative delay risk and the deadline of tasks, and the OPT algorithm gives priority to task completion rate. Figure 2(c) presents the tests results of resource utilization which indicates the ratio of resource utilization time to total task duration. With the increase of the number of tasks, the resource utilization of different algorithms all show a decreasing trend, and the resource utilization of OPT algorithm is smaller than that of WT algorithm and HC algorithm; and the resource utilization of HC algorithm gradually exceeds that of WT algorithm when the amount of tasks is larger than 3. The potential reason is that as the number of tasks increases, the number of tasks waiting for the same resource increases with the same amount of resources; thus it leads to the higher delay risk, the longer waiting time, and the lower resource utilization of tasks. The algorithm HC in this paper takes into account the cumulative delay risk and task deadline, so it allocate resources to tasks at critical vertices with higher priority, thus it can achieve a shorter total task execution time and a higher resource utilization.

6   Conclusions

To solve the human-machine resource scheduling problem in multiagent systems, we represent the complex constraint relationship between subtasks by a directed graph and model the transmission effect of uncertainty of task execution in the modeling of human-machine cooperative resource scheduling problem in this paper. Since we prove the problem is NP-hard, we propose a heuristic scheduling algorithm to solve the problem. The heuristic algorithm determines the task priority based on cumulative delay risk estimation and time period division, so as to produce the resource scheduling scheme. Through experiments employing PSPLIB dataset, we investigate the performance of the proposed heuristic algorithm from four aspects: the task completion rate, the algorithm running time, the average waiting time, and the resource utilization rate, and by comparing with OPT and WT algorithms, the proposed algorithm performs close to the OPT algorithm and have a much lower running time which can be applied into large scale collaboration scenarios.

Acknowledgement. This work was supported by the National Key Research and Development Project of China (2019YFB1405000), the National Natural Science Foundation of China (No. 61807008, 61806053, 61932007, 62076060, and 61703097); and the Natural Science Foundation of Jiangsu Province of China (BK20180369, BK20180356, BK20201394, and BK20171363).

References

1. PSPLIB. http://www.om-db.wi.tum.de/psplib/main.html
2. Abrishami, S., Naghibzadeh, M., Epema, D.H.: Deadline-constrained workflow scheduling algorithms for infrastructure as a service clouds. Fut. Gener. Comput. Syst. **29**(1), 158–169 (2013)
3. Cai, H., Mostofi, Y.: Human-robot collaborative site inspection under resource constraints. IEEE Trans. Rob. **35**(1), 200–215 (2018)
4. Habibi, F., Barzinpour, F., Sadjadi, S.: Resource-constrained project scheduling problem: review of past and recent developments. J. Proj. Manage. **3**(2), 55–88 (2018)
5. Jiang, Y., Zhou, Y., Li, Y.: Reliable task allocation with load balancing in multiplex networks. ACM Trans. Auton. Adapt. Syst. (TAAS) **10**(1), 1–32 (2015)
6. Jiang, Y., Zhou, Y., Wang, W.: Task allocation for undependable multiagent systems in social networks. IEEE Trans. Parallel Distrib. Syst. **24**(8), 1671–1681 (2012)
7. Johnson, D.S.: The NP-completeness column: an ongoing guide. J. Algorithms **6**(3), 434–451 (1985)
8. Lin, B., Guo, W., Xiong, N., Chen, G., Vasilakos, A.V., Zhang, H.: A pretreatment workflow scheduling approach for big data applications in multicloud environments. IEEE Trans. Netw. Serv. Manage. **13**(3), 581–594 (2016)
9. Lin, J., Zhu, L., Gao, K.: A genetic programming hyper-heuristic approach for the multi-skill resource constrained project scheduling problem. Exp. Syst. Appl. **140**, 112915 (2020)

10. Rezaei, F., Najafi, A.A., Ramezanian, R.: Mean-conditional value at risk model for the stochastic project scheduling problem. Comput. Ind. Eng. **142**, 106356 (2020)
11. Sprecher, A., Kolisch, R.: PSPLIB - a project scheduling problem library. Eur. J. Oper. Res. **96**, 205–216 (1996)
12. Tirkolaee, E.B., Goli, A., Hematian, M., Sangaiah, A.K., Han, T.: Multi-objective multi-mode resource constrained project scheduling problem using pareto-based algorithms. Computing **101**(6), 547–570 (2019)
13. Wu, B., Hu, B., Lin, H.: Toward efficient manufacturing systems: a trust based human robot collaboration. In: 2017 American Control Conference (ACC), pp. 1536–1541. IEEE (2017)
14. Zhou, Y., Di, K., Xing, H.: Hybrid multiagent collaboration for time-critical tasks: a mathematical model and heuristic approach. Algorithms **14**(11), 327 (2021)

Social Computing

Automatic Generation and Analysis of Role Relation Network from Emergency Plans

Hongkun Zhao, Qingtian Zeng$^{(\boxtimes)}$, Wenyan Guo, and Weijian Ni

Shan Dong University of Science and Technology, QingDao 266590, China
17864266938@163.com

Abstract. In order to improve the efficiency of emergency response and optimize the utilization of emergency resources, domain experts actively create role network of emergency response. Creating emergency role network manually is a time-consuming and labor-intensive task. An approach to extracting role networks from emergency plans is proposed, and then the extracted role relation network is made a quantitative analysis in this paper. First, role relation network is generated from emergency plan, which includes the emergency department and personnel are identified through a Bi-LSTM-CRF network, coreference resolution is implemented based on RoBERTa-E2E-Coref model, role relation is extracted based on the RoBRETa-CasRel model, and role relation network of emergency response is generated based on identified roles and their relationship. Second, role relation network from emergency plan with different levels were analyzed quantitatively by using the complex network analysis methods. Finally, experiment evaluation and a case study are given based on the real data sets, and the results show that the proposed approach can be used to assist emergency decision-makers to create role relation networks of emergency response. In addition, through the analysis of the extracted role relationship network, the quality of the emergency plan can be indirectly reflected.

Keywords: Emergency response · Role relation network · Coreference resolution · Relationship extraction

1 Introduction

In recent years, a series of emergencies have occurred, threatening people's lives and property security and social stability, such as COVID-19 and typhoon In-Fa. Emergency response participants do their best to reduce disaster loss when emergencies occur. A large number of emergency plans developed by government offices at all levels are used to instruct emergency participants to perform response tasks [1]. Specifically, the part of emergency response command system describes response departments and their response tasks, while the part of emergency response describes departmental interaction process [2]. These two parts together contain organization structure information which is the action basis of multi-department coordinated emergency response [3]. The diversity of emergency tasks and the dispersion of resources require multiple departments to cooperate and interact to deal with them. Domain experts actively create organizational network of emergency response to describe which emergency departments are involved and how they interact and collaborate [4].

The role relation network of emergency response is a relatively stable collaborative structure, which can meet the changing environment through collective decision-making and joint action [5]. Generally, social network methods are utilized to analyze connection characteristics and interaction patterns of emergency response organizational networks [6]. The connection characteristics can be reflected by network density, the number of organizations and the number of connections in the network [7]. Interaction patterns include cooperation relationship between superior and subordinate, cooperative relationship between same level, composition relationship and messaging relationship. Currently, emergency response role relation networks are manually constructed by domain experts with rich experience [8]. It is a time-consuming and labor-intensive task. Interorganizational networks arose in the process of multi-role coordination and cooperation [9]. An approach is proposed to automatically extract role relation network from emergency plans in this paper. Emergency response department and personnel elements are identified through a deep neural network. The identified departments and personals are used to perform coreference resolution operations. The role relationship is extracted through deep learning relational feature words. An emergency response role relation network is generated based on the extracted role and role relationships. The generated role relation network is quantitatively analyzed, which is used to reflect role characteristics of emergency plans.

The rest of this paper is arranged as follows: the related work is introduced in Sect. 2; relevant definitions are introduced in Sect. 3; the generation and analysis of role relation network for emergency plan is detailed in Sect. 4; the relevant experimental analysis is presented in Sect. 5 and a detailed case study is introduced; and the summary is in the Sect. 6.

2 Related Work

2.1 Generation of Role Relation Network for Emergency Plan

Department and personnel identification are regarded as named entity recognition task, it aims to extract and assign the entities of departments and personnels into predefined categories [10]. [11] proposed attention-based CNN-LSTM-CRF to recognize entities in Chinese clinical text. Coreference resolution identifies entity mentions and it refers to the same real-world entity in a document [12]. [13] proposed an end-to-end coreference resolution model and generated useful mention candidates from the space of all possible spans. [14] applied BERT to distinguish between related but distinct entities. Entity relationship extraction, as an important subtask of information extraction, aims to discover the relation between head entity and tail entity from large-scale unstructured text [15]. [16] proposed a novel cascade binary tagging framework (CASREL) and the model relations as functions that map subjects to objects in a sentence.

2.2 Analysis of Role Relation Network for Emergency Plan

Complex network analysis is introduced to analyze the relationship between roles and network distribution through centrality and network density. [17] was concluded that complexity can be found in the global structural of relation between syndrome differentiation and acupoint selection. [18] proposed the results of the complex network analysis showed that anxiety and sleep disorder were closely related to THI score, and anxiety was more important than sleep disorder. [19] used two complex network analysis methods, network meta-analysis and network pharmacology, to explore the curative effect observation of Traditional Chinese medicine injection in the treatment of acute cerebral infarction. [20] proposed the method of constructing the corresponding complex network dynamics model and it is proved that this kind of complex network dynamics model is uniformly asymptotically stable in a large range.

3 Preliminaries

In order to facilitate understanding, some definitions are given.

Definition 1. An emergency response organization system is 3-tuple $EROS = <D, R, \delta>$ where $D = \{d_0, d_1, \ldots, d_m\}$ is the set of emergency departments, d_0 is the command center, $d_1, d_2, \ldots, d_m$ are member units, $R = \{r_0, r_1, r_2, \ldots, r_n\}$ is the set of emergency roles, δ denotes subordinate superior relationship between emergency department and role, specifically $\delta(r) = d$ denotes the role r is subordinate to the department d.

Definition 2. Departmental relationship is defined as a 3-tuple $RD = <d_i, relationship, d_j>$, where d_i and d_j are emergency departments, and *relationship* represents the relationship between d_i and d_j. Four types of departmental relationship including *SL_cooperation*, *SS_cooperation*, *Composition* and *Message_passing*, are defined as follows:

- *SL_cooperation* describes a cooperative relationship between departments at the same level. $\forall d_i, d_j \in \{d_1, d_2, \ldots, d_m\}, d_i$ and d_j cooperate to complete the same emergency task, which is denoted as $< d_i, SL\_cooperation, d_j >$.
- *SS_cooperation* describes a cooperative relationship between superior and subordinate departments. $\forall d_i, d_j \in \{d_0, d_1, \ldots, d_m\}$, assuming that d_i is the superior department and d_j is the subordinate department, if d_i and d_j cooperate to complete the same emergency task, there is a *SS_cooperation* relationship between d_i and d_j, which is denoted as $< d_i, SS\_cooperation, d_j >$.
- *Composition* describes a composition relationship between two different departments. $\forall d_i, d_j \in \{d_0, d_1, d_2, \ldots, d_m\}$, if d_j is one of d_i's member departments, there is a *Composition* relationship between d_i and d_j, which is denoted as $< d_i, Composition, d_j >$.
- *Message_passing* describes a message passing relationship where d_i is a message sender and d_j is a message receiver, which is denoted as $< d_i, Message\_passing, d_j >$.

Both *SL_cooperation* and *SS_cooperation* indicated that there was a cooperative relationship between the two emergency departments, but the two departments in the former have the same level in the emergency plan, while the latter has obvious obedience relationship in the emergency plan, such as command relationship. The *Composition* relationship indicates that there is a composition relationship between the two departments. The two departments that have *Message_passing*, *SL_cooperation* or *SS_cooperation* may have *Composition* with the same department.

Definition 3. An interorganizational network of emergency response is defined as a 3-tuple $G = \{D, V, \varphi(D, V)\}$, where D is the set emergency departments, V is the set of the set of departmental relationships, and $\varphi(D, V)$ is a weight function specifying the frequency of interaction between different departments and $\varphi(D, V) \in \{1, 2, 3, 4\}$.

4   Generation and Analysis

The emergency plan role relation network is a structure that can intuitively reflect the relationship between the departments, which can reflect cooperation and common decisions between the departments, such as Fig. 1.

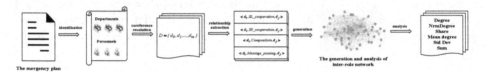

Fig. 1. The research framework

4.1   Generation of Role Relation Network

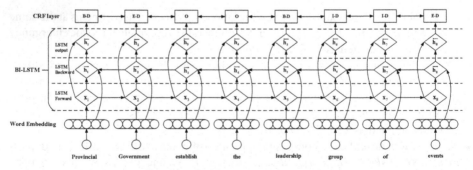

Fig. 2. Bi-LSTM-CRF model structure

The same emergency role entity can appear multiple times in different sentences in an emergency response plan and the context information is different. RNN is a classical neural network model for processing sequence data. RNN cannot solve the problem of long distance dependence well. LSTM makes up for the defect of RNN and overcomes the problem of long distance dependence. The information of each word in a sentence is closely related to the information of its context, while the output of each step in LSTM is only determined by the current input and the previous input, without considering the future input. Bi-LSTM can effectively solve this defect. CRF module can take into account the relationship between tags and output text corresponding prediction tag. The Bi-LSTM-CRF model as showed in Fig. 2 designed in this part can either excavate the internal configuration of the text and can obtain the dependence between long distance words. The characteristic vector enters to the BI-LSTM layer for training, using Bi-LSTM to model the context information. The number of invalid prediction labels is lowered after training through the CRF layer. For data labels, B means Begin indicating the start; I means intermediate indicating the middle; E means End indicating the end; O means other indicating other and used to mark independent characters.

In order to avoid repetition, habits, pronouns, title, and abbreviations to refer to the full name of the previous mentioned. Similarly, the same department will have different naming methods in the same text. In order to better reflect the relationship between different departments, this paper uses the coreference resolution method. In emergency plans, longer organizations are often given their full name when they first appear and only their abbreviation when they appear later. The RoBERTa-E2E-Coref does not rely on grammar analysis, and the core of the model is the vector representation of each span. Coreference resolution of roles is realized by considering all spans in the emergency plan and learning the possible referents of each span. The RoBERTa-E2E-Coref overall architecture is shown in Fig. 3.

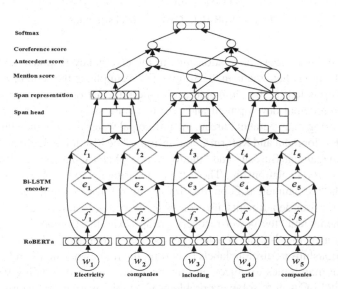

Fig. 3. RoBRETa-E2E-coref model

Such as Fig. 3, first, the Chinese pre-training model RoBERTa in used to obtain word embedding. Calculating potential entities refer to score, score-lower spans are discarded, and score-higher spans are reserved. Second, antecedent scores are calculated by a pair of spans. The coreference score of a pair of spans is computed by summing the mention scores of both spans and their pairwise antecedent score. For span representations, we use Bi-LSTM to encode internal and external information of each span, and add an attention mechanism to each span to model head words.

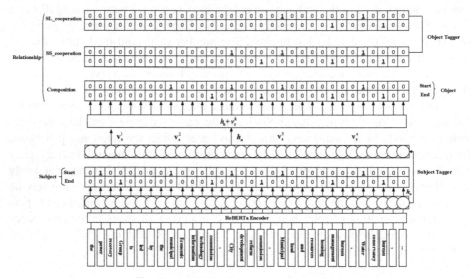

Fig. 4. RoBRETa-CasRel model structure

There may be a variety of relationships in the emergency response text, and there may be overlapping phenomena in the 3-tuple. For example, in the sentence "The power recovery group is led by the municipal economic information power committee, consists of the municipal development and reform commission, the municipal land and resources housing management bureau, the municipal water conservancy bureau.", "the Municipal Development and Reform Commission", "the Municipal Land and Resources Housing Management Bureau" and "the Municipal Water Conservancy Bureau" exist the *SL_cooperation* relationship. These three departments exist *SS_cooperation* relationship with "the Municipal Economic Information Power Committee", at the same time, the above four departments also compose "the power recovery group", the above four departments and "the power recovery group" exist the *Composition* relationship. The extraction of the 3-tuple in a new perspective is defined in Fig. 4. Rather than treating relationships as discrete labels as before, the framework model relationships as functions that map topics to objects in sentences, thus naturally dealing with overlap. Using RoBERTa-Casrel to solve the problem of 3-tuple overlap in the emergency plan text, and finally realize the extraction of the department relationship in the emergency plan text. This model extracts the relationship ternary group from the two levels steps. First, all the subjects in the input text which is a completed department entity should be detected. Then for each Subject, we check all our predefined relationships to find if there is a relationship that can pair the Subject and Object. So, the cascade decode consists of a subject tagger and a relation-object tagger. The model has two identical binary classifiers, the role of the binary classifier here is to detect and mark the start position and end position of the Subject. "The power recovery group is led by the Municipal Economic Information Power Committee, consists of the Municipal Development and Reform Commission, the Municipal Land and Resources Housing Management Bureau, the Municipal Water Conservancy Bureau" in the Fig. 4, first of all, "the power recovery group", "the Municipal Economic Information Power Committee", "the Municipal Development and Reform Commission", "the Municipal Land and Resources Housing Management Bureau", "the Municipal Water Conservancy Bureau" are detected subjects, when k = 3, "the Municipal Development and Reform Commission" and "the Municipal Land and Resources Housing Management Bureau" exist the *Cooperation* relationship, the result is shown as < *the Municipal Development and Reform Commission, Cooperation, the Municipal Land and Resources Housing Management Bureau* >.

4.2 Analysis of Role Relation Network

Neo4j are used for the role relation network and Ucinet6 are used for data analysis. In the construction of the departmental relationship network, the relationship between the form of social network diagrams is adopted, using departmental correlations, departmental density to measure the association of the network between emergency plans, and display two departments in action relationship and through the centrality degree to judge the role of departments in the emergency plan. Degree, Nrmdegree, Share, Mean degree, Std Dev and Sum are used to analyze and evaluate role relation network. Degree refers to the number of other points directly connected with a certain point in a network graph. A large number indicates that the point is closely connected with others and reflects the central position of the point in the network. Absolute point centrality reflects the power status and influence distribution of nodes in the network. The higher the centrality is, the more the nodes are in the core position and can effectively control and influence the activities of other actors in the network. On the contrary, nodes with lower centrality are more marginal, rarely participate in interaction and have little influence on other nodes. The Degree, Nrmdegree, Sum, Mean and Share are defined as follows:

$$C_{Degree}(N_i) = \sum_j^n x_{ij}(i \neq j)$$

$$C_{Nrmdegree}(N_i) = C_{degree}(N_i)/C_{degree}(N_j)_{max}$$

$$Sum = \sum_{m=1}^n C_{Degree}(N_m)$$

$$Mean = Sum/n$$

$$Share(N_i) = C_{Degree}(N_i)/Sum$$

where $C_{Degree}(N_i)$ indicates the degree of node i, $\sum_{j}^{n} x_{ij}$ is the sum of the relations between i and other nodes, $C_{Nrmdegree}(N_i)$ indicates the standard form of $C_{Degree}(N_i)$, Sum indicates the sum of role relations, Mean indicates the average number of relations for a role, Share indicates the proportion of N_i in the role relation network.

The analysis of the role relation network of emergency plan from two aspects. The first aspect is to analyze the network between the different provinces in the same type of emergency. The second aspect is to analyze the network from national, provincial and municipal perspectives.

5   Experimental Analysis

5.1   Data Set

This paper crawls out the emergency plan text as data from the public network of the government, municipal government, provincial government and national government. Among them, there are 1 national emergency plan, 11 provincial emergency plan and each level includes emergency plans for natural disasters and large-scale power failure.

5.2   Experimental Results Presentation

The recognition results of departments are shown in Table 1.

Table 1. Department and personnel recognition results of BIEO

Tags	CRF			Bi-LSTM			Bi-LSTM-CRF		
	P	R	F1	P	R	F1	P	R	F1
B-D	0.85	0.80	0.82	0.87	0.82	0.85	0.92	0.86	0.90
I-D	0.87	0.83	0.85	0.89	0.83	0.86	0.96	0.90	0.91
E-D	0.85	0.80	0.82	0.85	0.80	0.82	0.92	0.88	0.90
B-P	0.70	0.69	0.69	0.69	0.69	0.69	0.76	0.71	0.74
I-P	0.68	0.80	0.74	0.70	0.83	0.75	0.72	0.84	0.76
E-P	0.74	0.58	0.65	0.75	0.55	0.67	0.82	0.60	0.70
O	0.95	0.95	0.95	0.94	0.94	0.94	0.99	0.99	0.99

The precision, recall and F1 of data set constructed in this paper are shown in the Table 3 by CRF, Bi-LSTM and Bi-LSTM-CRF. The Bi-LSTM-CRF is higher than the CRF and Bi-LSTM in the precision, the recall, and F1 value. The method of CRF relies on the selection of the characteristics and identifies the complex department name, the method of BI-LSTM automatically learns contextual information in sentences, Bi-LSTM-CRF method automatically learned information in the sentence, combined with the contextual relationship of the current word and does not depend on the selection of features, improves the identification effect.

The experimental results of the coreference resolution are in Table 2.

Table 2. Results of the coreference resolution

Methods	P	R	F1
Mention-pair	0.85	0.80	0.82
RoBRETa-E2E-Coref	0.93	0.92	0.92

The RoBRETa-E2E-Coref model can be achieved by grouping all spans in a set of antecedent predicted results. Evaluate the vector representation of each span and score each potential Mention that is a different representation of the same entity in the text accordingly. For each span, combine each of its words such as matrix concatenation to get a vector representation of the span. Then, the vector representation of span is nonlinearly mapped to obtain the score of each potential mention, and a certain number of mentions is obtained by pruning the mention with the score size. The antecedent score is calculated for each pair of vector representations of spans. By summing up the two span mention scores and their paired antecedent scores, the final common reference scores of a pair of spans are obtained.

The results of role relationship extraction are in Table 3.

Table 3. Results of the relation extraction

Methods	P	R	F1
Bi-LSTM-CRF	0.72	0.84	0.76
RoBRETa-CasRel	0.80	0.80	0.80

The RoBRETa-CasRel solves the overlapping 3-tuple problem where multiple relational triples of the department relationship of the emergency plans in the same sentence share the same departments.

The role relation network of natural disaster emergency plan and large-scale power failure emergency plan in Shandong and Hubei provinces are showed in Fig. 5 and the centrality degree of some departments in natural disaster emergency plan of Shandong Province are shown in Table 4.

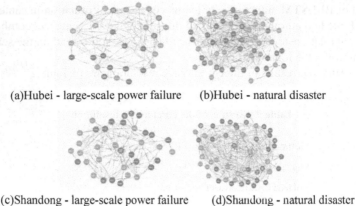

(a)Hubei - large-scale power failure   (b)Hubei - natural disaster

(c)Shandong - large-scale power failure   (d)Shandong - natural disaster

Fig. 5. Role relation relationship network

Table 4. Some roles in natural disaster emergency plan of Shandong Province

Emergency roles	Degree	NrmDegree	Share
Provincial disaster reduction committee	35.000	51.471	0.031
Provincial government	34.000	50.000	0.030
Health department	33.000	48.529	0.029
Provincial Development and Reform Commission	33.000	48.529	0.029
Provincial Disaster Reduction Commission Office	1.000	1.471	0.001

The interaction density in the network reflects the correlation between the department. The greater the network density between the two departments, the greater the interaction between the two departments. Different duties, different management privileges and capacity can show key departments in emergency plans. The more a department interacts with other departments, the more important the department is. In Fig. 5, it can directly represent the relationship and close connection between all participating roles in the natural disaster emergency plan and large-scale power failure emergency plan, role relation network density is used to measure the degree of interaction between roles and display the relationship between roles in emergency plans, the greater the network density around a role, the greater the role's responsibility in the contingency plan. Such as in Table 4, the max degree role in natural disaster emergency plan of Shandong Province is provincial disaster reduction committee so it can be seen that provincial disaster reduction committee plays a central role in the natural disaster emergency plan. When natural disasters occur, a lot of work inevitably revolves around provincial disaster reduction committee.

The indicators of role relation network are shown in Table 5.

Table 5. Indicators of role relation network from provincial emergency plans

Province	Natural disaster		Large-scale power failure	
	Mean degree	Sum	Mean degree	Sum
Shandong	32.1	1126	11.5	230
Hubei	33.9	1660	14.5	246
Anhui	30.0	986	12.8	200
Fujian	28.5	760	17.6	180
Henan	20.7	676	17.3	176
Heilongjiang	18.9	468	12.5	140
Jiangsu	32.9	1084	15.2	330
Shanxi	20.8	702	9.6	168
Sichuan	38.5	2238	26.8	368
Yunnan	38.4	2408	17.9	366
Hainan	17.8	322	7.5	108

Table 6. Indicators of role relation network from different levels of emergency plans.

Administrative level	Natural disaster		Large-scale power failure	
	Mean degree	Sum	Mean degree	Sum
Nation	40.5	1808	28.7	386
Province	32.1	1126	11.5	230
Municipality	25.6	978	9.7	186
District	18.5	624	4.8	82

In Table 5, in the first aspect, the number of roles' relation in emergency plans for large-scale power failure is much smaller than the number of roles' relation in emergency plans for natural disasters, is to analyze the network between the different provinces. The second aspect is to analyze the network from different levels of emergency plans. The sum and the mean degree of roles involved in emergency plans in Sichuan province and Yunnan Province are higher than those in other provinces, it shows that Sichuan province and Yunnan Province participate in a large number of role relations in the emergency plan and the relationship between the roles is very close. In the second aspect, such as in

Table 6, for the same type of contingency plan, the total number of relations and Mean degree among participating roles in emergency plans for Nation, Province, municipality and District gradually decreased, it shows that the higher the hierarchy, the more roles involved and the closer the connections between the roles.

5.3 A Case Study

1. 省自然灾害救助应急指挥部组成如下：指挥长：省政府分管副省长；副指挥长：省民政厅厅长；成员：省委宣传部、省台办。
2. 灾害发生后，省减灾委办公室认定灾情达到启动标准，向省减灾委提出启动响应的建议。
3. 省减灾委主任主持召开会商会议协调落实省委、省政府关于救灾工作的指示。
4. 省减灾委办公室及时掌握灾情和救灾工作动态信息，每日向省委、省政府和国家减灾委办公室、民政部报告一次灾情和救灾工作动态信息。
5. 省政府、省民政厅、省财政厅向国务院、民政部、财政部上报请拨救灾应急资金和救灾物资的请示。
6. 省外侨办、省台办协助做好救灾的涉外和涉港澳台工作。

Fig. 6. An example of emergency plan

Taking part of the text of the emergency plan for sudden natural disasters as an example, Fig. 6 shows an example of emergency plan, including 6 sentences, involving 14 departments, 4 relationships types and 53 relationships including 5 Composition, 16 SS_cooperation, 3 SL_cooperation, 14 Message_passing. The extraction results of the 14 roles identification are shown in Table 7, the result of role relation extraction is shown in Table 8, the role relation network of emergency plan as shown in Fig. 7 and the indicators of inter-role relationship network as shown in Table 9.

Table 7. The identified roles

Roles	Meaning of symbol
d_1	"省自然灾害救助应急指挥部"
d_2	"省政府"
d_3	"省民政厅"
d_4	"省委宣传部"
d_5	"省台办"
d_6	"省减灾委办公室"
d_7	"省减灾委"
d_8	"省委"
d_9	"国家减灾委办公室"
d_{10}	"民政部"
d_{11}	"省财政厅"

Table 8. The extracted role relationship results

Relationship	Role relationship
Composition	$<d_1$, Composition, $d_2>$, $<d_1$, Composition, $d_3>$, $<d_1$, Composition, $d_4>$, $<d_1$, Composition, $d_5>$, $<d_4$, Composition, $d_5>$
SS_cooperation	$<d_8$, SS_cooperation, $d_7>$, $<d_2$, SS_cooperation, $d_7>$, $<d_2$, SS_cooperation, $d_3>$, $<d_2$, SS_cooperation, $d_4>$, $<d_2$, SS_cooperation, $d_5>$, $<d_3$, SS_cooperation, $d_4>$, $<d_3$, SS_cooperation, $d_5>$, $<d_2$, SS_cooperation, $d_{12}>$, $<d_2$, SS_cooperation, $d_{10}>$, $<d_2$, SS_cooperation, $d_{13}>$, $<d_3$, SS_cooperation, $d_{12}>$, $<d_3$, SS_cooperation, $d_{10}>$, $<d_3$, SS_cooperation, $d_{13}>$, $<d_{11}$, SS_cooperation, $d_{12}>$, $<d_{11}$, SS_cooperation, $d_{10}>$, $<d_{11}$, SS_cooperation, $d_{13}>$
SL_cooperation	$<d_4$, SL_cooperation, $d_5>$, $<d_8$, SL_cooperation, $d_2>$, $<d_{14}$, SL_cooperation, $d_5>$
Message_passing	$<d_6$, Message_passing, $d_7>$, $<d_6$, Message_passing, $d_8>$, $<d_6$, Message_passing, $d_2>$, $<d_6$, Message_passing, $d_9>$, $<d_6$, Message_passing, $d_{10}>$, $<d_2$, Message_passing, $d_{12}>$, $<d_2$, Message_passing, $d_{10}>$, $<d_2$, Message_passing, $d_{13}>$, $<d_3$, Message_passing, $d_{12}>$, $<d_3$, Message_passing, $d_{10}>$, $<d_3$, Message_passing, $d_{13}>$, $<d_{11}$, Message_passing, $d_{12}>$, $<d_{11}$, Message_passing, $d_{10}>$, $<d_{11}$, Message_passing, $d_{13}>$

Table 9. Indicators of the generated role relation network

Roles	Degree	Nrm Degree	Share
Natural disaster relief and emergency response headquarters	13.000	100.000	0.186
Provincial government	9.000	69.231	0.129
Provincial civil affairs department	7.000	53.846	0.100
Provincial commission of disaster reduction office	6.000	46.154	0.086
Provincial Taiwan office	5.000	38.462	0.071
Provincial propaganda department	4.000	30.769	0.057
Provincial commission of disaster reduction	4.000	30.769	0.057
State council	4.000	30.769	0.057
Ministry of civil affairs	4.000	30.769	0.057
Ministry of finance	4.000	30.769	0.057
Provincial party committee	3.000	23.077	0.043
Provincial civil affairs department	3.000	23.077	0.043
Office of the national commission of disaster reduction	2.000	15.385	0.029
Provincial overseas Chinese affairs office	2.000	15.385	0.029

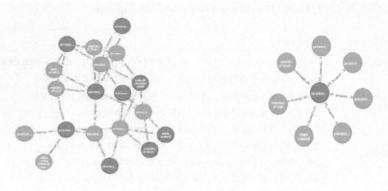

(a) Role relation network   (b) Sub-network about provincial government

Fig. 7. Inter-role network generated from Fig. 6

In Table 9, the role of max degree in the case is natural disaster relief and emergency response headquarters so it can be seen that natural disaster relief and emergency response headquarters plays a central role in the case emergency plan. The whole inter-role network of the case as shown in Fig. 7. (a), it intuitively reflects the relation between the roles and the degree of intimacy. Figure 7(b) is a local network diagrams of provincial government respectively. It can also be seen from Fig. 7 that provincial government have the higher network density and are more closely connected with other roles.

6 Summary

Based on the text of emergency plan, this paper obtained the interorganizational network of emergency plan through four steps: collection and annotation, department and role extraction, coreference resolution, and relationship extraction and through complex network analysis the role relation network in two aspects. Compared with the text, the interorganizational network built in this paper makes more specific and more intuitive reflection in the emergency plan, and provides great help to quickly understand the contents of the relevant plan. The proposed approach can quantify and visualize the organizational network structure and relationship patterns in emergency plans. At the same time, it also provides an effective reference for the preparation, revision, and specific implementation of the emergency plan, it provides a more comprehensive and effective method for analyzing the text of emergency plan and the role relation network, and it is very important in practical significance.

Acknowledgment. This work was supported by National Natural Science Foundation of China (No. U1931207 and No. 61702306), Sci. & Tech. Development Fund of Shandong Province of China (No. ZR2019LZH001, No. ZR2017BF015 and No. ZR2017MF027), Natural Science Foundation of Shandong Province (No. ZR202102250695), the Humanities and Social Science Research Project of the Ministry of Education (No. 18YJAZH017), Shandong Chongqing Science and technology cooperation project (No.cstc2020jscx-lyjsAX0008), Sci. & Tech. Development

Fund of Qingdao (No. 21-1-5-zlyj-1-zc), the Taishan Scholar Program of Shandong Province, SDUST Research Fund (No. 2015TDJH102 and No. 2019KJN024) and National Statistical Science Research Project (No. 2021LY053).

References

1. Kirschenbaum, A., Rapaport, C.: Informal social networks as generic contingency plans. J. Conting. Crisis Manag. **26**(4), 453–460 (2018)
2. Guo, W., Zeng, Q., Duan, H., et al.: Text quality analysis of emergency response plans. IEEE Access **8**, 9441–9456 (2020)
3. Jiang, Y.W., Wang, Q., Zhu, Y.B.: How occupational disease prevention and treatment apparatus to respond to public health emergency incidents. Zhonghua lao dong wei sheng zhi ye bing za zhi Zhonghua laodong weisheng zhiyebing zazhi Chinese J. Ind. Hyg. Occupat. Dis. **27**(5), 319–320 (2009)
4. Huang, X., Liu, Q.: Strategy of establishing the super network emergency plan system in coastal cities of China. Environ. Dev. Sustain. **23**(9), 13062–13086 (2021). https://doi.org/10.1007/s10668-020-01199-7
5. Uhr, C.: Multi-organizational Emergency Response Management. A Framework for Further Development. Department of Fire Safety Engineering and Systems Safety, Lund University, Lund, Sweden (2009)
6. Zhang, Y.C., Liu, Y., Zhang, H., et al.: The research of information dissemination model on online social network. Acta Physica Sinica **60**(5), 60–66 (2011)
7. Jiang-Tao, K., Jian, H., Jian-Xing, G., et al.: Evaluation methods of node importance in undirected weighted networks based on complex network dynamics models. Acta Physica Sinica **67**(9) (2018)
8. Tian, J.H., Shi, S.Z., Zhao, Y., et al.: Complex network analysis of law on Chinese herbal drugs intervention on radiation induced lung injury. Zhongguo Zhong yao za zhi Zhongguo zhongyao zazhi China J. Chin. Materia Medica **43**(14), 3018–3025 (2018)
9. Duan, M., Jiang, Y., Chen, X., et al.: Degree centrality of the functional network in schizophrenia patients. Sheng wu yi xue gong cheng xue za zhi J. Biomed. Eng. Shengwu yixue gongchengxue zazhi **34**(6), 837–841 (2017)
10. Li, J., Sun, A., Han, J., et al.: A survey on deep learning for named entity recognition. In: IEEE Transactions on Knowledge and Data Engineering, vol. 99, pp. 1–1 (2020)
11. Tang, B., Wang, X., Yan, J., et al.: Entity recognition in Chinese clinical text using attention-based CNN-LSTM-CRF. BMC Med. Inf. Dec. Mak. **19**(3), 89–97 (2019)
12. Le Thi, T., Phan Thi, T., Quan Thanh, T.: Machine learning using context vectors for object coreference resolution. Computing **1**, 20 (2021). https://doi.org/10.1007/s00607-021-00902-4
13. Lee, K., He, L., Lewis, M., et al.: End-to-end neural coreference resolution. arXiv preprint arXiv:1707.07045 (2017)
14. Joshi, M., Levy, O., Weld, D.S., et al.: BERT for coreference resolution: Baselines and analysis. arXiv preprint arXiv:1908.09091 (2019)
15. Li, Y.: Research on Chinese entity relation extraction method based on deep learning. In: 2021 International Conference on Communications, Information System and Computer Engineering (CISCE). IEEE, pp. 731–735 (2021)
16. Wei, Z., Su, J., Wang, Y., et al.: A novel hierarchical binary tagging framework for joint extraction of entities and relations. arXiv preprint arXiv:1909.03227 (2019)
17. Wang, Y.Y., Lin, F., Jiang, Z.L.: Pattern of acupoint selection based on complex network analysis technique. Zhongguo zhen jiu Chinese Acupunct. Moxib. **31**(1), 85–88 (2011)

18. Sun, H., Feng, G., Gao, Z.: Key factors of the severity of chronic subjective tinnitus: a complex network analysis. Lin Chuang J. Clin. Otorhinolaryngol. Head, Neck Surg. **35**(7), 586–592 (2021)
19. Hu, R.X., Yu, D.D., Li, H.M., et al.: Exploring efficacy of Chinese medicine injection for promoting blood circulation and removing blood stasis in treatment of acute cerebral infarction based on two complex network analysis methods. Zhongguo China J. Chinese Materia Medica **46**(14), 3722–3731 (2021)
20. Kong, J.T., Huang, J.G., Li, J.X.: Evaluation methods of node importance in undirected weighted networks based on complex network dynamics models. Acta Physica Sinica (2018)

Information Tracking Extraction for Emergency Scenario Response

Hua Zhao$^{(\boxtimes)}$ 🆔, Xiaoqian Li, Peixin Zhang, and Zhengguo Song

College of Computer Science and Engineering, Shandong University of Science
and Technology, Qingdao 266590, China
huamolin@163.com

Abstract. With the frequent occurrences of emergencies, scenario response is proposed by researchers for emergency management. On the one hand, extracting emergency-related information is necessary and important for describing emergency scenario correctly; On the other hand, some emergency-related information evolve dynamically with time going on. To this end, a method for information extraction based on event tracking (called as information tracking extraction) for emergency scenario response is proposed. Based on the emergency tracking, it firstly judges the type of the emergency; secondly extracts time, location, casualty and loss based on multi strategies; finally adopts E-charts to visualize the extraction results. Experimental results show the proposed method can achieve high precision and recall, and the visualization of the tracking extraction results can display the dynamic evolution process better, which is very helpful to the scientific decision-making in the emergency management.

Keywords: Emergency · Information extraction · Event track · Scenario response

1 Introduction

In recent years, there happed a series of emergencies, such as USA "911" terrorist incident, the Indian Ocean tsunami, the "5.12" Wenchuan earthquake and the "4.20" Lushan earthquake in China, which show that we are now in a social period with frequent emergencies. The frequent occurrence of emergency poses severe challenges to the emergency response and management. Many researches on emergency decision support have been carried out [1, 2]. Relevant researches showed that the traditional "prediction-response" management model is already difficult to adapt to the high timeliness, comprehensiveness, dynamic and interactive requirements of emergency management, and then proposed a new "scenario-response" emergency management model. The premise of the "scenario-response" management model is to monitor and analyze the development situation of emergency comprehensively, that is, to accurately depict the current "scenario" of emergency, in which the information related to emergency is a key dimension.

Z. Shi et al. (Eds.): IIP 2022, IFIP AICT 643, pp. 203–215, 2022.
https://doi.org/10.1007/978-3-031-03948-5_17

For the above-mentioned reasons, this paper aims to extract emergency-related information from unformatted news reports, including time, location, casualty, loss and so on, all of which are indispensable dimensions for describing emergency scenario accurately. Based on the summary of existing research results and the analysis of emergency news reports, we find that compared with traditional information extraction, emergency-related information extraction has its own characteristics. Firstly, the emergency information has a strong timeliness, and emergency news reports are often published on the day when the emergency occurs. Secondly, the format of ordinary text is often diversified, and cannot design uniform rules for extraction. But the format of emergency news reports are highly standardized, not only their contents generally conform to the news standard, but also their attributes are relatively uniform, which ensures that rule-based methods can be used for emergency-related information extraction.

The contributions of this paper are as follows:

(1) The concept of information tracking extraction is proposed. Existing studies neglect the continuity and dynamics of emergency, that is, an emergency usually lasts for a certain period of time after it occurs, and meanwhile, some emergency-related information (casualties, losses, etc.) evolves dynamically with time going on.
(2) Based on the topic tracking method, an emergency tracking algorithm is proposed. The tracking algorithm represents the emergency news report as a vector space model, and draws a conclusion whether they are relevant by comparing the similarity between news reports with the threshold.
(3) A multistrategy-based information extraction method is proposed and implemented, which mainly includes the extraction of the world, location, casualties, and economic losses and so on.

2 Related Work

The goal of information extraction is to obtain target information accurately and quickly from a large amount of data, thereby improving data utilization. Generally speaking, information extraction methods can be divided into statistical methods and rule-based methods [3]. With the frequent occurrence of emergency and the urgent need of emergency management in recent years, the research on emergency information extraction has gradually attracted extensive attentions of researchers at home and abroad.

Relevant studies abroad have been carried out earlier, for example, D Brunner [4] used emergency information extraction results in post-disaster loss assessment. Amailef et al. [5] extracted emergency information based on Ontology and maximum entropy statistical model, and then sent the results to an emergency response system based on mobile terminal.

Domestic research on emergency information extraction is relatively late, but some excellent results have been achieved. Chen et al. [6] proposed a method based on the combination of rules and machine learning to extract chemical emergency information. Michele et al. [7] first identified the three-level event framework system through the analysis of the composition of the main and auxiliary information structure chain, then identified the event keywords, and finally identified and classified the event attributes.

Jiang D. L. [8] implemented a rule matching-based method for extracting information from emergency news reports. Wang N. [9] introduced knowledge element into emergency field, designed customizable emergency case information extraction template, and then combined with rule matching, realized the emergency case information extraction method based on knowledge element.

3 Emergency Information Tracking Extraction Framework

The flow chart of our emergency information tracking extraction framework is shown in Fig. 1. It consists of three parts: data acquisition and pre-processing; information tracking extraction; and results visualization.

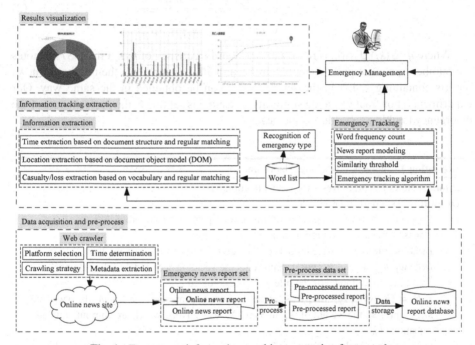

Fig. 1. Emergency information tracking extraction framework

Information Tracking Extraction. This is the core module of this paper, which is mainly responsible for information extraction, emergency type identification and event tracking. From Fig. 1, we can see that our proposed information tracking extraction method is to extract information based on emergency tracking. We will focus on this module in Sect. 4.

Results Visualization. This module visualizes the results of information tracking extraction. The main purpose of data visualization is to use graphical methods and means to clearly and effectively convey relevant information and express relevant data. This paper uses Baidu's open source E-Charts visualization library for data visualization.

4 Emergency Information Tracking Extraction Method

4.1 Emergency Tracking Method

Based on the idea of topic tracking [10], this paper designs and implements a simple and effective method for tracking incidents. The steps are shown in Algorithm 1.

Equation (1) is a kind of TFIDF method [11] and Eq. (2) is a classical cosine function. They are as follows:

$$sw_i = tf\_S(k_i) \times \log \frac{|ST|}{\delta(k_i)} \tag{1}$$

$$\cos(S, N_i) = \frac{\sum_{i=1}^{n}(sw_i \times sni_i)}{\sqrt{\sum_{i=1}^{n} sw_i^2} \times \sqrt{\sum_{i=1}^{n} sni_i^2}} \tag{2}$$

Where $tf\_S(k_i)$ tf_S(k_i) represents the word frequency of k_i k_i in S, $|ST|$ denotes the number of news reports contained in ST and $\delta(k_i)$ δ represents the number of news reports containing k_i k_i in the set ST. sni_i 〖can be obtained in the same way. Our experiments show that when the similarity threshold is set to 0.6, the performance of the emergency tracking algorithm is the best.

Algorithm 1 Emergency Tracking Algorithm

Input: A News Report S, News Report Collection ST
Output: News reports related to S
1. Repeat the following steps until all the news reports in ST are processed.
2. Choose a piece of news report from ST as $N_i(1 \leq i \leq |ST|)$.
3. Establish the vector space models of the news reports' title, assuming that $T\_S = (k_1, sw_1; k_2, sw_2; \dots; k_n, sw_n)$ represents the vector space model of the title of S, and the vector space model of the title of N_i is expressed as:
    $T\_N_i = (k_1, sni_1; k_2, sni_2; \dots; k_n, sni_n)$, where$k_i$ represents the keywords, sw_i and sni_i represent the weight of k_i in S and N_i respectively, which are computed using Equation (1).
4. Calculate the similarity between T_S and T_N_i using Equation (2) and mark the similarity as $\cos(S, N_i)$
5. If $\cos(S, N_i)$ is greater than or equal to the predetermined similarity threshold, then N_i is related to S, otherwise they are irrelevant.

4.2 Multi-strategy Based Information Extraction

Emergency Type Identification. Recognize emergency type precisely is the premise of other information extraction. Because we just focus on emergency-related information, so in order to improve the efficiency of the system, only when an event is judged as an emergency can the relevant information be extracted. In October 2012, the General Administration of Quality Supervision, Inspection and Quarantine and the National

Standardization Management Committee jointly issued the National Standard for Classification and Code of Natural Disasters, which was drafted by the National Disaster Reduction Center of the Civil Affairs Bureau. According to the standard, the natural disasters can by divided into 5 upper categories which include meteorological and hydrological disasters, geological and earthquake disasters, marine disasters, biological disasters and ecological environmental disasters. And these 5 upper natural disasters categories are then divided into 39 lower categories, which include drought, flood, and so on. Besides natural disasters, we add other three kinds of emergencies, which are accident, public health and social security, and then we collect the lower categories for these three emergencies, for example nuclear accident, poisoning and attack etc.

Type identification can be realized by classification method [12, 13] or cluster method [14]. Based on the keywords (emergency names) listed in Table 1, we use the following rules to indentify the emergency type: If one of the above keyword appears in a news report, the news report is considered to belong to the emergency to which the keyword belongs. On the contrary, if there isn't any keyword appears in the news report, the news report doesn't belong to any kind of emergency.

Time Extraction. In general, there are three kinds of time expressions in a news report, which are the time of the event occurred, the time of the event reported, and the time of the news report released. The time of the news report released can be directly obtained through the web crawler. And according to the news report writing specification and style, the time of the event reported is usually mentioned in the first sentence of the news report, so it also can be extracted easily. So, the difficulty of time information extraction is the extraction of the time of the event occurred.

Through the analysis of a large number of news reports, we find that in online news reports, there are usually the following kinds of formats for the time of the event reported, and the time of the news report released:

- YYYY-MM-DD, such as "2018-08-01"
- YYYY/MM/DD, such as "2018/08/01"
- YYYY.MM.DD, such as "2018.08.01"

Based on the above foundation, we use the regular "$\backslash d\{4\}(\backslash-|\backslash.|)\backslash d\{1,2\}\backslash/\backslash d\{1,2\}$" to extract the time of the event reported, and the time of the news report released in this paper, in which the meaning of symbols is shown in Table 1. And the symbols and their meaning are also applicable to the subsequent regulars appearing in this paper.

As mentioned earlier, there are no special fixed formats and rules about the time of the event occurred, and this paper designs the following regulars for its extraction:

$$((num)()) + (time)?((num)(time)) + (time)?$$

where,

num: one, time two, twice, three, four, five, six, seven, eight, nine, ten, 0, 1, 2, 3, 4, 5, 6, 7, 8, 9

time: year, month, day, hour, hour, minute, second, morning, before dawn, a. m, afternoon, evening, night, dusk.

Table 1. The regular expression syntax

Symbol	Meaning
\	Mark a character immediately following "\" as a special character, or as a literal character
*	Match the sub-expression before "*" 0 times or N times, which is equivalent to {0,}
+	Match sub-expressions in front of "+" once or N times, which is equivalent to {1,}
?	Match the sub-expression before "?" 0 times or 1 time, which is equivalent to {0,1}
{x, y}	Match the previous expression at least x times and at most y times
(text)	Match the content of text and get the match, and the brackets can be understood as grouping

Based on the above regulars, we adopt the following method to extract the time of the event occurred: all the time expressions appearing in the news report are extracted based on the above two rules, and then normalized into a unified format; and the earliest time is selected as the occurrence time of the emergency.

Location Extraction. Through analyzing a large number of news reports, we find out that location names usually appear in the following two places in news report:

- News headlines: the locations appearing in news headlines are usually the names of some provinces or municipalities;
- First sentence of news reports: the locations appearing in the first sentence are usually specific to the cities, districts, or counties.

In order to extract the locations, we create the hierarchical structure (provincial, municipal and district) of China administrative area, and use XML structure to store this hierarchy. Then we use the Document Object Model (DOM) to parse the above-mentioned location XML file, the steps are as follows:

- Create the object of DOM tree;
- Create the root node of DOM tree, that is, the national node, and use DOM object to add the root node;
- Use DOM objects to create the sub-nodes at next lower level, i.e. provincial and urban nodes;
- Add the next lower level child node to the object of the parent node to form the parent-child cascade relationship.

Based on the above DOM tree, we use the following method to extract the locations appearing in the news report:

- if the district (county) location name is found in the news report, the corresponding province/city/district (county) name is returned by searching the parent node in the DOM tree;

- if only the city location name is matched, the parent node in the DOM tree is searched, and return the province/city list, the district (county) part is blank;
- if only the provincial level place name is matched, the province list is returned, and the city/district (county) part is blank.

Personnel Casualty Extraction. Unexpected emergency would cause varying degree casualties, slight or serious. This is an important basis for launching different levels of emergency reserve plans. Accurately extracting casualty-related information is essential for emergency scientific decision-making. Through analysis, it is found that in the news reports, the format of casualty-related information is relatively fixed, such as "about 30 people with different degrees of injury", "two workers rescue invalid death". So it is suitable to use rule matching method to extract casualty-related information. To this end, this paper designed the following regular expressions, and the corresponding feature words are shown in Table 2.

    Death: (Degree adverbs)?(Numeral) + (Degree adverbs)?(Numeral)?(Disaster victims)?(Other words)?(Death keywords)

    Injured: (Degree adverbs)?(Numeral) + (Degree adverbs)?(Numeral)?(Disaster victims)?(Other words)?(Injury keywords)

Table 2. The feature vocabulary of casualty-related information extraction rules

Type	Characteristic words
Degree adverbs	about, almost, around, more than, at least......
Numeral	one, two, three, four, five, six, seven, eight, nine, ten, hundred, thousand, ten thousand, 0, 1, 2, 3, 4, 5, 6, 7, 8, 9....
Disaster victims	person, personnel, children, students, teachers, residents, teachers and students, workers, passengers......
Death keywords	dead, death, casualty, wreck, lose life, drowning, be buried, die in An accident, be murdered, suffocation, shoot dead, killing, no sign of life......
Injury keywords	wounded, injuries, serious injuries, minor injuries, infections, traps

The above casualty-related information extraction rules will result in a number of string, such as "One hundred and thirty people are injured, no one is dead". In order to facilitate subsequent statistical analysis, formatting is required to convert Chinese numbers and special words into Arabic numerals. For example, for the above results, "one hundred and thirty" needs to be converted to 130, and "no one" needs to be converted to 0.

Economic Loss Extraction. Emergency would also lead to a certain level of economic loss, which is a very important dimension for the correct assessment of the impact of disasters, and also an important consideration in emergency management. In the Web news report, the format of economic loss is relatively fixed, such as "the affected area is about 5.4 ha" and "the economic loss is 150 million yuan". Similar to the above casualty attribute extraction, this paper extracts economic loss information based on regular matching. The designed rules are as follows, and the corresponding feature vocabulary is shown in Table 3.

(Extent of loss) + (Degree adverbs)?(Numeral) + (\)?(Numeral)?(Degree adverbs)?(Quantifiers) +

Table 3. The feature vocabulary of economic loss information extraction rule

Type	Characteristic words
Degree adverbs	about, almost, around, more than, at least……
Numeral	one, two, three, four, five, six, seven, eight, nine, ten, hundred, thousand, ten thousand, 0, 1, 2, 3, 4, 5, 6, 7, 8, 9….
Extent of loss	economic losses, direct losses, indirect losses, collapsed houses, fields, livestock, poultry, landslides, damaged roads, affected areas, burned areas……
Quantifiers	dollars, yuan, RMB, hectares, square meters, mu, kilometers, households, heads……

5 Experiments and Analysis

5.1 Evaluation Metrics

In this paper, precision and recall are used as evaluation metrics for the results of emergency information extraction. Among them, the precision rate refers to the ratio of the correct amount of data extracted to the total number of extracted data. The recall rate refers to the correct amount of data extracted and the total number in database. The calculation equations for precision and recall are shown in Eq. (3) and Eq. (4), respectively.

$$Precision = \frac{A}{B} \times 100\% \tag{3}$$

$$Recall = \frac{A}{C} \times 100\% \tag{4}$$

Where A is the correct number in the information extraction result, B is the total number of extracted information, and C is the total number in database.

All our experiments are implemented in Python environment within Windows 10 operating system, and the main frequency is 3.3 GHz, memory is 8 GB.

5.2 Experimental Results and Analysis

Firstly, we evaluate our emergency tracking method. In order to evaluate the tracking performance, we randomly select 1,000 news reports from database, and then let three students to mark the emergency included in the each news report. And then, we select randomly 600 news reports from these 1,000 reports as the training corpus, and the other 400 news reports as the evaluation corpus. Based on training, we find that when the similarity threshold is set to 0.6, the performance of the emergency tracking method is best. We use this similarity threshold for the test, and experiments show that the tracking precision and recall are 0.8876 and 0.9023, respectively, which indicates that our proposed tracking method is simple and effective. The result of this experiment is better than that of the traditional topic tracking experiment. We think that this is because the format of emergency news report is more consistent and the news language is more standardized.

Secondly, we evaluate the performance of our method for emergency type identification and information tracking. Again, in order to evaluate, we randomly select 500 news reports from the database, and let three people to mark the emergency type, time, location, casualty and loss for each news report. The evaluation results are shown in Table 4.

Table 4. Experimental results of emergency type identification and information extraction

Information	Theoretical value	Actual value	Correct value	Precision	Recall
Type	500	478	466	0.9748	0.9320
Time	478	478	466	0.9748	0.9748
Location	478	477	341	0.7148	0.7133
Casualty	478	478	470	0.9832	0.9832
Loss	44	40	37	0.9250	0.8409

It can be seen from the results that:

(1) The precision and recall rate of emergency type identification are relatively high, which indicates that the types of keywords collected in this paper are comprehensive and can cover most types of emergency. Through the analysis of the experimental results, it is found that the reason for the identification error is mainly because some news reports contains keywords of cross-type emergencies, especially fire accidents. Some fires are caused by human factors and should belong to "accident disaster", while some others, such as forests fires, are caused by high temperatures and should be classified as "natural disasters", which lead to inaccurate type identification.

(2) The result of time extraction is better, which shows that the method of rule matching can play a very good role because the time expression format in Web news reports is relatively fixed and unified. The reason for the time extraction error is mainly because some related events are sometimes reviewed in the news report, so that

there will be multiple times in the news report other than the time of the current emergency, resulting in the extraction error.

(3) The precision and recall rate of location extraction is low. Based on analysis, it is found that the algorithm of the Chinese word segmentation has certain limitations and cannot identify the location nouns perfectly. For example, it is easy to divide "Xinhuanet" into "Xinhua" and "net", so the location extraction method will extract "Xinhua" as "Xinhua County", which results in extraction error.

(4) Casualty extraction got the highest precision and recall, both 98.32%. The high precision is mainly due to the uniformity of the description of casualty attributes in news reports, while the precision is not 100% mainly because some news reports don't describe casualties directly, such as "the casualty died unfortunately on the way to the hospital", in this case, the use of regular expressions cannot identify and derive a person's death.

(5) The performance of loss information extraction is also better, mainly due to the uniformity of loss description in news reports.

From the above experimental results, we can find that the rule-based information extraction method proposed in this paper is not only simple, but also can achieve good results.

5.3 Results Visualization

In order to display the information extraction results more intuitively, this paper uses E-charts as a tool for visualization. Based on the emergency type identification results of 1,634 news reports, a proportion statistical map of emergency types is obtained which is shown in Fig. 2. According to the identification results, accident disaster and natural disaster accounted for the largest proportion, which are 51% and 39% respectively; the proportions of public health accident and social safety accident are lower, which are 9% and 1%, respectively.

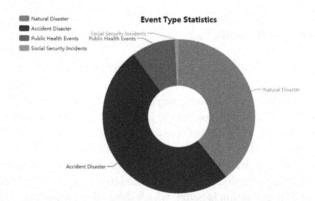

Fig. 2. The proportion chart of different type of emergency

Based on the location recognition results of 1,634 news reports, the statistical pro-portion map of each event type in each province is shown in Fig. 3. As can be seen from the figure, there are regional differences in the proportion of each type of emergency in each province. There are more natural disasters in Xinjiang and Sichuan Province, but more accident disasters in Hebei Province.

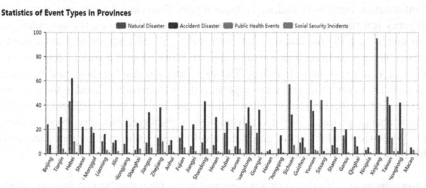

Fig. 3. The statistical charts of the occurrence of each event type in each province

Based on tracking "Taiwan Tourist Car Overturning Accident", the time extraction results and the death toll extraction results, a broken line graph shown in Fig. 4 is obtained. Using the broken line chart, we can see the dynamic changes of the relevant indicators with time more intuitively, which can better assist emergency decision-making.

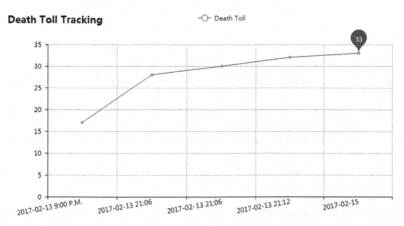

Fig. 4. An example chart of a broken line for tracking the number of deaths

6 Conclusions

In order to meet the high timeliness, comprehensiveness, dynamics and interactivity requirements of emergency management, a new "scenario-response" emergency management model was proposed. Accurate access to emergency-related information is an important dimension in building "scenario-response" emergency management model, and information such as casualties is dynamically changing. To this end, a method for emergency information tracking extraction is proposed. Based on the automatic tracking of emergency, the method first determines the type of emergency, and then extracts information such as time, location, casualty, and loss based on rule matching. Finally, results are displayed using E-charts. The experimental results show that because the news report has certain format when reporting the information related to the emergency, the extraction method based on rule matching can achieve good performance, and the dynamic change process of related information is displayed based on event tracking. It can help decision makers better grasp the development trend of emergency and provide technical support for scientific decision-making.

Acknowledgements. This research was supported by the Shandong Natural Science Foundation Project (No. ZR2021MG038); Special Study on Cultural Tourism of Shandong Social Science Planning (No. 21CLYJ32); 2019 Qingdao Philosophy and Social Science Planning Research Project (No. QDSKL1901124); Shandong Postgraduate Education Quality Improvement Plan (No. SDYJG19075); Shandong Education Teaching Research Key Project (No. 2021JXZ010); Qingdao City Philosophy and Social Science Planning Project (No. QDSKL2001128); National Statistical Science Research Project (No. 2021LY053) and Shandong University of Science and Technology Education and Teaching Research "Stars Plan" Project (No. QX2021M29).

References

1. Shi, W., Wang, H.W., He, S.Y.: Sentiment analysis of Chinese microblogging based on sentiment ontology: a case study of '7.23 Wenzhou Train Collision.' Conn. Sci. **25**(4), 161–178 (2013)
2. Tran, Q.K., Song, S.K.: Learning pattern of hurricane damage levels using semantic web resources. Int. J. Comput. Sci. Eng. **20**(4), 492–500 (2019)
3. Guo, X.Y., He, T.T.: Survey about research on information extraction. Comput. Sci. **42**(2), 14–17 (2015)
4. Brunner, D.: Advanced methods for building information extraction from very high resolution SAR data to support emergency response. Unpublished Ph.D. thesis, University of Trento, UniTrento, Italy (2009)
5. Amailef, K., Lu, J.: Mobile-based emergency response system using ontology-supported information extraction. In: Handbook on Decision, vol. 2, pp. 429–449 (2012). https://doi.org/10.1007/978-3-642-25755-1_21
6. Chen, Z., Zheng, S.: Research on chemical emergency information extraction based on multi algorithm fusion. Comput. Digit. Eng. **46**(2), 264–268 (2018)
7. Michele, B., Michael, J.C., Stephen, S., Matt, B., Oren, E.: Open information extraction from the web. In: Proceedings of the 2007 International Joint Conference on Artificial Intelligence, San Francisco, USA, pp. 2670–2676 (2007)

8. Jiang, D.L.: Research on extraction of emergency event information based on rules matching. Comput. Eng. Des. **31**(14), 3294–3297 (2010)
9. Wang, N., Chen, Y., Guo, W., Zhong, Q.Y., Wang, Y.Z.: A method for emergency case information extraction based on knowledge element. Syst. Eng. **32**(12), 133–139 (2014)
10. Zhao, H., Zhao, T.J., Yu, H., Zheng, D.Q.: English topic tracking research based on query vector. J. Comput. Res. Dev. **44**(8), 1412–1417 (2007)
11. Gu, Y.W., Wang, Y.R., Huan, J., Sun, Y.Q., Xu, S.K.: An improved TFIDF algorithm based on dual parallel adaptive computing model. Int. J. Embed. Syst. **13**(1), 18–27 (2020)
12. Li, X.O., Yu, W.: Imbalanced data classification via support vector machines and genetic algorithms Jair Cervantes. Conn. Sci. **26**(4), 335–348 (2014)
13. Wang, F.F., Liu, Z., Wang, C.D.: An improved kNN text classification method. Int. J. Comput. Sci. Eng. **20**(3), 397–403 (2019)
14. Zhang, D.B., Shou, Y.F., Xu, J.M.: An improved parallel K-means algorithm based on MapReduce. Int. J. Embed. Syst. **9**(3), 275–282 (2017)

Neighborhood Network for Aspect-Based Sentiment Analysis

Huan Liu and Quansheng Dou(✉)

School of Computer Science and Technology, Shandong Technology and Business University,
Yantai 264000, Shandong, China
li_dou@163.com

Abstract. Different aspects of a sentence may contain different sentiments, and sentiment descriptors for a given aspect exist in different places in the sentence, making it difficult to determine its sentiment polarity. Aiming at the above problems, a neighborhood network (Nenet) for aspect-based sentiment analysis is proposed. Firstly, the context information of the text is encoded, and the neighborhood information of the target aspect at the grammar level is extracted by using a graph convolutional neural network. At the same time, the convolutional neural network is used to extract the neighborhood information at the physical level, and the two extracted features are combined to improve the text expression ability. Finally, an attention mechanism is used to express the key information in sentences for judging sentiment polarity, and the final text representation is input to the sentiment analysis layer to predict sentiment polarity. Experiments are carried out on three standard datasets, and the experimental results show that the neighborhood network outperforms other baseline models in both index accuracy and F1 value.

Keywords: Aspect-based sentiment analysis · Sentiment polarity · Neighborhood network · Convolutional neural network · Attention mechanism

1 Introduction

With the development of society and the advancement of technology, social networks have become increasingly prosperous. How to mine the emotions expressed by users from massive text information has become a research hotspot in the field of Natural Language Processing (NLP). Sentiment analysis can be divided into three categories according to the granularity of research objects: document level, sentence level and aspect level. Document-level and sentence-level sentiment analysis take the entire document or specific sentences in the document as the analysis object, and are often used in scenarios such as product evaluation [1] or movie reviews. Aspect-based sentiment analysis (ABSA), also known as fine-grained sentiment analysis, uses the specified words or phrases in the sentence as the analysis object and judges their sentimental polarity in a specific context [2]. For example, in the sentence "The AMD Turin processor seems to always perform so much better than Intel." In terms of goals, the sentiment polarities of "AMD Turin processor" and "Intel" are positive and negative respectively.

Z. Shi et al. (Eds.): IIP 2022, IFIP AICT 643, pp. 216–227, 2022.
https://doi.org/10.1007/978-3-031-03948-5_18

In the past research, many scholars used traditional machine learning methods to solve the problem of text classification. This method manually marks part of the data as a training set, then extracts and learns the characteristics of the data on the training set to build a text classification model, and finally uses the model to predict the unlabeled data, so as to automatically realize text classification [3]. The method based on machine learning has made many achievements in the past research. This method usually depends on complex artificial rules, so the evaluation of model performance depends on the quality of text feature selection.

With the development of deep learning, aspect-based sentiment analysis based on deep neural networks has become the mainstream of research. At present, the commonly used methods are usually based on Long Short-Term Memory Networks (LSTM) [4] and Gated Recursive Unit (GRU) [5] etc. to transfer the information processed in front of the model and use it for subsequent processing. For aspect-based sentiment analysis, the key information that determines its sentiment polarity is often closer to the aspect word, but this type of model cannot effectively capture the neighborhood information of the aspect word.

This paper proposes an aspect-based sentiment analysis neighborhood network (Nenet), which adds an Aspect Neighborhood Information Representation (ANIR) layer after encoding the context of the sentence. The ANIR layer extracts the neighborhood information of the aspect word by adding the relative positional relationship between each word in the sentence and the target aspect word, and constructs a dependency syntax tree to capture the syntactic information between the words in the comment sentence. After the two parts of information being fused, the attention mechanism is used to focus on the key information in the sentence to improve the discriminative performance of the sentiment analysis model. The experimental results are significantly improved on three datasets, among which, on the 14Lap dataset, the accuracy and F1 value of the method are 76.15% and 72.52%, respectively, which are 1.54% and 2.38% higher than the previous model TNet-LF.

2 Related Work

Sentiment analysis is one of the most challenging tasks in the field of natural language processing, which makes it a current hot issue. There are some representative work in the early researches. Vo et al. [6] used sentiment word embeddings and sentiment dictionaries to obtain rich artificial features, and achieved good sentiment classification results on the dataset twitter. Yang et al. [7] used topic models to acquire new words and extended sentiment lexicons based on existing sentiment lexicons, achieving good results on multiple test datasets for sentiment analysis tasks. Reference [8] proposed a new domain-specific sentiment dictionary generation method, and proposed a sentiment analysis framework based on the generated domain-specific sentiment dictionary. The experimental results show that the sentiment analysis framework based on the new dictionary achieves better performance. Most of the early methods were based on emotional dictionaries. However, due to the complex context structure of natural language, it is not easy to build a relatively complete emotion dictionary. At the same time, the emotion dictionary built on one domain data can not be applied to other domains, which restricts the application of these methods in reality.

In recent years, deep learning has been widely used in the field of natural language processing and achieved good results in aspect-based sentiment analysis tasks. Representative work includes: reference [9] proposed a Recurrent Neural Network (RNN) model, which can process sequence data and learn long-term dependencies. RNN considered the relationship between the current output and the previous sequence output, which enabled it to fully learn the information between contextual texts, thereby got better sentence representations and complete sentiment analysis tasks. Therefore, many excellent methods for solving aspect-based sentiment analysis tasks are based on RNNs. Tang et al. [10] proposed Target-Dependent Long Short-Term Memory neural network (TD-LSTM) and Target-Connection Long Short-Term Memory neural network (TC-LSTM). This method associates target aspects with contextual features for aspect-based sentiment analysis, and obtains promising experimental results. Ruder et al. [11] used a Hierarchical Bidirectional Long Short-Term Memory (H-LSTM) network model to model the relationship between words in comment sentences, and proved that the hierarchical model can obtain better results compared with the other two non hierarchical baseline models. This type of model can effectively express the sequence information between words in a sentence, but the sentence is not a simple word stacking, and the key information that affects the sentimental polarity of an aspect is not necessarily the sequence information of all contexts.

In the sentiment analysis task, the attention mechanism is used to extract the key information affecting the sentiment polarity of words in the judgment aspect in the sentence to enhance the expressive ability of the sentence. Ma et al. [12] proposed Interactive Attention Network (IAN), in which two attention networks are used to obtain important features to correctly judge aspect-based sentiment polarity. Reference [13] proposes a Dyadic Memory Networks (DyMemNN) that synthesizes or integrates parameterized neural tensors into memory selection operations to achieve rich binary interactions between aspect words and word embeddings. Experimental results show that the model achieves better performance than other neural architectures on six standard datasets. Lin et al. [14] proposed a Multi-Head Self-Attention Transformation (MSAT) network to solve the target-sensitive sentiment analysis problem, which applies target-specific multi-head self-attention to capture global features and adds target-sensitive transfer to solve the problem. Secondly, part of speech (POS) is added to the model to obtain the part of speech features of words. The experimental results show that compared with other excellent models, the MSAT model obtains good sentiment analysis results. This kind of model can focus on the characteristic information of a given target, so as to improve the classification results. However, because this kind of model based on attention mechanism pays high attention to the target's own information, it can not accurately distinguish the emotional tendency containing implicit emotional information.

In view of the above defects based on the attention mechanism model, Huang et al. [15] used the parametric filter and gate mechanism to incorporate aspect information into the convolution neural network to effectively capture aspect specific features, and proposed a novel parametric convolution neural network model, which achieved excellent results on the data set semeval 2014. Literature [16] proposed a Convolution-based Memory Network (CMN) combined with attention mechanism to capture the word and multi word features in the evaluation sentence, so as to improve the classification results of aspect level emotion analysis model. To solve the problem of context dependence in sentences, Cheng Yan et al. [17] proposed a multi-channel CNN and BiGRU network model based on attention mechanism, which extracted local text information through CNN and fused the semantic features of long text captured by BiGRU to improve the information acquisition ability of the model. The network model based on CNN can effectively extract local features, which is conducive to identifying the emotional features related to the target aspect, but it often ignores the syntactic structure of the sentence.

Based on the inspiration and problems raised above, this paper proposes a neighborhood network for aspect-based sentiment analysis, and its aspect neighborhood information representation layer includes two modules: a physical-level representation module and a syntactic-level representation module. The physical-level features of aspect words are extracted through convolutional neural networks, and the grammatical-level feature representations of aspect words are captured using graph convolutional networks. After fusing the feature information of the two modules, the attention mechanism is used to obtain important information of sentences, and predict the final sentiment analysis result of the sentence. Experimental results showed that the network model improved the ability of sentiment analysis task.

3 Nenet Model

3.1 Neighborhood Network Model Architecture

Let $S = s_1 s_2 \cdots s_n$ represent an arbitrary natural sentence composed of n words, where $s_i, i = 1, 2, \cdots n$ is the i-th word in S, and $T = s_{asp} \cdots s_{asp+m}, m \geq 0$ is the word substring in the sentence S, which is continuous and has a single specific semantics is called Aspect. Let $y \in \{negative, positive, neutral\}$ be the emotional polarity of the predicted target. The low-dimensional embedding of S is denoted as $E = \left[e_1, e_2, \cdots, e_{asp}, \cdots, e_{asp+m}, \cdots, e_{n-1}, e_n\right]$, $e_i \in \mathbb{R}^{dim}$, $E \in \mathbb{R}^{n \times dim}$, where dim is the embedding dimension of the word vector.

As shown from Fig. 1, Nenet is divided into four layers. The first layer is contextual information representation. Because the Bidirectional Gated Recurrent Unit (GRU) model can obtain the contextual dependency information in the sentence as a whole, this layer uses the BiGRU model to represent the contextual information, which is $H = \left[h_1^\tau, h_2^\tau, \cdots, h_n^\tau\right] = BiGRU([e_1, e_2, \cdots, e_n])$.

The second layer is Aspect Neighborhood Information Representation (ANIR) layer.

Through the ANIR layer, you can obtain the neighborhood representation $q = \left[q_1, q_2, \cdots, q_{n-p+1}\right]$ at the aspect physical level and its neighborhood representation $H^K = \left[h_1^K, h_2^K, \cdots, h_{asp}^K, \cdots, h_{asp+m}^K, \cdots, h_{n-1}^K, h_n^K\right]$ at the syntactic level, and perform dot product operation on the two output representations. The calculation method is shown in (1).

$$\lambda_t = \sum_{i=1}^{n} h_i^K q_t \tag{1}$$

The third layer is important information extraction layer, which uses the attention mechanism to extract the important features related to the meaning of aspect words from the hidden state vector, and set the corresponding weight score for each context word accordingly, e.g. Eq. (2) is the calculation method of attention weight, and Eq. (3) is the final prediction expression.

$$\lambda'_t = \frac{\exp(\lambda_t)}{\sum\limits_{i=1}^{n} \exp(\lambda_i)} \tag{2}$$

$$\mathbf{f} = \sum_{t=1}^{n} \lambda'_t \mathbf{h}_t^\tau \tag{3}$$

where, λ'_t is the attention weight in formula (2), and $\mathbf{h}_t^\tau$ represents the encoding output of the first layer of serialized information in formula (3), $\mathbf{f}$ is the final representation of Nenet.

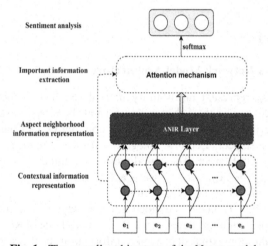

Fig. 1. The overall architecture of the Nenet model.

The fourth layer is sentiment analysis layer. The final text representation is input into the softmax function, as shown in Eq. (4), and the output of the sentiment polarity of the corresponding target in the comment sentence can be obtained.

$$\mathbf{z} = \text{softmax}(\mathbf{W}_z \mathbf{f} + \mathbf{b}_z) \tag{4}$$

where, $\mathbf{W}_z$ represents the weight that can be learned, and $\mathbf{b}_z$ represents the bias.

The above is the overall description of the Nenet structure, the following is a detailed introduction to the aspect neighborhood information representation (ANIR) layer.

3.2 Aspect Neighborhood Information Representation Layer

The distance between the aspect word and the descriptive word in the comment sentence is different. The key information for judging the emotional polarity is the neighborhood information of the aspect word at different levels. In order to solve this problem, this paper designs an aspect neighborhood information representation layer, and the specific structure is shown in Fig. 2.

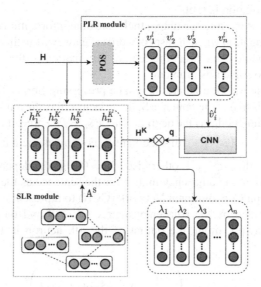

Fig. 2. ANIR layer.

The following is a detailed discussion of the aspect neighborhood information presentation layer, which can be obtained from Fig. 2. The ANIR layer includes a Physical Level Representation (PLR) module and a Syntax Level Representation (SLR) module.

The PLR module of this article first adds the position information of other words in the sentence relative to the aspect word, and then use the CNN module to extract the feature information at the physical level of the aspect word, as shown in Eqs. (5) and (6). Among them, $\mathbf{h}_i^l$ is the output representation after encoding of the BiGRU model, and $\mathbf{v}_i^l$ is the feature vector representation after adding position information.

$$u_i = \begin{cases} \dfrac{n - asp + i}{n} & 1 \leq i < asp \\ 0 & asp \leq i \leq asp + m \\ \dfrac{n - i + asp + m}{n} & asp + m < i \leq n \end{cases} \tag{5}$$

$$\mathbf{v}_i^l = u_i * \mathbf{h}_i^l, \ i \in [1, n] \tag{6}$$

After obtaining the relative position coding of aspect word and context word, the article uses CNN to further extract feature information, as shown in Eq. (7):

$$q_i = \delta\left(\mathbf{w}^\mathrm{T} \hat{\mathbf{v}}^l_{i:i+p-1} + \mathbf{b}\right) \tag{7}$$

In Eq. (7), $\hat{\mathbf{v}}^l_{i:i+p-1} \in \mathbb{R}^{p \cdot \dim_h}$ is the connection matrix of $\mathbf{v}^l_i, \cdots, \mathbf{v}^l_{i+p-1}$, p is the size of the kernel, $\delta(\cdot)$ is a nonlinear function, $\mathbf{w}^\mathrm{T} \in \mathbb{R}^{p \cdot \dim_h}$ and $\mathbf{b} \in \mathbb{R}$ are the learnable weights of the convolution kernel.

Although the PLR module can obtain the contextual information of the aspect word, it cannot solve the situation when the aspect word is far away from the relative description word. The SLR module can extract the feature information of the aspect words at the grammatical level to solve this problem.

The SLR module uses the natural language processing library Spacy to obtain the grammatical analysis tree of the sentence S. In the syntax tree, the number d_i of connected edges of corresponding nodes is the degree of node s_i, By the tree, it is easy to obtain the adjacency matrix $\mathbf{A}^S = \left(a^S_{i,j}\right)_{n \times n}$ of statement S. For any element $a^S_{i,j}$ in A, if node i is connected to node j, then $a^S_{i,j} = 1$, otherwise $a^S_{i,j} = 0$. Use the dependent syntax tree to generate the corresponding adjacency matrix for the sentence as the input of SLR, and use the L-layer Graph Convolutional Network (GCN) to represent non-Euclidean data.

GCN is represented by the adjacency matrix $\mathbf{A}^S$ of S and the output of BiGRU encoding as the network input, the output of the i-th neuron in the k + 1 layer is determined by Eq. (8):

$$\mathbf{h}^{k+1}_i = \varphi\left(\frac{1}{d_i + 1}\sum_{j=1}^{n}\mathbf{A}^S\mathbf{W}^k\mathbf{h}^k_j + \mathbf{b}^k\right) \tag{8}$$

Where $\mathbf{W}^k$ is the parameter matrix, $\mathbf{h}^k_j$ is the output representation of the j-th neuron in the k-th layer, and $\mathbf{b}^k$ is the corresponding bias. $\varphi(\cdot)$ is a nonlinear activation function. $\mathbf{h}^0_i$ represents the initial state of the i-th node, which is the output of the first context presentation layer. For layer K GCN, $k \in [1, 2, 3, \cdots, K]$, $\mathbf{h}^K_i$ is the final state of the i-th node.

As mentioned above, ANIR can extract the neighborhood information of a given aspect word in the text at different levels, aiming to improve the performance of the aspect-based sentiment analysis model.

4   Experiment Analysis

4.1   Dataset

Nenet was tested on three public datasets, where 14Lap and 14Rest were from SemEv-al 2014 task 4 [18], and the third is Twitter dataset [19]. These datasets are mainly used for fine-grained sentiment analysis, and can be roughly divided into three types of user comment data, as shown in Table 1, showing the statistics of these three datasets.

Table 1. The distribution of samples on the benchmark dataset by category labels.

Dataset	Positive		Neutral		Negative	
	Train	Test	Train	Test	Train	Test
14Rest	2163	725	637	195	805	196
14Lap	993	340	462	169	868	127
Twitter	1560	173	3122	343	1559	170

4.2 Parameter Setting and Evaluation Index

In this paper, the 300d GloVe [20] pretraining model is used to initialize the word embedding. and the experimental parameter settings are shown in Table 2.

Table 2. Parameter setting.

Parameter	Value
embed-dim	300
num-epoch	50
batch-size	32
d	0.6
lr	0.001

It can be seen from Table 2 that the dimension of the hidden state vector is set to 300. The batch size is set to 32. In this paper, the dropout layer loss rate is set to 0.6, Adam is used to optimizing the model, and the learning rate is 0.001. Set the epoch to 50, and perform the same experiment 5 times under random initialization. According to the results of the experiment report on the testset all indexes of average maximum.

Dropout Parameter Selection and Analysis. In this paper, the influence of dropout loss rate $d \in \{0.1, 0.2, \cdots 0.9\}$ on accuracy and F1 value is studied, and experiments are carried out on dataset 14Rest. The experimental results are shown in Fig. 3. when the value of d is 0.6, the accuracy and F1 value obtain the optimal value, because when the value of d is 0.6, the dropout can randomly generate the most network structures.

GCN Layer Number Setting Analysis. GCN layer parameter setting is important which affects the performance of the model. To study the impact of GCN layers on sentiment analysis tasks, the accuracy and F1 value are used as evaluation indicators to determine the reasonable number of layers in the Nenet of GCN in the article. The experimental results are shown in Fig. 4. The number of layers of GCN in the experimental setting ranges from 1 to 8. When k is 3, the two kinds of datasets reach the maximum in index accuracy and F1 value, and Nenet obtains the best performance.

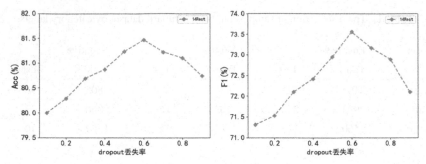

Fig. 3. The effect of dropout loss rate on the accuracy and F1 value on the dataset 14Rest.

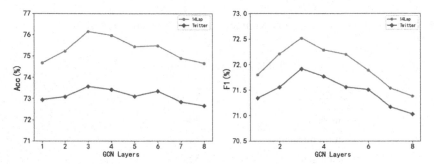

Fig. 4. The number of GCN layers has an impact on the accuracy and F1 value on the dataset 14Lap and Twitter.

4.3   Experimental Results and Analysis

This paper uses cross-entropy as the loss function of Nenet training. The ablation on three datasets and comparative experiments and analysis are carried out to verify the effectiveness of the proposed method, the results as stated below.

Ablation Experiment and Analysis. In order to verify the effectiveness of each component in Nenet for sentiment analysis tasks, this paper conducts corresponding ablation experiments on three datasets, and the results are shown in Table 3.

It can be seen from Table 3 that in the absence of any part, the Acc and F1 values of Nenet will decrease significantly on these three datasets. For the model being removed of the ANIR layer, the Acc and F1 values on the dataset 14Lap are 71.83% and 67.16% respectively, which is 4.32% and 5.36% lower than the Acc and F1 values of the Nenet model, respectively. It shows that adding the ANIR layer can better encode sentences and improve the experimental results of the emotion analysis task in the accuracy of the evaluation index and F1 value. For the model being removed of the PLR module and the model with the SLR module deleted, the accuracy and F1 value decreased to a certain extent compared with the Nenet model, which shows that the two modules in this method can enhance the text expression ability and improve the classification ability of the model.

Table 3. Comparison of ablation model accuracy and F1 value on three datasets. (Unit: %)

Model	14Rest		14Lap		Twitter	
	Acc	F1	Acc	F1	Acc	F1
Nenet	81.47	73.56	76.15	72.52	73.57	71.92
ANIR	80.45	70.50	71.83	67.16	71.76	70.47
-PLR	81.06	72.13	76.03	72.11	73.12	71.32
-SLR	81.13	72.21	75.11	70.89	72.63	71.01

Comparative Experiment and Analysis. In the experiments of sentiment analysis tasks on three different datasets, the baseline model listed below is compared with the Nenet proposed in this paper, and the accuracy and F1 value are used as evaluation indicators. The experimental results are shown in Table 4.

Table 4. Comparison results of different models on three datasets. (Unit: %)

Model	14Rest		14Lap		Twitter	
	Acc	F1	Acc	F1	Acc	F1
ATAE-LSTM	77.20	–	68.70	–	–	–
MemNet	79.61	69.64	70.64	65.17	71.48	69.90
IAN	79.26	70.09	72.05	67.38	72.50	70.81
TNet-LF	80.42	71.03	74.61	70.14	72.98	71.43
TransCap	78.84	69.70	72.65	68.77	–	–
Nenet	81.47	73.56	76.15	72.52	73.57	71.92

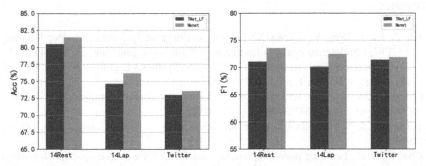

Fig. 5. On the different datasets, the accuracy and F1 value of the Nenet model are higher than that of the TNet-LF model.

The baseline model is as follows: (1) ATAE-LSTM [21] model is an attention-based LSTM for aspect-level sentiment analysis, where the attention mechanism can focus on different parts of the sentence when aspect words are used as input. (2) MemNet [22] introduces a deep memory network to implement an attention mechanism to learn the correlation between context words and aspects. (3) IAN [12] uses LSTM to represent aspects and contexts and uses attention mechanisms for aspects and contexts to capture important feature information. (4) TNet-LF [23] implements a Context-Preserving Transformation (CPT) mechanism to obtain the word representation of a specific aspect. (5) TransCap [24] network model encapsulates the semantic information in the sentence into a semantic capsule, and uses the semantic capsule to couple with the class capsule to implement aspect-based sentiment analysis.

It can be seen from Table 4 and Fig. 5 that the accuracy and F1 value of the Nenet model proposed in this paper on the three datasets are significantly higher than those of other models, and the accuracy and F1 value on the dataset 14Rest are 1.05 and 2.53 percentage points higher than that of the TNet-LF model. The above shows that the aspect neighborhood information extracted by Nenet and the grammatical dependence of sentences can improve the results of aspect sentiment analysis.

5   Conclusion and Further Work

In the sentiment analysis tasks, ignoring the neighborhood features of aspect words at different levels can lead to misjudgment of sentiment polarity. To solve the above problems, this paper proposes a neighborhood network for aspect-based sentiment analysis, and designs an aspect neighborhood feature representation layer to extract aspect neighborhood information from both physical and syntactic levels to improve the overall performance of the model. Experiments on three public datasets show that the Nenet model can effectively improve the results of sentiment analysis tasks. In future work, sentiment analysis in specific fields can be studied to meet the needs of sentiment analysis in different scenarios.

References

1. Hu, Z., Hu, J., Ding, W., Zheng, X.: Review sentiment analysis based on deep learning. In: 2015 IEEE 12th International Conference on e-Business Engineering, pp. 87–94 (2015)
2. Liu, B.: Sentiment Analysis and Opinion Mining. Synthesis Lectures on Human Language Technologies, vol. 5, no. 1, pp. 1–167 (2012)
3. Giachanou, A., Crestani, F.: Like it or not: a survey of twitter sentiment analysis methods. ACM Comput. Surv. (CSUR) **49**(2), 1–41 (2016)
4. Hochreiter, S., Schmidhuber, J.: Long short-term memory. Neural Comput. **9**(8), 1735–1780 (1997)
5. Cho, K., et al.: Learning phrase representations using RNN encoder-decoder for statistical machine translation. arXiv preprint arXiv:1406.1078 (2014)
6. Vo, D., Zhang, Y.: Target-dependent twitter sentiment classification with rich automatic features. AAAI Press (2015)
7. Chen, L., Yang, Y.: Emotional speaker recognition based on i-vector through Atom Aligned Sparse Representation. In: 2013 IEEE International Conference on Acoustics, Speech and Signal Processing, pp. 7760–7764. IEEE (2013)

8. Han, H., Zhang, J., Yang, J., Shen, Y., Zhang, Y.: Generate domain-specific sentiment lexicon for review sentiment analysis. Multimedia Tools Appl. **77**(16), 21265–21280 (2018). https://doi.org/10.1007/s11042-017-5529-5
9. Mikolov, T., Karafiát, M., Burget, L., Cernocký, J., Khudanpur, S.: Recurrent neural network-based language model. In: Interspeech, pp. 1045–1048 (2010)
10. Tang, D., Qin, B., Feng, X., Liu, T.: Effective LSTMs for target-dependent sentiment classification. In: Proceedings of COLING 2016, the 26th International Conference on Computational Linguistics: Technical Papers, pp. 3298–3307 (2016)
11. Ruder, S., Ghaffari, P., Breslin, J.G.: A hierarchical model of reviews for aspect-based sentiment analysis. In: Proceedings of the 2016 Conference on Empirical Methods in Natural Language Processing, pp. 999–1005 (2016)
12. Ma, D., Li, S., Zhang, X., Wang, H.: Interactive attention networks for aspect-level sentiment classification. In: IJCAI 2017 Proceedings of the 26th International Joint Conference on Artificial Intelligence, pp. 4068–4074 (2017)
13. Tay, Y., Tuan, L.A., Hui, S.C.: Dyadic memory networks for aspect-based sentiment analysis. In: Proceedings of the 2017 ACM on Conference on Information and Knowledge Management, pp. 107–116 (2017)
14. Lin, Y., Wang, C., Song, H., et al.: Multi-head self-attention transformation networks for aspect-based sentiment analysis. IEEE Access **9**, 8762–8770 (2021)
15. Huang, B., Carley, K.: Parameterized convolutional neural networks for aspect level sentiment classification. In: Proceedings of the 2018 Conference on Empirical Methods in Natural Language Processing, pp. 1091–1096. Association for Computational Linguistics, Brussels (2018)
16. Fan, C., Gao, Q., Du, J., et al.: Convolution-based memory network for aspect-based sentiment analysis. In: The 41st International ACM SIGIR Conference on Research & Development In Information Retrieval, pp. 1161–1164. ACM, New York (2018)
17. Yan, C., Leibo, Y., Guanghe, Z., et al.: Text sentiment orientation analysis of multi-channels CNN and BIGRU based on attention mechanism. J. Comput. Res. Dev. **57**(12), 2583–2595 (2020)
18. Pontiki, M., Galanis, D., Pavlopoulos, J., et al.: SemEval-2014 Task 4: aspect based sentiment analysis. In: Proceedings of the 8th International Workshop on Semantic Evaluation (SemEval 2014), pp. 27–35 (2014)
19. Dong, L., Wei, F., Tan, C., et al.: Adaptive recursive neural network for target-dependent twitter sentiment classification. In: Proceedings of the 52nd Annual Meeting of the Association for Computational Linguistics, pp. 49–54 (2014)
20. Pennington, J., Socher, R., Manning, C.D.: GloVe: global vectors for word representation. In: Proceedings of the 2014 Conference on Empirical Methods in Natural Language Processing (EMNLP), pp. 1532–1543 (2014)
21. Wang, Y., Huang, M., Zhu, X., Zhao, L.: Attention-based LSTM for aspect-level sentiment classification. In: Proceedings of the 2016 Conference on Empirical Methods in Natural Language Processing, pp. 606–615(2016)
22. Tang, D., Qin, B., Liu, T.: Aspect level sentiment classification with deep memory network. In: Proceedings of the 2016 Conference on Empirical Methods in Natural Language Processing, pp. 214–224 (2016)
23. Li, X., Bing, L., Lam, W., Shi, B.: Transformation networks for target-oriented sentiment classification. In: Proceedings of the 56th Annual Meeting of the Association for Computational Linguistics, pp. 946–956 (2018)
24. Chen, Z., Qian, T.: Transfer capsule network for aspect level sentiment classification. In: Proceedings of the 57th Annual Meeting of the Association for Computational Linguistics, pp. 547–556 (2019)

A Hybrid Parallel Algorithm
With Multiple Improved Strategies

Tingting Wang[1], Jeng-Shyang Pan[1,2], Pei-Cheng Song[1],
and Shu-Chuan Chu[1,3(✉)]

[1] College of Computer Science and Engineering,
Shandong University of Science and Technology, Qingdao, China
scchu0803@gmail.com
[2] Department of Information Management, Chaoyang University of Technology,
Taichung, Taiwan
[3] College of Science and Engineering, Flinders University, Bedford Park, Australia

Abstract. This paper proposes a novel hybrid parallel algorithm with multiple improved strategies. The whole population is divided into three subpopulations and each sub-population executes butterfly optimization algorithm, grey wolf optimization algorithm, and marine predator algorithm respectively. Meanwhile, they share information through three different communication strategies. And in order to improve the performance of the algorithm, the text uses the cubic chaotic mapping mechanism in the initialization stage. At the same time, the idea of adaptive parameter strategy is also introduced, so that some hyperparameters are changed along with the iteration. The results show that the algorithm can provide very competitive results, and is superior to the best algorithm in the literature on most test functions.

Keywords: Parallel · Cubic chaotic mapping · Adaptive parameter

1 Introduction

In recent years, in order to solve a variety of practical problems, a large number of meta heuristic algorithms have been proposed one after another. [21] and [1] use particle swarm optimization (PSO) [8,19,34] to find the best deployment of a group of sensors in the monitoring area to achieve the best coverage of the network [4,17,38]. [11] and [30] use quasi affine transformation evolutionary algorithm (Quatre) [24,25,35]. And an improved binary pigeon inspired optimization algorithm (PIO) [10,12,16] to solve the feature selection problem. Pan et al. [29] improved the states of matter search (SMS) [9,20,27] algorithm that hides the watermark in QR code [18,23,37]. Based on fractional micro product theory, an improved fish migration optimization (FMO) [15,31] is proposed to adjust PID controller [22,33,36]. There are many such examples, such as butterfly optimization algorithm (BOA) [5–7,39], grey wolf optimization algorithm (GWO) [13,26,28,32], and marine predator algorithm (MPA) [2,3,14] are also

© IFIP International Federation for Information Processing 2022
Published by Springer Nature Switzerland AG 2022
Z. Shi et al. (Eds.): IIP 2022, IFIP AICT 643, pp. 228–242, 2022.
https://doi.org/10.1007/978-3-031-03948-5_19

three commonly used intelligent optimization algorithms. The three algorithms are easy to implement in code and have achieved good results in test function, but there is still room for improvement. Therefore, we consider proposing a new algorithm combining the advantages of the three algorithms. The major contributions of this paper are as follows:

1. A population initialization method based on cubic chaotic mapping is proposed to replace the pseudo-random number generator to generate chaotic numbers between 0 and 1.
2. A parameter adaptive method is proposed to make the parameter setting more reasonable for the solution of the optimal value.
3. A parallel strategy combining three communication strategy is proposed to make the algorithm find the optimal solution more quickly and accurately.

The rest of the paper is arranged as follows. In the Sect. 2, we will briefly review the butterfly optimization algorithm, grey wolf algorithm and marine predator algorithm. Then, in Sect. 3, we will first describe the concepts of cubic chaotic mapping and adaptive parameter method and then describe how to combine parallel and cubic chaotic mapping and adaptive parameter strategies with three optimization algorithms to improve the performance of the proposed algorithm. The simulation experiment description and experimental results of the improved algorithm based on three improvement strategies will be displayed in the Sect. 4. In Sect. 5, we will summarize the paper.

2   Related Works

2.1   Butterfly Optimization Algorithm

The algorithm represents a solution in terms of the position of a butterfly and divides the process into three phases. The first phase of the algorithm initializes the position of each butterfly and gives the values of the required hyperparameters in the algorithm. Then the algorithm enters the loop iteration phase.

In this phase, the algorithm divides the evolutionary pattern of the population into two parts, global search and local search, according to the given threshold p area. In the global search mode, the positions of the butterflies are updated according to Eq. 1.

$$x_i^{t+1} = x_i^t + (r^2 \times g^* - x_i^t) \times f_i \tag{1}$$

where x_i^t denotes the position of the ith butterfly at the tth iteration, g^* denotes the global optimal solution that can be found so far, r is a random number belonging to the interval 0 to 1, and f_i denotes the odor produced by the ith butterfly and also the fitness of the ith solution,which is calculated using Eq. 2.

$$f = cI^a \tag{2}$$

In the local search mode, the position of butterfly i in the $(t+1)$th generation is determined using Eq. 3.

$$x_i^{t+1} = x_i^t + (r^2 \times x_j^t - x_k^t) \times f_i \tag{3}$$

where x_j and x_k are two different individuals in the population distinguished from x_i. The global search mode is switched with the local search mode by switching probability p. The threshold p is set a priori at the initialized individual.

The third stage is used to determine whether the algorithm satisfies the termination condition. If the algorithm satisfies the termination condition, the optimal value is returned. Otherwise, the loop iteration stage continues.

The above is the content of the butterfly optimization algorithm.

2.2   Grey Wolf Optimizer

Grey Wolf Optimizer (GWO) is a novel population intelligence optimization algorithm that simulates the social hierarchy and hunting behavior of the grey wolf population in nature.

In this algorithm, the social hierarchy of grey wolves can be divided into four levels:alpha wolf α, subordinate wolf β, common wolf δ and bottom wolf ω. Among them, α is responsible for leading the wolf pack, β assists α in making decisions, δ follows the instructions of α and β, and can also command the bottom individual ω. α, β and δ in the grey wolf optimization algorithm denote the historical optimal solution, the suboptimal solution and the third optimal solution, respectively, and ω denotes the remaining individuals.

When a prey is found, the iteration begins.There are mainly the best three wolves in each generation of the population (i.e. the three best solutions in the population) to guide the completion. The mathematical model of the behavior of the grey wolf, which gradually approaches the prey and encircles it when it lets the prey go, is represented in Eq. 4 to Eq. 8.

$$\vec{D} = \left| \vec{C} \cdot \overrightarrow{X_p(t)} - \overrightarrow{X(t)} \right| \tag{4}$$

$$\overrightarrow{X(t+1)} = \overrightarrow{X_p(t)} - \vec{A} \cdot \vec{D} \tag{5}$$

$$\vec{A} = 2\vec{a} \cdot \vec{r_1} - \vec{a} \tag{6}$$

$$\vec{C} = 2 \cdot \vec{r_2} \tag{7}$$

$$\vec{a} = 2 - \frac{2t}{t_{max}} \tag{8}$$

where t is the round of the current iteration, $\vec{X}$ is the position vector of the gray wolf, and the vector $\overrightarrow{X_p}$ represents the current position of the prey. $\vec{A}$ and $\vec{C}$ are the coefficient vectors. Eq. 6 and Eq. 7 give the calculation methods of $\vec{A}$ and $\vec{C}$. $\vec{a}$ is the convergence factor, and $\vec{r}_1$ and $\vec{r}_2$ obey a uniform distribution between $[0, 1]$ as the number of iterations decreases linearly from 2 to 0.

For simulating the search behavior of grey wolves(candidate solutions), during every iteration, the best three grey wolves (α, β, δ) in the present population are reserved, and then the locations of other search agents (including ω) are updated on the basis of their location information. We use Eq. 9 to Eq. 11 to simulate this behavior.

$$\begin{cases} \vec{D_\alpha} = |\vec{C_1} \cdot \vec{X_\alpha} - \vec{X}| \\ \vec{D_\beta} = |\vec{C_2} \cdot \vec{X_\beta} - \vec{X}| \\ \vec{D_\delta} = |\vec{C_3} \cdot \vec{X_\delta} - \vec{X}| \end{cases} \tag{9}$$

$$\begin{cases} \vec{X_1} = \vec{X_\alpha} - \vec{A_1} \cdot \vec{D_\alpha} \\ \vec{X_2} = \vec{X_\beta} - \vec{A_2} \cdot \vec{D_\beta} \\ \vec{X_3} = \vec{X_\omega} - \vec{A_3} \cdot \vec{D_\omega} \end{cases} \tag{10}$$

$$\overrightarrow{X(t+1)} = \frac{\vec{X_1} + \vec{X_2} + \vec{X_3}}{3} \tag{11}$$

Where, D_α, D_β and D_δ respectively represent α, β and δ distance from other individuals. X_α, X_β, X_δ respectively represent the current location of the α, β and δ. $\vec{C_1}$, $\vec{C_2}$ and $\vec{C_3}$ are vectors which elements are composed of random numbers, and X is the current grey wolf position. When $|\vec{A}| > 1$, the algorithm enters the global optimization stage, which also means that ω wolves will escape prey and explore more space. When $|\vec{A}| < 1$, the grey wolf will concentrate on the prey in one or some areas.

2.3   Marine Predator Algorithm

Marine predator algorithm was proposed by Afshin et al. in 2020. The algorithm simulates the process of catching prey by marine predators.

The marine predator algorithm begins with a random number evenly distributed in the search space. It is expressed by mathematical formula as Eq. 12:

$$X_0 = X_{min} + rand \times (X_{max} - X_{min}) \tag{12}$$

Where X_{min} and X_{max} represent the lower and upper boundaries of the population, and $rand$ represents a random number which the range of is $[0, 1]$. Finally, the d-dimensional population position matrix of n individuals is obtained, called the prey matrix:

$$\begin{bmatrix} X_{1,1} & X_{1,2} & \cdots & X_{1,d} \\ X_{2,1} & X_{2,2} & \cdots & X_{2,d} \\ \cdots & \cdots & \cdots & \cdots \\ \vdots & \vdots & \vdots & \vdots \\ X_{n,1} & X_{n,2} & X_{n,3} & X_{n,d} \end{bmatrix} \tag{13}$$

where $X_{i,j}$ describes the jth dimension for the ith prey. Then, for each individual $X_i = [X_{i1}, X_{i2}, ..., X_{id}]$, calculate its fitness, and then use the individual X_i with the best fitness to copy n copies to form the elite matrix:

$$
\begin{bmatrix}
X_{1,1}^1 & X_{1,2}^1 & \cdots & X_{1,d}^1 \\
X_{2,1}^1 & X_{2,2}^1 & \cdots & X_{2,d}^1 \\
\cdots & \cdots & \cdots & \cdots \\
\vdots & \vdots & \vdots & \vdots \\
X_{n,1}^1 & X_{n,2}^1 & X_{n,3}^1 & X_{n,d}^1
\end{bmatrix}
\tag{14}
$$

where d represents the dimension, X^1 represents the optimal predator vector with n simulation agents to bring the matrix, which is called *Elite*.

Then we began to optimize. There are three steps in the optimization process.

The step 1 (When the number of iterations is less than one third of the maximum number of iterations):

$$
\overrightarrow{stepsize_i} = \overrightarrow{R_B} \bigotimes (\overrightarrow{Elite_i} - \overrightarrow{R_B} \bigotimes \overrightarrow{P_i}), i = 1, 2, 3, ..., n \tag{15}
$$

$$
\overrightarrow{P_i} = \overrightarrow{P_i} + P \times \overrightarrow{R} \bigotimes \overrightarrow{stepsize_i} \tag{16}
$$

Where $\overrightarrow{stepsize_i}$ represents the moving step size, and $\overrightarrow{R_B}$ is a vector composed of random numbers which is generated by Brownian random walk. P is a constant with a value of 0.5. R is a vector of random number which is subject to a uniform distribution between 0 and 1, and its dimension is d. $\overrightarrow{R_B}$ is equivalent to the generalized Gaussian distribution. Each element $\overrightarrow{R_{Bi}}$ can be calculated by the following expression:

$$
R_{Bi} = \frac{1}{\sqrt{2\pi}} e^{-\frac{x^2}{2}} \tag{17}
$$

The step 2 (When the number of iterations is greater than one-third and less than two-thirds of the maximum number of iterations). The new rules for the first half of the population are as follows:

$$
\overrightarrow{stepsize_i} = \overrightarrow{R_L} \bigotimes (\overrightarrow{Elite_i} - \overrightarrow{R_L} \bigotimes \overrightarrow{P_i}), i = 1, 2, 3, ..., \frac{n}{2} \tag{18}
$$

$$
\overrightarrow{P_i} = \overrightarrow{P_i} + P \times \overrightarrow{R} \bigotimes \overrightarrow{stepsize_i} \tag{19}
$$

where $\overrightarrow{R_L}$ describes a random value that is distributed by the Lévy movement. Each element $\overrightarrow{R_{Li}}$ of $\overrightarrow{R_L}$ can be calculated from the following formula:

$$
R_{Li} = C \times \frac{x}{y^{\frac{1}{a}}} \tag{20}
$$

$$
x = Normal(0, \sigma_x^2) \tag{21}
$$

$$
y = Normal(0, \sigma_y^2) \tag{22}
$$

$$\sigma_x = [\frac{\Gamma(1+\alpha)sin(\frac{\pi\alpha}{2})}{\Gamma(\frac{1+\alpha}{2})\alpha2^{\frac{\alpha-1}{2}}}]^{\frac{1}{\alpha}} \tag{23}$$

$$\sigma_y = 1 \tag{24}$$

$$\alpha = 1.5 \tag{25}$$

Where, the value of C is 0.05 and the value of a is 1.5, the value of x and y are represented by the Eq. 21 and Eq. 22. The new rules for the second half of the population are as follows:

$$\overrightarrow{stepsize_i} = \overrightarrow{R_B} \bigotimes (\overrightarrow{Elitem_i} - \overrightarrow{R_B} \bigotimes \overrightarrow{P_i}), i = 1, 2, 3, ..., \frac{n}{2} \tag{26}$$

$$\overrightarrow{P_i} = \overrightarrow{Elitem_i} + P \times CF \bigotimes \overrightarrow{stepsize_i} \tag{27}$$

$$CF = (1 - \frac{iteration}{Maxiteration})^{\frac{2 \times iteration}{Maxiteration}} \tag{28}$$

The step 3 (When the number of iterations is greater than two-thirds of the maximum number of iterations):

In this stage, the population update rules are as follows:

$$\overrightarrow{stepsize_i} = \overrightarrow{R_L} \bigotimes (\overrightarrow{R_L} \bigotimes \overrightarrow{Elitem_i} - \overrightarrow{P_i}), i = 1, 2, 3, ..., n \tag{29}$$

$$\overrightarrow{P_i} = \overrightarrow{Elitem_i} + P \times CF \bigotimes \overrightarrow{stepsize_i} \tag{30}$$

Fish aggregation devices (FADS) or eddy current effect usually change the foraging behavior of marine predators. Hence, in order to avoid the algorithm falling into local optimization, jump operation is added in the paper. This is formulated as follows:

$$\begin{cases} \overrightarrow{P_i} = \overrightarrow{P_i} + CF[X_{min} + \overrightarrow{R_L} \bigotimes (X_{max} - X_{min})] \bigotimes \overrightarrow{U} \quad r \le FADs \\ \overrightarrow{P_i} + [FADs(1-r) + r](\overrightarrow{P_{r_1}} - \overrightarrow{P_{r_2}})r > FADs \end{cases} \tag{31}$$

where the (FADs) is the influence probability, taken as 0.2. U is the binary vector. r is the random value within $[0, 1]$. r_1, r_2 are the random indices of the prey matrix, respectively. The lower and upper bounds of a dimension are represented by X_{min} and X_{max}.

3   Our Proposed Hybrid Parallel Algorithm with Multiple Improved Strategies

In this section, we propose a hybrid algorithm called ACHBGM that combines the advantages of the butterfly optimization algorithm, the grey wolf optimization algorithm, and the marine predator optimization algorithm, and incorporates the idea of parallel mechanisms. At the same time, for improving the performance of the algorithm, we use cubic chaotic mapping in the initialization stage. In the iterative stage, some hyperparameters used in the algorithm are adaptively improved. The specific three strategies are as follows.

Table 1. The test function we use.

Function	Example	Range	f_{min}
F1	$\sum_{i=1}^{Dim} x_i^2$	$[-100, 100]$	0
F2	$\sum_{i=1}^{Dim} |x_i| + \prod_{i=1}^{Dim} |x_i|$	$[-10, 10]$	0
F3	$\sum_{i=1}^{Dim} (\sum_{j=1}^{i} x_j)^2$	$[-100, 100]$	0
F4	$\max\{|x_i|, 1 \le i \le Dim\}$	$[-10, 10]$	0
F5	$\sum_{i=1}^{Dim} (x_i + 0.5)^2$	$[-10, 10]$	0
F6	$\sum_{i=1}^{Dim} Dim \cdot x_i^2 + rand(0,1)$	$[-1.28, 1.28]$	0
F7	$\exp(0.5 \sum_{i=1}^{Dim} x_i)$	$[-10, 10]$	0
F8	$\sum_{i=1}^{Dim} |x_i|^{(i+1)}$	$[-1, 1]$	0
F9	$\sum_{i=1}^{Dim} (Dim \cdot x_i^2)$	$[-10, 10]$	0
F10	$\sum_{i=1}^{Dim} (100(x_{i+1} + x_i^2) + (x_i - 1)^2)$	$[-5, 10]$	0
F11	$\sum_{i=1}^{Dim} x_i^2 + (\sum_{i=1}^{Dim} 0.5ix_i)^2 + (\sum_{i=1}^{Dim} 0.5ix_i)^4$	$[-5, 10]$	0
F12	$(x_i - 1)^2 + \sum_{i=1}^{Dim} i \cdot (2x_i^2 - x_{i-1})^2$	$[-10, 10]$	0
F13	$\sum_{i=1}^{Dim} (10^6)^{(i-1)/(Dim-1)} \cdot x_i^2$	$[-100, 100]$	0
F14	$x_1^2 + 10^6 \sum_{i=2}^{Dim} x_i^2$	$[-100, 100]$	0
F15	$\sum_{i=1}^{Dim} [x_i^2 - 10cos(2\pi x_i) + 10]$	$[-5.12, 5.12]$	0
F16	$\sum_{i=1}^{Dim} [y_i^2 - 10cos(2\pi y_i) + 10]$	$[-5.12, 5.12]$	0
-	$y_i = \begin{cases} x_i, & |x_i| < 0.5 \\ round(2x_i)/2, & |x_i| > 0.5 \end{cases}$	000	0
F17	$-20\exp(-0.2\sqrt{\frac{1}{Dim}\sum_{i=1}^{Dim} x_i^2}) + \exp(\frac{1}{Dim} \sum_{i=1}^{Dim} cos(2\pi x_i)) + 20 + exp(1)$	$[-50, 50]$	0
F18	$\frac{1}{4000}\sum_{i=1}^{Dim} x_i^2 - \prod_{i=1}^{Dim} cos(\frac{x_i}{\sqrt{i}}) + 1$	$[-600, 600]$	0
F19	$\sum_{i=1}^{Dim} |x_i \cdot sin(x_i) + 0.1x_i|$	$[-10, 10]$	0
F20	$\frac{\pi}{Dim}\{\sum_{i=1}^{Dim-1} (y_i - 1)^2 [1 + 10sin^2(\pi y_{i+1})] + (y_{Dim}-1)^2 + 10sin^2(\pi y_1)\} + \sum_{i=1}^{Dim} u(x_i, 10, 100, 4)$	$[-100, 100]$	0
-	$y_i = 1 + (x_i + 1)/4, u_{y_i, a, k, m} = \begin{cases} k(x_i - a)^m, & x_i > a \\ 0, & -a \le x_i lea \\ k(-x_i - a)^m, & x_i < a \end{cases}$	000	0
F21	$\frac{1}{10}\{sin^2(\pi x_1) + \sum_{i=1}^{Dim-1} (x_i - 1)^2 [1 + sin^2(3\pi x_{i+1})] + (x_{Dim}-1)^2 (1 + sin^2(2\pi x_{i+1}))\} + \sum_{i=1}^{Dim} u(x_i, 5, 100, 4)$	$[-100, 100]$	0
F22	$\sum_{i=1}^{Dim} |x_i \cdot sin(\sqrt{|x_i|})|$	$[-100, 100]$	0
F23	$sin^2(3\pi x_i) + \sum_{i=1}^{Dim-1}(x_i - 1)^2 [1 + sin^2(3\pi x_{i+1})] + |x_{Dim} - 1| \cdot [1 + sin^2(2\pi x_{Dim})]$	$[-10, 10]$	0
F24	$\sum_{i=1}^{Dim} [\sum_{k=0}^{kmax} [a^k cos(2\pi b^k (x_i + 0.5))]] - Dim \cdot \sum_{k=0}^{k_{max}} [a^k cos(2\pi b^k \cdot 0.5)], a = 0.5, b = 3, k_{max} = 20$	$[-1, 1]$	0
F25	$1 - cos(2\pi \sqrt{\sum_{i=1}^{Dim} x_i^2}) + 0.1\sqrt{\sum_{i=1}^{Dim} x_i^2}$	$[-100, 100]$	0
F26	$\sum_{i=1}^{Dim} [x_i^2 + 2x_{i+1}^2 - 0.3 \cdot cos(3\pi x_i)]$	$[-10, 10]$	0

3.1   Cubic Chaotic Mapping

The cubic mapping method [40] with faster iteration speed to improve the coverage space of the initial solution. The calculation method is shown in Eq. 32.

$$z_{n+1} = \alpha z_n^3 - \beta z_n \tag{32}$$

where α and β represent chaotic factors. When β belongs to interval $(2.3, 3)$, cubic mapping shows chaotic phenomenon. When $\alpha = 1$, the cubic map is located in the interval $(-2, 2)$, and when $\alpha = 4$, the chaotic sequence is located in the interval $(-1, 1)$. Therefore, the chaotic sequence can also be written as:

$$z_{n+1} = \rho z_n (1 - z_n^2) \tag{33}$$

where ρ is the control parameter. In Eq. 32, the cubic mapping is located in the interval $(0, 1)$. When $\rho = 2.595$, the generation of chaotic variable Z_n has better ergodicity.

3.2   Parameter Adaptive Strategy

At the beginning of the iteration of butterfly optimization algorithm, the attraction of fragrance to each butterfly should be relatively large, and this attraction should decrease with the iteration. Therefore, in order to reflect the dynamic impact of fragrance on each butterfly, in this paper, the parameter a in Eq. 2 is processed adaptively. The mathematical expression of the improved parameter a is as Eq. 34:

$$a = 0.05 + 0.05 \times (1 - \frac{t}{T}) \tag{34}$$

where, t and T represent the current and the maximum value of iteration round of the algorithm respectively.

3.3   Parallel Strategy

Similar to most evolutionary calculations, at the beginning, we initialize the population $P = \{p_1, p_2, \ldots, p_n\}$. Then, the population was divided into three parts, namely $P_{butterfly}$, P_{wolf} and P_{prey}. The subpopulation $P_{butterfly}$ uses the evolutionary mechanism of BOA, i.e., Eq. 1, Eq. 2, and Eq. 3, to perform iterations to find the best solution. Similarly, subpopulations P_{wolf} and P_{prey} use the evolutionary approach of GWO and MPA to find the optimal solution, respectively. Then, the algorithm performs communication between different subpopulations every 50 iterations, and a total of three main communication strategies are used in this algorithm.

Algorithm 1. Proposed algorithm

1: Population P is initialized by cubic mapping using Eq. 33

2: Population P was divided into three subpopulations, $P_{butterfly}$, P_{wolf} and P_{prey}

3: **repeat**

4:    $n \leftarrow n + 1$

5:    Update the hyperparameter a in the BOA algorithm according to Eq. 34

6:    Update $P_{butterfly}$ based on BOA

7:    Update P_{wolf} based on GWO

8:    Update P_{prey} based on MPA

9:    **if** $n = R$ **then**

10:        Strategy 1, Strategy 2 and Strategy 3 are used for parallel communication among populations respectively

11:        **Strategy 1:**

12:            $P_{butterfly}^{worse} \leftarrow P_{wolf}^{best}$

13:            $P_{wolf}^{worse} \leftarrow P_{prey}^{best}$

14:            $P_{prey}^{worse} \leftarrow P_{butterfly}^{best}$

15:        **Strategy 2:**

16:            $P_{butterfly}^{worse} \leftarrow (P_{wolf}^{best} + P_{prey}^{best} + P_{butterfly}^{best})/3$

17:            $P_{wolf}^{worse} \leftarrow (P_{wolf}^{best} + P_{prey}^{best} + P_{butterfly}^{best})/3$

18:            $P_{prey}^{worse} \leftarrow (P_{wolf}^{best} + P_{prey}^{best} + P_{butterfly}^{best})/3$

19:        **Strategy 3:**

20:            $P_{butterfly}^{worse} \leftarrow (\alpha \cdot P_{wolf}^{best} + \beta \cdot P_{prey}^{best} + \gamma \cdot P_{butterfly}^{best})/3$

21:            $P_{wolf}^{worse} \leftarrow (\alpha \cdot P_{wolf}^{best} + \beta \cdot P_{prey}^{best} + \gamma \cdot P_{butterfly}^{best})/3$

22:            $P_{prey}^{worse} \leftarrow (\alpha \cdot P_{wolf}^{best} + \beta \cdot P_{prey}^{best} + \gamma \cdot P_{butterfly}^{best})/3.$

23:    **end if**

24: **until** The termination conditions are met.

25: Update $P^{best} \leftarrow \max\{P_{butterfly}^{best}, P_{wolf}^{best}, P_{prey}^{best}\}$

Output: P^{best}

Complementary Circle Communication Strategy. After the algorithm enters the iterative stage, three different subpopulations evolve independently according to their own evolution mechanism. All subpopulations share information every R generation. The communication strategy of complementary circle communication advantages aims to make the advantages of one sub-population compensate for the disadvantages of another subpopulation, which means that the best solution found in subpopulation $P_{butterfly}$ is used to improve the poor solution of P_{wolf}, and the individual with the best fitness in P_{wolf} is used to enhance the individual with the poor fitness in P_{prey}. Similarly, the best individual in P_{prey} replaces the best individual in $P_{butterfly}$.

Local Average Communication Strategy. Similar to the complementary circle communication strategy, the three subpopulations independently evolved to the R generation and communicated among the subpopulations. Different from the advantage complementary communication strategy, this strategy uses the arithmetic mean of the optimal solution in each subpopulation to improve the worse individuals in the three subpopulations. Considering that there is still

Table 2. The result of proposed algorithms on F1-F13.

F		BOA	GWO	MPA	ACHBGM-1	ACHBGM-2	ACHBGM-3
F1	AVG	8.20267E−11	4.05245E−15	3.2765E−19	7.70177E−45	0	3.40456E−69
	STD	5.6956E−12	4.7473E−15	2.57326E−19	1.34914E−44	0	1.5152E−68
	MIN	6.90818E−11	4.5932E−16	3.95248E−20	2.74006E−55	0	9.61134E−92
F2	AVG	4.31622E+49	1.60445E−09	2.05062E−11	2.15129E−39	0	2.0729E−108
	STD	1.11712E+50	5.86795E−10	1.52432E−11	2.36608E−39	0	9.0859E−108
	MIN	1.05202E+44	8.63671E−10	6.99273E−13	6.48284E−42	0	3.4981E−146
F3	AVG	5.84402E−11	0.920417496	0.046566631	1.54608E−44	0	7.47584E−66
	STD	5.34101E−12	1.112003472	0.086763663	2.11056E−44	0	2.68326E−65
	MIN	4.95193E−11	0.011445579	0.000958058	1.03969E−46	0	2.1551E−96
F4	AVG	3.00213E−08	0.015269914	2.96669E−08	6.25619E−39	1.0499E−262	2.61409E−91
	STD	2.36673E−09	0.025413454	1.00889E−08	6.30972E−39	0	8.04148E−91
	MIN	2.63649E−08	0.001234923	1.41054E−08	5.79104E−40	2.3903E−293	1.4696E−114
F5	AVG	22.10515943	7.464370166	1.239254488	4.12658E−08	4.22239E−08	4.48592E−08
	STD	0.79360213	0.952738108	0.409717154	1.44504E−08	1.13744E−08	1.60334E−08
	MIN	20.46727449	6.102047055	0.417215339	1.32913E−08	2.67848E−08	2.28834E−08
F6	AVG	0.001680654	0.004421525	0.001480682	1.47114E−05	3.11909E−05	6.47698E−06
	STD	0.000597359	0.002106161	0.000839343	1.06965E−05	1.99503E−05	5.9769E−06
	MIN	0.000666478	0.002321779	0.000540058	1.14752E−07	2.39528E−07	1.2051E−07
F7	AVG	1.53893E−23	4.558E−156	4.0478E−210	7.1246E−218	7.1246E−218	7.1246E−218
	STD	6.84765E−23	2.0176E−155	0	0	0	0
	MIN	4.28688E−72	6.799E−175	7.2796E−218	7.1246E−218	7.1246E−218	7.1246E−218
F8	AVG	6.17797E−14	2.56164E−86	1.08858E−62	6.18467E−54	2.6644E−186	5.13798E−50
	STD	2.51687E−14	7.5821E−86	3.25285E−62	1.16419E−53	0	2.20014E−49
	MIN	1.41682E−14	2.8828E−103	7.46253E−74	2.46334E−57	1.8133E−218	2.54353E−71
F9	AVG	8.11856E−11	1.64016E−15	1.17197E−19	1.42712E−44	0	3.01594E−68
	STD	5.42261E−12	1.4832E−15	8.49929E−20	2.04293E−44	0	1.24699E−67
	MIN	7.13377E−11	3.13488E−16	6.83108E−21	1.62396E−49	0	1.8251E−119
F10	AVG	98.88238924	97.32754713	96.31538166	90.7727665	91.83529037	90.81797196
	STD	0.03178052	1.050564781	0.578949312	0.251197016	0.515038682	0.21490587
	MIN	98.7901049	95.23559467	95.56895692	90.25036324	90.8265583	90.47588804
F11	AVG	7.89151E−11	1.86528E−15	9.86759E−20	2.35466E−44	0	4.21125E−64
	STD	6.23245E−12	1.20477E−15	1.80937E−19	3.78616E−44	0	1.79905E−63
	MIN	6.7448E−11	3.18422E−16	1.94037E−21	2.3268E−49	0	5.8041E−118
F12	AVG	0.997333524	0.666697243	0.666667641	0.666667904	0.666674412	0.666667555
	STD	0.000795827	2.97512E−05	6.01674E−07	3.97028E−07	2.24791E−05	3.23679E−07
	MIN	0.995990272	0.666682002	0.666666989	0.666667168	0.666667734	0.666667169
F13	AVG	8.08043E−22	0	1.5117E−247	3.2352E−127	0	3.9263E−121
	STD	2.37844E−21	0	0	1.0608E−126	0	1.2596E−120
	MIN	2.52239E−28	0	0	1.4376E−142	0	2.6542E−152
Sum of ranks		56	68	59	44	30	16

Table 3. The result of proposed algorithms on F14-F26.

F		BOA	GWO	MPA	ACHBGM-1	ACHBGM-2	ACHBGM-3
F14	AVG	1.1317E−17	1.6562E−248	6.62447E−92	2.03679E−66	0	1.62301E−64
	STD	1.44449E−17	0	2.94516E−91	8.2691E−66	0	7.25832E−64
	MIN	2.1006E−19	0	4.7309E−122	2.7606E−90	0	3.3786E−124
F15	AVG	7.14459E−20	0	5.4967E−114	2.51671E−94	0	9.38033E−92
	STD	1.21227E−19	0	2.458E−113	1.12545E−93	0	4.19377E−91
	MIN	9.26157E−24	0	8.6133E−145	1.3261E−116	0	1.1679E−111
F16	AVG	0	7.131474111	0	0	0	0
	STD	0	5.253730816	0	0	0	0
	MIN	0	3.22871E−10	0	0	0	0
F17	AVG	6.96471E−11	17.52327955	0	0	0	0
	STD	2.50725E−10	15.88307303	0	0	0	0
	MIN	0	3.000008061	0	0	0	0
F18	AVG	2.81675E−08	4.42485E−09	4.32296E−11	8.88178E−16	8.88178E−16	8.88178E−16
	STD	1.42709E−09	1.16068E−09	2.16022E−11	0	0	0
	MIN	2.52924E−08	2.67826E−09	9.40847E−12	8.88178E−16	8.88178E−16	8.88178E−16
F19	AVG	6.52919E−11	0.000733862	0	0	0	0
	STD	1.87636E−11	0.003281931	0	0	0	0
	MIN	3.00487E−11	2.9976E−15	0	0	0	0
F20	AVG	1.32828E−09	0.001499502	3.90313E−12	3.13406E−39	1.9055E−306	3.32752E−93
	STD	8.37764E−10	0.001208067	3.93902E−12	2.60546E−39	0	1.45374E−92
	MIN	2.45999E−10	7.97156E−09	1.3387E−13	1.38863E−41	0	6.7941E−114
F21	AVG	0.940142747	0.155537907	0.019995853	8.87375E−10	8.65685E−10	8.87682E−10
	STD	0.084449957	0.033668749	0.006444893	3.04724E−10	3.52543E−10	2.40168E−10
	MIN	0.779564979	0.110261225	0.007964981	4.40047E−10	4.70989E−10	5.38688E−10
F22	AVG	9.987075198	5.02108932	3.334885606	0.036033378	0.012635109	0.025118958
	STD	0.006545466	0.38362152	2.33191317	0.049367779	0.031738192	0.043405838
	MIN	9.969609571	4.227549961	0.738291234	2.10663E−08	2.87195E−08	2.19167E−08
F23	AVG	64.62313396	13.85256999	2.063384707	0.777461711	1.289235972	1.672479425
	STD	3.806873315	3.238347912	0.868292625	0.791874457	0.859140769	2.013159769
	MIN	57.91316802	6.155450601	0.926621119	0.05087255	0.162635606	0.075521182
F24	AVG	5.472455543	12.5501013	0	0	0	0
	STD	6.184780647	5.547453413	0	0	0	0
	MIN	0	3.870796175	0	0	0	0
F25	AVG	0.424870337	0.771090873	0.338285676	2.02948E−54	3.053E−176	3.33919E−81
	STD	0.110850249	0.221009959	0.122496568	9.0761E−54	0	1.4825E−80
	MIN	0.397983695	0.397983119	0.099495906	3.1523E−158	0	1.942E−163
F26	AVG	8.19317E−11	3.10862E−16	0	0	0	0
	STD	8.182E−12	4.10063E−16	0	0	0	0
	MIN	6.87764E−11	0	0	0	0	0
Sum of ranks		41	57	60	51	47	17

a small probability in the process of evolution, the local average communication strategy can effectively avoid this situation.

Global Average Communication Strategy. For solving the problem that the fitness gap between populations is too large, this paper introduces the global average communication strategy. The strategy no longer uses the arithmetic mean of the three best solutions, but gives weight to the optimal solution of each subpopulation, weights and sums the three solutions, and finally replaces the worse solution in each subpopulation. It can be seen that the local average communication strategy is a special case of this strategy.

4 Experiments and Results

In order to test the effectiveness of our proposed algorithm, we use 26 test functions to verify the performance of the algorithm, which are listed in Table 1. The running results of all algorithms on 26 test functions are sorted, and then the sorted sum of each algorithm is accumulated, and the accumulated results are compared. In order to show the experimental data more clearly, we divided 26 test functions into two groups. The first group contains functions $F1$–$F13$, and the second group contains functions $F14$–$F26$. We use two sets of test functions to test all algorithms and count the final results respectively. This paper makes three groups of comparative experiments on 26 test functions.

4.1 Comparative Experiment Based on Adaptive Strategy

In this subsection, the BOA algorithm with parameter adaptive strategy is compared with the original BOA algorithm. The experimental results show that the BOA algorithm with parameter adaptive strategy performs well on 22 functions.

4.2 Comparative Experiment Based on Cubic Chaotic Mapping

In this subsection, in order to prove the effectiveness of cubic chaotic mapping initialization, the three original algorithms BOA, GWO and MPA are compared with the three algorithms after cubic chaotic map initialization. Experimental results show that the algorithm after cubic mapping initialization performs well on 20 test functions. In order to make the results more visual, then we sort the running results of all algorithms on 26 test functions, and accumulate the sorting and of each algorithm to get the ranking.

4.3 Comparative Experiments of Proposed Algorithms

In this subsection, we run all the algorithms involved in the comparison 20 times independently. Firstly, the optimal fitness value is used as the evaluation standard. ACHBGM with elite negotiation strategy has advantages over other functions in 19 test functions. If the average value of fitness value is taken as the evaluation standard, ACHBGM with elite negotiation strategy has achieved good results in 15 test functions. The experimental data are shown in Table 2 and 3. ACHBGM-1 represents the hybrid algorithm with complementary communication strategy, ACHBGM-2 represents that the hybrid algorithm adopts elite negotiation strategy, and ACHBGM-3 means that the communication strategy in the algorithm uses elite team leader strategy.

Overall, we rank the results of all algorithms on each test function, and judge the advantages and disadvantages of different algorithms by adding the ranking of each algorithm on two sets of test functions separately. Similarly, I also discuss from two indicators, one is the average fitness value, and the other is the best fitness value. Firstly, from the perspective of average fitness value, the best is ACHBGM with elite team leader strategy, the second best is ACHBGM with elite negotiation strategy, and the third is ACHBGM with complementary advantage strategy. Secondly, the best fitness value is used as the evaluation standard, ACHBGM-3 is still the top algorithm, followed by ACHBGM-1 and then ACHBGM-2. Experimental results show that the proposed hybrid algorithm is better than the relevant original algorithm under the two evaluation criteria.

5   Conclusion

This work proposes a novel hybrid algorithm ACHBGM, which integrates the idea of parallelism and combines the advantages of BOA, GWO and MPA. The introduction of cubic chaotic mapping initialization and adaptive parameter method also improves the performance of the algorithm. During the iterative process, three different populations share information with three communication strategies, so that the algorithm can jump out of the local optimization. Finally, their effectiveness of proposed algorithm is illustrated by experiments.

References

1. Aziz, N.A.B.A., Mohemmed, A.W., Alias, M.Y.: A wireless sensor network coverage optimization algorithm based on particle swarm optimization and Voronoi diagram. In: 2009 International Conference on Networking, Sensing and Control, pp. 602–607 (2009)
2. Abdel-Basset, M., Mohamed, R., Chakrabortty, R.K., Ryan, M., Mirjalili, S.: New binary marine predators optimization algorithms for 0–1 knapsack problems. Comput. Ind. Eng. **151**, 106949 (2021)
3. Abdel-Basset, M., Mohamed, R., Elhoseny, M., Chakrabortty, R.K., Ryan, M.: A hybrid covid-19 detection model using an improved marine predators algorithm and a ranking-based diversity reduction strategy. IEEE Access **8**, 79521–79540 (2020)
4. Abdollahzadeh, S., Navimipour, N.J.: Deployment strategies in the wireless sensor network: a comprehensive review. Comput. Commun. **91**, 1–16 (2016)

5. Arora, S., Singh, S.: An effective hybrid butterfly optimization algorithm with artificial bee colony for numerical optimization. Int. J. Interact. Multimedia Artif. Intell. **4**(4), 14–21 (2017)
6. Arora, S., Singh, S.: An improved Butterfly Optimization Algorithm with chaos. J. Intell. Fuzzy Syst. **32**(1), 1079–1088 (2017)
7. Arora, S., Singh, S.: Butterfly Optimization Algorithm: a novel approach for global optimization. Soft. Comput. **23**(3), 715–734 (2018). https://doi.org/10. 1007/s00500-018-3102-4
8. Bratton, D., Kennedy, J.: Defining a standard for particle swarm optimization. In: 2007 IEEE Swarm Intelligence Symposium, pp. 120–127 (2007)
9. Cuevas, E., Echavarría, A., Ramírez-Ortegón, M.A.: An optimization algorithm inspired by the states of matter that improves the balance between exploration and exploitation. Appl. Intell. **40**(2), 256–272 (2014)
10. Cui, Z., et al.: A pigeon-inspired optimization algorithm for many-objective optimization problems. Sci. Chin. Inf. Sci. **62**(7), 1–3 (2019). https://doi.org/10.1007/ s11432-018-9729-5
11. Du, Z.-G., Pan, T.-S., Pan, J.-S., Chu, S.-C.: QUasi-Affine TRansformation Evolutionary Algorithm for feature selection. In: Wu, T.-Y., Ni, S., Chu, S.-C., Chen, C.-H., Favorskaya, M. (eds.) Advances in Smart Vehicular Technology, Transportation, Communication and Applications. SIST, vol. 250, pp. 147–156. Springer, Singapore (2022). https://doi.org/10.1007/978-981-16-4039-1_14
12. Duan, H., Qiao, P.: Pigeon-inspired optimization: a new swarm intelligence optimizer for air robot path planning. Int. J. Intell. Comput. Cybern. **7**(1), 24–37 (2014)
13. Emary, E., Zawbaa, H.M., Hassanien, A.E.: Binary grey wolf optimization approaches for feature selection. Neurocomputing **172**, 371–381 (2016)
14. Faramarzi, A., Heidarinejad, M., Mirjalili, S., Gandomi, A.H.: Marine predators algorithm: a nature-inspired metaheuristic. Exp. Syst. Appl. **152**, 113377 (2020)
15. Guo, B., Zhuang, Z., Pan, J.S., Chu, S.C.: Optimal design and simulation for PID controller using fractional-order fish migration optimization algorithm. IEEE Access **9**, 8808–8819 (2021)
16. Hu, Y., et al.: A self-organizing multimodal multi-objective pigeon-inspired optimization algorithm. Sci. Chin. Inf. Sci. **62**(7), 1–17 (2019). https://doi.org/10. 1007/s11432-018-9754-6
17. Huang, C.F., Tseng, Y.C.: The coverage problem in a wireless sensor network. Mob. Netw. Appl. **10**(4), 519–528 (2005)
18. Kan, T.W., Teng, C.H., Chou, W.S.: Applying qr code in augmented reality applications. In: Proceedings of the 8th International Conference on Virtual Reality Continuum and its Applications in Industry, pp. 253–257 (2009)
19. Kennedy, J., Eberhart, R.: Particle swarm optimization. In: Proceedings of ICNN'95-International Conference on Neural Networks, vol. 4, pp. 1942–1948. IEEE (1995)
20. Khanduja, N., Bhushan, B.: Chaotic state of matter search with elite opposition based learning: a new hybrid metaheuristic algorithm. Optim. Control Appl. Meth. **2021**, 1–16. (2021) https://doi.org/10.1002/oca.2810
21. Li, Z., Lei, L.: Sensor node deployment in wireless sensor networks based on improved particle swarm optimization. In: 2009 International Conference on Applied Superconductivity and Electromagnetic Devices, pp. 215–217 (2009)
22. Mann, G.K., Hu, B.G., Gosine, R.G.: Analysis of direct action fuzzy PID controller structures. IEEE Trans. Syst. Man Cybern. Part B (Cybern.) **29**(3), 371–388 (1999)

23. Masalha, F., Hirzallah, N., et al.: A students attendance system using QR code. Int. J. Adv. Comput. Sci. Appl. **5**(3), 75–79 (2014)
24. Meng, Z., Chen, Y., Li, X., Yang, C., Zhong, Y.: Enhancing quasi-affine transformation evolution (QUATRE) with adaptation scheme on numerical optimization. Knowl. Based Syst. **197**, 105908 (2020)
25. Meng, Z., Pan, J.S., Xu, H.: Quasi-affine transformation evolutionary (QUATRE) algorithm: a cooperative swarm based algorithm for global optimization. Knowl. Based Syst. **109**, 104–121 (2016)
26. Mirjalili, S., Mirjalili, S.M., Lewis, A.: Grey wolf optimizer. Adv. Eng. Softw. **69**, 46–61 (2014)
27. Mohamed, A.A.A., El-Gaafary, A.A., Mohamed, Y.S., Hemeida, A.M.: Multi-objective states of matter search algorithm for TCSC-based smart controller design. Electr. Power Syst. Res. **140**, 874–885 (2016)
28. Niu, P., Niu, S., Chang, L., et al.: The defect of the grey wolf optimization algorithm and its verification method. Knowl. Based Syst. **171**, 37–43 (2019)
29. Pan, J.S., Sun, X.X., Chu, S.C., Abraham, A., Yan, B.: Digital watermarking with improved SMS applied for QR code. Eng. Appl. Artif. Intell. **97**, 104049 (2021)
30. Pan, J.-S., Tian, A.-Q., Chu, S.-C., Li, J.-B.: Improved binary pigeon-inspired optimization and its application for feature selection. Appl. Intell. **51**(12), 8661–8679 (2021). https://doi.org/10.1007/s10489-021-02302-9
31. Pan, J.S., Tsai, P.W., Liao, Y.B.: Fish migration optimization based on the fishy biology. In: 2010 4th International Conference on Genetic and Evolutionary Computing, pp. 783–786 (2010)
32. Pradhan, M., Roy, P.K., Pal, T.: Grey wolf optimization applied to economic load dispatch problems. Int. J. Electr. Power Energy Syst. **83**, 325–334 (2016)
33. Rivera, D.E., Morari, M., Skogestad, S.: Internal model control: PID controller design. Ind. Eng. Chem. Process Des. Dev. **25**(1), 252–265 (1986)
34. Shi, Y., et al.: Particle swarm optimization: developments, applications and resources. In: Proceedings of the 2001 Congress on Evolutionary Computation, vol. 1, pp. 81–86. IEEE (2001)
35. Sung, T.W., Zhao, B., Zhang, X.: Quasi-affine transformation evolutionary with double excellent guidance. Wirel. Commun. Mob. Comput. **2021**, 5591543 (2021)
36. Tang, K.S., Man, K.F., Chen, G., Kwong, S.: An optimal fuzzy PID controller. IEEE Trans. Ind. Electron. **48**(4), 757–765 (2001)
37. Tiwari, S.: An introduction to QR code technology. In: 2016 international Conference on Information Technology (ICIT), pp. 39–44 (2016)
38. Wang, B., Lim, H.B., Ma, D.: A survey of movement strategies for improving network coverage in wireless sensor networks. Comput. Commun. **32**(13–14), 1427–1436 (2009)
39. Yıldız, B.S., Yıldız, A.R., Albak, E.İ, Abderazek, H., Sait, S.M., Bureerat, S.: Butterfly optimization algorithm for optimum shape design of automobile suspension components. Mater. Test. **62**(4), 365–370 (2020)
40. Zhang, M., Long, D., Qin, T., Yang, J.: A chaotic hybrid butterfly optimization algorithm with particle swarm optimization for high-dimensional optimization problems. Symmetry **12**(11), 1800 (2020)

Blockchain Technology

Research on Blockchain Privacy Protection Mechanism in Financial Transaction Services Based on Zero-Knowledge Proof and Federal Learning

Maoguang Wang, Tianming Wang[✉], and Haoyue Ji

College of Information, Central University of Finance and Economics, Beijing 10000, China
595575614@qq.com

Abstract. In the financial transaction system centering on blockchain technology, institutions at different levels have different powers and roles, so that they have dissimilar private contents to protect. Taking supply chain financing as an example, a multi-level blockchain system is proposed in this paper. The main steps of building the system are as follows: Firstly, commercial banks and regulatory authorities cooperatively establish a risk control model by Federal Learning. Secondly, the private transaction information will be preserved by zero-knowledge proofs for downstream suppliers. Finally, an architecture of multi-level blockchain is designed to supervise the financial trading for guaranteeing credibility. The experimental results show that the system is more beneficial to privacy protection. By incorporating Federal Learning, it can provide stronger security and more reliable risk control. Further, that can also improve the efficiency and performance of the financial transaction system.

Keywords: Blockchain · Federal learning · Zero-knowledge proof · Privacy protection · Supply chain

1 Introduction

With the global development of blockchain represented by cryptocurrency, blockchain has received extensive attention from the Internet industry, financial institutions, and academia. Blockchain 3.0 has penetrated various industries. The essence of blockchain reduces the cost of trust. As a result, Internet giants and international financial institutions have started to invest heavily in blockchain. Issues such as consensus mechanism and privacy protection continue to be popular topics of current research.

Blockchain is widely used in the financial industry because of its characteristics such as non-tamperability. These financial applications based on blockchain have different functions so that they face different privacy-preserving issues. In this paper, we take the privacy protection of accounts receivable financing in the supply chain as an entry point, solving two problems. One is that how to preserve the privacy of transaction information between suppliers. Another is that how to train the risk control model when the lending institutions such as commercial banks store their private data on local devices.

Firstly, to prevent counterparties from stealing trade secrets in transaction information, it is necessary to establish a transaction mechanism for privacy protection. One way to enhance privacy protection is to generate many random account addresses for each user [1, 2] and every address only be used once. However, it is troublesome for the user to maintain a large number of addresses. Therefore, in this paper, we will hide the transaction amount, which could preserve private data while there is only one address/account per user.

Second, a large number of commercial banks apply AI technology to train a more accurate and intelligent risk control model. However, due to the factors such as economic utility, legal policies, and standard systems, data sharing among participants faces the dilemma of "unwillingness, fear, and inability", which forms "data silos" [3, 4]. This has seriously hindered the training and enhancement of risk control models. Therefore, it can not wait to protect the private data of all parties while satisfying the data requirements of risk control models [5]. Federal Learning has the characteristics of "data available but not visible, data not moved but model moved". So we use this technology to achieve collaborative training among participants. The combination of Federated Learning and blockchain ensures a shared ledger smart contracts and collaborative training of model while considering the privacy of data. The main works of this paper consist of three aspects:

1) We design a multi-level blockchain architecture. The architecture is divided into two levels. Especially, commercial banks are viewed as the link between the two levels. The first level is a management blockchain consisting of regulators and commercial banks, which is mainly used to build risk control models and give credit ratings. Another level is the blockchain between commercial banks and suppliers, which can record transaction information in the supply chain.
2) We propose a financial transaction mechanism by incorporating zero-knowledge proof. Particularly, a double balance model is designed to hide the transaction amount, which could protect the private transaction information between suppliers.
3) We propose a secure data-sharing framework that combines blockchain with Federal Learning. Specifically, an algorithm POQ (Proof of Quality) is designed to determine how to select the participants in Federal Learning.

2   Related Work

Zero-Knowledge Proof (ZKP) means that a prover can make a verifier believe that a certain assertion is correct without providing any useful information. In recent years, ZKP has been developed rapidly. It is viewed as a very promising solution to protect blockchain privacy. For UTXO (unused transaction output model), the existing privacy-preserving projects are included Zerocash [6], Monero [7], Zerocoin [8], Dash [9], and CoinJoin [10]. However, there are few schemes with effective privacy protection like DSC [11] in the account model. For the blockchain, the most popular zero-knowledge proof system is zk-SNARK. Zk-SNARK have also been used in the literature [12, 13] to achieve privacy protection. Among them, the initialized settings of traditional zk-SNARK are disposable trusted settings for a specific circuit. After the circuit changed, the initialized settings need to be reset [8]. For better reuse of the initialized settings, several new schemes have recently been proposed in academia [14, 15]. Among them, Fractal [16], Halo [17], and Supersonic [18] design the publicly transparent initialized settings that can generate a common reference string (CRS) without additional variables. However, it is still inappropriate to apply these new schemes to blockchains. Because their proof sizes are much larger than these of traditional schemes. Moreover, Sonic [19], Marlin [20] and PLONK [21] design the generic initialized settings that could create a shared and updatable structured reference string (SRS) using additional variables. Therefore, they theoretically support an unlimited number of arbitrary circuits. Besides, Bulletproof [22] is also an effective zero-knowledge proof that does not require the trusted initialized settings. Zether [13] implements a variant mechanism of Bulletproof to hide the transaction amount and addresses with the help of ElGamal encryption. But the computational and verification costs of its provers are still much higher than those of zk-SNARKs. We found that Groth16 [24] can generate proofs with low time complexity and space complexity. Therefore, we utilize the Groth16 proof system to achieve zero-knowledge proofs [25].

Federated Learning provides a possibility to construct a global model while preserving the training data. The literature [5, 25, 26] propose the distributed frameworks by combining blockchain with federated learning while maintaining the security and trustworthiness of blockchain. At the same time, the communication efficiency in the blockchain is also optimized. Some scholars [5] propose a secure architecture authorized by blockchain for sharing data, which stores the federated models through blockchain and ensures the security of the data sharing process. The article [26] proposes a new privacy-preserving mechanism and designs a two-stage solution that includes the transformation of intelligent data and detection of collaborative data leakage. The work is proven to be high accuracy, efficiency, and reliability. Inspired by the above works, we propose the proof of quality, i.e., POQ, to improve the efficiency of federated training.

3   Multi-level Blockchain System Privacy Protection Mechanism

3.1   Privacy Protection Based on Zero-Knowledge Proof and Double Balance

The architecture of this system includes three types of nodes: regulators, commercial banks, and suppliers who need the loan. Two types of blockchains are composed from those nodes. Different types of nodes publish different content by their roles. The constructed architecture of the system is shown in Fig. 1.

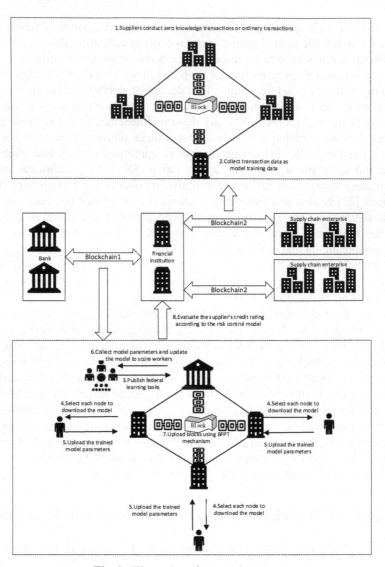

Fig. 1. Illustration of transaction system

Blockchain 1 is the blockchain between commercial bank and lender supplier: it consists of commercial banks and lender suppliers. And it is used to maintain the transaction records among enterprises. In addition, it can hide important transaction information through zero-knowledge proof and protect supplier privacy by setting up a double-balanced transaction model. Meanwhile, reputation rating is introduced. The suppliers with different reputation scores have different rights when posting transactions. Suppliers with low reputation scores will be faced to cancel the permission of zero-knowledge proof. Vendors with a very poor reputation will have their transaction privileges removed.

Blockchain 2 is the blockchain between commercial bank and regulator: its function is mainly to give a reputation score to each lender. This chain combines the features of federal learning and blockchain. The regulator acts as a task publisher and the commercial banks are viewed as participants in Federal Learning. The publisher first sends the initial global risk control model to the participants in the form of outsourcing. Then, during per round of collaborative training, each participant iteratively trains his local model without uploading his private training data to the publisher. In contrast, the parameters of the local model are sent to the publisher. Then the publisher aggregates the parameters from all participants to update the global model. After that, the publisher uploads the global model to Blockchain 2 forguaranteeing the global model to be immutable. We also introduce a quality metric to select participants according to the quality scores by POQ That can avoid some malicious nodes affecting the performance of the overall model. All commercial banks form a consensus committee, which uses the PBFT consensus algorithm to verify the blocks.

3.2 Privacy Protection Based on Zero Knowledge Proof and Double Balance

This section introduced in detail how to protect transaction privacy of the transaction system in blockchain 1 based on ZKP and double-balance technology. Common symbols used in the paper are shown in Table 1 below.

Table 1. Symbol definition

Expression	Description
A	Sender Alice
B	Recipient Bob
sk_A	The private key of A
pk_A	The public key of A
$addr_A$	The address of A
$pt\_balance_A$	The plaintext balance of A
$zk\_balance_A$	Zero knowledge balance of A
$Ledger_T$	Account book
TDSet	Global data table
SNSet	Serial number table
CRH	Anti-collision hash function
$COMM_{bc}$	A non-interactive commitment scheme for hiding account balances
$COMM_{tc}$	A non-interactive commitment scheme for hiding transfer amounts
cmt_A	Express balance commitment of A
$value_A$	The plaintext balance of A
sn_A	Serial number associated with cmt_A
r_A	Random number confusing sn_A
PRF	Pseudorandom function
cmt_v	Commitment to transfer the amount

Entities are defined as follows:

- Ledger
  Anyone can access Ledger at any time. It is a block containing all transactions.
- Address key pair
  Each user has a pair of address keys (sk, pk). Account address:addr: $= CRH\ (pk)$.
- Commitment
  Balance commitment refers to the commitment to account balance, i.e. $cmt_A = COMM_{bc}(addr_A, value_A, sn_A, r_A).COMM_{bc}$ is a non interactive commitment scheme for statistical hiding of account balance, with hidden and bound attributes.
- Public data Table
  The public data table is used to store one-time variables including $TDSet$ and $SNSet$. $TCMSet_N$ represents the data sheet of all publicly announced fund transfer commitments cmt_v in block $block_N$.

Definition of zk-SNARK

The zk-SNARKs scheme [12–14] can be represented as the following polynomial tuple:

$$\Pi_Z(\text{Setup, KeyGen, GenProof, VerProof})$$

The transaction algorithm are as follows:

- Setup $(1^\lambda) \rightarrow pp_Z$: Preset a random security parameter λ, the algorithm will generate and output a public parameter list $pp_Z = (\mathbb{F}_p, p, \mathbb{G}_1, \mathcal{P}_1, \mathbb{G}_2, e, \mathcal{P}_2, \mathbb{G}_T)$, where $\mathbb{F}_P$ is a finite field and p is a prime number; $(\mathbb{G}_1, \mathbb{G}_2, \mathbb{G}_T)$ are cyclic groups of order p; $\mathbb{G}_T$ is derived from $\mathbb{G}_1 \times \mathbb{G}_2$; e is a bilinear pair; $\mathcal{P}_1$ and $\mathcal{P}_2$ are generators of $\mathbb{G}_1$ and $\mathbb{G}_2$ respectively; $\mathbb{F}_P$ is a finite field.
- Keygen (c) $\rightarrow (pk_Z, vk_Z)$: Preset a circuit C, and the algorithm generates a key pair (pk_Z, vk_Z) via the public parameter pp_Z as the proof key and verification key of the zero-knowledge proof.
- Genproof $(pk_z, \overrightarrow{x}, \overrightarrow{a}) \rightarrow \pi$: Preset key pk_Z, a state declaration $\overrightarrow{x}$ and a private evidence $\overrightarrow{a}$, this algorithm is used to generate a zero knowledge proof π, and returns $\bot$ if it fails. Among the input parameters, pk_z is the proof key to generating the zero-knowledge proof; $\overrightarrow{x}$ and $\overrightarrow{a}$ are used as the inputs of circuit C; π is the zero-knowledge proof, which can prove that $\overrightarrow{x}$ and $\overrightarrow{a}$ indeed meet the relationship constructed by circuit C.
- Verproof $(vk_Z, \overrightarrow{x}, \pi) \rightarrow$ B: Preset key vk_Z, the state declaration $\overrightarrow{x}$ and zero knowledge proof π, this algorithm can verify the correctness of zero knowledge proof. If zero knowledge verification is successful, output B $= 1$; Otherwise, output B $= 0$.

The Main functions are as follows:

- Setup(1^λ) $\rightarrow$ pp;Preset the security parameter λ, the algorithm generates the system public parameter pp with number of λ bits by a trusted third party, and the parameter pp is public.
- CreateAccount(pp) $\rightarrow$ {$addr,(sk,pk),tt$}; Preset the public parameter pp, the algorithm creates an account address $addr$ for the user and generates a key pair (sk, pk), in which the private key sk is used to access private data and decrypt the ciphertext data in the transaction, and the public key pk is used to encrypt the transaction data to be submitted, and tt is adopted as a traceable label, which is shared with commercial banks and regulatory authorities, and enables them to track the transaction.
- Mint $(pp,\ zk\_balance_A,\ sk_A,\ v)$ $\rightarrow$ {$zk\_balance_A^*,\ tx_{Mint}$}; This algorithm enables account A to convert plaintext amount v into-zero knowledge amount and merge it with the current zero-knowledge balance.
- Redeem($pp,zk\_balance_A,\ sk_A,\ v$) $\rightarrow$ {$zk\_balance_A^*,\ tx_{Redeem}$}; This algorithm enables account A to send zero-knowledge balance into plaintext balance and merge it with the current plaintext balance. The operation is similar to Mint.
- Send($pp,zk\_balance_A,\ sk_A,\ pk_B,\ v,\ tt$) $\rightarrow$ {$zk\_balance_A^*,\ tx_{Send}$}; This algorithm enables sender a to send zero-knowledge amount to receiver B. After tx_{Send} transaction is generated by hiding the transaction amount and receiver address, account A informs account B offline of the transaction hash value $h_{tx_{send}} := CRH(tx_{Send})$, so that account B can retrieve and parse tx_{Send}. At the same time, the regulator can track the receiver through the tracking tag ta_B. The process is shown in Fig. 2.
- Deposit
  ($Ledger_T$, pp, (sk_B, pk_B), $h_{tx_{Send}}$, $zk\_balance_B$, tt) $\rightarrow$ {$zk\_balance_B^*,\ tx_{Deposit}$}; This algorithm allows recipient B to check the collection and deposit the received amount into its own account. Preset the current Ledger, public parameter pp, the account key pair (sk_B, pk_B), the hash value $h_{tx_{send}}$ of tx_{Send} and current zero-knowledge balance of account B$zk\_balance_B$, It is possible for receiver B to call the Deposit algorithm to make a collection deposit to obtain a new zero-knowledge balance $zk\_balance_B^*$ and generate the transaction $tx_{Deposit}$, According to the transaction hash value $h_{tx_{send}}$ generated by sender A, receiver B is allowed to retrieve and parse tx_{Send} to construct $tx_{Deposit}$ for deposit. The operation is similar to Send.
- Vertx ($Ledger_T, pp, tx$) $\rightarrow$ b; Preset the current ledger, public parameter pp, transaction tx. It is possible for verifier to use this algorithm to check whether all zero-knowledge transactions are valid. If valid, output 1, invalid output 0.

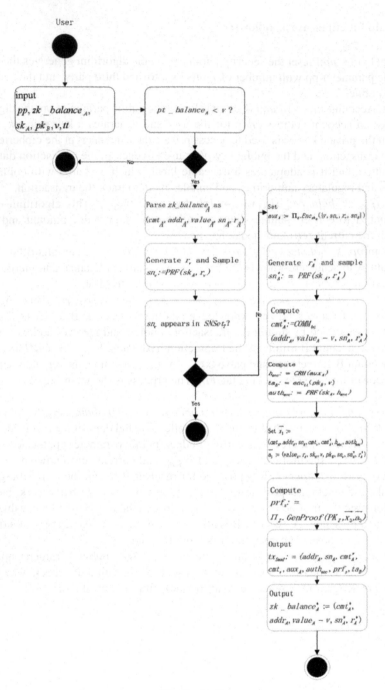

Fig. 2. Send

3.3   Construction of Federal Learning Risk Control Model

Federated learning can ensure that the training data of participants are not out of the local while training the global model, so as to protect the data privacy effectively. The federated learning system architecture in this thesis includes task publishers, task participants and blockchain 2. Publishers and participants need to register accounts on the blockchain to obtain their own public-private key pairs.

Definition of Quality Score

Because the scheme proposed in this thesis is open, an effective management mechanism is needed to evaluate the quality of federated learning between nodes, so as to eliminate the situation that malicious nodes may destroy the whole federated learning task. Here a quality scoring algorithm POQ is established to score each node.

In this quality scoring algorithm POQ, the task publisher scores the participants according to the impact of the participants on the model quality in each task. Among them, the model uploaded by participants after training through local data which improves the accuracy of the overall model, is recorded as a positive interaction event, on the contrary, the model which reduces the accuracy of the model is recorded as a negative interaction event. α_i represents the number of positive interaction events made by participant i, and the initial value is 1. β_i represents the number of negative interaction events made by participant i, and the initial value is 0. b_i indicates the credibility of participant I. Because both positive interaction events and negative interaction events will occur in federal learning tasks. However, from the actual results, negative interaction events can usually lead to serious consequences. Therefore, negative interaction events have high weights. So let K and t be the weights of positive interaction events and negative interaction events respectively, where $k = 2$ and $T = 3$, so

$$b_i = \frac{ka_i}{ka_i + t\beta_i} \tag{1}$$

Suppose the initial score of each node as p = 20 and the reliability weight as μ = 50. Considering that some nodes cannot participate in the following training due to the vicious circle caused by the poor training effect of the model at the beginning, a compensation score is added to each node (suppose s as the training number, y_i as the last training number of participant i, the weight h = 0.8, and the compensation is $((s-y_i) * h) \le 30$), so as to ensure that each node has the opportunity to participate in training. Therefore, the quality score S_i of participant i by the s time training is:

$$S_i = p + \left(s - y_i * h + \frac{\mu ka_i}{ka_i + t\beta_i} \right) \tag{2}$$

The federal learning algorithm is as follows:

Algorithm 1 federated learning algorithm

input:

The current quality score of all nodes $(S_1, S_2, S_3, .. S_n)$, n is the total number of all nodes in blockchain 1.

A set of participants w requesting participation in federal learning;

Global iteration times of Federated learning task, N;

output:

Final accuracy of federal learning tasks, a;

Quality score of all participants $(S_1, S_2, S_3, .. S_n)$;

1: The federal learning task publisher publishes the task and receives the W;

2: The task publisher obtains the quality score of each node in W;

3: The task publisher selects K nodes with the highest scores as participants according to the quality score S_i of all participants in W or special requirements to obtain the final participant set n

4: for $i = 0; i < k; i + +$ do

5:    The task publisher publishes the global model to the participants in the;

6:    Participants in set n download the model and train the model through local data.

7:    After training, upload the trained model;

8:    The task publisher updates the global model from the collected model data;

9   end for

10: After this task, update the quality scores of all nodes $(S_1, S_2, S_3, .. S_n)$ according to the POQ algorithm;

11: return A and $(S_1, S_2, S_3, .. S_n)$;

Steps 1 to 3: Release federated learning tasks. The task publisher broadcasts the federated learning tasks it needs and specific data requirements. After receiving the broadcast, each participant node decides whether to apply to the federal learning task. Then the publisher calculates the quality score of the participant node requested to apply, and selects an appropriate number of participants to participate in federal learning and training according to the quality score or special requirements.

Steps 4 to 10: Conduct federated learning. The task publisher publishes an initial machine learning model as a global shared model. After each participant trains his own local data and uploads new model parameters, the task publisher tests the accuracy of the model through the test set and updates its quality score.

Step 11: Update the final model and upload the model and training records to the blockchain. The publisher submits the legal but unconfirmed relevant data generated in this round of asynchronous global model training to the block. The publisher digitally signs and broadcasts the packaged blocks and enters the block verification stage. Finally, the consensus committee verifies the effectiveness of the blocks through the PBFT consensus mechanism.

4 Experimental Design and Evaluation

Construction of Accounts Receivable Financing Scheme

Accounts receivable financing is a type of financing arrangement in which suppliers who need funds (i.e. financiers and general suppliers) conditionally transfer or pledge accounts receivable, and commercial banks and other lending institutions provide financial services such as financing funds to enterprises. Here, we set the following 8 nodes:

The blockchain network consists of four users and four administrators. The accounts receivable financing process is as follows: first, the upstream suppliers in the supply chain sign a purchase agreement with the core enterprise, stipulating that the upstream suppliers provide with goods, and the core enterprise pays within a certain time after receiving the goods. Every transaction between suppliers and the core enterprise goes up the chain. Secondly, upstream suppliers, as financiers, apply for loans from commercial banks and other financial institutions, and then the core enterprises make repayment/repurchase commitments. Banks and credit rating agencies can check the capital transactions between suppliers and the core enterprise, and finally commercial banks decide whether to lend loans according to the evaluation results.

We build an 8-node multi-layer blockchain through FISCO alliance chain [27], and each organization has two nodes. Node A is the commercial bank node. Node B is the regulatory authority node. Node C and node D are upstream supplier nodes. Blockchain 1 establishes a risk control model through federated learning in the form of smart contract, and scores nodes C and D through the risk control model. This thesis sets up three virtual machines (Ubuntu 20.04LTS system AMD Ryzen 5 2600x, 32gNvidia1650SUPER), and carries out cooperative training of federal learning through the federal learning platform FATE [28].

Federated Learning Experiment Design

Blockchain 1 is used in the federal learning experiment, and the horizontal federal learning experiment is carried out by using the built-in online loan data set of FATE federal learning platform. The logistic regression model is used as the training model. Set 1 task publisher and 2 task participants. Figure 3 shows the results:

Zero-Knowledge Proof Experiment Design

Organization C and organization D are supplier nodes. Here, they use the double balance transaction model based on zero-knowledge proof to hide the transaction amount and the other party's address, so as to achieve privacy protection. At the same time, commercial bank node A has the right to cancel the zero-knowledge proof transaction permission of C or D. Here, we use Libsnark cryptography library to implement zk-SNARK scheme. zk-SNARK are used to generate zero-knowledge proofs for the circuits constructed by these transactions. The key pair used for zk-SNARK generation or verification proof is preinstalled on each node.

For example, supplier A and supplier B register accounts and obtain account addresses and key pairs respectively. When A wants to initiate an account transfer to B, A transfers the plaintext balance X to zero-knowledge balance by generating a balance

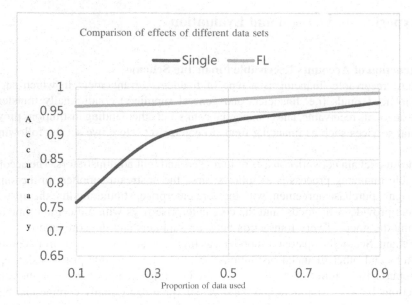

Fig. 3. Federal learning results

commitment and initiates a Mint transaction. Each node links the transaction after verifying that the commitment is valid through the BPFT consensus mechanism. Then A generates a new zero-knowledge balance commitment and transfers the zero-knowledge amount v to B through Send. The transaction is linked, and A informs B of the hash value of the transaction offline. Therefore, node B can analyze the transaction with its own key and transfer the zero-knowledge amount transferred by A to its own zero-knowledge balance (Fig. 4).

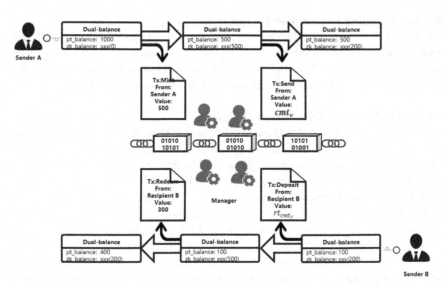

Fig. 4. Transaction workflow

Blockchain 2 is used in the transaction experiment. We compared the zero-knowledge proof application Zerocash on the market. The test is conducted from the two dimensions of time and space, and the results are shown in Table 2. The above experiment shows that our privacy protection mechanism can effectively improve the operation efficiency of most systems while ensuring account privacy, and federated learning can improve the model training efficiency while protecting data privacy.

Table 2. Comparison Experiment of zero knowledge proof transaction

Zero-knowledge proof system			Zerocash system		
Setup	Time	97.4 s	274.3 s	Time	**Setup**
	pp	266MB	1.87GB	pp	
Create Account	Time	1 ms	743 ms	Time	**Create create** your own Address
	Pk	64B	343B	Addr	
Mint	Time	4.82 s	1 μs	Time	**Mint**
	Tx	357B	72B	tx	
Redeem	Time	4.73 s	104.2 s	Time	Pour
	Tx	357B			
Send	Time	8.51 s	1004B	tx	
	Tx	509B			
Deposit	Time	18.75 s	2.14 ms	Time	Receive
	Tx	433B			
Vertx	Time	14.52 ms	28.63 ms	Time	**Verify**

5 Conclusion

In the financial transaction system, a single blockchain system cannot meet the actual needs. Therefore, this thesis constructs a multi-level blockchain system to meet the application needs. Aiming at the privacy protection problems involved in blockchain transactions, a double balance transaction model based on zero knowledge is adopted to ensure the transaction privacy between suppliers. In addition, federal learning is used to solve the problem of "data island" between financial institutions and protect data privacy. Finally, through theoretical analysis and a series of comparative experiments, the effectiveness of the scheme is verified and the potential applications are fantastic.

References

1. Nakamoto, S.: Bitcoin: a peer-to-peer electronic cash system (2009)

2. Chao, L., He, D., Huang, X., et al.: BSeIn: a blockchain-based secure mutual authentication with fine-grained access control system for industry 4.0. J. Netw. Comput. Appl. **116**, 42–52 (2018)
3. Wang, H., Song, X., Junming, K.E., et al.: Blockchain and privacy preserving mechanisms in cryptocurrency. Netinfo Secur. **7**, 32–39 (2017)
4. Zhang, Y., Lu, Y., Huang, X., et al.: Blockchain empowered asynchronous federated learning for secure data sharing in internet of vehicles. IEEE Trans. Veh. Technol. **69**(4), 4298–4311 (2020)
5. You, J.K., Hong, C.S.: Blockchain-based node-aware dynamic weighting methods for improving federated learning performance. In: 2019 20th Asia-Pacific Network Operations and Management Symposium (APNOMS). IEEE (2019)
6. Sasson, E.B., Chiesa, A., Garman, C., et al.: Zerocash: decentralized anonymous payments from bitcoin. In: 2014 IEEE Symposium on Security and Privacy (SP). IEEE (2014)
7. Nicolas Saberhagen, N.: Cryptonote v2.0 [EB/OL] (2013). https://cryptonote.org/whitepaper.pdf
8. Miers, I., Garman, C., Green, M., et al.: Zerocoin: anonymous distributed e-cash from bitcoin. In: 2013 IEEE Symposium on Security and Privacy (SP). IEEE (2013)
9. Duffield, E., Diaz, D.: Dash: a payments-focused cryptocurrency [EB/OL] (2016). https://github.com/dashpay/dash/wiki/Whitepaper
10. Maxwell, G.: CoinJoin: bitcoin privacy for the real world [EB/OL] (2013). https://bitcointalk.org/index.php?Topic=279249.0
11. BitInfoCharts: Cryptocurrency statistics [EB/OL]. https://bitinfocharts.com/
12. Parno, B., et al.: Pinocchio: nearly practical verifiable computation. Commun. ACM **59**(2), 103–112 (2016)
13. Groth, J., Maller, M.: Snarky signatures: minimal signatures of knowledge from simulation-extractable SNARKs. In: International Cryptology Conference (2017)
14. Buterin, V.: Ethereum white paper: a next generation smart contract & decentralized application platform. First version (2014)
15. Fleder, M., Kester, M.S., Pillai, S.: Bitcoin transaction graph analysis. Comput. Sci. (2015)
16. Chiesa, A., Ojha, D., Spooner, N.: Fractal: post-quantum and transparent recursive proofs from holography. In: Canteaut, A., Ishai, Y. (eds.) EUROCRYPT 2020. LNCS, vol. 12105, pp. 769–793. Springer, Cham (2020). https://doi.org/10.1007/978-3-030-45721-1_27
17. Boew, S., Grigg, J., Hopwood, D.: Halo: recursive proof composition without a trusted setup. IACR Crptology ePrint Archieve (2019)
18. Bünz, B., Fisch, B., Szepieniec, A.: Transparent SNARKs from DARK compilers (2020)
19. Maller, M., Bowe, S., Kohlweiss, M., et al.: Sonic: zero-knowledge SNARKs from linear-size universal and updatable structured reference strings. In: The 2019 ACM SIGSAC Conference. ACM (2019)
20. Chiesa, A., Hu, Y., Maller, M., Mishra, P., Vesely, N., Ward, N.: Marlin: preprocessing zkSNARKs with universal and updatable SRS. In: Canteaut, A., Ishai, Y. (eds.) EUROCRYPT 2020. LNCS, vol. 12105, pp. 738–768. Springer, Cham (2020). https://doi.org/10.1007/978-3-030-45721-1_26
21. Gabizon, A., Williamson, Z.J., Ciobotaru, O.: PLONK: Permutations over LAgrange-bases for Oecumenical Noninteractive arguments of Knowledge. IACR Crptology ePrint Archieve (2019)
22. Bunz, B., Bootle, J., Boneh, D., et al.: Bulletproofs: short proofs for confidential transactions and more, pp. 315–334 (2018)
23. Bünz, B., Agrawal, S., Zamani, M., Boneh, D.: Zether: towards privacy in a smart contract world. In: Bonneau, J., Heninger, N. (eds.) FC 2020. LNCS, vol. 12059, pp. 423–443. Springer, Cham (2020). https://doi.org/10.1007/978-3-030-51280-4_23

24. Zhangshuang, G.: Research on privacy protection of account model blockchain system based on zero knowledge proof. Shandong University, ShanDong (2020)
25. Lu, Y., Huang, X., Dai, Y., et al.: Blockchain and federated learning for privacy-preserved data sharing in industrial IoT. IEEE Trans. Ind. Inform. **16**(6), 4177–4186 (2019)
26. Lu, Y., Huang, X., Dai, Y., et al.: Federated learning for data privacy preservation in vehicular cyber-physical systems. IEEE Netw. **34**(3), 50–56 (2020)
27. Webank-FISCO-BCOS: Cryptocur. An alliance blockchain underlying technology platform [EB/OL]. https://github.com/FISCO-BCOS/FISCO-BCOS
28. Webank-fate: An open source federated learning platform [EB/OL]. https://github.com/FederatedAI/FATE

A Distributed Supply Chain Architecture Based on Blockchain Technology

Peng Zhao and Shiren Ye[✉]

Changzhou University, Changzhou 213000, Jiangsu, China
yes@cczu.edu.cn

Abstract. Traditional supply chain management systems use centralized servers and centralized databases, which exhibit disadvantages such as opaque transaction information, difficult information sharing, high maintenance costs, low database security, and poor anti-risk capabilities. Here we develop a supply chain transaction architecture based on blockchain technology. It stores data on decentralized blockchains, and these distributed data are traceable and antitampering under low maintenance costs. We take the alliance chain as the underlying architecture and adopts the "blockchain + business database" double-layer data storage structure to ensure the safety and convenience of transaction data, which will protect the security of transaction data and ensure the speed of data processing. We conduct simulation experiments and performance tests on the system. The experimental results show that the supply chain system using this architecture achieves high efficiency, transparency and security, as well as it could be utilized in the real applications.

Keywords: Blockchain · Supply chain · Consortium blockchain · Hyperledger fabric · Smart contract · Chaincode

1 Introduction

The concept of supply chain began to be proposed in the 1980s, with the advent of economic globalization, the flow of information between enterprises, the interaction between capital flow and logistics has become more frequent and complex, the data scale of the supply chain is growing geometrically in the competition of enterprises [1]. The traditional supply chain model dominated by core enterprises has problems such as poor information sharing, low collaboration efficiency, difficulty in product traceability, lack of trust between enterprises, and excessive voice of core enterprises. At the same time, most of the supply chain management and control system load limit is severely restricted by the performance of the central server. It is very expensive to maintain a high-performance server. Once the centralized server and database are compromised, it will bring serious security threats to the entire supply chain [2].

© IFIP International Federation for Information Processing 2022
Published by Springer Nature Switzerland AG 2022
Z. Shi et al. (Eds.): IIP 2022, IFIP AICT 643, pp. 260–273, 2022.
https://doi.org/10.1007/978-3-031-03948-5_21

The essence of blockchain is a distributed database (ledger), which has the characteristics of decentralization, tamper-proof and traceability. It has been widely used in digital currency, anti-counterfeiting and traceability, electronic deposit certificates, intellectual property protection, Internet of Things and other fields. The data stored on the blockchain is tamper-resistant, providing a new mode for information sharing between enterprises in the supply chain. Companies on the chain can build a decentralized or multi-center supply chain network to avoid the potential risk of excessive power of the core company.

Based on summarizing the problems of traditional supply chain management systems and analyzing some deficiencies in the existing blockchain-based supply chain management architecture, this paper constructs a supply chain management architecture based on alliance chains. The architecture uses Hyperledger Fabric as the underlying framework to isolate private data through channel isolation. Under the premise of protecting privacy, companies in the supply chain can quickly reach consensus and trusted transactions, and achieve massive transactions that meet actual application scenarios. The "blockchain + business database" distributed storage accounting mode overcomes many of the problems of low transaction speed and low data throughput of classic blockchain technology.

2 Related Work

Blockchain was proposed as the underlying technology of Bitcoin [3]. Taking Bitcoin as an example of the blockchain model, the blockchain is divided into data layer, network layer, consensus layer, incentive layer, contract layer and application layer [4]. Each block is composed of a block header and a block body. The blocks that are generated one after another are linked together to form a block chain. Smart contract [5] is a kind of script running on the blockchain, which realizes the automation of contract content and rule execution by computer coding the script language. On the basis of Bitcoin, the addition of Turing's complete smart contract is the technical core of Ethereum [6].

The blockchain network based on the Proof of Work consensus mechanism has problems such as low transaction speed, low data throughput, and high hardware cost [7], which will cause energy waste and environmental pollution, and cannot meet the supply chain. The needs of a large number of business scenarios. Pedrosa et al. [8] designed the lightning network and used it as a side chain of Bitcoin to increase the transaction speed of the Bitcoin network. With the introduction of Byzantine Fault Tolerance into the blockchain, the hardware and energy costs required to achieve consensus have been greatly reduced. However, as the number of nodes increases, the time required for the Byzantine algorithm to reach a consensus has also greatly increased. For this issue, Androulaki et al. [9] proposed an expandable Hyperledger Fabric alliance chain system, which achieved an end-to-end throughput of more than 3,500 transactions per second, and can be well extended to more than 100 peers.

Today's competition among enterprises has shifted from individual product competition to supply chain competition. In the industry, Wal-Mart uses barcode (UPC) technology and radio frequency data communication (RFDC) technology to build a low-cost and high-efficiency replenishment system [10], which has greatly increased its gross profit margin. JD.com completed the electronic transformation of the entire supply chain, and data shows that only in the warehousing handover stage, it saves about 100 million yuan in expenses every year. Real-time dynamics and precise arrangement of logistics are the core of supply chain development.

The traditional supply chain system integrates transaction, transportation and warehousing, spans multiple steps and hundreds of locations, and generates huge amounts of data. This may cause data to be tampered with, illegal transactions cannot be monitored, and default costs are low. The application of blockchain technology to the supply chain system helps to solve the problems of supply chain decentralization, traceability, information security, and maintenance costs. For example, Feng Tian [11] combined the traceable supply chain with RFID tags and blockchain technology, and classified and stored the RFID tag data generated during production, processing, transportation and other processes in the blockchain, which improved the traceability of the supply chain. Figorilli et al. [12] implemented a blockchain-based timber chain traceability system through RFID sensor technology and blockchain technology, which use the characteristics of decentralization and distributed storage of blockchain technology to safely store data information and transaction records, and realize the electronic traceability of timber from standing timber to end users. However, this solution does not support the two-way update of the blockchain and the database, and it has poor support for data persistence. Caro et al. [13] combined the Internet of Things technology to propose a blockchain solution for agricultural product supply chain management, AgriBlockIoT, which realizes the traceability of information in the whole process of production and sales of agricultural products, but this solution has the problem of insufficient computing power at the edge nodes. Resulting in low overall system throughput. This paper adopts the "blockchain + business database" distributed storage accounting mode to control the size of the unit block. Compared with the literature [12], the efficiency of data storage is improved, and the Kafka consensus mechanism is introduced to achieve rapid consensus of trustless nodes. It reduces the computing overhead of nodes, overcomes the problem of insufficient computing power of edge nodes in the literature [13], and improves the availability of low computing power computing nodes.

3 System Design

3.1 Supply Chain Transaction Architecture Design

The supply chain transaction architecture of this article is developed based on Hyperledger Fabric 1.4, as shown in Fig. 1. It consists of a data layer, a consensus layer, and an application layer. The main function of the data layer is to store business data such as business registration information and transaction data in the blockchain and the hash value of these data. In the consensus layer, each organization in the alliance has a peer node for information exchange and a node for sorting, and Kafka consensus is used to package and sort transactions. The application layer allows web services to interact with the blockchain network through the SDK interface to facilitate data query and product traceability.

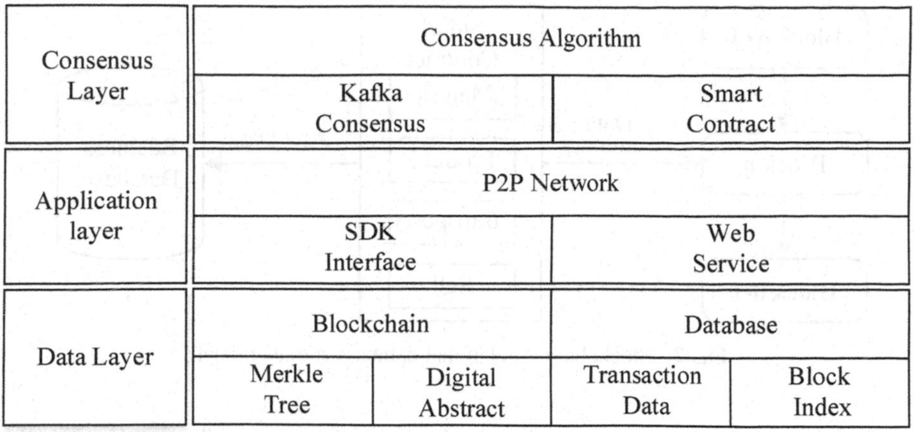

Consensus Layer	Consensus Algorithm	
	Kafka Consensus	Smart Contract
Application layer	P2P Network	
	SDK Interface	Web Service
Data Layer	Blockchain		Database	
	Merkle Tree	Digital Abstract	Transaction Data	Block Index

Fig. 1. Supply chain transaction architecture

3.2 Multi-tier Database Design

With the increase of network nodes, the speed of consensus on the blockchain becomes slow. In order to accelerate the speed of consensus and increase the throughput of data per unit time of the system, the block size is often limited to a small range. In a supply chain transaction system, a transaction often involves a large amount of data, and it is obviously difficult to store all the data involved in the transaction on the blockchain network. In order to solve this problem and improve the throughput of the network, this paper adopts a two-layer database design of "blockchain + business database". As shown in Fig. 2, in the supply chain, the data generated during the procurement of raw and auxiliary materials, production, circulation and use of finished products is submitted to the smart contract for verification by the node. The smart contract authenticates and processes the data and then hashes the data. After that it upload the data summary generated by the hash operation to the blockchain network, and store the original data and the block location information stored in the data summary in the business database. This paper reduces the block size through the design of a multi-layer database, improves the system throughput per unit time, and ensures the reliability of the data through smart contract verification.

The simulation platform in this paper uses CouchDB database to store actual business data. CouchDB is a document-based database system. Data is stored in a key-value pair format to store specific transaction information in the ledger. The CouchDB database supports two-way synchronization. When the data in the blockchain is changed through transactions, the corresponding data in CouchDB will also be updated synchronously. When adding, modifying and deleting data in CouchDB, all operations will be simultaneously appended to the blockchain ledger.

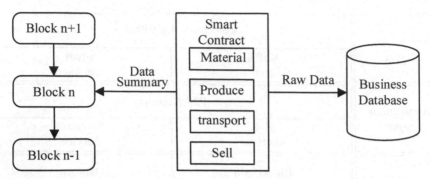

Fig. 2. Blockchain + relational database storage model

The data verification process of this article is as follows, when the data needs to be verified, the original data and the block location information stored in the data summary are retrieved from the database. Hash the data in the database and compare it with the data on the block. If it is consistent with the data on the block, the data has not been tampered with, otherwise, the data has tampered.

3.3 Kafka Consensus Configuration

This paper adopts Apache Kafka consensus mechanism. Compared with the traditional consensus mechanism based on workload proof, Kafka consensus speed is faster, and the hardware overhead is small and will not cause energy waste.

Compared with the consensus algorithm based on Byzantine fault tolerance, Kafka consensus still has better system throughput when it accommodates more nodes. Compared with Proof of Work and Proof of Stake, Kafka consensus has sufficient fault tolerance but poor resistance to malicious attacks. Considering that general enterprise databases are deployed in the intranet, and only enterprises with a foundation of trust can join. Therefore, this paper selects the more powerful Kafka consensus mechanism without considering the existence of external attacks.

The simulation platform of this paper adopts the consensus mechanism based on Kafka cluster as shown in Fig. 3, and the nodes in the following Table 1 are configured on 16 virtual machines. The hardware platform of the system is as follows: Intel Core i9 10900k 4.7 GHz processor, NVIDIA RTX3070 graphics card, DDR4 32G memory, 1T solid state drive. The software platform is as follows: Ubuntu 16.04 operating system, Hyperledger Fabric1.4, Golang 1.8, Docker 2.0. The server configuration information is shown in the table below. A total of 16 nodes run on 16 virtual machines. It includes three organizations: Organization 1/2/3. Each organization has two nodes. The first node of each organization is the anchor node that joins the public channel and interacts with other organizations. In addition, 3 Zookeeper clusters, 4 Kafka clusters, and 3 Orderer nodes for sorting are included.

Table 1. Kafka cluster configuration

Name	IP Address	Quantity	Organization
Zookeeper	192.168.247.1/2/3	3	/
Kafka	192.168.247.4/5/6/7	4	/
Orderer	192.168.247.8/9/10	3	/
Org1	192.168.247.11/12	2	Org1
Org2	192.168.247.13/14	2	Org2
Org3	192.168.247.13/14	2	Org3

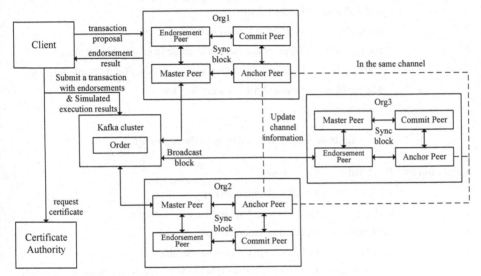

Fig. 3. Kafka consensus architecture

3.4 Smart Contract Design

The smart contract in this simulation experiment is written in Golang language and uses the shim API interface provided by the Hyperledger Fabric team. The data structure of the smart contract defines a user information table and a product information table. The user information table is shown in Table 2, which is used to maintain the user's personal information and a list of products owned by the user. The product information table is shown in Table 3, which is used to maintain various information of the product. When the product is made of chain materials, the product information table also maintains the raw material table of the product. Table 4 is the function description in the following smart contract Algorithm 1–3.

Table 2. User information form

Serial number	Field name	Description
1	userName	User's name
2	userId	User Unique Id number
3	productArr	productArrUser's product list

Table 3. Product information sheet

Serial number	Field name	Description
1	productName	Product name
2	productId	Product unique Id number
3	madeInChian	Whether the product is made from on-chain materials
4	productInfo	Product information such as production date, quantity, etc.
5	rMaterialArr	productArr User's product list

Table 4. Function description in the algorithm

Serial number	Field name	Description
1	isExist	Check if the input exists
2	getState	Get the current value of a state variable
3	putState	Update the specified state variable
4	delateState	Delete the specified state variable
5	madeInChain	Determine whether it is made from raw materials on the chain

In this paper, three contracts are designed, among which Algorithms 1 and 2 are the registration and transaction algorithms of smart contracts, and Algorithm 3 is used to verify the reliability of data on the supply chain. Algorithm 1 is a smart contract algorithm used by companies in the blockchain for product registration. Before product registration, the user needs to define the structure of the product and store it in a json file in string format. After the definition is completed, the smart contract will determine the format of the written data. After the determination is passed, the product will be registered under the corresponding owner's name and written into the blockchain network.

```
Algorithm_1 Product_Grade
Input productId, productInfo, ownerId
Output return Shim.Success else Except
Begin:
1.type Product struct
2.if input is empty or error struct
3.      return input error
4.else
5.      if isExist(productId) is true
6.           return productId is exist
7.      else
8.           if isExist(ownerId) is false
9.             return user not exist
10.          else
11.             ownerId.product.PutSate(productId)
12.             productId.putState(productInfo)
13.             return put product success
End
```

Algorithm 2 introduces product transaction between enterprises. During the transaction, the smart contract will determine the input data. When all the determination conditions are passed, the smart contract will change the asset owner and put the transaction on the chain.

```
Algorithm_2 Product_Trading
Input preownerId, productId, ownerId
Output return Shim.Success else Except
Begin:
1.if isExist(preownerId or productId or ownerId)
is false
2.   return input error
3.else
4.   getState(preownerId)
4.   for i in perownerId.productArr
5.      if perownerId.product[i] == productId
6.         preownerId.deleteState(product.productId)
7.         ownerId.putState(product.productId)
8.      else
9.         return preownerId not have this productId
End
```

Algorithm 3 is an algorithm called when companies consume some raw materials or materials recorded on the chain to manufacture products. It is mainly used to determine whether there are illegal operations such as raw materials that have passed the shelf life and ingredients measurement inconsistent during the production process.

```
Algorithm_3 Production_Monitoring
Input productId, productInfo, ownerId
Output Return Shim.Success else Except
Begin:
1.type Product struct
2.if isExist(productId) is true
3.    return productId is exist
4.else
5.    if madeInChain(productInfo) is true
6.        get rMaterialArr from productInfo
7.        for rMaterial in rmArr.num
8.            if rMaterial.Exp<Now.date
9.                return rMaterial out of date
10.   else
11.       ownerId.deleteState(product. rMaterial)
12.       ownerId.putState(productId)
13.       productId.putState(productInfo)
End
```

4 System Performance Analysis

4.1 Parameter Introduction

After completing the construction of the supply chain transaction system, the supply chain transaction system needs to be tested. This article uses the load testing tool Tape to evaluate the throughput of the system by analyzing the response to the gRPC request. The test mainly calls the query function and the call function in the smart contract, and measures the system performance by testing the system transaction throughput, transactions per second, TPS, under different parameter settings. In the process of blockchain transactions, transaction data throughput, transaction success rate, and transaction delay are the key factors for measuring system performance.

In the process of transaction packaging, the ordering node needs to digitally sign each transaction. Digital signatures for a large number of transactions in a unit time occupy a large amount of system performance. Therefore, this article introduces the concept of batch signature, which is to package a group of data into one bag. The ordering node only needs to sign each packet once, thereby achieving the goal of saving system performance and improving data throughput per unit time. Also, to prevent the number of transactions in the blockchain within a period of time from being too small to meet the packaging requirements, resulting in too long a single package generation time, this article sets a maximum block time for each package. The system performance test in this article will provide the system throughput under the query operation and call operation of the system under the adjustment of packet size, maximum block time, and block size.

4.2   System Performance Analysis Under Query Operation

When performing a query operation on the blockchain, there is no need to call an additional ordering node of the system, and no record will be left on the blockchain.

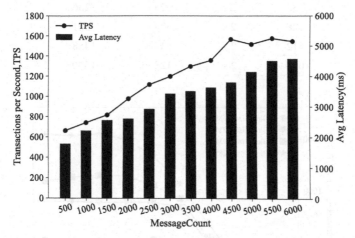

Fig. 4. System Throughput (TPS) under query operation

Figure 4 shows the change in system throughput with the increase of the request volume under the query operation. When the number of requests is 500, the throughput of the system is 603TPS, when the number of requests is 1000, the throughput of the system reaches 1080TPS, and when the number of requests is more than 2000, the throughput of the system reaches more than 1600TPS and tends to be stable. This shows that the blockchain-based supply chain platform proposed in this article can basically meet the needs of most small and medium-sized enterprises for supply chain management when deployed on ordinary servers.

4.3   System Performance Analysis Under Call Operation

The call operation needs to call the ordering node to order the transaction, and the endorsing node is required to endorse the transaction. Among them, the batch size, maximum block time, block size and other parameters will affect the performance of the system under the call operation. This article chooses to adjust other parameters to test the system performance based on controlling the maximum block time. Table 5 records the size of the system throughput under different parameter settings.

Figure 5 shows the effect of batch size and block size on system throughput when the maximum block time is fixed.

As the unit block size and batch size increase, the throughput of the network also increases. When the block size is set to 32M, as the batch size increases, the system throughput gradually rises. When the batch size reaches 2048, the system throughput reaches 880TPS. When the batch size is 1024 and the block size reaches 128M, the system throughput reaches 1500TPS. At this time, increasing the block and batch size

Table 5. System throughput under different parameter settings

BatchSize	Timeout	BlockSize	TPS
8	2 s	8 m	57
32	2 s	32 m	236
128	2 s	32 m	501
512	2 s	64 m	1458
1024	2 s	128 m	1539

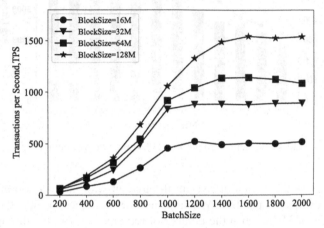

Fig. 5. System throughput under call operation

cannot improve the system performance. Through the analysis of log files, it is found that the number of transactions per unit time processed by the sorting node has not reached the upper limit, that is, a bottleneck has appeared in the I/O performance of the computer. Limited by the computer's hardware, there is still room for improvement in the performance of this system. The final data throughput under the current hardware platform is 1500TPS, which can basically meet the transaction processing needs of medium-sized enterprises.

4.4   Analysis of the Influence of the Number of Nodes on the System Performance

As the number of nodes on the blockchain network increases, where a large number of nodes make data calls simultaneously, it will also lead to an increase in system resource overhead, furthermore affecting system latency and system throughput. We also need to consider how to perform concurrent testing among multiple nodes and how to select the appropriate number of peak nodes for the system.

We simulate the impact of the number of nodes on the system throughput when the batch size is set to 2048, the block size is set to 128M, and the call operation is performed in the public channel. Table 6 shows the number of nodes in the experiment and the system delay time and system throughput of 50,000 transactions completed by the call operation under the current settings. It can be seen from Fig. 6 that with the increase in the number of nodes, the overhead of the system gradually increases, the throughput of the system does not increase indefinitely, and the system delay continues to rise. When the number of nodes exceeds 60, the performance of the system begins to drop significantly. When there are 100 nodes in the call operation at the same time, the system throughput can still reach 1326TPS. Through experiments, it can be found that the system performance can still meet the basic application requirements when multiple nodes are called at the same time.

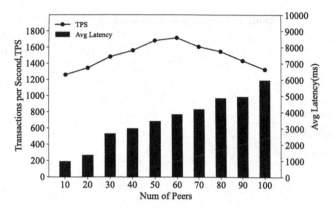

Fig. 6. The impact of the number of users on throughput

Table 6. System throughput under different parameter settings

Numbers of peer	Number of transactions	Latency	TPS
10	50000	0.97 s	1442
20	50000	1.34 s	1562
60	50000	3.48 s	1684
80	50000	4.82 s	1547
100	50000	5.96 s	1326

4.5 Comparison with Existing Systems

The scheme in this paper is a supply chain management scheme based on blockchain, which adopts Kafka consensus mechanism to reach the consensus of network nodes. Compared with the traditional supply chain management system based on central-ized service, this scheme has certain advantages in data tamper proof, independent of central server and data traceability. Compared with the Ref. [17], which takes azure SQL blockchain platform to build supply chain management system, our scheme uses

CouchDB database to store business data and supports bidirectional modification of data modification of data, which has certain advantages in data storage. Compared with the Ethereum platform and sawtooth platform adopted in document [18], the supply chain management system based on Ethereum platform has the problem of insufficient computing power of edge nodes. The Kafka consensus used in our scheme has lower requirements for node computing power, better compatibility with low configuration computers, and higher efficiency of consensus. Table 7 shows the comparison between our scheme and the above two schemes in decentralization, computing overhead, tamper proof, fault tolerance and data storage.

Table 7. Comparison with existing systems

Function	This paper	Literature [12]	Literature [13]
Decentralization	✓	✓	✓
Tamper proof	✓	✓	✓
Support fault tolerance	✓	✓	✓
Low computational cost	✓	×	✓
Bidirectional data storage	✓	×	×

5 Conclusions

With the advent of the era of blockchain 3.0, the concept of blockchain + business database has received extensive attention from all walks of life in society, and the blockchain network has been applied to various fields as a trust network. This paper designs a supply chain transaction processing architecture based on blockchain technology, and uses experiments to demonstrate the feasibility and efficiency of this architecture. This article uses the Hyperledger Fabric framework to design, realizes the transaction processing in the supply chain, uses the channel isolation method to realize the protection of private data in the transaction process, and guarantees the transaction processing speed and data storage efficiency through the multi-layer database design. The simulation experiment test results show that the final throughput of the blockchain architecture in this paper has reached 1500TPS, which proves that the solution can meet the needs of small and medium-sized enterprises' supply chain management.

This solution still has some problems to be solved later, such as how to achieve rapid product traceability on the chain under the premise of meeting privacy data protection is still difficult, and how to further improve the efficiency of the consensus algorithm. These issues are worthy of further study.

References

1. Wuxue, J.: An intelligent supply chain information collaboration model based on Internet of Things and big data. IEEE Access 7, 58324–58335 (2019)

2. Kim, H.M., Laskowski, M.: Toward an ontology-driven blockchain design for supply-chain provenance. Intell. Syst. Account. Finance Manag. **25**(1), 18–27 (2018)
3. Wang, R.J., Tang, Y.C., Zhang, W.Q., et al.: Privacy protection scheme for Internet of vehicles based on homomorphic encryption and block chain technology. Chin. J. Netw. Inf. Secur. **6**(1), 46–53 (2020)
4. Huang, C.Y., Wang, Z.Y., Chen, H.X., et al.: RepChain: a reputation-based secure, fast, and high incentive blockchain system via sharing. IEEE Internet Things J. **8**(6), 4291–4304 (2021)
5. Hassan, E.R., Tahoun, M., Eltaweel, G.S.: A robust computational DRM framework for protecting multimedia contents using AES and ECC. Alex. Eng. J. **59**(3), 1275–1286 (2020)
6. Luu, L., Chu, D.H., Olickel, H., et al.: Making smart contracts smarter. In: ACM SIGSAC Conference on Computer and Communications Security, pp. 254–269 (2016)
7. Leonhard, R.D.: Developing renewable energy credits as cryptocurrency on ethereum's blockchain. Soc. Sci. Electron. Publ. **14**(12), 1–15 (2016)
8. Pedrosa, A.R., Potop-Butucaru, M., Tucci-Piergiovanni, S.: Scalable lightning factories for Bitcoin. In: ACM/SIGAPP Symposium on Applied Computing, pp. 302–309 (2019)
9. Androulaki, E., Manevich, Y., Muralidharan, S., et al.: Hyperledger fabric: a distributed operating system for permissioned blockchains. In: The 13th EuroSys Conference, pp. 1–15 (2018)
10. Ali, S., Wang, G., White, B., Fatima, K.: Libra critique towards global decentralized financial system. In: Wang, G., El Saddik, A., Lai, X., Martinez Perez, G., Choo, K.-K. (eds.) iSCI 2019. CCIS, vol. 1122, pp. 661–672. Springer, Singapore (2019). https://doi.org/10.1007/978-981-15-1301-5_52
11. Tian, F.: An agri-food supply chain traceability system for China based on RFID & blockchain technology. In: 2016 13th International Conference on Service Systems and Service Management (ICSSSM), pp. 1–6. IEEE (2016)
12. Caro, M.P., Ali, M.S., Vecchio, M., et al.: Blockchain-based traceability in agri-food supply chain management: a practical implementation. In: 2018 IoT Vertical and Topical Summit on Agriculture, pp. 1–4 (2018)
13. Figorilli, S., Antonucci, F., Costa, C., et al.: A blockchain implementation prototype for the electronic open source traceability of wood along the whole supply chain. Sensors **18**(9), 3133 (2018)

Game Theory and Emotion

A Game-Theoretic Analysis of Impulse Purchase

Kaili Sun and Xudong Luo[✉]

Guangxi Key Lab of Multi-source Information Mining and Security,
School of Computer Science and Engineering, Guangxi Normal University,
Guilin 541001, China
luoxd@mailbox.gxnu.edu.cn

Abstract. There are a dazzling array of various products on a big e-commerce platform. So, the sales competition for the same goods has become increasingly fierce. In this paper, to help sellers attract customers, we study how to stimulate consumers to purchase impulsively. Specifically, we define a utility function. It can reflect that logistics, pre-sale and after-sale service quality, product rate, product sales volume, source reliability, product prices, and product discounts positively impact impulse buying. More importantly, we use game theory to analyse the equilibria of the trading game between a seller and a buyer under these factors' impact so that the seller can make a competitive marketing strategy.

Keywords: Game theory · e-commerce · Impulse purchase · Prospect theory · Transaction utility theory

1 Introduction

In commerce, the utility of a commodity reflects its ability to satisfy people's desires or their satisfaction degree when consuming the item. Usually, consumers calculate the utility of a commodity brought by different commodity attributes to determine the final commodity to be purchased for the same type of commodity. Consumers' preferences over commodity attributes are subjective judgments based on specific objective criteria or psychological feelings. For example, one store has a better logistics service when choosing schoolbags, while the other has a more reliable after-sale service. If consumers want to get them as soon as possible when buying schoolbags, then the satisfaction of logistics has a more significant impact on purchasing decisions than after-sale service. Hence consumers will, of course, choose the store with faster logistics under the same conditions.

To analyse people's impulse purchase behaviour, in our previous work [11], we developed a theoretical framework of factors affecting consumers' shopping desires, and then verified the model via a questionnaire survey of human participants. Now in this paper, we define a consumer utility function regarding these factors. Moreover, based on the utility function, we establish a trading game model between a seller and a buyer, and analyse how various factors affect

© IFIP International Federation for Information Processing 2022
Published by Springer Nature Switzerland AG 2022
Z. Shi et al. (Eds.): IIP 2022, IFIP AICT 643, pp. 277–289, 2022.
https://doi.org/10.1007/978-3-031-03948-5_22

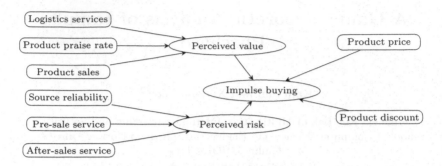

Fig. 1. The structure model of impulse purchasing factor

Table 1. Sample demographics

Measure	Item	Frequency	Percentage
Gender	Male	532	44%
	Female	687	56%
Age	<20	274	22%
	20–30	764	63%
	>30	181	15%
Education level	Below university degree	222	18%
	Undergraduate	689	57%
	Master degree and above	308	25%
Income in RMB (monthly)	<1500	544	45%
	1500–3000	502	41%
	>3000	173	14%

the equilibria of the game, which the seller can use to make their marketing strategies appropriately.

The rest of this paper is structured as follows. Section 2 recaps the online impulsive purchasing behaviour model using online questionnaires. Section 3 proposes a function for consumers to calculate their commodity utility according to these factors. Section 4 establishes a game model of trading between a seller and a buyer and finds its equilibria under various conditions. Section 5 discusses the related work. Finally, Sect. 6 concludes this paper with future work.

2   Structure Model and Questionnaire Data Analysis

This section will recap our work [11] of identifying which factors that may impact online impulsive purchasing behaviour using online questionnaires and statistics.

Consumers often make impulse purchases in real shopping scenarios because they can get a higher utility than not buying. To study the reasons for this phenomenon, we construct a structural model of factors that stimulate consumers

Table 2. Results of reliability analysis

Measurement items	Cronbach's α after deletion of terms
Source reliability	.719
Logistics services rate	.730
Product sale volume	.728
Product praise	.723
Pre-sales services	.713
After-sales service	.714
Product price	.724
Product discounts	.737
Overall	.750

Table 3. Results of validity analysis

KMO		.803
Bartlett's test	Approximate Chi-Square	1759.342
	Df.	28
	Sig.	.000

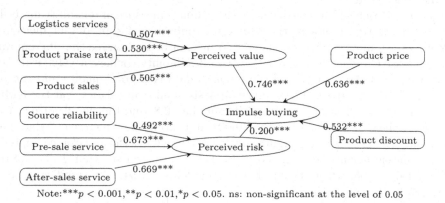

Note:***$p < 0.001$,**$p < 0.01$,*$p < 0.05$. ns: non-significant at the level of 0.05

Fig. 2. The research model text result

to purchase impulsively, as shown in Fig. 1. We use a questionnaire to find: 1) logistics services, commodity praise rate, and commodity sale volume indirectly affect impulse purchases by affecting the perceived value of a commodity; 2) commodity source reliability, pre-sale service, and after-sale service indirectly affect impulsive purchases by affecting perceived risk of purchasing a commodity; and 3) commodity price and discount rate directly affect impulse purchases. We put our questionnaire on the "Questionnaire Star" platform and advertise the questionnaire for online shoppers through its links and QR code on social

Table 4. ANOVA

Model		Quadratic sum	Df.	Mean-square	F	Sig.
1	Regression	255	.539 7	36.506	83.816	.000
	Residual	3713.461	8526	.436		
	Sum	3969.000	9751	.456		

Table 5. The scores of all the attributes

Attribute	Logistics services	Product praise rate	Product sales	Source reliability	Pre-sale service	After-sale service	Product price	Product discount
Score	11.72%	12.83%	11.42%	12.62%	12.93%	13.14%	13.14%	11.82%

media such as WeChat and QQ. We got 1,260 responses, from which we screened out a total of 1,219 valid questionnaires (see Table 1 for sample demographics), with an effective recovery rate of 96.75%. Then we use Harman's single factor test to test the standard method deviations among the collected sample data. Specifically, we use SPSSAU (a statistical analysis tool) to analyse these valid questionnaires.

Tables 2 and 3 show the result of our analysis on the reliability and validity of the collected data.

We use Cronbach's α coefficient as the primary measure of reliability analysis of scale data. After removing the item, the Cronbach coefficient of each measurement factor is more significant than 0.7. It has not been observed that its removal will increase Cronbach's α value. The overall reliability coefficient value is 0.750, indicating that the reliability of the research data is of good quality and can be used for further analysis. The validity analysis of all scales shows that the KMO value of the overall scale is more significant than 0.8, and the significance of the Bartlett sphere test value is less than 0.001, indicating that the research data has good validity and reached a significant level. After we perform variance analysis on the measurement data, as shown in Table 3, we can see that $F = 83.816$, $P = 0.000 < 0.05$, which means that our model is statistically significant, so it is worth further analysis.

We use SPSSAU to verify the structure model proposed in this paper, and the test result of the structure model is shown in Fig. 2. The test includes the coefficients and their significance, verifying all the hypotheses we have made. Table 4 shows the results of the hypothesis verification.

Logistics services, product praise rate, product sale volume, source reliability, pre-sale service, after-sale service, product price, and product discount can all be regarded as different attributes of a product. So, when designing the questionnaire, we set four scoring items for each factor: no impact, slight impact, comparative impact, and extraordinary impact on impulse purchasing, corresponding to 1–4 points, respectively. Then, according to the calculations, we obtain general consumers' preference over these attributes, as shown in Table 5.

3   Consumer Utility Function

This section will present the consumer utility function of a product regarding the factors we identify in the previous section. We also discuss some properties of the utility function in real-life.

As mentioned in the previous section, consumers determine the final product they purchase by comparing the utility satisfaction of all the product attributes. By fusing the factors that affect impulse purchases and the resulting preference over these attributes, we can obtain the overall utility. Based on consumer scores and ratings on impact factors, as well as through word-of-mouth on the internet for their products, sellers can have the utility of the six subsidiary attributes of the product they sell: logistics service, product rating, product sales, source reliability, and pre-sale and after-sale service. Let the utilities of these six attributes are $v_1, \cdots, v_6$, and the utilities from the commodity price and commodity discount are denoted as v_7 and v_8, respectively. According to prospect theory [7], utility v_7 resulting from the commodity price is

$$v_7 = v(\bar{p}, -p) = \bar{p} - p. \tag{1}$$

The transaction utility arising from the discounted goods v_8 is

$$v_8 = v(-p : p^*) = p^* - p, \tag{2}$$

where p is the actual price paid for the product and p^* is its reference price. The reference price of a product can also be called the expected or fair price and indicates the product's actual value. Product prices are crucial for browsing and purchasing goods in both the traditional consumer and e-commerce spheres. For price-oriented customers, online shopping is more attractive. Donovan [4] find that price discounts can induce consumers to make unplanned purchases, a phenomenon that transaction utility theory [13] can well explain. The price difference between the discounted price of a product and its reference price causes consumers to perceive transaction utility. The greater the perceived transactional utility, the more likely the consumer is willing to purchase.

Let the utility of a commodity on attribute $i \in \{1, \cdots, 8\}$ be v_i and the consumer's preference over attribute $i \in \{1, \cdots, 8\}$ be p_i.

Then the utility generated by the consumer's transaction process is given by:

$$u = \sum_{i=1}^{8} p_i v_i. \tag{3}$$

We assume that the value of each p_i obtained is fixed. What can influence consumer utility is the magnitude of the utility generated by each attribute of the fixed good. Sellers can improve their reputation and achieve long term growth based on these attributes at the beginning of the sale of their products.

Theorem 1. *Improving the quality of logistics services for goods helps to increase consumer utility.*

Proof. Assume that the same functional product with two different brands B_1 and B_2 has two choices of logistics companies L_1 and $L2$, respectively. The qualities of service provided by the two logistics companies are different. Let the utility due to the quality of company L_1 be v_1' and the one due to company L_2's be v_1''. If $v_1' > v_1''$ and $p_1 > 0$, we have $u_1' > u_1''$ by formula (3).   □

Logistics is an adjunct to goods in online shopping transactions, creating additional value and meeting customer expectations. Uvet [14] shows that time utility is the most traditional and vital feature of logistics service quality and that timeliness increases customer satisfaction. For example, a girl wants to attend a party in a few days and thus buy a dress. If she gets the dress before the party, she will look great at the party. So the logistics service contributes some utility to the girl. However, if the dress is delivered after the party, then the utility of logistics must be negative. There is more to logistics than just timeliness; it has many dimensions, including return and exchange, damage rates, and last-mile delivery. In particular, in fresh food e-commerce, timeliness and low loss rates are critical for marketing products and maintaining market competitiveness. Also, consumers usually consider strong brands when choosing to shop online for better logistics services [12]. Meanwhile, the quality of logistics services affects the perceived quality of the goods, which is one of the main reasons consumers make purchasing decisions. So, when selling products, the seller must not ignore the utility generated by the quality of logistics services.

Theorem 2. *The higher the praise rating and sale volume of an item, the higher the utility the consumer gains from purchasing the item.*

Proof. Assume that brand B_1 has a greater positive rating and higher sale volume than brand B_1. Let their utilities from positive ratings and sales volume be v_2', v_3' and v_2'', v_3'' respectively. Since both p_2 and p_3 are greater than 0, $p_2 v_2' > p_2 v_2''$, $p_3 v_3' > p_3 v_3''$. By formula (3), we have $u_2' + u_3' > u_2'' + u_3''$.   □

In the Internet era, consumers often comment online on their shopping experience and product quality, among other things. These comments are essential for users of e-commerce platforms to understand what customers think of their products. With the diversification of consumer needs and the growth of rational consumer awareness, it has become more difficult than ever to attract consumers simply by lowering prices [8]. So, most consumers obtain and analyse the corresponding online reviews before purchasing a product as an essential reference for their purchasing decision [5,6]. Chevalier [3] investigated the relative sales of books on Amazon.com and Barnesandnoble.com and found that consumer reviews had a positive impact on product sales.

Meanwhile, the higher the sales volume, the more reliable the positive reviews are because the proportion of false reviews is reduced. The higher the positive review rate and sales volume of an item, the more people approve of the item, leading to a blind trust mood among consumers. So, the buyer's perceived value of the item may consequently increase, and thus the utility gained from purchasing the item may increase as well.

Theorem 3. *The higher the source reliability the higher the consumer utility.*

Proof. Assume that the co-producer of brand B_1 is more reliable than the co-producer of brand B_2. Let the utilities arising from the source reliability of brands B_1 and B_2 be v_4' and v_4'', respectively. Let the customers' utilities of brands B_1 and B_2 be u' and u'', respectively. Then $v_4' > v_4''$. Since $p_4 > 0$, by formula (3), we have $u' > u''$.   □

As people's living standards increase, they are no longer satisfied with basic food and clothes. Instead, they need quality food and clothes. They would not be happy with a product as if it works. Brand and shop reputation have an increasing influence on consumers' propensity to buy, and Chen *et al.* [2] show that emotional trust determines impulse buying. In the internet area, advertising is everywhere, from TV commercial breaks and ad inserts in TV dramas and variety shows to promoting ads in small videos in apps such as Jitterbug and Racer. Nowadays, advertising is more or less exaggerated. Some unscrupulous businessmen may even add false propaganda in their advertisements. So, consumers need to judge what is reliable and not among the various claims. If it is an uncontactable product, it is hard for consumers to judge whether it is good or bad. Trial and error by purchase is too costly and may even result in additional losses. So, most consumers use source reliability as a basis for judgement. For example, if the personal reputation of the anchor is high, consumers usually consider the product they recommend to be more reliable. Alternatively, if an item's manufacturer is a credible company, people will assume that the item's quality is over the top. When people believe that the product they want to buy is unreliable, its utility to them is low. Conversely, when people believe that the product they want to buy is more reliable, it must bring positive utility to them.

Theorem 4. *Improved customer service systems can increase consumer utility.*

Proof. Let the utility from pre-sale and after-sale services of brands B_1 and B_2 be v_5', v_6' and v_5'', v_6'', respectively. Let the customers' utilities of brands B_1 and B_2 be u' and u'', respectively. Assuming $v_5' > v_5''$ and $v_6' > v_6''$, since $p_5 > 0$ and $p_6 > 0$, we have $u' > u''$ by formula (3).   □

The virtual nature of online goods deprives consumers of the opportunity to experience the goods in person, making it possible to buy worse goods than they are willing to pay. This information asymmetry in the transaction process increases the perceived risk to the consumer. At the same time, even though the general public's awareness of their rights has increased considerably at present, in many cases, the rights are not always met with losses. At the same time, the defence of rights inevitably entails a loss of time. To solve these problems, e-commerce platforms employ customer service systems. If the customer service system does not solve these problems well and thus leads to losses for the consumer, the utility contributed by the customer service system is low and may even be harmful. In particular, for entertainment-oriented shoppers, a warm, patient, and professional attitude of the customer service staff and rules such as hassle-free returns and exchanges can provide a pleasant shopping experience and significantly increase the utility generated by the customer service system.

Theorem 5. *Adjusting the price can change the magnitude of the utility of money, thus affecting the consumer's shopping utility.*

Proof. Based on the results of the questionnaire, we have a value of $p_7 = 13.14\%$ for consumer preference for price and $p_8 = 11.82\%$ for discount. By formulas (1) and (2), we have the pecuniary utility function as follows:

$$u = p_7 \cdot v_7 + p_8 \cdot v_8 = p_7 \cdot (\bar{p} - p) + p_8 \cdot (p^* - p). \tag{4}$$

By formula (4), we know that the actual value of the commodity $\bar{p}$ and the reference price p^* are certain. The smaller the actual sale price p of the commodity, the larger v_7 and v_8, so the larger u. If p is increased, the result goes the opposite. □

In general, the actual sale price of an item is higher than its actual value, *i.e.*, $p > \bar{p}$, so the value of v_7 is usually negative. However, the lower the actual price at which the good is sold, the smaller the resulting negative value. Sellers can reduce the negative utility associated with the acquisition utility by reducing the actual sale price of the good. On the other hand, to attract consumers, the actual sale price of a good should generally be lower than the reference price of the good, or at least not higher than the reference price of the good. In other words, $p^* \geq p$. Thus, v_8 is greater than or equal 0. With the reference price as a pair of ratios, the seller can lower the actual sale price of the good through a discount, increasing the positive utility from the transaction utility. The larger the price difference, the higher the transaction utility. Since both p_7 and p_8 are positive, then under this strategy, the total pecuniary utility can be positive even though the acquisition utility in the pecuniary utility is negative. This can explain the phenomenon that most people make impulse purchases during promotions such as Tmall's Double Eleven and Jingdong's 618. For a seller, if the other six attributes of his product have relatively high overall utility, then he can achieve a lower discount to enhance his advantage. If, on the other hand, some of the product's attributes are of low utility and there is no way to change this in the short term, then the only way to increase utility is to increase the monetary utility. At this point, the seller must make discounts big enough to offset the lack of utility of other attributes while still delivering additional positive utility to entice consumers to purchase competitive conditions.

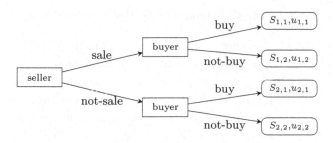

Fig. 3. The game tree

In summary, our consumer utility formula can help companies and sellers understand the psychological factors that make consumers make impulse purchases. At the same time, it is possible to explain the reasons behind the success of a brand or a shop in the e-commerce platform.

4 Game Model and Game Equilibria

In the case of certain product logistics service quality, product sale volume, product praise rate, source reliability, pre-sale service, and after-sale service, merchants want their products to be more attractive to consumers than other products of the same type. Otherwise, consumers' utility can be increased by adjusting commodity prices and discounts. This section will discuss how the game's outcome is affected by monetary factors. This result can tell the marketing manager, for the general consumer group, what price and how much discount they should set to attract consumers to buy their products.

Theorem 6. *Let the total utility from the quality of logistics services, product sales volume, positive product feedback, source reliability, pre-sale service and after-sale service be $C = p_1v_1 + \cdots + p_6v_6$. Assume that the sale price of a good is equal to the market reference price p^*, and the actual sale price of a good sold by a seller is denoted as p'. The utility of these six attributes is denoted as C'. Then Table 6 shows various equilibria of the trading game between the seller and the buyer under different conditions.*

Proof. The process of trading between buyers and sellers is, in fact, a dynamic game. It proceeds in this order: first, the seller takes a discount or no discount strategy, and then the buyer takes a buy or not-buy decision after knowing the strategy made by the seller. We use a game tree to show the exact process of the game, as shown in Fig. 3. $(1, 1)$ stands for discount and buy, $(1, 2)$ for the discount but not buy, $(2, 1)$ for no discount and buy, and $(2, 2)$ for no discount and not-buy. S represents the seller's utility, and w represents the buyer's utility. Next, we discuss the eight cases included in Table 6.

Table 6. The Equilibriums under Different Conditions

C' and C	p' satisfies	Equilibrium
$C' < C$	$p' > \frac{C-C'}{P_7+P_8} + P^*$ and $P' > \bar{p}$	(sale, buy)
	$\frac{C-C'}{P_7+P_8} + P^* < p' < \bar{p}$	(not-sale, buy)
	$\bar{p} < p' < \frac{C-C'}{P_7+P_8} + P^*$	(sale, not-buy)
	$p' < \frac{C-C'}{P_7+P_8} + P^*$ and $P' < \bar{p}$	(not-sale, not-buy)
$C' > C$	$\bar{p} < p' < P^* - \frac{C-C'}{P_7+P_8}$	(sale, buy)
	$p' < P^* - \frac{C-C'}{P_7+P_8}$ and $P' < \bar{p}$	(not-sale, buy)
	$p' > P^* - \frac{C-C'}{P_7+P_8}$ and $P' > \bar{p}$	(sale, not-buy)
	$P^* - \frac{C-C'}{P_7+P_8} < p' < \bar{p}$	(not-sale, not-buy)

In the case of $C' < C$, the seller must make a concession on p' if he wants to attract consumers. The exact value of p' takes into account both $\bar{p}$ and p'. By formulas (3) and (4), 1) if $p' > \frac{C-C'}{P_7+P_8} + P^*$ and $p' > \bar{p}$, for the seller, $S_{1,i} > S_{2,i}$. So the seller chooses to discount. At this point, $u_{1,1} > u_{1,2}$, so the buyer chooses to buy. 2) If $\frac{C-C'}{P_7+P_8} + P^* < p' < \bar{p}$, then $u_{1,1} > u_{1,2}$. So the buyer chooses to buy. However, since $S_{1,i} < S_{2,i}$, the seller chooses not to make a discount decision. 3) If $\bar{p} < p' < \frac{C-C'}{P_7+P_8} + P^*$, $S_{1,i} > S_{2,i}$. A positive utility can be gained by the seller, so the seller chooses to discount. However, in this case the buyer chooses not to buy. 4) If $p' < \frac{C-C'}{P_7+P_8} + P^*$, then $S_{1,i} < S_{2,i}$ and $u_{j,1} < u_{j,2}$. So the seller chooses not to discount and the buyer chooses not to buy.

In the case of $C' > C$, if p^* does not change, then p' can still be competitive without a price reduction, even if it is higher than within a certain range. 1) If $\bar{p} < p' < P^* - \frac{C-C'}{P_7+P_8}$, then $S_{1,i} > S_{2,i}$. So the seller chooses sell at such a price. Then since $u_{1,1} > u_{1,2}$, the buyer chooses to buy. 2) If $p' < P^* - \frac{C-C'}{P_7+P_8}$ and $P' < \bar{p}$, then $u_{1,1} > u_{1,2}$. Thus, the buyer chooses to buy. However, $S_{1,i} < S_{2,i}$, so the seller chooses not to make such a big discount. 3) If $p' > P^* - \frac{C-C'}{p_7+p_8}$ and $p' > \bar{p}$, then $S_{1,i} > S_{2,i}$. So, the seller choose to sell at a suitably higher price. However, since $u_{1,1} < u_{1,2}$, the buyer chooses not to buy. 4) If $p^* - \frac{C-C'}{p_7+p_8} < p' < \bar{p}$, then $S_{1,i} < S_{2,i}$ and $u_{j,1} < u_{j,2}$. So the seller chooses not to discount and then the buyer chooses not to buy. □

We can put the above game process into a practical example. Support there are now two brands (B_1 and B_2) of umbrellas that meet a buyer's needs. The buyer needs to make a purchase decision by calculating and comparing the benefits of his purchase. B_1 chooses SF Express as the partner, while B_2 chooses Yuan Tong Express as the partner. The overall service quality of SF Express is higher than that of Yuan Tong Express, so the utility of logistics service quality is 100 and 90 for B_1 and B_2, respectively. Both brands are recognised as being relatively reliable, and their promotional methods and efforts are equally divided, so the utility from source reliability is recorded as 100. B_1's pre-sale and after-sale service quality ratings are higher than B_2's, so the utility from pre-sale and after-sale service for B_1 and B_2 are recorded as 100, 100 and 90, 90 respectively. With the same price and no discounts, the utility gained by the buyer from purchasing these two brands of umbrellas is: $u_{B_1} = 11.72\% \times 100 + 12.83\% \times 95 + 11.42\% \times 90 + 12.62\% \times 100 + 12.93\% \times 100 + 13.14\% \times 100 + u_A$; $u_{B_2} = 11.72\% \times 100 + 12.83\% \times 95 + 11.42\% \times 97 + 12.62\% \times 100 + 12.93\% \times 90 + 13.14\% \times 90 + u_{B_2}$. So, $u_{B_1} > u_{B_2}$. We assume that the actual value of both umbrellas is RMB 90, and the reference price is RMB 100 for both. Then by formula (4), brand B_2 has to make at least a discount of 9.5% for consumers to obtain the same utility and be able to attract them to make a purchase decision. However, at the same time, the net profit of brand B_2 is reduced. So, the marketing manager needs to consider all the factors such as cost and sales volume before making a reasonable discount strategy.

5 Related Work

Although many investigations and studies on factors that may influence consumers' online impulse purchasing behaviour, our work differs from them. Chen et al. [2] use signalling theory to investigate how information cues influence online purchasers' trust, product attitudes and impulse purchases. Zafar et al. [15] use partial least squares structural modelling and fuzzy set qualitative comparative analysis to investigate the effect of social media celebrity. Chen et al. [1] analyse the effect of emotions such as visual appeal and pleasure on impulse purchases and the effect of emotional dissonance on the willingness to return products. Our work in this paper differs from theirs in the following ways. 1) We used an online questionnaire to examine the factors that directly or indirectly influence impulse buying. 2) We constructed a model using the S-O-R paradigm and used a standard statistics tool to validate the model. And 3) we argue that perceived risk and value act as mediators that influence impulse buying.

On the other hand, we need to note that the transaction process is a dynamic game. Srinivasan et al. [10] propose a dynamic pricing algorithm based on game theory that significantly reduces the peak load on intelligent grids and increases profits. Shari and Shamsudin [9] argue that game theory is a tool for predicting competitive behaviour and can be used to make pricing decisions and identify goods to be sold. Zhou and Luo [16] treat sellers and buyers as two players in a trading game, where the latter's decisions are the result of the former's strategic choices. They use transaction utility to calculate the utility of both buyers and sellers, helping them to make utility-maximising decisions. However, these studies either pay little attention to the monetary utility induced by price or ignore the utility derived from the collateral properties of the good. In this paper, we consider pecuniary utility and the additional utility arising from various aspects of the commodity's attributes. As a result, our model and utility function can explain and predict consumers' impulse purchasing behaviour more accurately.

6 Summary

Nowadays, online shopping is trendy, but there are still many open issues. In this paper, according to our previous finding of which factors can stimulate consumers to shop impulsively, we define a consumer utility function. The function reflects that the quality of logistics services, positive product reviews, product sales volume, source reliability, pre-sale services, after-sale services, and product prices and discounts positively impact impulse buying. Moreover, we analyse the transaction process as a dynamic game. Our analysis confirms that consumers need to compare the small utility that comes from buying different goods when making a purchase decision, while sellers need to consider the additional utility of each attribute of the product when pricing it. Only in this way can a brand or shop achieve more long-term development. So, sometimes the service quality of logistics, pre-sale and after-sale, customer product rating, the product's sales amount, and the source's reliability cannot change in a short period. In that case, the marketing manager needs to make a reasonable discount to stimulate consumer spending quickly. Precisely, using our model, the marketing manager can determine a discount to comprise one attribute of a product they operate are deficient. The parameters in our model are already set to quantitative based on the questionnaire, the only variable is the net price after the discount. The sales manager can price a product reasonably according to Table 6 to attract more customers to buy while ensuring their effectiveness.

However, our work still has some issues, which are worthy of addressing in the future. First, it is worth considering the regret behaviour of consumers after impulse purchase. This study may reduce consumers' return behaviour after impulse purchase because ignoring the results of impulse buying may waste social resources and hurt the company's reputation. Second, according to the framing effect, consumers' purchasing intents depend on how discounts are offered (*e.g.*, percentages and absolute values, more extensive and more minor discounts). So, after using our utility function to determine the new sales price, the seller should choose the appropriate promotion form. Finally, we set the consumer attribute preference value as an average result obtained from the questionnaire data. However, preferences are individual and not applicable to all people. So, enterprises can analyse the big data of e-commerce websites, such as historical order analysis, overall consumption level analysis, browsing history analysis, to get the specific preference set of target consumers for various attributes of products.

Acknowledgment. This work was supported by National Natural Science Foundation of China (No. 61762016) and Graduate Student Innovation Project of School of Computer Science and Engineering, Guangxi Normal University (JXXYYJSCXXM-2021-001).

References

1. Chen, W.K., Chen, C.W., Lin, Y.C.: Understanding the influence of impulse buying toward consumers' post-purchase dissonance and return intention: an empirical investigation of apparel websites. J. Ambient Intell. Humanized Comput., 1–14 (2020). https://doi.org/10.1007/s12652-020-02333-z
2. Chen, Y., Lu, Y., Wang, B., Pan, Z.: How do product recommendations affect impulse buying? An empirical study on WeChat social commerce. Inf. Manage. **56**(2), 236–248 (2019)
3. Chevalier, J.A., Mayzlin, D.: The effect of word of mouth on sales: online book reviews. J. Mark. Res. **43**(3), 345–354 (2006)
4. Donovan, R.J., Rossiter, J.R., Marcoolyn, G., Nesdale, A.: Store atmosphere and purchasing behavior. J. Retail. **70**(3), 283–294 (1994)
5. Gao, B., Hu, N., Bose, I.: Follow the herd or be myself? An analysis of consistency in behavior of reviewers and helpfulness of their reviews. Decis. Support Syst. **95**, 1–11 (2017)
6. Gavilan, D., Avello, M., Martinez-Navarro, G.: The influence of online ratings and reviews on hotel booking consideration. Tour. Manage. **66**, 53–61 (2018)
7. Kahneman, D., Tversky, A.: Prospect theory: an analysis of decision under risk. In: Handbook of the Fundamentals of Financial Decision Making, pp. 99–127. World Scientific (2013)
8. Liu, C., Wang, S., Jia, G.: Exploring e-commerce big data and customer-perceived value: an empirical study on Chinese online customers. Sustainability **12**(20), 8649 (2020)
9. Shari, N.S.M., Shamsudin, M.F.: Can game theory solve marketing problems? J. Postgrad. Curr. Bus. Res. **5**(1), 1–4 (2020)
10. Srinivasan, D., Rajgarhia, S., Radhakrishnan, B.M., Sharma, A., Khincha, H.: Game-theory based dynamic pricing strategies for demand side management in smart grids. Energy **126**, 132–143 (2017)
11. Sun, K., Luo, X.: An empirical analysis of consumer impulse purchases. In: ICEB 2021 Proceedings, Nanjing, China (2021). Paper no. 55. https://aisel.aisnet.org/iceb2021/55
12. Sürücü, E., Özispa, N.: Measuring the effect of perceived logistics service quality on brand factors in the e-commerce context. Mark. Branding Res. **4**, 112–128 (2017)
13. Thaler, R.: Transaction utility theory. Adv. Consum. Res. **10**, 229–232 (1983)
14. Uvet, H.: Importance of logistics service quality in customer satisfaction: an empirical study. Oper. Supply Chain Manage. Int. J. **13**(1), 1–10 (2020)
15. Zafar, A.U., Qiu, J., Li, Y., Wang, J., Shahzad, M.: The impact of social media celebrities' posts and contextual interactions on impulse buying in social commerce. Comput. Hum. Behav. **115**, 106178 (2021)
16. Zhou, X., Luo, X.: An irrationally rational game model. In: ICEB 2016 Proceedings, Xiamen, China (2016). Article no. 76

A Self-supervised Strategy for the Robustness of VQA Models

Jingyu Su, Chuanhao Li, Chenchen Jing, and Yuwei Wu[✉]

Beijing Laboratory of Intelligent Information Technology, School of Computer Science, Beijing Institute of Technology (BIT), Beijing, China
{3120195500,lichuanhao,chenchen.jing,wuyuwei}@bit.edu.cn

Abstract. In visual question answering (VQA), most existing models suffer from language biases which make models not robust. Recently, many approaches have been proposed to alleviate language biases by generating samples for the VQA task. These methods require the model to distinguish original samples from synthetic samples, to ensure that the model fully understands two modalities of both visual and linguistic information rather than just predicts answers based on language biases. However, these models are still not sensitive enough to changes of key information in questions. To make full use of the key information in questions, we design a self-supervised strategy to make the nouns of questions be focused for enhancing the robustness of VQA models. Its auxiliary training process, predicting answers for synthetic samples generated by masking the last noun in questions, alleviates the negative influence of language biases. Experiments conducted on VQA-CP v2 and VQA v2 datasets show that our method achieves better results than other VQA models.

Keywords: Visual question answering · Language bias · Self-supervised learning

1 Introduction

The visual question answering (VQA) task requires a model to make comprehensive use of both visual information in images and linguistic information in questions to provide correct answers (Antol et al. 2015). It has attracted lots of interest in the computer vision and natural language processing communities.

During training, most early models learn spurious correlations between question types and answers (i.e., language biases). However, the other parts of the question and the visual information are overlooked, although the model needs to combine the nouns outside of the question type and the image to make inferential region localization. For example, we know a question with the type "What color is the" should be answered by color. It seems that this correlation will provide a set of candidate answers and help the model predict the correct answer. However, if most samples with a question type "What color is the" in the training set have the answer "Red" and the model learned this

© IFIP International Federation for Information Processing 2022
Published by Springer Nature Switzerland AG 2022
Z. Shi et al. (Eds.): IIP 2022, IFIP AICT 643, pp. 290–298, 2022.
https://doi.org/10.1007/978-3-031-03948-5_23

spurious statistical correlation in training, the model may be able to answer correctly based on "What color is the" alone when we ask "What color is the train?" as depicted in Fig. 1a. In this case, the models will ignore the visual information and the rest parts of the question. These models have been validated to perform poorly on the VQA-CP dataset (Agrawal et al. 2018) in which the training set has different answer distributions to the test set.

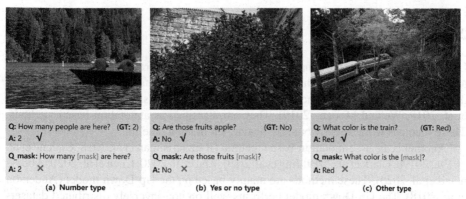

Q: How many people are here? (GT: 2)
A: 2   √

Q_mask: How many [mask] are here?
A: 2   ✗

(a) Number type

Q: Are those fruits apple?   (GT: No)
A: No   √

Q_mask: Are those fruits [mask]?
A: No   ✗

(b) Yes or no type

Q: What color is the train?   (GT: Red)
A: Red   √

Q_mask: What color is the [mask]?
A: Red   ✗

(c) Other type

Fig. 1. A model learned language biases cannot respond to the changes (i.e., [mask]) in question-image pairs although it can give the correct answer when the questions are complete. However, when keywords are masked, a robust model will not give the original answers for the lack of key information pointing to a particular answer.

Recent approaches have attempted to address this issue. A popular method is to generate a different input question-image pair and supervise whether the model has learned the bias by seeing if it still predicts the same answer (Zhu et al. 2020; Chen et al. 2020). For example, Zhu et al. (2020) proposed a self-supervised framework, called SSL, that generates samples by randomly replacing the image in original samples and achieves a good result because their framework helps the model recognize the importance of the visual part in question answering. However, the important regions in questions are not located in the SSL framework. The model still lose sight of some keywords in the question and performs the task well only with the information from the question type in the training process. In this paper, we propose a self-supervised framework based on SSL with an auxiliary task helping the model pay attention to the important parts of the question other than the question type when predicting the answer. In particular, the important parts refer to those keywords which are directly related to visual objects. And we empirically found that they are always the nouns that come later in the sentence.

We introduce an auxiliary self-supervised training process to the conventional training process. The self-supervised training process requires the model to predict the "false" answers for the "wrong" image-question pairs. The "wrong" pairs are generated by masking the nouns and replacing the image, which will be detailed described in Sect. 3.2. Such a self-supervised task can help the model be aware of not only the importance of image but also the differences between partially masked questions and original questions. This encourages the model to pay more attention to the nouns at the end of sentences and consider the information in question more fully when predicting answers.

To sum up, we propose a self-supervised framework based on UpDn (Anderson et al. 2018) to avoid the model learning language biases and design a strategy to generate samples for the self-supervised training progress. Experiments conducted on VQA-CP v2 (Agrawal et al. 2018) and VQA v2 (Goyal et al. 2017) datasets demonstrate the effectiveness of our method.

2 Related Work

Language bias has become a major challenge for VQA researchers. Existing algorithms to solve this problem can be divided into two categories. One is based on highlighting the important visual regions under the guidance of external visual supervision (Selvaraju et al. 2019; Wu and Mooney 2019). They are classified as annotation-based methods. These methods work directly but rely heavily on manual labeling.

Another is the no-annotation-based method (Ramakrishnan et al. 2018; Cadene et al. 2019a, 2019b; Clark et al. 2019; Jing et al. 2020; Zhu et al. 2020; Chen et al. 2020; Abbas-nejad et al. 2020). These methods are mainly based on the Up-Down model (Anderson et al. 2018). The Up-Down model performs well on non-inversely distributed datasets like VQA v1 (Antol et al. 2015) and VQA v2 (Goyal et al. 2017). As with other early models like SAN (Yang et al. 2016), MCB (Fukui et al. 2016), and GVQA (Agrawal et al. 2018), its accuracy is decreased on the inverse distributed datasets, VQA-CP (Agrawal et al. 2018), because of language biases.

A popular solution proposed so far is to generate some auxiliary samples for the training process. For example, SSL (Zhu et al. 2020) generates auxiliary samples by randomly replacing images in the original sample and requires models to distinguish auxiliary samples and origin samples. CSS (Chen et al. 2020) generates auxiliary samples by masking critical objects in images or words in questions and assigning with different ground-truth answers. These works help the model to be aware of the importance of both images and questions but did not directly indicate which part of the questions should be the focus. The model can still answer only based on the "type" information in questions. In this paper, we generate a group of auxiliary samples by masking the nouns in questions to help models be aware of their importance of them.

Besides generating auxiliary samples, there are also some other effective methods (Clark et al. 2019; Jing et al. 2020). These methods usually use auxiliary branches or delicate structures to eliminate biases.

3 Method

3.1 The Basic VQA Training

A VQA dataset with N samples can be denoted as $D = \{I^i, W^i, A^i\}_{i=1}^N$, where I^i and W^i represent the image and question of the ith sample, and A^i is the corresponding answer. The training target for models is to predict A^i for (I^i, W^i). We build our model upon

UpDn (the part of the dashed box in Fig. 2). It is used for basic training. The model uses an image encoder and question encoder, respectively, to embed (I^i, W^i) to (V^i, Q^i) by

$$\begin{cases} V^i = \{o_1^i, ..., o_{n_{Ii}}^i\}, \\ Q^i = \{w_1^i, ..., w_{n_{Wi}}^i\} \end{cases}, \tag{1}$$

where o_j^i is the j-th object feature of I^i, and w_j^i is the j-th word feature of W^i.

The target of basic VQA training is to learn a model which can output the correct answer when inputting the image-question pair. The model can be described as

$$y^i = softmax(\mathcal{F}(V^i, Q^i)), \tag{2}$$

where y^i is a vector with dimensions equal to the total number of answers and represents the probability distribution of the answer prediction. A commonly used loss function for this training is the multi-label soft loss

$$\mathcal{L}_{vqa_{ml}} = -\frac{1}{N}\sum_i^N \left[t_i \log\left(\sigma\left(\mathcal{F}(A^i|V^i, Q^i)\right)\right) + (1 - t_i)\log\left(1 - \sigma\left(\mathcal{F}(A^i|V^i, Q^i)\right)\right)\right], \tag{3}$$

where $\sigma(\cdot)$ represents the sigmoid function and $\mathcal{F}(A^i|V^i, Q^i)$ is the value of answer distribution function $F(A^i) = \mathcal{F}(V^i, Q^i)$ at A^i.

3.2 Sample Generation

We generate two kinds of self-supervised samples for the self-supervised task during the training process. They are named as "question partially masked sample", (V^i, Q_{mask}^i), and "image randomly replaced sample", (V_{rand}^i, Q^i). The input of generating process is the original sample (V^i, Q^i). To distinguish it from the synthetic sample, we note it as (V^{i0}, Q^{i0}).

To generate (V^i, Q_{mask}^i), we first tagged the Part-Of-Speech tagging (POS_tag) of each word in Q^{i0} by NLTK (Bird et al. 2009). Then we masked the last k nouns in each question to get Q_{mask}^i. And V^i is equal to original V^{i0}. In the actual experimental environment, we found that multiple masks would lead to unstable training results, since it would make the whole sentence meaningless. It makes no sense to force the model to learn from such an example. To maximize the information available in the sentence, we set $k = 1$, which means that only the last noun in the sentence of Q^{i0} would be masked to get Q_{mask}^i.

The sample generation of (V_{rand}^i, Q^i) is the same as SSL. The V_{rand}^i means feature of the image which is randomly chosen from the image set to replace the original one (i.e. $V_{rand}^i \in \{V^i\}_{i=1}^N$ and $V_{rand}^i \neq V^{i0}$). And Q^i is equal to origin Q^{i0}.

3.3 Self-supervised Training

After generating new samples, we can use them for our self-supervised training in conjunction with basic VQA training. The self-supervised training uses the two kinds of synthetic samples as input and shares the same model used in basic training to predict answers. Different from basic training, the target for this training is not to let the model output the correct answer. While the input is the synthetic samples, the model should no longer output the original correct answer. Therefore, the loss function for self-supervised training should be positively related to the value of the output probability on the origin label. For those two kinds of synthetic samples, the loss function can be defined as.

$$\mathcal{L}_q = \frac{1}{N} \sum_i^N P\left(A^i \big| V^i, Q^i_{mask}\right), \mathcal{L}_v = \frac{1}{N} \sum_i^N P\left(A^i \big| V^i_{rand}, Q^i\right), \tag{4}$$

where $P\left(A^i \big| V^i, Q^i\right) = softmax(\mathcal{F}(A^i | V^i, Q^i))$ denotes the predicted probability at the answer annotation. These loss functions mean that the model shall not predict the "correct" answers through "wrong" inputs.

The self-supervised training process can be synchronized with basic training. We only need to let the model predict the label and calculate the loss for the original sample and two synthetic samples respectively, and sum the three losses with different weights. The total loss of training becomes

$$\mathcal{L} = \mathcal{L}_{vqa} + \alpha \mathcal{L}_v + \beta \mathcal{L}_q, \tag{5}$$

where α and β are hyper-parameters that adjust the weights of self-supervised losses. The $\mathcal{L}_{vqa}$ here can be any VQA loss included mentioned in Sect. 3.1.

Algorithm 1. Model Training with auxiliary self-supervised task

Input: Training sample $D = \{I^i, W^i, A^i\}_{i=1}^N$, model $\mathcal{F}$ in Eq. (2), and maximum iteration T.

Output: Updated model $\mathcal{F}$.

---

1. **while** $t < T$ **do**
2.   Encode training sample to the form in Eq. (1).
3.   Generate auxiliary samples in **Section 3.2**.
4.   Predict answer for original sample and synthetic sample respectively
5.   through the same model $\mathcal{F}$.
6.   Compute loss for original sample in Eq. (3).
7.   Compute loss for synthetic sample in Eq. (4).
8.   Backpropagation.
9. **end while**

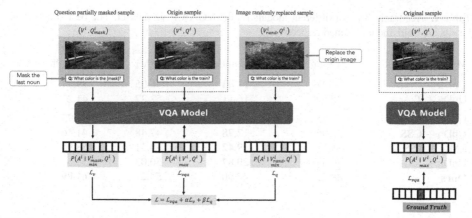

Fig. 2. Self-supervised framework (left) and base model (right). The base model predicts answers for original question-image pairs. And its loss function aims to maximize the probability of producing the answer "Red". In the dashed box we use the original input the same as the base model. The auxiliary branches outside the dashed box answer the question for the auxiliary sample question partially masked input and the image randomly replaced input generate by the progress depicted in Sect. 3.2, respectively. In contrast to the original branch, their loss functions (Eq. (4) in Sect. 3.3) aim to minimize the probability of producing the answer "Red".

4 Experiments

4.1 Performance on VQA Dataset Under Changing Prior

We compared our model with state-of-the-art models on the VQA-CP v2 dataset to evaluate whether our method can effectively avoid language biases problem.

For the first 21 epochs, our model is trained with only $\mathcal{L}_{vqa_{ml}}$, which is set as the multi-label VQA loss, to get a basic ability for the VQA task. Then we add $\mathcal{L}_v$ and $\mathcal{L}_q$ to adjust the model for the last 19 epochs. The hyper-parameter α and β are set to 12.6 and 0.09, respectively. Usually, in our environment, accuracy on the validation set gets the most significant increase at the certain epoch we add the two self-supervised losses.

The results are shown in Table 1. The **best** and the second performance are highlighted in each column. **UpDn + $\mathcal{L}_{vqa_{ml}}$** is different from **UpDn** for its using $\mathcal{L}_{vqa_{ml}}$ replace of the origin VQA loss that **UpDn** used. **UpDn + SSL** and **UpDn + Ours** also use the $\mathcal{L}_{vqa_{ml}}$. It can be observed that our method gets the best overall accuracy and get the best score for the "Yes or No" and "Other" type. For the "Number" type, we achieved a +35.97% improvement over **UpDn** and a +18.03% improvement over **SSL**. It is comparable with **UpDn + LMH + CSS**, which performed best in this particular category.

Table 1. Accuracies (%) of different models on the VQA-CP v2 dataset. The best and second results are bold and underlined respectively.

Method	Yes or No	Number	Other	Overall
UpDn	42.27	11.93	46.05	39.74
UpDn + $\mathcal{L}_{vqa_{ml}}$	45.66	16.11	<u>52.27</u>	41.27
UpDn + LMH	72.95	31.90	47.79	52.73
UpDn + CSS	43.96	12.78	47.48	41.16
LMH + CSS	84.37	**49.42**	48.21	<u>58.95</u>
UpDn + SSL	<u>86.53</u>	29.87	50.03	57.59
Ours	**88.62**	<u>47.90</u>	**54.21**	**61.09**

4.2 Performance on Traditional VQA Dataset

On the VQA dataset without inverse distribution, our model can also reach state-of-the-art performance. It was evaluated on the VQA v2 dataset. The results are shown in Table 2. The hyper-parameter α and β are set to 0.1 and 0.5, respectively. After training with only $\mathcal{L}_{vqa_{ml}}$ for 20 epochs, the model reaches the highest overall accuracy 65.51% for the base. The model at this stage is the same as UpDn + $\mathcal{L}_{vqa_{ml}}$. Then, the accuracy drops a little bit by 0.22% in the last 20 epochs since we add $\mathcal{L}_v$ and $\mathcal{L}_q$ to the total loss. This is an acceptable price to pay for improving the robustness of the model by getting rid of language biases.

Table 2. Accuracies (%) of different models on VQA v2 datasets. The best and second results are bold and underlined respectively.

Method	Yes or No	Number	Other	Overall
UpDn	63.79	<u>42.51</u>	55.78	63.79
UpDn + $\mathcal{L}_{vqa_{ml}}$	<u>78.48</u>	**44.98**	<u>57.12</u>	**65.51**
UpDn + LMH	65.06	37.63	54.69	56.35
UpDn + CSS	72.97	40.00	55.13	59.21
LMH + CSS	73.25	39.77	55.11	59.91
UpDn + SSL	–	–	–	63.73
Ours	**80.51**	42.39	**57.20**	<u>65.29</u>

5 Conclusions

In this paper, we have presented a self-supervised strategy to help the VQA model focus on the important nouns in the questions hence avoiding the model learning language biases. In addition, we have proposed an efficient method to generate samples for the self-supervised training. And a series of experiments have verified the effectiveness of the proposed self-supervised method. The operation of masking the last noun, while effective, is simplistic and subjective. A more flexible rule of masking should further improve the accuracy of the model at the expense of more complex structures and more hyper-parameters. This should be considered in future works.

References

Antol, S., et al.: VQA: visual question answering. In: Proceedings of the IEEE International Conference on Computer Vision, pp. 2425–2433 (2015)

Ramakrishnan, S., Agrawal, A., Lee, S.: Overcoming language priors in visual question answering with adversarial regularization. In: Advances in Neural Information Processing Systems, pp. 1541–1551 (2018)

Cadene, R., Ben-Younes, H., Cord, M., Thome, N.: Murel: multimodal relational reasoning for visual question answering. In: Proceedings of the IEEE Conference on Computer Vision and Pattern Recognition, pp. 1989–1998 (2019)

Zhu, X., Mao, Z., Liu, C., Zhang, P., Wang, B., Zhang, Y.: Overcoming language priors with self-supervised learning for visual question answering. In: International Joint Conference on Artificial Intelligence, pp. 1083–1089 (2020)

Chen, L., Yan, X., Xiao, J., Zhang, H., Pu, S., Zhuang, Y.: Counterfactual samples synthesizing for robust visual question answering. In: Proceedings of the IEEE/CVF Conference on Computer Vision and Pattern Recognition, pp. 10800–10809 (2020)

Clark, C., Yatskar, M., Zettlemoyer, L.: Don't take the easy way out: ensemble based methods for avoiding known dataset biases. In: Conference on Empirical Methods in Natural Language Processing and the 9th International Joint Conference on Natural Language Processing, pp. 4060–4073 (2019)

Abbasnejad, E., Teney, D., Parvaneh, A., Shi, J., Hengel, A.V.D.: Counterfactual vision and language learning. In: Proceedings of the IEEE/CVF Conference on Computer Vision and Pattern Recognition, pp. 10044–10054 (2020)

Jing, C., Wu, Y., Zhang, X., Jia, Y., Wu, Q.: Overcoming language priors in VQA via decomposed linguistic representations. In: AAAI Conference on Artificial Intelligence, vol. 34, no. 07, pp. 11181–11188 (2020)

Anderson, P., et al.: Bottom-up and top-down attention for image captioning and visual question answering. In: Proceedings of the IEEE Conference on Computer Vision and Pattern Recognition, pp. 6077–6086 (2018)

Yang, Z., He, X., Gao, J., Deng, L., Smola, A.: Stacked attention networks for image question answering. In: Proceedings of the IEEE Conference on Computer Vision and Pattern Recognition, pp. 21–29 (2016)

Fukui, A., Park, D.H., Yang, D., Rohrbach, A., Darrell, T., Rohrbach, M.: Multimodal compact bilinear pooling for visual question answering and visual grounding. In: Empirical Methods in Natural Language Processing, pp. 457–468 (2016)

Agrawal, A., Batra, D., Parikh, D., Kembhavi, A.: Don't just assume; look and answer: overcoming priors for visual question answering. In: Proceedings of the IEEE Conference on Computer Vision and Pattern Recognition, pp. 4971–4980 (2018)

Selvaraju, R.R., et al.: Taking a hint: leveraging explanations to make vision and language models more grounded. In: Proceedings of the IEEE International Conference on Computer Vision, pp. 2591–2600 (2019)

Wu, J., Mooney, R.J.: Self-critical reasoning for robust visual question answering. In: Advances in Neural Information Processing Systems, pp. 8601–8611 (2019)

Cadene, R., Dancette C., Cord M., Parikh D.: Rubi: reducing unimodal biases for visual question answering. In: Advances in Neural Information Processing Systems, pp. 841–852 (2019)

Goyal, Y., Khot, T., Summers-Stay, D., Batra, D., Parikh, D.: Making the V in VQA matter: elevating the role of image understanding in visual question answering. In: Proceedings of the IEEE Conference on Computer Vision and Pattern Recognition, pp. 6904–6913 (2017)

Bird, S., Klein, E., Loper, E.: Natural Language Processing with Python: Analyzing Text with the Natural Language Toolkit. O'Reilly Media Inc., Newton (2009)

Employing Contrastive Strategies for Multi-label Textual Emotion Recognition

Yangyang Zhou⍟, Xin Kang⍟, and Fuji Ren⁽⍟⁾⍟

Tokushima University, Tokushima, Japan
{kang-xin,ren}@is.tokushima-u.ac.jp

Abstract. Textual emotion recognition is an important part of the human-computer interaction field. Current methods of textual emotion recognition mainly use large-scale pre-trained models fine-tuning. However, these methods are not accurate enough in the semantic representation of sentences. Contrastive learning has been shown to optimize the representation of vectors in the feature space. Therefore, we introduce the contrastive strategies to the textual emotion recognition task. We propose two approaches: using self-supervised contrastive learning before fine-tuning the pre-trained model, and using contrastive training on the same inputs during fine-tuning. We experiment on two multi-label emotion classification datasets: Ren-CECps and NLPCC2018. The experimental results demonstrate that the latter contrastive approach effectively improves the accuracy of emotion recognition.

Keywords: Textual emotion recognition · Multi-label classification · Large-scale pre-trained models · Contrastive learning · Fine-tuning

1 Introduction

Emotion recognition is the process by which a machine identifies human emotion. The response of the machine based on the user's emotional state can enhance the user's experience. Emotion recognition can be applied in many realistic scenarios. For example, obtaining user satisfaction with a product can help a sales platform develop a better sales strategy [25]. Machines usually recognize the emotion by acquiring emotion-induced physiological signals or behavioral information. In this paper, we focus on emotion recognition from the text.

According to the level of the content, emotion analysis of the text can be divided into word level, sentence level, chapter level and target level [32]. Building an emotion dictionary is a common method for word-level emotion analysis [14]. The information of each word in a sentence/chapter is pooled or concatenated to represent the sentence-level/chapter-level emotion as a whole [21]. The target-level target refers to the emotion of an entity or an attribute [16]. Regardless of the level, words that contain emotional tendencies are the most critical factors in the emotion analysis process [22].

© IFIP International Federation for Information Processing 2022
Published by Springer Nature Switzerland AG 2022
Z. Shi et al. (Eds.): IIP 2022, IFIP AICT 643, pp. 299–310, 2022.
https://doi.org/10.1007/978-3-031-03948-5_24

Treating pooled or concatenated word vectors as sentence vectors will inevitably lose information. To solve this problem, some language models tend to design semantic tasks to train feature representations of whole sentences [20]. Large-scale pre-trained language models, such as bidirectional encoder representations from transformers (BERT), predict whether the sentences are contextually relevant at the first token position [7]. Semantic text similarity measures the meaning similarity of sentences. In this kind of task, the state-of-the-art results are almost obtained by large-scale pre-trained language models [4].

In large-scale pre-trained language models, the representation of word vectors is correlated with word frequency, resulting in uneven distribution of word vectors in the feature space [12]. The idea of contrastive learning is to represent the features uniformly in the feature space [29]. Therefore, Gao et al. introduce contrastive learning into the training process of large-scale pre-trained language models, which in turn achieves uniform distribution of sentence vectors in the feature space [8].

This paper is devoted to investigating how contrastive strategies affect the accuracy of multi-label emotion recognition from text. Using unsupervised contrastive learning to adjust parameters before fine-tuning a large-scale pre-trained language model has no significant benefit for emotion recognition. In contrast, adding a supervised contrastive learning approach to fine-tune the large-scale pre-trained language model is beneficial for accuracy improvement. We experiment on two multi-label textual emotion classification datasets based on our methods.

The main contribution of this paper is to introduce contrastive strategies in the training phase of multi-label emotion recognition from text to further improve the recognition accuracy based on large-scale and training language models. The remainder of this paper is organized as follows. Section 2 presents a review of the related work. Section 3 gives the details of the mechanism of the proposed methods. The experimental setup is presented in Sect. 4. The system performance analysis is presented in Sect. 5. Finally, Sect. 6 presents the conclusion and future work of this study.

2 Related Work

Textual emotion recognition has recently become a hot topic due to its commercial and academic potential[6]. In tasks such as product comments analysis, sentiment analysis is generally performed with positive and negative [19]. We classify emotion more fine-grained into multiple categories. Some scholars regard text analysis as a single-label classification task [3], which is different from the complex emotional states in real-world conditions. In this article, we regard textual emotion analysis as a multi-label classification task, with the goal of recognizing all possible emotions in the textual expression [17].

Approaches for emotion recognition from the text can be classified into 4 categories: rule-based approaches, classical learning-based approaches, deep learning approaches, and hybrid approaches [1]. The emotion rules are usually extracted by statistics or linguistic concepts. These rules rely heavily on pre-processing steps including tokenization, lemmatization, POS tagging, and stop words removal. Udochukwu et al. proposed a rule-based emotion recognition model called Ortony, Clore, and Collins model [28]. The results show that the rule-based approach is very sensitive to text quality. Support vector machine is a common classification algorithm used in classical learning-based approaches. This algorithm relies on extracting and selecting features with the most information gain and then outputting the optimal hyperplane. Experiments by Anusha et al. show that the important part of the sentence is essential for improving the results [2]. The convolutional neural network, recurrent neural network and transformer are the commonly used frameworks for deep learning approaches. With a large amount of data information and automatic feature engineering, deep learning approaches achieve better results. Hybrid approaches inherit the advantages and disadvantages of the above methods.

Most of the datasets involve a specific domain rather than an open domain, so there is also some work to make up for the limitations of the datasets by introducing background knowledge or prior information [24]. Recently, language models pre-trained on large-scale datasets have been shown to be effective in capturing contextual information and benefiting various downstream tasks through fine-tuning [9]. Language models have been classified into autoregressive and autoencoder language models based on whether there is information leakage. Autoregressive language models, represented by Generative Pre-Training 2 [23], predict words using frameworks such as unidirectional transformers. The autoencoder language model, represented by BERT [7], uses a framework such as bidirectional transformers to incorporate contextual information into the model. Since different mask strategies for autoencoder language models during training and testing lead to errors, we try to reduce this error by the contrastive strategy. In this paper, we introduce two different contrastive strategies based on the autoencoder language model BERT.

At first, contrastive learning used a self-supervised approach to avoid the cost of annotating large-scale datasets in the field of computer vision [10]. Contrastive learning constructs positive and negative samples by means of data augmentation and adjusts the distribution of features in space. Later, contrastive learning was also gradually used in the field of natural language processing. The most commonly used methods of text data augmentation are replacement, insertion, deletion and swap [26]. Gao et al. used the property of dropout to implicitly construct positive samples and achieved state-of-the-art results on several semantic text similarity tasks [8]. Liang et al. added a regularization strategy to improve the robustness of the model based on the inconsistency of dropout output [15]. Inspired by the above work, we use dropout and construct two large-scale pre-trained models based on fine-tuning to explore the influence of contrastive strategies on emotion recognition.

3   Model Architecture

In this paper, we explore how the contrastive strategy can be introduced into the textual emotion recognition model to achieve better results. The process of textual emotion recognition is described as follows. Given a sentence s, we use an encoder to map s to a representation s'. Then, we use a classifier to transform s' into the emotion e.

3.1   Dropout and Contrastive Strategy

Contrastive learning adjusts the representation of features by decreasing the distance between similar samples and increasing the distance between different samples. Similar samples are generally transformed from the original sample, and we use the dropout method to transform in this article.

Dropout is a method commonly used to prevent overfitting of neural networks [27]. By dropping some neurons randomly during the training process, the model can be prevented from over-relying on some neurons and dependencies. Since dropout has randomness, the model will produce similar but not the same output each time with the same input. According to the property of dropout, it is easy to construct two similar samples.

3.2   Encoder and Classifier

We construct a framework consisting of an encoder and a classifier.

For encoding, we use a large-scale pre-trained model, load the weights, and fine-tune them. In this paper, we use BERT as an encoder. To be unified with BERT, each sentence is prefixed with a [cls] token at first before it is fed into the model. BERT is designed with two pre-training tasks. The text involves the masked language modeling task, while the [cls] token involves the next sentence prediction task. Thus, the first token of the output contains the sentence semantics to some extent. We use this token for classification.

We take the fully connected network with bias as a classifier. Since the first token does not contain the sequence axis, we can directly map it to the emotion state e.

$$e = (e_1, e_2, ..., e_n) \tag{1}$$

in which n is the number of emotion categories. When the output of emotion e_i exceeds the threshold, we believe that sentence s expresses the emotion e_i.

We introduce the contrastive strategy into the encoding and classification parts separately to get two different recognition models.

3.3   Model with Contrastive Strategy Added to the Encoding Part

The semantics represented by sentence vectors is the most critical part of emotion recognition. Different sentence vectors represented by [cls] token in BERT have been confirmed to be very similar and do not represent the semantics well

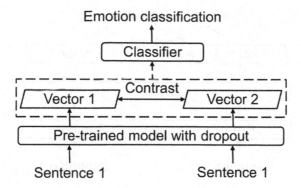

Fig. 1. Overall framework of the model with contrastive strategy added to the encoding part.

[12]. We try to enhance the semantic representation of sentence vectors with a contrastive strategy.

According to the description above, contrastive learning is a self-supervised training process, the same as what large-scale pre-trained models do. We continue to train the weights of the model with similar samples constructed by dropout on the basis of BERT. We expect that this weight for fine-tuning will improve the accuracy of emotion recognition.

As shown in Fig. 1, we fine-tune the encoder before classification. The encoder predicts two similar representations Vector1 and Vector2 by dropout from the same input Sentence 1. Using unsupervised contrastive learning, the parameters of the encoder can be fine-tuned so that the distribution of the encoded results in the feature space is more favorable for emotion classification. Based on this, we add the classifier at the top for supervised training.

3.4 Model with Contrastive Strategy Added to the Classification Part

In addition to self-supervised training, we can use the contrastive strategy for supervised training. Dropout only works at training time, i.e., the model is not consistent at training and prediction. To reduce the gap of the model between training and prediction, we close the distance between the outputs of the model after randomly dropping neurons.

Specifically, we take input during training twice through the model and add a Kullback-Leibler (KL) divergence between the two outputs. KL divergence is a metric used to estimate the distance between distributions [11]. When calculating the loss function, adding KL divergence ensures that the model outputs are closer after each random drop of neurons to reduce the effect of dropout on the results.

As shown in Fig. 2, we supervised train the classifier and the encoder at the same time. Due to dropout, the same input Sentence 1 has similar results Vector 3 and Vector 4 when prediction. For the stability of results, we introduce the KL loss function during training to make Vector 3 and Vector 4 as close as possible.

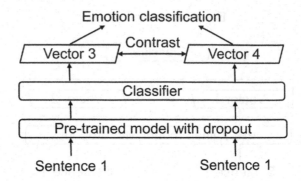

Fig. 2. Overall framework of the model with contrastive strategy added to the classification part.

4   Experiments Setup

4.1   Datasets

To verify that the contrastive strategy is effective in the emotion recognition from text, we select two multi-label emotion classification datasets as follows.

The Ren-CECps dataset selects Chinese blog texts and annotates 8 kinds of emotions: joy, hate, love, sorrow, anxiety, surprise, anger and expect. Emotions are in range [0, 1]. We labeled data points with emotion scores over 0 as 1 and others as 0 during preprocessing. We labeled the data points with all 0 emotion scores as neutral. The dataset can be regarded as a multi-label classification task where the average number of emotions expressed per sentence is about 1.45. This dataset includes a total of 27,091 sentences of training data and 7,681 sentences of test data. The details of this dataset can be found in the article [13].

The NLPCC2018 dataset contains 5 kinds of emotions: happiness, sadness, anger, fear and surprise. As with the Ren-CECps dataset, we added the neutral to the labels. Compared to the Ren-CECps dataset, the average number of emotions expressed per sentence in the NLPCC2018 dataset is less (about 1.15). This dataset includes a total of 4,611 sentences of training data and 955 sentences of test data. The details of this dataset can be found in the article [30].

4.2   Evaluation Metrics

Unlike the evaluation metrics for single-label classification tasks, the commonly used accuracy does not reflect the effectiveness of multi-label classification models well. To compare with other public models, we use the following evaluation metrics.

The F1 score is a combination of precision and recall. Micro F1 score is calculated overall for all categories, with errors when it is used for imbalanced datasets. Macro F1 score is calculated separately for different categories with the same weights and is strongly influenced by extreme precision and recall.

Average precision (AP) is the average score of accuracy for recall from 0 to 1. For the metrics of micro-F1, macro-F1 and AP, higher values indicate better performance. Coverage error (CE) indicates the average number of labels that can cover the ground truth labels. Ranking loss (RL) is the proportion of misclassifications after weighting by the number of relevant labels. For the metrics of CE and RL, lower values indicate better performance.

4.3 Model for Comparison

We choose the model with the best-published results on both datasets to compare with our proposed models. The multi-label emotion detection architecture from sentence (MEDA-FS) [5] is a multichannel hierarchical model. MEDA-FS captures the underlying emotion-specified features through a multi-channel feature extractor and then predicts emotion sequences through an emotion correlation learner.

Commonly used baseline models for multi-label classification such as binary relevance and backpropagation for multi-label learning have been compared in the article of the MEDA-FS and will not be repeated in this paper.

To better control the variables, in addition to the MEDA-FS model that uses the pre-trained model as a feature extractor, we also compare fine-tuned models that do not use the contrastive strategy.

4.4 Experimental Details

We used the hugging face open source large-scale pre-training model BERT (chinese-bert-wwm-ext) as our backbone [31]. For the model with contrastive strategy added to the encoding part, 0.1M news titles are used for contrastive learning to adjust the semantic expressiveness of sentence embedding. For the model with contrastive strategy added to the classification part, we add KL loss between the replicated data points in a batch.

We used AdamW [18] optimizer to train the model. The learning rate of the classifier is $1e-2$ and the learning rate of the backbone is $1e-5$. When predicting, if the output result of an emotion is greater than the boundary threshold, we assume that the emotion is expressed.

5 Experimental Results and Discussion

5.1 Experimental Results

Table 1 shows the results of the Ren-CECps dataset. MEDA-FS uses the feature extraction approach for downstream tasks. BERT FT refers to fine-tuning approach with BERT on the dataset. The BERT FT improves from 60.76/48.31 to 65.42/53.57 in f1 scores compared to MEDA-FS. CE model means that the weights are adjusted with the self-supervised contrastive learning approach before fine-tuning. This method makes the evaluation metrics worse, especially

Table 1. The results of the Ren-CECps dataset. For the metrics of Micro F1, Macro F1 and AP, higher values indicate better performance. For the metrics of CE and RL, lower values indicate better performance.

	Micro F1	Macro F1	AP	CE	RL
MEDA-FS	60.76	48.31	76.51	2.2226	0.1062
BERT FT	65.42	53.57	81.99	1.9046	0.0871
CE model	61.78	45.80	79.58	2.0187	0.1008
CC model	**66.16**	**53.75**	**82.00**	**1.9021**	**0.0868**

the macro f1 score of 45.80 which is even lower than that of the MEDA-FS. CC model refers to the addition of supervised contrastive training to fine-tuning. This method improves the f1 score from 65.42/53.57 to 66.16/53.75 compared to the BERT FT. CC model also performs better in AP, CE and RL metrics.

Table 2. The results of the NLPCC2018 dataset. For the metrics of Micro F1, Macro F1 and AP, higher values indicate better performance. For the metrics of CE and RL, lower values indicate better performance.

	Micro F1	Macro F1	AP	CE	RL
MEDA-FS	**63.02**	49.42	77.12	1.7288	0.1681
BERT FT	59.05	49.94	**85.13**	1.2883	0.1114
CE model	60.67	43.40	84.74	1.2958	0.1137
CC model	58.68	**50.57**	85.09	**1.2775**	**0.1090**

Table 2 shows the results of the NLPCC2018 dataset. The results are similar to those in Table 1. In terms of evaluation metrics, the fine-tuning approach outperforms the feature extraction approach to a certain extent. BERT FT achieves scores of 85.13 on the AP metrics, which is the best results in the comparison. Compared to BERT FT, the macro f1 score of the CE model decrease from 49.94 to 43.40. Compared to BERT FT, the macro f1 scores of the CC model improve to 50.57. CC model also achieves scores of 1.2775 and 0.1090 on the CE and RL metrics. It proves that the model with a contrastive strategy added to the classification part is more effective in the textual emotion recognition task than to the encoding part.

5.2   Discussion

Compared to feature extraction, fine-tuning has better performance in downstream tasks. The large-scale pre-trained model utilizes a large corpus for self-supervised learning, and this corpus may deviate a little from the corpus used for the downstream task. The fine-tuning approach adaptively adjusts the model weights to make it more accurate in feature representation for downstream tasks. This is reflected in both Tables 1 and 2. However, fine-tuning requires supervised learning, so the computational overhead is greater.

The self-supervised contrastive learning is adopted before fine-tuning, but the results become worse. We intended to represent the sentence semantics that was slighted in the pre-training task better by contrastive learning. However, this approach was not effective enough in the textual emotion classification task. The CE model does not perform well in all metrics for both datasets.

We originally thought the possible reason was that emotion classification did not depend entirely on sentence semantics. However, after fine-tuning by replacing the [cls] token with pooled word vectors, the results slightly decreased. This suggests that sentence semantics plays a bigger role in emotion classification than word embeddings. Therefore, the reason for the worse results may be that the semantics compared to contrastive learning is not exactly related to emotion. That is, a better comparison scheme may improve the results.

Another possible reason is the inconsistent training goals of the model at different stages. The CE model focuses on sentence similarity rather than classification when encoding. Compared to the CE model, the CC model has better performance because it adds the comparison of hidden states similarity to the classification part.

We tried fine-tuning the pre-contrastive training with data from the unlabeled training set. We combined the textual parts of Ren-CECps and NLPCC2018 (excluding labels) for unsupervised training. The results were worse than the classification results obtained with the additionally found title data. This indicates that the self-supervised learning corpus affects the training results. A more general, larger corpus facilitates parameter fine-tuning during unsupervised learning.

The contrastive training on the same sample representation is adopted during fine-tuning and the results are improved. This suggests that the contrastive strategy used in models with dropout is beneficial to the textual emotion classification task.

We experimented with the effect of different drop rates on the results. In this kind of task, the classification results get worse as the drop rate increases. We believe that dropout is a regularization method, so the larger the drop rate, the stronger the constraint on the model and the more unstable results predicted by the model. Under the contrastive strategy, stability training becomes more difficult as the drop rate increases. If the amount of data is large enough, a larger drop rate may have a better performance. However, in our experiment, the best result is achieved by the BERT model with a default rate of 0.1.

We also tried both contrastive learnings before and during fine-tuning. The results are better than the CE model but worse than the CC model. We believe that the two contrastive strategies are independent and do not affect each other. Overall, the strategy of contrastive training during fine-tuning is a better choice for the textual emotion classification task.

6 Conclusions

In this article, we introduce the contrastive strategies for multi-label textual emotion classification tasks. Based on the large-scale pre-trained model BERT, we propose two approaches: using self-supervised contrastive learning before fine-tuning the model, and using contrastive training on the same inputs during fine-tuning. We experiment with the effectiveness of the strategies on two multi-label emotion classification datasets: Ren-CECps and NLPCC2018. The experimental results demonstrate that using the contrastive strategy in the classification part is more effective in improving the accuracy of emotion recognition than using the contrastive strategy in the encoding part.

We use the $[cls]$ token of the pre-trained model for classification in the experiments. In the future, we will investigate the relationship between word embeddings and $[cls]$ token to minimize the loss of emotional information contained in sentences during training.

Acknowledgements. This research has been supported by JSPS KAKENHI Grant Number 19K20345 and Grant Number 19H04215.

References

1. Alswaidan, N., Menai, M.E.B.: A survey of state-of-the-art approaches for emotion recognition in text. Knowl. Inf. Syst. **62**(8), 2937–2987 (2020). https://doi.org/10.1007/s10115-020-01449-0
2. Anusha, V., Sandhya, B.: A learning based emotion classifier with semantic text processing. In: El-Alfy, E.-S.M., Thampi, S.M., Takagi, H., Piramuthu, S., Hanne, T. (eds.) Advances in Intelligent Informatics. AISC, vol. 320, pp. 371–382. Springer, Cham (2015). https://doi.org/10.1007/978-3-319-11218-3_34
3. Bandhakavi, A., Wiratunga, N., Padmanabhan, D., Massie, S.: Lexicon based feature extraction for emotion text classification. Pattern Recogn. Lett. **93**, 133–142 (2017)
4. Chandrasekaran, D., Mago, V.: Evolution of semantic similarity-a survey. ACM Comput. Surv. (CSUR) **54**(2), 1–37 (2021)
5. Deng, J., Ren, F.: Multi-label emotion detection via emotion-specified feature extraction and emotion correlation learning. IEEE Trans. Affect. Comput. (2020)
6. Deng, J., Ren, F.: A survey of textual emotion recognition and its challenges. IEEE Trans. Affect. Comput. (2021)
7. Devlin, J., Chang, M.W., Lee, K., Toutanova, K.: BERT: pre-training of deep bidirectional transformers for language understanding. arXiv preprint arXiv:1810.04805 (2018)
8. Gao, T., Yao, X., Chen, D.: SimCSE: simple contrastive learning of sentence embeddings. arXiv preprint arXiv:2104.08821 (2021)
9. Han, X., et al.: Pre-trained models: past, present and future. AI Open **2**, 225–250 (2021)
10. Jaiswal, A., Babu, A.R., Zadeh, M.Z., Banerjee, D., Makedon, F.: A survey on contrastive self-supervised learning. Technologies **9**(1), 2 (2021)
11. Kullback, S., Leibler, R.A.: On information and sufficiency. Ann. Math. Stat. **22**(1), 79–86 (1951)

12. Li, B., Zhou, H., He, J., Wang, M., Yang, Y., Li, L.: On the sentence embeddings from pre-trained language models. arXiv preprint arXiv:2011.05864 (2020)
13. Li, J., Ren, F.: Creating a Chinese emotion lexicon based on corpus Ren-CECps. In: 2011 IEEE International Conference on Cloud Computing and Intelligence Systems, pp. 80–84. IEEE (2011)
14. Li, J., Xu, Y., Xiong, H., Wang, Y.: Chinese text emotion classification based on emotion dictionary. In: 2010 IEEE 2nd Symposium on Web Society, pp. 170–174. IEEE (2010)
15. Liang, X., et al.: R-drop: Regularized dropout for neural networks. arXiv preprint arXiv:2106.14448 (2021)
16. Liu, B.: Sentiment analysis and opinion mining. Synth. Lect. Hum. Lang. Technol. **5**(1), 1–167 (2012)
17. Liu, S.M., Chen, J.H.: A multi-label classification based approach for sentiment classification. Expert Syst. Appl. **42**(3), 1083–1093 (2015)
18. Loshchilov, I., Hutter, F.: Decoupled weight decay regularization. arXiv preprint arXiv:1711.05101 (2017)
19. Mai, L., Le, B.: Joint sentence and aspect-level sentiment analysis of product comments. Ann. Oper. Res. **300**(2), 493–513 (2020). https://doi.org/10.1007/s10479-020-03534-7
20. Majumder, G., Pakray, P., Gelbukh, A., Pinto, D.: Semantic textual similarity methods, tools, and applications: a survey. Computación y Sistemas **20**(4), 647–665 (2016)
21. Majumder, N., Poria, S., Gelbukh, A., Cambria, E.: Deep learning-based document modeling for personality detection from text. IEEE Intell. Syst. **32**(2), 74–79 (2017)
22. Quan, C., Ren, F.: An exploration of features for recognizing word emotion. In: Proceedings of the 23rd International Conference on Computational Linguistics (Coling 2010), pp. 922–930 (2010)
23. Radford, A., Wu, J., Child, R., Luan, D., Amodei, D., Sutskever, I., et al.: Language models are unsupervised multitask learners. OpenAI Blog **1**(8), 9 (2019)
24. Ren, F., Deng, J.: Background knowledge based multi-stream neural network for text classification. Appl. Sci. **8**(12), 2472 (2018)
25. Satrio, D., Priyanto, S.H., Nugraha, A.K.: Viral marketing for cultural product: the role of emotion and cultural awareness to influence purchasing intention. Montenegrin J. Econ. **16**(2), 77–91 (2020)
26. Shorten, C., Khoshgoftaar, T.M., Furht, B.: Text data augmentation for deep learning. J. Big Data **8**(1), 1–34 (2021)
27. Srivastava, N., Hinton, G., Krizhevsky, A., Sutskever, I., Salakhutdinov, R.: Dropout: a simple way to prevent neural networks from overfitting. J. Mach. Learn. Res. **15**(1), 1929–1958 (2014)
28. Udochukwu, O., He, Y.: A rule-based approach to implicit emotion detection in text. In: Biemann, C., Handschuh, S., Freitas, A., Meziane, F., Métais, E. (eds.) NLDB 2015. LNCS, vol. 9103, pp. 197–203. Springer, Cham (2015). https://doi.org/10.1007/978-3-319-19581-0_17
29. Wang, T., Isola, P.: Understanding contrastive representation learning through alignment and uniformity on the hypersphere. In: International Conference on Machine Learning, pp. 9929–9939. PMLR (2020)
30. Wang, Z., Li, S., Wu, F., Sun, Q., Zhou, G.: Overview of NLPCC 2018 shared task 1: emotion detection in code-switching text. In: Zhang, M., Ng, V., Zhao, D., Li, S., Zan, H. (eds.) NLPCC 2018. LNCS (LNAI), vol. 11109, pp. 429–433. Springer, Cham (2018). https://doi.org/10.1007/978-3-319-99501-4_39

31. Wolf, T., et al.: Transformers: state-of-the-art natural language processing. In: Proceedings of the 2020 Conference on Empirical Methods in Natural Language Processing: System Demonstrations, pp. 38–45 (2020)
32. Zhang, L., Wang, S., Liu, B.: Deep learning for sentiment analysis: a survey. Wiley Interdisc. Rev. Data Mining Knowl. Discov. 8(4), e1253 (2018)

Pattern Recognition

Fault Localization Based on Deep Neural Network and Execution Slicing

Wei-Dong Zhao[1], Xin-Ling Li[1], and Ming Wang[2(✉)]

[1] Shandong University of Science and Technology, Qingdao 266590, China
[2] Qingdao Customs Technology Center, Qingdao 266590, China
wangm415@163.com

Abstract. Aiming at the problems that the existing fault localization techniques cannot meet the requirements for the effectiveness of locating faults, and the effectiveness of the method is sensitive to the number of sample data, this paper proposes a fault localization method that combines deep neural network (DNN) and execution slicing. In this method, coverage data and test case results are used as input to train the deep neural network model iteratively until convergence. Then inputs virtual test cases to obtain the suspiciousness of each execution statement. To further reduce the number of statements to be checked and improve the effectiveness of the method, we propose a new execution slice metric function, which can select the key execution slices by putting the suspiciousness into the formula. Taking the intersection of the key execution slices and the suspiciousness table to get the final suspicion table in descending order. After theoretical analysis and experimental verification, the effectiveness of our approach in this paper improves 6.09%–28.35% compared with Tarantula, 3.32%–11.42% compared with the BPNN-based technique, and 1.19%–9.67% compared with the DNN-based technique.

Keywords: Fault localization · Deep learning · Execution slicing

1 Introduction

Software testing is important to improve software quality. It exists in the whole life cycle of software development. According to statistics, the cost of software testing accounts for about 50%–75% of the total cost of software development and maintenance. Program debugging refers to the process of finding faults in a program and analyzing them to fix them. It usually takes the most time during testing. Fault localization, which is one of the most tedious, time-consuming, and extremely important activities in program debugging, aims to locate faults in the program. It is a hot topic in recent years. Any improvement of its process can greatly improve the efficiency of program debugging and reduce the cost of software testing.

© IFIP International Federation for Information Processing 2022
Published by Springer Nature Switzerland AG 2022
Z. Shi et al. (Eds.): IIP 2022, IFIP AICT 643, pp. 313–326, 2022.
https://doi.org/10.1007/978-3-031-03948-5_25

1.1 Research Status

In recent years, Techniques for locating software faults mainly include the following research directions: spectrum-based fault localization methods (SFL), machine learning-based methods, and slice-based methods.

SFL technique intends to construct a program spectrum and use a suspicious evaluation formula to measure the suspicious value of each statement, J. A. Jones et al. proposed the Tarantula coefficient, which uses coverage and results to calculate the suspiciousness, the method is fast, but loses dependency information. Later many research scholars worked in this direction and proposed Ochiai, Ochiai2, Crosstab, DStar, etc.

Machine learning-based approaches mainly combine fault localization with neural networks, and the more far-reaching one is a BP neural network-based technique proposed by Wong et al. [2] The BP-based technique was extended to object-oriented programs by Ascari et al. [3] Wong et al. also proposed a method based on RBF networks [4]. Briand et al. successfully introduced the C4.5 decision tree algorithm to locate faults [5].

Slice-based methods include static slicing, dynamic slicing, and execution slicing. Static slicing was first proposed by Weiser et al. and is commonly used to reduce the search domain; dynamic slicing was proposed by Korel et al. and since then many researchers have worked on dynamic slicing and published hundreds of related papers [6–11]. In recent years, neither static nor dynamic slicing, but execution slicing dominates [12].

All of the above methods have problems that are difficult to solve: first, SFL has received extensive attention and intensive research, and has shown theoretically the maximum effectiveness it can achieve, i.e., its potential has been fully exploited and it is difficult to further improve the effectiveness, and, these techniques strongly rely on deformation relations derived from the program specification, and the correct identification of such relations is not only difficult but also time-consuming in practice. Second, among the machine learning-based methods, the BP neural network-based methods lead to problems such as local minima. The RBF network-based method requires a large amount of data to train the neural network, and it is difficult to obtain such a scale of sample data in practice, resulting in the method failing to meet the requirements in terms of effectiveness. The search domain of the DNN-based method is the whole program, which is too large in scope and time-consuming. Third, the result of slicing is a subset of the whole program, which can narrow the search domain, but ignores the information about the suspiciousness of different statements in that subset.

1.2 Research Status

Using DNN is important to solve the problems that existing methods cannot meet the requirements in terms of the effectiveness of locating faults and that the effectiveness of the method is sensitive to the amount of sample data. DNN model is better than the shallow learning model in terms of its ability to express nonlinear relationships, and it can still obtain high effectiveness with limited sample data. To reduce the search domain and further improve the effectiveness of the method, this paper combines DNN with execution slicing and proposes a metric function for evaluating the effectiveness of execution slices corresponding to failed test cases to select key execution slices, the results of which are a subset of all executable statements in the whole program. It reduces the number of statements to be checked, reduces the scope of debugging, and improves the effectiveness of the method.

2 Related Work

2.1 DNN-Based Techniques

DNN refers to a deep learning model containing multiple hidden layers, which is a deep network structure obtained by deep learning. The DNN model is shown in Fig. 1.

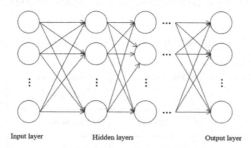

Fig. 1. Depth neural network model diagram

In recent years, machine learning techniques have been successfully applied to numerous fields [13–16], including the field of fault localization. We chose DNN for the following reasons: First, it contains multiple hidden layers, so deep learning models tend to have a better representation of nonlinear relationships than shallow learning models. Second, instead of relying on manual extraction of sample features, deep learning models automatically learn by transforming the input data layer by layer to obtain a hierarchical feature representation. The method iteratively trains the DNN model until it converges, using the results of coverage data and test cases as input. The trained model already contains a complex nonlinear mapping relationship between coverage data and execution results, and a set of virtual test cases are input to obtain the suspicion of each executed statement.

2.2 Slice-Based Techniques

Program slicing is a program analysis technique for decomposing programs, the basic idea of which was developed by M. Weiser was first proposed in his Ph.D. thesis. The idea of program slicing is based on the theory that a particular output of a program is related to only some of the statements and control predicates in the source program, and that deleting other statements and predicates does not affect that output.

A program slice is essentially a subset of the executable statements of the entire program, roughly comprising static, dynamic, and execution slices.

Static slicing is a static analysis of dependencies to obtain a slice of the program that may have an impact on the variables to be tested, without running the program, and the results of the slice are independent of the specific test case, with a high time complexity and possible false positives (false positives).

Dynamic slicing was created to locate faults by using information from successful and failed test cases. Dynamic slices are obtained dynamically along the execution path to obtain the dependencies that may have an impact on the variables to be tested in a given execution and need to be obtained by executing the program for a failed test case, which is costly.

Execution slicing is a lightweight program slicing that is constructed by collecting coverage data information from test cases for a given test case and is less expensive than static and dynamic slicing.

A comparison of the three program slicing techniques is shown in Table 1.

Table 1. Comparison table of static, dynamic, and execution slices

Line number	Source Program	Static slicie	Dynamic slice x=1,y=5	Execution slice x=1,y=5
1	int tmp,sum,res;	int tmp,sum,res;	int tmp,sum,res;	int tmp,sum,res;
2	read(x,y);	read(x,y);	read(x,y);	read(x,y);
3	if(x<y)	if(x<y)	if(x<y)	if(x<y)
4	tmp=2*x;	tmp=2*x;	tmp=2*x;	tmp=2*x;
5	sum=x;		sum=x;	sum=x;
6	else	else		
7	tmp=3*y;	tmp=3*y;		
8	sum=y;			
9	sum=sum+x+y;			sum=sum+x+y;
10	res=tmp+x+y;	res=tmp+x+y;	res=tmp+x+y;	res=tmp+x+y;
11	print(sum);			print(sum);
12	print(res);	print(res);	print(res);	print(res);

Between 2004 and 2007, articles related to static slicing and dynamic slicing techniques dominated program slicing-based techniques. In contrast, since a few years ago, execution slicing has replaced static and dynamic slicing techniques as the dominant player in the field.

3   Related Work

The previous section gives an overview of DNN-based techniques and slice-based techniques, and this section will introduce in detail the method based on DNN and execution slicing proposed in this paper. There are two parts in this section, the first part is DNN modeling and training, and the second part is the algorithm combining DNN and execution slicing.

3.1   DNN Modeling and Training

In the first step, the training matrix used to train the DNN model is constructed as shown in (1), based on the statement coverage, decision coverage, etc. in the software test.

$$
\begin{bmatrix}
x_{11} & x_{12} & \cdots & x_{1N} \\
x_{21} & x_{22} & \cdots & x_{2N} \\
\vdots & \vdots & \ddots & \vdots \\
x_{M1} & x_{M2} & \cdots & x_{MN}
\end{bmatrix}
\begin{bmatrix}
e_1 \\
e_2 \\
\vdots \\
e_M
\end{bmatrix}
\tag{1}
$$

Where N is the number of executable statements of program P, M is the number of test cases, and x_{ij} indicates the coverage data of the ith test case on the jth executed statement, and if x_{ij} is 1, then the statement is executed, otherwise, the statement is not executed in this test.

In the second step, the DNN model is constructed, as shown in Fig. 2.

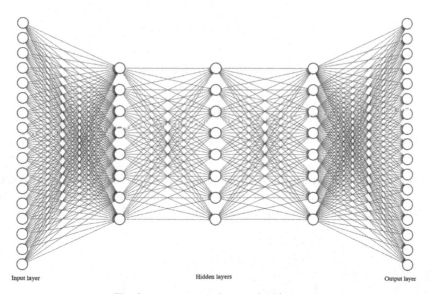

Input layer   Hidden layers   Output layer

Fig. 2. DNN model diagram in this paper

Where the number of nodes in the input and output layers is N. The number of hidden layers is determined to be 3 according to the scale of the experiment, and the transfer function is shown in (2).

$$Sigmoid(x) = \frac{1}{1 + e^{-x}} \tag{2}$$

In the third step, the training matrix (1) is fed into the DNN model as a row vector until the coverage data of M test cases in the group and their execution results are fed into the DNN model, and then the training set of the next group is fed iteratively, and the DNN model is continuously optimized until convergence.

3.2 Fault Localization Based on DNN and Execution Slicing

The previous subsection shows the modeling process, and this subsection shows the specific algorithm, and the algorithm flowchart is shown in Fig. 3.

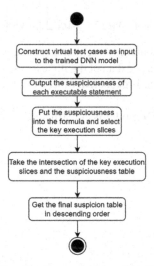

Fig. 3. Flowchart of fault localization method based on DNN and execution slicing

First, after the training is completed, to obtain the suspicion of each executed statement, it is necessary to construct an identity matrix that simulates that only one test statement is executed for each case, as shown in (3).

$$\begin{bmatrix} x_{11} & x_{12} & \cdots & x_{1N} \\ x_{21} & x_{22} & \cdots & x_{2N} \\ \vdots & \vdots & \ddots & \vdots \\ x_{N1} & x_{N2} & \cdots & x_{NN} \end{bmatrix} = \begin{bmatrix} 1 & 0 & \cdots & 0 \\ 0 & 1 & \cdots & 0 \\ \vdots & \vdots & \ddots & \vdots \\ 0 & 0 & \cdots & 1 \end{bmatrix} \tag{3}$$

The unit matrix (3) is fed into the trained DNN model to obtain a suspicion table containing all statements.

In the second step, the key execution slices are selected according to the metric function proposed in this paper.

Execution slicing, as a lightweight slice, is consistent with a very important idea in program debugging - suggesting that programmers analyze program behavior under failed test cases rather than under general test cases - and has a smaller cost compared to static and dynamic slicing, but its ability to reveal bugs in programs has not been fully explored has not been fully explored.

In the process of software testing, multiple slices are obtained, and to find the slice with the greatest possible utility for locating faults and further explore the ability of slices to reveal program faults, scholars have proposed various methods for selecting slices: Xiaolin Ju et al. proposed four selection strategies for execution slices by constructing a slice spectrum for execution slices and full slices [17], similarly, Wanzhi Wen et al. constructed a conditional execution slice spectrum based on fault-related conditional execution slices with high time cost; Lei Wang proposed a utility metric function for failure slices, but when the slice similarity is high, the function value gap is small and the screening effect is not satisfactory.

In this paper, we propose a new metric function $f(T_i)$, which fully takes into account the ability of failed test cases to reveal faults compared to the above methods, especially in scenarios where multiple slicing paths are similar, with relatively higher discrimination and relatively lower time cost. $f(T_i)$ As shown in (4).

$$f(T_i) = \frac{n}{\sqrt{\sum_{j=1}^{N} x_{ij} \times \left(100 \times sus_j\right)^2}}, i = 1, 2, \ldots, M \tag{4}$$

Where T_i is the execution slice corresponding to the failed test cases, and sus_j is the suspiciousness of the jth statement, and n is the number of statements in the execution slice corresponding to the failed test case.

By calculating the execution slice metric function value, the key slices are selected from the execution slices corresponding to multiple failed test cases to obtain a subset of executable statements. Since faults in the program are bound to appear in the execution slices of the failed test cases, selecting the appropriate critical slices can effectively remove the noise in the suspiciousness ranking table and greatly improve the accuracy of the approach.

In the third step, after obtaining a subset of executable statements by execution slicing technique, the intersection of this subset and the suspiciousness table obtained by DNN is taken to obtain the reduced suspiciousness ranking table.

The advantages of the method combining DNN and execution slicing proposed in this paper include the following.

First, DNN is able to learn more essential features from a small amount of sample data, overcoming the problem that RBF has a limited ability to express complex relationships with a limited amount of sample data. Second, compared to static slicing and dynamic slicing, execution slicing is more lightweight and less expensive, neither ignoring the importance of failed test cases for locating faults as static slicing does, nor does dynamic. Third, the DNN-based method eventually obtains a suspiciousness table of all executable statements of the entire program, which needs to be ranked in descending order of suspiciousness until the fault statement is located, while the execution slicing technique can obtain a subset of all executable statements in the program, and by combining with the execution slicing technique, it can eliminate a portion of By combining with the execution slicing technique, a part of the program fragments that are not related to the fault can be eliminated and only some of the more suspicious statements can be retained, thus narrowing the range of statements to be checked and thus improving the effectiveness of the method.

4   Empirical Studies

4.1   Methods Indicators

Validity is a key indicator of the fault localization approach. Since faults in a program may span multiple lines of code and may even be in different modules, and the purpose of fault localization is to help the programmer determine a location of a fault and thus begin to fix the fault in the program, the location can be stopped as soon as a location is found. With this in mind, the effectiveness of techniques is defined as the percentage of code to be checked before the location of the first fault is found.

The effectiveness evaluation criteria for mislocation include the following two main categories.

(1) Score method. Renieres et al. proposed the use of T-score to evaluate the effectiveness at the 18th IEEE International Conference on Automation Software Engineering. The T-score metric is the number of nodes detected by the first layer of depth-first traversal as a percentage of the total number of nodes in the program dependency graph. In 2009, Zhang Z et al. proposed the P-score evaluation metric [18]. The N-score, proposed by Gong C et al. in 2012, calculates the number of erroneous versions as a percentage of the total number of versions [19]. In addition to the above evaluation metrics, the EXAM metric is also widely used to evaluate the effectiveness of methods. The EXAM metric calculates the number of unchecked statements as a percentage of the total number of statements when the programmer locates a fault statement, and the higher the score, the better the result. In 2012, Wong et al. changed the EXAM metric to calculate the number of statements that must be checked before reaching the first fault position as a percentage of the total number of statements in the entire program Percentage [20].

(2) Cumulative Number of Statements Examined (Cumulative Number of Statements Examined). This metric is the total number of statements to be examined to detect all faults in all fault versions, focusing on the global perspective. The smaller the value of the Cumulative Number of Statements Examined, the more effective the method is.

The effectiveness evaluation criterion used in this paper is the EXAM index, and the higher the score, the better the effect.

4.2   The Example of Fault Localization Based on DNN and Execution Slicing

The experimental language of this method is Python, which implements the model construction of DNN and executes the slicing of the program to finally obtain the suspicion report of descending order.

The procedures to be tested are shown in Table 2.

Table 2. Procedures to be tested

Program P		
S_1: int res = 0, x = 0, y = 0, z = 0;	S_6: }else if(x < z && z < 0){	S_{11}: res += y; S_{16}: res = -1; }
S_2: read(x, y, z);	S_7: res += z;}	S_{12}: }else if(y < z && S_{17}: output(res);
S_3: if(x > y){	S_8: res *= y;	z > 0){
S_4: if(x > z && x > 0){	S_9: }else{	S_{13}: res += z; }
S_5: res += x;	S_{10}: if(y > z && y > 0){	S_{14}: res *= x; }
		S_{15}: if(res == 0)
Description	S_6 is an error statement, the correct one should be: }else if{x < z && z > 0}	

Table 3. Execution results of test cases, coverage data, and test cases (0 is a success, 1 is failure)

Test cases	t_1	t_2	t_3	t_4	t_5	t_6	t_7	t_8	t_9	t_{10}
x, y, z	2, -2, 0	2, 1, 0	1, -2, 2	2, -2, 3	-2, -3, -1	0, 2, 1	1, 2, 1	0, 1, 2	1, 2, 3	-2, -1, -1
S_1	1	1	1	1	1	1	1	1	1	1
S_2	1	1	1	1	1	1	1	1	1	1
S_3	1	1	1	1	1	1	1	1	1	1
S_4	1	1	1	1	1	0	0	0	0	0
S_5	1	1	0	0	0	0	0	0	0	0
S_6	0	0	1	1	1	0	0	0	0	0
S_7	0	0	1	1	0	0	0	0	0	0
S_8	1	1	1	1	1	0	0	0	0	0
S_9	0	0	0	0	0	1	1	1	1	1
S_{10}	0	0	0	0	0	1	1	1	1	1
S_{11}	0	0	0	0	0	1	1	0	0	0
S_{12}	0	0	0	0	0	0	0	1	1	1
S_{13}	0	0	0	0	0	0	0	1	1	0
S_{14}	0	0	0	0	0	1	1	1	1	1
S_{15}	1	1	1	1	1	1	1	1	1	1
S_{16}	1	0	1	0	1	1	0	1	0	1
S_{17}	1	1	1	1	1	1	1	1	1	1
error	0	0	0	1	1	0	0	0	0	0

The test cases, coverage data, and test case execution results are shown in Table 3.

In the first step, a training matrix is constructed based on the test cases, coverage data, and the results of the test case execution, as shown in (5).

$$\begin{bmatrix} 1\ 1\ 1\ 1\ 1\ 0\ 0\ 1\ 0\ 0\ 0\ 0\ 0\ 1\ 1\ 1 \\ 1\ 1\ 1\ 1\ 1\ 0\ 0\ 1\ 0\ 0\ 0\ 0\ 0\ 1\ 0\ 1 \\ 1\ 1\ 1\ 1\ 0\ 1\ 1\ 1\ 0\ 0\ 0\ 0\ 0\ 1\ 1\ 1 \\ 1\ 1\ 1\ 1\ 0\ 1\ 1\ 1\ 0\ 0\ 0\ 0\ 0\ 1\ 0\ 1 \\ 1\ 1\ 1\ 1\ 0\ 1\ 0\ 1\ 0\ 0\ 0\ 0\ 0\ 1\ 1\ 1 \\ 1\ 1\ 1\ 0\ 0\ 0\ 0\ 0\ 1\ 1\ 1\ 0\ 0\ 1\ 1\ 1 \\ 1\ 1\ 1\ 0\ 0\ 0\ 0\ 0\ 1\ 1\ 1\ 0\ 0\ 1\ 1\ 0\ 1 \\ 1\ 1\ 1\ 0\ 0\ 0\ 0\ 0\ 1\ 1\ 0\ 1\ 1\ 1\ 1\ 1 \\ 1\ 1\ 1\ 0\ 0\ 0\ 0\ 0\ 1\ 1\ 0\ 1\ 1\ 1\ 0\ 1 \\ 1\ 1\ 1\ 0\ 0\ 0\ 0\ 0\ 1\ 1\ 0\ 1\ 0\ 1\ 1\ 1 \end{bmatrix} \begin{bmatrix} 0 \\ 0 \\ 0 \\ 1 \\ 1 \\ 0 \\ 0 \\ 0 \\ 0 \\ 0 \end{bmatrix} \tag{5}$$

In the second step, the DNN model includes: 1 input layer with 17 nodes; 3 hidden layers, the number of nodes in the hidden layer is determined as 8 according to the information of problem size and sample data volume; 1 output layer with 17 nodes.

In the third step, (5) is fed into the DNN model and trained iteratively until convergence.

In the fourth step, a set of virtual test cases is constructed, each test case in the set should cover only one execution statement and should be a 17-dimensional unit matrix as shown in (6).

$$\begin{bmatrix} 1\ 0 \cdots 0 \\ 0\ 1 \dots 0 \\ \vdots\ \vdots\ \ddots\ \vdots \\ 0\ 0 \dots 1 \end{bmatrix} \tag{6}$$

In the fifth step, the virtual test cases are fed into the trained DNN model, and the output obtained is the suspiciousness of each executed statement of the program P, sorted in descending order, and the results are shown in Sect. 4.3.

In the sixth step, the key metric function is selected based on the execution of the slice metric function (4). From Table 2, we can see that the test cases t_5, and t_6 are the failed test cases, and their corresponding execution slices are $T_5 = \{s_1, s_2, s_3, s_4, s_6, s_7, s_8, s_{15}, s_{17}\}$ and $T_6 = \{s_1, s_2, s_3, s_4, s_6, s_8, s_{15}, s_{17}\}$ The corresponding function values can be derived from the slice metric function, which are $f(T_5) = 0.0627$, and $f(T_6) = 0.2241$ The key execution slices are $T_6 = \{s_1, s_2, s_3, s_4, s_6, s_8, s_{15}, s_{17}\}$.

In the seventh step, the intersection operation is done on the set of utterances contained in the key slices and the descending table of suspicion obtained by the DNN model to obtain the reduced suspicion report.

4.3   Results and Discussion of the Example

The results of the validation experiments are shown in Table 4.

Table 4. Suspectiveness report table after narrowing the search field

x, y, z	Susceptibility	Sort by	Combine and sort
S_1	0.267	8	7
S_2	0.265	9	8
S_3	0.27	5	5
S_4	0.478	3	2
S_5	0.134	13	
S_6	0.609	2	1
S_7	0.613	1	
S_8	0.477	4	3
S_9	0.102	17	
S_{10}	0.102	16	
S_{11}	0.136	11	
S_{12}	0.114	15	
S_{13}	0.135	12	
S_{14}	0.16	10	
S_{15}	0.267	7	6
S_{16}	0.118	14	
S_{17}	0.27	6	4

As can be seen from the table, for this experiment, the effectiveness evaluation index EXAM-score of the method based on DNN is 88.235%, while the effectiveness evaluation index EXAM-score of the fault location method based on DNN and execution slicing is 94.118%. The effectiveness of our method is increased by 5.883%.

4.4 Contrast Experiment

The evaluation standard dataset used in this experiment is the Siemens Suite, which was first created to demonstrate the effectiveness of control flow and data flow coverage based methods for fault detection on real programs at the IEEE International Conference on Software Engineering by Hutchins et al. and has since been widely used for research in the field of software testing. The evaluation dataset consists of seven sets of programs written in C. Each set contains one correct version and several fault versions obtained by implantation and can be downloaded from the SIR (Software-artifact Infrastructure Repository) website. descriptive statistics of Siemens Suite are shown in Table 5.

The method based on DNN and execution slicing proposed in this paper is used to perform comparison experiments on the commonly used test dataset Siemens-suite with several of the most commonly used and widely accepted methods in this field (SFL, BPNN-based method and DNN-based method).

Table 5. Siemens suite statistical information table

Program	Faulty Versions	Lines of Code	Test cases	Description
print_tokens	7	565	4130	lexical analyzer
print_tokens2	10	510	4115	lexical analyzer
schedule	9	412	2650	priority scheduler
schedule2	10	307	2710	priority scheduler
replace	32	563	5542	pattern replacement
tcas	41	173	1608	altitude separation
tot_info	23	406	1052	Information measure

4.5   Results and Discussion of the Contrast Experiment

The results of the comparison experiments are shown in Fig. 4.

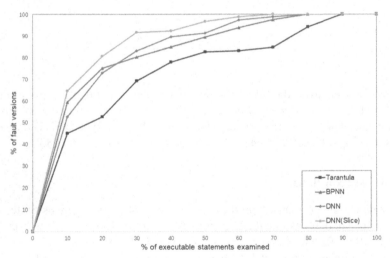

Fig. 4. Comparison of experimental results

After theoretical analysis and experiments, the results show that the overall effectiveness of the method in this paper outperforms the SFL technique, the BPNN-based technique, and the DNN-based technique of the mainstream methods for fault localization. For checking the same number of utterances, the proposed method in this paper can identify fault versions that are 6.09%–28.35% better than Tarantula, 3.32%–11.42% better than BPNN-based technique, and 1.19%–9.67% better than DNN-based technique.

Since the method proposed in this paper uses a combination of DNN and execution slicing, the time cost in program execution increases compared to other methods mentioned above, but the rise in time cost is within tolerable limits.

5 Conclusions

Locating faults is a very important part of program debugging, and program debugging is one of the most time-consuming and labor-intensive activities in software testing. In order to learn more essential features from limited sample data, and to improve the effectiveness of method, this paper proposes a method that combines DNN and execution slicing. This method introduces DNN, which has excellent ability to express complex nonlinear relationships, and is the most essential feature of deep learning data. In addition, the method also narrows the scope of the test by executing the slicing technique, and further improves the effectiveness of the fault location. Although the combination of the two will pay a certain time and space price, it is still within an acceptable range. The effectiveness of this method in the case of limited sample data has been significantly improved, but it still has certain limitations for the case of multiple faults in the program. The next step will be to further study the case of multiple faults.

References

1. Yu, K., Lin, M.: Advances in fault localization techniques for automation software. Chin. J. Comput. **34**(008), 1411–1422 (2011)
2. Wong, W.E., Qi, Y.: BP neural network-based effective fault localization. Int. J. Softw. Eng. Knowl. Eng. **19**(04), 573–597 (2009)
3. Ascari, L.C., Araki, L.Y., Pozo, A.R.T., Vergilio, S.R.: Exploring machine learning techniques for fault localization, pp. 1–6. IEEE (2009)
4. Wong, W.E., Debroy, V., Golden, R., Xu, X., Thuraisingham, B.: Effective software fault localization using an RBF neural network. IEEE Trans. Reliab. **61**(1), 149–169 (2012)
5. Briand, L.C., Labiche, Y., Liu, X.: Using machine learning to support debugging with Tarantula, pp. 137–146. IEEE (2007)
6. Sterling, C.D., Olsson, R.A.: Automated bug isolation via program chipping. Softw. Pract. Experiance **37**(10), 1061–1086 (2010)
7. Wang, Y., Patil, H., Pereira, C., Lueck, G., Gupta, R., Neamtiu, I.: DrDebug: deterministic replay based cyclic debugging with dynamic slicing, pp. 98–108. ACM (2014)
8. Ju, X., Jiang, S., Xiang, C., Wang, X., Zhang, Y., Cao, H.: HSFal: effective fault localization using a hybrid spectrum of full slices and execution slices. J. Syst. Softw. **90**, 3–17 (2014)
9. Chao, L., Zhang, X., Han, J., Yu, Z., Bhargava, B.K.: Indexing noncrashing failures: a dynamic program slicing-based approach. IEEE (2015)
10. Mao, X., Yan, L., Dai, Z., Qi, Y., Wang, C.: Slice-based statistical fault localization. J. Syst. Softw. **89**, 51–62 (2014)
11. Alves, E., Gligoric, M., Jagannath, V., D'Amorim, M.: Fault-localization using dynamic slicing and change impact analysis (2011)
12. Wong, W.E., Gao, R., Li, Y., Abreu, R., Wotawa, F.: A survey on software fault localization. IEEE Trans. Software Eng. **42**(8), 707–740 (2016)
13. Mao, Y., Gui, X., Li, Q., He, X.: Deep learning applied technology research. Application Research of Computers (2016)

14. Zhou, L., Pan, S., Wang, J., Vasilakos, A.V.: Machine learning on big data: opportunities and challenges. Neurocomputing (Amsterdam) **237**, 350–361 (2017)
15. Jordan, M.I., Mitchell, T.M.: Machine learning: trends, perspectives, and prospects. Science **349**(6245), 255–260 (2015)
16. Chen, M., Challita, U., Saad, W., Yin, C., Debbah, M.: Artificial neural networks-based machine learning for wireless networks: a tutorial. IEEE Commun. Surv. Tutorials **21**(4), 3039–3071 (2017)
17. Ju, X., Jiang, S., Chen, X., Zhang, Y., Shao, H.: **51**(12), 16 (2014)
18. Zhang, Z., Chan, W.K., Tse, T.H., Hu, P., Wang, X.: Is non-parametric hypothesis testing model robust for statistical fault localization? Inf. Softw. Technol. **51**, 1573–1585 (2009)
19. Gong, C., Zheng, Z., Li, W., Hao, P.: Effects of class imbalance in test suites: an empirical study of spectrum-based fault localization, pp. 470–475. IEEE (2012)
20. Wong, W.E., Debroy, V., Li, Y., Gao, R.: Software fault localization using DStar (D*) (2012)

Defect Detection and Classification of Strip Steel Based on Improved VIT Model

Lina Xing[1,2], Tinghui Li[1,2], Honghui Fan[1,2], and Hongjin Zhu[1,2(✉)]

[1] Jiangsu University of Technology, Changzhou 213001, China
zhuhongjin@jsut.edu.cn
[2] 1801 Zhongwu Avenue, Changzhou, Jiangsu, China

Abstract. With the further development of industry, strip steel occupies an important position in industrial production and is widely used in various manufacturing fields. It is especially important to monitor the quality of strip steel production. In order to improve the detection rate of defective strip steel for its complex and varied surface defects and other characteristics, this paper proposes a defect classification algorithm based on the SFN-VIT (Improved Shuffle Network Unite Vision Transformer) model to classify six types of defects in strip steel and compare it with other classification algorithms based on convolutional neural network. The experimental data show that the proposed SFN-VIT model outperforms the traditional machine learning algorithm model and achieves an average accuracy of 91.7% for defect classification on the NEU-CLS dataset (Tohoku University strip steel surface defect categories dataset), which is a 5.1% improvement compared to the traditional classification algorithm.

Keywords: Defect classification · Strip steel · Transformer · Machine vision

1 Introduction

Strip steel is widely used in aerospace, automotive manufacturing, building structures, machinery manufacturing, household appliances and electronic instrumentation production because of its high surface flatness and good mechanical properties [1]. With the increasing requirements of industrial production, the total demand and production quality of strip steel is also increasing [2]. Due to the influence of cold rolling process, production materials, processing equipment and many other technologies, the surface of strip steel will inevitably produce defects such as inclusions, scratches, pressed-in oxide, cracks, pockmarks, patches and so on, which directly affect the corrosion resistance and wear resistance of strip steel, so the detection of surface defects on strip steel is an important part of product quality monitoring. The research on strip steel surface defect detection at home and abroad is mainly based on traditional machine vision and based on deep learning, while in recent years deep learning algorithms gradually show high performance in computer vision tasks beyond traditional machine vision algorithms, and the research on strip steel surface defect detection based on deep learning has become

© IFIP International Federation for Information Processing 2022
Published by Springer Nature Switzerland AG 2022
Z. Shi et al. (Eds.): IIP 2022, IFIP AICT 643, pp. 327–335, 2022.
https://doi.org/10.1007/978-3-031-03948-5_26

mainstream and achieved better results. Therefore, the SFN-Vision Transformer model is used to detect strip steel surface defects according to their characteristics.

The Vision Transformer model is based on the following considerations for the detection and classification of cold-rolled strip surface defects: Vision Transformer is an image classification algorithm based on the Transformer model, while Transformer lacks inductive preferences such as translation invariance and locality. In other words, Vision Transformer lacks a priori experience that convolutional structures have, therefore it requires more data to learn such structures. When the Vision Transformer model is pre-trained on a large-scale dataset and then migrated to a small-scale dataset, the results achieved are comparable to most outstanding convolutional neural networks and are suitable for small-scale cold-rolled strip defect datasets. To the greatest extent, it avoids the prone to overfitting of convolutional neural networks to small data sets. Furthermore, the strip surface defect dataset has a large variation of intra-class defects, while inter-class defects have many similarities. Moreover, the strip surface defect image will be affected by the image sensor itself and the surrounding environment such as high temperature and bright light, these characteristics bring challenges to the strip surface defect category recognition. We optimize the defect classification algorithm for the above problem as follows: sparse representation technique is used to denoise the strip surface defect images, which enhances the feature extraction effect of the subsequent network model.

2 Related Work

To improve the detection rate of defective strips, many scholars have studied it in recent years and proposed various methods for improving the performance of classification models [3]. Literature [4] proposed a new semi-supervised learning method based on convolutional self-encoder and semi-supervised generative adversarial network, which improved the performance of SGAN with limited training samples as a solution to the situation that strip steel sample images exist mostly unlabeled, and improved the classification rate by about 16% compared with traditional detection methods; literature [5] used YOLOv3 as the feature extraction network, and the DenseNet Block for feature fusion and reuse before predicting the whole layer of features, and detected on six strip steel surface defect datasets with a detection accuracy of 85.7%, achieving good results; literature [6] proposed a tree neural network classifier, consisting of four different neural networks, which divided the defects into specific defects by area type, disk type, and area and linear detail types, and used the SFFS algorithm to select the optimal features for the classifier and achieved better results; literature [7] established a lightweight search algorithm using dominant non-uniform patterns (DNUPs), proposed a mixed-mode code mapping mechanism for encoding, and performed feature extraction in the framework of local binary patterns (GCLBP), and finally used a nearest neighbor classifier to achieve histogram matching, and experimental data showed that better experimental results were achieved; literature [8] first binarized the image data, combined with the original defective image for the extraction of geometric features, grayscale features and shape features, and based on the support vector machine classification model with Gaussian radial basis as the kernel function, and determined the model parameters through cross-validation, the experimental classification accuracy was better than that of the traditional BP neural network-based classification model.

3   Research Methods

In this paper, the strip steel surface defect detection model is improved based on the Vision Transformer model. The image data are denoised using a sparse representation technique before being fed into the classification model, and the VIT (Vision Transformer) model is improved using a modified ShuffleNetv2 network as a feature extraction network.

3.1   De-Noise Processing

The images acquired during the actual production of strip steel can generate noise due to environmental factors such as the image sensor itself, high temperature, and bright light [9]. Noise can interfere with the classification results and affect the effect of feature extraction, so it is essential to perform noise reduction on the images before performing the detection [10]. The sparse representation technique is introduced to denoise cold rolled strip images. While removing the image noise, the noise is not a sparse component of the signal, it can minimize the damage to the original image information [11]. The sparse representation technique mainly consists of two parts: sparse coding and dictionary learning. In other words, the dictionary atoms that can linearly represent the image data are generated in the data set, thus forming an overcomplete dictionary that can extract the multidimensional features of the image, and the sparse vector is obtained by sparse coding of the image with the trained overcomplete dictionary, while the noise is not linearly represented by the overcomplete dictionary and cannot be sparse, so the noise is discarded in the form of residuals in the reconstruction process.

In this paper, KSVD algorithm is used for denoising, and the sparse representation model is used to optimize the minimum error by fixing the number of sparse coefficients. K-means and SVD algorithms are integrated in KSVD algorithm, and after determining the number of iterations K, each iteration is decomposed using SVD algorithm, and in the process of updating the dictionary, only one atom in the dictionary and its corresponding sparse coding vector are updated each time, the other atoms remain unchanged. The other atoms are kept unchanged, and the sparse coding factor is also updated when all the atoms in the dictionary are updated to complete this iterative process. The algorithm steps are as follows:

(1)   Randomly select n atoms in the strip defect dataset to initialize the learning dictionary.
(2)   Based on the determined sparse representation model, the sparse encoding matrix X is calculated using the OMP algorithm.
(3)   Optimize the error matrix using the SVD algorithm as in Eq. (1) and update the atoms in the dictionary.
(4)   Determine whether all the atoms in the dictionary have been updated, if not continue to step (3); if all the atoms in the dictionary have been updated, determine whether the number of iterations has been reached, if not continue to step (2); if the number of iterations has been reached, get the updated dictionary, use the updated dictionary to calculate the sparse encoding and reconstruct the image with steel defects, and

then perform weighted superposition on the image blocks to get the denoised image.

$$E_k = Y - \sum_{j \neq k} d_j x_T^j \tag{1}$$

3.2 SFN-Vision Transformer

Convolutional neural network models have been the dominant model in computer vision since the explosion of deep learning [12]. Convolution has a natural advantage in image problems by virtue of equivalence and localization, but by continuously stacking convolutional layers to obtain large perceptual fields, while Transformer has a long memory length and can parallelize processing [13, 14]. Vision Transformer applies Transformer to image classification tasks [15]. VIT model consists of three main modules, Linear Projection of Flattened Patches, Transformer Encoder, and MLP Head. The Transformer Encoder module requires a vector matrix as input, thus mapping patches divided into images into one-dimensional vectors by linear mapping, adding category vectors and position encoding, feeding them into the Transformer Encoder module of the repetitive stack Encoder Block module L times, and getting classification results according to the corresponding data generated by extracting category vectors.

The VIT model will be optimized in the following two aspects: before reshaping the image data into a flattened two-dimensional fragment sequence, feature extraction is performed on the image data, and we replace the feature extraction network with a lighter ShuffleNetv2 network and improve the ShuffleNetv2 model. Combining the SE unit with Shuffle Block, we add the SE module on the shortcut branch of Shuffle Block. That is, a squeezing operation is first performed on it by global average pooling, compress the channel feature information into weight factors, normalize them with two fully connected layers, and finally multiply the normalized weight factors with the weighted input features to achieve weight rescaling. The structure of Shuffle Block with a step of 1 is shown in Fig. 1. By adding SE unit modules to suppress the feature channel information on the Shuffle Block shortcut branch that has little effect on the current task, strengthening important feature information, and further enhancing the performance of the network model. The optimized SFN-Vision-Transformer network model is shown in Fig. 2.

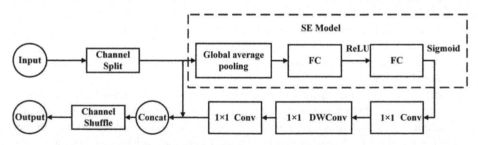

Fig. 1. Shuffle Blockc structure diagram

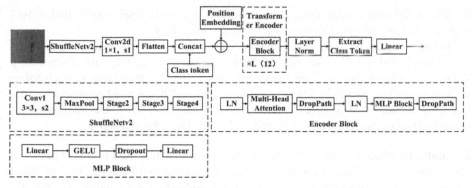

Fig. 2. SFN-Vision Transformer network structure diagram

4 Experimental Results and Analysis

4.1 Data Set

The strip surface defect dataset used in this paper is a NEU-CLS image file for defect classification task disclosed by Tohoku University, containing six typical strip surface defects, namely, inclusions, scratches, pressed-in oxide, cracks, pockmarks and patches, each containing 300 images, each with the size of 299 × 299, Fig. 3 shows the sample images of six strip defects. Due to the lack of positive samples in the NEU-CLS dataset, 300 images of qualified strip steel were obtained as positive samples by the camera with the size of 299 × 299.

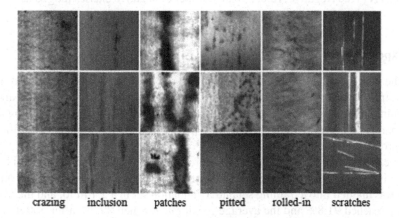

crazing   inclusion   patches   pitted   rolled-in   scratches

Fig. 3. Strip surface defect map

4.2 Experimental Setup and Evaluation Indexes

Experimental Environment and Model Parameters. The experiment is conducted based on the following platform and environment: code implementation using Python, specific experimental environment configuration is: processor Intel Core i5-10400, 16G memory devices, operating system Win10 Professional 64-bit.

In order to reduce the number of parameters of the model, the Vision Transformer model is selected as VIT-Base, and the Patch Size is 32 × 32, The time of repeatedly stacked Encoder Blocks in Transformer Encoder is 12, the dimension of each token sequence after passing through the Embedding layer is 768, the number of nodes of the first fully connected MLP Block in Transformer Encoder is 3072, and the number of heads in Transformer The number of heads of Multi-Head Attention is 12.

Evaluation Indicators. Since the strip surface defect dataset used in this experiment contains six defects, which is a multi-classification task, the multi-classification problem is transformed into multiple binary classification problems for evaluation, specifically containing Accuracy and Recall rate of each defect, where Accuracy is the proportion of the number of correctly classified samples to the total number of samples, as in Eq. (2), and Recall rate is the proportion of all positive classes that are predicted to be positive, as in Eq. (3) [16].

$$Accuracy = \frac{TP + TN}{TP + TN + FP + FN} \tag{2}$$

$$Recall = \frac{TP}{TP + FN} \tag{3}$$

Among them, TP (True Positive) refers to the number of positive classes judged as positive; FN (False Negative) refers to the number of positive classes misjudged as negative; FP (False Positive) refers to the number of negative classes misjudged as positive; TN (True Negative) refers to the number of negative classes judged as negative [17].

4.3 Experimental Results

Since the VIT model can get better results on large datasets, thus the proposed model was pre-trained on ImageNet dataset, and after obtaining the pre-training parameters, the training was carried out using the strip surface defect dataset, and the tuning of the model parameters was completed. The final partial results of strip defect classification on the proposed model are shown in Fig. 4.

The experiments were conducted in the context of a dataset containing six types of defective images, 300 images of each defective and qualified image strips, and the dataset was divided into a training set and a validation set in a 2:1 ratio, and the average accuracy reached 91.8% and the average recall rate reached 89.2% after 500 iterations with batch-size set as 5, as shown in Table 1.

The proposed algorithm is compared with other classification model algorithms based on the average accuracy and average recall rate evaluation metrics, and the results are shown in Fig. 5. After pre-training on large ImageNet datasets, the generalization ability of the Vision Transformer model is greatly improved, large-scale data trained on Vision Transformer can outperform the inherent inductive bias that convolutional neural

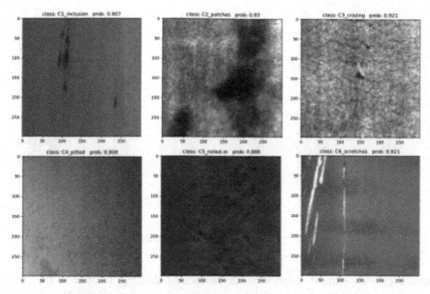

Fig. 4. Some strip steel surface defects detection results

Table 1. Various types of defects detection and evaluation table

Type of defect	Accuracy/%	Recall rate/%
Crazing	92.1	90.4
Inclusion	91.6	88.7
Patches	92.9	90.8
Pitted	91.7	89.7
Rolled-in	89.8	85.3
Scratches	92.4	90.2

networks have, such as localization and translational covariance, and the required computational resources are also significantly reduced, and its detection capability is better compared with the convolutional neural network model. The SFN-VIT model based on the combination of convolutional neural network and Transformer can be calculated in parallel using Transformer and the number of operations required to calculate the correlation between different positions does not increase with the increase of distance, which can produce the advantages of a more explanatory model. At the same time, the use of convolution characteristics can have the advantage of better expressiveness in structured data such as images, so as to learn image features more efficiently, and its detection results are better than those of the convolution network model and the improved Vision Transformer Model.

The traditional industrial methods for detecting defects in strip steel are eddy current detection, infrared detection and magnetic leakage detection. Eddy current inspection

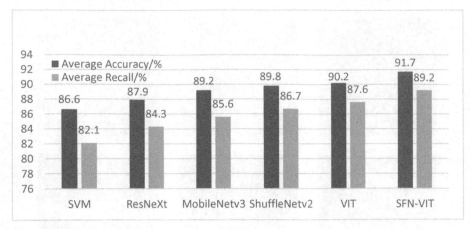

Fig. 5. Comparison chart of classification models

method uses eddy current detector on the surface of the strip to observe the changes in the induced current to determine the presence or absence of defects. However, using this method for inspection requires a long period of heating to process the strip to be inspected into a uniform temperature field, so the method has great limitations and is very difficult to achieve for cold rolled strip. Infrared detection method uses electric current through the surface of the detected object to produce different temperatures, resulting in infrared differences to achieve defect detection. When passing through the defective area, a difference in temperature and infrared light is generated that is different from the normal area. But the method is not adapted to large depth defects, and limited types of defects can be detected. Leakage detection method uses the change in magnetic flux density to detect defects, and this technology can detect the size of defects, but the method can only detect ferromagnetic materials and the influence of the surrounding environment is large. There are limitations in the detection occasions. The machine vision-based inspection method can solve the above problems, so the improved VIT model of strip steel surface defect detection method proposed in this paper has some practical significance.

5 Summary

In this paper, the classification of strip steel surface defects was performed based on the NEU-CLS dataset. By improving the Vision Transformer model, pre-training on ImageNet data, and optimizing the parameters of the network model, a classification model with high accuracy is obtained. It can be seen that using the attention mechanism can make the model pay more attention to the features of the defective part, and at the same time, noise reduction is performed on the image to achieve the purpose of improving the classification accuracy. Many improvements need to be made in the future, such as the introduction of BackBone for feature extraction to the VIT model, which will increase the number of parameters of the network model, and further optimization of the algorithm, which will be completed in future work.

Acknowledgements. This work was supported by the National Natural Science Foundation of China (61806088), by the Natural science fund for colleges and universities in Jiangsu Province (20KJA520007), by Graduate Practice Innovation Project Fund for Jiangsu university of Technology (XSJCX21_51).

References

1. Tang, M., Li, Y., Yao, W., Hou, L., Sun, Q., Chen, J.: A strip steel surface defect detection method based on attention mechanism and multi-scale maxpooling. Measure. Sci. Technol. **32**(11), 115401 (2021)
2. Wang, W., et al.: Surface defects classification of hot rolled strip based on improved convolutional neural network: instrumentation, control and system engineering. ISIJ Int. **61**(5), 1579–1583 (2021)
3. Support Vector Machines; New Support Vector Machines Study Findings Have Been Reported from University of Science and Technology (Multi-class classification method for strip steel surface defects based on support vector machine with adjustable hyper-sphere). J. Robot. Mach. Learn. (2019)
4. Di, H., Ke, Z., Peng, Z., Dongdong, Z.: Surface defect classification of steels with a new semi-supervised learning method. Optics Lasers Eng. **117**, 40–48 (2019)
5. Jiaqiao, Z.: Surface defect detection of steel strips based on classification priority YOLOv3-dense network. Ironmaking Steelmaking **48**, 547–558 (2020)
6. Moon, C.I., Choi, S.H., Kim, G.B., et al.: Classification of surface defects on cold rolled strip by tree-structured neural networks. Trans. Korean Soc. Mech. Eng. A **31**(6), 651–658 (2007)
7. Luo, Q., Sun, Y., Li, P., et al.: Generalized completed local binary patterns for time-efficient steel surface defect classification. IEEE Trans. Instrum. Measure. **68**(3), 667–679 (2018)
8. Hu, H., Li, Y., Liu, M., et al.: Classification of defects in steel strip surface based on multiclass support vector machine. Multimedia Tools Appl. **69**(1), 199–216 (2014)
9. Wan, X., Zhang, X., Liu, L.: An improved VGG19 transfer learning strip steel surface defect recognition deep neural network based on few samples and imbalanced datasets. Appl. Sci. **11**(6), 2606 (2021)
10. Dongyan, C., Kewen, X., Aslam, N., Jingzhong, H.: Defect classification recognition on strip steel surface using second-order cone programming-relevance vector machine algorithm. J. Comput. Theor. Nanosci. **13**(9), 6141–6148 (2016)
11. Classification of surface defects of hot rolled strips: effectiveness of SVM over HOG and combined features GLCM. Int. J. Innov. Technol. Explor. Eng. **9**(3) (2020)
12. Engineering; Researchers at Central South University Target Engineering (Surface defect classification for hot-rolled steel strips by selectively dominant local binary patterns). J. Eng. (2019)
13. Wang, C., Liu, Y., Yang, Y., Xu, X., Zhang, T.: Research on classification of surface defects of hot-rolled steel strip based on deep learning. In: Proceedings of 2019 2nd International Conference on Informatics, Control and Automation (ICA 2019), pp. 375–379 (2019)
14. Science - Science and Engineering; Investigators at University of Putra Malaysia Report Findings in Science and Engineering (Surface defects classification of hot-rolled steel strips using multi-directional Shearlet features). J. Eng. (2019)
15. Ashour, M.W., Khalid, F., Halin, A.A., Abdullah, L.N., Darwish, S.H.: Surface defects classification of hot-rolled steel strips using multi-directional Shearlet features. Arab. J. Sci. Eng. **44**(4), 2925–2932 (2019)
16. Luo, Q., et al.: Surface defect classification for hot-rolled steel strips by selectively dominant local binary patterns. IEEE Access **7**, 23488–23499 (2019)
17. Brendan, K., Isaac, H., Farhana, Z.: Condition-CNN: A hierarchical multi-label fashion image classification model. Expert Syst. Appl. **182**, 11595 (2021)

Roses: A Novel Semi-supervised Feature Selector

Xiaoyu Zhang[1], Keyu Liu[1,2], Jing Ba[1], Xin Yang[3], and Xibei Yang[1(✉)]

[1] School of Computer, Jiangsu University of Science and Technology,
Zhenjiang 212003, China
jsjxy_yxb@just.edu.cn
[2] School of Computing and Artificial Intelligence, Southwest Jiaotong University,
Chengdu 611756, China
[3] School of Economic Information Engineering, Southwestern University of Finance
and Economics, Chengdu 611130, China

Abstract. In this study, a novel ROugh set based Semi-supervised fEature Selector (Roses) was developed to pre-process partially labeled data. The main innovations of our Roses are: 1) the selected features over labeled samples laid the foundation for further searching qualified features over unlabeled samples; 2) a new granularity related measure was designed to quickly evaluate features. Through testing four different ratios (20%, 40%, 60%, 80%) of labeled samples, the experimental results over 15 UCI datasets demonstrated that our framework is superior to the other five popular partially labeled data feature selectors: 1) the feature subsets identified by Roses offer competitive classification performances; 2) Roses is good at seeking a balance between efficiency of searching features and effectiveness of the selected features.

Keywords: Feature selection · Granularity · Partially labeled · Roses · Rough sets

1 Introduction

Attribute reduction is the key in the filed of rough set [1]. It can be regarded as a valuable technique to perform feature selection. Though such a technique has been conventionally explored over samples with complete labels, i.e., labeled data, much attention has recently been paid to samples unlabeled data or samples with missing labels, which are required for practical applications.

Generally speaking, a data contains samples with missing labels can be termed as the partially labeled data [2,3]. Such a type of data is more complicated than labeled data and unlabeled data. As far as the topic of feature selection is concerned, it may be argued that both the techniques related to labeled and unlabeled data should be fully taken into account if partially labeled data is studied.

Presently, many pioneering researchers have developed various rough set based feature selection strategies over partially labeled data. For example,

© IFIP International Federation for Information Processing 2022
Published by Springer Nature Switzerland AG 2022
Z. Shi et al. (Eds.): IIP 2022, IFIP AICT 643, pp. 336–347, 2022.
https://doi.org/10.1007/978-3-031-03948-5_27

Dai et al. [4] have proposed a semirough-P which fuses the evaluations of features over both labeled and unlabeled samples; Pang and Zhang [5] have introduced the neighborhood discrimination index [6] into partially labeled data, which aims to evaluate the significance of features more exactly; Liu et al. [7] have completed the missing labels in partially labeled data by using LPA [8], and then introduced an ensemble selector [9] into such a revised data for evaluate features.

Nevertheless, most of the previous studies about feature selection over partially labeled data are focused on evaluating features by either new measures or new angles. In other words, the keys of the employed feature selectors are similar to those which have been exploited over labeled and unlabeled data. From this point of view, the difference between the structures inherent in labeled and unlabeled samples may be overlooked. For instance, in Ref. [7], LPA is used to complete the labels of unlabeled samples, it follows that the raw structure of unlabeled samples may be disturbed because the performance of LPA relies heavily on the structure of labeled data.

From discussions above, we want to work out how to make full use of labeled and unlabeled data while maintaining a certain speed, in the context of this study, a novel feature selection framework called ROugh set based Semi-supervised fEature Selector (ROSES) will be developed. Different from existing approaches, our framework divides the whole process of feature selection over partially labeled data into two phases: 1) selecting qualified features over labeled samples and then derive a temporary result; 2) based on the information provided by unlabeled samples, further adding qualified features into such a temporary result.

Obviously, the above two phases imply an efficient guidance mechanism which is useful in speeding up the process of feature selection over partially labeled data. Furthermore, a new measure related to the concept called granularity is proposed in the second stage of searching. The calculation of such a measure is low cost and it can also be used to quickly identify qualified features over unlabeled samples. Such two points demonstrate the main contributions of our ROSES.

The remainder of this paper is organized as follows. In Sect. 2, we will briefly review some basic notions related to partially labeled data. Our framework are introduced in Sect. 3. In Sect. 4, comparative experimental results are presented, as well as corresponding analyses. The paper is ended with conclusions and perspectives for future work in Sect. 5.

2   Preliminary Knowledge

In this section, we will briefly review some basic notions related to partially labeled data. Without loss of generality, a partially labeled data can be denoted by $DS = \langle U^l \cup U^{ul}, AT, d^l \rangle$: U^l is a set of labeled samples; U^{ul} is a set of unlabeled samples; AT is a set of features for characterizing samples in both U^l and U^{ul}; d^l is used to record the labels of samples in U^l.

In rough set, an indiscernibility relation or some other binary relations are frequently constructed for the convenience of granulating samples [10], which are based on the information provided by features. For instance, Hu et al. [11] have developed a neighborhood relation: $\delta_{AT}^{U} = \{(x_i, x_j) \in U \times U : dis_{AT}(x_i, x_j) \leq \delta\}$ in which $dis_{AT}(x_i, x_j)$ is the distance between samples x_i and x_j over AT, $U \subseteq U^l \cup U^{ul}$, $\delta \geq 0$ is a given radius.

Following δ_{AT}^{U}, $\forall x_i \in U$, the neighborhood of x_i is then obtained by $\delta_{AT}^{U}(x_i) = \{x_j \in U : (x_i, x_j) \in \delta_{AT}\}$. Such a process can be regarded as an information granulation over U. To further characterize the degree of information granulation, the following definition of granularity can be used.

Definition 1. *Given a partially labeled data DS, $\delta \geq 0$ is a radius, the neighborhood relation related granularity over $U \subseteq U^l \cup U^{ul}$ is:*

$$G_{AT}^{\delta}(U) = \frac{|\delta_{AT}^{U}|}{|U|^2} = \frac{\sum_{x_i \in U} \delta_{AT}^{U}(x_i)}{|U|^2}, \tag{1}$$

$|X|$ denotes the cardinal number of set X.

Based on Definition 1, it is not difficult to conclude that a finer neighborhood relation indicates a small value of granularity, a coarser neighborhood relation will generate a great value of granularity.

Furthermore, by considering the labels of samples in U^l, from the viewpoint of rough set, we can induce a partition over U^l such that $U^l/\text{IND}_{d^l} = \{X_1, \cdots, X_t\}$. $\forall X_s \in U^l/\text{IND}_{d^l} (1 \leq s \leq t)$, X_s is regarded as the s-th decision class which contains all samples with same label. Immediately, the following neighborhood rough set can be defined over U^l.

Definition 2. *Given a partially labeled data DS, $\forall X_s \in U^l/IND_{d^l}$, $\delta \geq 0$ is a radius, the neighborhood based lower and upper approximations of X_s are:*

$$\underline{X_s}_{AT}^{\delta} = \{x_i \in U : \delta_{AT}^{U^l}(x_i) \subseteq X_s\}; \tag{2}$$

$$\overline{X_s}_{AT}^{\delta} = \{x_i \in U : \delta_{AT}^{U^l}(x_i) \cap X_s \neq \emptyset\}. \tag{3}$$

Following Definition 2, a crucial concept called approximation quality [12] can be formed for the measurement of degree of certain belongingness.

Definition 3. *Given a partially labeled data DS, $\delta \geq 0$ is a radius, the neighborhood based approximation quality over U^l is:*

$$\gamma_{AT}^{\delta}(U^l) = \frac{|\underline{d^l}_{AT}^{\delta}|}{|U^l|} = \frac{|\bigcup_{s=1}^{t} \underline{X_s}_{AT}^{\delta}|}{|U^l|}. \tag{4}$$

Obviously, the above rough set and approximation quality are only defined over labeled samples. Furthermore, to analyze unlabeled samples in partially labeled data by rough set, the following unsupervised relevance [13] can be used.

Definition 4. *Given a partially labeled data DS, $\delta \geq 0$ is a radius, the neighborhood based unsupervised relevance over U^{ul} is defined as:*

$$\gamma_{AT}^{\delta}(U^{ul}) = \frac{1}{|AT|} \sum_{a \in AT} \frac{|\underline{d_a^{ul}}_{AT}^{\delta}|}{|U^{ul}|}, \tag{5}$$

d_a^{ul} is used to record the pseudo labels of unlabeled samples in U^{ul}, which is generated by single attribute a.

In Definition 4, each single attribute is required to generate the pseudo labels of unlabeled samples in U^{ul} and then the neighborhood relation $\delta_{AT}^{U^{ul}}$ can be constructed for rough characterization of decision classes related to those pseudo labels. Therefore, the number of approximation qualities which will be generated is $|AT|$, a mean value of those approximation qualities is regarded as the unsupervised relevance.

3 Proposed Framework

Following the above section, it is not difficult to draw the following conclusions.

1) Approximation quality shown in Definition 3 can be directly used to select qualified features over labeled samples. In such a mechanism, the value of approximation quality related to AT is regarded as the feature evaluation criterion and then features which provide higher value of approximation quality will be selected.
2) Unsupervised relevance shown in Definition 4 can be employed to construct feature selection criterion for selecting qualified features over unlabeled samples. In such a mechanism, features which provide higher value of unsupervised relevance will be selected.

However, our objective in this study is to select qualified features over partially labeled samples instead of mere labeled samples or unlabeled samples, and then we have been faced with the problem of making a bridge between the above two mechanisms of selecting features. To this end, we will design a novel framework to perform feature selection over partially labeled data. The detailed steps of our framework are shown as follows.

1) Select qualified features over labeled samples based on measure shown in Definition 3. In this case, the widely accepted forward greedy searching [14] can be employed.
2) Determine whether the above selected features satisfies the criterion related to unsupervised relevance shown in Definition 4. If so, then terminate the procedure; otherwise, go to next step.
3) By calculating unsupervised relevances in terms of all candidate features, select some other valuable features step by step until the required criterion is satisfied.

From discussions above, a detailed algorithm can be designed as follows. The main structures of our algorithm is categorized into the following two aspects: 1) labeled and unlabeled samples in partially labeled data are processed separately; 2) the selected features over labeled samples may guide a further searching of features over unlabeled samples.

Furthermore, in the process of searching features over unlabeled samples, a new measure $\dfrac{G_a^\delta(U^{ul})}{dis(a,c)}$ is proposed for evaluating candidate features and then identifying an appropriate feature for each iteration. By comparing with unsupervised relevance, the computation of such a measure is simple and low cost. This is mainly because the time complexity of computing $\dfrac{G_a^\delta(U^{ul})}{dis(a,c)}$ is $\mathcal{O}(|U^{ul}|^2)$, the time complexity of computing unsupervised relevance is $\mathcal{O}(|U^{ul}|^2 \cdot |A|^2)$ in which $|A|$ keeps increasing with the increasing of the number of iterations.

Algorithm 1: ROugh set based Semi-supervised fEature Selection (ROSES).

Input: A Decision system DS, radius $\delta \geq 0$.
Output: One subset A of selected features.
1 $A = \emptyset$;
   // **Select qualified features over labeled samples**
2 Calculate $\gamma_{AT}^\delta(U^l)$;
3 $\gamma_A^\delta(U^l) = -\infty$;
4 **while** $\gamma_A^\delta(U^l) < \gamma_{AT}^\delta(U^l)$ **do**
5 $\quad$ $\forall a \in AT - A$, evaluate a by calculating $\gamma_{A \cup \{a\}}^\delta(U^l)$;
6 $\quad$ Select a feature $b \in AT - A$ with the maximal value of evaluation;
7 $\quad$ $A = A \cup \{b\}$;
8 $\quad$ Calculate $\gamma_A^\delta(U^l)$;
9 **end**
   // **Select qualified features over unlabeled samples**
10 Calculate $\gamma_A^\delta(U^{ul})$ and $\gamma_{AT}^\delta(U^{ul})$;
11 **if** $\gamma_A^\delta(U^{ul}) \geq \gamma_{AT}^\delta(U^{ul})$ **then**
12 $\quad$ go to step 21;
13 **else**
14 $\quad$ **while** $\gamma_A^\delta(U^{ul}) < \gamma_{AT}^\delta(U^{ul})$ **do**
15 $\quad\quad$ $\forall a \in AT - A$, evaluate a by calculating $\dfrac{G_a^\delta(U^{ul})}{dis(a,c)}$;
   $\quad\quad$ // c is the latest feature in A.
   $\quad\quad$ // $dis(a,c)$ is the distance between two features.
16 $\quad\quad$ Select a feature $b \in AT - A$ with the maximal value of evaluation;
17 $\quad\quad$ $A = A \cup \{b\}$;
18 $\quad\quad$ Calculate $\gamma_A^\delta(U^{ul})$;
19 $\quad$ **end**
20 **end**
21 **return** A;

4   Experiments

In this section, all experiments are conducted on a personal computer powered with Window 10, intel(R) Core(TM) i7-7700HQ CPU @ 2.80 GHz and 16.00 GB memory. Additionally, 15 public data sets from UCI Machine Learning Repository have been employed to conduct the experiments. The detailed statistics of these data are shown in the following Table 1.

Table 1. Details of data sets

ID	Data sets	# Samples	# Features	# Labels
1	Breast Cancer Wisconsin (Diagnostic)	569	30	2
2	Cardiotocography	2126	21	10
3	Diabetic Retinopathy Debrecen	1151	19	2
4	Forest Type Mapping	523	27	4
5	German	1000	24	2
6	Ionosphere	351	34	2
7	Libras Movement	360	90	15
8	Musk (Version 1)	476	166	2
9	Parkinson Multiple Sound Recording	1208	26	2
10	QSAR Biodegradation	1055	41	2
11	Seeds	210	7	3
12	Statlog (Image Segmentation)	2310	18	7
13	Statlog (Vehicle Silhouettes)	846	18	4
14	Ultrasonic Flowmeter Diagnostics-Meter D	180	43	4
15	Urban Land Cover	675	147	9

To ensure the reliability and stability of comparative studies, 10-fold cross validation is used. That is, given one data set, it is divided into 10 groups with same size. Then, for each round of computation, 9 groups compose the training data and the remainder is taken as the testing data. Furthermore, for each training data, we have also set the proportions of unlabeled samples as 20%, 40%, 60% and 80%, respectively.

Regarding the parameter of neighborhood rough set, we have appointed 20 different radii such that $0.02, 0.04, \cdots, 0.4$ for calculating granularity, approximation quality and unsupervised relevance.

In what follows, our algorithm (ROSES) will be compared with other five state-of-the-art methods, they are: 1) semirough-P [4] (Attribute Selection for Partially Labeled Data); 2) RSES [7] (Rough set based Semi-supervised feature selection via Ensemble Selector); 3) FW-SemiFS [15] (Forward Semi-supervised Feature Selection); 4) RRPC [16] (Max-Relevance and Min-Redundancy via Pearsons Correlation Coefficient); 5) SSNDI [5] (Semi-supervised Neighborhood Discrimination Index).

4.1   Comparisons Among Classification Accuracies

In this subsection, classification accuracies related to the selected features will be compared among six different algorithms. To obtain the classification results over partially labeled data, a graph-based semi-supervised classifier [17] was used. When used, the test data is imported into the semi-supervised classifier along with the results of the training data. The detailed results are shown in the following Figs. 1, 2, 3 and 4.

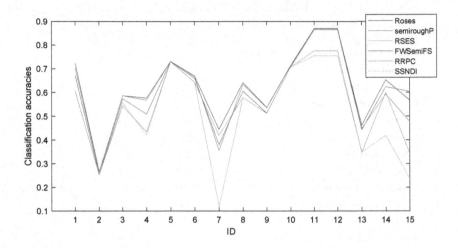

Fig. 1. Classification accuracies (20% of unlabeled samples)

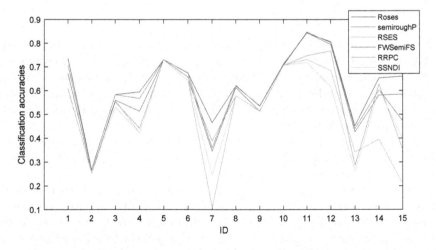

Fig. 2. Classification accuracies (40% of unlabeled samples)

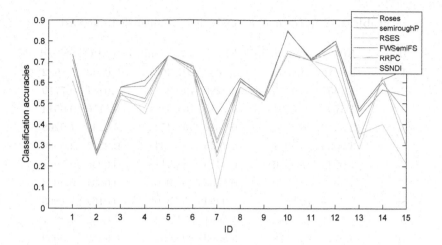

Fig. 3. Classification accuracies (60% of unlabeled samples)

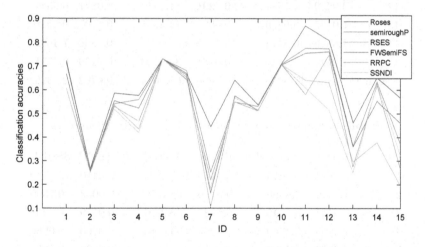

Fig. 4. Classification accuracies (80% of unlabeled samples)

With a thorough investigation, it is not difficult to reveal: for the four different ratios of unlabeled samples we have tested, because we made full use of the labeled data, and then processed the unlabeled data based on it features identified by our approach provide competitive classification performances and have good classification ability for different data.

4.2   Comparisons Among Time Consumptions

Besides the effectiveness of selected features, efficiency of the process of selecting features is another index which should be paid much attention to. Therefore, the following Tables 2, 3, 4 and 5 show detailed time consumptions of searching features in terms of 6 different algorithms.

Table 2. Elapsed time (Seconds, 20% of unlabeled samples)

ID	ROSES	semirough-P	RSES	FW-SemiFS	RRPC	SSNDI
1	9.8410	34.7805	2.3042	807.9025	0.0473	7.8902
2	1.8457	6.4650	0.4296	140.2531	0.0131	0.7719
3	1.5791	5.5891	0.1473	57.3781	0.1156	0.6514
4	2.3610	8.4731	0.1828	131.4534	0.0247	1.0268
5	3.9058	45.5061	0.2805	187.6341	0.2571	2.1024
6	1.0944	6.3066	0.0436	28.9118	0.0236	0.1971
7	4.9920	24.3230	0.1202	257.9602	0.0631	0.9288
8	3.6975	15.2654	0.9464	251.5692	0.0162	1.1063
9	5.7617	25.9482	1.7091	371.5844	0.0192	1.4837
10	9.0672	33.5578	3.8300	892.9948	0.0312	7.0059
11	0.0660	0.1449	0.0141	2.5931	0.0094	0.1048
12	0.9459	3.1381	0.2291	81.8578	0.0221	0.6346
13	1.0135	6.0669	0.0860	14.4555	0.1107	0.2025
14	8.3566	46.5414	0.3952	656.1304	0.2852	7.4682
15	1.2416	4.9355	0.0931	36.9320	0.0139	0.4151
Average	3.7180	17.8028	0.7208	261.3074	0.0702	2.1326

Table 3. Elapsed time (Seconds, 40% of unlabeled samples)

ID	ROSES	semirough-P	RSES	FW-SemiFS	RRPC	SSNDI
1	6.7874	21.8645	3.5453	810.5540	0.0410	12.2549
2	1.1446	3.8866	0.5136	95.7897	0.0053	0.7390
3	0.9715	3.2948	0.0985	32.2797	0.0179	0.4251
4	1.3665	5.2340	0.1967	93.0061	0.0063	0.9060
5	3.8372	45.5269	0.2033	153.5287	0.3036	2.8257
6	0.8592	4.5758	0.0368	20.7222	0.0147	0.2157
7	4.4509	38.7812	0.1478	199.8708	0.0472	0.8501
8	2.0530	8.6184	0.8815	180.8451	0.0075	1.2125
9	4.0983	16.5857	1.7082	272.5337	0.0150	1.3748
10	5.2193	17.1016	3.9603	699.0257	0.0233	8.3030
11	0.0607	0.1294	0.0106	2.3041	0.0028	0.0191
12	0.6514	2.1407	0.2227	63.4573	0.0116	0.5791
13	0.8384	4.9821	0.0677	12.8724	0.0220	0.1150
14	7.6571	57.9956	0.4045	402.2444	0.2343	7.4535
15	0.9882	3.7313	0.0941	29.9364	0.0081	0.4103
Average	2.7322	15.6299	0.8061	204.5980	0.0507	2.5122

Table 4. Elapsed time (Seconds, 60% of unlabeled samples)

ID	ROSES	semirough-P	RSES	FW-SemiFS	RRPC	SSNDI
1	5.1207	12.9354	3.7267	601.2517	0.0367	11.5602
2	0.8078	2.4154	0.4824	60.4513	0.0051	0.6070
3	0.9002	2.7397	0.0981	28.3272	0.0143	0.3110
4	1.0775	3.8580	0.5605	67.3118	0.0063	0.9177
5	4.7934	35.7112	0.1810	125.8219	0.2391	1.4298
6	0.9625	4.4285	0.0398	21.3258	0.0115	0.1472
7	4.6988	50.0832	0.1902	169.6717	0.0444	0.7432
8	1.4130	5.7734	0.9541	113.1499	0.0076	1.2112
9	3.6194	13.3789	2.1563	198.5682	0.0127	1.7350
10	3.9326	8.9997	3.5265	478.6376	0.0200	6.0474
11	0.0643	0.1185	0.0107	2.1276	0.0030	0.0182
12	0.5153	1.4163	0.2095	46.0624	0.0113	0.6397
13	0.7623	4.3229	0.0526	11.3633	0.0236	0.1150
14	7.9060	47.9627	0.3922	315.8386	0.2555	7.1038
15	0.9295	3.1501	0.0954	24.9964	0.0085	0.4483
Average	2.5002	13.1529	0.8451	150.9937	0.0467	2.2023

Table 5. Elapsed time (Seconds, 80% of unlabeled samples)

ID	ROSES	semirough-P	RSES	FW-SemiFS	RRPC	SSNDI
1	6.5311	8.9779	3.6702	386.8968	0.0336	9.5654
2	0.8539	1.6771	0.4879	29.7393	0.0052	0.6067
3	0.9414	2.4550	0.0926	20.7566	0.0149	0.2893
4	1.2292	3.4281	0.3964	50.5998	0.0059	0.8620
5	5.5429	29.2371	0.2123	82.8208	0.2144	1.3173
6	0.9992	3.7063	0.0350	16.6370	0.0086	0.1424
7	5.6846	55.8450	0.2565	140.8585	0.0444	0.7144
8	1.5969	5.1384	0.8884	70.9006	0.0074	1.1608
9	4.5283	13.6170	2.1100	149.4086	0.0136	1.6328
10	5.5023	6.4261	4.0925	324.9634	0.0230	7.1872
11	0.0764	0.1210	0.0110	1.9730	0.0031	0.0174
12	0.5845	1.3412	0.2069	21.5483	0.0112	0.5788
13	0.7890	3.8177	0.0662	9.4349	0.0232	0.1135
14	9.5079	37.7121	0.3505	228.4705	0.2183	5.8929
15	1.1010	2.9981	0.0937	19.8349	0.0075	0.3938
Average	3.0312	11.7665	0.8647	103.6562	0.0423	2.0316

Based on the above results, we can draw the following conclusions.

1) For the four approaches which have been constructed based on neighborhood, i.e., ROSES, semirough-P, RSES and FW-SemiFS, our ROSES ranks the second. In other words, our approach is slower than RSES while it is faster than both semirough-P and FW-SemiFS. The reason may be contributed to the fact that RSES is realized by using a measure called neighborhood decision error rate [18]. Such a measure is over-relaxation and then fewer iterations are required to terminate RSES.

   However, though RESE is efficient, the selected features by such an approach are powerless if the classification performances are concerned (see Figs. 1, 2, 3 and 4). Obviously, the corresponding classification accuracies rank behind the other comparative algorithms.

2) For the other two comparative methods, i.e., RRPC and SSNDI, both of them are faster than our ROSES. Firstly, RPRC uses only the Pearsons Correlation Coefficient to evaluate candidate features and then identify the qualified features, such a calculation implies a lower computational cost. Secondly, SSNDI is designed based on the measure called neighborhood discrimination index, such a measure has been demonstrate to be an efficient measure in the field of rough set [6].

   Nevertheless, following Figs. 1, 2, 3 and 4, we can also observe that the effectiveness of selected features based on RPRC and SSNDI are also significantly inferior to those based on our ROSES.

5   Conclusions and Future Plans

In this research, we have developed a novel strategy–ROSES for searching qualified features over partially labeled data. Different from previous researches, our strategy divides the procedure of searching features into two stages. Firstly, the qualified features are selected based on conventional measures related to rough set over labeled samples. Secondly, such a subset of qualified features is further checked over unlabeled samples. If the corresponding constraint in terms of unsupervised relevance can not be satisfied, then more features will be selected by using a new granularity related measure which is equipped with lower computational cost. The framework proposed in this paper gives a new and better perspective to solve related problems in the future.

The following topics will be our further investigations.

1) How the ratio of unlabeled samples in data will affect the performances of our framework.
2) The robustness of the selected features is another interesting issue which will be addressed.

Acknowledgments. This work is supported by the Natural Science Foundation of China (Nos. 62076111, 62076088, 62006128, 61876157).

References

1. Pawlak, Z.: Rough sets. Int. J. Comput. Inform. Sci. **11**(3), 341–356 (1982)
2. Zhang, G.B., Yang, Z.Y., Huo, B., Chai, S.D., Jiang, S.: Multiorgan segmentation from partially labeled datasets with conditional NNU-Net. Comput. Biol. Med. **136**, Article 104658 (2021)
3. Gao, C., Zhou, J., Miao, D., Wen, J., Yue, X.: Three-way decision with co-training for partially labeled data. Inf. Sci. **544**, 500–518 (2021)
4. Dai, J.H., Hu, Q.H., Zhang, J.H., Hu, H., Zheng, N.G.: Attribute selection for partially labeled categorical data by rough set approach. IEEE Trans. Cybern. **47**(9), 2460–2471 (2017)
5. Pang, Q.Q., Li, Z.: Semi-supervised neighborhood discrimination index for feature selection. Knowl.-Based Syst. **204**, Article 106224 (2020)
6. Wang, C.Z., Hu, Q.H., Wang, X.Z., Chen, D.G., Qian, Y.H., Dong, Z.: Feature selection based on neighborhood discrimination index. IEEE Trans. Neural Netw. Learn. Syst. **29**(7), 2986–2999 (2018)
7. Liu, K.Y., Yang, X.B., Yu, H.L., Mi, J.S., Wang, P.X., Chen, X.J.: Rough set based semi-supervised feature selection via ensemble selector. Knowl.-Based Syst. **165**, 282–296 (2019)
8. Zhang, Z.-W., Jing, X.-Y., Wang, T.-J.: Label propagation based semi-supervised learning for software defect prediction. Autom. Softw. Eng. **24**(1), 47–69 (2016). https://doi.org/10.1007/s10515-016-0194-x
9. Yang, X.B., Yao, Y.Y.: Ensemble selector for attribute reduction. Appl. Soft Comput. **70**, 1–11 (2018)
10. Qian, Y.H., Cheng, H.H., Wang, J.T., Liang, J.Y., Pedrycz, W., Dang, C.Y.: Grouping granular structures in human granulation intelligence. Inf. Sci. **382–383**, 150–169 (2017)
11. Hu, Q.H., Yu, D.R., Liu, J.F., Wu, C.X.: Neighborhood rough set based heterogeneous feature subset selection. Inf. Sci. **178**(18), 3577–3594 (2008)
12. Wu, Z., Wang, B., Chen, N., Luo, J.: Semi-monolayer covering rough set on set-valued information systems and its efficient computation. Int. J. Approximate Reasoning **130**(2), 83–106 (2021)
13. Yuan, Z., Chen, H.M., Li, T.R., Yu, Z., Sang, B.B., Luo, C.: Unsupervised attribute reduction for mixed data based on fuzzy rough sets. Inf. Sci. **572**, 67–87 (2021)
14. Chen, Z., Liu, K.Y., Yang, X.D., Fujita, H.: Random sampling accelerator for attribute reduction. Int. J. Approximate Reasoning **140**, 75–91 (2022)
15. Ren, J.T., Qiu, Z.Y., Fan, W., Chen, H., Yu, P.S.: Forward semi-supervised feature selection. In: Proceedings of the 12th Pacific-Asia Conference on Advances in Knowledge Discovery and Data Mining, Osaka, Japan, pp. 970–976 (2008)
16. Jin, X., Tang, B., He, H.B., Man, H.: Semisupervised feature selection based on relevance and redundancy criteria. IEEE Trans. Neural Netw. Learn. Syst. **28**(9), 1974–1984 (2017)
17. Zhu, X., Ghahramani, Z., Lafferty, J.: Semi-supervised learning using Gaussian fields and harmonic functions. In: Proceedings of the Twentieth International Conference on Machine Learning, pp. 912–919 (2003)
18. Hu, Q.H., Pedrycz, W., Yu, D.R., Lang, J.: Selecting discrete and continuous features based on neighborhood decision error minimization. IEEE Trans. Syst. Man Cybern. Part B **40**(1), 137–150 (2010)

Improving Speech Emotion Recognition by Fusing Pre-trained and Acoustic Features Using Transformer and BiLSTM

Zheng Liu, Xin Kang, and Fuji Ren[✉]

School of Information Faculty of Engineering, Tokushima University, Tokushima 770-8506, Japan
{kang-xin,ren}@is.tokushima-u.ac.jp

Abstract. With the emergence of machine learning and the deepening of human-computer interaction applications, the field of speech emotion recognition has attracted more and more attention. However, due to the high cost of speech emotion corpus construction, the speech emotion datasets are scarce. Therefore, how to obtain higher accuracy of recognition under the condition of limited corpus is one of the problems of speech emotion recognition. To solve the problem, we fused speech pre-trained features and acoustic features to enhance the generalization of speech features and proposed a novel feature fusion model based on Transformer and BiLSTM. We fused the speech pre-trained features extracted by Tera, Audio Albert, and Npc with the acoustic features of the voice, and conducted experiments on the CASIA Chinese voice emotion corpus. The results showed that our method and model achieved 94% accuracy in the Tera model.

Keywords: Speech emotion recognition · Speech representation learning · Feature fusion · Transformer

1 Introduction

Speech emotion recognition refers to a signal processing task that extracts emotional features from speech digital signals and recognizes the specified emotions. The research on making robots expresses emotion has attracted the attention of many researchers (Ren 2009). Emotion recognition plays an important role in the application of human-computer interaction (Ren and Bao 2020). Speech not only contains textual information, but also contains rich emotional information. Therefore, speech emotion recognition has gradually become one of the topics that has received widespread attention in the field of speech signal processing. Limited by the high cost of constructing speech emotion corpus, it is a challenging task facing current speech emotion recognition to obtain a higher recognition rate on a limited speech emotional corpus.

In the past ten years, the emergence of machine learning has greatly promoted the development of various fields of signal processing including image, text, and speech (Liu et al. 2020; Deng and Ren 2020; Huang 2020). For machine learning, the feature

© IFIP International Federation for Information Processing 2022
Published by Springer Nature Switzerland AG 2022
Z. Shi et al. (Eds.): IIP 2022, IFIP AICT 643, pp. 348–357, 2022.
https://doi.org/10.1007/978-3-031-03948-5_28

processing engineering of data is indispensable, and excellent feature construction is very important for the improvement of recognition accuracy. Data and features determine the upper limit of recognition accuracy, and machine learning models and algorithms constantly approach this upper limit. Regarding the commonly used features in the field of speech emotion recognition, after many literature surveys (Akay and Ouz 2020; Swain et al. 2018), we found that the speech features used for speech emotion recognition usually include speech acoustic features, deep features, and hybrid features. Among them, the acoustic features of speech include traditional speech parameters such as F0, formant, signal energy, waveform MFCC, Mel cepstrum, and Fbank. Deep features refer to the features extracted from the original speech waveform or spectrum using deep learning neural network models such as CNN, RNN, DNN, or the pre-trained models. Hybrid features refer to features that are combined with language context, combined with other modal features such as facial expressions, text, and voice features for speech recognition.

Due to the high cost of constructing speech emotion data sets, the emotion data sets are scarce. Improving recognition accuracy on a small amount of data sets has always been a challenging task in the field of speech emotion recognition. At present, more and more researches are no longer satisfied with the construction of a single emotional feature. These studies have enriched the diversity of the features of a single sample in the construction of feature engineering, but still cannot solve the problem of poor generalization of voice features caused by the rare corpus.

To solve the excessive dependence of deep learning on data, many feature extraction schemes based on transfer learning technology have appeared in recent years (Zhuang et al. 2020). Transfer learning learns new knowledge using existing knowledge, and then finds the similarities between existing knowledge and new knowledge, focusing on storing existing problem-solving models, and using them for other different but related problems. Using the idea of transfer learning, a pre-trained model built on a large-scale data set can effectively improve the generalization ability of features in a small data set. Our work combines the voice transfer learning method and proposes a novel deep learning model that combines traditional acoustic features and pre-trained features and achieved excellent results in the CASIA dataset experiment.

Our work mainly has the following contributions:

1. To improve the recognition rate of speech emotion recognition, we used speech transfer learning technology for the first time, combined pre-trained features and acoustic features, and made relevant explorations to improve the generalization ability of features.
2. Based on the Transformer and BiLSTM models, we proposed a novel feature fusion model, which effectively fuses pre-trained features and acoustic features of different maximum lengths and dimensions.
3. After experiments on the CASIA dataset, the Chinese emotional speech dataset, our proposed approach achieved excellent results.

The rest of our paper is arranged as follows. The second section introduces related work on speech emotion recognition, speech pre-trained models, and the model used in our experiment. The third part describes the details of the models and methods we proposed. The fourth part shows the details of our experiment, including CASIA dataset, feature extraction, and experimental results. The last part summarizes our work and describes plans for future work.

2   Related Work

In the speech emotion recognition system, speech feature extraction and processing, as well as the construction of algorithm models, are very important for improving the ability of speech emotion recognition. In recent years, speech acoustic features and acoustic low-level feature descriptors using statistical methods have been widely used in various recognition models (Byun and Lee 2021). Ho et al. (2020a) used opensmile to extract the features of LLDs, combined with RNN and attention mechanism, and achieved good recognition results. Deep features are mainly built around various spectrograms such as Mel spectrogram and MFCC spectrum of speech, combined with deep learning model learning. Chung and Glass (2018) and Kwon (2021) proposed the MLT-DNet model, which took the original waveform of the speech as input, and achieved a high recognition rate on the IEMOCAP and EMODB data sets. To enhance the diversity of voice features and solve the single problem of voice features, some methods related to speech feature fusion are constructed. The paper (Ho et al. 2020b) combines the attention mechanism and the RNN model to fuse speech features and text features to enhance the accuracy of emotion recognition.

The features used in traditional speech emotion recognition are all based on the extraction of individual speech samples. In the case of insufficient data set size, over-fitting is prone to occur, which will lead to the problem of low speech emotion recognition rate. In recent years, to improve the robustness of speech features, research on speech unsupervised representation learning has become more and more active (Chung and Glass 2018; Schneider et al. 2019; Anonymous et al. 2020; Chorowski et al. 2019). The main motivation of this research is to extract higher-level feature expressions of speech. The features of speech itself are learned in a large-scale data set, and the trained representation model can be used for many downstream tasks.

The speech features extracted through representation learning enhance the generalization of traditional features. In this paper, we use voice pre-trained features and fuse individual acoustic features to improve the performance of the neural network model. The model feature fusion is roughly divided into two categories, pre-fusion and post-fusion. The papers (Wang et al. 2020; Zhang et al. 2021) only used simple feature splicing after extracting features of different types and dimensions of speech, which is insufficient to express the corresponding relationship between the features. The emergence of transformer (Vaswani et al. 2017) can focus on the correspondence of local information between sentences, so it is more efficient for different types of feature fusion.

This paper proposes a novel feature fusion model based on transformer and BiLSTM model. The model we proposed can effectively fuse the pre-trained features of different maximum lengths and feature dimensions with traditional acoustic features, which greatly improves the prediction accuracy of emotion recognition.

3 Method

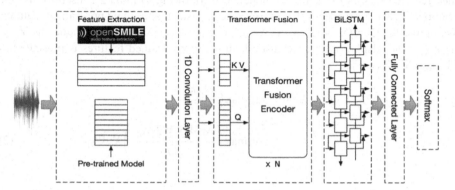

Fig. 1. Overall architecture for fusing pre-trained features and acoustic features

In this section, we will introduce our new framework for speech emotion recognition. Our framework combines the acoustic features of traditional speech with pre-trained features. After the proposed feature fusion model, the two features are fully fused, and finally achieve the purpose of improving the accuracy of speech emotion recognition. As shown in the Fig. 1, the entire framework mainly includes a feature construction part, a 1D convolution module, a Transformer-based feature fusion module, a BiLSTM modle, the final fully connected layer and Softmax module.

In the feature extraction part, we used the OpenSmile tool to split each utterance into segments with a length of 200 ms. Each sub-segment was extracted to features of 1583 dimensions, and a total of n * 1583 feature blocks were constructed, where n is the number of speech segments. In addition, to make up for the limitations of traditional features, we fused the traditional acoustic features and pre-trained features extracted from the latest speech representation learning models NPC, Audio Albert, Tera, which are trained in the large-scale corpus.

The feature fusion part will first undergo 1D convolution processing, and the two features will be unified into vectors of different lengths but the same dimension, and then sent to the Transformer attention fusion model for further fusion. As shown in the Fig. 2, Transformer abandons the traditional CNN and RNN structure. The entire network structure is entirely composed of Attention mechanism, which increases the training speed and can effectively capture the relationship between the input units. In our experiment, we used a 6-layer Transformer encoder to fuse the pre-trained and acoustic features. The attention mechanism for a sentence in the traditional Transformer is represented by formula 1, where Q represents the query vector, and KV represents the vector being queried.

$$\text{Attention}(Q, K, V) = \text{Softmax}\left(\frac{QK^T}{\sqrt{d_k}}\right)V \tag{1}$$

In our method, since speech pre-trained features and traditional acoustic features have different maximum lengths and dimensions, we first use 1D convolutional network to convert the acoustic features and pre-trained features to the same dimensional features, then feed the vectors to the fusion model. The following formula 2 is used to fuse the features. X_α and X_β respectively represent the acoustic features and pre-trained features. We define the Querys as $Q_\alpha = X_\alpha W_{Q\alpha}$, Keys as $K_\beta = X_\beta W_{K\beta}$ and Values as $V_\beta = X_\beta W_{V\beta}$. The adaptation from acoustic features to pre-trained features is presented as $PF_{\beta \to \alpha}(X_\alpha, X_\beta)$.

$$\begin{aligned} PF_{\alpha \to \beta}(X_\alpha, X_\beta) &= \text{Softmax}\left(\frac{Q_\beta K_\alpha^T}{\sqrt{d_k}}\right)V_\alpha \\ &= \text{Softmax}\left(\frac{X_\beta W_{Q_\beta} W_{K_\alpha}^T X_\alpha^T}{\sqrt{d_k}}\right)X_\alpha W_{V_\alpha} \end{aligned} \tag{2}$$

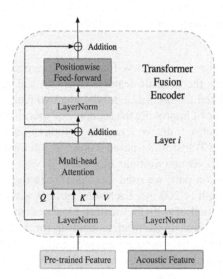

Fig. 2. Transformer fusion module of pre-trained features and traditional acoustic features

After the feature fusion of the Transformer mechanism, to further enhance the spatial timing relationship of the hidden features, we send the output hidden vectors of the Transformer to the BiLSTM, as shown in the Fig. 3. The LSTM model solves the problem of gradient disappearance and gradient explosion caused by the long-time sequence segment in the back propagation process of the traditional RNN model. We use the BiLSTM to further process the features outputted by the Transformer and finally use softmax for emotional classification.

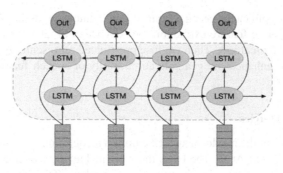

Fig. 3. Struction of BiLSTM model

4   Experiments and Discussion

To verify the effectiveness of our proposed method, we fused the pre-trained features and traditional acoustic features using three pre-trained models respectively. We conducted experiments on the CASIA dataset, and the results showed that our proposed method framework achieved excellent results.

4.1   CASIA Dataset

The CASIA dataset was recorded by the Institute of Automation, Chinese Academy of Sciences. A total of 2 males and 2 females participated in the recoding of this dataset. In a pure recording environment with a signal-to-noise ratio of about 35 db, based on 5 different emotions, happy, sad, angry, frightened, and neutral, it was obtained from a performance of 500 sentences of text. For voice quality, a 16 kHz sampling rate and 16 bit quantization standard are used. Finally, after listening and screening, a total of 9600 utterances were retained. In our experiment, 6000 utterances were used and divided into training set, validation set, and test set of 5440, 280, and 280 respectively.

4.2   Feature Extraction

In the experiment, we used three speech representation models, Tera, Audio Albert, and NPC, combined with traditional acoustic features to improve the accuracy of speech emotion recognition.

TERA is a self-supervised speech pre-training model, its full name is Transformer Encoder Representations from Alteration, which is used for pre-training on many unlabelled speech to obtain the Transformer encoding model by masking the speech spectrum along three orthogonal axes (Liu et al. 2021). AUDIO ALBERT, also called AALBERT, uses the ALBERT self-supervised learning model, which is trained on a large-scale speech dataset, and can be used for feature extraction of downstream tasks such as speech-related tasks, or as a fine-tuning participation model training (Chi et al. 2021). The full name of NPC is Non-Autoregressive Predictive Coding, which is also a self-supervised learning method. It only relies on the local information of the voice to represent the voice in a non-autoregressive manner. It has achieved good results in the voice speaker classification experiment (Liu et al. 2020).

In addition, we split each speech utterance into segments with the 200 ms length and then use the opensmile feature extraction tool (Eyben et al. 2010) to extract for 1582 dimensional acoustic features. Then we fuse pre-trained representations and traditional speech features to enhance the generalization ability of speech features by using the proposed model.

4.3   Evaluation Metrics

In this experiment, for the results of speech emotion recognition, we used two evaluation metrics, namely F1 and ACC. The F1 is the weighted average of precision and recall, and the F1 formula is expressed as formula 3. Among them, TP (True Positive) indicates that the model prediction result is positive, and the sample is also positive, TN (True Negative) indicates that the model prediction result is positive, but the sample is negative, FP (False Positive) indicates that the prediction is negative, and the sample is positive, FN (False Negative) indicates that the prediction is negative, and the sample is also negative.

$$F1 = \frac{2 * \text{Precision} * \text{Recall}}{\text{Precision} + \text{Recall}} = \frac{2 * TP}{2 * TP + FP + FN} \tag{3}$$

Ac is the classification accuracy score, which refers to the percentage of all classifications that are correct. The formula is as follows:

$$Ac = \frac{TP + TF}{TP + TF + FP + FN} \tag{4}$$

4.4   Result and Analysis

Table 1 shows the performance results of our proposed model with different pre-trained models. The performance is the worst when the acoustic features are used alone. After the pre-trained features are added, a better recognition rate is obtained. Among them, the fusion of Tera pre-trained features and acoustic features achieved the best results with F1 value of 0.942 and Ac value of 0.943.

Table 1. Performance of different pre-trained features and acoustic features on CASIA

Dataset	CASIA	
Metric	F1	Ac
Acoustic Only	0.789	0.789
Acoustic + Npc	0.861	0.861
Acoustic + Audio Albert	0.915	0.914
Acoustic + Tera	**0.942**	**0.943**

Figure 4 shows the detailed results of different emotion recognition of our model on the CASIA dataset. Among them, a high recognition rate of 100% was obtained on Angry, and a recognition rate of 82.14% was obtained on Happy. Some samples of Happy were incorrectly recognized as Angry.

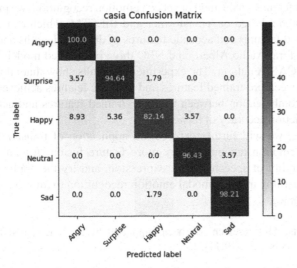

Fig. 4. Detailed results of using Tera pre-trained features and acoustic features on CASIA

Figure 5 is the loss value change curve of different feature combinations during the training process. Due to the singularity of acoustic features, the fitting effect of the model is not good. The model combined with pre-trained features enhances the generalization ability of data features, making the model better fit the data. Compared with other loss curves, the fusion of Tera pre-trained features and acoustic features achieved the best results. It can better improve the generalization ability of features, and make the model achieve a better recognition rate.

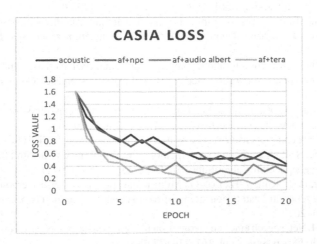

Fig. 5. Loss value of different feature combinations

5   Conclusions

To solve the problem of low recognition accuracy caused by insufficient generalization ability of speech features in the field of speech emotion recognition, we proposed a novel feature fusion model based on Transformer and BiLSTM, which can effectively fuse speech pre-trained features and acoustic features of different lengths and dimensions.

We utilized Tera, Audio Albert, and NPC three pre-trained models and conducted experiments on CASIA dataset. The experimental results show that all the combinenation features between pre-trained features and acoustic features achieved better results. Especially the combineation between Tera pre-trained features and acoustic features, achieved a prediction accuracy of 94%.

In the future, we will further explore the application of transfer learning in the field of speech emotion recognition, try more feature fusion structures, enhance the generalization ability of speech feature expression, and try the application of speech representation learning in multi-modal emotion recognition to improve speech emotion recognition accuracy.

Acknowledgments. This research has been supported by JSPS KAKENHI Grant Number 19K20345 and Grant Number 19H04215.

References

Ren, F.: Affective information processing and recognizing human emotion. Electron. Notes Theor. Comput. Sci. **225**, 39–50 (2009)

Ren, F., Bao, Y.: A review on human-computer interaction and intelligent robots. Int. J. Inf. Technol. Decis. Mak. **19**(1), 5–47 (2020)

Liu, Z., et al.: Vowel priority lip matching scheme and similarity evaluation model based on humanoid robot Ren-Xin. J. Ambient Intell. Humaniz. Comput. 1–12 (2020)

Deng, J., Ren, F.: Multi-label emotion detection via emotion-specified feature extraction and emotion correlation learning. IEEE Trans. Affect. Comput. (2020)

Huang, Z., et al.: Facial expression imitation method for humanoid robot based on smooth-constraint reversed mechanical model (SRMM). IEEE Trans. Hum. Mach. Syst. **50**(6), 538–549 (2020)

Akçay, M.B., Oğuz, K.: Speech emotion recognition: emotional models, databases, features, preprocessing methods, supporting modalities, and classifiers. Speech Commun. **116**, 56–76 (2020)

Swain, M., Routray, A., Kabisatpathy, P.: Databases, features and classifiers for speech emotion recognition: a review. Int. J. Speech Technol. **21**(1), 93–120 (2018)

Zhuang, F., et al.: A comprehensive survey on transfer learning. Proc. IEEE **109**(1), 43–76 (2020)

Byun, S.-W., Lee, S.-P.: A study on a speech emotion recognition system with effective acoustic features using deep learning algorithms. Appl. Sci. **11**(4), 1890 (2021)

Ho, N.-H., Yang, H.-J., Kim, S.-H., Lee, G.: Multimodal approach of speech emotion recognition using multi-level multi-head fusion attention-based recurrent neural network. IEEE Access **8**, 61672–61686 (2020)

Kwon, S.: MLT-DNet: speech emotion recognition using 1D dilated CNN based on multi-learning trick approach. Expert Syst. Appl. **167**, 114177 (2021)

Ho, N.-H., et al.: Multimodal approach of speech emotion recognition using multi-level multi-head fusion attention-based recurrent neural network. IEEE Access **8**, 61672–61686 (2020)

Chung, Y.-A., Glass, J.: Speech2vec: a sequence-to-sequence framework for learning word embeddings from speech. Interspeech **2018** (2018)

Schneider, S., Baevski, A., Collobert, R., Auli, M.: wav2vec: unsupervised pre-training for speech recognition. Interspeech (2019)

Anonymous Authors. vq-wav2vec: self-supervised learning of discrete speech representations. In: ICLR 2020 Conference Blind Submission (2020)

Chorowski, J., Weiss, R.J., Bengio, S., van den Oord, A.: Unsupervised speech representation learning using wavenet autoencoders. IEEE/ACM Trans. Audio Speech Lang. Process. **27**(12), 2041–2053 (2019)

Wang, W., Watters, P.A., Cao, X., Shen, L., Li, B.: Significance of phonological features in speech emotion recognition. Int. J. Speech Technol. **23**(3), 633–642 (2020)

Zhang, S., et al.: Learning deep multimodal affective features for spontaneous speech emotion recognition. Speech Commun. **127**, 73–81 (2021)

Vaswani, A., et al.: Attention is all you need. Adv. Neural Inf. Process. Syst. (2017)

Liu, A.T., Li, S.-W., Lee, H.: Tera: selfupervised learning of transformer encoder representation for speech. IEEE/ACM Trans. Audio Speech Lang. Process. **29**, 2351–2366 (2021)

Chi, P.-H., et al.: Audio albert: a lite bert for self-supervised learning of audio representation. In: 2021 IEEE Spoken Language Technology Workshop (SLT). IEEE (2021)

Liu, A.H., Chung, Y.-A., Glass, J.: Non-autoregressive predictive coding for learning speech representations from local dependencies. arXiv preprint arXiv:2011.00406 (2020)

Eyben, F., Wöllmer, M., Schuller, B.: Opensmile: the munich versatile and fast open-source audio feature extractor. In: Proceedings of the 18th ACM International Conference on Multimedia (2010)

A Pear Leaf Diseases Image Recognition Model Based on Capsule Network

Zhida Jia[1], Wenqian Mu[1], Junhua Gong[2], Yi Zong[3], and Yongjie Liu[4(✉)]

[1] College of Information Science and Engineering, Shandong Agricultural University, Taian, China
[2] ShiKeFeng Ecological Agriculture Engineering Co., Ltd., Linyi, China
[3] Feicheng Bianyuan Town Agricultural Comprehensive Service Center, Taian, China
[4] College of Plant Protection, Shandong Agricultural University, Taian, China
lyj@sdau.edu.cn

Abstract. Image recognition of pear leaf diseases is an important task of plant protection. The lesion area of pear leaf diseases is not fixed in the whole leaf, which has the characteristics of randomness. The convolution neural network is used to identify the images of pear leaf diseases, due to its rotation and translation invariance, the generalization ability of the model is weak. The capsule network uses feature vectors to replace feature value, and uses dynamic routing to replace pooling to obtain spatial information between entities. However, the size of lesion area of pear leaf diseases is random, and the capsule network cannot fully extract features, resulting in a decrease in recognition rate. To solve the problem, a pear leaf diseases image recognition model based on capsule network was proposed, which uses conditional convolution to customize specific convolution kernels for each input to adapt to pear leaf diseases images of different sizes. The experimental results show that the recognition accuracy, precision, recall and F1score of the proposed algorithm are 91.33%, 91.40%, 91.33% and 91.36%, which are better than capsule network.

Keywords: Capsule network · Conditional convolution · Image recognition · Images of pear leaf diseases

1 Introduction

Pear is the third largest fruit in China, accounting for about 80% of the world's planting area [1]. However, due to the occurrence of pear leaf diseases, resulting in pear branches withered, fruit decay, less fruit, the yield and quality of pear have a serious impact. The prevention and control of pear leaf diseases is mainly divided into two steps. Firstly, the leaf diseases of pear are identified, and then the appropriate pesticides are selected according to the identification results. At present, the leaf diseases of pear are mainly identified manually by plant protection experts based on their experience, which are subjective and prone to errors. At the same time, plant protection experts and technical personnel are limited, which is difficult to timely diagnose the occurrence of early

© IFIP International Federation for Information Processing 2022
Published by Springer Nature Switzerland AG 2022
Z. Shi et al. (Eds.): IIP 2022, IFIP AICT 643, pp. 358–368, 2022.
https://doi.org/10.1007/978-3-031-03948-5_29

diseases, resulting in missing the best prevention period and causing serious economic losses to fruit farmers. Therefore, automatic identification of pear leaf diseases is an urgent problem to be solved in plant protection.

Plant leaf diseases image recognition mainly includes classical machine learning and deep learning. Image recognition algorithm based on classical machine learning mainly includes Bayesian classification, support vector machine (SVM) and other algorithms. Its advantage is that it can use a small amount of data samples to train, but requires manual extraction of features. Image recognition algorithm based on deep learning, especially convolution neural network, is widely used in the field of image recognition. The convolutional neural network has strong feature extraction ability, but it has rotation and translation invariance, and its training needs massive data. The capsule network [2] is a new attractive neural network structure. Its feature vector can represent the size and direction of the target, and solve the problem of rotation and translation invariance. However, the feature extraction ability of capsule network is weak, resulting in low recognition accuracy. To solve this problem, this paper proposes a capsule network based on conditional convolution [3], which uses the characteristics of conditional convolution to customize convolution kernel for each input sample to adapt to different sizes of diseases characteristics and improve the recognition accuracy.

2 Related Work

Automatic identification of plant leaf diseases images is an urgent problem to be solved for plant protection. Early, with the development of machine learning, many researchers used the combination of image processing and machine learning to achieve plant diseases image recognition. Almadhor et al. [4] took pomegranate leaf and fruit diseases images as the research object, used color difference to segment the diseases area, and extracted the RGB and HSV color histogram and LBP texture features of the diseases. Finally, the extracted features are classified using Bagged Tree. Padol et al. [5] uses K-means clustering to segment the diseases area, and then extracts color and texture features. Finally, SVM is used to classify grape leaf diseases images. Later, with the rapid development of deep learning, it has been widely used in agriculture. Hang et al. [6] proposed a model combining Inception module, squeeze-and-excitation module and global pooling layer to realize plant leaf diseases image recognition. The model has the advantages of less parameters and easy training. Wu et al. [7] proposed a dual-channel model based on ResNet50 and VGG16 to identify maize leaf diseases. Bansal et al. [8] proposed integrating DenseNet and EfficientNet to detect apple diseases images. The purpose of capsule network is to replace convolution neural network, which has been widely used in agriculture due to its less parameters and easy training. Verma et al. [9] used capsule network to achieve potato diseases image classification. Patrick et al. [10] proposed capsule network based on K-Means routing to realize tomato diseases image recognition. Kwabena et al. [11] proposed Gabor capsule network, which combines global Gabor filters and convolution kernels to extract features to identify blurred and deformed tomato and citrus diseases images. Wang et al. [12] proposed a capsule network based on attention mechanism. The attention module was added to the capsule to reduce the influence of noise and realize the fine-grained identification of crop pests.

3   Proposed Method

3.1   Capsule Network

Capsule network [2] (CapsNet) is a new vector neural network, whose input and output are vectors. The direction of the vector can represent the spatial information of the target, such as attitude, position, size, direction and deformation. The length of the vector represents the probability of the existence of the target. The structure of capsule network mainly includes convolution layer, Primarycap layer, Digitcaps layer and Decoder layer. The convolution layer is used to extract features. Primarycap converts the extracted features into vector capsules, and then converts them into digital capsules through dynamic routing. Finally, the class of images is obtained according to ‖L2‖ of digital capsules.

The dynamic routing structure of the capsule network as shown in Fig. 1. The capsule network uses dynamic routing to combine the key features in the feature map. In the dynamic routing, high-level capsules and low-level capsules are fully connected, and the output V_j of high-level capsules is shown in (1).

$$v_j = \frac{\|s_j\|^2}{1 + \|s_j\|^2} \cdot \frac{s_j}{\|s_j\|} \tag{1}$$

Where V_j is the output of high-level capsule, S_j is the weighted sum of all low-level capsule prediction vectors, as shown in (2).

$$s_j = \sum_i c_{ij} \hat{u}_{j|i} \tag{2}$$

Where C_{ij} is the coupling coefficient of each low-level capsule i connected to the high-level capsule j, as shown in (3). $\hat{u}_{j|i}$ is the prediction vector of low-level capsules, as shown in (4).

$$c_{ij} = \frac{\exp(b_{ij})}{\sum_k \exp(b_{ik})} \tag{3}$$

$$\hat{u}_{j|i} = W_{ij} u_i \tag{4}$$

Where W_{ij} is the weight matrix, u_i is the output vector of low-level capsules, and b_{ij} is the prior probability of coupling capsule i and capsule j.

Similar to convolution neural network, capsule network measures the gap between the predicted results of the model and the actual results through the loss function in the training process. However, the difference is that the capsule network allows multiple classes to exist at the same time, so the cross-entropy loss function cannot be simply used, but is composed of margin loss and reconstruction loss. For each class by a margin loss, the margin loss of the k class is shown in (5).

$$L_k = T_k \max(0, m^+ - \|v_k\|)^2 + \lambda(1 - T_k) \max(0, \|v_k\| - m^-)^2 \tag{5}$$

Where Tk denotes whether class k exists. If k class exists, the value is 1, else k class does not exist, the value is 0. m+ is the upper bound of 0.9 to punish false positives.

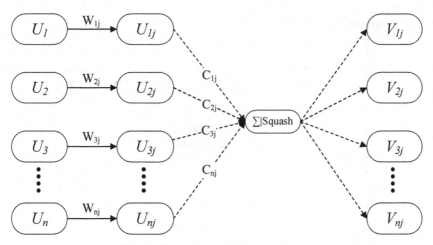

Fig. 1. The structure of dynamic routing

When k class exists but not predicted, the loss value increases. m- is the lower bound of 0.1 to penalize false negatives. λ is a proportional coefficient, which is used to balance the upper and lower bounds, and the value is 0.5. If class k exists, $\|v_k\|$ is greater than 0.9, and if class k does not exist, $\|v_k\|$ is less than 0.1.

The reconstruction loss is composed of 32×32 pixels of the input image minus 32×32 pixels of the reconstructed image, and the square is multiplied by the coefficient 0.005. The margin loss is the main component of the loss function.

3.2 Conditional Convolution

Conditional convolution [3] (CondConv) breaks the limitation of using the same convolution kernel parameters for all input samples by traditional convolution, and realizes the customization of specific convolution kernel parameters for each sample input. In traditional convolutional neural networks, in order to extract sufficient features, the network is generally deepened, resulting in a sharp increase in model parameters and difficult training. By increasing the number of experts, conditional convolution achieves the purpose of extracting sufficient features with a small number of parameters, as shown in Fig. 2. By learning the input sample features, the convolution kernel is parameterized conditionally to achieve the effect of multiple convolutions.

The convolution kernel of conditional convolution is customized for each input sample, and the output is calculated using the customized convolution kernel, as shown in (6).

$$y = \sigma((\alpha_1 \cdot W_1 + ... + \alpha_n \cdot W_n) * x) \qquad (6)$$

Where y is the convolution kernel output, x is the convolution kernel input, W is the standard convolution kernel, α is the scalar calculated by each expert according to the input, a total of n experts, $\alpha = r(x)$, as shown in (7).

$$r(x) = Sigmoid(GlobalAveragePool(x)R) \qquad (7)$$

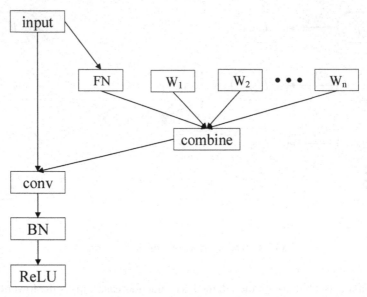

Fig. 2. The structure of conditional convolution

Where R is a full connection layer with n neurons, and n expert weights are obtained. The values are constrained to [0,1] by Sigmoid as the weights of n convolution kernels.

3.3 CondConv CapsNet

Although CapsNet has the ability to capture the spatial information of features, such as the relative position relationship, relative size relationship and feature direction of features, which effectively solves the problem of rotation and translation invariance of CNN, its recognition accuracy still needs to be further improved. Due to the randomness of the lesion size of pear leaf diseases, the convolution kernel receptive field in CapsNet is fixed, and the diseases characteristics cannot be fully extracted, resulting in the decrease of recognition accuracy. Therefore, this paper introduces conditional convolution into the capsule network and proposes a capsule network model based on conditional convolution, and its structure as shown in Fig. 3. The $32 \times 32 \times 3$ pear leaf diseases images were input, and the diseases characteristics of different sizes were fully extracted by conditional convolution with 256 channels, 9×9 size and 1 stride. Then, through the Primarycap layer, each capsule contains a conditional convolution with 8 channels, 9×9 size and 2 stride, and a total of 32 capsules, of which low-level capsules and high-level capsules are connected by dynamic routing. Then, through the Digitcap layer, each class contains one 16D capsule, a total of three classes. Finally, through the Decoder layer, it is composed of three fully connected layers. Each layer contains 512, 1024 and $32 \times 32 \times 3$ neurons, and finally the classification results are output.

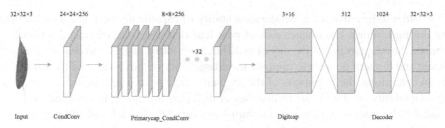

Fig. 3. The structure of CondConv CapsNet

4 Experiment

4.1 Data Construction and Processing

In this paper, pear leaf diseases images were taken as the research object. There is no public pear leaf disease image dataset. So, the pear leaf diseases images were collected in Xiazhang pear orchard of Taian City, Shandong Province. A total of 900 images were collected, including 491 images of brown spot, 333 images of gray spot and 76 images of ring rot.

In order to improve the efficiency of model training and facilitate batch processing, the images size are unified to 32 × 32. In order to reduce the influence of complex background on recognition results, disease images under single background are collected. The constructed leaf diseases images of pear as shown in Table 1, where the size and location of lesion are random.

Table 1. Image samples of pear leaf diseases.

Classes	Sample 1	Sample 2	Sample 3	Sample 4
Brown Spot				
Gray Spot				
Ring Rot				

In order to improve the generalization ability of capsule network and avoid overfitting during training, the images data of pear leaf diseases were enhanced. In order to enhance the adaptability of the model to different shooting angles, the original image is rotated and flipped. In order to improve the adaptability of the model to different illumination conditions, the brightness of the original image is adjusted. In order to improve the adaptability of the model to diseases at different locations, the original image is translated. In order to improve the anti-noise ability of the model, salt and pepper noise is added to the original image. At the same time, in order to reduce the impact of data imbalance on the performance of the model, each kind of diseases images are expanded to 5000, a total of 15000. The image enhancement method example is shown in Table 2. The enhanced data are divided into training set, verification set and test set according to the ratio of 6:2:2. Among them, 9000 training sets are used to train model parameters, 3000 verification sets are used to optimize model parameters, and 3000 test sets are used to evaluate model performance.

Table 2. Image enhancement methods.

Artwork	Flip	Rotated	Translation	Brightness	Noise

4.2 Evaluation Standard

In order to quantify the performance of the model, Accuracy, Precision, Recall and F1score were used as evaluation criteria in this experiment, as shown in (8)–(11).

$$Accuracy = \frac{TP + TN}{TP + TN + FP + FN} \tag{8}$$

$$Precision = \frac{TP}{TP + FP} \tag{9}$$

$$Recall = \frac{TP}{TP + FN} \tag{10}$$

$$F1score = \frac{2 \times Precision \times Recall}{Precision + Recall} \tag{11}$$

Where TP is the number of positive samples predicted as positive samples, TN is the number of negative samples predicted as negative samples, FP is the number of negative samples predicted as positive samples, and FN is the number of positive samples predicted as negative samples.

4.3 Environment and Parameter

The hardware environment of this experiment is Intel Core i7-8700K CPU @ 3.70 GHz, 16 GB memory, NVIDIA GeForce GTX 1080Ti GPU 12 G memory. The software environment is Windows 7 system, Python 3.6, TensorFlow 2.3.0. The hyperparameters of model training as shown in Table 3.

Table 3. Hyper-parameter setting.

Model	Learn rate	Batch size	Epoch	Lr_decay	Experts
CapsNet	0.0002	20	100	0.9	4

4.4 Results and Analysis

In order to verify the proposed method, the experimental scheme is designed as shown in Table 4, and the model in the experimental scheme is used to train the pear leaf diseases images. Where the structure of CapsNet is convolution layer, Primarycap layer based on convolution, Digitcap layer and Decoder layer. CondConv_CapsNet1 replaces the convolution layer with the conditional convolution layer, and the other structures are the same as CapsNet. CondConv_CapsNet2 replaces the Primarycap layer based on convolution with the Primarycap layer based on conditional convolution, and the other structures are the same as CapsNet. CondConv_CapsNet3 replaces the convolution layer with the conditional convolution layer, and the Primarycap layer based on convolution with the Primarycap layer based on conditional convolution, and the other structures are the same as CapsNet.

Table 4. Experimental schemes.

Model	Layer			
CapsNet	Conv	Primarycap_conv	Digitcap	Decoder
CondConv_CapsNet1	CondConv	Primarycap_conv	Digitcap	Decoder
CondConv_CapsNet2	Conv	Primarycap_condconv	Digitcap	Decoder
CondConv_CapsNet3	CondConv	Primarycap_condconv	Digitcap	Decoder

Four groups of models are trained, and the loss changes in the training process as shown in Fig. 4. CapsNet and the improved CapsNet converge after 40 rounds of training. The loss after convergence of CapsNet is 0.1, and the loss after convergence of the three groups of improved CapsNet is 0.084, 0.082 and 0.080, respectively, which is significantly lower than that of CapsNet, where the loss value of CondConv_CapsNet3 is the lowest, indicating that the prediction results of CondConv_CapsNet3 are closer to the real results.

Four groups of models are trained, and the accuracy, precision, recall and F1score change curve of the four groups of models on the verification set are shown in Fig. 5.

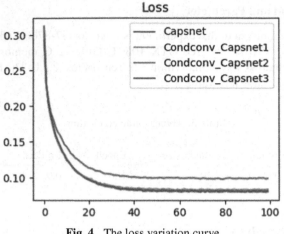

Fig. 4. The loss variation curve

It can be seen from the four groups of change curves that the recognition effect of the three groups of improved CapsNet is significantly better than that of CapsNet, and Condconv_CapsNet3 has the highest accuracy, recall and F1score.

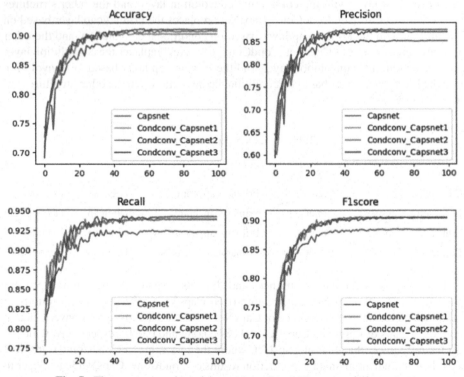

Fig. 5. The accuracy and precision and recall and F1score variation curve

The four groups of convergent models are tested on the test set respectively. The test results as shown in Table 5. The three groups of improved CapsNet are higher than CapsNet in four evaluation criteria. Among them, CondConv_CapsNet3 has the best recognition effect, which is 2.4%, 2.35%, 2.4% and 2.37% higher than CapsNet in accuracy, precision, recall and F1score, respectively.

Table 5. Test results of different models.

Model	Accuracy/%	Precision/%	Recall/%	F1score/%
CapsNet	88.93	89.05	88.93	88.99
CondConv_CapsNet1	90.40	90.55	90.40	90.47
CondConv_CapsNet2	91.00	91.09	91.00	91.04
CondConv_CapsNet3	91.33	91.40	91.33	91.36

The identification accuracy of the four models for different diseases is shown in Table 6. The four models have the highest recognition accuracy for Gray Spot. Because of its obvious characteristics and the sufficient original data. The recognition accuracy of Brown Spot and Ring Rot is low, because the color and texture features of the two diseases are similar. The recognition accuracy of Ring Rot is the lowest, because the original data are less. The improved model has improved the recognition accuracy of the three diseases, and the model proposed in this paper has the highest recognition accuracy. Compared with the capsule network, the recognition accuracy of Brown Spot, Gray Spot and Ring Rot is increased by 1.9%, 2.2% and 3.1%, respectively, indicating that the proposed model has strong generalization ability.

Table 6. The accuracy of different diseases.

Model	Brown spot/%	Gray spot/%	Ring rot/%
CapsNet	90.80	92.60	83.40
CondConv_CapsNet1	92.70	93.80	84.70
CondConv_CapsNet2	92.80	93.80	86.40
CondConv_CapsNet3	92.70	94.80	86.50

5   Conclusion

In this paper, the advantages and disadvantages of capsule network were analysed, and the characteristics of capsule network adapting to the rotation and translation of diseases spots were used to solve the problem of randomness in the location of diseases incidence area of pear leaves. At the same time, in view of the problem that the receptive field of the capsule network is fixed, and the size of the diseased area of the pear leaf is random, and the capsule network cannot fully extract the characteristics, a capsule network based on conditional convolution is proposed to realize the image recognition of pear leaf diseases. The convolution layer of the first layer is replaced by conditional convolution, and the conditional convolution is used to customize the specific convolution kernel for each input to fully extract the characteristics of different lesions. At the same time, the convolution of Primarycap is replaced by conditional convolution to enhance the feature expression ability of the whole network. The experimental results show that the proposed model has higher accuracy on the same test set, which provides a solution for automatic identification of pear leaf diseases images.

Acknowledgements. This study was funded by College Students' Innovative Entrepreneurial Training Plan Program—the research on pear leaf diseases image recognition and fruit counting method based on deep learning and the project of introducing urgently needed talents in key support areas of Shandong Province in 2021—the key technology research and application of intelligent water and fertilizer integration based on big data.

References

1. Bagheri, N., Mohamadi-Monavar, H., Azizi, A., et al.: Detection of fire blight disease in pear trees by hyperspectral data. Eur. J. Remote Sens. **51**(1), 1–10 (2018)
2. Sabour, S., Frosst, N., Hinton, G.E.: Dynamic routing between capsules. arXiv preprint arXiv:1710.09829 (2017)
3. Yang, B., Bender, G., Le, Q.V., et al.: Condconv: conditionally parameterized convolutions for efficient inference. arXiv preprint arXiv:1904.04971 (2019)
4. Almadhor, A., Rauf, H.T., Lali, M.I.U., et al.: AI-driven framework for recognition of guava plant diseases through machine learning from DSLR camera sensor based high resolution imagery. Sensors **21**(11), 3830 (2021)
5. Padol, P.B., Yadav, A.A.: SVM classifier based grape leaf disease detection. In: 2016 Conference on Advances in Signal Processing (CASP), pp. 175–179. IEEE (2016)
6. Hang, J., Zhang, D., Chen, P., et al.: Classification of plant leaf diseases based on improved convolutional neural network. Sensors **19**(19), 4161 (2019)
7. Wu, Y.: Identification of maize leaf diseases based on convolutional neural network. J. Phys. Conf. Ser. IOP Publ. **1748**(3), 032004 (2021)
8. Bansal, P., Kumar, R., Kumar, S.: Disease detection in apple leaves using deep convolutional neural network. Agriculture **11**(7), 617 (2021)
9. Verma, S., Chug, A., Singh, A.P.: Exploring capsule networks for disease classification in plants. J. Stat. Manag. Syst. **23**(2), 307–315 (2020)
10. Patrick, M.K., Weyori, B.A., Mighty, A.A.: Capsule network with K-means routingfor plant disease recognition. J. Intell. Fuzzy Syst. (Preprint) 1–12 (2021)
11. Kwabena, P.M., Weyori, B.A., Mighty, A.A.: Gabor capsule network for plant disease detection. Int. J. Adv. Comput. Sci. Appl. **11**(10) (2020)
12. Wang, X., Wang, X., Huang, W., Zhang, S.: Fine-grained recognition of crop pests based on capsule network with attention mechanism. In: Huang, D.-S., Jo, K.-H., Li, J., Gribova, V., Bevilacqua, V. (eds.) Intelligent Computing Theories and Application: 17th International Conference, ICIC 2021, Shenzhen, China, August 12–15, 2021, Proceedings, Part I, pp. 465–474. Springer International Publishing, Cham (2021). https://doi.org/10.1007/978-3-030-84522-3_38

Software Defect Prediction Method Based on Cost-Sensitive Random Forest

Wei-Dong Zhao[1], Sheng-Dong Zhang[1], and Ming Wang[2]($\boxtimes$)

[1] Shandong University of Science and Technology, Qingdao 266590, China
[2] Qingdao Customs Technology Center, Qingdao 266590, China
wangm415@163.com

Abstract. In this paper, a new method was proposed to reduce the misclassification cost of software defect prediction under the condition of imbalanced classes. The effectiveness of the method was evaluated by the correct rate of sample classification, precision rate, recall rate, and F-Measure index. The main results of this research were as follows: (1) The proposed method can maintain a high accuracy rate while maintaining a relatively low cost of misclassification; (2) In the data preprocessing stage, a median assignment method is proposed, Used to deal with the field missing value problem of a reasonable sample in the data set; (3) In the classification stage of the decision tree and the voting classification stage of the formed random forest, the cost-sensitive factors defined according to different objects are introduced respectively, and the training is based on the cost-sensitive The improved random forest model. Experimental results show that this method can reduce the cost of misclassification while maintaining a high accuracy rate.

Keywords: Software defect prediction · Class imbalance · Cost-sensitive · Random forest

1 Introduction

With the rapid change and development of software projects, software development technology continues to improve and improve. However, in the development process of the entire software project, due to the increasing scale of the software and the increasing complexity of internal logic, it leads to it becomes more difficult to manually judge software defects. If these problems cannot be discovered in time, it will increase the cost of software development, cause waste of human and material resources. Software defect prediction technology is an effective means to find defects in software projects. Therefore, the research of software defect prediction technology is of great significance.

Software defect prediction (SDP) has always been one of the most active areas in software engineering research. According to the different granularity of prediction, it mainly includes module-level, file-level, and change-level defect prediction [1]. This article is research on defect prediction technology for module-level software entities. This technology uses the existing software defect public data set to train a defect prediction model to predict whether there are defects in the software modules.

© IFIP International Federation for Information Processing 2022
Published by Springer Nature Switzerland AG 2022
Z. Shi et al. (Eds.): IIP 2022, IFIP AICT 643, pp. 369–381, 2022.
https://doi.org/10.1007/978-3-031-03948-5_30

In the early stage of the development of software defect prediction technology, Nagappan N, Compton BT, T. Menzies and others generated defect prediction models based on statistical methods [2–4]. However, due to the serious class imbalance and high feature dimension in the acquired data set, the performance of the model based on statistics may not always achieve the expected effect. F. Xing, Kechao Wang et al. used support vector machine (SVM) [5, 6], Haijin Ji et al. used Naive Bayes (NB) method [7], K. Ayan, J. Zheng used neural network [8, 9], T.M. Khoshgoftaar used decision tree [10], Zhou L, Sun Z et al. used ensemble learning [11, 12] to build a software defect prediction model, although they improved the prediction accuracy of unknown category modules, however, most of these constructed classifiers did not consider the impact of the serious class imbalance in the data set, which increased the cost of misclassification. In addition, Michael J, M. Liu, Ling Xu and others used cost-sensitive learning [13–15] to create software defect prediction models. Although it reduced the cost of misclassification, it also reduced the prediction accuracy. However, in the field of software defect prediction (SDP), the construction of classifiers is often aimed at minimizing the classification cost, which is the cost associated with the classification [13].

To construct a software defect prediction model that can minimize the cost of misclassification while ensuring high prediction accuracy, this paper proposes a software defect prediction method based on cost-sensitive and improved random forest. This method mainly improves the forecasting work in three aspects. First, in the data preprocessing stage, for the field missing value problem of a reasonable sample in the data set, use the median assignment processing of the column where the missing value is located; second, divide the sample in the ID3 tree when classifying, introduce cost-sensitive factors, and use the best model discriminant index that is customized according to the error rate, recall rate, and precision rate indicators to filter the generated ID3 tree; third, in the constructed random forest, the performance and number of the selected ID3 trees are secondarily limited, and in the stage of voting and classification, the cost-sensitive factor is introduced again. Overall, reduce the impact on prediction accuracy and increase the tendency of predictions to be defective.

2   Related Work

2.1   Classification Error Type

According to current research, there are two types of errors in the environment of software defect prediction (SDP) [15]. When the classification model predicts a non-defective module as a defective module, Type I misclassification occurs. Similarly, when a defective module is incorrectly classified as non-defective, Type II misclassification occurs. In practical applications, Type II will cause more serious prediction errors, because software defects have not been discovered, causing more serious damage to the software after it is put into use. Therefore, the cost of Type II is much higher than that of Type I. Therefore, to avoid only Type II misclassification, the frequency of Type I misclassification can be appropriately increased. This cost conversion is considered worthwhile in the field of software defect prediction and can effectively reduce the cost of misclassification [14].

2.2 ID3 Tree

The ID3 algorithm [16] proposed by Quinlan J R has a simple structure, strong learning ability, and is easy to understand. It is a classic decision tree algorithm. The algorithm uses information gain as the basis for division and selects the attribute with the largest information gain as the split node to generate a decision tree. At present, there are many optimizations on the ID3 algorithm [17–19].

The ID3 algorithm selects the current best feature to segment the data set each time. There are two ways of segmentation: First, segment according to all possible values of the feature; Secondly, use the binary segmentation method to divide the data set into two parts each time.

In software defect prediction, ID3 trees based on binary segmentation are mostly used. Generally, two aspects need to be considered, on the one hand, select the best segmentation attribute and attribute value. First, calculate the expected information. The expected information indicates the degree of fluctuation of the attribute's influence on the result. The smaller the expected information, the smaller the fluctuation, and the greater the information gain, assuming that there are k categories in the data set D, and the occupancy rate of the i-th category in the total data is pi, the calculation formula for the expected information is as (1); secondly, find the information entropy of each attribute and attribute value. It is a measure of the uncertainty of random variables. The greater the uncertainty, the greater the entropy. Assuming that feature A has m categories or values, and Dj is a subset of D, the information entropy is calculated as formula (2); then, solve for information gain according to formula (3), which is determined by the expected information and information of the attribute Entropy is jointly determined, and it is also the criterion for selecting partition attributes, generally, the attribute and attribute value with the largest information gain is selected as the split node. Finally, under this attribute, put the value less than or equal to this attribute in the left subtree, and vice versa put it in the right subtree.

On the other hand, set the conditions for the ID3 tree to stop splitting. In the process of constructing the ID3 tree, to reduce the impact of model overfitting and the complexity of tree growth, the minimum number of nodes and a single type of child nodes are used as general conditions for the ID3 tree nodes to stop splitting. When the data volume of the node is less than a specified amount or when the data in the node is all of the same types, the split will not continue. Finally, complete the construction of the ID3 tree.

$$Info(D) = -\sum_{i=1}^{k} pi \log_2 pi \tag{1}$$

$$Ent(D, A) = -\sum_{j=1}^{m} Info(Dj) \tag{2}$$

$$Gain(A) = Info(D) - Ent(D, A) \tag{3}$$

2.3 Random Forest

The random forest algorithm proposed by Breiman [20] is an extended variant of Bagging, which is composed of multiple independent decision trees. When judging the category of a new sample, each tree in the random forest will judge the classification result of the sample, and finally vote for judgment. The category with more votes is the final result of the prediction. The formula is as (4):

$$H(x) = \arg \max_j \sum_{i=1}^{T} h_j^i(x) \tag{4}$$

Specific experimental steps: assuming that the original data set has n samples, use data disturbance sampling to form the training set; from the d attributes of the sample, use attribute perturbation to randomly select a subset containing k (k < d) attributes, and use the attribute subset to construct a decision tree model; input the sample, each tree gets its result, vote on the result, and choose the classification result of the sample with more votes.

Owing to the random forest [21] being simple to implement and easy to understand, it has good advantages in processing high-dimensional data, detection feature importance, anti-noise ability, and classification accuracy, making this model a widely used software defect prediction method. However, because the data set used for software defect prediction is usually unbalanced, the random forest has defects in the prediction and classification process.

3   Method of this Article

3.1   Method Flow

Figure 1 is a flowchart of the proposed software defect prediction model. The process of the method is mainly divided into two parts. The first part builds a prediction model, including data preprocessing and training cost-sensitive ID3 trees. The second part is the prediction algorithm, a cost-sensitive random forest is constructed from the trained ID3 tree, for each test module entered, the proposed prediction algorithm divides it into defective or non-defective. The specific process is as follows:

(1)   Data preprocessing

   Step 1. For the software defect prediction data set Data, delete the duplicate and contradictory data; use the median of the missing value column to fill in the missing values of a reasonable piece of data to obtain the preprocessed data set Data';

   Step 2. Use the minimum-maximum normalization method to normalize Data', and map the value of each attribute to the interval [0,1] to obtain Data'';

   Step 3. According to the size of Data'', randomly divide it into a training set TrainD and test TestD according to a custom ratio.

(2)   Training cost-sensitive ID3 tree

   Step 1. Use Bagging technology to perturb the data of TrainD, randomly extract samples from TrainD with replacement, use the extracted samples as the training set TrainD_train of the training ID3 tree, and use the remaining samples as the test set TrainD_test in the training set;

   Step 2. Introduce attribute disturbance, perform attribute disturbance on TrainD_train, and generate TrainD_trainM after attribute disturbance;

Step 3. Use TrainD_trainM, adopt the binary segmentation method, introduce the cost-sensitive factor Acost, and build a cost-sensitive ID3 tree;

Step 4. Use the constructed ID3 tree to predict the samples in TrainD_test and determine whether each sample is a defective module;

Step 5. Calculate and analyze the performance of the improved ID3 tree;

Step 6. Set the best model discriminating index value Ψ, and select the ID3 tree with better overall performance.

(3) Build a cost-sensitive random forest

Step 1. Set the conditions for the secondary screening of ID3 trees and the limit on the number of ID3 trees in the forest, introduce the cost-sensitive factor Bcost, and construct a cost-sensitive random forest (RF);

Step 2. Use the constructed RF to predict the samples in TestD, and each test sample is predicted to be one of two categories (i.e., defective or non-defective);

Step 3. Calculate and analyze the predictive performance of RF;

Step 4. Output the final prediction result of the sample.

3.2 Cost-Sensitive ID3 Tree

Use binary segmentation method to construct ID3 tree. In the process of building an ID3 tree, a single type of child node and the minimum number of nodes are used as the general conditions for the ID3 tree node to stop splitting. When it is found that the number of remaining samples SN is the same category or SN is less than or equal to the minimum number of nodes, that is, the split threshold ε, stop splitting and classify all of them as a leaf node to reduce the impact of overfitting.

When selecting the category of the leaf node, the cost-sensitive factor Acost related to the number of different categories in the data set is introduced as the weight of the defect module in the leaf node to increase the tendency of predicting the defect category, as in formula (5). The general denominator num_y is the number of true defective samples in the data set, the numerator num_x is the number of true non-defective samples, and η and λ represent auxiliary parameters. Without loss of generality, add 1 to both the numerator and denominator.

$$Acost = (num_x + 1)/(num_y + 1) \times \eta \pm \lambda \tag{5}$$

To filter the ID3 tree with better overall performance, for the constructed ID3 tree, the pros and cons model threshold Ψ is introduced, which is set according to the custom values of the error rate, recall rate, and precision rate indicators. Use the test set to test the trained ID3 tree to obtain test indicators such as error rate. If the test index is lower than the defined Ψ, the decision tree is considered unqualified and cannot be included in the number of decision trees specified by the user.

3.3 Cost-Sensitive Random Forest

The cost-sensitive ID3 tree is used as the decision tree in the random forest. Before adding the constructed ID3 tree to the random forest, the conditions for the secondary screening of the ID3 tree are introduced. The numTrees refers to the total number of ID3 trees trained. When the performance of the ID3 tree satisfies: error $\leq$ $\sum_{i=1}^{numTrees} error_i/numTrees$, recall $\geq$ $\sum_{i=1}^{numTrees} recall_i/numTrees$, precision $\geq$ $\sum_{i=1}^{numTrees} precision_i/numTrees$, the ID3 trees will be added to the forest.

Secondly, the random forest will limit the number of ID3 trees added. The number of ID3 trees in the random forest needs to meet: $(numTrees \times 1/2) \leq numF \leq (numTrees \times 4/5)$, numF is the number of ID3 trees in the random forest.

Finally, in the stage of voting to determine the sample category, the cost-sensitive factor Bcost is introduced, which is limited by the number of decision trees in the random forest with different sample prediction results and the number of samples in different categories in the data set. Let it be the weight of the number of decision trees that predict the sample category as a defect to increase the tendency to predict the defect category. The solution of Bcost is as formula (6), where, $trees_x$ is the number of ID3 trees that predict the sample as a non-defect category, $trees_y$ is the number of ID3 trees that predict the sample as a defect category, t_x is the number of real non-defective samples in the data set, t_y is the number of real defective samples, η, λ, γ ($\gamma > 0$, generally take 1) are auxiliary parameters.

$$Bcost = \frac{trees_x}{trees_y + \gamma} \times \sqrt{(t_x + 1)/(t_y + 1)} \times \eta \pm \lambda \tag{6}$$

4 Experiment

4.1 Experimental Data Set and Processing

The experimental data comes from the KC3 and CM1 data sets of the NASA MDP data warehouse. They are a collection of modules after software measurement, which can be downloaded from the website.

In the data set, faced with the problem of missing values of reasonable data, this paper proposes to use the median of the column where the missing value is located to fill the missing value of this data. For example, there are n samples in a certain data set Data, and each sample is represented as $d_i(i = 0, 1, 2, ..., n - 1)$, There are m attributes (including label attributes), and each attribute is represented as $p_j(j = 0, 1, 2, ..., m - 1)$, The j-th attribute of the i-th sample is expressed as dp_{ij}, When the dp_{ij} of a piece of data is missing, after sorting this column of data, use formula (7) to assign value to dp_{ij}.

$$value = \begin{cases} dp^{n/2^j}, n为偶数 \\ dp^{n+1/2^j}, n为奇数 \end{cases} \tag{7}$$

4.2 Method Evaluation Index

The binary classification results of software defect prediction are represented by a confusion matrix, as shown in Table 1. In Table 1, TP means that positive cases are correctly predicted as positive cases; FN means that positive cases are incorrectly predicted as negative cases (Type II misclassification); FP means that negative cases are incorrectly predicted as positive cases (Type I misclassification); TN means that a negative case is correctly predicted as a negative case. The actual number of positive (defective) samples is $P = TP + FN$; the actual number of negative (non-defective) samples is $N = FP + TN$; the total number of all samples is $C = P + N$.

This paper uses correct rate, recall rate, precision rate, F-Measure index to measure the predictive ability of the software defect prediction model and verify the effectiveness of the proposed method. The calculation methods of these performance indicators are described in detail as follows. And, on any given data set, each performance index takes the average of 15 running results as the final performance index value of the method.

(1) Accuracy refers to the proportion of modules that are correctly classified in all modules.

$$Accuracy = \frac{TP + TN}{C} \tag{8}$$

(2) Recall refers to the proportion of all correctly classified defective modules to all truly defective modules.

$$Recall = \frac{TP}{P} \tag{9}$$

(3) Precision refers to the proportion of all correctly classified defective modules to all predicted defective modules.

$$Precision = \frac{TP}{TP + FP} \tag{10}$$

(4) F1-Measure is a weighted harmonic average of precision and recall and is often used to evaluate the quality of a classification model.

$$F1 = \frac{2 \times Precision \times Recall}{Precision + Recall} \tag{11}$$

Table 1. Confusion matrix for software defect prediction

Instance category		Forecast category	
		Defective	Non-defective
	Defective	TP (True positive)	FN (False negative)
	Non-defective	FP (False positive)	TN (True negative)

4.3 Verification Experiment

This paper mainly conducts two sets of experiments. Through verification experiments, the feasibility of the cost-sensitive random forest method is verified, and the effectiveness of the proposed method is verified through comparative experiments. In the two data sets of the experiment, take the KC3 data set as an example, and repeat similar operations on the other data sets.

Input: public data set KC3, public data set division ratio Ex = 7:3, number of decision trees constructed by the user numTrees = 200.

Output: predicted defect label for each test module.

Step 1. Data preprocessing is performed on the public data set KC3, and the data volume of TrainD in the data set KC3 is 135 and that of TestD is 59;

Step 2. Perform data perturbation on trained to obtain the training set TrainD_train and the test set TrainD_test of the training ID3 tree;

Step 3. Calculate the number of attributes ms = 7 after attribute disturbance by formula (12), randomly select the sample containing only 7 attributes from TrainD_train to generate a training set TrainD_trainM;

$$ms = \log(\sqrt{m})*10 - 1 (ms < m, m : \text{Total number of attributes}) \tag{12}$$

Step 4. Set $\varepsilon = 5$, $\eta = 0.5$, $\lambda = 0.4$, and use formula (5) to get Acost ≈ 1.75 is used as the weight of the defect category to construct a cost-sensitive ID3 tree;

Step 5. Use the constructed ID3 tree to predict the samples in TrainD_test and determine whether each sample is defective;

Step 6. Calculate various performance values to obtain the predictive performance of the ID3 tree;

Step 7: Set the best model identification index value Ψ (that is, $\Psi_{error} = 34\%$, $\Psi_{recall} = 25\%$, $\Psi_{accuracy} = 22\%$), and select ID3 trees with better overall performance;

Step 8: Screen ID3 trees again, and limit the number of ID3 trees in the random forest. In the random forest, the number of ID3 trees is $100 \leq numF \leq 160$, and the constructed random forest is obtained.

Step 9. Set $\gamma = 1$, $\eta = 2.5$, $\lambda = 0.35$, and use the formula (6) to obtain Bcost ≈ 1.62 as the voting weight of the defect category to construct a cost-sensitive random forest (cost-RF);

Step 10: Use the constructed improved random forest model to vote and predict the sample categories in TestD;

Step 11: Calculate various performance values to obtain the predicted performance of RF, as shown in Table 2;

Step 12. Output the final prediction result of the sample.

Table 2. Average experimental results of cost-RF 15 runs.

Data set	Accuracy (%)	Precision (%)	Recall (%)	F-Measure (%)
KC3	88.20	65.49	73.51	69.27
CM1	88.62	67.85	73.63	70.62

4.4 Comparative Experiment

To verify the prediction performance of the cost-sensitive random forest method, this paper compares the experimental results of this method with the traditional ID3-based random forest, SVM, and LASSO-SVM. To avoid losing generality, all experiments are compared under the same experimental environment, the data set, and the data preprocessing steps to verify the effectiveness of the cost-sensitive random forest method.

To make the experimental results more reliable, the average value of all performance indicators of 15 runs is taken as the final performance indicator value of each prediction model. Table 3 shows the accuracy (ACC), the precision (PRE), the recall (REC), and the F-Measure values of the traditional random forest model (t-RF), SVM, and LASSO-SVM on the two test sets (KC3, CM1).

Table 3. Average experimental results of 15 runs of other models.

Data set	KC3				CM1			
	ACC (%)	PRE (%)	REC (%)	F-Measure (%)	ACC (%)	PRE (%)	REC (%)	F-Measure (%)
t-RF	69.65	60.31	52.18	55.95	74.60	62.10	56.02	58.90
SVM	74.28	64.67	60.18	62.34	74.32	62.25	59.34	60.76
LASSO-SVM	88.22	65.79	73.01	69.21	90.02	65.23	76.35	70.35

5   Experimental Results and Discussion

5.1   Analysis of Verification Experiment Results

According to the verification experiment results in Table 3, it can be found that the cost-sensitive improved random forest model (cost-RF) is in the above data set. As the imbalance rate increases, the number of data increases. It can ensure that the precision rate will not change significantly, and the recall rate will be improved to a certain extent. Figure 2 shows the comparison of experimental results. Among them, in the KC3 data set, due to the low imbalance rate, this model increases the occurrence of Type I in the prediction process, that is, by reducing the precision, to improve the recall rate index. But the overall results also confirm the effectiveness of this model from the side. Under the CM1 data set, it can be seen that under a certain imbalance rate and data volume, the precision rate is relatively stable, and the recall rate has been improved. At the same time, the F-Measure indicator has exceeded 70%. Further, the feasibility of this model is verified.

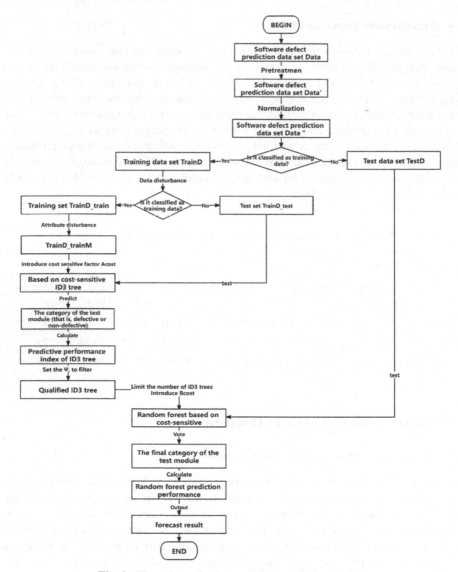

Fig. 1. Flow chart of software defect prediction model.

5.2 Comparative Test Results Analysis

According to the comparative experimental results in Table 3 and the comparison results of all models in the correct, precision, recall, and F-Measure, the results are shown in Fig. 2. It can be found that cost-RF is superior to the random forest model and SVM composed of traditional ID3 trees in any index, especially in the index of recall rate, cost-RF is much higher than them. Compared with the LASSO-SVM model, it can be seen from Fig. 3 that due to the cost-sensitive factor introduced in the cost-RF twice, the accuracy index is weaker than that of the LASSO-SVM. However, F-Measure is better than LASSO-SVM, and cost-RF is less than 8% in the difference between precision and recall. According to the above experimental data, cost-RF can effectively increase the weight of predicting defect categories while maintaining a high accuracy rate, reduce the frequency of Type II misclassification, and minimize the cost of misclassification.

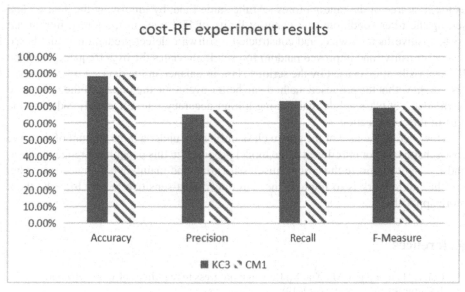

Fig. 2. Average experimental results of 15 runs of Cost-RF on different data sets.

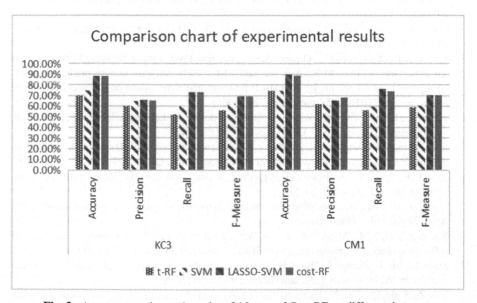

Fig. 3. Average experimental results of 15 runs of Cost-RF on different data sets.

6 Conclusion

This paper proposes a software defect prediction method based on cost-sensitive and improved random forest. Specifically, this method makes full use of the advantages that the random forest is not affected by high-dimensional data, can extract important features, and has stable performance and the ID3 tree with binary segmentation is used as the base tree of the random forest. At the same time, by improving the data set and setting the filter conditions and quantity limits of ID3 trees in the forest, introduced cost-sensitive factors twice, and constructed a software defect prediction model based on cost-sensitive and improved random forests. It alleviates the high frequency of Type II misclassification caused by the serious class imbalance in the data set. Experimental results show that the proposed method can better overcome the impact of the imbalance of the data set class, while maintaining a high accuracy rate, effectively reducing the cost of misclassification.

However, in the face of the severe class imbalance under a large amount of data, the cost-sensitive factor introduced in the model proposed in this paper has a reduced effect, and it cannot minimize the cost of misclassification and maintain a high accuracy rate. So, the future work is to improve the introduced cost-sensitive factors to make them more applicable.

References

1. Cai, L., Fan, Y., Yan, M., Xia, X.: Research progress in real-time software defect prediction. J. Softw. **30**(5), 1288–1307 (2019)
2. Nagappan, N., Ball, T.: Use of relative code churn measures to predict system defect density. In: Proceedings of the 27th International Conference on Software Engineering (ICSE 2005), pp. 284–292 (2005)
3. Compton, B.T., Withrow, C.: Prediction and control of ADA software defects. J. Syst. Softw. **12**, 199–207 (1990)
4. Menzies, T., DiStefano, J.S., Orrego, A.S.: Assessing Predictors of Software Defects (2004)
5. Xing, F., Guo, P., Lyu, M.R.: A novel method for early software quality prediction based on support vector machine. In: 16th IEEE International Symposium on Software Reliability Engineering (ISSRE 2005), vol. 10, p. 222 (2005)
6. Wang, K., Liu, L., Yuan, C., Wang, Z.: Software defect prediction model based on LASSO–SVM. Neural Comput. Appl. **33**(14), 8249–8259 (2020)
7. Ji, H., Huang, S., Wu, Y., Hui, Z., Zheng, C.: A new weighted naive Bayes method based on information diffusion for software defect prediction. Softw. Qual. J. **27**(3), 923–968 (2019)
8. Arar, Ö.F., Ayan, K.: Software defect prediction using cost-sensitive neural network. Appl. Soft Comput. **33**, 263–277 (2015)
9. Zheng, J.: Cost-sensitive boosting neural networks for software defect prediction. Expert Syst. Appl. **37**(6), 4537–4543 (2010)
10. Khoshgoftaar, T.M., Allen, E.B., Jones, W.D., Hudepohl, J.P.: Classification-tree models of software-quality over multiple releases. IEEE Trans. Reliab. **49**(1), 4–11 (2000)
11. Zhou, L., Li, R., Zhang, S., Wang, H.: Imbalanced data processing model for software defect prediction. Wirel. Person. Commun. **102**(2), 937–950 (2018)
12. Sun, Z., Song, Q., Zhu, X.: Using coding-based ensemble learning to improve software defect prediction. IEEE Trans. Syst. Man Cybern. C Appl. Rev. **42**(6), 1806–1817 (2012)

13. Siers, M.J., Islam, M.Z.: Software defect prediction using a cost sensitive decision forest and voting, and a potential solution to the class imbalance problem. Inf. Syst. **51**, 62–71 (2015)
14. Liu, M., Miao, L., Zhang, D.: Two-stage cost-sensitive learning for software defect prediction. IEEE Trans. Reliab. **63**(2), 676–686 (2014)
15. Xu, L., Wang, B., Liu, L., Zhou, M., Liao, S., Yan, M.: Misclassification cost-sensitive software defect prediction. In: 2018 IEEE International Conference on Information Reuse and Integration (IRI), pp. 256–263 (2018)
16. Quinlan, J.R.: Induction of decision trees. Mach. Learn. **1**(1), 81–106 (1986)
17. Zhu, L., Yang, Y.: Improvement of decision tree ID3 algorithm. In: Wang, S., Zhou, A. (eds.) CollaborateCom 2016. LNICSSITE, vol. 201, pp. 595–600. Springer, Cham (2017). https://doi.org/10.1007/978-3-319-59288-6_59
18. Kraidech, S., Jearanaitanakij, K.: Improving ID3 algorithm by combining values from equally important attributes. In: 2017 21st International Computer Science and Engineering Conference (ICSEC), pp. 1–5 (2017)
19. Zhang, H., Zhou, R.: The analysis and optimization of decision tree based on ID3 algorithm. In: 2017 9th International Conference on Modelling, Identification and Control (ICMIC), pp. 924–928 (2017)
20. Breiman, L.: Bagging predictors. Mach. Learn. **24**(2), 123–140 (1996)
21. Belgiu, M., Drăguţ, L.: Random forest in remote sensing: a review of applications and future directions. ISPRS J. Photogram. Remote Sens. **114**, 24–31 (2016)

Fault Diagnosis of Sewage Treatment Equipment Based on Feature Selection

Mingzhu Lou[✉]

School of Information Engineering, Nanchang Institute of Technology, Nanchang 330099, Jiangxi, People's Republic of China
minzhulou@163.com

Abstract. There are many factors that affect the operation state in the wastewater treatment process. Generally, the probability of failure is much less than the probability of normal operation. Fault diagnosis of wastewater treatment is a high-dimensional unbalanced data classification. In this study, we propose a feature selection-based method to improve the classification performance of wastewater treatment fault diagnosis. Two filter-based feature selection methods and one wrapper-based feature selection method were used for experiments. Three classifiers of C4.5, Naive Bayes, and RBF-SVM were used to evaluate the proposed method. Experimental results show that the proposed method can significantly improve the overall classification accuracy and AUC value on the wastewater treatment fault diagnosis dataset.

Keywords: Fault diagnosis · Wastewater treatment · Imbalanced classification · Feature selection

1 Introduction

Wastewater treatment plants are a key infrastructure to build ecological civilization and improve the quality of the water environment. The wastewater treatment process is extremely complex, and there are many influencing factors, which will cause problems such as failure, normal and stable operation, and environmental pollution in the treatment process [1]. Therefore, fault diagnosis and corresponding management of wastewater treatment plants are of great importance [2].

In recent years, many scholars have researched wastewater treatment fault diagnosis and achieved some results [3–6]. In the process of sewage treatment, the data collected by sensors have the characteristics of high-dimensional and unbalanced, that is, the samples of normal data are much more than the samples of fault data [7]. The distribution of samples in different feature space is different. There are certain features that are beneficial to the classification of small categories. The main idea of our study is to select features with significant distinguishing power to improve the classification performance of unbalanced sewage treatment faults.

Feature selection methods can be divided into three categories of filter, wrapper, and embedded [8–10]. Filter methods filter out irrelevant features independent of the subsequent learning process. The filter feature selection method is universal, straightforward in principle, and fast in operation [11, 12]. Wrapper methods determine the optimal feature subset according to the evaluation result of the feature subset by using a classifier [13, 14]. In the process of feature selection, the wrapper method requires classifier training and testing of candidate subsets, so the algorithm complexity is high. Embedded feature selection is the integration of the feature selection process and the classifier training process [15, 16].

In this study, two filter-based feature selection methods and one wrapper-based feature selection method were used for wastewater treatment fault diagnosis. Three classifiers of C4.5 [17], Naive Bayes [18], and RBF-SVM [19] were used to evaluate the proposed method. Experimental results demonstrate that the proposed method can significantly improve the overall classification accuracy and AUC value on the wastewater treatment fault diagnosis dataset.

The remainder of the paper is organized as follows. In Sect. 2, we provide a brief review of existing work on imbalanced classification problems. In Sect. 3, we describe two types of filter feature selection algorithms and a wrapper feature selection algorithm used in this paper. Section 4 presents the experimental results and analysis of real sewage equipment processing data. Finally, Sect. 5 concludes the paper.

2 Related Work

Wastewater treatment fault diagnosis belongs to an imbalanced classification. Considerable work has been done to deal with the problem of unbalanced classification. At the preprocessing, this work is mainly included sampling-based methods and feature selection-based methods. In this paper, we focus on the application of the feature selection method in fault diagnosis of wastewater treatment equipment. Feature selection can effectively remove redundant features and irrelevant features in the dataset, reduce the impact of irrelevant data on the classifier, make the final generated classifier more concise and easier to understand, and effectively improve the performance of the classifier. Feature selection can be effective for some imbalanced classification since the distribution of samples in different feature space is different and some features are beneficial to the classification of small categories.

The filter method requires a criterion to evaluate correlations between features and categories. The filter method assumes that features that are more relevant to the category contribute more to the classification, so these features are preferentially selected. The wrapper approach uses the classification performance of the learning algorithm as the evaluation criteria for feature subsets. In the process of subset evaluation, the data corresponding to the feature subset to be evaluated is used as the training set training classifier, and then the cross-validation method is used to evaluate the performance of the feature subset.

In addition to feature evaluation, a key problem of feature selection technology is how to search from feature subset space. The common search strategies include global optimal search, random search, and heuristic search. Global optimal search is to determine the global optimal subset by enumerating all feature combinations. Time complexity is exponential in terms of data dimensionality for optimal search algorithms. Due to its extremely high time complexity, global optimal search is rarely used. Heuristic search is divided into deterministic heuristic and nondeterministic heuristic algorithms. Deterministic heuristic search mainly includes sequence forward selection, sequence backward selection, and two-way selection. Sequence forward selection starts with an empty feature set, evaluates each feature individually to find the best feature, and places the feature into the feature set. The search then tries each of the remaining features to find the best single feature and places it into the feature set again. This process continues until no improvement is achieved when adding a new feature. Sequence backward selection is the opposite of the sequence forward selection. Sequence backward selection starting with the original feature set, remove the feature at a time that results in the most improvement in the evaluation index. Bidirectional selection combines sequence forward selection and sequence backward selection. In this study, we focus on a forward search rather than a backward search. The main reason for this choice is that forward selection is much more efficient than backward deletion.

3   Feature Selection Methods

For filter methods, feature selection and classification algorithms do not interfere with each other. The filter method needs a relevance measure to assess the correlation between the features and categories. In this paper, we focus on two widely used feature correlation assessment criteria: information gain and ReliefF.

3.1   Information Gain

Information gain is one of the most widely used feature evaluation methods based on information entropy theory. Information entropy can measure the diversity of variables. The higher the value of a variable, the greater its uncertainty. Information entropy is descriptive information uncertainty, and is defined as:

$$Info(D) = -\sum_{i=1}^{m} p_i \log_2(p_i) \tag{1}$$

Where D denotes a variable, p_i represents the probability of the ith event in variable D. $Info(D)$ is the information entropy of variable D. Conditional Entropy is defined as follows.

$$Info_A(D) = -\sum_{j=1}^{y} \frac{|D_j|}{|D|} \times Info(D_j) \tag{2}$$

$Info_A(D)$ is the conditional entropy of variable D under a given variable A. Variable D is needed to be divided to multiple categories according to the value of variable A. On the basis above, information gain $Gain(A)$ is defined as:

$$Gain(A) = Info(D) - Info_A(D) \tag{3}$$

Information gain $Gain(A)$ measures the decrease in the uncertainty of variable D under given a variable A.

In a classification problem, D can be regarded as the class labels of all samples and A can be regarded as a feature. According to Eq. (3), the significance of feature A can is obtained.

3.2 ReliefF

ReliefF is a nearest-neighbor-based feature evaluation algorithm. ReliefF algorithm is a feature weighting algorithm that assigns different weights to features according to the correlation of each feature and class. The features with a weight less than a certain threshold will be removed. The flow of ReliefF is as follows:

Input : Training dataset D, Sample sampling times m , Feature weight threshold, Number of nearest neighbor samples k

Output : The weight of each feature W(i)

---

1   All feature scores set to 0, T is the empty set

2   for i=1 to m do

3   Randomly select a sample R from D

4   Find the k nearest neighbor samples $H_j(j=1,2,...k)$ of R from the sample set of the same class of R, and find the k nearest neighbor samples $M_j(C)$ from each sample set of different classes;

5   for A=1 to N , // Calculate the weight of each feature, where N is the number of features

---

6    $W(A)=W(A)-\sum_{j=1}^{k} diff(A,R,H_j)/(mk)+ \sum_{C\neq Class(R)}\left[\frac{p(C)}{1-p(Class(R))}\sum_{j=1}^{k} diff(A,R,M_j(C))\right]/(mk)$

$diff(A, R_1, R_2)$ represents the distance between sample and sample according to feature A. $M_j(C)$ represents the jth nearest neighbor sample in class C.

According to a feature, if the distance between a sample and its nearest neighbor of a different category is greater than the distance between the sample and its nearest neighbor of the same category, the feature has a strong ability to identify the sample. ReliefF method outputs ranking scores according to the weight of each feature.

3.3 Wrapper Evaluation

In the wrapper approach, the importance of a subset of features is evaluated using an inductive algorithm. In this study, we use a sequence forward selection search strategy for the wrapper method named WrapperEval. WrapperEval starts with the empty set of features and searches forward for the optimal feature subset from the original dataset by greedy hill-climbing augmented. The selection of the classification algorithm is not fixed. Three classical classification algorithms: C4.5, naïve Bayes, and RBF-SVM were used to evaluate feature subsets. Five-fold cross-validation was used to evaluate the accuracy of the learning scheme on a candidate feature subset. In addition, the termination condition

386   M. Lou

we set *searchTermination* = 5 means that the program terminates when optimal features are added five consecutive times without any improvement in classification performance. Chart flow of WrapperEval is shown in Fig. 1.

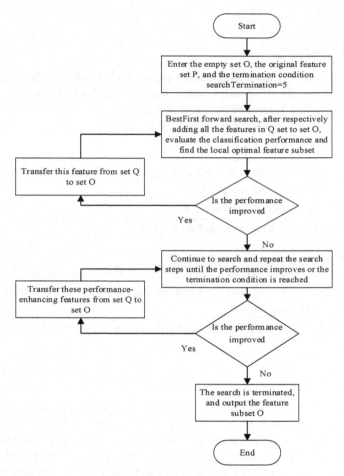

Fig. 1. Flow of WrapperEval

4   Experimental Results and Analysis

In this section, we evaluate the effectiveness of three feature selection algorithms for fault diagnosis of sewage treatment equipment. We first present the experimental framework, including the benchmark dataset, classification algorithms, and assessment metrics. The results and discussions are presented subsequently.

4.1 Water Treatment Plant Dataset

We used the real dataset Water Treatment Plant from the UCI machine learning library [20] for experiments. The Water Treatment Plant dataset comes from the daily measures of sensors in an urban wastewater treatment plant. The objective is to classify the operational state of the plant to predict faults through the state variables of the plant at each of the stages of the treatment process. The dataset contains 527 samples, each corresponding to one day of operational monitoring. Each sample has 38 features, including flow rate, pH value, conductivity, etc.

According to the operating status of the wastewater treatment process, all samples are divided into 13 classes. The operating states corresponding to each class are shown in Table 1. We are focused on studying the imbalanced two-classification problem. Therefore, we combined the categories of similar states to obtain 6 imbalanced datasets, namely, water1, water2, water3, water4, water5, and water6, respectively. Table 2 lists in detail the number of samples in the 6 datasets, the proportion of minority samples, and the imbalance ratio.

Table 1. The status of Water Treatment Plant

ClassIndex	Status (Class)
1	Normal situation1
2	Secondary settler problems-1
3	Secondary settler problems-2
4	Secondary settler problems-3
5	Normal situation with performance over the mean
6	Solids overload-1
7	Secondary settler problems-4
8	Storm-1
9	Normal situation with low influent
10	Storm-2
11	Normal situation2
12	Storm-3
13	Solids overload-2

Table 2. Description of the datasets

Dataset	Minority Class	Majority class	Attributes	Instances	Minority	Majority	%Minority	Imbalance ratio
Water1	All other classes	Class of '1, 5, 9, 11'	38	527	14	513	2.66%	0.03:0.97
Water2	Class of '5'	Class of '1, 11'	38	513	116	397	22.61%	0.230.77
Water3	Class of '9'	Class of '1, 11'	38	513	69	444	13.45%	0.13:0.87
Water4	Class of '5'	Class of '1'	38	391	116	275	29.67%	0.30:0.70
Water5	Class of '9'	Class of '5'	38	185	69	116	37.30%	0.37:0.63
Water6	Class of '5, 9'	Class of '1, 11'	38	513	185	328	36.06%	0.36:0.64

4.2 Classification Algorithms

Three classical classifiers of C4.5, naïve Bayes, and RBF-SVM were used to evaluate the performance of feature selection algorithms.

C4.5 is a classical decision tree algorithm. The C4.5 classifier can generate pruned or unpruned decision trees, because unpruned decision trees may lead to overfitting of the model, so the C4.5 classification algorithm in this article utilizes pruned decision trees.

The Naive Bayes classification algorithm is a probabilistic classification algorithm based on the Bayes theorem and features independence hypothesis. Equation (4) is the Bayesian formula, which is also the posterior probability, which represents the probability that the sample is classified into this class.

$$P(c_i|x) = \frac{P(x|c_i)P(c_i)}{P(x)} \tag{4}$$

$$h(x) = argmaxP(c_i|x) \tag{5}$$

Equation (5) indicates that the sample is regarded as the class with the largest posterior probability.

SVM is a learning machine that minimizes structural risks based on statistical learning theory. Because it can establish nonlinear decision boundaries, it has high accuracy. In our experiments, we choose the radial basis function kernel as the kernel function of the support vector machine. Compared with other kernel functions, the radial basis function kernel has higher performance and lower computational cost.

4.3 Assessment Metric

For a two-class classification problem, in which the outcomes are labeled as either positive or negative. Given a testing dataset comprising P positive and N negative samples, the task of any classification model is to assign a class label to each sample. If the outcome of a prediction is positive and the actual value is also positive, then it is called a true positive. However, if the actual value is negative, then it is regarded as a false positive. Conversely, a true negative occurs when both the prediction outcome and the actual value are negative, and a false negative when the prediction outcome is negative while the actual value is positive. The confusion matrix is shown in Table 3.

Table 3. Confusion matrix

Class	Predict positive	Predict negative
Actual positive	TP	FN
Actual negative	FP	TN

$$Accuracy = \frac{TP + TN}{P + N} \tag{6}$$

$$Precision = \frac{TP}{TP + FP} \tag{7}$$

$$TPR = Recall = \frac{TP}{TP + FN} \tag{8}$$

$$FPR = \frac{FP}{TN + FP} \tag{9}$$

$$F - measure = \frac{(\beta^2 + 1)Precision * Recall}{\beta^2(Precision + Recall)} \tag{10}$$

The accuracy represents the proportion of samples that were correctly classified. For an imbalanced dataset, the cost of misclassification of a minority class sample is higher, therefore, higher overall accuracy cannot represent better classification performance. AUC (Area Under Curve) refers to the area under the ROC characteristic curve and the horizontal and vertical axis. AUC is the area under the Receiver Operating Characteristics graph that is plotted on a two-dimensional graph, with pairs of true positive rate TPR over false positives rate FPR. AUC is a reliable performance measure; it has been widely used to evaluate classifier performance regardless of the severity of the class imbalance. Therefore, we take the AUC value as the most important evaluation index for the fault diagnosis performance of wastewater treatment. In addition, we also examine other performance indexes such as the overall classification accuracy (Accuracy).

In the experiment, a 10-fold cross-validation technique was used to measure the classification performance of the algorithm. In 10-fold cross-validation, the dataset is equally divided into 10 subsets, one subset is taken as the test set, and the remaining nine subsets are used as the training set. Each subset is selected as the test dataset of the other 9 training subsets, and the average of the 10 test results is calculated as the final result.

4.4   Results and Analysis

We compared four methods of InfoGain, ReliefF, WrapperEval, and Original (means no feature selection) in our experiments.

Filter methods (InfoGain and ReliefF) output the feature subsets according to the ranking score of the feature. In the experiment, we did not set a fixed threshold value but obtained 18 feature subsets within the interval with step size 2 as the unit [2]. That is, the top-2 in the ranker sequence features as the first feature subset, the top-4 features as the second feature subset, … and the top-36 features as the last feature subset. Then, three classification algorithms are adopted to evaluate the performance of all these feature subsets. The feature subset with the best performance as the optimal feature subset is then compared with other algorithms. The number of features of the resulting optimal feature subset is shown in parentheses following the accuracy. The results of the best performance of each evaluation index are shown in bold.

Tables 4, 5 and 6 show the classification performance results of the two Filter type feature selection algorithms under the three classification algorithms.

As shown in Table 4 that for the C4.5 classification algorithm, the InfoGain algorithm has improved the overall classification accuracy on 5 datasets including Water2, Water3, Water4, Water5, and Water6. Among them, the InfoGain algorithm is better than the ReliefF algorithm on Water4 and Water6 datasets. AUC value is improved on all datasets. And InfoGain algorithm is better than the ReliefF algorithm of the Water1 and Water4 datasets. The ReliefF algorithm has improved the overall classification accuracy on four datasets of Water1, Water3, Water4, and Water6. Among them, it is better than the InfoGain algorithm on the three datasets of Water1, Water3, and Water5. AUC has been enhanced on all datasets. Among them, Water3, Water5, Water6, and the other three datasets are best if InfoGain algorithm. It is shown that the classification performance of the ReliefF algorithm based on the C4.5 classification algorithm is better than the compared algorithm.

One can see from Table 5 that for the NaiveBayes classification algorithm, the Info-Gain algorithm has improved the overall classification accuracy on 4 datasets including Water2, Water3, Water4, and Water6. Among them, the InfoGain algorithm is preferable to the ReliefF algorithm on the Water4 dataset. AUC value is improved on all datasets. The ReliefF algorithm has improved the overall classification accuracy on four datasets of Water2, Water3, Water5, and Water6, and is better than the InfoGain algorithm. AUC value has been improved on all datasets. In the data of Water3, Water5, and Water6, the ReliefF algorithm is better than InfoGain algorithm. It is shown that the classification performance of the ReliefF algorithm under the Naïve Bayes classification algorithm is better than the comparison algorithm.

It can be seen from Table 6 that for the RBF-SVM classifier, the InfoGain algorithm has improved the overall classification accuracy on the Water2, Water4, and Water5 datasets. InfoGain algorithm is preferable to the ReliefF algorithm on the Water5 dataset. AUC value has been improved on the datasets of Water2, Water4, Water5, and Water6. Among which the datasets of Water5 and Water6, the InfoGain algorithm is better than the ReliefF algorithm. The ReliefF algorithm has improved the overall classification accuracy and AUC value on two datasets such as Water2 and Water4. However, the ReliefF algorithm is not significantly better than the InfoGain algorithm on all datasets, indicating that the InfoGain algorithm is better than the comparison algorithm under the RBF-SVM classification algorithm.

Based on the C4.5 and NaiveBayes classification algorithms, the ReliefF algorithm has better performance, and under the RBF-SVM classification algorithm, the InfoGain algorithm has better performance.

Tables 7, 8 and 9 list the experimental results of the Original and the WrapperEval algorithm for three classification algorithms. One can see that the AUC values of all datasets under the three classification algorithms have improved for the WrapperEval algorithm. For the Water1, Water3, Water4, and Water6 datasets, the experimental results of the WrapperEval on the accuracy index for the three classification algorithms have improved to different degrees compared with the Original. Among the 18 groups of TP Rate comparisons, WrapperEval has 14 groups increased; the increase of TP Rate indicates that the correct classification of minority classes is improved. The experimental results show that the WrapperEval algorithm has significantly improved the classification performance.

Table 4. Comparison of classification performance between filter methods and Original based on C4.5 classification algorithm

Algorithm		Water1	Water2	Water3	Water4	Water5	Water6
Original	Accuracy	0.9810	0.8460	0.8928	0.8363	0.7892	0.7817
	AUC	0.869	0.785	0.788	0.800	0.826	0.774
InfoGain	Accuracy	0.9829(10)	0.8324(2)	0.9006(2)	**0.8670**(4)	0.8270(2)	**0.7992**(2)
	AUC	**0.915**	**0.851**	0.874	**0.870**	0.866	0.8435
ReliefF	Accuracy	**0.9848**(10)	0.8324(2)	**0.9123**(4)	0.8465(12)	**0.8595**(10)	0.7778(4)
	AUC	0.870	**0.851**	**0.887**	0.862	**0.878**	**0.885**

Table 5. Comparison of classification performance between filter methods and Original based on NaiveBayes classification algorithm

Algorithm		Water1	Water2	Water3	Water4	Water5	Water6
Original	Accuracy	0.9658	0.8713	0.8713	0.8977	0.8595	0.8129
	AUC	0.920	0.893	0.923	0.934	0.921	0.8975
InfoGain	Accuracy	0.9658(12)	**0.8772**(10)	0.8928(4)	**0.9028**(10)	0.8486(36)	0.8382(16)
	AUC	0.990	0.921	0.943	0.958	0.922	0.923
ReliefF	Accuracy	0.9564(12)	**0.8772**(10)	**0.8967**(10)	0.8926(8)	**0.8757**(10)	**0.8460**(12)
	AUC	**0.992**	**0.927**	**0.947**	**0.962**	**0.930**	**0.9375**

Tables 10, 11 and 12 list the experimental results of the InfoGain, ReliefF, and WrapperEval for three classification algorithms respectively.

For the C4.5 classification algorithm, the WrapperEval is better than the two filter feature selection algorithms in the accuracy and AUC value on the datasets of Water2,

Table 6. Comparison of classification performance between filter methods and Original based on RBF-SVM classification algorithm

Algorithm		Water1	Water2	Water3	Water4	Water5	Water6
Original	Accuracy	0.9734	0.7739	0.8655	0.7033	0.6270	0.6394
	AUC	0.5	0.5	0.5	0.5	0.5	0.5
InfoGain	Accuracy	0.9734(4)	**0.7797**(2)	0.8655(4)	**0.7877**(2)	**0.6378**(2)	0.6257(2)
	AUC	0.5	**0.601**	0.5	**0.697**	**0.514**	**0.5045**
ReliefF	Accuracy	0.9734(2)	**0.7797**(2)	0.8655(4)	**0.7877**(2)	0.6270(6)	0.6394(4)
	AUC	0.5	**0.601**	0.5	**0.697**	0.5	0.5

Table 7. Comparison of classification performance between WrapperEval and Original based on C4.5 classification algorithm

Dataset	Methods	Accuracy	TP rate	FP rate	Precision	F-measure	AUC
Water1	Original	0.9810	0.571	**0.008**	0.667	0.615	0.869
	WrapperEval	**0.9829**	**0.643**	**0.008**	**0.692**	**0.667**	**0.908**
Water2	Original	0.8460	0.629	0.091	0.67	0.649	0.785
	WrapperEval	**0.8616**	**0.647**	**0.076**	**0.714**	**0.679**	**0.853**
Water3	Original	0.8928	**0.638**	0.068	0.595	0.615	0.788
	WrapperEval	**0.9181**	0.623	**0.036**	**0.729**	**0.672**	**0.895**
Water4	Original	0.8363	0.681	0.098	0.745	0.712	0.800
	WrapperEval	**0.8824**	**0.750**	**0.062**	**0.837**	**0.791**	**0.912**
Water5	Original	0.7892	0.681	**0.147**	0.734	0.707	0.826
	WrapperEval	**0.8432**	**0.826**	**0.147**	**0.770**	**0.797**	**0.852**
Water6	Original	0.7817	**0.619**	0.089	0.602	0.6105	0.774
	WrapperEval	**0.7934**	0.609	**0.071**	**0.6475**	**0.6275**	**0.8335**

Table 8. Comparison of classification performance between WrapperEval and Original based on NaiveBayes classification algorithm

Dataset	Methods	Accuracy	TP rate	FP rate	Precision	F-measure	AUC
Water1	Original	0.9658	0.857	0.031	0.429	0.571	0.92
	WrapperEval	**0.9848**	**0.929**	**0.014**	**0.65**	**0.765**	**0.995**
Water2	Original	0.8713	**0.776**	0.101	0.692	**0.732**	0.893
	WrapperEval	0.8713	0.69	**0.076**	**0.727**	0.708	**0.937**
Water3	Original	0.8713	0.841	0.124	0.513	0.637	0.923
	WrapperEval	**0.9220**	**0.899**	**0.074**	**0.653**	**0.756**	**0.968**

(*continued*)

Table 8. (*continued*)

Dataset	Methods	Accuracy	TP rate	FP rate	Precision	F-measure	AUC
Water4	Original	0.8977	0.862	0.087	0.806	0.833	0.934
	WrapperEval	**0.9182**	**0.871**	**0.062**	**0.856**	**0.863**	**0.974**
Water5	Original	**0.8595**	0.913	0.172	0.759	**0.829**	0.921
	WrapperEval	0.8486	**0.928**	**0.198**	**0.736**	0.821	**0.955**
Water6	Original	0.8129	0.761	0.089	0.6435	0.6855	0.8975
	WrapperEval	**0.8674**	**0.794**	**0.0535**	**0.7555**	**0.7695**	**0.9505**

Table 9. Comparison of classification performance between WrapperEval and Original based on RBF-SVM classification algorithm

Dataset	Methods	Accuracy	TP rate	FP rate	Precision	F-measure	AUC
Water1	Original	0.9734	0	**0**	0	0	0.5
	WrapperEval	**0.9772**	**0.143**	**0**	**1**	**0.25**	**0.571**
Water2	Original	0.7739	0	**0**	0	0	0.5
	WrapperEval	**0.8421**	**0.56**	0.076	**0.684**	**0.616**	**0.742**
Water3	Original	0.8655	0	**0**	0	0	0.5
	WrapperEval	**0.9025**	**0.362**	0.014	**0.806**	**0.5**	**0.674**
Water4	Original	0.7033	0	**0**	0	0	0.5
	WrapperEval	**0.8696**	**0.716**	0.065	**0.822**	**0.765**	**0.825**
Water5	Original	0.6270	0	**0**	0	0	0.5
	WrapperEval	**0.7730**	**0.667**	0.164	**0.708**	**0.687**	**0.751**
Water6	Original	0.6394	0	0	0	0	0.5
	WrapperEval	**0.7602**	**0.345**	0.0535	**0.336**	**0.3405**	**0.6455**

Water3, and Water4. For the Water5 dataset, the ReliefF algorithm obtains the best result. For the naïve Bayes classifier, the AUC value of the WrapperEval is the highest for all datasets; and accuracy is the highest on the four datasets of Water1, Water3, Water4, and Water6. Therefore, in the performance comparison of NaiveBayes and RBF-SVM classification algorithms, the WrapperEval is better than other comparison algorithms.

To further illustrate the classification performance of the WrapperEval, Figs. 2, 3 and 4 provide an overall intuitive comparison of the Accuracy value; Figs. 5, 6 and 7 provide an overall intuitive comparison of the AUC value. As can be seen from the figures, the three feature selection algorithms have significantly improved compared to the Original, and the WrapperEval algorithm performs the best.

Table 10. Comparison of classification performance of InfoGain, ReliefF, and WrapperEval based on C4.5 classification algorithm

Algorithm		Water1	Water2	Water3	Water4	Water5	Water6
InfoGain	Accuracy	0.9829(10)	0.8324(2)	0.9006(2)	0.8670(4)	0.8270(20)	**0.7992(6)**
	AUC	**0.915**	0.851	0.874	0.870	0.866	0.8435
ReliefF	Accuracy	**0.9848(10)**	0.8324(2)	0.9123(4)	0.8465(12)	**0.8595(10)**	0.7778(4)
	AUC	0.870	0.851	0.887	0.862	**0.878**	**0.885**
WrapperEval	Accuracy	0.9829(8)	**0.8616(15)**	**0.9181(6)**	**0.8824(5)**	0.8432(10)	0.7934(5)
	AUC	0.908	**0.853**	**0.895**	**0.912**	0.852	0.8335

Table 11. Comparison of classification performance of InfoGain, ReliefF, and WrapperEval based on NaiveBayes classification algorithm

Algorithm		Water1	Water2	Water3	Water4	Water5	Water6
InfoGain	Accuracy	0.9658(12)	**0.8772(10)**	0.8928(4)	0.9028(10)	0.8486(36)	0.8382(16)
	AUC	0.990	0.921	0.943	0.958	0.922	0.923
ReliefF	Accuracy	0.9564(12)	**0.8772(10)**	0.8967(10)	0.8926(8)	**0.8757(10)**	0.8460(12)
	AUC	0.992	0.927	0.947	0.962	0.930	0.9375
WrapperEval	Accuracy	**0.9848(7)**	0.8713(12)	**0.9220(11)**	**0.9182(15)**	0.8486(18)	**0.8674(14)**
	AUC	**0.995**	**0.937**	**0.968**	**0.974**	**0.955**	**0.9505**

Table 12. Comparison of classification performance of InfoGain, ReliefF, and WrapperEval based on RBF-SVM classification algorithm

Algorithm		Water1	Water2	Water3	Water4	Water5	Water6
InfoGain	Accuracy	0.9734(4)	0.7797(2)	0.8655(4)	0.7877(2)	0.6378(2)	0.6257(2)
	AUC	0.5	0.601	0.5	0.697	0.514	0.5045
ReliefF	Accuracy	0.9734(2)	0.7797(2)	0.8655(4)	0.7877(2)	0.6270(6)	0.6394(4)
	AUC	0.5	0.601	0.5	0.697	0.5	0.5
WrapperEval	Accuracy	**0.9772(1)**	**0.8421(8)**	**0.9025(5)**	**0.8696(7)**	**0.7730(7)**	**0.7602(9)**
	AUC	**0.571**	**0.742**	**0.674**	**0.825**	**0.751**	**0.6455**

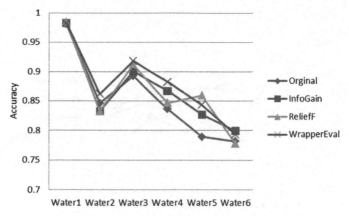

Fig. 2. Comparison of accuracy based on C4.5

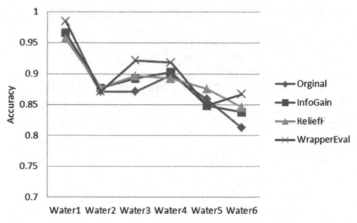

Fig. 3. Comparison of accuracy based on NaivBayes

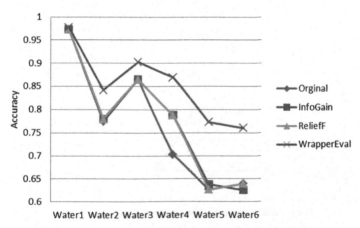

Fig. 4. Comparison of accuracy based on RBF-SVM

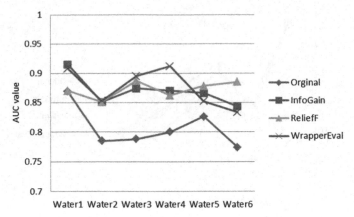

Fig. 5. Comparison of AUC based on C4.5

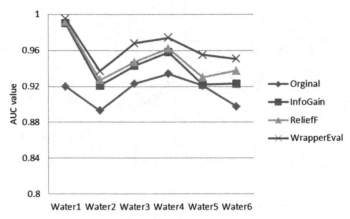

Fig. 6. Comparison of AUC based on NaivBayes

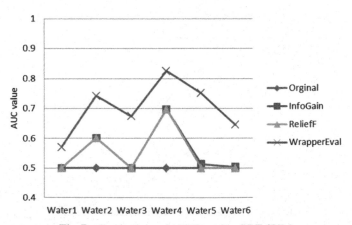

Fig. 7. Comparison of AUC based on RBF-SVM

5 Conclusion

Wastewater treatment fault diagnosis belongs to high-dimensional imbalanced data classification problem. In this study, we adopt feature selection algorithms to reduce the dimensionality of the data and improve the fault diagnosis of wastewater treatment equipment. Two filter-based feature selection methods and one wrapper-based feature selection method were used for experiments. Experimental results demonstrate that, compared with the original feature set classification data, the three feature selection algorithms have a significant improvement in the overall classification accuracy and AUC value. In addition, our experiments show that WrapperEval is better than InfoGain and ReliefF. The conclusions obtained have definite application value in the fault diagnosis of wastewater treatment equipment. Future work is to examine the distribution of samples while considering the feature attributes of the dataset and to change the spatial distribution of samples by sampling algorithm to further improve the classification performance of fault diagnosis of wastewater treatment equipment.

Acknowledgments. Research on this work was partially supported by the funds from Jiangxi Education Department (No. GJJ211919).

References

1. Speece, R.E.: Anaerobic biotechnology for industrial wastewater treatment. Environ. Sci. Technol. **17**(9), 416A (1983)
2. Shrestha, P.R., Shrestha, S.: Troubleshooting for improved bio P at Lundåkraverket wastewater treatment plant, Landskrona, Sweden (2008)
3. Villegas, T., Fuente, M.J., Sainz-Palmero, G.I.: Fault diagnosis in a wastewater treatment plant using dynamic Independent Component Analysis. In: Control and Automation. IEEE (2010)
4. Xu, Y., Deng, W., Chen, L.: Online fault diagnosis in wastewater treatment process by kernel-based weighted extreme learning machine. CIESC J. **67**, 3817–3825 (2016)
5. Tao, E.P., Shen, W.H., Liu, T.L., et al.: Fault diagnosis based on PCA for sensors of laboratorial wastewater treatment process. Chemom. Intell. Lab. Syst. **128**, 49–55 (2013)
6. Ribeiro, R., Pinheiro, C.C., Arriaga, T., et al.: Model based fault diagnosis for performance control of a decentralized wastewater treatment plant. Comput. Aided Chem. Eng. **33**, 691–696 (2014)
7. He, H., Garcia, E.A.: Learning from imbalanced data. IEEE Trans. Knowl. Data Eng. **21**(9), 1263–1284 (2009)
8. Yin, L., Ge, Y., Xiao, K., et al.: Feature selection for high-dimensional imbalanced data. Neurocomputing **105**(3), 3–11 (2013)
9. Shang, C., Li, M., Feng, S., Jiang, Q., Fan, J.: Feature selection via maximizing global information gain for text classification. Knowl. Based Syst. **54**, 298–309 (2013)
10. Guyon, I., Elisseeff, A.: An introduction to variable and feature selection. J. Mach. Learn. Res. **3**(6), 1157–1182 (2013)
11. Li, Y., Liang, X., Lin, J., et al.: Train axle bearing fault detection using a feature selection scheme based multi-scale morphological filter. Mech. Syst. Sig. Process. **101**, 435–448 (2018)
12. Hancer, E., Xue, B., Zhang, M.: Differential evolution for filter feature selection based on information theory and feature ranking. Knowl. Based Syst. **140**, 103–119 (2018)

13. Ma, L., Li, M., Gao, Y., et al.: A novel wrapper approach for feature selection in object-based image classification using polygon-based cross-validation. IEEE Geosci. Remote Sens. Lett. **14**(3), 409–413 (2017)
14. Tran, C.T., Zhang, M., Andreae, P., et al.: Improving performance for classification with incomplete data using wrapper-based feature selection. Evol. Intel. **9**(3), 1–14 (2016)
15. Ma, S., Song, X., Huang, J.: Supervised group Lasso with applications to microarray data analysis. BMC Bioinform. **8**(1), 1–17 (2017)
16. Mistry, K., Zhang, L., Neoh, S.C., et al.: A micro-GA embedded PSO feature selection approach to intelligent facial emotion recognition. IEEE Trans. Cybern. **47**(6), 1496–1509 (2017)
17. Salzberg, S.L.: Book review: C4.5: Programs for Machine Learning by J. Ross Quinlan. Morgan Kaufmann Publishers, Inc., 1993. Mach. Learn. **16**(3), 235–240 (1994). https://doi.org/10.1023/A:1022645310020
18. Guo, H., Zhou, L.: A framework for titled document categorization with modified multinomial NaiveBayes classifier. In: Alhajj, R., Gao, H., Li, J., Li, X., Zaïane, O.R. (eds.) ADMA 2007. LNCS (LNAI), vol. 4632, pp. 335–344. Springer, Heidelberg (2007). https://doi.org/10.1007/978-3-540-73871-8_31
19. Zhang, J., Ji, R., Yuan, X., et al.: Recognition of pest damage for cotton leaf based on RBF-SVM algorithm. Nongye Jixie Xuebao/Trans. Chin. Soc. Agric. Mach. **42**(8), 178–183 (2011)
20. UC Irvine Machine Learning Repository. http://archive.ics.uci.edu/ml/2009

Attention Adaptive Chinese Named Entity Recognition Based on Vocabulary Enhancement

Ping Zhao[1], Quansheng Dou[2](✉), and Ping Jiang[2]

[1] School of Information and Electronic Engineering, Shandong Technology and Business University, Yantai 264000, China
[2] School of Computer Science and Technology, Shandong Technology and Business University, Yantai 264000, China
li_dou@163.com

Abstract. To deal with the lack of word information in character vector embedding and the problem of Out-of-Vocabulary in Named Entity Recognition, an attention adaptive chinese named entity recognition (CNER) model based on vocabulary enhancement (ACVE) is proposed. The mechanism of potential information embedding is designed, which acquires word-level potential information by constructing semantic vectors, and the fusion embedding of character information and word-level information realizes the enhancement of semantic features; We also propose an attention mechanism for adaptive distribution, which adaptively adjusts the position of attention by introducing a dynamic scaling factor to obtain the attention distribution suitable for NER tasks. Experiments on a special field dataset with a large number of out-of-vocabulary (OOV) words show that, compared with state-of-the-art methods, our method is more effective and achieves better results.

Keywords: Chinese named entity recognition · Attention mechanism · Adaptive distribution · Scaling factor

1 Introduction

Named entity recognition (NER) is used to identify the entities with specific meanings in natural languages, such as names of people, places, organizations and proper nouns, etc. NER is related to the oriented natural language. Compared with English, Chinese characters, words, and grammatical structures are more complex, so it is more difficult to identify named entities. When there are OOV words in the text, the model is not sufficiently learned, which often leads to entity recognition errors due to ambiguity. What's more, in Chinese sentences, there are no natural separators between words, and the boundaries are not clear. CNER based on character-level embedding can avoid word segmentation errors, but this method cannot make full use of word information and the recognition effect is not satisfactory.

In this paper, the ACVE model is proposed with the following contributions: Potential information embedding (PIE) mechanism is implemented, which uses the new word

© IFIP International Federation for Information Processing 2022
Published by Springer Nature Switzerland AG 2022
Z. Shi et al. (Eds.): IIP 2022, IFIP AICT 643, pp. 399–406, 2022.
https://doi.org/10.1007/978-3-031-03948-5_32

discovery strategy to extract entities from related texts and expand the dictionary, to reduce the influence of OOV words on the performance of the model. The semantic vector of related words is obtained by matching characters and dictionary, which increases the utilization rate of potential information and helps the model to capture deep features; An attention mechanism for adaptive distribution (ADM) is implemented. By introducing a dynamic scaling factor, the model obtains the attention distribution suitable for NER tasks. It can dynamically adjust the attention position and adaptively focuses on the entity part.

2 Related Work

For the CNER problem, the most common deep learning method is to segment the input sentence with the CWS system and then apply the word-level sequence labeling model [1]. This framework makes the task easy to perform, but if the word segmentation is wrong, the sequence labeling will also cause errors. Luo and Yang [2] used multiple word segmentation results as additional features of the NER model, but they did not realize the incorrect segmentation problem caused by the CWS system. Zhang and Yang [3] proposed the Lattice LSTM model, which integrated the matching vocabulary information into the character sequence. Although it showed good results, there was a problem of information loss in the process of fusion. To reduce this problem, some scholars [4, 5] transformed the word information fusion process from chain structure to graph structure and encoded it with graph neural networks (GNN), and proposed cooperative graph network (CGN) and lexicon-based graph neural (LGN) model to enhance the ability of global information capture. Although CGN and LGN models can capture the sequence structure of NER, they usually required RNN as the underlying encoder to capture the sequence, and the model structure was more complex. Liu et al. [6] introduced several simple selection strategies to match words for the model from a pre-prepared dictionary. However, these strategies did not consider sentence context.

3 ACVE Model

3.1 Symbols and Definitions

Let $C = \{c_1, c_2, \cdots, c_m\}$, $W = \{w_1, w_2, \cdots, w_D\}$ represent Chinese characters and vocabulary sets respectively. $\forall w_i \in W$, $w_i = c_1 c_2 \cdots c_k$, $k \geq 1$, $c_j \in C$, $j = 1, \cdots, k$.

Suppose $S = w_1 w_2 \cdots w_N = c_1 c_2 \cdots c_T$ is a natural sentence, $w_i \in W$, $c_j \in C$, $N \leq T$. A segment of consecutive characters in S is called a substring of S, and all the substrings of S constitute a set:

$$\Omega_s = \{c_i c_{i+1} \cdots c_{i+h} | i \geq 1, \ i + h \leq T\} \tag{1}$$

Suppose z is a continuous character string in the corpus and all the character sets adjacent to the left and right of z in the corpus are respectively denoted as N_{left}^z and N_{right}^z, which are called the left and right-adjacent character set of z.

Definition 1. Suppose S is a natural sentence, Ω_s is the set of S substrings, for $\forall x, y \in \Omega_s$, let $x = c_k \cdots c_{k+h}$ and $y = c_j \cdots c_{j+l}$. If $k + h < j$ or $j + l < k$, then the substrings x and y are not intersected, i.e. $x \cap y = \emptyset$.

Definition 2. Based on Definition 1, x, y are two substrings of S and $x \cap y = \emptyset$, $MI(x, y)$ called the mutual information (MI) of x and y.

$$MI(x, y) = \log_2 \frac{p(x, y)}{p(x)p(y)} \tag{2}$$

Where $p(x)$ and $p(y)$ represent the probability for x and y appearing in the corpus separately, and $p(x, y)$ is the probability for x and y simultaneously appearing in the corpus.

Definition 3. Let z be a continuous string in the corpus, N_{left}^z and N_{right}^z be the left and right adjacent character sets of the string z respectively. Left and right adjacency entropy of substring z is calculated in formula (3), where $p(c|z)$ represents the conditional probability that c is the left and right adjacent characters of the string z.

$$BE_L(z) = - \sum_{c \in N_{left}^w} p(c|z) \log p(c|z) \; BE_R(z) = - \sum_{c \in N_{right}^w} p(c|z) \log p(c|z) \tag{3}$$

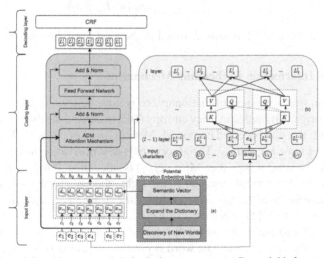

Fig. 1. ACVE model architecture mainly includes two parts: (a) Potential information embedding mechanism. (b) Attention mechanism of adaptive distribution.

3.2 Overall Architecture

The ACVE model is divided into three layers, including the input layer, encoding layer, and decoding layer, as shown in Fig. 1. Given statement $S = c_1 c_2 \cdots c_T, c_i \in C$,

$i = 1, \cdots, T$. The input layer obtains the word embedding vector $X = \{x_{c_1}, \cdots, x_{c_T}\}$ corresponding to the sentence S through BERT [7]. For $\forall c_i \in S$, the corresponding semantic vector d_{c_i} is generated by the PIE mechanism and $d_{c_i} = \text{PIE}(c_i)$. The semantic vector d_{c_i} contains the word-level potential information related to the character. The word embedding vector x_{c_i} is merged with the semantic vector d_{c_i} to obtain the embedding vector h_i. The formula is as follows:

$$h_i = x_{c_i} + W_{c_i} d_{c_i} \tag{4}$$

Matrix $H \in \mathbb{R}^{T \times H_c}$ is denoted as $H = \{h_1, \cdots, h_T\}$. The matrix H contains character features and word-level information. The next step will be to extract features of H through the coding layer. The coding layer uses a Transformer as the encoder, and an attention mechanism of adaptive distribution (ADM) is proposed based on this encoder. ADM attention mechanism introduces a scaling factor to adjust the probability distribution of the output. Matrix $H = \{h_1, \cdots, h_T\}$ passes through the encoding layer to get the hidden output $L^l = \{L_1^l, \cdots, L_T^l\}$. The matrix L^l contains the local and global features of the input characters. The hidden output L^l is sent to CRF. The calculation is shown in formula (5). The above formula $w_k \in \mathbb{R}^{H_c}$ and b_k are trainable parameters specific to the k - th label and r is the number of different NER labels.

$$p(k|c_i) = \frac{\exp(w_k^T L_i^l + b_k)}{\sum_{j \in \{1, \ldots, r\}} \exp(w_j^T L_i^l + b_j)} \tag{5}$$

The PIE and ADM mechanisms involved in the model will be introduced below.

3.3   Potential Information Embedding Mechanism

PIE mechanism needs the help of dictionary, so we use new word discovery based on mutual information (MI) and adjacency entropy (BE) to expand the dictionary. The input of the algorithm is a preprocessed corpus M, $M = c_1, \cdots, c_N, c_j \in C$. The MI and BE threshold are set to be MI_{th}, BE_{th}. The algorithm is described as follows.

If the current character is c_i, then $\text{MI}(c_i, c_{i+1})$ is calculated. If $\text{MI}(c_i, c_{i+1})$ is greater than MI_{th}, connect the current character to the right adjacent character to form a string $c_i c_{i+1}$, and calculate the $\text{MI}(c_i c_{i+1}, c_{i+2})$ value of the string $c_i c_{i+1}$ and the right adjacent character c_{i+2} until the MI between the string $c_i c_{i+1} \cdots c_k$ and c_{k+1} is less than the MI_{th}, and stop extending to the right and mark $c_i c_{i+1} \cdots c_k$ as a candidate. Filter candidate words by BE. If the current candidate word is $c_i c_{i+1} \cdots c_k$, then $\text{BE}_L(c_i c_{i+1} \cdots c_k)$ and $\text{BE}_R(c_i c_{i+1} \cdots c_k)$ of the $c_i c_{i+1} \cdots c_k$ are calculated. If both are greater than BE_{th}, the candidate word is retained, otherwise it is deleted. A new word set *CanList* is obtained by the algorithm. We remove the common words from the jieba8 dictionary and merge the remaining words with the *CanList* to obtain dictionary ε_{ent}. If $\exists wd \in \varepsilon_{ent}$ and c_i is at the beginning, middle or end of wd, set the first, second, or third component of semantic vector d_{c_i} to be 1, otherwise 0. If there is no word containing c_i in ε_{ent}, set the fourth component of d_{c_i} to be 1, otherwise 0. The purpose of the PIE mechanism is to obtain a semantic vector d_{c_i}. It contains word-level potential information related to the character.

3.4 Attention Mechanism of Adaptive Distribution

For scaled dot-product attention, Yan [8] had proved that this attention had a poor effect on NER. Therefore, we designed an ADM attention mechanism, which adjusted the probability distribution by introducing a dynamic scaling factor to prevent the inner product from being too large and adaptively weighted the position of the attention.

We used the same attention transformation as in literature [9] to achieve entity enhancement. Given the hidden representation of a sequence $\left\{ L_1^{l-1}, \cdots, L_T^{l-1} \right\}$ for the $(l-1)$th layer and packed together as the matrix $\{L_t^{l-1}\}_{t=1}^T \in \mathbb{R}^{T \times H_c}$. The query matrix $Q^l = \left\{ q_t^l \right\}_{t=1}^T$ is obtained by multiplying the matrix $\{L_t^{l-1}\}_{t=1}^T$ by $W_{L,q}^l$. The key matrix $K^l = \left\{ k_t^l \right\}_{t=1}^T$ and value matrix $V^l = \left\{ v_t^l \right\}_{t=1}^T$ of the lth layer of the attention mechanism is calculated as follows formula (6), where $W_{L,q}^l, W_{L,k}^l, W_{L,v}^l \in \mathbb{R}^{T \times H_c}$ is the trainable parameter of lth layer and $W_{e,k}^l, W_{e,v}^l \in \mathbb{R}^{H_e \times H_c}$ is the trainable parameter of related entities. E_{ent} is an entity embedded query table.

The probability distribution of Softmax output is adjusted by the dynamically learnable scaling factor η. A set of entity embedding $\{E_{ent}[e_1], \cdots, E_{ent}[e_l]\}$ is represented by $e \in \mathbb{R}^{T \times H_e}$ integration, and the attention score of the i - th character in the lth layer is calculated as shown in formula (7), where $w_1 \in \mathbb{R}^{H_c}, \delta \in \mathbb{R}$ is a trainable parameter.

$$k_t^l = \begin{cases} L_t^{l-1\,\mathrm{T}} W_{L,k}^l & \text{if } e_t = 0, \\ \frac{1}{2}(L_t^{l-1\,\mathrm{T}} W_{L,k}^l + E_{ent}^{\mathrm{T}}[e_t] W_{e,k}^l) & \text{else;} \end{cases} \quad v_t^l = \begin{cases} L_t^{l-1\,\mathrm{T}} W_{L,v}^l & \text{if } e_t = 0, \\ \frac{1}{2}(L_t^{l-1\,\mathrm{T}} W_{L,v}^l + E_{ent}^{\mathrm{T}}[e_t] W_{e,v}^l) & \text{else;} \end{cases} \tag{6}$$

$$S_i^l = softmax\left\{ \frac{q_i^l K^{l\,\mathrm{T}}}{\sqrt{\eta}} \right\} = softmax\left\{ \frac{q_i^l (L^{l-1} W_{L,k}^l + e W_{e,k}^l)^{\mathrm{T}}}{2\sqrt{\eta}} \right\} \tag{7}$$

$$\eta = \min(ReLu(w_1 L^{l-1\,\mathrm{T}} + \delta), \sqrt{H_c/n}) + 1; \tag{8}$$

In formula (8), the dynamic scaling factor η linearly activates the matrix L^{l-1} containing feature information through the $ReLU$ function. The output value is in the range of $[0, \infty)$ and η is bounded in the range of $\left[1, 1 + \sqrt{H_c/n}\right]$. By using the sparse activation of the $ReLU$ function, the scaling factor can be adjusted without increasing the computational cost.

4 Experiments

4.1 Experimental Setup

This article conducts experiments on 4 datasets, including Novel, Medicine (CCKS2018), Weibo, and Resume dataset. "The Legend of the Condor Heroes" is selected as the novel corpus. Weibo dataset contains four types of entities, all entities are also divided into named entities (NE) and generic entities (NM). The hyperparameter settings are as follows: coding layers $l = 12$, self-attention $A = 12$, character hiding size $H_c = 768$, entity hiding size $H_e = 64$, initial learning rate $3e^{-5}$, epoch number 3, max sentence length 200, and batch size 32.

4.2 Ablation Study

To verify the effectiveness of PIE and ADM, we use the LSTM+CRF as the baseline model and carried out experiments on Weibo and Novel datasets. By adding PIE and ADM mechanisms to the baseline model, the effectiveness of the two structures is proved step by step. The experimental results of the control group are shown in Table 1.

On the Weibo dataset, after Step1"+PIE" ("+" means adding a model), compared with the baseline, the F1 value increased by 7.5%, and the recall rate increased by 3.84%. When Step2 "+ADM" is completed, compared with the baseline, the recall rate increased by 9.14%, and the F1 value increased by 8.2%. On the Novel dataset, after Step1"+PIE", the F1 value increased by 6.68%, and the recall rate increased by 1.9%. When Step2 "+ADM" is completed, compared with the baseline, the F1 value increases by 8.09%, the recall rate increases by 4.24%. From the perspective of decomposition, Step1 "+PIE" has a greater effect on improving the F1 value, and step2 "+ADM" is very important for improving the recall rate. Therefore, the two parts of PIE and ADM are complementary.

Table 1. Ablation experiment results of WeiboNER dataset and MSRA dataset.

Models	Weibo			Novel		
	P	R	F1	P	R	F1
Character embedding (baseline)	69.45	58.47	61.2 ± 0.42	66.45	60.23	59.10 ± 0.21
+Potential Information Embedding	70.10	62.31	68.7 ± 0.34	70.35	62.13	65.78 ± 0.04
+Adaptive Distribution Selection	72.07	67.61	69.4 ± 0.21	68.14	64.47	67.19 ± 0.24
FWPI+BERT	72.62	70.13	71.5 ± 0.20	77.75	73.67	75.26 ± 0.12

Table 2. Performance comparison table of different models.

Models	Medicine	Novel	Resume	NE	NM	Overall
Char-based (LSTM) [10]	84.71	59.11	92.41	50.25	55.29	52.77
BiLSTM+CRF [11]	85.09	62.74	93.26	53.95	62.63	58.96
Lattice LSTM [3]	87.90	63.89	94.46	58.04	61.25	59.79
FWPI	92.21	72.43	95.10	71.21	69.45	69.33

Table 3. Experimental results of F1 value of various attention mechanisms.

Models	Attention	Novel	Weibo	Models	Attention	Novel	Weibo
NER-only	Soft [11]	62.70	59.15	Joint	Soft [11]	70.05	69.72
	Self+Scaled [3]	63.93	60.12		Self+Scaled [3]	70.20	69.98
	Self+Uscaled [6]	64.73	61.54		Self+Uscaled [6]	71.09	70.14
	ADM	65.98	62.48		ADM	72.43	71.33

4.3 Comparison with Existing Methods

We conducted experiments on the four datasets mentioned above and compared the experimental results with the current common models. The experimental results are listed in Table 2. Although the BiLSTM+CRF model shows good results on the Resume dataset, it has not made significant improvements on the Novel and Weibo corpus. In addition to word segmentation errors on social media, another important reason is that the semantic expression of colloquial texts limits their performance. In contrast, our model has better advantages and performance in adapting to spoken texts. The ACVE model has a significant increase in the F1 value on the Novel and Weibo datasets.

4.4 Verification of Effectiveness of ADM Attention Mechanism

To verify the effectiveness of the ADM, Weibo and Novel datasets are selected for experiments, and BiLSTM+CRF(NER-only) and FWPI-ADM(Joint) are used as baseline models; Based on the NER-only and Joint models, various attention mechanisms are added to the experiment. The experimental results are shown in Table 3. Experimental results show that the Joint model is always better than the NER-only model. In the NER-only model, the recognition effect of ADM is better than that of Self+Scaled and Self+Unscaled. For all experiments, Self+Unscaled attention produced a better F1 value than Self+Scaled attention, which indicated that clear attention distribution was helpful to the NER task. The ADM attention mechanism adds a dynamic scaling factor based on Self+Unscaled attention, and its value is also increased by about 1% on the basis of Self+Unscaled attention, which proves the effectiveness of the ADM.

5 Conclusions

This paper proposed an ACVE model integrated with potential information. The PIE mechanism provides word-level deep features, and the semantic vector and character embedding vector are merged as the input layer to realize the enhancement of information features; The ADM mechanism obtains an attention distribution suitable for CNER and extracts entity features without increasing calculation cost.

References

1. He, H., Sun, X.: A unified model for cross-domain and semi-supervised named entity recognition in chinese social media. In: Proceedings of the AAAI Conference on Artificial Intelligence, vol. 31, no. 1 (2017)
2. Luo, W., Yang, F.: An empirical study of automatic chinese word segmentation for spoken language understanding and named entity recognition. In Proceedings of the 2016 Conference of the North American Chapter of the Association for Computational Linguistics: Human Language Technologies, pp. 238–248 (2016)
3. Zhang, Y., Yang, J.: Chinese NER using lattice LSTM. In: Proceedings of the 56th Annual Meeting of the Association for Computational Linguistics (Volume 1: Long Papers), vol. 1, pp. 1554–1564 (2018)
4. Sui, D., Chen, Y., Liu, K., Zhao, J., Liu, S.: Leverage lexical knowledge for chinese named entity recognition via collaborative graph network. In: Proceedings of the 2019 Conference on Empirical Methods in Natural Language Processing and the 9th International Joint Conference on Natural Language Processing EMNLP-IJCNLP, pp. 3828–3838 (2019)

5. Gui, T., Zou, Y., Zhang, Q.: A lexicon-based graph neural network for Chinese NER. In: Proceedings of the 2019 Conference on Empirical Methods in Natural Language Processing and the 9th International Joint Conference on Natural Language Processing (EMNLP-IJCNLP), pp. 1040–1050 (2019)
6. Liu, W., Xu, T., Xu, Q., Song, J., Zu, Y.: An encoding strategy based word character LSTM for Chinese NER. In: Proceedings of the 2019 Conference of the North American Chapter of the Association for Computational Linguistics: Human Language Technologies, pp. 2379–2389 (2019)
7. Devlin, J., et al.: BERT: pre-training of deep bidirectional transformers for language understanding. In: Proceedings of the 2019 Conference of the North American Chapter of the Association for Computational Linguistics: Human Language Technologies, Volume 1 (Long and Short Papers), vol. 2019, pp. 4171–4186 (2019)
8. Yan, H., Deng, B., Li, X., Qiu, X.: TENER: adapting transformer encoder for named entity recognition. arXiv Preprint arXiv:1911.04474 (2019)
9. Jia, C., Shi, Y., Yang, Q., Zhang, Y.: Entity enhanced BERT pre-training for Chinese NER. In: Proceedings of the 2020 Conference on Empirical Methods in Natural Language Processing (EMNLP), November 2020, pp. 6384–6396 (2020)
10. Lample, G., et al.: Neural architectures for named entity recognition. In: 2016 Conference of the North American Chapter of the Association for Computational Linguistics: Human Language Technologies, NAACL HLT 2016-Proceedings of the Conference, pp. 260–270 (2016)
11. Huang, Z., Xu, W., Yu, K.: Bidirectional LSTM-CRF models for sequence tagging. arXiv preprint arXiv:1508.01991 (2015)

Image Processing

A HEp-2 Cell Image Classification Model Based on Deep Residual Shrinkage Network Combined with Dilated Convolution

Chen Wang[1,2](✉), Tao He[2], Jiansheng Liu[2], Dapeng Li[2], and Yingyou Wen[1,2]

[1] Northeastern University, Shenyang 110004, China
wangchen-neu@neusoft.com
[2] Neusoft Research, Shenyang 110179, Liaoning, China
het@neusoft.com

Abstract. Detection of antinuclear antibodies (ANA) in human epithelial cells (HEp-2) is a common method for the diagnosis of autoimmune diseases. The recognition of fluorescence images of human epithelial cells obtained using Indirect Immunofluorescence (IIF) is a key step in the classification of ANA. To address the problems of low efficiency and high labor intensity caused by manual evaluation methods, a HEp-2 cell fluorescent image classification model based on the depth residual shrinkage network combined with dilated convolution is proposed. First, The model accomplish feature extraction by expanding the field of sensation through dilated convolution. Secondly, a 50-layer deep residual network is build, and each residual module embeds a soft threshold learning sub-network to shrink the output data of the original residual module by the automatically learned soft threshold to achieve the purpose of noise removal. Finally, the multi-scale feature fusion module and fusion of features at different scales are used to complete the classification of HEp-2 cell. Experiments show that this model has good performance and is superior to other depth neural network methods.

Keywords: Deep residual shrinkage network · Soft threshold · ANA · HEp-2

1 Introduction

Autoimmune disease refers to the immune system mistakenly attacking healthy cells in human tissues. In this case, the body will release various antibodies, one of which is antinuclear antibody (ANA). The specificity of the type of antinuclear antibody varies with different autoimmune diseases. Therefore, the identification of ANA can be used as a means to assist medical treatment and evaluate the degree of damage in patients, which has important medical value. Indirect immunofluorescence (IIF) [1] is the most commonly used method to detect ANAs. IIF imaging has good specificity and sensitivity. Recognition of IIF fluorescence images can classify different antinuclear antibody in patients' serum, it plays an important role in the diagnosis of specific autoimmune diseases.

© IFIP International Federation for Information Processing 2022
Published by Springer Nature Switzerland AG 2022
Z. Shi et al. (Eds.): IIP 2022, IFIP AICT 643, pp. 409–418, 2022.
https://doi.org/10.1007/978-3-031-03948-5_33

According to the cell nuclear fluorescence imaging features, ANA are usually divided into 9 categories as shown in Fig. 1: (1) cytoplasmic granular type, (2) cytoplasmic fibrous type, (3) nuclear dot type, (4) nuclear granular type, (5) nuclear membrane type, (6) nucleolar type, (7) homogeneous type, (8) centromere type and (9) negative control type. Each type of picture has great similarity in morphology, which makes it difficult to extract picture features.

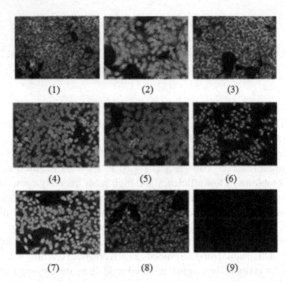

Fig. 1. ANA categories according to the cell nuclear fluorescence imaging features

The traditional HEp-2 cell image recognition [2, 3] method not only requires experienced doctors to spend a lot of time on manual discrimination, but also different doctors' judgment methods for cell types are relatively subjective, and different doctors' judgments will be inconsistent [4]. Therefore, building an automatic and reliable HEp-2 image recognition model has become an important research topic.

2   HEp-2 Cell Classification

At present, in-depth research has been carried out in the field of HEp-2 cell classification, especially convolutional neural network is more widely used in this field. Manju C [5] proposed an improved convolutional neural network to effectively classify HEp-2 cells by using the optimization concept. Rahmans [6] reviewed the existing Hep-2 cell image classification methods based on deep learning, and analyzed the core idea, remarkable achievements, key advantages and disadvantages of each method. Foggia [7] comprehensively summarized the development of HEp-2 cell classification methods. Hobson [8] proposed classification methods on large datasets, and analyzed algorithms and their performance at different levels of cells and samples. Manivannan [9] extracted root sieve features and multi-resolution local patterns from HEp-2 cell images and classified them according to the set of support vector machines. Lei [10] proposed a cross modal transfer learning strategy to automatically identify HEp-2 cells. Xie [11] designed a deep monitoring network based on ResNet, which can directly guide the training of the upper and lower layers of the network and offset the impact of unstable gradient changes on the training process. However, most of the existing HEp-2 cell recognition methods are for the processing of single cell samples, and the actual demand is often the whole picture containing many different forms. Therefore, this paper proposes a picture level HEp-2 image recognition model based on deep residual shrinkage network combined with dilated convolution (DRSN-DC). This model uses the ResNet model as the base network, extracts features by expanding the perceptual field through dilated convolution [12], removes noise and redundant data using a deep residual shrinkage network [13], and finally goes through a multi-scale [14] feature fusion module and fuses features from different scales to improve the classification accuracy.

3 HEp-2 Image Classification Model Based on DRSN-DC

3.1 Model Architecture

The HEp-2 classification model proposed in this paper mainly consists of dilated convolution module, depth residual shrinkage module and multi-scale feature fusion module. The dilated convolution module automatically extracts feature information at different scales in the hep-2 cell images by using a dilated convolution network with expansion rates of 1, 2 and 3, respectively, through three convolution operations with different sensory fields. The deep residual shrinkage module removes noise and redundant data from the features extracted by the dilated convolution network through soft thresholding to enhance the weights of effective features and improve the classification accuracy of hep-2 cell images. The multi-scale feature fusion module takes the obtained multi-scale feature information, performs feature fusion, and outputs the classification results. The model architecture is shown in Fig. 2.

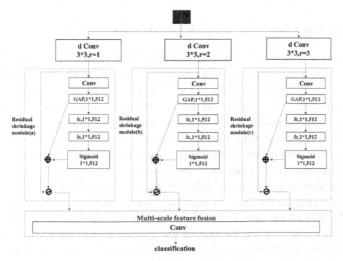

Fig. 2. Model architecture

3.2 Dilated Convolution Network Construction

Traditional convolutional neural networks have better performance in image classification, but they also have some drawbacks. For example, although the pooling operation can increase the perceptual field, it can lead to information loss. Dilated convolution defines the spacing of the convolution kernel processing data values during the convolution operation by introducing the expansion rate in the convolution layer, thus increasing the perceptual field, which can improve the segmentation effect of small object recognition in tasks such as target detection and semantic segmentation. HEp-2 cell fluorescence images have the characteristics of small targets, dense distribution and irregular distribution, etc. With the increase of the number of layers in the network, the local information is lost during the down sampling process, resulting in small cells cannot be recognized. The dilated convolution network can increase the perceptual field of feature extraction to capture more detailed features without losing local information. In this paper, three dilated convolutional networks with kernel of 3 * 3 and dilation rate r of 1, 2, and 3 are used, as shown in Fig. 3.

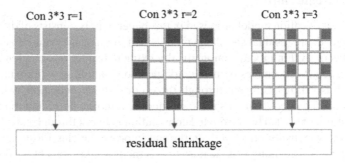

Fig. 3. Three dilated convolutional networks with kernel of 3 * 3

3.3 Deep Residual Learning Network Construction

Deep residual learning [15] is a very effective method to solve the problem of network degradation. This method does not directly use several layers of networks to fit the desired actual mapping relationship, but to fit a residual mapping. This way makes the output change have a greater effect on the adjustment of weight, so it is easier to train.

This paper uses a 50 layer depth residual network, and its overall network structure is shown in Fig. 4. This network includes 3-layer residual learning units, including three residual units that output 256 feature maps, four residual units that output 512 feature maps, six residual units that output 1024 feature maps, and three residual units that output 2048 feature maps. In the middle 3 × 3 use before and after convolution 1 × 1, the purpose is to reduce the dimension and reduce the amount of calculation.

For the layers with the same size of the output feature map, there are the same number of convolution kernels. When the size of the feature map is halved, it is necessary to double the number of filters to maintain the time complexity of each layer. The output of the network includes a global mean pooling layer and a fully connected layers (FC) containing 1000 neurons, which are classified by softmax.

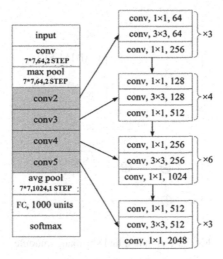

Fig. 4. Depth residual network structure

3.4 Deep Residual Shrinkage Network Construction

In a HEp-2 cell fluorescence image, only part of the cell morphology and connection can reflect the type of the ANA, while other part of the cells cannot be used as the basis for category determination and be seen as noise. How to remove noise and redundant data has become an important problem affecting the performance of the model.

Soft threshold is the most commonly used technology in signal denoising algorithm. It sets the feature of signal smaller than a certain threshold to 0. The traditional method of setting soft threshold needs experts in the business field to select an appropriate soft threshold through continuous debugging according to their professional knowledge. This method has no learning ability and lack of scalability. Therefore, combining soft threshold learning and depth residual network, through automatic learning and adjustment, a way to effectively eliminate noise information and construct high discriminant features is formed, and its transformation formula is as follows:

$$y = \begin{cases} x - \tau & x > \tau \\ 0 & -\tau \leq x \leq \tau \\ x + \tau & x < -\tau \end{cases} \quad (1)$$

Where x is the input characteristic and y is the output characteristic, τ is a positive threshold. After the feature is calculated, the absolute value is less than τ all features will be set to 0, and features with an absolute value greater than τ shrink toward the center, so it is called depth residual shrinkage network. The soft threshold does not set

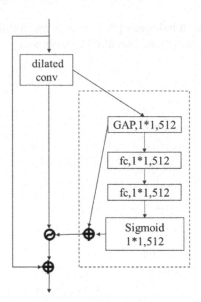

Fig. 5. Depth residual shrinkage module

the negative value to 0 like the ReLu activation function, which can retain useful negative value characteristics. A depth residual shrinkage module structure is shown in Fig. 5.

The depth residual shrinkage network is an improvement of the depth residual network. The soft threshold is inserted into the residual learning unit as a nonlinear transformation layer. The soft threshold learning module is shown in the dotted box in Fig. 5. In this module, firstly, the absolute value of the last layer network output of the residual unit is global average pooling (GAP) to obtain a one-dimensional vector with the same number of convolution kernels as the previous layer. Input the one-dimensional vector into the two-layer fully connected network, apply a sigmoid function at the end of the two-layer FC network, and normalize the scaling parameters.

3.5 Multi-scale Feature Fusion

The semantic features extracted from small target images in the shallow network are weak. Due to the small and concentrated targets in hEp-2 cell fluorescence images, if the traditional target detection and classification model is used to obtain strong semantic features, the feature maps can only be output at the last layer to complete the classification of the images. However, the last layer is the down sampling process, which will cause the HEp-2 cell fluorescence images with small target to have less effective information on the last feature map, resulting in the loss of local information, thus leading to the degradation of recognition and classification accuracy. Multi-scale feature fusion solves the above problems well. In this paper, the model fuses the features extracted after convolution of three different scales of dilated convolution and features after removing noise and redundant data, and uses Concatenate to stitch the multi-channel extracted feature maps into a complete feature map, and then completes the cell image classification. The multi-scale feature fusion module is shown in Fig. 6.

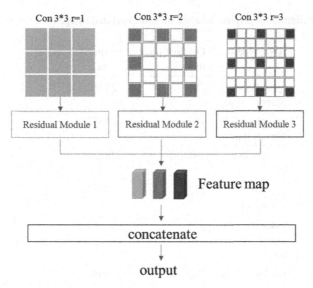

Fig. 6. The multi-scale feature fusion module

4   Test Results and Analysis

The hardware environment for the model experiments in this paper is a Dell R740 server with two NVIDIA Tesla P40 GPU cards mounted; the deep learning framework uses TensorFlow version 1.12.0.

4.1   Experimental Data Set

Due to the cumbersome picture acquisition process, laboratory doctors need to take pictures manually under the microscope, resulting in a scarcity of each type of HEp-2 cell fluorescence image, which is far from meeting the requirements of in-depth learning. It is necessary to enhance the training data set and test data set of HEp-2 cell images through technical means, In order to expand the sample data set and enhance the data characteristics. In order to facilitate training, the original image is cut to 2 24 × 224 pixel size.

According to the characteristics of HEp-2 cell fluorescence image imaging and application, rotation and flip are selected for expansion. (1) With the center of the picture as the origin, rotate the picture clockwise for 5°, which can be rotated 72 times, that is, 72 pictures with the same label are derived from one picture; (2) While rotating, flip with the y-axis as the centerline to double the amount of data.

The dataset used in this paper is from the real data of the hospital LIS system, and the annotation and review of the cytofluorescence images are done by professional doctors. Since the number of samples was not sufficient, some methods such as rotation and flip were used to expand the dataset. After removing some unusable data, the distribution of original image data and expanded image data for each ANA type is shown in Table 1.

Table 1. Distribution of original image data and expanded image data for each ANA type

ANA type	Original image data	Expanded image data
cytoplasmic granular type	208	29952
cytoplasmic fibrous type	183	26352
nuclear dot type	196	28224
nuclear granular type	213	30672
nuclear membrane type	223	32112
nucleolar type	209	30096
homogeneous type	188	27072
centromere type	215	30960
negative control type	220	31680

4.2 Results and Analysis

The error rate is the ratio of the number of misclassified samples to the total number of samples. The curves in Fig. 7 show how the overall error rate of the deep learning network constructed in this paper varies with the number of iterations.

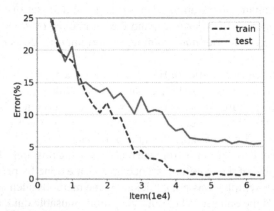

Fig. 7. The error rate of the training set and the test set

From the results, it can be seen that using the deep residual shrinkage network, the error rate of the training set and the test set can decrease quickly with the number of iterations, which better solves the network degradation problem. In this paper, P, R and F_1 score are used to evaluate the performance of the proposed model, and Fig. 8 shows the F_1 score for each type of ANA recognition on the test image dataset.

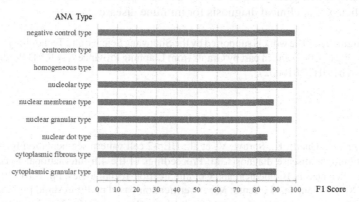

Fig. 8. F_1 score for each type of ANA recognition on the test image dataset

The proposed recognition models in this paper were compared with AlexNet, GoogLeNet, VGGNet and ResNet models on the same dataset for experiments, and the ANA recognition performance of each model is shown in Table 2.

Table 2. ANA recognition performance of each model

Model	P	R	F_1
AlexNet	0.7081	0.7233	0.7156
GoogLeNet	0.8883	0.7759	0.8283
VGG-19	0.7912	0.8331	0.8116
Resnet50	0.8477	0.8699	0.8587
DRSN-DC	**0.9310**	**0.9451**	**0.9282**

By comparing with other models experimentally, the F1 score of the model proposed in this paper reaches 93%, which is about 7% better than the residual network with the same depth, and about 10% better than the F_1 scores of GoogLeNet and VGG-19, showing a significant improvement in performance.

5 Conclusion

In this paper, we propose a HEp-2 cell image classification model based on deep residual shrinkage network combined with dilated convolution. The model embeds soft thresholds as trainable systolic functions into the deep residual network, expands sensory field and accomplish feature extraction by dilated convolution, removes noise and redundant data by using deep residual shrinkage network, and finally fuses features of different scales. Experiments show that the model in this paper outperforms classical CNN networks such as GoogLeNet and Resnet50 in HEp-2 cell fluorescence image recognition and ANA classification, which greatly improves the speed of clinical fluorescence image analysis and the efficiency of clinical diagnosis for immune diseases.

Acknowledgments. The work is supported by the Shenyang Science and Technology Plan Project (Grant Nos. 2021RC003) and in part by Grants from Liaoning Province Key R&D Program Project (Grant Nos. 2019JH2/10100027).

References

1. Creemers, C., Guerti, K., Spruyt, V., et al.: HEp-2 cell pattern segmentation for the support of autoimmune disease diagnosis. In: Proceedings of the 4th International Symposium on Applied Sciences in Biomedical and Communication Technologies, pp. 1001–1015 (2011)
2. Jiang, X., Percannella, G., Vento, M.: A verification-based multithreshold probing approach to HEp-2 cell segmentation. Comput. Anal. Images Patterns 5(10), 266–276 (2015)
3. Percannella, G., Soda, P., Vento, M.: A classification-based approach to segment HEp-2 cells. In: Computer-Based Medical Systems International Symposium on IEEE, pp. 956–955 (2012)
4. Cheng, C.C., Taur, J.S., Hsieh, T.Y., et al.: Segmentation of anti-nuclear antibody images based on the watershed approach. In: IEEE Conference on Industrial Electronics and Applications, pp. 1695–1700 (2010)
5. Manju, C.C., Jose, M.V.: HEp-2 cell classification by adaptive convolutional layer based convolutional neural network. Biomed. Eng. Appl. Basis Commun. **31**, 1950041 (2019)
6. Rahman, S., Wang, L., Sun, C., et al.: Deep learning based HEp-2 image classification: a comprehensive review. Med. Image Anal. **65**, 101764 (2020)
7. Foggia, P., Percannella, G., Saggese, A., et al.: Pattern recognition in stained HEp-2 cells. Pattern Recogn. **47**(7), 2305–2314 (2014)
8. Hobson, P., Lovell, B., Percannella, G., et al.: Benchmarking human epithelial type 2 interphase cells classification methods on a very large dataset. Artif. Intel. Med. **65**(3), 239–250 (2015)
9. Manivannan, S., Li, W., Akbar, S., et al.: An automated pattern recognition system for classifying indirect immunofluorescence images of HEp-2 cells and specimens. Pattern Recogn. **5**(51), 12–26 (2016)
10. Lei, H., Han, T., Huang, W., et al.: Cross-modal transfer learning for HEp-2 cell classification based on deep residual network. In: 2017 IEEE International Symposium on Multimedia, pp. 465–468 (2017)
11. Xie, H., He, Y., Lei, H., et al.: Deeply supervised residual network for HEp-2 cell classification. In: 2018 24th International Conference on Pattern Recognition (ICPR), Beijing, pp. 699–703(2018)
12. Yu, F., Koltun, V.: Multi-scale context aggregation by dilated convolutions (2016)
13. Zhao, M., Zhong, S., Fu, X., et al.: Deep residual shrinkage networks for fault diagnosis. IEEE Trans. Ind. Inf. **16**, 4681–4690 (2020)
14. Wang, P., Song, L., Guo, X., Wang, H., Cui, L.: A high-stability diagnosis model based on a multiscale feature fusion convolutional neural network. IEEE Trans. Instrum. Measur. **70**, 1–9 (2021). https://doi.org/10.1109/TIM.2021.3102745
15. He, K., Zhang, X., Ren, S., et al.: Deep residual learning for image recognition. IEEE (2016)

A Method on Online Learning Video Recommendation Method Based on Knowledge Graph

Xin Chen[1]([✉]) [iD], Yuhong Sun[1] [iD], Tong Zhou[2]([✉]) [iD], Qingtian Zeng[1] [iD], and Huafang Qi[1] [iD]

[1] College of Computer Science and Engineering, Shandong University of Science and Technology, Qingdao 266590, People's Republic of China
`xxwar@163.com`
[2] College of Civil Engineering and Architecture, Shandong University of Science and Technology, Qingdao 266590, People's Republic of China
`768279353@qq.com`

Abstract. The MOOC platforms usually recommend online course resources to users among a large number of courses on platform whose users are almost college students or students by selves. However, the entire course as the recommendation results may ignore student interests in some specific knowledge points, and so may reduce student learning interests. The recommendation not courses but online learning videos of course are researched. The connection between a single learning video and other entities is considered to construct learning video knowledge graph. Based on the end-to-end deep learning framework, a convolutional neural network KGCN-LV is applied in learning videos recommendation, which is integrated learning video knowledge graph. Experimental results on public data set MOOCCube show that the learning video recommendation method based on knowledge graph is up to 5% better than the traditional collaborative filtering method. The recommendation performance is effectively improved, and the recommendation effect is interpretable.

Keywords: Recommendation system · Knowledge graph · Convolutional neural network · Learning video

1 Introduction

1.1 A Subsection Sample

The popularity and development of MOOC platforms (such as Xuetang X, Chinese University MOOC, iCourse, etc.) has promoted development to Online education. Students usually study by the way of online learning on Internet especially during the COVID-19 pandemic which is gradually becoming a popular education mode. Faced with massive online course resources, it becomes extremely difficult for students to choose the courses

© IFIP International Federation for Information Processing 2022
Published by Springer Nature Switzerland AG 2022
Z. Shi et al. (Eds.): IIP 2022, IFIP AICT 643, pp. 419–430, 2022.
https://doi.org/10.1007/978-3-031-03948-5_34

they need, which also reduces student interests in learning. The current overall course completion rate for MOOC platforms is less than 5%. In order to capture and understand student interests on the MOOC platforms, researchers have done a lot of work, including course recommendation [1], behavior prediction [2], user intention understanding [3], etc. In these works, the MOOC platform applies a recommendation system to recommend courses to students. However, a course is composed of lots of knowledge points, and a course online usually contains severallearning videos. Each video is focus on a specific knowledge point and the length of time is about 10–20 min. The whole course recommendation may ignore student interests in some specific knowledge points. Each course is constructed by different teacher or different university and so there are some similar knowledge points between different courses. For example, if a student wants to learn "the loss function of the neural networks", the course recommendation maybe recommends the entire course to him or her but the videos about "the loss function of the neural networks" cannot be focused on. He or she has to find the videos corresponding from the course indexes. The whole process is tedious and the student may lose interest. Therefore, MOOC platforms need to capture student learning interests and the recommendation results are not the courses but the specific videos which contains knowledge points that students just need.

Traditional recommendation strategies, such as collaborative filtering (CF), utilize user-item (student-learning video) historical interactions and make recommendations based on the common preferences of potential users (students). However, CF has problems of data sparsity and cold start, which limit the performance of the recommendation. In order to solve this problem, the recommended method considers the integration of auxiliary information (such as social network [4], user project attributes [5], and context [6]) into collaborative filtering, and has achieved good results. On the MOOC platform, we observe that in addition to users and learning videos, there are also relationships between entities of various types, such as schools, teachers, courses and knowledge points. Based on these relationships, rich semantic information between entities can be obtained. Therefore, this paper considers the construction of Learning Video Knowledge Graph (LVKG), which can be used as auxiliary information to capture rich semantic information between different types of entities and incorporate them into the presentation learning process. Convolutional Networks (KGCN-LV), an end-to-end Learning Video Knowledge Graph framework proposed in this paper, aggregates the neighborhood information of a given entity representation when computing it. To conduct high-level modeling to capture students' potential interests. KGCN-LV uses knowledge graph as auxiliary information to recommend learning videos to students, which effectively improves data sparsity and cold start problems in recommendation and makes recommendation interpretable.

The main contributions of this paper are as follows. Firstly, we construct the learning video knowledge graph (LVKG) from the MOOC platform to capture the auxiliary information from entities and connections to identify the potential interactions. Secondly, a convolutional neural network based on the knowledge graph of learning video (KGCN-LV) is proposed, and the experiments on MOOCCube public dataset contains the methods of KGCN-LV, SVD, LibFM, RippleNet, MKR.

2 Related Work

2.1 Traditional Recommendation Strategy

Traditional recommendation strategies are mainly collaborative filtering (CF), which considers the historical interaction between students and learning videos and recommends student common preferences based on potential similar interests, such as matrix decomposition method [7] and factor decomposition method libFM [8]. CF has effectiveness and universality in practical recommendation scenes, but it cannot model auxiliary information, such as learning video attributes, student profiles and context. Therefore, the recommendation effect is extremely poor when the interaction matrix between students and courses is extremely sparse. In order to solve this problem, the neural network method is introduced to convert student ID and learning video ID into a general feature vector, which is input into the supervised learning model to predict scores, such as neural network-based collaborative filtering recommendation NCF [9], neural factor decomposition machine NFM [10], and Wide&Deep model [11]. These methods all provide powerful performance for recommendation systems, but they model each student course interaction as an independent data instance without considering the relationships between them, which makes them inadequate to extract collaborative signals from students' collective behavior.

2.2 Existing KG-Aware Methods

As a semantic network, knowledge graph has strong expression ability and modeling flexibility, and can model entities, concepts, attributes and their relationships in the real world [12]. Properly utilizing knowledge graph to model the real world can make computers have a stronger ability to understand the real world. The concept of knowledge graph was proposed and released by Google on May 17, 2012, and it announced to build the next generation of intelligent search engine based on the knowledge graph. The key technologies include extracting entities, entity attribute information and relationship between entities from the Web pages of the Internet [13]. Recently, researchers have proposed several academic knowledge graphs, such as NELL, DBpedia and Google Knowledge Graph and Microsoft Satori. The knowledge graph method used in recommendation systems is now used in films, books, music, news and other fields. Collaborative Knowledge Base Embedding (CKE) [14] combines collaborative filtering (CF) module with knowledge embedding, text embedding and image embedding of projects in a unified Bayesian framework. CKE is suitable for knowledge graph completion and link prediction, but not for recommendation. Based on deep knowledge perception network (DKN) [15], entity embedding and word embedding are regarded as different channels, and then the convolutional neural network (CNN) framework is used to combine them together for news recommendation. However, before using DKN, entity embedding is required, which results in the lack of end-to-end training mode for DKN. Another disadvantage of DKN is that it contains little information other than text. RippleNet [16] is a model similar to memory network, which propagates users' potential preferences in KG and explores their hierarchical interests. However, the importance of relationships in

RippleNet is weakly characterized. MKR [17] is a multi-task deep learning framework for knowledge graph embedding tasks to assist in enhancing recommendation tasks. In the recommendation process, entities and projects update their vector representations to each other. Ignoring the importance of relationships in the knowledge graph.

3 Model and Method

A learning video knowledge graph LVKG is constructed to support the KGCN-LV model for the learning video recommendation.

3.1 Problem Formulation

The single learning video recommendation problem is to recommend learning videos (projects) to students (users). In the course recommendation scenario, there is a group of M studentsas $\mathcal{U} = \{u_1, u_2, \ldots, u_M\}$ and a group of N learning videos $\mathcal{V} = \{v_1, v_2, \ldots, v_N\}$. The interaction matrix is constructed according to the implicit feedback of students, which is expressed as $Y = \{y_{uv}|u \in \mathcal{U}, v \in \mathcal{V}\}$, if students interact with the learning video (such as learning, browsing, etc.), $y_{uv} = 1$, otherwise $y_{uv} = 0$, which is

$$y_{uv} = \begin{cases} 1, & \text{if interaction } (u, v) \text{ is observed} \\ 0, & \text{otherwise} \end{cases} \tag{1}$$

The learning video knowledge graph is composed of a large number of entity-relation-entity triples (h, r, t), where $h \in \mathcal{E}, r \in \mathcal{R}, t \in \mathcal{E}$ represent the head entity, relation and tail entity in the knowledge graph. $\mathcal{E}$ and $\mathcal{R}$ respectively represent the entity set and relationship set in the knowledge graph. For example, the triple (V_e88505, teacher, T_Liu Boli) means that the teacher of the learning video 'V_e88505' is Liu Boli.

The purpose of the learning video recommendation problem is to predict whether the student u is potentially interested in the learning video v that has not been interacted before, given the interaction matrix Y and the knowledge graph $\mathcal{G}$. The goal of the model is to learn $\hat{y}_{uv} = F(u, v; \Theta)$, $\hat{y}_{uv}$ represents the possibility that student u clicks on the learning video v, and Θ represents the model parameter of the function F.

3.2 Construction of KG for Learning Videos

This paper adopts a bottom-up construction method to add structured data in the MOOC-Cube dataset [18] to the data layer, and then process these knowledge elements to construct a knowledge graph LVKG.KG construction method is shown as Fig. 1.

The data used in this article already has a certain data structure. For preliminary knowledge representation, knowledge processing is required. For example, for the same entity, there may be different descriptions, and the different descriptions of entities can be accurately and completely expressed by the coreference resolution. When constructing a knowledge graph, entities with the same name may be ambiguous. For example, the

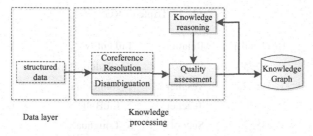

Fig. 1. KG construction method

entity "operating system" can be either a knowledge point or the name of a computer course. The entity disambiguation is used to accurately identify it by understanding the context. After data knowledge processing, a series of examples are obtained. In order to obtain a more accurate knowledge system than before, quality evaluation and knowledge reasoning are carried out, and finally the construction of LVKG is completed.

For the actual application scenario of the MOOC platform, the extracted entities include video id, course id, school name, teacher name, and related knowledge points. The relationship includes the course, school, teacher, and knowledge points to which the video belongs. The data fragment is shown as follows as Table 1. According to the knowledge graph construction method, the triple form of the knowledge graph LVKG is obtained as shown as Table 2. For example, a triple (V-297bc3, knowledge point, KMP algorithm) means that 'KMP algorithm' is the knowledge point contained in video 'V-297bc3'.

Table 1. MOOCCube Data fragment

Video	Point	Teacher	School	Course
V_a37950	KMP algorithm	T_DengJunhui	S_TsinghuaX	Data structure
V_7b6672	White box testing	T_JohnGuttag	S_MITx	Software test
V_4ab7bf	Encoder	T_LiuBoli	S_HBNU	Programming
V_c1857a	Concurrency	T_Chen Yu	S_TsinghuaX	Programming
V_40268a	Operating system	T_Xiang Yong	S_TsinghuaX	Operating system
...	...	...	...	...

According to the obtained triples, we use the graph database Neo4j to visualize the knowledge graph LVKG shown in Fig. 2.

3.3 Framework

In this paper, the KGCN-LV model is proposed to implement student-oriented learning video recommendation. The model captures the high-order connections between entities in the knowledge graph, aggregates the entity representation of learning video and its

Table 2. Triple of KG.

Head entity	Relation	Tail entity
V_a37950	Points	KMP algorithm
V_7b6672	Teacher	T_JohnGuttag
V_4ab7bf	Teacher	T_LiuBoli
V_c1857a	School	S_TsinghuaX
V_40268a	Course	Operating system
V_40268a	Teacher	T_Xiang Yong
...	...	...

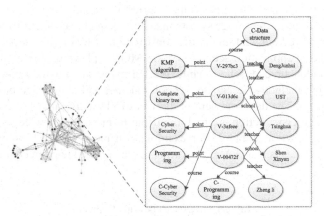

Fig. 2. Learning Video Knowledge Graph-LVKG

neighborhood nodes (green nodes), and forms the representation of the next iteration (dark blue nodes). The KGCN-LV model is shown in Fig. 3.

In the first-order connection of KGCN-LV, for student u and learning video (entity) v, use $N_{(v)}$ to represent the entity set directly connected to v, and r_{e_i,e_j} to represent the relationship between e_i and e_j. The model uses the function $g : \mathbb{R}^d \times \mathbb{R}^d \to \mathbb{R}$ to calculate the student's interest in the relationship. For example, in the learning process, the student pays more attention to which teacher teaches. Here, the inner product of the student and the relationship is used to express the interest.

$$\pi_r^u = g(\boldsymbol{u}, \boldsymbol{r}), \tag{2}$$

$\mathbf{u} \in \mathbb{R}^d$ and $\mathbf{r} \in \mathbb{R}^d$ are the vector representation of the student u and the relation r, and d is the vector dimension. In order to characterize the neighboring structure of the learning video, the linear combination of its neighbors is expressed as:

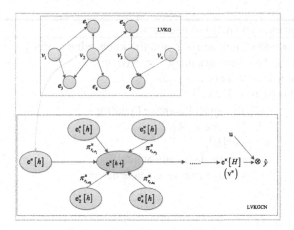

Fig. 3. Framework of KGCN-LV

$$v_{\mathcal{N}(v)}^{u} = \sum_{e \in \mathcal{N}(v)} \tilde{\pi}_{r_{v,e}}^{u} e, \tag{3}$$

and $\tilde{\pi}_{r_{v,e}}^{u}$ is the normalized representation of the user's interest in the relationship,

$$\tilde{\pi}_{r_{v,e}}^{u} = \frac{\exp\left(\pi_{r_{v,e}}^{u}\right)}{\sum_{e \in \mathcal{N}(v)} \exp\left(\pi_{r_{v,e}}^{u}\right)}, \tag{4}$$

where e is the vector representation of the entity e. When calculating the neighborhood representation of the entity, $\tilde{\pi}_{r_{v,e}}^{u}$ is used as a personalized filter to capture the learning interest of students.Finally, the entity representation and its neighborhood representation are aggregated into a single vector, and the two representation vectors are added together to perform a nonlinear transformation.

The final representation of an entity is its own representation and its neighborhood representation. In order to maintain computational efficiency, a fixed-size neighbor is used for each entity. The first-order representation is extended to the multiple-order, and user preferences are explored in more depth. The formal description of the above steps is presented in Algorithm 1. H denotes the maximum depth of receptive field (orequivalently, the number of aggregation iterations), and a suffix $[h]$ attached by a representation vector denotes h-order. For a given user-item pair (u, v) (line 2), we first calculate the receptive field $\mathcal{M}$ of v in an iterative layer-by-layer manner (line 3, 11–16).The final H-order entity representation is denoted as v^{u}(line 5), which is fed into a function F together with user representation u for predicting the probability $\hat{y}_{uv}$.

Algorithm 1:KGCN-LV algorithm

Input: Interaction matrix Y and the knowledge graph $\mathcal{G}$.

Output: Prediction function$\hat{y}_{uv} = F(u, v; \Theta)$

1 **while** KGCN not converge **do**

2   **for** (u, v) in Y **do**

3          $\mathcal{M}[i]_{i=0}^{H}$ ←Get Receptive Field(v);

4          $e^{u}[0] \leftarrow e, \forall e \in \mathcal{M}[0]$;

5          $v^{u} \leftarrow e^{u}[H]$;

6   Calculate predicted probability $\hat{y}_{uv}$;

7   Update parameters by gradient descent;

8   end for

9 end while

10 return F

11 **Function** Get Receptive Field(v);

12      $\mathcal{M}[H] \leftarrow v$

13   for $h = H - 1, ..., 0$

14          $\mathcal{M}[h] \leftarrow \mathcal{M}[h + 1]$

15   end for

16 return $\mathcal{M}[i]_{i=0}^{H}$;

In order to improve computational efficiency, a non-negative sampling strategy is used during training [19], and the complete loss function is as follows:

$$\mathcal{L} = \sum_{u \in \mathcal{U}} \left(\sum_{v:y_{uv}=1} \mathcal{J}(y_{uv}, \hat{y}_{uv}) - \sum_{i=1}^{T^{u}} \mathbb{E}_{v_i \sim P(v_i)} \mathcal{J}(y_{uv_i}, \hat{y}_{uv_i}) \right) + \lambda \|\mathcal{F}\|_2^2, \quad (5)$$

Where $\mathcal{J}$ is the cross-entropy loss function, P is the negative sampling distribution, and T^{u} is the negative sampling number of student u. In this article, $T^{u} = |\{v : y_{uv} = 1\}|$ and P obey a uniform distribution, the last term is the L2 regularization term to prevent overfitting. λ is the balance parameter.

4 Experiment

4.1 Dataset

The experiment uses the Q&A dataset in MOOCCube. The MOOCCube dataset is a large-scale data repository containing more than 700 MOOC courses, 38k videos, 200,000 students, 100k points, and 300k relationship examples. The large data set supports model experiments well. The twelve courses in the Q&A dataset all come from the field of computer science. They cover different levels of computer science courses.

According to the recommendation algorithm, the four attributes of the data set, such as video id, teacher, course id, school, and knowledge points, used in the experiment are extracted. The basic statistics of the data set are shown in Table 3.

The experimental environment is Inteli7-6700HQ CPU @ 2.60 GHz, 16 GB memory, Window10 operating system, and the software tools include PyCharm, Anaconda3 and TensorFlow framework.

Table 3. Basic statistics of the dataset.

Dataset	#students	#videos	#interactions	#entities	#relation	#KG triples
MOOCCube	4361	1401	450724	4700	4	8777

4.2 Baselines

SVD [7] decomposes the high-dimensional student course scoring matrix into low-dimensional student feature vector matrix, course feature matrix and diagonal matrix of singular values. The parameters can be updated according to the existing scoring data, once the student eigenvector matrix and the course eigenvector matrix is acquired. SVD takes the student's course scoring matrix as input.

LibFM [8] is a widely used feature-based decomposition model that takes the original features of students and courses as the input of LibFM. The dimension is $\{1, 1, 8\}$, and the number of training epochs is 50.

RippleNet [16] is a method similar to a memory network, which can spread student's preferences on the KG for a recommendation. The hyperparameters are set to $d = 8$, $H = 2$, $\lambda_1 = 10^{-6}$, $\lambda_2 = 0.01$, $\eta = 0.02$.

MKR [17] is a multi-task feature learning method for knowledge graph enhancement recommendation, and knowledge graph embedding tasks can be used to assist the recommendation.

4.3 Experiments Setup

The experiment adopts a negative sampling strategy to establish a student-learning video interaction matrix. This matrix is a sparse matrix. The positive examples are examples of students interacting with the learning video, and the negative examples are sampled from examples that the students have not interacted with. The ratio of training set, validation set to test set is 6:2:2. Each experiment is repeated four times, and the average performance is reported. The method is evaluated in two experimental scenarios: (1) In click-through rate (CTR) prediction, we apply the trained model to predict each interaction in the test set. We use AUC and ACC to evaluate CTR prediction. (2) In top-K recommendation, we use the trained model to select K items with highest predicted click probability for each user in the test set, and choose Presicion@K, Recall@K to evaluate the recommended sets. All trainable parameters are optimized by Adam algorithm. For KGCN-LV, set functions g and f as inner product, $K = 4$, aggregator as sum, batch size $= 65536$, and other hyperparameters $H = 2$, $d = 32$, $\lambda = 10^{-7}$ are validation set is determined by optimizing AUC.

4.4 Results

CTR prediction and top-K recommendation results of all methods are presented in Table 4 and Fig. 4 respectively. It can be observed from the experimental results: (1) The experimental effect of MKR and RippleNet models that add knowledge graph to learning video recommendation is 3% higher than that of SVD and LibFM, and they can perform well even in the case of sparse student course interaction. This shows that the use of knowledge graphs as auxiliary information captures rich semantic information between different types of entities, and effectively improves the data sparseness and cold start problems in the recommendation system. (2) KGCN-LV performed the best, improved by about 1% compared to the strongest baseline MKR. MKR is a multi-task learning method recommended for knowledge graph enhancement. It does not aggregate the neighborhood information between knowledge graph entities, but only represents the entity itself. KGCN-LV aggregates the neighborhood information of learning video entities and enriches the representation of the entities themselves. This shows that when computing the representation of a given entity, the neighborhood information is aggregated to perform high-level modeling to capture the potential interest of students and enhance the recommendation effect.

Table 4. Learn videos click rate prediction probability.

Model	AUC	ACC
SVD	0.9322	0.9113
LibFM	0.9303	0.9045
RippleNet	0.9611	0.9246
MKR	0.9665	0.9270
KGCN-LV	**0.9753**	**0.9319**

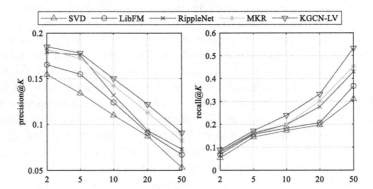

Fig. 4. Top-K recommendation *Persicion@K* and *Recall@K*

5 Conclusions and Future Work

In order to solve the problem that student interest in specific knowledge points may be ignored for course recommendation on the MOOC platform, as well as the data sparsity and cold start problems of traditional recommendation algorithms CF. A single online learning video recommendation method using knowledge graph is researched. The connection between a single learning video and other entities, such as courses, teachers, schools, knowledge points is considered to build a learning video knowledge graph LVKG. A convolution neural network KGCN-LV is proposed, which integrates learning video knowledge graphs. By gathering neighborhood information, it can obtain potential personalized student interests. Through experiments on MOOC Cube, KGCN-LV is always better than the baseline. In future work, the establishment of a student-end knowledge graph would be considered to improve the recommendation performance, and the optimized algorithm is designed to combine the knowledge graphs between the student-end and the course-end.

Acknowledgement. This work is partially supported by the Open Fund of the National Virtual Simulation Experimental Teaching Center for Coal Mine Safety Mining (SDUST 2019), the 2018 Postgraduate Tutors' Guidance Ability Improvement Project of Shandong Province (SDYY18084), the Teaching Reform Research Project of the Teaching Steering Committee of Electronic Information Specialty in Higher Education and Universities of the Ministry of Education, the Special Project of China Association of Higher Education, the Education and Teaching Research Project of Shandong Province, and Excellent Teaching Team Construction Project of Shandong University of Science and Technology.

References

1. Zhang, J., Hao, B., Chen, B., Li, C., Chen, H., Sun, J.: Hierarchical reinforcement learning for course recommendation in MOOCs. In: The 33rd AAAI Conference on Artificial Intelligence (2019). https://doi.org/10.1609/aaai.v33i01.3301435
2. Xie, S.-T., He, Z.-B., Chen, Q., Chen, R.-X., Kong, Q.-Z., Song, C.-Y.: Predicting learning behavior using log data in blended teaching. Sci. Program. **2021**, 1–14 (2021). https://doi.org/10.1155/2021/4327896
3. Zhang, H., Song, Z., Sun, M., Tang, J., Wang, X., Sun, J.: Smart jump: automated navigation suggestion for videos in MOOCs. In: International World Wide Web Conference Committee (2017). https://doi.org/10.1145/3041021.3054166
4. Liu, J., Fu, L., Wang, X., Tang, F., Chen, G.: Joint recommendations in multilayer mobile social networks. IEEE Trans. Mob. Comput. **19**, 2358–2373 (2020). https://doi.org/10.1109/TMC.2019.2923665
5. Wang, H., Zhang, F., Hou, M., Xie, X., Guo, M., Liu, Q.: SHINE: signed heterogeneous information network embedding for sentiment link prediction. In: Proceedings of the 11th ACM International Conference on Web Search and Data Mining, February 2018, pp. 592–600 (2018)
6. Xie, R., Qiu, Z., Rao, J., et al.: Internal and contextual attention network for cold-start multichannel matching in recommendation. In: IJCAI 2020, pp. 2732–2738 (2020)
7. Matrix, N.F.: SVD Recommendation model based on positive and negative feedback matrix (2015)
8. Rendle, S.: Factorization machines with libFM. ACM Trans. Intell. Syst. Technol. **3**(3), 1–22 (2012). https://doi.org/10.1145/2168752.2168771
9. He, X., Liao, L., Zhang, H., Nie, L., Hu, X., Chua, T.S.: Neural collaborative filtering. In: 26th International World Wide Web Conference, WWW 2017 (2017)

10. He, X., Chua, T.S.: Neural factorization machines for sparse predictive analytics. In: International Conference on Research and Development in Information Retrieval (2017). https://doi.org/10.1145/3077136.3080777
11. Cheng, H.T., et al.: Wide & deep learning for recommender systems. In: ACM International Conference Proceeding Series (2016). https://doi.org/10.1145/2988450.2988454
12. Qi, G.L.: The research advances of knowledge graph. Technol. Intell. Eng. (2017).https://doi.org/10.3772/j.issn.2095-915x.2017.01.002
13. Qiao, L.: Knowledge graph construction techniques. J. Comput. Res. Develop. **53**(3), 582–600 (2016)
14. Zhang, F., Yuan, N.J., Lian, D., Xie, X., Ma, W.Y.: Collaborative knowledge base embedding for recommender systems. In: Proceedings of the ACM SIGKDD International Conference on Knowledge Discovery and Data Mining, 13–17 August 2016, pp. 353–362 (2016)
15. Wang, H., Zhang, F., Xie, X., Guo, M.: DKN: deep knowledge-aware network for news recommendation, pp. 1835–1844. International World Wide Web Conference Committee (2018). https://doi.org/10.1145/3178876.3186175
16. Wang, H., et al.: RippleNet: propagating user preferences on the knowledge graph for recommender systems. In: International Conference on Information and Knowledge Management, pp. 417–426 (2018). https://doi.org/10.1145/3269206.3271739
17. Wang, H., Zhang, F., Zhao, M., Li, W., Xie, X., Guo, M.: Multi-task feature learning for knowledge graph enhanced recommendation, pp. 2000–2010. International World Wide Web Conference Committee (2019). https://doi.org/10.1145/3308558.3313411
18. Yu, J., et al.: MOOCCube: a large-scale data repository for NLP applications in MOOCs. In: Annual Conference of the Association for Computational Linguistics (2020). https://doi.org/10.18653/v1/2020.acl-main.285
19. Wang, H., Zhao, M., Xie, X., Li, W., Guo, M.: Knowledge graph convolutional networks for recommender systems. In: World Wide Web Conference (2019). https://doi.org/10.1145/3308558.3313417

Data Transformation for Super-Resolution on Ocean Remote Sensing Images

Yuting Yang[1,2,3], Kin-Man Lam[2], Xin Sun[3], Junyu Dong[3,4,5(✉)], Muwei Jian[6], and Hanjiang Luo[1]

[1] Shandong University of Science and Technology, Qingdao 266590, China
[2] Department of Electronic and Information Engineering, The Hong Kong Polytechnic University, Hong Kong 999077, China
enkmlam@polyu.edu.hk
[3] Department of Information Science and Engineering, Ocean University of China, Qingdao 266100, China
sunxin1984@ieee.org, dongjunyu@ouc.edu.cn
[4] Haide College, Ocean University of China, Qingdao 266100, China
[5] Institute of Advanced Ocean Study, Ocean University of China, Qingdao 266100, China
[6] School of Computer Science and Technology, Shandong University of Finance and Economics, 7366 Li Xia, Jinan 250000, China

Abstract. High-resolution ocean remote sensing imaging is of vital importance for research in the field of ocean remote sensing. However, the available ocean remote sensing images are often averaged data, whose resolution is lower than the instant remote sensing images. In this paper, we propose a data transformation method to process remote sensing images in different locations and resolutions. We target satellite-derived sea surface temperature (SST) images as a specific case-study. In detail, we use a modified very deep super-resolution (VDSR) model as our baseline model and propose a data transformation method to improve the robustness of the model. Furthermore, we also illustrates how the degree of difference in the data distribution influences the model's robustness and also, how our proposed data transformation method can improve the model's robustness. Experiment results prove that our method is effective and our model is robust.

Keywords: Deep learning · Super-resolution · Sea surface temperature · Data transformation · Ocean-front

1 Introduction

Sea surface features are an important factor in oceanography and can be applied to many fields, such as air-sea interaction, severe weather prediction, ocean engineering, etc. The sea surface features include, but are not limited to, sea surface

© IFIP International Federation for Information Processing 2022
Published by Springer Nature Switzerland AG 2022
Z. Shi et al. (Eds.): IIP 2022, IFIP AICT 643, pp. 431–443, 2022.
https://doi.org/10.1007/978-3-031-03948-5_35

temperature, sea surface chlorophyll, and sea surface height. It has been a popular topic for many years, bringing together a large amount of remote sensing sea surface feature data with different resolutions, thus allowing for new insights in small-scale processes at a larger-scale area coverage. Based on these feature images, we can further research some important marine environmental characteristics, such as vortex, ocean-fronts, etc. However, research on sea surface features is limited by the resolution of the weekly, or monthly, averaged remote sensing images, and the cloud contamination of the instant remote sensing images. Thus, how to increase the resolution of remote sensing images and eliminate the cloud contamination are of great valuable for various ocean-related research works.

In this paper, we take one of the most famous marine environmental characteristics, named ocean-front as a specific case-study to analyze the effectiveness of our super-resolution method and data transformation method. Ocean-front is one of the most well-studied ocean mesoscale characteristics. It is usually expressed as open streamline in high-resolution remote sensing images that separates water masses with different physical properties, for example, water masses that contain distinct amount of salt, heat, and chemicals. It can be transported by currents, and mix with surrounding water masses. Usually, jets and strong currents will engender ocean-front, and the existence of ocean-front makes it difficult for particles to cross. Thus, the water masses separated by long-living ocean-fronts could maintain its biogeochemical properties for a long time. They stand a show of becoming the best living environments for various kinds of fish species and forming into a complicated ecological system.

There are mainly two kinds of ocean-front detection methods, one is a data analysis method based on the physical characteristics of ocean-front images [1,2], and the other one is a data-learning method based on the mapping relationship between the input and the ground-truth images [3,4]. In our research, we use one of the state-of-the-art ocean-front detection methods, named Microcanonical Multiscale Formalism (MMF), to detect ocean fronts. The method has been used to extract ocean fronts in sea surface temperature (SST) images in our former work [5–7]. Under the microcanonical framework, the algorithm analyzes the critical transitions in oceanographic satellite data by calculating the Singularity Exponents (SE), and transforms SST images into clean and simple line drawings of ocean fronts. The method has been validated by oceanographers and has an advantage over traditional edge extraction methods in dealing with satellite oceanographic images [8].

In this paper, we focus on the super-resolution of remote sensing SST images, in consideration of the noise caused by clouds. The state-of-the-art super-resolution methods can be roughly divided into two categories. One is the traditional method based on EOF or analog schemes, and the other one is the data-driven approach, such as neural networks and machine learning methods. Ducournau et al. [9] were the first to apply super-resolution methods, based on the super-resolution convolutional neural network (SRCNN) proposed in [10], to SST images. The experiment results showed an obvious improvement of the super-resolution performance based on a convolutional network, compared to those traditional methods. However, shallow convolutional networks have been surpassed by deep neural networks in many tasks. Deep neural network is a key breakthrough in the field of computer vision and pattern recognition. For the past decade, deep networks have enabled machines to classify images with accuracy as high as humans can. The most important breakthrough is "residuals learning", which can reconstruct the learning process and redirect the flow of information in deep neural networks effectively. It improves the performance of deep neural network without increasing the computing cost. For this reason, the Very Deep Super-Resolution network (VDSR) proposed in [11], is employed as our baseline model. We improve its performance by enhancing its ability to integrate low-level features with high-level features. VDSR is a deep learning approach proposed for image super-resolution. It has 20 convolutional layers, which is much deeper than SRCNN, which contains 3 convolutional layers only. The modified VDSR network proposed in our previous work [6] can help us to reconstruct high-resolution images with high quality from low-resolution ones. The Enhanced Deep Super-Resolution network (EDSR) proposed in [12], is a more complex and deeper residual network, compared with VDSR, whose performance on low-resolution images, for example, the Set5 database proposed in [13], is better than that of the VDSR model. In this paper, we compare the performance of these two deep neural networks with the modified VDSR model for SST images.

The rest of this paper is organized as follows. In the second section, we propose our data transformation method. We introduce the databases used in our experiments in Section 3. A detailed description on the experimental setup and evaluation methods is given in Sect. 4. In Sect. 5, we analysis the experiment results. Then, we conclude this paper and give our future research plan in Sect. 6.

2   Data Transformation

Unlike standard images, whose pixel values range from 0 to 255, SST images typically range from 0 to 5000. Consequently, the VDSR and EDSR networks cannot process remote sensing or SST images directly. As the dynamic range of SST images is more than 10 times that of standard image, this makes it difficult to use existing deep neural networks to learn the mapping between the input and the ground-truth data.

200	220	330	0	20	30
200	50	10	0	50	10
340	50	100	40	50	0

Fig. 1. The effect of data transformation. The input image is shown on the left, while the processed image is displayed on the right. We set the data domain within [0–100]. Then, the data domain of the input image is transferred from [0–340] to [0–100].

Data transformation is to transfer the data domain from one to another. The deep neural network trained on one data domain can hardly be adapted to another data domain. The data transformation method can solve the domain adaptation problem. The effect of the method is shown in Fig. 1.

Before feeding SST images into EDSR and VDSR, their data domain has to be compressed. The common compression operation can blur the SST images. In this situation, even though the network is deep and its structure is well designed, it is still a great challenge to reconstruct high-resolution image from the blurred SST image. We trained and tested EDSR and VDSR on the compressed images from the ocean SST database. The experimental results show that the network fails to improve the resolution of the SST images.

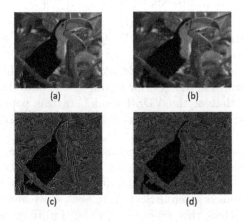

Fig. 2. The effect of data transformation on the Set5 database. (a) The y channel of a ground-truth image (data domain 0–255), (b) the y channel of the bicubic image (data domain 0–255), (c) the transformed ground-truth image, with data domain [0–100], and (d) the transformed bicubic image, with data domain [0–100].

To improve the performance, we propose a data transformation method, which transforms the SST data from one domain to another, while the data is not blurred. In order to verify the impact of the data transformation method, we trained and tested EDSR and VDSR on the transformed data from the low-resolution and high-resolution ocean SST databases. The experiment results proved the effectiveness of the proposed method. Moreover, to evaluate the robustness of the data transformation method, we also applied the same data transformation method to the 291 database. Then, we trained VDSR on the 291 database, but tested it on Set5. The experiment results proved that the data transformation method is robust.

As shown in Fig. 2, we transform the data domain of the bicubic interpolation image to 0–100. We also apply the same operation to the ground-truth images. In this way, we can keep the difference between the input image and the ground-truth image unchanged, so as to maintain the data dependence of the input and the ground-truth images. Transforming the data domain also makes the difference between the ground-truth and bicubic images more obvious. According to the experiments, the best data domain for standard images to be transformed is from the domain 0–50 to the domain 0–150, larger or smaller will make the performance worse.

Figure 3 presents a SST image before and after the transformation. The ground-truth image is chosen from the low-resolution ocean SST database. Similarly, the SST image can maintain its dependence between data after the data domain transformation. According to experiments, the best data domain that the original database can be transformed is from the domain 0–5 to the domain of 0–250, larger or smaller makes the performance worse.

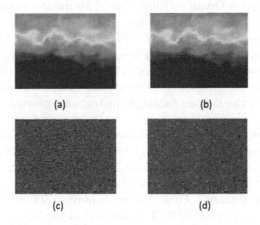

Fig. 3. The effect of data transformation on the Ocean SST database. (a) The ground-truth image (data domain 0–3000) (b) the bicubic image (data domain 0–3000) (c) the transformed ground-truth image (data domain 0–5) and (d) the transformed bicubic image (data domain 0–5)

3 Databases

In this work, we compare the difference in data distribution between standard and remote sensing images. Specifically, we use the 291 database as a case-study for standard images and the China Ocean SST database for remote sensing images.

As well, we also used another four databases for comparison and evaluation, including the Ocean SST database, the High-resolution Ocean SST database, the Low-resolution Ocean SST database and the SST Ocean-Front database. We propose the Ocean SST database, the high-resolution and low-resolution ocean SST databases, for comparing the performance of different methods on coastal and ocean areas in high-resolution and low-resolution SST images. Furthermore, we also propose a SST ocean-front database to evaluate the performance of different models on the SST ocean-front super-resolution task. In the following, we will introduce these databases in detail.

The China Ocean SST database: This database is proposed in our previous paper [1]. This database contains a total of 600 daily-averaged AVHRR SST images, covering China's coastal waters (112.5E–135E, 10N–40N) with a spatial resolution of 5 km approximately. The waters considered in the database are highly dynamic, and contains complex turbulence structures. This is because the waters are in a part of the Kuroshio Current system, which can convey a great amount of mass and power, such as heat, from low-latitude to mid-latitude waters [14]. In this paper, we consider the time series from January to April, between 2007 and 2011 as the training data, and the time-series from January to April, in 2012 as the evaluation data.

The High-resolution Ocean SST database: This database contains 150 images, captured from 1st January 2011 to 30st May 2011. This database covers the intersection waters (155E–180E, 30N–50N), where the Kuroshio, Oyashio and North Pacific warm currents cross. These currents have great implications on the global climate and marine fisheries [14,15]. Image super-resolution in these areas may increase the prediction accuracy on marine climate change, give a better guidance for the marine fishing industry, and prevent the occurrence of marine disasters.

The Low-resolution Ocean SST database: This database corresponds to the low-resolution counterpart of the High-resolution Ocean SST database, so it covers the same waters, with a downsampling factor of 5. This database is used for comparison with the high-resolution database.

The Ocean SST database: This database contains 1500 SST images, captured from January 2008 to December 2011. Each pixel in the image represents an area with a spatial resolution of 5 km approximately. The database covers the intersection waters (155E–180E, 30N–50N), where the Kuroshio, Oyashio and North Pacific warm currents cross. This database is used to evaluate the performance of different methods.

The SST Ocean-Front database: This database consists of ocean-front images processed by the MMF method, on the Ocean SST database. This database is also used for the performance evaluation of different methods.

Before training and testing the networks, all the data in the databases are processed using the data transformation method. All the output data are also processed by our data transformation method, before evaluating the performance.

4   Experimental Setup and Evaluation Methods

The data domain difference between the databases often make a deep model trained on one database unable to achieve satisfactory performance on another database. Thus, the domain adaptation problem is a great challenge for training a robust deep model, and this problem inspires our research. On the one hand, we want to know whether or not the data domain difference between the two databases can influence the model performance and the degree. On the other hand, we need to identify which properties of the data contribute most to the difference.

Besides, deeper networks usually gain better performance. Since EDSR is deeper than VDSR, we want to know whether or not EDSR can achieve better performance than VDSR.

Furthermore, since the ocean-front is one of the most important factors in ocean biogeochemical environment, can we upsample the ocean-front images directly?

4.1   Experimental Setup

We compare the VDSR model trained on the 291 database to the same model trained on SST databases. We aim at evaluating whether or not the data-distribution difference between these two database will influence the model performance and the degree. Then, we can gain an insight into the robustness of the VDSR model for databases with different data distribution. This suggests that we can design more effective experiments. Thereby, we further compare the performance of VDSR and the modified VDSR model, so as to figure out which model is more robust.

In another aspect, since the domain adaptation problem exists, we intend to find out what makes the difference. More specifically, we aim to find out which part of the data contributes most to the difference. Through careful analysis on the SST data and the natural image data, we can have a general guess that the coastal waters is the key factor that makes the difference. Under this point, we should design an experiment to verify this conjecture. Then, two sets of experiments are carried out. One experiment will use the SST images, with the coastal waters, as the evaluation database, and another experiment will use images without coastal waters, for comparison.

To evaluate the influence of different resolution on the model performance and to find out the better way to upsample ocean front, two sets of comparison experiments will be conducted, based on four representative databases. The first set of experiments makes use of the High-resolution and Low-resolution SST databases, and is conducted to display the effect of the resolutions of low-resolution images on the super-resolution performance. To make sure that the only variable is the resolution, we set the location, model, upsampling factor, and the number of training samples the same. The second set uses different kinds of input images to identify the best way to obtain high-resolution ocean-front image. One type of the input is SST images, selected from the Ocean SST database, another type of input is ocean-front images, selected from the SST ocean-front database. To evaluate their effect on ocean-front super-resolution, we use the ocean-front images rather than the SST images in the evaluation. Besides, we also control the variables in this set of experiments.

4.2   Evaluation Methods

We evaluate the model performance in terms of PSNR and Perceptual Loss, with upsampling factor set at 3. The equation of PSNR is defined as follows:

$$PSNR = 10 \times \log_{10}(\frac{1}{\sum_{i=1}^{n} \frac{|I(i)-\widehat{I}(i)|^2}{n}})$$ (1)

where $I(i)$ and $\widehat{I}(i)$ denote the ith pixel of the ground-truth SST image and the output image, respectively, and n is the number of pixels in the images. The pixel-wise losses between the reconstructed and the ground-truth images are averaged to evaluate the reconstruction quality.

In addition to PSNR, we further analyze the reconstruction quality with the Perceptual Loss. The Perceptual Loss is defined as follows:

$$L_X = \frac{1}{\mathbf{W_{i,j}H_{i,j}}} \sum_{x=1}^{\mathbf{W_{i,j}}} \sum_{y=1}^{\mathbf{H_{i,j}}} (\phi_{i,j}(\mathbf{I^G})_{x,y} - (\phi_{i,j}(M(\mathbf{I^B}))_{x,y})^2$$ (2)

where the model M is trained for the super-resolution task. $\mathbf{I^B}$ represents the input obtained upsampling with the bicubic method, and is compared with the corresponding ground-truth $\mathbf{I^G}$. $\phi_{i,j}$ represents the feature maps extracted from a convolutional layer, whose layer depths are indexed as i and j. All the convolutional layers are chosen from the VGG19 network, which is pretrained on the ImageNet database [16]. We extract feature maps using $VGG_{3,3}$ convolutional layers. $\mathbf{W_{i,j}}$ and $\mathbf{H_{i,j}}$ represent the height and width of the feature maps. Note that deeper convolutional layer extracts more abstract features [17–19]. The perceptual loss function pays attention to the content and overall spatial structure of the input images [18], rather than the texture and exact shape, while the PSNR is just the opposite.

We evaluate the PSNR and Perceptual Loss for the models trained on the 291 and China Ocean SST databases. For the China Ocean SST database, the coastal waters (keep the coastline) and the marine waters (delete the coastline) are tested respectively.

5   Analysis on the Experiment Results

Finally, Tables 1 and 2 tabulate the performance of the different models on the China Ocean SST images. As shown in Table 1, the modified model trained on the 291 database has a higher PSNR and Perceptual Loss than VDSR and bicubic methods, while the same model trained on the China Ocean SST database gains a slightly higher PSNR value, but a much lower Perceptual Loss. This proves the existence of data distribution difference. Then, Table 2 reveals the key factor that causes the difference. The results show a significant difference in the PSNR and Perceptual Loss achieved by the different models trained on different databases. Thus, the fact that the coastal waters make the data distribution of SST images different from standard images can be proved.

Table 1. The PSNR and Perceptual Loss of the different methods on the 291 and China Ocean SST database with coastline removed.

Method	PSNR	Perceptual loss
Bicubic (291)	36.83	5.34
VDSR (291)	45.68	**3.05**
Modified VDSR (291)	46.29	6.92
Modified VDSR (SST)	**46.94**	3.79

Table 2. The PSNR and Perceptual Loss of the different methods on the China Ocean SST database.

Method	PSNR	Perceptual loss
Bicubic	17.04	21.07
VDSR (SST)	17.67	53.77
Modified VDSR (SST)	**21.53**	**5.89**

Table 3. The VDSR network trained on the 291 database, the down-sample factor set at 3

PSNR	Bicubic	VDSR
Low resolution	33.52	**36.06**
High resolution	32.67	**38.25**

Figure 4 displays a SST image, captured on 1st January 2011, from the high-resolution Ocean SST database. The ground-truth image is first downsampled by 3 times, using the bicubic method, and then upsampled using the bicubic and the VDSR methods. It is hard for humans to figure out which method performs better from the output images. Therefore, we present the loss images. It is easy to tell that the loss between the VDSR output and the ground-truth image is smaller than that between the bicubic output and the ground-truth image. In other words, the VDSR model performs better than the bicubic method. We not only apply the VDSR model on high-resolution SST images, but also apply it to low-resolution images. The results are tabulated in Table 3.

As shown in Table 3, the VDSR model performs better than the bicubic method on both the high-resolution and low-resolution SST images, especially on the high-resolution SST images. The reason for this can be that the high-resolution images contain more textures and sharper edges, which are hard for the bicubic method to reconstruct.

For comparison, we also apply EDSR, trained with the same databases. However, as presented in Table 4, the results are complicated. On the one hand, the performance of EDSR, in terms of PSNR, is 5.67 dB and 7.19 dB higher than that of the bicubic method, on the low-resolution and high-resolution SST images,

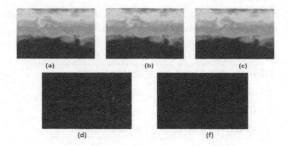

Fig. 4. Super-resolution effect using different methods on SST images. (a) An image from the high-resolution SST database, labeled as the ground-truth image (data domain 0–5000) (b) Its bicubic up-sampled image (c) The output image of the VDSR model (d) The loss between the ground-truth image and the bicubic image (data domain 0–30) (e) the loss between the ground-truth image and the model output image

Table 4. The EDSR model trained on the Ocean SST databases, the down-sample factor set at 3

PSNR	Bicubic	EDSR
Low resolution	33.52	**39.19**
High resolution	32.67	**39.86**

Table 5. The models trained on the Ocean SST and SST ocean-front databases.

PSNR	SST	Ocean-front
Bicubic	43.15	27.40
EDSR	31.85	34.55
VDSR	45.89	**34.78**
Modified VDSR	**46.04**	34.77

respectively. These relative improvement is higher than that of VDSR, whose performance is 2.54 dB and 5.58 dB higher than bicubic, on the two datasets.

As shown in Fig. 5, we choose the first image of the database to demonstrate the performance of the different methods on upsampling ocean front on SST images and SST ocean-front images. In our experiment, we choose the biggest 10% Singular Exponent (SE) pixels as the ocean front. From Fig. 5 (b) to (g), we can hardly judge the best and the worst methods. Therefore, we present the loss images from Fig. 5 (h) to (m). It can be seen from these images that the bicubic method achieves the worst performance on the SST ocean-front images, while VDSR achieves the best performance, with the SST images as input. The performances, in terms of PSNR, are presented in Table 5.

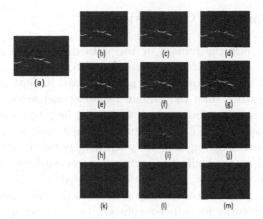

Fig. 5. Super-resolution effect using different methods on ocean front images. (a) The ground-truth image is chosen from the SST ocean-front database (data domain 100–350) (b) The bicubic up-sampled ocean-front image on the Ocean SST database (c) The bicubic up-sampled ocean-front image on the SST ocean-front database (d) The output ocean-front image of VDSR, trained on the Ocean SST database (e) The output ocean-front image of VDSR trained on the SST ocean-front database (f) The output ocean-front image from EDSR, trained on the Ocean SST database (g) The output ocean-front image of EDSR on the SST ocean-front database (h–m) Loss images between a ground-truth image and the output image, based on the bicubic, VDSR, EDSR methods on the Ocean SST database and SST ocean-front database respectively (data domain 0–30)

Table 5 shows the experiment results based on the different methods for upsampling SST ocean-front images from the Ocean SST database and the SST ocean-front database. In this set of experiments, we use MMF to calculate the ocean fronts from the SST images. We set the downsampling scale at 3, for both the Ocean SST database and the SST ocean-front database. Then, these images are sent to the networks to obtain the upsampled SST images and upsampled ocean-front images. After that, on the one hand, we extract ocean fronts from the upsampled SST image using MMF. Comparing with the ground-truth ocean-front images, which are also calculated by using MMF, the modified VDSR achieves the best performance for the SST ocean-front super-resolution task in terms of PSNR, which is 46.07. On the other hand, the output ocean-front images of the different methods are compared with the ground-truth ocean-front images. It can be easily observed that the best performance is achieved by the VDSR method. Although EDSR takes downsampled images as the input, and it has better performance on standard databases, its domain adaption ability is worse than the VDSR network. The results reveal that the best way to reconstruct ocean front is to upsample the SST image rather than the ocean-front image. The reason for this may be that the ocean-front images are sparser than the SST image, which makes it harder to reconstruct features from the down-sampled ocean-front images.

6   Future Work and Conclusion

This paper points out the impact of the data distribution difference on the robustness of some deep learning models and also draws an interesting conclusion that the data distribution of SST and standard images differs the most in the ocean areas, rather than the sea-land intersection areas. Besides, we also propose a data transformation method, which can help to handle data from different databases, such as SST images and standard images. This work may be useful for further investigating new deep learning networks for super-resolution in geophysical fields, especially for zooming in sea surface features in remote sensing images. What's more, we propose four databases for two sets of experiments, which may promote oceanography community to validate their method and ameliorate networks for super-resolution task on remote sensing images. The experiment results prove that our data transformation method can not only improve the performance on the SST images, with different resolutions and locations, but also can improve the performance on standard images.

In the future, we will train a super-resolution network, based on the Low-resolution Ocean SST database, and take the High-resolution Ocean SST database as the ground-truth data. Then, we will also evaluate its performance on the Ocean SST database and SST ocean-front database. We believe that the future work will be more challenging and meaningful.

Acknowledgments. This work was jointly supported by the National Natural Science Foundation of China (No. U1706218, 61971388, 62072287).

References

1. Yuting, Y., Junyu, D., Xin, S., Redouane, L., Muwei, J., Xinhua, W.: Ocean front detection from instant remote sensing SST images. IEEE Geosci. Remote Sens. Lett. **13**(12), 1960–1964 (2016)
2. Yuting, Y., Junyu, D., Xin, S., Estanislau, L., Quanquan, M., Xinhua, W.: A CFCC-LSTM model for sea surface temperature prediction. IEEE Geosci. Remote Sens. Lett. **15**(2), 207–211 (2018)
3. Estanislau, L., Xin, S., Junyu, D., Hui, W., Yuting, Y., Lipeng, L.: Learning and transferring convolutional neural network knowledge to ocean front recognition. IEEE Geosci. Remote Sens. Lett. **14**(3), 354–358 (2017)
4. Estanislau, L., Xin, S., Yuting, Y., Junyu, D.: Application of deep convolutional neural networks for ocean front recognition. J. Appl. Remote Sens. **11**(4), 042610 (2017)
5. Yuting, Y., Kin-Man, L., Xin, S., Junyu, D., Hanjiang, L.: An efficient algorithm for ocean-front evolution trend recognition. Remote Sens. **14**(2), 259 (2022)
6. Yuting, Y., Lam, K.M., Junyu, D., Xin, S., Jian, M.: Super-resolution on remote sensing images. In: Proceedings of the International Workshop on Advanced Image Technology, pp. 1–5. SPIE (2021)
7. Yuting, Y., Lam, K.M., Junyu, D., Xin, S., Jian, M.: Application of GoogLeNet for ocean-front tracking. In: Proceedings of the International Workshop on Advanced Image Technology, pp. 1–5. SPIE, Hong Kong (2022)

8. Oriol, P., Antonio, T., Hussein, Y.: Singularity analysis of digital signals through the evaluation of their unpredictable point manifold. Int. J. Comput. Math. **90**(8), 1693–1707 (2013)
9. Aurélien, D., Ronan, F.: Deep learning for ocean remote sensing: an application of convolutional neural networks for super-resolution on satellite-derived SST data. In: 9th IAPR Workshop on Pattern Recogniton in Remote Sensing (PRRS), Cancun, Mexico, pp. 1–6. IEEE (2016)
10. Chao, D., Chen Change, L., Kaiming, H., Xiaoou, T.: Image super-resolution using deep convolutional networks. IEEE Trans. Pattern Anal. Mach. Intell. **38**(2), 295–307 (2016)
11. Jiwon, K., Jung Kwon, L., Kyoung Mu, L.: Accurate image super-resolution using very deep convolutional networks. In: Proceedings of the IEEE Conference on Computer Vision and Pattern Recognition (CVPR), Las Vegas, Nevada, USA, pp. 1646–1654. IEEE (2016)
12. Bee, L., Sanghyun, S., Heewon, K., Seungjun, N., Kyoung Mu, L.: Enhanced deep residual networks for single image super-resolution. In: Proceedings of the IEEE Conference on Computer Vision and Pattern Recognition (CVPR), Florida, USA, pp. 136–144. IEEE (2017)
13. Marco, B., Aline, R., Christine, G., Marie, l., Alberi M.: Low-complexity single-image super-resolution based on nonnegative neighbor embedding. In: Proceedings of the British Machine Vision Conference, Surrey, England, pp. 135.1–135.10. BMVA Press (2012)
14. Yu-Heng, T., Mao-Lin, S., Sen, J., David, E.D., Chia-Ping, C.: Validation of the Kuroshio current system in the dual-domain Pacific Ocean model framework. Prog. Oceanogr. **105**, 102–124 (2012)
15. II, L., Chun-Chieh, W., Iam-Fei, P., Dong-Shan, K.: Upper-ocean thermal structure and the western north pacific category 5 typhoons. Part I: ocean features and the category 5 typhoons intensification. Mon. Weather Rev. **136**(9), 3288–3306 (2008)
16. Jia, D., Wei, D., Richard, S., Li-Jia, L., Kai, L., Fei-Fei, L.: ImageNet: a large-scale hierarchical image database. In: 2009 IEEE Conference on Computer Vision and Pattern Recognition (CVPR), Florida, USA, pp. 248–255. IEEE (2009)
17. Zeiler, M.D., Fergus, R.: Visualizing and understanding convolutional networks. In: Fleet, D., Pajdla, T., Schiele, B., Tuytelaars, T. (eds.) ECCV 2014. LNCS, vol. 8689, pp. 818–833. Springer, Cham (2014). https://doi.org/10.1007/978-3-319-10590-1_53
18. Christian, L., et al.: Photo-realistic single image super-resolution using a generative adversarial network. In: Proceedings of the IEEE Conference on Computer Vision and Pattern Recognition (CVPR), Florida, USA, pp. 4681–4690. IEEE (2017)
19. Junyu, D., Ruiying, Y., Xin, S., Qiong, L., Yuting, Y., Xukun, Q.: Inpainting of remote sensing SST images with deep convolutional generative adversarial network. IEEE Geosci. Remote Sens. Lett. **16**(2), 173–177 (2019)

A Novel RGBD Image Superpixel Segmentation Intergrated Depth Map Quality

Weiyi Wei, Wenxia Chen[✉], and Hong Tao

College of Computer Science and Engineering, Northwest Normal University, Lanzhou, Gansu, China
2020211950@nwnu.edu.cn

Abstract. Superpixel segmentation is to gather adjacent pixels into sub-regions with certain semantics, which can greatly reduce the computational complexity of subsequent image processing. The existing SLIC-D algorithm of RGBD image is a superpixel segmentation method that integrates depth information based on SLIC algorithm. However, for some images with complex background, it cannot stick to the weak edge of the image, and even has the defect of wrong segmentation. Therefore, this paper proposes a novel RGBD image superpixel segmentation intergrated depth map quality. Firstly, RGB map is enhanced by bilateral filtering to suppress and smooth noise, joint bilateral filtering is used to fill the depth map hole. Secondly, Holistically-Nested Edge Detection method based on convolutional neural network is used to obtain the RGB contour map, the edge consistency map is obtained by Hadamard product operation with depth gradient map. Finally, superpixel segmentation is performed by clustering based on LAB color space, spatial location and high-quality depth information similarity. Through the verification on NYU dataset, the advantages of this algorithm in edge fit degree are fully demonstrated.

Keywords: Superpixel segmentation · RGBD · Depth map quality · Clustering

1 Introduction

As an image preprocessing step, superpixel segmentation gathers adjacent pixels with similar attributes into a class of sub-regions, which reduces the computational complexity of subsequent image processing. Superpixel segmentation has been widely used in image segmentation [1], target recognition and tracking [2], and saliency detection [3–6]. Among the algorithms for generating superpixels, the SLIC (Simple Linear Iterative Clustering) algorithm proposed by Achanta et al. [7] often achieves the best results, the algorithm generates regular shape and controllable number of superpixel blocks based on the 5-dimensional features of CIELAB color space and pixel position. LSC [8] (Linear Spectral Clustering) developed from SLIC, replaces clustering pixels with high-dimensional features. Guo et al. [9] based on the SLIC algorithm, proposed an improved algorithm combining adaptive multi-threshold LBP texture features, which solved the

© IFIP International Federation for Information Processing 2022
Published by Springer Nature Switzerland AG 2022
Z. Shi et al. (Eds.): IIP 2022, IFIP AICT 643, pp. 444–456, 2022.
https://doi.org/10.1007/978-3-031-03948-5_36

inaccurate segmentation problem of the SLIC algorithm considering only color and spatial information. In view of the time-consuming problem of SLIC algorithm, Lei et al. [10] proposed a fast SLIC superpixel segmentation method. Liao et al. [11] aiming at the fact that the above superpixel segmentation algorithm cannot automatically determine the appropriate number of superpixels, proposed a superpixel segmentation method using local information. Xiao et al. [12] proposed an adaptive content-based superpixel segmentation method, which can iteratively evaluate the importance of color, contour, texture and spatial location features based on the discriminant method of clustering, and adaptively adjust the weight of each feature.

With the development of imaging technology, many researchers began to turn to the RGBD image superpixel segmentation method for research. In the depth map, the depth sensor may not detect some pixels of depth information, and these pixels constitute depth map holes. Zhang et al. [13] proposed a joint filtering method to fill the hole and up-sampled depth information to generate RGBD image capture system. The depth map quality was often neglected in previous work, Zhao et al. [14] mentioned the importance of depth map quality and introduced contrast loss of RGB stream into depth stream to improve the quality of depth map. Wang et al. [15] proposed three quality assessment methods of depth map, the selective fusion of these three depth qualities improves the accuracy of saliency detection in RGBD image. In the case of very low light, can't rely on color information for superpixel segmentation, Agoes [16] proposes a superpixel generation algorithm rely on depth information, the depth and gradient direction as an alternative LAB color space features, to solve the problem of semantic inconsistency in depth map segmentation due to the same depth value near the boundary. Li et al. [17] proposed RGBD image superpixel segmentation, namely, SLIC-D algorithm, the depth information is not only used to solve the image with similar foreground and background color, but also to achieve the co-segmentation of multiple images. Therefore, this paper proposes a novel RGBD image superpixel segmentation method intergrated depth map quality. Firstly, the quality of depth map is evaluated according to the edge consistency of RGB contour map and depth gradient map. In this paper, HED (Holistically-Nested Edge Detection method) [18] based on convolutional neural network is used to extract RGB contour map. Secondly, the results of depth map quality evaluation are weighted and fused with depth map to obtain high-quality depth map. Finally, superpixel segmentation is achieved by clustering based on LAB color space, spatial location and high-quality depth information similarity. The main contributions are summarized as follows.

- This paper proposes a high-quality depth map generation method. The edge consistency map is obtained from RGB contour map and depth gradient map by Hadamard product operation, high-quality depth map is obtained by weighted fusion of edge consistency map and depth map.
- This paper proposes a novel superpixel segmentation method for RGBD images. Superpixels are generated by clustering with the similarity of color, similarity of space location and similarity of high-quality depth information.

2   RGBD Image Superpixel Segmentation Intergrated Depth Map Quality

In this paper, firstly, the RGB map is enhanced by bilateral filtering, and the hole of depth map is filled by joint bilateral filtering enhancement. Secondly, Depth map quality assessment method was carried out based on the edge consistency map between RGB profile map and depth gradient map, however, in the space weighting operation, to reduce the computational complexity, considering neighborhood information at the same time, this paper uses an adaptive nonlocal random walk algorithm for segmenting superpixel proposed by Wang et al. [19]. Thirdly, edge consistency map are weighted and fused with the depth map to obtain a high-quality depth map. Lastly, the color, space location and high-quality depth information are integrated for clustering to obtain the RGBD image superpixel segmentation method. The algorithm flow is shown in Fig. 1.

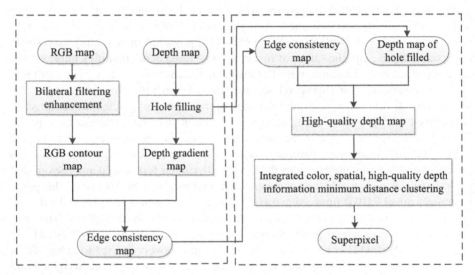

Fig. 1. The algorithm flow of the proposed superpixel segmentation.

2.1   Color Map Bilateral Filtering Enhancement

Bilateral filtering enhancement can not only eliminate image noise, but also preserve image edge information, which is convenient for subsequent image superpixel segmentation. Its principle is to calculate the gaussian function of the space distance and gray distance between two pixels, determine the weight size through the range of the Gaussian kernel function, and then multiply the two weight coefficients for filtering. The expression is as follows.

$$g(x, y) = \frac{\sum\limits_{(k,m) \in S(x,y)} I(k, m) w(x, y, k, m)}{w(x, y, k, m)} \tag{1}$$

$$w(x, y, k, m) = w_s(x, y, k, m) * w_r(x, y, k, m) \tag{2}$$

$$w_s(x, y, k, m) = \exp(-\frac{(k - x)^2 + (m - y)^2}{2\delta_s^2}) \tag{3}$$

$$w_r(x, y, k, m) = \exp(-\frac{||I(k, m) - I(x, y)||^2}{2\delta_r^2}) \tag{4}$$

where $g(x,y)$ is the image processed by bilateral filtering, $S(x,y)$ is the collection of $(2N + 1)(2N + 1)$ neighborhood pixels centered on pixel point (x,y), $I(k,m)$ denotes the pixel value at (k,m). $w(x,y,k,m)$ denotes the value calculated by two gaussian functions, $w_s(x,y,k,m)$ is based on the similarity of spatial distance, which decreases with the increase of the distance between pixels. $w_r(x,y,k,m)$ is the gray value similarity calculated by square of the absolute value difference between two pixels, which decreases with the increase of the gray value difference. The larger the δ_s is, the more weighted pixels will lead to the more blurred the image. The limit of δ_r will keep the edge information of the image, so as to eliminate the image noise and preserve the edge information of the image, making the image prepare for the subsequent superpixel segmentation.

2.2 Depth Map Hole Filling

To fill depth map hole using joint bilateral filtering algorithm, joint bilateral filter is developed by the bilateral filtering, the difference between them is that the joint bilateral filtering algorithm uses color map as guide map to calculate the domain weight, and the filtering results of the bilateral filtering algorithm are optimized to have the unstable effect of flipping near the edge. The expression is as follows.

$$U_y = \frac{\sum\limits_{x \in \Omega} w_c(x, y).w_s(x, y).O_x}{\sum\limits_{x \in \Omega} w_c(x, y).w_s(x, y)} \tag{5}$$

$$w_c(x, y) = \exp(-\frac{||D_y - N_x||^2}{2\delta_c^2}) \tag{6}$$

$$w_s(x, y) = \exp(-\frac{||y - x||^2}{2\delta_s^2}) \tag{7}$$

where U_y is the pixel depth value after joint filtering, O_x is the depth value of the processed depth map, and Ω denotes the filtering neighborhood range, $W_c(x,y)$ is the color similarity weight, $W_s(x,y)$ is the spatial position similarity weight, D_y is the pixel depth value of the position y of the point to be filled in the color map, and N_x is the pixel value of the position x in the neighborhood. δ_c is the color similarity weight parameter, and δ_s is the spatial location similarity weight parameter. Color similarity means that the more similar the pixels to be filled are in the color image, the more weight the pixels to be filled will have. Spatial location similarity means that the closer the pixels to be filled are, the more weight they will have.

2.3 High-Quality Depth Map Generation Algorithm

In the D (Depth) map of RGBD image, the area around the edge of the image is a high-quality depth area. Therefore, in this paper, RGB contour map and depth gradient map are used to obtain edge consistency map, and it is weighted and fused with depth map to obtain high-quality depth map. The algorithm steps are as follows.

Algorithm 1. High-quality depth map generation algorithm.

Input: RGB map, Depth map.
Output: High-quality depth map.
Step 1. RGB contour map and depth gradient map are generated to obtain the rough edge consistency map, and then gaussian smoothing operation is carried out to roughly locate high-quality depth areas.

In this paper, the HED method based on convolutional neural network is used to obtain RGB contour map. Compared with the traditional edge detection method, this method can not only show the object boundary, but also suppress the irrelevant edges inside the object. *EC* (Edge Consistency map) of *HED* (RGB contour graph) and *DG* (Depth gradient map) can be expressed as Eq. (8).

$$EC = HED \odot DG \tag{8}$$

where $\odot$ denotes the Hadamard product operation of the elements corresponding to image matrix *HED* and image matrix *DG*, and the resulting of edge consistency map is shown in Fig. 2.

Since high-quality depth regions tend to be located near those pixels with large edge consistency values, a defined threshold is used to determine a subgroup of "anchor pixels", the APC in Fig. 2. and these anchor pixels are used to roughly locate high-quality D regions (EC^-) through Eq. (9).

$$EC^- = G(f(EC - Tc)) \tag{9}$$

where, T_c is the determined threshold, G denotes Gaussian smoothing operation, f is a function that assigns its negative value to zero.

Step 2. In this paper, the adaptive non-local random walk algorithm is used for super-pixel segmentation to replace image pixels and generate a complete edge consistency map.

The depth map quality feature map should be complete, so a novel spatial weighting operation is used for regions not near the edge, it mainly includes similarity measure and space weighted range of features, exp is the similarity measure of features, it is implemented with the common thread [20]. The euclidean distance is used to determine the spatial weighted range (11) in Eq. (10), that is, APA in Fig. 2. is determined adaptively by Eq. (11), where T_c is set to 20, T_a is set to 30. In this paper, in order to consider the global neighborhood relationship between image pixels and reduce time complexity, an adaptive nonlocal random walk algorithm is used to generate superpixel blocks.

$$EC(P_i) \leftarrow \frac{\sum P_j \phi EC^-(P_j).\exp(w||V(P_i), V(P_j)||_2)}{\sum P_j \in \exp(w|||V(P_i), V(P_j)||_2)} \tag{10}$$

$$\phi : ||c(p_i, p_j)||_2 \leq \min(\{||p_i, f(DG - T_a)||_2\}) \tag{11}$$

where P_i denotes the i-th superpixel, T_a is determined threshold, w is the weight parameter, $||.||$ is l_2 norm, $V(.)$ and $P(.)$ returns the average and center of the given RGB image respectively. The final edge consistency map (EC) is at the lower right corner of Fig. 2.

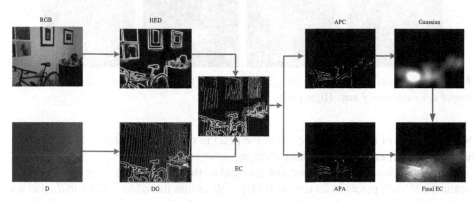

Fig. 2. Edge consistency map

Step 3. The complete edge consistency map is weighted and fused with depth map to obtain high-quality depth map, as the Eq. 12.

$$h(x) = (1 - \partial)f_0(x) + \partial f_1(x) \tag{12}$$

where ∂ sets to 0.6, namely, the weight of edge consistency map is set to 0.6, and the weight of depth map is set to 0.4 will get high-quality depth map to extract the high-quality depth information, combined with the similarity of high-quality depth information, color similarity, similarity of space location clustering, get superpixel segmentation results will be more accurate, $f_0(x)$ and $f_1(x)$ respectively denote the depth map and the corresponding edge consistency map, $h(x)$ denotes the weighted fusion of the depth map and edge consistency map, high-quality depth map generation process is shown in Fig. 3.

2.4 Superpixel Segmentation Intergrated Depth Map Quality

The method in this paper is to transform the 5-dimensional feature composed of CIELAB color space and pixel position from the traditional SLIC algorithm to the 6-dimensional feature composed of CIELAB color space, the depth information after quality evaluation and pixel position to cluster adjacent pixels. The algorithm steps are as follows.

Algorithm 2. Superpixel segmentation intergrated depth map quality.

Input: RGB map, high-quality depth map.
Output: Superpixel block.
Step 1. The interval S is used to initialize the cluster center C_k, in order to prevent the clustering center from being at the edge of the image, the clustering center was moved

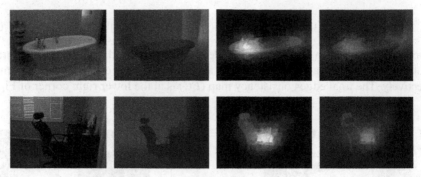

Fig. 3. The process of generating high-quality depth map. From left to right are RGB map, Depth map, Edge consistency map, High-quality depth map.

to the position of the lowest gradient of the pixel in the 3 neighborhood. Set each pixel label $l(i)$ to -1, and set the distance d_i to ∞.

Step 2. For each clustering center C_k, calculate the distance $D_{i,k}$ from the clustering center C_k to each pixel i in 2S region. If $D_{i,k} < d_i$, assign the values of $D_{i,k}$ to d_i, and set the label $l(i)$ is k, the pixels are divided into the central region with the highest similarity in turn. Where interval S and the similarity distance formula can be calculated as.

$$S = \sqrt{Num/K} \tag{13}$$

$$d_{\text{lab}} = \sqrt{(l_i - l_k)^2 + (a_i - a_k)^2 + (b_i - b_k)^2} \tag{14}$$

$$d_{\text{d}} = \sqrt{(d_i - d_k)^2} \tag{15}$$

$$d_{xy} = \sqrt{(x_i - x_k)^2 + (y_i - y_k)^2} \tag{16}$$

where *Num* denotes the total number of pixels in an image, and K denotes the number of presegmented pixels. d_{lab} denotes the distance measurement from i to k in the Lab color space, d_{d} denotes the distance calculation of high-quality depth value from i to k, d_{xy} denotes the calculation of the spatial distance from i to k pixel coordinate values. The final similarity distance measure D_{ik} is shown in Eq. (17).

$$D_{i,k} = \sqrt{\left(\frac{d_{\text{lab}}}{m}\right)^2 + \left(\frac{d_d}{n}\right)^2 + \left(\frac{d_{xy}}{S}\right)^2} \tag{17}$$

where m, n and S are weight coefficients, which are used to balance the proportion of color information, high-quality depth information and spatial location information in similarity measurement.

3 Experimental Results and Analysis

3.1 Datasets and Evaluation Metrics

This paper selects 654 images contained in NYU dataset, which are composed of video sequences of various indoor scenes recorded by RGB and Depth cameras of Microsoft Kinect.

Both UE (Under-segmentation Error) [7] and ASA (Achievable segmentation Accuracy) [21] are used for experimental verification of the proposed algorithm. UE and ASA are indexes to evaluate the edge fitting ability of superpixel segmentation results, where UE denotes the percentage of pixels that overflow from the truth boundary, and ASA denotes the upper limit of segmentation accuracy, which is the highest accuracy that can be obtained when using superpixels as basic units for image segmentation, its definition is shown in Eqs. (18, 19).

$$UE = \frac{\sum\limits_{m}(\sum\limits_{C_k \cap G_m > B}|C_k|) - N}{N} \tag{18}$$

$$ASA(S) = \frac{\sum\limits_{k}\max\limits_{m}(C_k \cap G_m)}{\sum\limits_{m}|G_m|} \tag{19}$$

where $C_1, C_2, C_3 ... C_n$ denotes n superpixel blocks generated by the superpixel segmentation algorithm, N is the number of pixels in the image, G represents the truth segmentation region, B is 5%, m denotes the number of truth segmentation regions, and k denotes the number of superpixel segmentation regions.

3.2 Influence of Parameters

Given that the number of superpixels is 300 and n is 500, the influence of m on the result of superpixel segmentation is shown in Table 1.

Table 1. The influence of m on the result of superpixel segmentation.

m	ASA	UE
10	0.893	0.216
20	**0.898**	**0.212**
30	0.892	0.222
40	0.897	0.243

It can be observed from Table 1 that when m is 20, ASA takes the maximum value and UE takes the minimum value. When the value of m is greater than or less than 20, the segmentation accuracy will decrease and the under-segmentation error will increase compared with that when m is 20. So m is going to take 20.

Table 2. The influence of n on the result of superpixel segmentation.

N	ASA	UE
50	0.848	0.297
200	0.854	0.286
500	**0.869**	**0.254**
600	0.865	0.354

When the given number of superpixels is 300 and m is 20, the influence of n on the result of superpixel segmentation is shown in Table 2.

As can be seen from Table 2, when n is less than 500, the accuracy of superpixel segmentation increases with the increase of n value, and the under-segmentation error decreases with the increase of n value. When the value is an integer above 500, the segmentation accuracy will decrease and the under-segmentation error will increase compared with that when n is 500. So n is going to take 500 in this paper.

3.3   Comparation Experiment

On the one hand, the method in this paper has the advantages of fast running speed and clear contour of SLIC algorithm. On the other hand, for some images with complex background, by incorporating high-quality depth information, the superpixel segmentation region of the image stick to the image boundary better. The comparison algorithms involved in verification in this paper are: the SLIC algorithm [7] and the SLIC-D algorithm [17].

Visually Compare.   In Fig. 4 shows the comparison of the superpixel segmentation results visual effect map in NYU dataset when the number of superpixels is set to 300. The original map and the superpixel segmentation result map are given, and local magnification of them is also given.

From Fig. 4 the first group of picture, as can be seen from the superpixel segmentation result of hand sanitizer on the wash table, the algorithms in Reference [7] and Reference [17] do not distinguish the outer contour edges of hand sanitizer, while Our algorithm can not only segment the rough contour of the outer contour of the hand sanitizer, but also it can separate the weak edges of the target object inside the image. The second group of picture, it can be seen from the superpixel segmentation result of the left chair, Reference [7] algorithm and Reference [17] algorithm do not stick to the edge of chair, and only Our algorithm can stick to the edge of chair closely. The third group of picture can be observed that Reference [7] algorithm can only divide the outer contour of the stool, but the weak edge part of the internal target in the image cannot be recognized, Reference [17] algorithm mistakenly regarded the contour of the internal target of the stool as the outer contour of the stool. The algorithm in this paper not only segmented the rough edges of the outer contour of the stool, but also accurately segmented the weak edge part of the internal target of the stool. In conclusion, RGBD image superpixel segmentation method intergrated depth map quality has more advantages in edge fitting

Fig. 4. Visual effect map. From left to right are Origin, Reference [7], Reference [17], Ours.

degree. We are analyzed theoretically, RGB profile map and depth gradient map by Hadamard product operation to get edge consistency map, high-quality depth map is obtained by weighted fusion between edge consistency map and depth map, because clustering is based on high-quality depth information, color information and spatial location information, therefore, compared with the SLIC algorithm and the SLIC-D algorithm, the algorithm in this paper can significantly improve the image edge fitting degree.

Objective Evaluation. *UE* and *ASA* are indicators to evaluate the edge fitting ability of superpixel segmentation results. in this paper, under the condition that the number of pixels is given, the mean value of the superpixel segmentation results on *ASA* and *UE* indexes of all images is selected (Fig. 5).

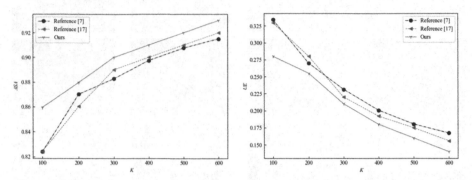

Fig. 5. Contrast data diagram. From left to right are *ASA, UE*.

In general, when the number of superpixels is given, Our algorithm has higher segmentation accuracy and lower under-segmentation error than Reference [17] algorithm, Reference [17] algorithm has higher segmentation accuracy and lower under-segmentation error than Reference [7] algorithm. However, when the number of superpixels is set to 200, the average segmentation accuracy of Reference [7] algorithm is 0.870, and the under-segmentation error is 0.269, the average segmentation accuracy of Reference [17] algorithm is 0.861, and the under-segmentation error is 0.280. However, the segmentation accuracy of the proposed algorithm is 0.879 and the under-segmentation error is 0.255. That is to say, when the number of superpixels is set to 200, Reference [17] algorithm has lower segmentation accuracy and higher under-segmentation error than Reference [7] algorithm, while the proposed algorithm has higher segmentation accuracy and lower under-segmentation error than the previous two algorithms. It shows that the proposed algorithm can not only stick to the weak edge of the image with a given number of superpixels, but also improve the image edge fitting degree. For example, the proposed algorithm can well stick to the weak boundary region of hand sanitizer and stool, so the proposed algorithm can maintain good contour details and have a good edge fit degree.

4 Conclusion

In this paper, firstly, the RGB map is enhanced by bilateral filtering to suppress and smooth the noise, joint bilateral filtering enhancement is used to fill the depth map hole. Secondly, contour map was obtained from the enhanced RGB map, and depth gradient map was obtained from the hole filled depth map. Then the edge consistency map and depth map are weighted and fused to get a high-quality depth map. Finally, clustering is based on the similarity of color, spatial location and high-quality depth information, a novel superpixel segmentation method for RGBD image was obtained. The algorithm is verified by experiments on NYU dataset and compared with the existing SLIC algorithm and SLIC-D algorithm. The results show that for images with complex background, the superpixel blocks generated by the algorithm in this paper can not only recognize the weak edges of the image, but also closely stick to the edges of the image.

Acknowledgement. This work was supported by the Science and Technology Plan-natural Science Foundation project of Gansu (grant numbers 20JR5RA518), and the Cultivation plan of major Scientific Research Projects of Northwest Normal University (grant numbers NWNU-LKZD2021-06).

References

1. Arbelaez, P., Maire, M., Fowlkes, C., et al.: Contour detection and hierarchical image segmentation. IEEE Trans. Pattern Anal. Mach. Intell. **33**(5), 898–916 (2010). https://doi.org/10.1109/TPAMI.2010.161
2. Yang, F., Lu, H., Yang, M.: Robust superpixel tracking. IEEE Trans. Image Process. **23**(4), 1639–1651 (2014). https://doi.org/10.1109/TIP.2014.2300823
3. Li, C., Cong, R., Hou, J., et al.: Nested network with two-stream pyramid for salient object detection in optical remote sensing images. IEEE Trans. Geosci. Remote Sens. **57**(11), 9156–9166 (2019). https://doi.org/10.1109/TGRS.2019.2925070
4. Cong, R., Lei, J., Fu, H., et al.: An iterative co-saliency framework for RGBD images. IEEE Trans. Cybern. **49**(1), 233–246 (2017). https://doi.org/10.1109/TCYB.2017.2771488
5. Cong, R., Lei, J., Fu, H., et al.: Video saliency detection via sparsity-based reconstruction and propagation. IEEE Trans. Image Process. **28**(10), 4819–4831 (2019). https://doi.org/10.1109/TIP.2019.2910377
6. Cong, R., Lei, J., Fu, H., et al.: Going from RGB to RGBD saliency: a depth-guided transformation model. IEEE Trans. Cybern. **50**(8), 3627–3639 (2019). https://doi.org/10.1109/TCYB.2019.2932005
7. Achanta, R., Shaji, A., Smith, K., et al.: SLIC superpixels compared to state-of-the-art superpixel methods. IEEE Trans. Pattern Anal. Mach. Intell. **34**(11), 2274–2282 (2012). https://doi.org/10.1109/TPAMI.2012.120
8. Li, Z., Chen, J.: Superpixel segmentation using linear spectral clustering. In: Proceedings of the IEEE Conference on Computer Vision and Pattern Recognition. IEEE Press, Boston, pp. 1356–1363 (2015). https://doi.org/10.1109/CVPR.2015.7298741
9. Guo, Y.J., Yang, M., Hou, Y.C.: Application of an improved SLIC algorithm in color image segmentation. J. Chongqing Univ. Technol. Nat. Sci. **34**(2), 158–164 (2020). https://doi.org/10.3969/j.issn.1674-8425(z).2020.02.022
10. Lei, T., Lian, Q., Jia, X.H., et al.: Fast simple linear iterative clustering for image superpixel algorithm. Comput. Sci. **47**(2), 143–149 (2020)
11. Liao, M., Li, Y., Zhao, Y.Q., et al.: A new method for image superpixel segmentation. J. Electron. Inf. Technol. **42**(2), 83–89 (2020)
12. Xiao, X., Zhou, Y., Gong, Y.J.: Content-adaptive superpixel segmentation. IEEE Trans. Image Process. **27**(6), 2883–2896 (2018). https://doi.org/10.1109/TIP.2018.2810541
13. Zhang, Y., Ding, L., Sharma, G.: Local-linear-fitting-based matting for joint hole filling and depth upsampling of RGB-D images. J. Electron. Imaging. **28**(3), 033019 (2019). https://doi.org/10.1117/1.JEI.28.3.033019
14. Zhao, J.X., Cao, Y., Fan, D.P., et al.: Contrast prior and fluid pyramid integration for RGBD salient object detection. In: Proceedings of the IEEE/CVF Conference on Computer Vision and Pattern Recognition. IEEE Press, Long Beach, pp. 3927–3936 (2019). https://doi.org/10.1109/CVPR.2019.00405

15. Wang, X., Li, S., Chen, C., et al.: Depth map quality-aware selective saliency fusion for RGB-D image salient object detection. Neurocomputing **432**, 44–56 (2021). https://doi.org/10.1016/j.neucom.2020.12.071

16. Agoes, A.S., Hu, Z., Matsunaga, N.: DSLIC: A Superpixel Based Segmentation Algorithm for Depth Image. In: Chen, C.-S., Lu, J., Ma, K.-K. (eds.) ACCV 2016. LNCS, vol. 10117, pp. 77–87. Springer, Cham (2017). https://doi.org/10.1007/978-3-319-54427-4_6

17. Li, X.Y., Wan, L.L., Li, H.N., et al.: RGBD image co-segmentation via saliency detection and graph cut. J. Simul. **30**(7), 2558 (2018). https://doi.org/10.16182/j.issn1004731x.joss.201807016

18. Xie, S., Tu, Z.: Holistically-nested edge detection. In: Proceedings of the IEEE International Conference on Computer Vision. IEEE Press, Santiago, pp. 1395–1403 (2015). https://doi.org/10.1109/ICCV.2015.164

19. Wang, H., Shen, J., Yin, J., et al.: Adaptive nonlocal random walks for image superpixel segmentation. IEEE Trans. Circ. Syst. Vid. **30**(3), 822–834 (2019). https://doi.org/10.1109/TCSVT.2019.2896438

20. Chen, C., Li, S., Wang, Y., et al.: Video saliency detection via spatial-temporal fusion and low-rank coherency diffusion. IEEE Trans. Image Process. **26**(7), 3156–3170 (2017). https://doi.org/10.1109/TIP.2017.2670143

21. Stutz, D., Hermans, A., Leibe, B.: Superpixels: an evaluation of the state-of-the-art. Comput. Vis. Image Underst. **166**, 1–27 (2018). https://doi.org/10.1016/j.cviu.2017.03.007

Super-Resolution of Defocus Thread Image Based on Cycle Generative Adversarial Networks

Pengfei Jiang[1,2,3] (iD), Wangqing Xu[1,2,3], and Jinping Li[1,2,3](✉)

[1] School of Information Science and Engineering, University
of Jinan, Jinan 250022, China
ise_lijp@ujn.edu.cn
[2] Shandong Provincial Key Laboratory of Network Based Intelligent Computing, University of
Jinan, Jinan 250022, China
[3] Shandong College and University Key Laboratory of Information Processing and Cognitive
Computing in 13th Five-Year, Jinan 250022, China

Abstract. The dual camera calibration measurement method can realize low-cost and high-precision bolt dimension measurement by using two microscope cameras. But the height difference between the thread crest and root exceeds the depth of field, and the thread image becomes defocus, which seriously affects the measurement accuracy. For this reason, a super-resolution method for defocus thread image based on cyclic generative adversarial networks is proposed. We collected focus thread images and defocus thread images as training data. Two encoders are used in the generation network to extract image defocus features and content features. And a sub-pixel convolution layer is added to the decoder to achieve image super-resolution. A loss function based on adversarial loss and cycle-consistent loss is constructed to realize unsupervised training of the network, thereby achieve super-resolution of defocus thread images. The experimental results show that, in the simulated defocus images, the method has superiority in image detail preservation, sharpness improvement and peak signal to noise ratio. In the bolt dimension measurement task, it can effectively reconstruct the clear thread image and thus provide the measurement accuracy to 0.01 mm.

Keywords: Bolt · Dimension measurement · Defocus image · Super-resolution · Cyclic generative adversarial networks

1 Introduction

Bolts are an important part of industrial products and represent the country's basic industrial level. Bolt dimension parameters determine the degree of stability of industrial products, among which the major diameter, minor diameter and pitch are the most important. At present, the dimension measurement methods of bolt are mainly based on three measurement methods: manual, laser and machine vision. Among them, manual measurement method is the most common, but this method has low accuracy, poor

© IFIP International Federation for Information Processing 2022
Published by Springer Nature Switzerland AG 2022
Z. Shi et al. (Eds.): IIP 2022, IFIP AICT 643, pp. 457–472, 2022.
https://doi.org/10.1007/978-3-031-03948-5_37

consistency, time-consuming and labor-intensive, and easily leads to bolt damage. The laser measurement method has high precision, but the cost is very high, so it is difficult to apply in a large range. The bolt dimension measurement method based on machine vision collects the bolt image using a camera, then establishes the conversion model between the size in pixel and the size in millimeter, and finally locates the thread edge to calculate the bolt size in pixel, and combines the conversion model to obtain the bolt size in millimeter. Compared with other measurement methods, it has significant advantages of high precision, high efficiency, low cost, and non-contact. Modern industry has higher and higher requirements for bolt size measurement accuracy, and the accuracy requirements of some enterprises have reached 0.01 mm. But limited by the spatial resolution of the camera and the field of view, if the diameter of the bolt exceeds 10 mm, it can't achieve high measurement accuracy. The width of the lens field of view of the microscope camera is about 3 mm. Using the microscope camera and the dual camera calibration dimension measurement method [1, 2] to realize the bolt dimension measurement can ensure that the measurement accuracy can reach more than 0.01 mm. Due to the small depth of field of the microscope camera, the height difference between the thread crest and root bottom exceeds the range of the depth of field, and there is a certain degree of defocus blur on the edge of the thread in the collected bolt image. This will widen the bolt edge transition area, cause the edge location algorithm to be misaligned, and severely reduce the bolt dimension measurement accuracy. Therefore, removing defocus blur and improving thread image quality are of great significance for

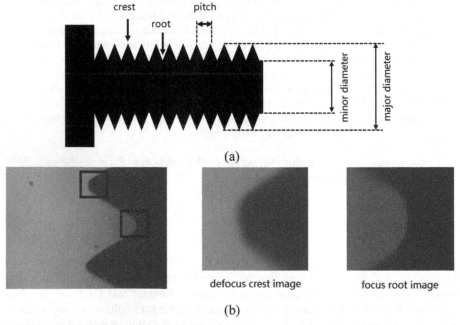

Fig. 1. The schematic diagram of the bolt dimension measurement and the thread image. (a) Bolt structure and bolt dimension measurement items. (b) Thread image taken by microscope camera.

bolt dimension measurement. The schematic diagram of the bolt dimension measurement and the thread image are shown in Fig. 1.

The current methods to improve image quality mainly include traditional deblurring methods based on defocus models, image deblurring methods based on deep learning, and super-resolution (SR) methods based on deep learning. The traditional deblurring method based on the defocus model represents the defocus blur process as the result of the convolution of the original clear image and the point spread function under random noise. The point spread function can be approximately described as the disc defocus model and the gaussian defocus model [3, 4]. These methods first estimate the point spread function, and then uses inverse filtering [5], Wiener filtering [6], Lucy-Richardson [7] and other algorithms to estimate a clear image. These methods can improve the image quality to a certain extent, but they are very computationally intensive and prone to ringing. Not only does it fail to recover effectively, but it also caused damage to a certain extent, and it is difficult to apply it to dimension measurement tasks. The image deblurring method and super-resolution method based on deep learning use convolutional neural network (CNN) to directly learn the best mapping of the image from the blurry domain to the clear domain, which can effectively restore the high-frequency details of the image. The difference between the super-resolution method and the image deblurring method is that the super-resolution method can improve the defocus image quality and increase the image resolution, which can theoretically increase the single pixel accuracy of the dimensional measurement system and improve the dimensional measurement accuracy, and is more valuable for research. In the bolt dimension measurement task, only the edge features of the image are extracted, so only the super-resolution of the thread edge image is needed, and for the other parts, the bicubic linear interpolation is performed to enlarge the image resolution and the edge image is stitched. In the bolt dimension measurement task, only extract the image edge features. Therefore, it is only necessary to achieve thread edge image super-resolution, and for the other parts, using bilinear interpolation to enlarge the image resolution and stitching with edge images.

The biggest problem with the super-resolution of the defocus thread image is that the degree of defocus is unknown, and because the image acquisition equipment needs to be adjusted during the process of acquiring the real thread defocus and focus image, the acquired bolt defocus image and focus image can't be guaranteed It is completely spatially aligned, and paired dataset can't be obtained. However, most of the existing super-resolution methods use paired dataset for supervised training. This paper starts from the real defocus thread image, proposes a super-resolution method of defocus thread image based on cyclic generative adversarial networks (CycleGAN), constructs a CycleGAN to realize the mutual conversion from blurry domain to clear domain for unpaired defocus and focus threaded images. In the generation network, two encoders are used to extract the image defocus feature and content feature respectively to improve the network's adaptability to different defocus degrees, and a sub-pixel convolutional layer is added to the decoder to achieve image super-resolution. The defocus thread images and focus thread images collected by the industrial camera are used as the dataset for model training, and the super-resolution result is used to measure the bolt dimension to verify the effectiveness of the method in this paper.

2 Related Work

The super-resolution of the defocus thread image in the task of bolt dimension measurement belongs to the real-world single image super-resolution. This section will introduce two parts: single image super-resolution and real-world super-resolution.

2.1 Single Image Super-Resolution

CNN has achieved great success in low-level vision tasks with their powerful representation capabilities. The most advanced super-resolution methods at present use CNN to learn to reconstruct high-resolution images from low-resolution images. SRCNN [8] first applied the CNN to super-resolution, using only three convolutional layers to learn the mapping from low-resolution images to high-resolution images, and achieved a leapfrog performance improvement in peak signal to noise ratio (PSNR) and structural similarity (SSIM). ESPCN [9] proposes a sub-pixel convolutional layer, which realizes end-to-end learning from low-resolution images to high-resolution images. In order to further improve the effect of super-resolution, researchers extract more image information by increasing the depth or width of the network, such as a deeper network with residual learning [10], Laplacian pyramid structure [11], recursive learning [12], deep back projection network [13] and residual dense network [14]. In addition, the EDSR [15] removes unnecessary batch normalization layers (BN) layers in the residual block, enlarges the model size, and the performance has been significantly improved. The innovation of SRGAN and its improved method [16, 17] lies in the application of a generative adversarial network (GAN) to achieve super-resolution, which combines pixel loss and adversarial loss, and uses the generation network and the discriminant network to confront each other to improve the clarity of the image, and the reconstructed image is in the texture details and visual perception are more real.

2.2 Real-World Super-Resolution

There are two major problems in real-world super-resolution. One is that the degradation of the real blurred image doesn't follow the bicubic degradation model, and the other is that the real blurred image lacks the corresponding high-definition image. Although single image super-resolution has powerful performance in dealing with bicubic degradation, it is difficult to apply to actual degraded images. The paired training data is obtained by sampling high-definition images, but the degradation of real blurred images doesn't follow the bicubic degradation model, and the results obtained by inputting real images are not reliable. Literature [18] proposes a dimensionality extension strategy, which takes different degrees of blur kernels as input to improve the applicability to real images. Literature [19] trains a network that converts high-definition images into low-resolution blurred images firstly, and then uses the synthesized low-resolution blurred images and high-definition images to form a pair of training data for network training. ZSSR [20] trains a small model for each image separately, but its training time is too long to be applied to actual scenes. Literature [21] constructed a dataset by means of optical zoom, but it still can't guarantee complete alignment. After the CycleGAN [22] is proposed, there are effective methods to solve the learning problem of unpaired data.

However, there are few researches on real-world super-resolution using CycleGAN at present. This paper starts from the defocus thread image in the bolt dimension measurement system, and uses the CycleGAN to learn the mapping from low-resolution defocus thread image to high-resolution focus thread image to enhance the sharpness of the thread edge and improve the measurement accuracy of bolt dimension measurement system.

3   Dual Camera Calibration Measurement

The principle of 2-D measurement based on machine vision is to establish a conversion model from size in pixel to size in millimeter by calibrating the internal and external parameters of the camera, that is, to calculate the single pixel accuracy of the image at the working distance of the lens, and then calculate the size in pixel of the object to be measured by extracting the edge features of the image to achieve two-dimensional size measurement. Single-pixel accuracy A_p is generally calculated by standard part, and its calculation formula is:

$$A_p = \frac{L_r}{L_p}, \tag{1}$$

where L_r is the size in millimeter of the standard part, and L_p is the size in pixel of the standard part. The single pixel accuracy is affected by the camera resolution and the field of view of the lens. Generally, the larger the camera resolution, the smaller the field of view of the lens, and the higher the single pixel accuracy. The field of view of a single camera is restricted by the camera's resolution, and it is difficult to cover the entire bolt under the premise of ensuring the measurement accuracy. Therefore, it is necessary to use the dual camera calibration measurement method to achieve bolt dimension measurement. This method uses two cameras to collect images at both ends of the size to be measured, and then accurately calibrates the positions of the two cameras to obtain the camera spacing L_1, then locates the edge of the image, calculates the relative distances L_2 and L_3 between the edge and the camera center line. Measurement result L is equal to $L_1 + L_2 + L_3$. The schematic diagram of the dual camera calibration measurement method is shown in Fig. 2.

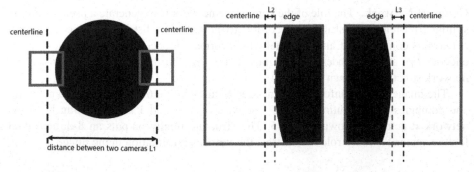

Fig. 2. Schematic diagram of dual camera calibration measurement method.

4   Method

Since the measurement system parameters need to be adjusted in the process of acquiring real thread defocus and focus images, the defocus images and the focus images can't achieve complete spatial alignment. Therefore, we choose to use a CycleGAN to learn the mapping from low-resolution defocus images to high-resolution focus images. The overall structure of the network is shown in Fig. 3. The CycleGAN contains two generative adversarial networks, one is applied to the forward process of learning the image from the blurry domain to the clear domain, and the other is applied to the reverse process of learning the image from the clear domain to the blurry domain. The super-resolution network takes the low-resolution defocus image x as input, and obtains the high-resolution output hr through the generation network G_H; then inputs hr into second generation network G_L to obtain the low-resolution composite image lr, finally uses the discriminant network D_H and D_L to determine whether hr and lr are true.

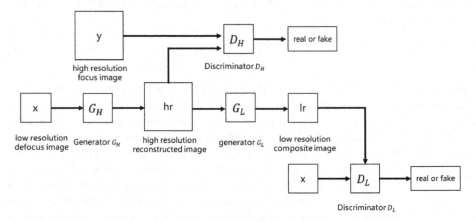

Fig. 3. Overview of the super-resolution method for defocus thread image.

4.1   Network Structure

Generate Network. The role of the generative network is to generate a pseudo sample similar to the real data distribution according to the input data distribution. The generation network is composed of an image defocus information encoder E_S, an image content encoder E_C, and a decoder D_{L2H} (replaced by D_{H2L} in the reverse process), and its network structure is shown in Fig. 4.

The image defocus information encoder E_S uses VGG16 as the backbone network, and combines 1 convolutional layer, 1 activation layer and 1 mean pooling layer. Its network structure is shown in Fig. 5. The structure finally outputs an 8-dimensional feature vector S, whose role is to extract the defocus information in the image.

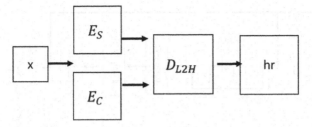

Fig. 4. Generate network.

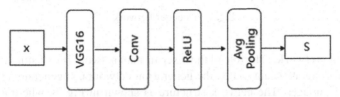

Fig. 5. Image defocus information encoder.

The role of the image content encoder E_C is to extract the content information in the image. In order to better extract the multi-scale information in the image, the image content encoder adopts the Res2Net [23] structure, and its network structure is shown in Fig. 6.

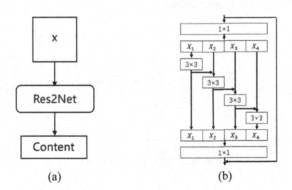

       (a)   (b)

Fig. 6. Image content encoder and Res2Net.

The decoder network structure is shown in Fig. 7. In the forward loop of reconstructing a high-resolution clear image from a low-resolution defocus image, the image defocus feature and image content feature extracted from the encoder are input to the decoder for feature fusion and use sub-pixel convolutional to achieve 2 times magnification of image resolution, and finally output high-resolution results. In the reverse process of synthesizing a high-resolution clear image into a low-resolution defocus image, the sub-pixel convolution layer is changed to a maximum pooling layer to reduce the image resolution by half.

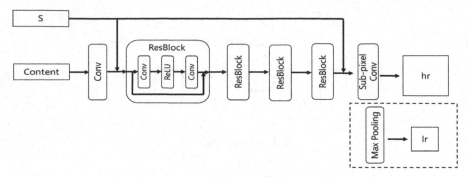

Fig. 7. Decoder network.

Discriminant Network. The role of the discriminant network is to distinguish between real data and generated data so that the generation network can generate more realistic target domain images. The network structure is shown in Fig. 8, where k represents the size of the convolution kernel in the convolution layer, n represents the number of output feature maps, s represents the step size of the convolution kernel. The discriminant network consists of 8 convolutional layers, and each convolutional layer uses a 3×3 size convolution kernel. In the calculation process, the number of feature maps is gradually increased from 64 to 512, each time the feature map is doubled, a convolution kernel with a step size of 2 is used to reduce the size of the output feature map. Finally, the binary adaptive mean convergence layer and the sigmoid activation function are used to judge the authenticity of the input image.

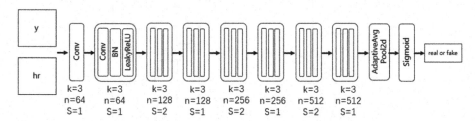

Fig. 8. Discriminant network.

4.2 Loss Function

The loss function is very important to the network performance, and the essence of the network model training process lies in the continuous optimization of the loss function. For paired dataset, the loss function usually uses pixel domain loss, that is, using mean square error (MSE) loss or perceptual loss [24] in the pixel domain, by comparing the two types of images pixel by pixel to ensure a higher PSNR. Since the defocus image and the focus image can't be completely aligned in space, the loss function in the pixel domain can't be used to optimize the network model. Therefore, the cyclic consistency loss function is introduced in this method to realize the optimization of the super-resolution network. The overall network loss function l_t is

$$l_t = l_H(G_H, D_H, x, y) + l_L(G_L, D_L, y, x) + \lambda l_C(G_H, G_L, x, y), \tag{2}$$

where l_H is the loss of the generation network G_H from low-resolution defocus image to high-resolution focus image and its discriminant network D_H; l_L is the loss of the generation network G_L from high-resolution focus image to low-resolution defocus image and its discriminant network D_H; l_C is the cyclic consistency loss; λ is the weight of l_C. The loss function l_H is defined as

$$l_H(G_H, D_H, x, y) = E_{y-P_{data}(y)}\big[logD_H(y)\big] + E_{x-P_{data}(x)}\big[log(1 - D_H(G_H(x)))\big], \tag{3}$$

where E is the mathematical expectation function, ~represents the obey relationship, $P_{data}(y)$ is the distribution of the focus high-resolution image y. The purpose of the loss function is to make the generated high-resolution clear image and the focus image as similar as possible. Similarly, the loss function l_L can also be constructed.

$$l_L(G_L, D_L, y, x) = E_{x-P_{data}(x)}\big[logD_L(x)\big] + E_{y-P_{data}(y)}\big[log(1 - D_L(G_L(y)))\big]. \tag{4}$$

The cyclic consistency loss function l_C is defined as

$$l_C(G_H, G_L, x, y) = E_{x-P_{data}(x)}\big[\|G_L(G_H(x)) - x\|_1\big] + E_{y-P_{data}(y)}\big[\|G_H(G_L(y)) - y\|_1\big]. \tag{5}$$

5   Experiment and Analysis

Since the method in this paper is aimed at unpaired defocus thread image and can't directly quantitatively analyze the super-resolution results, this experiment will first construct a paired simulated defocus image datasets to analyze the performance of the method, and then the method in this paper is applied to the bolt dimension measurement to test its influence on the measurement accuracy.

In this experiment, the hardware configuration is Inter I5-9600KF CPU with RTX-3060Ti GPU, and the software uses OpenCV image processing library and PyTorch deep learning framework.

5.1   Super-Resolution Experiment of Simulated Defocus Image

Dataset. In this part of the experiment, the DIV2K dataset is used as the experimental data. First, we crop the high-resolution clear images in the DIV2K dataset to obtain a clear image with a size of 512×512, and then apply different degrees of defocus blur with a blur kernel size of 3, 4, 5 to the clear image, then apply a defocus blur with blur kernels size of 3, 4, 5 to the clear image to obtain 3 defocus images, and the shape of the blur kernel is as shown in Fig. 9. Finally, we reduce the resolution of defocus images to 256×256 to obtain low-resolution defocus images and form 3 pairs of paired data. The number of images in the training set is 3000, and the number of images in the test set is 600.

Fig. 9. The shape of the blur kernel.

Experimental Results and Analysis. In order to compare the performance of the methods in this paper, the methods of EDSR, SRGAN, and ESRGAN are introduced for comparison. Because these methods use pixel domain loss functions in the training process, in order to ensure fairness, in this part of the experiment, the method in this paper also adds the pixel domain mean square error loss and the perceptual loss to optimize the network. The square error loss l_{mse} and the perceptual loss l_p are defined as

$$l_{mse} = \frac{1}{mn} \sum_{i=0}^{m-1} \sum_{j=0}^{n-1} \|I(i,j) - K(i,j)\|^2, \tag{6}$$

$$l_p = \frac{1}{uv} \sum_{i=0}^{u-1} \sum_{j=0}^{v-1} \|V_I(i,j) - V_K(i,j)\|^2, \tag{7}$$

where I is the label image, $I(i,j)$ is the pixel value in the i-th row and j-th column of the label image, K is the super-resolution result, $K(i,j)$ is the pixel value in the i-th row and j-th column of the label image, V_I is the output of I input VGG16, $V_I(i,j)$ is the value in the i-th row and j-th column of V_I, V_K is the output of K input VGG16, $V_K(i,j)$ is the value in the i-th row and j-th column of V_K.

The result of super-resolution of the simulated defocus images is shown in Fig. 10. The first column is the low-resolution defocus images, the second column is the high-resolution clear images, the third column, the fourth column, the fifth column, the sixth column, and the seventh column are the results of Bicubic, EDSR, SRGAN, ESRGAN and the method in this paper.

In order to be able to compare several methods more fairly, we use PSNR and SSIM to quantitatively evaluate the image quality. The calculation formula of PSNR is

$$MSE = \frac{1}{mn} \sum_{i=0}^{m-1} \sum_{j=0}^{n-1} \|I(i,j) - K(i,j)\|^2, \tag{8}$$

$$PSNR = 10 * log_{10} \left(\frac{MAX_I^2}{MSE} \right), \tag{9}$$

where I is the label image, K is the super-resolution result, MSE is the mean square error between the label image and the super-resolution result, MAX is the maximum value of the pixel color.

The calculation formula of SSIM is

$$l(I, K) = \frac{2\mu_I \mu_K + C_1}{\mu_I^2 + \mu_K^2 + C_1}, \tag{10}$$

Defocus Image   Ground Truth   Bicubic   EDSR   SRGAN   ESRGAN   Ours

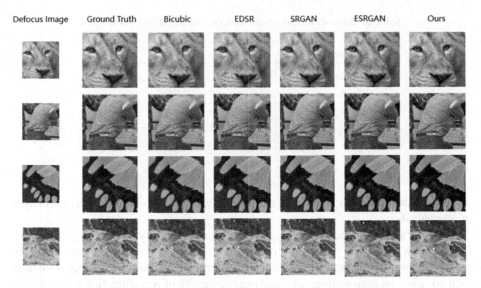

Fig. 10. Super-resolution results of simulated defocus images.

$$c(I, K) = \frac{2\sigma_I \sigma_K + C_2}{\sigma_I^2 + \sigma_K^2 + C_2}, \tag{11}$$

$$s(I, K) = \frac{\sigma_{IK} + C_3}{\sigma_I \sigma_K + C_3}, \tag{12}$$

$$SSIM = l(I, K) * c(I, K) * s(I, K), \tag{13}$$

where $l(I, K)$, $c(I, K)$, $s(I, K)$ represents the similarity of the two images in terms of brightness, contrast, and structure, μ_I, μ_K represent the mean values of I and K, σ_I, σ_K represent the variances of I and K, σ_{IK} represents the covariance of I and K, C_1, C_2, and C_3 are constants, usually $C_1 = (k_1 * l)^2$, $C_2 = (k_2 * l)^2$, $C_3 = C_2/2$, where $k_1 = 0.01$, $k_2 = 0.01$, $l = 255$. The calculation formula of mean μ_I, variance σ_I^2 and covariance σ_{IK} is

$$\mu_I = \frac{1}{H \times W} \sum_{i=1}^{H} \sum_{j=1}^{W} I(i, j), \tag{14}$$

$$\sigma_I^2 = \frac{1}{H \times W - 1} \sum_{i=1}^{H} \sum_{j=1}^{W} (I(i, j) - \mu_I)^2, \tag{15}$$

$$\sigma_{IK} = \frac{1}{H \times W - 1} \sum_{i=1}^{H} \sum_{j=1}^{W} (I(i, j) - \mu_I)(K(i, j) - \mu_K), \tag{16}$$

where I and K are the target image, H and W are the height and width of the image, μ_I and μ_K are the average values of I and K.

Table 1. Super-resolution evaluation on simulated defocus images.

Methods	PSNR	SSIM
Bicubic	25.96	0.8193
EDSR	29.12	0.8563
SRGAN	31.79	0.8762
ESRGAN	32.19	0.8968
Ours	32.74	0.9182

The following Table 1 gives super-resolution evaluation on simulated defocus images of all methods.

It can be seen from the visual comparison, the image quality produced by the bicubic interpolation method is poor, high-frequency information is seriously lost, and even artifacts appear. Compared with the bicubic interpolation image, the super-resolution method based on deep learning can improve the quality of reconstruction and make the image clearer. It can be seen from Table 1 that the super-resolution method based on deep learning all achieve high performance in terms of PSNR and SSIM. Among them, the methods with the generative adversarial structure are able to better recover high-frequency information in defocus images. Compared with other methods, the method in this paper obtains higher values, which means that the method in this paper can generate better reconstructed images.

5.2 Super-Resolution Experiment of Defocus Thread Image

Experiment Platform. In order to verify the effectiveness of the method in this paper, a bolt dimension measurement platform is built to conduct experiments, and a laser rangefinder is used to calibrate the experimental platform. The experimental platform is shown in Fig. 11. The camera is MER2-1800-32U3M, and its resolution is 4912 × 3684. The lens is MML3-ST40D, and the light source is a forward point light source matching the lens.

Experimental Results and Analysis. In this part of the experiment, this method is applied to the bolt dimension measurement task. First, the defocused thread images and the focused thread images are collected through the experimental platform, and then the edge images of the thread crest and root are intercepted, their size is 640 * 640. Finally the defocused thread images are down-sampled by 2 times to obtain low-resolution defocus images for super-resolution model training. The number of training sets is 600. The visualization results of super-resolution of the defocus thread images are shown in Fig. 12.

Fig. 11. Experimental platform.

The bolt dimension measurement results are shown in Table 2. Taking the standard bolts of known size as the measurement object, the method in this paper is used to measure the dimensions of 5 different positions. The measurement items are the major diameter, minor diameter and thread spacing of the bolt. The results are shown in Table 2. In order to test the stability of the method, 10 repeated experiments were carried out for the major diameter, minor diameter and pitch of the No. 1 position, and the results are shown in Fig. 13.

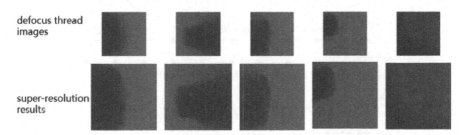

Fig. 12. Super-resolution results of defocus thread images.

It can be seen from Fig. 12 that the method in this paper effectively restores the edge details of the thread image and reconstructs a clear thread image. It can be seen from Table 2 and Fig. 13 that the method in this paper reduces the edge positioning error by about 15 pixels, greatly reduces the measurement error, and can effectively improve the measurement accuracy of the bolt dimension. It can basically ensure that the measurement accuracy is within 0.01 mm and can maintain good stability in repeated experiments, which is of great significance to the task of bolt dimension measurement.

Table 2. Results of bolt dimension measurement.

Position	Item	Real value	Measurement results (no SR)	Error (no SR)	Measured value (SR)	Error (SR)
No. 1	Major diameter	10.0052	9.9928	−0.0124	9.9990	−0.0052
	Minor diameter	8.8003	8.7924	−0.0079	8.7962	−0.0041
	Pitch	1.0034	1.0002	−0.0032	1.0050	0.0016
No. 2	Major diameter	10.0012	10.0245	0.0233	10.0104	0.0092
	Minor diameter	8.7954	8.8007	0.0053	8.8008	0.0054
	Pitch	0.9941	0.9972	0.0031	0.9960	0.0019
No. 3	Major diameter	9.9978	10.0016	0.0038	10.0013	0.0035
	Minor diameter	8.7967	8.8359	0.0392	8.8006	0.0039
	Pitch	1.0060	1.0067	0.0007	1.0067	0.0007
No. 4	Major diameter	10.0102	9.9903	−0.0199	10.0079	−0.0023
	Minor diameter	8.8505	8.8534	0.0029	8.8530	0.0025
	Pitch	1.0032	0.9937	−0.0095	1.0023	−0.0009
No. 5	Major diameter	10.0081	10.0491	0.0338	10.0183	0.0102
	Minor diameter	8.8223	8.8286	0.0063	8.8274	0.0051
	Pitch	9.9921	9.9983	0.0062	9.9994	0.0073

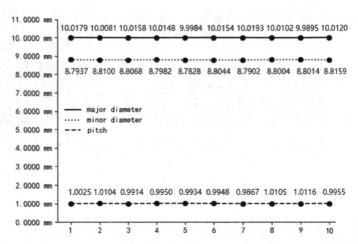

Fig. 13. Repeated measurement results of major diameter, minor diameter and pitch at position No. 1.

6   Conclusion

In this paper we have proposed a super-resolution method for defocus thread image based on CycleGAN in bolt dimension measurement. This method utilizes CycleGAN to solve the problem of the lack of paired data in defocus thread images. In the generative network, two encoders are used to extract the defocus feature and content feature of the image respectively to increase the adaptability to different degrees of defocus blur, and the sub-pixel convolutional layer is used to achieve image resolution enlargement. The results show that this method can effectively reconstruct a clear thread image in the bolt dimension measurement task, improve the edge positioning accuracy, and effectively improve the bolt dimension measurement accuracy. However, the calculation of this method is slightly complicated. In the next step, we will simplify the network to improve the efficiency of bolt dimension measurement.

Funding. This research was supported by the Department of Science & Technology of Shandong Province (2017CXGC0810).

References

1. Zhang, P.J.: Research on High-Precision Measurement Technology of Complex Workpiece Shape and Size Based on Machine Vision. University of Jinan (2019)
2. Lan, J.F.: Design and Implementation of a High-Precision Detection System for Piston Shape and Position Based on Machine Vision. University of Jinan (2021)
3. Yang, Y., Geng, Z., Wang, R., Li, J.: Defocusing and deblurring of traditional cameras with spatial variation. Electr. Opt. Contr. **22**(9), 91–95 (2015)
4. Yang, Y.: Research on Image Restoration Algorithm. Sichuan University (2004)
5. Gonzalez, R.C., Wentz, P.: Digital Image Processing. Science Press (1981)
6. Xiaoping, H., Chen, G., Mao, Z., et al.: Research on wiener filter restoration of defocused images. J. Instrum. **28**(3), 479–482 (2007)
7. Yan, H., Yan, W., Li, W.W.: Image restoration based on Lucy-Richardson algorithm. Comput. Eng. **36**(15), 204–205 (2010)
8. Dong, C., Loy, C.C., He, K., Tang, X.: Learning a deep convolutional network for image super-resolution. In: Fleet, D., Pajdla, T., Schiele, B., Tuytelaars, T. (eds.) ECCV 2014. LNCS, vol. 8692, pp. 184–199. Springer, Cham (2014). https://doi.org/10.1007/978-3-319-10593-2_13
9. Shi, W., Caballero, J., Huszár, F., et al.: Real-time single image and video super-resolution using an efficient sub-pixel convolutional neural network. In: IEEE Conference on Computer Vision and Pattern Recognition 2016, LNCS, pp. 1874–1883. IEEE, Las Vegas (2016)
10. Kim, J., Lee, J.K., Lee, K.M.: Accurate image super-resolution using very deep convolutional networks. In: IEEE Conference on Computer Vision and Pattern Recognition 2016, LNCS, pp. 1646–1654. IEEE, Las Vegas (2016)
11. Lai, W.S., Huang, J.B., Ahuja, N., et al.: Deep laplacian pyramid networks for fast and accurate super-resolution. In: IEEE Conference on Computer Vision and Pattern Recognition 2017, LNCS, pp. 5835–5843. IEEE, Hawaii (2017)
12. Kim, J., Lee, J.K., Lee, K.M.: Deeply-recursive convolutional network for image super-resolution. In: IEEE Conference on Computer Vision and Pattern Recognition 2016, LNCS, pp. 1637–1645. IEEE, Las Vegas (2016)
13. Haris, M., Shakhnarovich, G., Ukita, N.: Deep back-projection networks for super-resolution. In: IEEE Conference on Computer Vision and Pattern Recognition 2018, LNCS, pp. 1664–1673. IEEE, Salt Lake City (2018)

14. Zhang, Y., Tian, Y., Kong, Y., et al.: Residual dense network for image super-resolution. In: IEEE Conference on Computer Vision and Pattern Recognition 2018, LNCS, pp. 2472–2481. IEEE, Salt Lake City (2018)
15. Lim, B., Son, S., Kim, H., et al.: Enhanced deep residual networks for single image super-resolution. In: IEEE Conference on Computer Vision and Pattern Recognition 2017, LNCS, pp. 1132–1140. IEEE, Hawaii (2017)
16. Ledig, C., Theis, L., Huszar, F., et al.: Photo-realistic single image super-resolution using a generative adversarial network. In: IEEE Conference on Computer Vision and Pattern Recognition 2017, LNCS, pp. 105–114. IEEE, Hawaii (2017)
17. Wang, X., et al.: ESRGAN: enhanced super-resolution generative adversarial networks. In: Leal-Taixé, L., Roth, S. (eds.) ECCV 2018. LNCS, vol. 11133, pp. 63–79. Springer, Cham (2019). https://doi.org/10.1007/978-3-030-11021-5_5
18. Zhang, K., Zuo, W., Zhang, L.: Learning a single convolutional super-resolution network for multiple degradations. In: IEEE Conference on Computer Vision and Pattern Recognition 2018, LNCS, pp. 3262–3271. IEEE, Salt Lake City (2018)
19. Bulat, A., Yang, J., Tzimiropoulos, G.: To learn image super-resolution, use a GAN to learn how to do image degradation first. In: Ferrari, V., Hebert, M., Sminchisescu, C., Weiss, Y. (eds.) ECCV 2018. LNCS, vol. 11210, pp. 187–202. Springer, Cham (2018). https://doi.org/10.1007/978-3-030-01231-1_12
20. Shocher, A., Cohen, N., Irani, M.: Zero-shot super-resolution using deep internal learning. In: IEEE Conference on Computer Vision and Pattern Recognition 2018, LNCS, pp. 3118–3126. IEEE, Salt Lake City (2018)
21. Zhang, X., Chen, Q., Ren, N., et al.: Zoom to learn, learn to zoom. In: IEEE Conference on Computer Vision and Pattern Recognition 2019, LNCS, pp. 3757–3765. IEEE, Long Beach (2019)
22. Zhu, J.Y., Park, T., Isola, P., et al.: Unpaired image-to-image translation using cycle-consistent adversarial networks. In: IEEE International Conference on Computer Vision 2017, LNCS, pp. 2242–2251. IEEE, Venice (2017)
23. Gao, S.H., Cheng, M.M., Zhao, K., Zhang, X.Y., Yang, M.H., Torr, P.: Res2Net: a new multi-scale backbone architecture. IEEE Trans. Pattern Anal. Mach. Intell. 43(2), 652–662 (2021)
24. Johnson, J., Alahi, A., Fei-Fei, L.: Perceptual losses for real-time style transfer and super-resolution. In: Leibe, B., Matas, J., Sebe, N., Welling, M. (eds.) ECCV 2016. LNCS, vol. 9906, pp. 694–711. Springer, Cham (2016). https://doi.org/10.1007/978-3-319-46475-6_43

Multi-instance Learning for Semantic Image Analysis

Dongping Tian[1(✉)] and Ying Zhang[2]

[1] Institute of Computer Software, Baoji University of Arts and Sciences, No. 1 Hi-Tech Avenue, Hi-Tech District, Baoji 721013, Shaanxi, China
422588370@qq.com
[2] Hangtian Primary School, No. 44 Baoguang Road, Weibin District, Baoji 721007, Shaanxi, China

Abstract. Semantic image analysis is an active topic of research in computer vision and pattern recognition. In the last two decades, a large number of works on semantic image analysis have emerged, among which the multi-instance learning (MIL) is one of the most commonly used methods due to its theoretical interest and its applicability to real-world problems. However, compared with various MIL methods and their corresponding applications in the field of semantic image analysis, there is a lack of surveys or review researches about MIL related studies. So the current paper, to begin with, elaborates the basic principles of multi-instance learning, subsequently summarizes it with applications to semantic based- image annotation, image retrieval and image classification as well as several other related applications comprehensively. At length, this paper concludes with a summary of some important conclusions and several potential research directions of MIL in the area of semantic image analysis for the future.

Keywords: Multi-instance learning · Image annotation · CBIR · Image classification · PLSA · GMM · SVM

1 Introduction

With the explosive growth of the world wide web and rapidly growing number of available digital color images, much research effort is devoted to the development of efficient and reliable semantic image analysis (SIA) systems. It is witnessed that a considerable progress in SIA has been obtained in the past few years, yet, it still confronts with many challenges and limitations. One of the main handicaps is the well-known semantic gap between low-level visual features and high-level semantic concepts. Fortunately, a huge number of advanced machine learning techniques have been proposed in the literature as a promising solution to fill the semantic gap. In general, current automatic image annotation (AIA) methods existed in the literature can be roughly divided into three categories: (i) generative model based AIA. Note that this kind of methods is dedicated to maximizing the generative likelihood of image features and labels. For an unlabeled

© IFIP International Federation for Information Processing 2022
Published by Springer Nature Switzerland AG 2022
Z. Shi et al. (Eds.): IIP 2022, IFIP AICT 643, pp. 473–484, 2022.
https://doi.org/10.1007/978-3-031-03948-5_38

image, the generative model based AIA methods provide the probability of an image label by computing a joint probabilistic model of image features and words from training datasets. Classic work includes cross-media relevance model (CMRM) [1], multiple Bernoulli relevance model [2] and probabilistic topic model [3], etc. (ii) discriminative model based AIA. This approach views image annotation as a multi-label classification problem, which is solved by first learning an independent binary classifier for each label and then to use the binary classifiers to predict labels for unlabeled images. Representative work involves Bayes point machine [4], label ranking [5] and support vector machine [6]. (iii) nearest-neighbour based AIA. This method assumes that those visually similar images are more likely to share common labels. For a given query image, the nearest neighbor model based AIA techniques usually search for a set of similar images firstly, and then the labels of the query image are derived based on the labels of the similar images. Note that the notable works [7, 8] and [9] belong to this category. Alternatively, it should be noted that the multi-instance learning (MIL), as another kind of supervised learning method, has also been widely used in the community of computer vision [10–33].

As briefly reviewed above, most of these approaches can achieve promising performance and motivate us to explore better semantic image analysis methods with the help of their excellent experiences and knowledge. So in this paper, instead of a specific model, we provide a brief survey of MIL that related to the semantic image analysis in the last two decades. The primary purpose is to illustrate the benefits and limitations of MIL and how to further improve its applications in the field of computer vision and pattern recognition. The rest of this paper is organized as follows. Section 2 elaborates the basic principles of MIL. In Sect. 3, the MIL with applications to image annotation, image retrieval, image classification and some other applications are reviewed respectively. Finally, we conclude this paper in Sect. 4 with a summary of some important conclusions and highlight the potential research directions of MIL in semantic image analysis for the future.

2   Multi-instance Learning

Multi-instance learning (MIL) [10] is a variation of supervised learning, where the task is to learn a concept given positive and negative bags of instances. Each bag may contain many instances, but a bag is labeled positive even if only one of the instances in it falls within the concept. On the contrary, a bag is labeled negative only if all the instances in it are negative. Hence, learning focuses on finding the actual positive instances in the positive bags. In other words, the goal of MIL is to generate a classifier that can classify unseen bags correctly. Formally, the task of MIL is to learn a function as follows [11]:

$f_{MIL}:2^\chi \to \{-1, +1\}$ from a given data set $\{(X_1, y_1),(X_2, y_2),...,(X_m, y_m)\}$, where $X_i \subseteq \chi$ denotes a set of instances $\left\{x_1^{(i)}, x_2^{(i)}, \cdots, x_{n_i}^{(i)}\right\}$ and $x_j^{(i)} \in \chi$ is the label of X_i.

In the context of automatic image annotation, an image is usually described by multiple semantic labels (or keywords) and these labels are often highly related to respective regions rather than the entire image itself. As a result, it is unclear which region in an image is associated with which class label assigned to the image. From this sense, the problem of AIA can be effectively solved by a more rational and natural strategy, i.e., the multi-instance learning method. To summarize, the task of AIA can be formulated as a MIL problem based on the following two aspects. On one hand, each segmented region is treated as an instance and all of them are grouped to form an image as a bag of instances. On the other side, at least one label should be assigned on each bag. Given an image labeled by keyword w_i, it is expected that at least one region will correspond to w_i even if segmentation may not be perfect. Hence, the AIA problem is in essence identical to MIL setting.

3 MIL for Semantic Image Analysis

From the literature, it can be seen that MIL is one of the recent machine-learning paradigms that is well suited to semantic image analysis tasks. Thus in this section, MIL will be summarized from the aspects of image annotation, image retrieval, image classification and other specific applications, respectively. Note that it is not possible to list all the existing MILs. Instead, we mainly focus on various MIL methods associated with semantic image analysis and attempt to look into them through a unified view.

3.1 MIL for Image Annotation

Image annotation has been an active topic of research in computer vision for decades due to its potentially large impact on both image understanding and web image search. In this subsection, we will review some classic works for automatic image annotation by using MIL related models. Note that during the past decade, many MIL algorithms have been proposed for AIA [10–17]. As a pioneer work, the point-wise diverse density (PWDD) approach [10] was the first probability model of MIL, which has been widely used to look for the target concept. The diverse density (DD) method measured a co-occurrence of similar instances from different bags with the same label. A feature point with large DD value indicated that it was close to at least one instance from every positive bag and far away from every negative instance. A gradient ascent method was in general adopted to search the instance feature space for points with high diverse density. In particular, PWDD was very useful for image annotation since it can return the most representative regions for a label, which makes it possible to explicitly observe the correspondence between the regions and labels. In the work of [12], the mi-SVM and MI-SVM algorithms were presented for instance-level classification and bag-level classification respectively by modifying the SVM formation. Note that mi-SVM explicitly treats the label instance labels y_i as unobserved hidden variables subject to constraints defined by their bag labels Y_I, whose goal is to maximize the usual instance margin jointly over the unknown instance labels and a linear or kernelized discriminant function, given below:

$$\min_{\{y_i\}} \min_{w,b,\zeta} \frac{1}{2}\|w\|^2 + C \sum_i \zeta_i$$

$$s.t. \forall i : y_i(< w, x_i > +b) \geq 1 - \zeta_i, \zeta_i \geq 0 \tag{1}$$

$$\sum_{i \in I} \frac{y_i + 1}{2} \geq 1, \forall I : Y_I = 1; y_i = -1, \forall I : Y_I = -1$$

where the second part of the constraint enforces the relations between instance labels and bag labels. In comparison, MI-SVM aims at maximizing the bag margin, which is defined as the margin of the "most positive" instance in case of positive bags, or the margin of the "least negative" instance in case of negative bags, given as:

$$\min_{w,b,\zeta} \frac{1}{2}\|w\|^2 + C\sum_I \zeta_I$$

$$s.t. \forall_I : Y_I \max_{i \in I}(< w, x_i > +b) \geq 1 - \zeta_I, \zeta_I \geq 0 \tag{2}$$

Note that in mi-SVM the margin of every instance matters, and one has the freedom to set the instance label variables under the constraints of their bag labels to maximize the margin. In comparison, in MI-SVM only one instance per bag matters since it determines the margin of the bag. The former is suitable for tasks where users care about instance labels whereas the latter is suitable for tasks where only the bag labels are concerned. Both methods are implemented using mixed integer quadratic programming (MIQP). However, unlike the standard SVM, they would lead to the non-convex optimization problems that suffer from local minima. As a result, the deterministic annealing is utilized to solve this non-convex optimization problem and the corresponding AL-SVM is proposed which could find better local minima of the objective function [13].

On the other hand, note that as the pioneer work of MIL for region-based image annotation, Yang et al. [14] proposed to learn an explicit correspondence between image regions and keywords through the sequential PWDD multi-instance learning. Subsequently they modeled AIA as a problem of image classification with the help of Bayesian framework. In order to find an optimal nonlinear decision boundary for each concept, they developed the asymmetrical support vector machine based MIL that extended the conventional SVM in the MIL framework by introducing asymmetrical loss functions for false positives and false negatives [15]. Besides, Feng et al. [16] formulated an improved citation-kNN (ICKNN) MIL algorithm for AIA. The main difference between PWDD and ICKNN lies in that the latter avoids learning the target instance (region) to represent a given keyword from the collection of training bags (images) and the labels are annotated on the whole image instead of image regions. In other words, the testing bag's labels are directly decided by its neighbor training bags. Followed by they put forward a reinforced DD method to search instance prototypes in an efficient and effective way (abbreviated as TMIML) to solve the issue of AIA [17]. The advantages of this method mainly lie in twofold: First, a more robust DD method was utilized, which is more resistant to the presence of outliers. Second, this reinforced DD algorithm can work directly with the MI data, which precluded the need for the multiple starts that are necessary in most existing EM-based algorithms, thus the running speed was markedly improved. Compared with previous MIML algorithm [11], the TMIML framework is much more effective due to the fact that the large amount of unlabeled samples were taken into account to resolve the small samples problem that often appears in the context of image auto-annotation task. Figure 1 illustrates the generalized framework of the MIL based AIA.

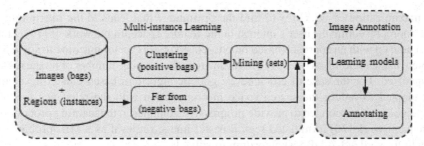

Fig. 1. Generalized framework of the MIL-based AIA models

As reviewed above, the MIL based methods for image annotation are concept-clear and structure-intuitive, and most of them have been proved to be quite successful for image annotation. However, improvements are still needed because of some inherent shortages. First, how to formulate an appropriate bag generator for MIL problems should be paid special attention to by researchers. Second, due to the multi-instance representation allows for concept descriptions that are defined upon the interaction of instance-level concepts, which is a natural way to describe visual concepts. As a consequence, how to find more effective and generally applicable algorithms for learning visual concepts is also well worth exploring.

3.2 MIL for Image Retrieval

In the past years, content-based image retrieval (CBIR) has been one of the most hot research topics in computer vision. Much work has been done in applying MIL to localized content-based image retrieval since the CBIR fits well the MIL framework as an image can be seen as a bag comprised of smaller regions/patches (i.e., instances). Given a query for a particular object, one may be interested in deciding only whether the image contains the queried object or not, instead of solving the more involved problem of labeling every single patch in the image. As the pioneer work of MIL for image retrieval, Maron et al. [18] firstly formulated CBIR as a multiple instance learning problem. In their framework, each image was deemed as a labeled bag with multiple instances and the segmented regions in the images corresponded to the instances in the bags. Specifically, they developed the DD method to solve MIL problem by converting the goal of MIL to a maximization problem. That is, with the assumption of n labeled bags and the hypothesis t, the DD value is calculated as:

$$DD(t) = \prod_{i=1}^{n} Pr(B_i, l_i|t) = \prod_{i=1}^{n} (1 - |l_i - Label(B_i|t)|) \tag{3}$$

$$Label(B_i|t) = \max_{j}\{exp[-\sum_{d=1}^{m} (s_d(B_{ijd} - t_d))^2]\} \tag{4}$$

where B_i denotes the i-th bag, l_i denotes the actual label of the i-th bag, B_{ij} is the j-th instance of bag i, B_{ijd} represents the feature value of instance B_{ij} on dimension d, S_d denotes the value of feature weight vector S on dimension d, t_d denotes the value of t on dimension d, n denotes the number of instances, and m denotes the number of features.

The maximization of Eq. (3) is to find the optimum t that leads to the maximum DD value for representing the user's interest in the feature space. In the work of [19], Zhang et al. came up with an approach based on one-class support vector machine to solve MIL problem in the region-based CBIR. This is an area where a huge number of image regions are involved. For the sake of efficiency, a genetic algorithm based clustering method was adopted to reduce the search space in conjunction with the relevance feedback technique was incorporated to provide progressive guidance to the learning process. The subsequent work [20] formulated region-based image retrieval as a MIL problem and brought forward MI-AdaBoost algorithm to solve it.

In spite of many MILs applied to CBIR, most of them only have a supervised manner using bag-level labels instead of the information of unlabeled data which do not belong to any labeled bag. In view of this, a multiple-instance semi-supervised learning (MISSL) method was proposed to solve the object-based image retrieval problem [21]. Unlike the loosely coupled manner exhibited in previous studies, a graph-based multiple-instance learning (GMIL) model was developed based on the regularization framework of MISSL by explicitly taking into account labelled data, semi-labeled data and unlabeled data simultaneously to propagate information on a graph. Here, it should be noted that the object-based image retrieval is related but different from the concept of region-based image retrieval. In addition, Li et al. [22] utilized relevant and irrelevant training web images rather than image regions to generate bags as well as instances for MIL formulation. They constructed a new model called MIL-CPB to effectively exploit the constraints that each positive bag contained at least a portion of positive instances on positive bags and predicted labels of test instances (images). What's more, they also developed a progressive scheme called progressive MIL-CPB to further improve the retrieval performance by iteratively partitioning the top-ranked training web images from the current MIL-CPB classifier to construct more confident positive bags and then added these new bags as training data to learn the subsequent MIL-CPB classifiers. Meanwhile, LSASVM-MIL model [23] was formulated for image retrieval based on the latent semantic analysis (LSA) and support vector machine (shown in Fig. 2). Specifically, a LSA based method was first utilized to convert bags in the MIL problem into a single representation vector, and then combining with SVM in the framework of a MIL algorithm for image retrieval. Experimental results on Corel datasets validated the effectiveness and efficiency of this model. To summarize, it is worth noting that MIL techniques can be incorporated into various CBIR systems to deal with the ambiguity existing in the user queries. But one of the key problems in developing a practical MIL-based CBIR system is to obtain a nice bag generator. Moreover, how to efficiently integrate MIL with other methods based on the trade-off between the computational complexity and the model reconstruction error is still an open issue and evidently worth studying.

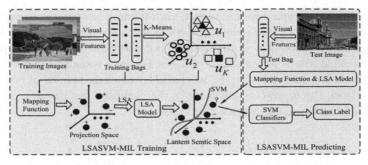

Fig. 2. Framework of the LSASVM-MIL model

3.3 MIL for Image Classification

Image classification is an important research topic due to its potential impact on both the image processing and understanding. However, it actually becomes a challenge problem due to the inherent ambiguity of image-keyword mapping. From the viewpoint of machine learning, image classification fits the MIL framework very well owing to the fact that a specific keyword is often relevant to an object in an image rather than the entire image. So far there has been much work on applying MIL to the task of image classification [24–26]. As a classic work, Chen et al. [24] developed the DD-SVM for mapping every bag to a point in a new feature space defined by the instance prototypes selected from local maxima of DD function, and then a SVM was trained based on the bag features. Note that the maximum margin formulation of MIL in the bag feature space was given as the following quadratic optimization problem:

$$\alpha^* = \underset{\alpha_i}{argmax} \sum_{i=1}^{l} \alpha_i - \frac{1}{2} \sum_{i,j=1}^{l} y_i y_j \alpha_i \alpha_j K(\phi(B_i), \phi(B_j)) \tag{5}$$

$$s.t. \begin{cases} \sum_{i=1}^{l} y_i \alpha_i = 0 \\ 0 \leq \alpha_i \leq C, i = 1, \cdots, l. \end{cases}$$

Here, it is worth noting that the representation feature of DD-SVM was very sensitive to noise and could easily incur very high computation cost.

As can be seen from the existed literatures, the single-instance supervised learning algorithm can be adapted to multi-instance learning as long as its focus is shifted from the discrimination on the instances to the discrimination on the bags. In actual fact, most current MIL algorithms can be viewed as going along this way, which is adapting single-instance learning algorithms to the multi-instance representation. In [25], an EM based learning algorithm was proposed to provide a comprehensive procedure for maximizing the measurement of diverse density on the given multiple instances. In essential, this method converted the multi-instance problem into a single-instance treatment by using EM to maximize the instance responsibility for the corresponding label of each bag. In recent work [26], a MIL algorithm was constructed to address image classification involving three steps, i.e., a new instance prototype extraction method was proposed to construct projection space for each label, each training sample was mapped to this potential projection space as a point and a SVM was trained for each label to implement image classification. It is worth noting that the proposed new instance prototype extraction method can be formulated as follows. For each instance I in positive bags, the DD value of I is defined by Eq. (6), where $|L^+|$ denotes the number of positive bags for a given label, $P_r((B_i, y_i)|I)$ is a measure of the likelihood that bag B_i receives label y_i given that I belongs to the instance prototypes.

$$DD(I, L) = \sum_{i=1}^{|L^+|} P_r((B_i, y_i)|I) \tag{6}$$

$$P_r((B_i, y_i)|I) = \max_j \{1 - |y_i - exp(dist^2(B_{ij}, I))|\} \tag{7}$$

$$dist^2(B_{ij}, I) = \sqrt{\sum_{k=1}^{d} (B_{ij}^k - I^k)^2} \tag{8}$$

In a nutshell, the MIL based methods have been successfully applied in image classification, effective features still need to be further researched because the time complexities in these models are often very expensive. Furthermore, that lacking enough qualified labeled training images can also limit the performance of them in real-world applications. Hence, semi-supervised learning method, which aims at learning from labeled and unlabeled data simultaneously, can be employed to boost the quality of the training image data with the help of unlabelled data in the presence of the small sample size problem, in particular, to solve MIL issues for partially labeled data by leveraging informative yet unlabeled data.

3.4   MIL for Other Applications

Except for the content described above, many MIL algorithms have also been intensively studied and applied in many other applications during the last decade, such as object detection [27], visual tracking [28], text annotation [29] and medical image analysis [30], etc. Besides, we refer the readers to two recent works [31, 32] as well as a very classic book [33] recently published for more details on a comprehensive and extensive survey on multi-instance learning. Meanwhile, a MIL library developed by prof. Yang of Carnegie Mellon University can also be publicly accessible[1]. In the following, several MIL related semantic image analysis approaches involved in this paper are concisely summarized in Table 1, mainly including the methods adopted, datasets employed and their corresponding websites.

---

[1] http://www.cs.cmu.edu/~juny/MILL/.

Table 1. Summary of MIL related semantic image analysis models

Refs. no.	Methods adopted	Datasets applied	Datasets websites
[11]	MIMLSVM, MIMLBOOST	COREL Dataset	http://corel.digitalriver.com/
[12, 13, 19, 23, 26]	MIL, SVM	COREL/MUSK Datasets	https://archive-beta.ics.uci.edu/
[14]	MIL, Bayesian Classifiers	COREL Dataset	http://corel.digitalriver.com/
[15]	Asymmetrical SVM-MIL	COREL/MUSK Datasets	https://archive-beta.ics.uci.edu/
[16]	ICKNN MIL	COREL Dataset	http://corel.digitalriver.com/
[17]	TMIML	COREL Dataset	http://corel.digitalriver.com/
[18]	MIL	COREL/SIMPLIcity Datasets	http://corel.digitalriver.com/
[20]	MI-AdaBoost	COREL/MUSK Datasets	https://archive-beta.ics.uci.edu/
[21]	GMIL,GMIL-M	SIVAL/MUSK Datasets	https://archive-beta.ics.uci.edu/
[25]	MIL	OTHER Dataset	/

4 Conclusions and Future Work

Multi-instance learning has become an active area of investigation in machine learning and computer vision since it was first formulized in the context of drug activity prediction. In this paper, we present a brief review of MIL related studies in semantic image analysis. The primary purpose is to illustrate the pros and cons of MIL combined with a great deal of existing researches as well as to point out the promising research directions of MIL for semantic image analysis in the future. A lot of very interesting topics have not been included here but would be worth exploring more in depth in the future. It should be noted that the following issues remain to be investigated. First, the most serious problem encumbering the advance of MIL is that there is only one popularly used real-world benchmark data, i.e. the Musk data sets. Although some application data have been used in some works, they can hardly act as benchmarks for some reasons. So how to build some publicly available challenging datasets that can estimate the performance of MIL pretty well is a worthy research direction. Second, MIL techniques can be incorporated into CBIR systems to deal with the ambiguity existing in the user queries. One of the key problems in developing a practical multi-instance learning based CBIR system is to obtain a nice bag generator. Thus how to formulate an appropriate bag generator for MIL problems should be paid special attention to. Third, how to efficiently integrate MIL with other methods based on the tradeoff between computational complexity and model reconstruction error is a valuable research direction in the future. Fourth, due to the multi-instance representation allows for concept descriptions that are defined upon the interaction of instance-level concepts, which is a natural way to describe visual concepts. As a consequence how to find more effective and generally applicable algorithms for learning visual concepts is also a promising research direction. Fifth, since labeled images are often hard to obtain or create in large quantities in practical applications while the unlabeled ones are easier to collect from the image repository. Thus semi-supervised learning method, which aims at learning from the labeled and unlabeled data simultaneously, can be employed to boost the quality of the training image data with the help of unlabelled data in the presence of the small sample size problem. Particularly, how to solve MIL issues for partially labeled data has become a promising research direction to leverage informative yet unlabeled data. Last but not the least, for the future work, MIL should be applied in more wider ranges to deal with more multimedia related tasks, such as speech recognition, action recognition, music information retrieval and other multimedia event detection tasks, etc.

Acknowledgement. This work is supported by the National Natural Science Foundation of China (No. 61971005) and the Key Research and Development Program of the Shaanxi Province of China (No. 2022GY-071).

References

1. Jeon, L., Lavrenko, V., Manmantha, R.: Automatic image annotation and retrieval using cross-media relevance model. In: Proceedings of the 26th International ACM SIGIR Conference on Research and Development in Information Retrieval, pp. 119–126 (2003)
2. Feng, S., Manmatha, R., Lavrenko, V.: Multiple Bernoulli relevance models for image and video annotation. In: Proceedings of the International Conference on Computer Vision and Pattern Recognition, pp. 1002–1009 (2004)
3. Tian, D., Shi, Z.: A two-stage hybrid probabilistic topic model for refining image annotation. Int. J. Mach. Learn. Cybern. **11**(2), 417–431 (2020)
4. Chang, E., Goh, K., Sychay, G., et al.: CBSA: content-based soft annotation for multimodal image retrieval using bayes point machines. IEEE Trans. Circuits Syst. Video Technol. **13**(1), 26–38 (2003)
5. Grangier, D., Bengio, S.: A discriminative kernel-based approach to rank images from text queries. IEEE Trans. Pattern Anal. Mach. Intell. **30**(8), 1371–1384 (2008)
6. Ciocca, G., Cusano, C., Santini, S., et al.: Halfway through the semantic gap: prosemantic features for image retrieval. Inf. Sci. **181**(22), 4943–4958 (2011)
7. Guillaumin, M., Mensink, T., Verbeek, J., et al.: TagProp: discriminative metric learning in nearest neighbor models for image auto-annotation. In: Proceedings of the 12th International Conference on Computer Vision, pp. 309–316 (2009)
8. Verma, Y., Jawahar, C.: Image annotation using metric learning in semantic neighbourhoods. In: Fitzgibbon, A., Lazebnik, S., Perona, P., Sato, Y., Schmid, C. (eds.) ECCV 2012. LNCS, vol. 7574, pp. 836–849. Springer, Heidelberg (2012). https://doi.org/10.1007/978-3-642-33712-3_60
9. Kalayeh, M., Idrees, H., Shah, M.: NMF-knn: image annotation using weighted multi-view non-negative matrix factorization. In: Proceedings of the International Conference on Computer Vision and Pattern Recognition, pp. 184–191 (2014)

10. Maron, O., Lozano-Perez, T.: A framework for multiple-instance learning. In: Advances in Neural Information Processing Systems, pp. 570–576 (1998)
11. Zhou, Z., Zhang, M.: Multi-instance multi-label learning with application to scene classification. In: Advances in Neural Information Processing Systems, pp. 1609–1616 (2007)
12. Andrews, S., Hofmann, T., Tsochantaridis, I.: Multiple instance learning with generalized support vector machines. In: Proceedings of the 18th AAAI Conference on Artificial Intelligence, pp. 943–944 (2002)
13. Gehler, P., Chapelle, O.: Deterministic annealing for multiple-instance learning. In: Proceedings of the 11th International Conference on Artificial Intelligence and Statistics, pp. 123–130 (2007)
14. Yang, C., Dong, M., Fotouhi, F.: Region-based image annotation through multiple-instance learning. In: Proceedings of the 13th International Conference on Multimedia, pp. 435–438 (2005)
15. Yang, C., Dong, M., Hua, J.: Region-based image annotation using asymmetrical support vector machine-based multiple-instance learning. In: Proceedings of the International Conference on Computer Vision and Pattern Recognition, pp. 2057–2063 (2006)
16. Feng, S., Xu, D., Li, B.: Automatic region-based image annotation using an improved multiple-instance learning algorithm. Chin. J. Electron. **17**(1), 43–47 (2008)
17. Feng, S., Xu, D.: Transductive multi-instance multi-label learning algorithm with application to automatic image annotation. Expert Syst. Appl. **37**(1), 661–670 (2010)
18. Maron, O., Ratan, A.: Multiple-instance learning for natural scene classification. In: Proceedings of 15th International Conference on Machine Learning, pp. 341–349 (1998)
19. Zhang, C., Chen, X.: Region-based image clustering and retrieval using multiple instance learning. In: Leow, W.-K., Lew, M.S., Chua, T.-S., Ma, W.-Y., Chaisorn, L., Bakker, E.M. (eds.) CIVR 2005. LNCS, vol. 3568, pp. 194–204. Springer, Heidelberg (2005). https://doi.org/10.1007/11526346_23
20. Yuan, X., Hua, X., Wang, M., et al.: A novel multiple instance learning approach for image retrieval based on Adaboost feature selection. In: Proceedings of the International Conference on Multimedia and Expo, pp. 1491–1494 (2007)
21. Wang, C., Zhang, L., Zhang, H.: Graph-based multiple-instance learning for object-based image retrieval. In: Proceeding of the International Conference on Multimedia Information Retrieval, pp. 156–163 (2008)
22. Li, W., Duan, L., Xu, D., et al.: Text-based image retrieval using progressive multi-instance learning. In: Proceedings of the 13th International Conference on Computer Vision, pp. 2049–2055 (2011)
23. Li, D., Peng, J., Li, Z., et al.: LSA based multi-instance learning algorithm for image retrieval. Signal Process. **91**(8), 1993–2000 (2011)
24. Chen, Y., Wang, J.: Image categorization by learning and reasoning with regions. J. Mach. Learn. Res. **5**(8), 913–939 (2004)
25. Pao, H., Chuang, S., Xu, Y., et al.: An EM based multiple instance learning method for image classification. Expert Syst. Appl. **35**(3), 1468–1472 (2008)
26. Xi, X., Xu, X., Wang, X.: A novel multi-instance learning algorithm with application to image classification. In: Proceedings of the Asia-Pacific Signal & Information Processing Association Annual Summit and Conference, pp. 1–6 (2012)
27. Yuan, T., Wan, F., Fu, M., et al.: Multiple instance active learning for object detection. In: Proceedings of the International Conference on Computer Vision and Pattern Recognition, pp. 5330–5339 (2021)
28. Li, D., Wen, G., Kuai, Y., et al.: Spatio-temporally weighted multiple instance learning for visual tracking. Optik **171**, 904–917 (2018)
29. Qiao, M., Liu, L., Yu, J., et al.: Diversified dictionaries for multi-instance learning. Pattern Recogn. **64**, 407–416 (2017)

30. Wang, Q., Zou, Y., Zhang, J., et al.: Second-order multi-instance learning model for whole slide image classification. Phys. Med. Biol. **66**(14), 34181583 (2021)
31. Carbonneau, M., Cheplygina, V., Granger, E., et al.: Multiple instance learning: a survey of problem characteristics and applications. Pattern Recogn. **77**, 329–353 (2018)
32. Tian, Y., Hao, W., Jin, D., et al.: A review of latest multi-instance learning. In: Proceedings of the 4th International Conference on Computer Science and Artificial Intelligence, pp. 41–45 (2020)
33. Herrera, F., et al.: Multiple Instance Learning. Springer, Cham (2016). https://doi.org/10.1007/978-3-319-47759-6

High-Resolution Remote Sensing Image Semantic Segmentation Method Based on Improved Encoder-Decoder Convolutional Neural Network

Xinyu Zhang$^{(\boxtimes)}$, Ying Zhang, Jianfei Chen, and Huijun Du

State Grid Shandong Electric Power Company Tai'an Power Supply Company, 8 Dongyue Street, Taishan District, Tai'an, Shandong, China
Weike.liu@163.com

Abstract. In recent years, Convolutional neural network with encoder-decoder structure is a kind of image semantic segmentation method with high accuracy. However, the characteristics of large amount of parameters and high requirements for computing power restrict its application in the fields of limited computing power and high real-time requirement, such as unmanned driving, road monitoring, remote sensing classification and mobile object detection. To solve the above problems, this thesis firstly designs the dilated convolution combination module, which solves the gridding problems while ensuring large receptive field; then, a double-channel encoder-decoder convolutional neural network is built by using the dilated convolution module combined with the depth separable convolution. Using this network, the parameters and computation of semantic segmentation convolution model of high resolution remote sensing image are greatly reduced while maintaining high segmentation accuracy. Through experiments on GID data sets, and compared with a variety of semantic segmentation methods, this thesis verifies the effectiveness and light-weight of this method.

Keywords: Semantic segmentation · Dilated convolution combination · Receptive field · Gridding problems · Depthwise separable convolution

1 Introduction

With the development of remote sensing technology, high-resolution remote sensing images have become the key research object in the field of remote sensing because they have more abundant and accurate ground object information. High resolution remote sensing images have the characteristics of changeable spectral characteristics, detailed texture characteristics, obvious geometric structure and clear context information, which provides more convenience for automatic classification of high resolution remote sensing images. However, because it contains more semantic and detailed information, some traditional methods, such as SVM [1], Watershed, Random-Forest and so on, do not

Z. Shi et al. (Eds.): IIP 2022, IFIP AICT 643, pp. 485–492, 2022.
https://doi.org/10.1007/978-3-031-03948-5_39

perform well in the classification of high-resolution remote sensing images. The inter-ference factors of the task are mostly the same spectrum foreign matter and the same object different spectrum. Therefore, we need to find a more accurate classification algorithm.

In 2014, using the deep learning, LONG [2] proposed the first image semantic seg-mentation network: Full convolutional networks (FCN) [3], and then advanced semantic segmentation networks such as SegNet [3], U-Net [4, 5], DeepLab [6] series and ESPNet [7] series were proposed. The encoder-decoder structure [3, 8] network represented by U-Net has attracted the attention of scholars because of its high segmentation accuracy, such as U-Net++ [9], Refine-net, SegNet and Deeplab-v3+ [10]. The convolutional neu-ral network of encoder decoder structure is divided into two parts. The encoding part obtains the feature expression from detail to whole through convolution and pooling, and the decoding part obtains the semantic label from whole to detail through deconvolution. However, this kind of network has large volume, many parameters and high requirements for computing power. In order to reduce the computational power requirements, a variety of lightweight semantic segmentation networks have been proposed, such as Refine Net-LW [11], LiteSeg [12], ESPNet-v2 [13], which greatly improves the network training speed, but this performance is obtained at the cost of reducing the accuracy of semantic segmentation. To solve this problem, on the premise of ensuring the accuracy, in order to improve the convolution efficiency and reduce the amount of network parameters, this thesis designs the dilated convolution combination based on the encoder-decoder struc-ture convolution neural network structure and aiming at expanding the receptive field, and solves the gridding problem in the dilated convolution by standardizing the dilation rate in the dilated convolution combination, The deep separable convolution is used to reduce the parameters of the model, and the learning of feature details is improved by establishing the double connection structure of long connection and pooled index of the corresponding codec layer. And finally, the encoder-decoder structure network is built, and an efficient light-weight semantic segmentation method is obtained.

2   Network Structure

In view of the excellent performance of convolutional neural network of the encoder-decoder structure in the field of semantic segmentation, it can be used for ground object classification and extraction with high-resolution remote sensing images. In order to better deal with the problem of large parameters and large amount of calculation of convolution neural network caused by large spatial size and rich detailed features of high-resolution remote sensing images, this thesis establishes a double connection between encoder-decoder structure by using deep separable convolution [14], and combines the dilated convolution non-gridding problem, and has large receptive field, It enhances the learning ability of encoder-decoder network to detail features and large-scale features, and reduces the amount of network parameters and computation (Fig. 1).

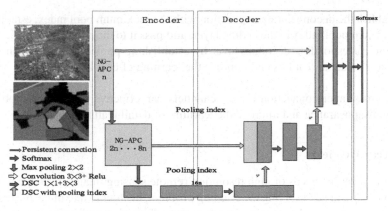

Fig. 1. Structure the encoder decoder network

2.1 Light-Weight

In order to realize light-weight convolution neural network, it is an effective method to transform convolution into deep separable convolution. Its principle is to decouple the mapping of correlation and spatial correlation between channels in convolution layer, and map them separately, which can achieve the same convolution effect, and the amount of parameters can be greatly reduced. Deep separable convolution is used in lightweight semantic segmentation models such as Xception [16], Mobile-Net [17], ShuffleNet [18], Squeeze-Net [19]. Therefore, a deep separable convolution encoder-decoder network structure is proposed, which not only improves the network training speed, but also reduces the amount of parameters and calculation of the network.

Specifically, the standard convolution (except the input layer) in the encoder-decoder network is improved to a separable two-steps convolution structure. Firstly, the characteristic diagram of each input channel is spatially convoluted, and the characteristic combination of an input channel is obtained through the training of the parameter value of the convolution kernel. Secondly, the small convolution kernel is used to confuse the channel dimension to obtain the combined characteristics of the channel dimension. And the parameters fell from $M \times N \times n^2$ to $M \times n^2 + M \times N \times 1^2$, which the number of input channels is M, the number of output channels is N, and the kernel size is n^2.

2.2 Double Connection

According to the convolutional neural network of various codec structures, it can be seen that the key of codec structure is how to accurately complete the sampling on the image and the feature extraction after sampling. To solve this problem, two channel connection is adopted in the network:

i. Establish the feature splicing of the corresponding coding layer and decoding layer. The long connection structure is a larger scale cross layer connection, which can effectively solve the problem of gradient disappearance and improve the learning of detailed features.

ii. Establish the deconvolution connection with the maximum pool index, establish the maximum pool index in the coding layer, and pass it to the deconvolution operation of the corresponding decoding layer by establishing pooled index, we can reduce the loss of detail features and improve the learning of detail features.

The cross layer connection of two channels can effectively solve the problem of gradient disappearance and improve the learning of detail features.

2.3 Receptive Fields

In order to meet the needs of high resolution remote sensing images for large receptive fields, on the premise of solving the gridding problem, in order to maximize the receptive fields and keep the number of parameters unchanged, we designed a three-layer cascade and multi branch parallel dilated convolution combination [20]. The first part is the cascade part, which is the cascade dilated convolution with a dilation rate of 3, after the standard convolution. If the dilated convolution is selected for the first layer, the characteristics around the sampling center point will be missed. After the cascade, this phenomenon of missing sampling will be exacerbated and cannot be completely no-gridding. So the standard convolution [21] is selected for the first layer, the dilated convolution with a dilation rate of 3 is selected for the second layer. The third layer is two branch Parallel Grouping convolution. The first branch is the dilated convolution with a dilation rate of 9, which can achieve the dilated convolution of the non-gridding problem. The receptive field is 27 pixels. In order to further expand the receptive field, the second branch is the dilated convolution with a dilation rate of 18, and the characteristics of the missing sampling part are supplemented by the first branch. Thus, the gridding problem can be maximized, and the dilation convolution combination of receptive field is 45 pixels. After the activation function and feature splicing, a convolution module is formed, and the module structure is shown in Fig. 2.

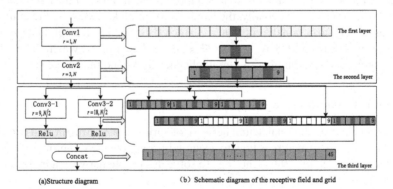

(a)Structure diagram   (b) Schematic diagram of the receptive field and grid

Fig. 2. Three layers and two branches of NG-APC module diagram

3   Experiment Verification and Analysis

In order to verify the effectiveness of the method proposed in this thesis in high resolution remote sensing image classification, this paper uses the GID dataset [22] with GF-2 images as the data source for training and testing.

3.1   Dataset and Training Process

The feature classification dataset released by Wuhan University, 2018, using GF-2 images, is a large dataset for land use and land cover classification. It contains over of the 150 images, whose images including more than 50,000 km^2 of 60 different cities in China, the high-precision land cover includes 10 images of 15 types with the size of 7200 * 6800 * 3 pixels.

In the experiment, an image from southern China is selected, as shown in Fig. 3 (No.gf2_pms2_l1a0001471436-mss2). Because the image is too large, direct training using the original image will lead to computer overload, and the positive sample ratio is low (the effective data ratio is very low), so a series of processing such as atmospheric correction, orthographic correction, image registration and image fusion should be carried out first, Then, the fused high resolution image is preprocessed with a series of data, such as annotation, cutting and data amplification. After the preprocessing operation of the above process, the learning data set that can be used to identify the model is obtained, including training set, verification set and test set, with a total of about 10000 samples. Among them, there are 10000 training sets, 1000 verification sets and tests, the sample size is 600 * 600, and 12 pixels are overlapped between adjacent samples to avoid damaging small target objects. The sample includes image data and annotation data, as shown in Fig. 3(a) and Fig. 3(b).

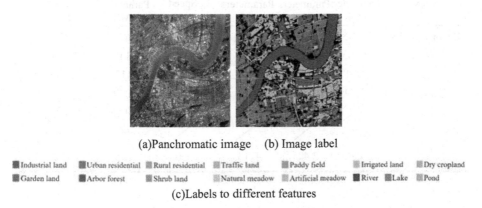

(a)Panchromatic image   (b) Image label

■ Industrial land   ■ Urban residential   ■ Rural residential   ■ Traffic land   ■ Paddy field   ■ Irrigated land   ■ Dry cropland
■ Garden land   ■ Arbor forest   ■ Shrub land   ■ Natural meadow   ■ Artificial meadow   ■ River   ■ Lake   ■ Pond

(c)Labels to different features

Fig. 3. Experimental image of GID datasets

3.2   Experiment Results and Analysis

The parameters and computation quantity are compared with the classical encoder-decoder network DeconvNet, U-Net, SegNet, and lightweight encoder-decoder network

ESP-Netv2, LiteSeg and RefineNet-LW. The result of comparison is shown in Table 1 (Fig. 4).

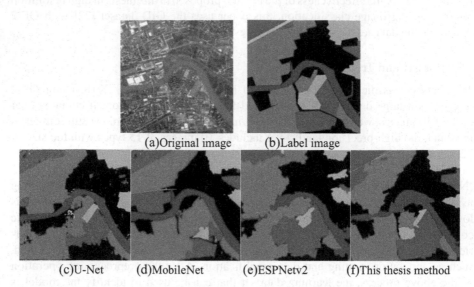

(a)Original image   (b)Label image

(c)U-Net   (d)MobileNet   (e)ESPNetv2   (f)This thesis method

Fig. 4. Comparison of classification results of first GID images by different methods

Table 1. Comparison of operation results of different image semantic segmentation algorithms

CNN	Encoder Parameters /MB	Decoder Parameters /MB	Softmax Parameters /KB	Training Speed Frames/S	Total Parameters /MB	Calculation Quantity GFLOPs
DeconvNet[16]	131.3	131.3	0.13	0.1	262.7	1814
U-Net	18.85	12.18	0.13	0.3	31.03	217.
SegNet	64.1	52.9	0.13	0.2	117	218
ESPNetv2	3.49	3.28	0.13	1.3	6.79	22.6
LightSeg	\	\	\	\	20.55	57.4
RefineNet-LW	\	\	\	\	46	52
This thesis method	4.96	2.42	0.13	1.0	7.39	43.27

It can be seen from the Table 1 that among a variety of encoder decoder convolutional neural networks, the parameters and computation quantity of this thesis method belong to lightweight networks, which are much smaller than DeconvNet, U-Net and Segnet, and are equivalent to lightweight ESPNetv2. At the same time, it is not far from the current mainstream lightweight convolutional neural networks LightSeg and RefineNet-LW networks. Therefore, in general, this thesis method is a lightweight encoder decoder convolutional neural network.

Table 2. Accuracy list of the first GID image classification results by different methods

	U-Net	MobileNet	ESPNetv2	This thesis method
Accuracy/%	68.68	67.51	69.29	78.84
mIoU/%	52.9	50.8	54.5	60.0

The accuracy and mIou value are compared with the classical encoder-decoder network U-Net, lightweight encoder-decoder network ESP-Netv2, LiteSeg and RefineNet-LW. The result of comparison is shown in Table 2. It can be seen from the segmentation results in Table 2 that this method can distinguish high resolution images well. Compared with U-Net, MobileNet and ESPNetv2, the accuracy of this method is improved by 10.16%, 11.33% and 9.55% respectively, and the mIou value is improved by 7.1%, 9.2% and 5.5% respectively, which verifies the advantages of the new method in algorithm accuracy.

4 Conclusion

Based on the U-Net model, using dilated convolution combination and depthwise separable convolution, this thesis method constructs a lightweight semantic segmentation model based on convolution neural network. At the encoder part, the NG-APC dilated convolution combination module is used to solve the gridding problem in dilated convolution combination. At the decoder part, depthwise separable convolution is used to reduce the amount of parameters and calculation of this model, and reduce the dependence of the model on computational power. Through experimental verification on GF-2 image dataset, accuracy reaches 78.84%, and the parameter quantity is only 7.39M, which is smaller than U-Net model and many lightweight semantic segmentation models based on U-Net. The results show that this thesis method is a lightweight and efficient image semantic segmentation method with encoder-decoder structure.

References

1. Madan, S., Pranjali, C.: A review of machine learning techniques using decision tree and support vector machine. In: International Conference on Computing Communication Control & Automation, Piscataway, Pune, India, pp. 1–7. IEEE (2017)
2. Long, J., Shelhamer, E., Darrell, T.: Fully convolutional networks for semantic segmentation. IEEE Trans. Pattern Anal. Mach. Intell. **39**(4), 640–651 (2014)
3. Badrinarayanan, V., Kendall, A., Cipolla, R.: SegNet: a deep convolutional encoder-decoder architecture for image segmentation. IEEE Trans. Pattern Anal. Mach. Intell. **39**(12), 2481–2495 (2017)
4. Ronneberger, O., Fischer, P., Brox, T.: U-Net: convolutional networks for biomedical image segmentation. In: Navab, N., Hornegger, J., Wells, W.M., Frangi, A.F. (eds.) MICCAI 2015. LNCS, vol. 9351, pp. 234–241. Springer, Cham (2015). https://doi.org/10.1007/978-3-319-24574-4_28
5. Nanjun, H., Leyuan, F., Plaza, A.: Hybrid first and second order attention U-Net for building segmentation in remote sensing images. Inf. Sci. **63**(140305), 69–80 (2020)

6. Liang, C., George, P., Iasonas, K., et al.: DeepLab: semantic image segmentation with deep convolutional nets, atrous convolution, and fully connected CRFs. IEEE Trans. Pattern Anal. Mach. Intell. **40**(4), 834–848 (2018)

7. Mehta, S., Rastegari, M., Caspi, A., Shapiro, L., Hajishirzi, H.: ESPNet: efficient spatial pyramid of dilated convolutions for semantic segmentation. In: Ferrari, V., Hebert, M., Sminchisescu, C., Weiss, Y. (eds.) ECCV 2018. LNCS, vol. 11214, pp. 561–580. Springer, Cham (2018). https://doi.org/10.1007/978-3-030-01249-6_34

8. Huihui, H., Weitao, L., Jianping, W., et al.: Semantic segmentation of encoder-decoder structure. J. Image Graph. **25**(02), 255–266 (2020)

9. Norman, B., Pedoia, V., Majumdar, S.: Use of 2D U-Net convolutional neural networks for automated cartilage and meniscus segmentation of knee MR imaging data to determine relaxometry and morphometry. Radiology **288**(1), 1109–1122 (2018)

10. Wang, Y., Sun, S., Yu, J., et al.: Skin lesion segmentation using atrous convolution via DeepLab v3. arXiv, vol. 1, pp. 1 4 (2018)

11. Nekrasov, V., Shen, C., Reid, I.: Light-weight refine-net for real-time semantic segmentation. In: BMVC, Newcastle upon Tyne, England, pp. 1–15 (2018)

12. Emara, T., Hossam, E., Abd, E.: LiteSeg: a novel lightweight ConvNet for semantic segmentation. In: 2019 Digital Image Computing: Techniques and Applications (DICTA), Perth, Australia, pp. 1–7 (2019)

13. Mehta, S., Rastegari, M., Shapiro, L., et al.: ESPNetv2: a light-weight, power efficient, and general purpose convolutional neural network. In: CVPR, CA, USA, pp. 1–10. IEEE (2019)

14. Xiaoqing, Z., Yongguo, Z., Weike, L., et al.: An improved architecture for urban building extraction based on depthwise separable convolution. J. Intell. Fuzzy Syst. **38**(11), 1–9 (2020)

15. Noh, H., Hong, S., Han, B.: Learning deconvolution network for semantic segmentation. In: 2015 IEEE International Conference on Computer Vision (ICCV), Santiago, pp. 1520–1528. IEEE (2015)

16. Francois, C.: Xception: deep learning with depthwise separable convolutions. In: CVPR, Honolulu, HI, USA, pp. 1800–1807. IEEE (2017)

17. Akay, M., Du, Y., Sershen, C.L., et al.: Deep learning classification of systemic sclerosis skin using the MobileNetV2 model. IEEE Open J. Eng. Med. Biol. **99**, 104–110 (2021)

18. Zhang, X., Zhou, X., Lin, M., et al.: ShuffleNet: an extremely efficient convolutional neural network for mobile devices. In: Proceedings of the IEEE Computer Society Conference on Computer Vision and Pattern Recognition, Salt Lake City, USA, pp. 6848–6856. IEEE (2018)

19. Qi, Z., Nauman, R., Shuchang, L., et al.: RSNet: a compact relative squeezing net for image recognition. In: VCIP, NSW, Australia, pp. 1–4. IEEE (2019)

20. Zhang, X., Zheng, Y., Liu, W., Wang, Z.: A hyperspectral image classification algorithm based on atrous convolution. EURASIP J. Wirel. Commun. Netw. **2019**(1), 1–12 (2019)

21. Chen, L.C., Papandreou, G., Kokkinos, I., et al.: Semantic image segmentation with deep convolutional nets and fully connected CRFs. Comput. Sci. **22**(4), 357–361 (2014)

22. Zhang, Y., Chi, M.: Mask-R-FCN: a deep fusion network for semantic segmentation. IEEE Access **8**, 155753–155765 (2020)

Applications

A Method for AGV Double-Cycling Scheduling at Automated Container Terminals

Hongchang Zhang[1], Liang Qi[1(✉)], and Huijuan Ma[2]

[1] College of Computer Science and Engineering, Shandong University of Science and Technology, Qingdao 266590, China
qiliangsdkd@163.com
[2] Qingdao New Qianwan Container Terminal Company Ltd., Qingdao 266500, China

Abstract. Automated container terminal (ACT) plays an important role in the modern logistics and transportation industry. The utilization of automated guided vehicles (AGV) can be effectively promoted by reducing their empty running. The existing scheduling strategies of AGVs for most ACTs cannot ensure their full load, leading to underutilization. This work proposes a double-cycling AGV path planning model to maximize the loading rate of AGVs by scheduling their loading and unloading tasks. The randomness of the quay crane's operational time is considered. By allocating time intervals of AGVs arriving at the quayside, it determines a loading sequence of containers based on a genetic algorithm with a penalty function. Experimental results show that the model can realize double-cycling transport with AGVs and effectively reduce the operational cost of ACTs.

Keywords: Logistics · Automated container terminals (ACTs) · Automatic guided vehicles (AGVs) · Double-cycling scheduling · Genetic algorithm

1 Introduction

As a basic logistic model, maritime transportation plays a vital role in the global economy, trade, and cultural exchanges. Automated container terminals (ACTs) have been developed as critical components in modern logistic transportation systems. ACTs consist of three major facilities: quay cranes (QCs), yard cranes (YCs), and automatic guided vehicles (AGVs). AGVs cooperate with the operations of QCs and YCs. Effective AGVs' scheduling is the key to reducing the operating cost of ACTs. In ACTs, the container transportation process has an AGV transport chain and a crane transport chain. In the former topic, Mohammad and Saeed propose a mathematical model composed of a job shop scheduling problem and a conflict-free routing problem [1]. The objective is to minimize AGVs' delay time and achieve multi-AGV integrated scheduling. A two-stage ant colony algorithm is proposed to solve it. Angeloudis and Bell study job assignments of AGVs in container terminals under various uncertainty conditions [2]. A flexible algorithm for real-time AGV scheduling is proposed. Most studies have significantly improved the utilization of AGVs and the operational efficiency of container terminals,

© IFIP International Federation for Information Processing 2022
Published by Springer Nature Switzerland AG 2022
Z. Shi et al. (Eds.): IIP 2022, IFIP AICT 643, pp. 495–507, 2022.
https://doi.org/10.1007/978-3-031-03948-5_40

but they cannot guarantee the full load of AGVs during transportation. In the crane transport chain, Huang and Li propose a bounded two-level dynamic programming algorithm aiming at a quay crane scheduling problem (QCSP) [3]. A method is proposed to evaluate the practicability of the algorithm. Ji et al. consider optimizing a loading sequence in container terminals [4]. A model is established to integrate the loading sequence and a re-handling strategy under parallel operations of multi-quay cranes. An improved genetic algorithm is proposed to solve the model. Tidal fluctuation and other factors will cause ship instability, resulting in QC operations not being fully automated. At present, most QC operations need manual assistance, resulting in the uncertainty of QC's operational time. The major problem is that most of the existing QC scheduling methods fail to fully consider the impact of uncertain factors, including tide fluctuation and manual operation on QC transportation tasks.

A double-cycling scheduling model requires that a crane transports a container, unloads it, and returns by taking another container. Meanwhile, AGVs transport a container to its destination and bring another one back. At present, double-cycling strategies have been used in QCSP, Yard Crane Scheduling Problem (YCSP), Yard Truck Scheduling Problem (YTSP), and Container Sequencing Problem (CSP), where the related studies are shown in Table 1. Most of these studies considering a double-cycling scheduling

Table 1. The problems solved by using double-cycling strategies

Studies	Scheduling Problem	Uncertainty Considered?	AGV scheduling sequence obtained?
Luo and Wu (2015) [5]	QCSP with YCSP	No	Yes
Zheng et al. (2019) [6]	QCSP with CSP	No	No
Cao et al. (2018) [7]	Integrated QCSP-YTSP	No	Yes
Liu et al. (2015) [8]	QCSP with CSP	No	No
Wang and Li (2015) [9]	QCSP with CSP	No	No
Nguyen and Kim (2010) [10]	YTSP	Yes	No
Meisel and Wichmann (2010) [11]	QCSP with CSP	No	No
Zhang and Kim (2009) [12]	QCSP	No	No
Goodchild and Daganzo (2006) [13]	QCSP	Yes	No
Ahmed et al. [14]	Integrated QCSP-YTSP-YCSP	Yes	No
Our Work	Integrated QCSP-YCSP	Yes	Yes

mode do not specifically consider the uncertainty of QC operation. In this work, a double-cycling model is proposed to realize the full load of AGVs by scheduling the loaded and unloaded tasks. Its objective is to minimize the waiting time of AGVs. A genetic algorithm with a penalty function is used to find a loading sequence of containers for each AGV.

The rest of this paper is organized as follows. Section 2 formulates a double-cycling AGV route planning model, which maximizes the loading rate of AGVs during their transportation by scheduling the loaded and unloaded tasks. Section 3 proposes a container scheduling sequence based on a genetic algorithm with a penalty function and gets the shortest waiting time of AGVs. Section 4 shows experimental results. Section 5 concludes this paper and discusses the future work.

2 AGV Double-Cycling

2.1 Problem Description

In an ACT, QCs, YCs, and AGVs are responsible for loading/unloading containers on ships, loading/unloading containers on the yard, and transporting containers between the quayside and the yard. This work proposes an AGV double-cycling scheduling model. AGV carries a container at the quayside, drives to the yard to unload it, takes another one from the yard, returns to the quayside for unloading, and repeats such a process. Firstly, we give the following assumptions:

1) Tidal fluctuation and other factors will cause ship instability, resulting in QC operations not being fully automated. At present, most QC operations need manual assistance, resulting in the uncertainty of QC's operational time. Etsuko mentions that the transportation time of containers on QC roughly conforms to a Gaussian distribution [15], which is adopted in our work. The probability that the distributed value in $(\mu - 2\sigma, \mu + 2\sigma)$ is 0.9544, and a time interval $(t + \mu - 2\sigma, t + \mu + 2\sigma)$ is adopted to the completion time of QC operation.
2) YC can prepare in advance for the arrival of containers [16], and we assume that YC can obtain the information of a container and move to it in advance.

AGVs are fully loaded in and out of the yard and quayside, thus realizing the double-cycling of AGVs. It is a basic constraint of our double-cycling model. Figure 1 shows the flow chart.

Another constraint is that no delay of QC should be guaranteed. QC operations' uncertainty leads to the uncertain time when an AGV arrives at the quayside. Thus, the latest time when an AGV arrives at the quayside (LTAQ) is defined. As mentioned above, the time of QC transporting containers conforms to the Gaussian distribution with parameters (μ, σ^2). Therefore, the LTAQ is the moment for QC to finish transporting the previous container.

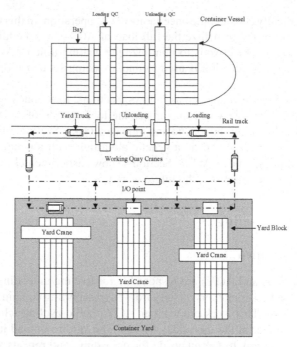

Fig. 1. A double-cycling AGV scheduling mode.

2.2 Mathematical Model

Let $N = \{1, 2, \cdots\}$ represent the set of natural numbers, and $N_m = \{1, 2, \cdots, m\}$. The related symbolic definitions are given as follows:

M: $M = \{m_1, m_2, \ldots, m_n\}$ is a set of task points, where $m_i = \{P_1^i, w, P_2^i, T_i\}$, P_1^i represents the location of container i on the ship, w represents the number of the yards, P_2^i represents the location of container i on the yard, and T_i represents the LTAQ of container i;

X: a set of unloading task points that represent unloading the containers from the ship to the yard;

Y: a set of loading task points that represent loading the containers in the yard onto the ship;

n: the number of AGVs, $n \in N$;

k: the index of the k-th AGV, $k \in N_n$, remember as A_k;

m_s: a virtual start task point;

m_e: a virtual end task point;

T_i^q: time taken to transport container i by QC;

V_Q: the average movement speed of QC;

C_i: a time-interval conforming to the Gaussian distribution, including the minimum and maximum time taken by QC to transport the container, $C_i = (C_1^i, C_2^i)$, where C_1^i and C_2^i are the minimum time and maximum time for QC to transport container i, respectively;

V_Y: moving speed of YC;

D_{ij}^Y: the moving distance of the YC from the position of container i to the position of container j. It represents the distance from the I/O point to the position of container j when $i = 0$; it represents the distance moved from the position of container i to the I/O point when $j = 0$;

V_y: movement speed of a spreader;

D_{ij}^y: the distance that the YC's spreader moves from the position of container i to the position of container j. It represents the distance of the spreader moved from the I/O point to the position of container j when $i = 0$; it represents the distance moved from the position of container i to the I/O point when $j = 0$;

G_y: the speed at which the spreader moves up and down;

T_y: time required by spreader to transport a container at the I/O point;

T_k: a set of waiting time of AGV, where $T_k = \{t_1, t_2, \ldots, t_n\}$, t_k $(1 \le k \le n)$ is the waiting time of A_k.

V_A: the speed of AGV;

D_q: the distance between two QCs;

T: the time interval between two consecutive AGVs exiting the quayside;

T_i^{q1}: the waiting time before task point i is unloaded at the quayside;

T_i^{q2}: the waiting time before task point i is loaded at the quayside;

T_i^{y1}: the waiting time before task point i is unloaded in the yard;

T_i^{y2}: the unloading time of task point i in the yard;

T_i^{y3}: the waiting time before task point i is loaded in the yard;

T_i^{y4}: the loading time of task point i in the yard;

H_{ij}: the empty running time of AGV loading task point v_i after unloading task point v_j in the yard.

Symbols used in the genetic algorithm are given next.

q: initial population size;

q': offspring population size;

t: current iteration index;

t_{max}: maximum iteration;

P_u: a penalty factor on full loading;

P_q: a penalty factor on LTAQ;

P_c: crossover probability;

P_v: mutation probability;

P_r: reverse probability;

P: individual fitness value.

Our double-cycling model focuses on the efficiency of the QC, and AGV should meet the full load constraint and the LTAQ constraints. Hence, the waiting time of AGV is a metric to evaluate the efficiency of the double-cycling model. The objective function of the model is to minimize the waiting time of AGVs:

$$\min \sum\nolimits_1^n T_k \tag{1}$$

The decision variables are defined as follows:

$$x_j^i = \begin{cases} 1, & \text{an AGV transports task point } j \text{ after task point } i \\ 0, & \text{otherwise} \end{cases} \tag{2}$$

$$\alpha^k = \begin{cases} 1, & \text{AGV } k \text{ drives out of the yard being fully loaded} \\ 0, & \text{otherwise} \end{cases} \tag{3}$$

$$\beta^k = \begin{cases} 1, & A_k \text{ drives out of the quayside being fully loaded} \\ 0, & \text{otherwise} \end{cases} \tag{4}$$

$$\gamma_i^w = \begin{cases} 0, & \text{the YC cannot be prepared in advance.} \\ 1, & \text{the YC can be prepared in advance.} \end{cases} \tag{5}$$

where w is the number of the yard.

$$\delta_i = \begin{cases} 1, & \text{task point } i \text{ is transported to the quayside} \\ 0, & \text{task point } i \text{ is transported to the yard} \end{cases} \tag{6}$$

$$\varepsilon_w^i = \begin{cases} 1, & \text{container } i \text{ is loaded in yard } w \\ 0, & \text{container } i \text{ is unloaded in yard } w \end{cases} \tag{7}$$

$$\epsilon = \begin{cases} 1, & \text{AGV loads at the same yard after unloading} \\ 0, & \text{AGV loads at the different yard after unloading} \end{cases} \tag{8}$$

The constraints are defined as follows:

$$\sum x_i^j = 1, \quad \forall M_i \in M + \{m_e\} \tag{9}$$

$$\sum x_i^j = 1, \quad \forall M_i \in M + \{m_s\} \tag{10}$$

$$\sum x_{x'}^x = 0, \quad \forall M_x, M_{x'} \in X \tag{11}$$

$$\sum x_{y'}^y = 0, \quad \forall M_y, M_{y'} \in Y \tag{12}$$

$$\alpha^k = 1, \quad \forall k \in N_m \tag{13}$$

$$\beta^k = 1, \quad \forall k \in N_m \tag{14}$$

$$C_1^i = (\mu - 2\sigma) + V_Q/D_i^q + \Delta t_i \tag{15}$$

$$C_2^i = (\mu + 2\sigma) + V_Q/D_i^q + \Delta t_i \tag{16}$$

$$C_1^i < T_i < C_2^i \tag{17}$$

$$T_i = \sum_{0}^{i-2} T_k^q + C_2^{i-1}, \; \delta_i = 1 \tag{18}$$

$$T_j^i = T_j^q + \frac{D_i^q}{V_Q} \tag{19}$$

$$T_i^{q1} = T_{i-1}^{q1} + T_{i-1}^q + \frac{D_i^q}{V_Q} \tag{20}$$

$$T_i^{q2} = T_{i-1}^{q2} + T_{i-1}^q + \frac{D_i^q}{V_Q} \tag{21}$$

$$T_i^{y1} = \begin{cases} 0, & \gamma_i^w = 1 \\ \max(T_{i-1}^3 + T_{i-1}^4 - T, 0), & \varepsilon_w^{i-1} = 1, \gamma_i^w = 0 \\ \max\left(T_{i-1}^{y1} + T_{i-1}^{y2} + \frac{D_{(i-1)0}^Y}{V_y} - T, 0\right), & \varepsilon_w^{i-1} = 0, \gamma_i^w = 0 \end{cases} \tag{22}$$

$$T_i^{y3} = \begin{cases} max\left(\frac{D_{0(i-1)}^Y}{V_Y}, \frac{D_{0(i-1)}^y}{V_y}\right) + \frac{d_i}{G_y} + T_G, \epsilon = 1 \\ H_{ij}, \gamma_i^w = 1, \epsilon = 0 \\ max(T_j^{y3} + T_j^{y4} - P_{ij}, 0), \varepsilon_w^j = 1, \gamma_i^w = 0, \epsilon = 0 \\ max(T_j^{y1} + T_j^{y2} - P_{ij}, 0), \varepsilon_w^j = 0, \gamma_i^w = 0, \epsilon = 0 \end{cases} \tag{23}$$

Equations (9)–(12) describe the container transportation mode at ACTs, where (9) denotes that all task points, including the virtual end task point, have only one prefix task point. Equation (10) suggests that all task points, including the virtual start task point, have only one suffix task point. Equation (11) indicates that all the unloading task points' prefix and suffix cannot be unloading task points. Equation (12) requires that all loading task points' prefix and suffix cannot be loading task points. Equations (13) and (14) describe the double-cycling mode, where (13) indicates that all AGVs driving out of the yard must be fully loaded and (14) requires that all AGVs moving out of the quayside must be fully loaded. Equations (15) and (16) describe the minimum and maximum time for QC to transport container i. The minimum time is the average time needed by the QC transporting container i minus a time-interval conforming to the Gaussian distribution; The maximum time is the average time needed by the QC transporting container i plus a time-interval conforming to the Gaussian distribution. Equation (17) describes the uncertainty of the QC operation, indicating that no matter the loading operation or unloading operation, the QC completes the transportation of container i within the time interval $[C_1^i, C_2^i]$. Equation (18) describes the LTAQ. When container i is transported to the quayside, the LTAQ is the latest time when the QC completes transporting the previous container. Equations (19)–(21) describe the situation of AGVs entering and leaving the quayside, where (19) indicates the time interval between two consecutive AGVs driving out of the quayside. The time interval is the second AGV's loading time in quayside. (20) indicates the waiting time before task point i is unloaded at the quayside. The waiting time is the previous task point's waiting time before unloading plus the unloading time of the previous task point. (21) indicates the waiting time before task point i is loaded at the quayside. The waiting time is the previous task point's waiting time before loading plus the loading time of the previous task point. Equations (22) and (23) describe the specific situation of AGVs entering and leaving the yard, where (22) indicates the waiting time before task point i is unloaded in the yard. It has two cases: 1) when the YC is prepared in advance, the waiting time is 0; 2) when the YC cannot be prepared in advance, there are two situations: if the YC is loading a container, the waiting time is the waiting time of previous task point plus the loading time of the previous task point and minus the time interval between two consecutive AGVs driving out of the quayside. It may be less than zero, and we use 0 instead; If the YC is unloading container, the waiting time is the waiting time of unloading at the previous task point plus the unloading time of task point minus the time interval from the arrival at the yard at the previous task point. (23) describes the waiting time before task point i is loaded in the yard. Specifically, 1) If AGVs are loaded in the same yard, the waiting time is the time needed by YC moving to the I/O Point after the unloading operation. 2) If the AGVs are loaded in another yard, there are two situations. When the next target yard's YC can be prepared in advance, the waiting time before the loading is when the AGV runs empty to the target yard; When the next target yard's YC cannot be prepared in advance, there are also two situations. If the yard is conducting a loading operation, the waiting time is the waiting time of the previous task point plus the loading time of the task point minus the empty running time of the AGV. If the yard is conducting an unloading operation, the waiting time is the waiting time of the previous task point plus the unloading time of the task point minus the empty running time of the AGV.

3 Genetic Algorithm with Penalty Value

This model is to find a container transport sequence. It minimizes the total waiting time of AGV in the transport process and satisfies the double-cycling requirement and the LTAQ constraints.

A penalty function is used to search for the optimal solution. The number of non-conforming double-cycling task points is k, the number of non-conforming LTAQ task points is a, the penalty coefficient at the LTAQ is P_q, and the penalty coefficient at the double-cycling value is P_u. Then, we have

$$P = \begin{cases} a * P_q + T, & k = 0 \\ k * P_u, & k > 0 \end{cases} \tag{24}$$

Individual fitness value P includes 1) all AGVs' waiting time and 2) the penalty value of task points in the scheduling sequence that do not conform to the LTAQ. The final individual fitness value is the sum of them. During the generation of solutions, the generated solutions may not meet the conditions of double-cycling, so before calculating the fitness, the scheduling sequence should be judged whether it meets the basic condition of double-cycling. If not, the fitness value is adjusted to the $k*Pu$ to speed up eliminating the generated solution.

Algorithm 1 AGV double-cycling model solving algorithm

Input:

Unloading task point set X, loading task point set Y, AGV number m, initial population number q, offspring population number q', maximum iteration number t_{max}, the LTAQ penalty coefficient P_q, the double-cycling penalty coefficient is P_u, crossover probability P_c, mutation probability P_v, and reversal probability P_r.

Output:

A legitimate scheduling sequence with minimum fitness P.

Step 1:

Individual coding. For q individuals, arrange a scheduling sequence in an ascending order according to the LTAQ of X and Y, add n-1 AGV segmentation number at the end of the sequence, and set the current iteration times t =1.

Step 2:

Calculate the fitness and select the generation of progeny population. For each individual, its fitness P is calculated, and the smaller the fitness is set, the greater the probability of being selected. q' individuals are assigned according to roulette to generate offspring population.

Step 3:

Perform crossover, mutation, and reversal operators. The offspring population is combined in pairs, and the crossover operation is carried out with probability P_c, and then the mutation and reversal operation is carried out with probabilities P_v and P_r, respectively, for each individual.

Step 4:

Elite reserve iteration and output the solution. Re-insert q' children into the original population to generate a new population, and select p individuals from the new population. If $t=t_{max}$, the optimal individuals will be output; Otherwise, $t=t+1$, return to **Step 2**.

---

4   Simulation Experiment

In this paper, Matlab_R2019a is used to solve the double-cycling model. In this work, a queue is formulated for each quay or yard. The task points are arranged in the queue according to transportation order. The waiting time of the task point and the number of task points that do not meet the LTAQ are calculated according to the relationship among the task points in the queue. Then the scheduling sequence with the least number of task points that do not meet the LTAQ and the least AGV waiting time is obtained using a genetic algorithm. We now discuss the critical parameters to determine the influence of double-cycling mode in practical application.

Corresponding waiting areas are set up at the quayside and the yard for storing AGVs that need to wait. AGVs in the waiting area can choose to turn off the engine or keep starting the engine for waiting according to the estimated waiting time. The waiting time of the AGV that remains in the starting the engine is the key object to be considered in the double-cycling model. Table 2 shows the experimental results under multiple experiments, including the total waiting time of AGVs (Total Waiting Time), the number of task points that do not conform to LTAQ (Not Conform LTAQ), the number of task points that do not conform to double-cycling (Not Conform Doble-cycling), the fitness value, and the number of iterations.

Table 2. Results of multiple experiments in our double-cycle model

Experiment number	Not Conform Doble-cycling	Not Conform LTAQ	Fitness Value	Number Of Iterations	Total Waiting Time
1	0	0	971	265	971
2	0	0	978	356	978
3	0	0	964	151	964
4	0	0	1003	135	1003
5	0	2	21039	255	1039
6	0	0	1004	115	1004
7	0	0	906	164	906
8	0	0	987	206	987
9	0	0	978	307	978
10	0	0	944	139	944
11	0	0	976	191	976
12	0	0	989	311	989

In the experimental results, we can get some valuable conclusions. First of all, a time disturbance that conforms to Gaussian distribution is randomly added to the time of QC operation, so the experimental results are highly likely to be different each time. In the double-cycling model, the experimental results show that most scheduling schemes satisfy both double-cycling and LTAQ. This work simulates the time disturbance existing in the QC operator, so a few experimental results cannot meet LTAQ in all task points based on double-cycling. A few experimental results show that the number of task points that do not conform to LTAQ differs significantly from other experimental results. This situation is generally caused by the significant difference between the QC operation time and other experiments' QC operation time, leading to the algorithm not normally converging to an appropriate fitness value. Therefore, we believe the AGV cannot reach the quayside in time due to the operator's operation error. This part of the data should be discarded or recalculated. The operator's status should be adjusted in actual situations. However, according to the experimental results in Table 3, there exists the phenomenon that the number of task points is 0 in the optimal scheduling sequence, which leads to resource waste. To further improve the efficiency of the double-cycling system, this work continues to consider the influence of the number of AGVs on the efficiency of the double-cycling system. Tables 3 and 4 show the experimental results of changing the number of AGVs under a different number of task points, including the total waiting time of AGV and the number of task points that do not conform to LTAQ.

Table 3. The experimental results of different number of AGVs at 20 task points

Number of AGV	Number of task points	Experiment number	Total Waiting Time	Not Conform LTAQ
3	20	1	1054	8
		2	1039	10
		3	1007	8
4	20	1	980	0
		2	1038	0
		3	1032	2
5	20	1	981	0
		2	964	0
		3	984	0
6	20	1	1089	0
		2	1094	0
		3	1098	0

Table 4. The experimental results of different number of AGVs at 30 task points

Number of AGV	Number of task points	Experiment number	Total Waiting Time	Not Conform LTAQ
4	30	1	1595	4
		2	1575	6
		3	1537	2
5	30	1	1504	0
		2	1507	2
		3	1550	0
6	30	1	1588	0
		2	1602	0
		3	1726	0
7	30	1	1859	0
		2	1884	4
		3	1805	2
8	30	1	2134	0
		2	1809	2
		3	2133	0

For the different number of task points, we set different numbers of AGVs. The number of AGVs is gradually reduced until AGVs cannot meet the requirement of all task points conforming to LATQ, and the number of AGVs is set as the lower bound to transport the number of task points successfully. The number of AGVs is gradually increased until the number of task points of some AGVs is still 0 in the AGV scheduling sequence after several experiments, and the number of AGVs is regarded as the upper bound under the number of task points. Tables 3 and 4 show that for different numbers of task points, there is a corresponding number of AGV to ensure that all task points meet LTAQ and have the minimum waiting time. Fewer AGVs will increase the number of task points that do not conform to LTAQ, and more AGVs will cause a significant rise in waiting time and fluctuations in the number of task points that do not conform to LTAQ. Therefore, only a certain number of AGVs can improve the efficiency of the double-cycling model and make full use of transportation resources.

5   Conclusions

To improve the utilization rate of AGV in the process of ACTs, this work proposes a double-cycling model of AGV, which specifies that AGV should enter and exit the yard and quayside with the full load during transportation. By considering the uncertainty of the QC's operational time. To not affect the QC work efficiency, the LTAQ is stipulated. The AGV needs to arrive at the quayside before the earliest time that the previous task point is completed. Considering the different situations when AGV arrives at the yard, the container scheduling sequence is reasonably arranged to prevent AGV from accumulating. AGV should meet the constraints of LTAQ and pursue the shortest waiting time. Experiments are designed to obtain the scheduling sequence satisfying the double-cycling conditions and LTAQ constraints. Furthermore, to adjust the number of AGVs and the time disturbance of QC operation followed different Gaussian distributions, obtaining the optimal scheduling sequence, proving the feasibility of the double-cycling mode in practical application.

Although the experimental results successfully prove the feasibility of the double-cycling mode in practical application. There are still some improvements. To further improve the transport efficiency of the double-cycling mode, the scheduling problem of multiple QC can be continued to be considered so that it can simultaneously load and unload multiple bays in a ship.

References

1. Saidi-Mehrabad, M., Dehnavi-Arani, S., Evazabadian, F., Mahmoodian, V.: An ant colony algorithm (ACA) for solving the new integrated model of job shop scheduling and conflict-free routing of AGVs. Comput. Ind. Eng. **86**, 2–13 (2015)
2. Angeloudis, P., Bell, M.G.H.: An uncertainty-aware AGV assignment algorithm for automated container terminals. Transp. Res. E Logist. Transp. Rev. **46**(3), 354–366 (2010)
3. Huang, S.Y., Li, Y.: A bounded two-level dynamic programming algorithm for quay crane scheduling in container terminals. Comput. Ind. Eng. **123**, 303–313 (2018)

4. Ji, M., Guo, W., Zhu, H., Yang, Y.: Optimization of loading sequence and rehandling strategy for multi-quay crane operations in container terminals. Transp. Res. E Logist. Transp. Rev. **80**, 1–19 (2015)
5. Luo, J., Wu, Y.: Modelling of dual-cycle strategy for container storage and vehicle scheduling problems at automated container terminals. Transp. Res. E Logist. Transp. Rev. **79**, 49–64 (2015)
6. Zheng, F., Pang, Y., Liu, M., Xu, Y.: Dynamic programming algorithms for the general quay crane double-cycling problem with internal-reshuffles. J. Comb. Optim. **39**(3), 708–724 (2019)
7. Cao, J.X., Shang, X., Yao, X.: Integrated quay crane and yard truck schedule for the dual-cycling strategies. In: CICTP 2017: Transportation Reform and Change—Equity, Inclusiveness, Sharing, and Innovation, pp. 1346–1357 (2018)
8. Liu, M., Chu, F., Zhang, Z., Chu, C.: A polynomial-time heuristic for the quay crane double cycling problem with internal-reshuffling operations. Transp. Res. E Logist. Transp. Rev. **81**, 52–74 (2015)
9. Wang, D., Li, X.: Quay crane scheduling with dual cycling. Eng. Optimiz. **47**(10), 1343–1360 (2015)
10. Nguyen, V.D., Kim, K.H.: Minimizing empty trips of yard trucks in container terminals by dual cycle operations. Indust. Eng. Manag. Syst. **9**(1), 28–40 (2010)
11. Meisel, F., Wichmann, M.: Container sequencing for quay cranes with internal reshuffles. OR Spectrum **32**(3), 569–591 (2010)
12. Zhang, H., Kim, K.H.: Maximizing the number of dual-cycle operations of quay cranes in container terminals. Comput. Ind. Eng. **56**(3), 979–992 (2009)
13. Goodchild, A.V., Daganzo, C.F.: Double-cycling strategies for container ships and their effect on ship loading and unloading operations. Transp. Sci. **40**(4), 473–483 (2016)
14. Ahmed, E., El-Abbasy, M.S., Zayed, T., Alfalah, G., Alkass, S.: Synchronized scheduling model for container terminals using simulated double-cycling strategy. Comput. Indust. Eng. **154**, 107118 (2021)
15. Nishimura, E.: Yard and berth planning efficiency with estimated handling time. Maritime Bus. Rev. **5**(1), 5–29 (2020)
16. Guo, X., Huang, S.Y., Hsu, W.J., Low, M.Y.H.: Yard crane dispatching based on real time data driven simulation for container terminals. In: Proceedings of the 2008 Winter Simulation Conference, pp. 2648–2655 (2008)

Predicting Student Performance in Online Learning Using a Highly Efficient Gradient Boosting Decision Tree

Chang Wang[2], Liang Chang[1,2], and Tieyuan Liu[2,3]([⊠])

[1] Guangxi Key Laboratory of Trusted Software, Guilin 541004, China
[2] School of Computer Science and Information Security, Guilin University of Electronic Technology, Guilin 541004, China
`lty205@guet.edu.cn`
[3] School of Information and Communication, Guilin University of Electronic Technology, Guilin 514000, China

Abstract. Online learning has become a popular way of learning due to the rapid development of informatization of education, the rise of online learning platforms has provided great convenience to students' learning, breaking the limitations of time and space, enabling students to study various courses anytime, anywhere. However, due to the lack of an effective supervision mechanism, online learning undermined by low quality tutoring and a substantial dropout rate of students. In this study, we used an efficient ensemble learning algorithm, LightGBM, to develop a student performance prediction model. Basing on the interaction behavior data of students' online learning, the prediction model can predict whether a student will be able to pass the course. As a result of identifying at-risk students, teachers can provide targeted interventions to improve the learning performance of these students. During the experiments, we compared with ten classical machine learning algorithms on a public dataset. It reflected that LightGBM outperformed in predicting student performance. The study also analyzed the impact of different interaction behaviors on students' online learning performance, which will help teachers and educational researchers to better understand the relationship between students' online learning behavior and students' learning performance. This will help teachers guide students in online learning and optimize the design of online learning courses.

Keywords: LightGBM · Student performance prediction · Learning analytics

1 Introduction

In recent years, in conjunction with the rapid development of Internet technology, a large number of online learning systems have emerged. These include Virtual Learning Environments (VLEs), Massive Open Online Courses (MOOCs), etcetera. This innovation enables there to be intellectual freedom and also allows students to take courses

© IFIP International Federation for Information Processing 2022
Published by Springer Nature Switzerland AG 2022
Z. Shi et al. (Eds.): IIP 2022, IFIP AICT 643, pp. 508–521, 2022.
https://doi.org/10.1007/978-3-031-03948-5_41

without going to an educational institution. However, online learning faces a multitude of challenges. The number of students studying online far exceeds that of those taking traditional courses, and it is difficult for teachers to track student learning, which makes many under-performing students drop out of courses due to lack of timely guidance [1]. Fortunately, these online learning platforms widely store a large amount of student learning data, which benefits educational research immensely [2]. As a result of analyzing the learning data of students during the online learning process, it is possible to predict students' learning performance, help teachers identify at-risk students, and provide targeted additional help and interventions to improve students' academic performance.

Predicting student performance as an effective measure to identify at-risk students has been recognized as an important research problem in online learning [4]. Accurate predictions of student performance will help provide students with personalized guidance to help them pass the course, all the while, obtaining effective predictions requires powerful predictive models [5]. Therefore, many researchers have used various machine learning methods to develop the best predictive models of student performance. Among these methods, ensemble learning can often achieve better prediction results. As an algorithm of ensemble learning, random forest has been widely used in student performance prediction research and achieved excellent prediction results [6].

The student performance prediction task in the online learning environment faces new challenges which are different from the student performance prediction task in the traditional course learning environment. Due to the convenience and freedom of learning, online platforms attract a large number of students, which makes online platforms record a large amount of data related to student learning. However, due to the lack of constraints on student learning, this data often exhibits high-dimensional and sparse characteristics. It is difficult for traditional ensemble learning algorithm to analyze quickly and efficiently. LightGBM not only can handle large datasets, but also has high predictive ability, as an efficient ensemble algorithm. The algorithm can also utilize the sparsity of features to perform lossless merging of features, which is suitable for processing high-dimensional and sparse data. Therefore, we use the LightGBM algorithm to build a student performance prediction model, which predicts students' performance by analyzing their interaction data with the platform during their online learning process. In addition to that, we analyze the importance of different features in prediction and the correlation of features to explore the relationship between students' different interaction behaviors in the learning process and student performance. Based on these explorations, it can provide effective assistance to teachers to guide students' learning, and provide meaningful reference for the design of online courses.

2   Literature Review

In the field of student performance prediction, students' learning performance prediction tasks are generally divided into two categories: classification tasks and regression tasks. The classification task is to predict whether a student will pass a course or predict a student's final grade. The regression task is the prediction of the most likely score a student will get in the final exam [7]. Traditional machine learning methods are widely used to predict student performance with good results, such as regression analysis [8], decision trees [9, 10], Bayesian [11], support vector machines [12–14], neural network [15, 16] and other methods. These algorithms are often based on a single model for predicting student performance, which may perform differently for different datasets, making it difficult to identify a generally accepted prediction algorithm [17]. As a result of widespread application of ensemble learning in other fields, more and more researchers apply ensemble learning to student performance prediction. Compared with single model prediction methods, ensemble learning can assemble multiple weak classifiers into a strong classifier, improve the performance of prediction, and can achieve good prediction results on datasets of different scales.

The most commonly used ensemble learning in student performance prediction is random forest, an ensemble learning algorithm developed by Breiman and Adele Cutler, which uses a large number of decision tree models to improve accurate predictions. It does this by reducing the bias and variance of estimate [18]. Its essence is a random combination of freely growing decision trees in a random subspace through Bagging. Trakunphutthirak et al. [19] collected students' online logs for one week during the exam, which included 90 students' online activities during the exam, including 120 Internet access activities and 25 browsing categories. Process logs into two distinct datasets by visit activity and browsing category. On the two datasets, students' learning performance is predicted based on the student's usage time and the student's usage frequency, respectively. The experimental results show that the random forest is the best method for predicting the risk of students' failure compared to decision trees, naive Bayes, logistic regression and neural networks. Hasan et al. [20] used video learning data and data mining techniques to predict whether a student would be able to pass a course. The dataset consists of academic data in SSI, activity data in Moodle, and video clickstream data in eDify for 772 students during an academic year. The commonly adopted classification algorithms in the existing literature are used: random forest, k-nearest neighbor, support vector machine, etc. The results show that random forest is the best amongst the other methods with an accuracy rate of 88.3%.

As a meta-algorithm in ensemble learning, bagging can combine different models to reduce the generalization error and effectively improve the prediction accuracy [21]. Injada et al. [22] proposed a method to systematically build a bagging ensemble learner for multiple segments, which selects appropriate weak classifiers according to the Gini coefficient and the target classification score. Basing on this method, six basic machine learning algorithms were used to combine the optimal bagging ensemble learner to predict the performance of students in different stages of the course in the e-learning environment. As a result of conducting sufficient experiments on different undergraduate datasets from two universities, the established Bagging ensemble learner has higher prediction accuracy compared with the classical classification techniques. In order to predict the performance of students in academic competitions, Yan et al. [23] used support vector machines, random trees and AdaBoost as basic learners to predict students' performance respectively, and used a simple logistic regression algorithm as a voter to integrate the prediction results of different base learners. On the experimental data set, through the comparison of five evaluation indicators, the model not only outperforms the commonly used single machine learning algorithm, but also outperforms other ensemble learning algorithms.

As another major class of ensemble learning algorithms, Boosting algorithms have also been used in student performance prediction research. Contrast to Bagging, the Boosting algorithm assembles weak classifiers into a strong classifier by reducing bias. Han et al. [24] used a decision tree-based AdaBoost algorithm to predict the final grades of students in compulsory courses. The ensemble algorithm was evaluated using performance data from 123 undergraduate students in 20 compulsory courses over four years. The experimental results show that the algorithm has better prediction accuracy compared with decision tree, neural network, random forest and other models. Ahmed et al. [25] proposed the use of the GBDT algorithm to predict student performance on final exams, comparing with support vector machines, logistic regression, and naive bayes on a dataset containing 450 undergraduate students. The experimental results show that the algorithm has better performance than other algorithms, and the prediction accuracy is 89.1%.

In the existing research on student performance prediction, the prediction effect of ensemble learning is often better than that of single machine learning algorithms. However, when the dataset features are high-dimensional and the number of samples is large, the efficiency and scalability of the existing ensemble learning algorithms are unsatisfactory. As an efficient ensemble learning method, LightGBM can be applied to large-scale datasets with high feature dimensions, and achieves higher accuracy on multiple public datasets. So in this article, we will use LightGBM to predict student performance. Although Vultureanu-Albişi et al. [26] used different ensemble learning algorithms based on tree models to predict student performance, they found that decision trees outperformed other ensemble learning algorithms including LightGBM. However, the two datasets used in this study are both small, with only a few hundred students, and cannot well demonstrate the predictive performance of the ensemble learning algorithm in the online learning environment. We used LightGBM to predict student online learning performance with a dataset containing several thousand students. Furthermore, it will be compared with a variety of classic machine learning algorithms to evaluate the performance of the algorithm in the task of predicting student performance.

3   Methodology

LightGBM is an efficient ensemble learning algorithm proposed by Guolin et al. [27]. The purpose is to solve the problem that the efficiency and scalability of the existing GBDT algorithm are still unsatisfactory when the feature dimension is high and the amount of data is large. From the perspective of reducing the number of data instances and features during model training, two new techniques in the LightGBM, Gradient-based One-Side Sampling (GOSS) and Exclusive Feature Bundling (EFB), are proposed to improve GBDT.

3.1   Gradient-Based One-Side Sampling

In GBDT, the gradient information of each data instance can provide valuable information for data sampling. Instances with larger gradients (that is, instances with insufficient training) contribute more to the information gain. However, reducing the data training size by discarding data instances with small gradients will change the data distribution and affect the accuracy of the trained model. The GOSS algorithm can randomly remove instances with small gradients without changing the original data distribution immensely. When the algorithm determines the sample set for a new round of training, it will sort the samples by the absolute value of the gradient according to the current training result. All instances with large gradients are used as selected samples, and a certain proportion of instances with small gradients are randomly selected as the ideal ones, thus selected. In order not to change the original distribution by a great margin, the ratio of the number of selected small gradient samples to all small gradient samples needs to be used as the weight coefficient of the selected small gradient samples.

Algorithm 1 Gradient-based One-Side Sampling

Input: I: training data, d: iterations
Input: a: Sampling ratio of large gradient data
Input: b: Sampling ratio of small gradient data
Input: $loss$: loss function, L: weak learner
$models \leftarrow \{\}, fact \leftarrow \frac{1-a}{b}$
$topN \leftarrow a \times len(I), randN \leftarrow b \times len(I)$
for $i = 1$ **to** d **do**
    $preds \leftarrow models.predict(I)$
    $g \leftarrow loss(I, preds), w \leftarrow \{1,1,...\}$
    $sorted \leftarrow$ GetSortedIndices(abs(g))
    $topSet \leftarrow sorted[1:topN]$
    $randSet \leftarrow RandomPick(sorted[topN:len(I)], randN)$
    $usedSet \leftarrow topSet + randSet$
    $w[randSet] \times= fact$ ▷Assign weight fact to the small gradient data
    $newmodel \leftarrow L(I[usedSet], -g[usedSet], w[usedSet])$
    $models.$append$(newModel)$

3.2 Exclusive Feature Bundling

Since it is evident in many cases that the data is sparse with high feature dimension, EFB can reduce the number of features without loss, and can speed up the training speed of GBDT under the premise of ensuring accuracy. EFB consists of two parts: Identification of features that should be bundled together and construction of the bundle.

In the first part, it is not only necessary to find suitable bundling features, but the number of bundles should be minimal, therefore a reasonably greedy algorithm is ideal and used. Since there are more non-zero values of the features, there may be more conflict, therefore the greedy algorithm will sort in descending order according to the number of non-zero values of the features, and then check each feature according to the sorted sequence, and assign it to a smaller conflicting bundle or create a new one.

Algorithm 2 Greedy Bundling

Input: F: features, K: max conflict count
Non zero statistical set S
$searchOrder \leftarrow S.\text{sortByNumberOfNonZero}()$
$bundles \leftarrow \{\}, bundlesConflict \leftarrow \{\}$
for i **in** $searchOrder$ **do**
  needNew$\leftarrow$True
  for $j = 1$ **to** $len(bundles)$ **do**
    cnt$\leftarrow$conflictCnt($bundles[j], F[i]$)
    if $cnt + bundlesConflict[i] \leq k$ **then**
      $bundles[j].add(F[i])$,needNew $\leftarrow$False
      break
  if $needNew$ **then**
    Add $F[i]$ as a new bundle to $bundles$
Output: $bundles$

In the second part, in order to reduce the training complexity and be able to identify the original features from the feature bundles, a feature bundle is constructed by increasing the offset of the original value of the feature.

Algorithm 3 Merge Exclusive Features

Input: $numData$: number of data
Input: F: One bundle of exclusive features
$binRanges \leftarrow \{0\}, totalBin \leftarrow 0$
for f **in** F **do**
  $totalBin += f.\text{numBin}$
  $binRanges.\text{append}(totalBin)$
$newBin \leftarrow$ new Bin($numData$)
for $i = 1$ **to** $numData$ **do**
  $newBin[i] \leftarrow 0$
  for $j = 1$ **to** $len(F)$ **do**
    if $F[j].bin[i] \neq 0$ **then**
      $newBin[i] \leftarrow F[j].bin[i] + binRanges[j]$
Output: $newBin, binRanges$

Compared with other ensemble learning algorithms, when the feature dimension is high and the amount of data is large, LightGBM is more suitable and often achieves better prediction results. So, we use LightGBM to predict whether students would be able to pass the online course. We use ten classic machine learning algorithms to evaluate the predictive performance of LightGBM on student performance tasks, including Logistic Regression (LR), K-Nearest Neighbors(KNN), Decision Trees(DT), Naive Bayes(NB), Support Vector Machines(SVM), Multi-layered Perceptron(DNN), Random Forests(RF), Adaboost, GBDT, XGBoost. Among these algorithms, XGBoost and

LightGBM are implemented based on the Sklearn interface in their respective python packages, while other algorithms are implemented using the Sklearn toolkit.

4 Experiments

4.1 Experimental Setup

Dataset

The Open University Learning Analytics Dataset (OULAD) is a dataset containing aggregated clickstream data of student interactions with the learning environment in a virtual learning environment (VLE) [28]. This dataset is often used to evaluate the predictive performance of student performance prediction models [29, 30]. In order to avoid the influence of course type and effectively evaluate the performance of the model, we use the data of the FFF courses with the largest number of students and the most frequent interaction behaviors for experimental evaluation.

The course's original dataset contains more than 4 million interactions generated by 7,762 students. Among them, some students participated in courses multiple times, some students also participated in other courses, and some students' interaction data with the platform was not recorded. Therefore, we deleted the data of these students, and finally generated an experimental data set containing 6455 students and their interaction data with the platform. We aggregated the interaction data of students during the learning process by interaction type to generate 18 features for prediction.

Evaluation Metrics

In this experiment, we use five categories of metrics, Accuracy, Precision, Recall, F1-Score, and AUC to evaluate the performance of the student performance prediction method.

Accuracy: The percentage of students who predict the correct performance of the total students. Although the accurate rate can judge the correct rate of the prediction, it cannot be used as a good measure when the sample is unbalanced.

Precision: The percentage of students who actually passed the course among all the students who were predicted to pass the course.

Recall: The percentage of students who passed the course that were correctly predicted in the real world.

F1-Score: The harmonic mean of precision and recall. The calculated value is between 0 and 1. The larger the F1 value, the better the classification quality.

AUC: The area under the ROC curve. Generally, the AUC is between 0.5 and 1. The larger the value, the better the effect. It is often used to measure the pros and cons of learners.

4.2 Comparison of LightGBM and the Single Machine Learning Algorithms

To achieve this research goal, we used six single machine learning classification algorithms commonly used in student performance prediction research to separately predict whether students will pass the course, and the results are shown in Table 1.

Table 1. Comparison with the single machine learning algorithms

	Accuracy	Precision	Recall	F1-Score	AUC
NB	0.783	0.906	0.671	0.771	0.794
KNN	0.869	0.914	0.837	0.874	0.871
DT	0.904	0.922	0.899	0.91	0.904
LR	0.907	**0.924**	0.903	0.914	0.907
SVM	0.931	0.901	**0.979**	0.939	0.926
DNN	0.937	0.916	0.973	0.944	0.934
LightGBM	**0.941**	**0.924**	0.972	**0.947**	**0.938**

From Table 2, we can find that in the single algorithm model, the NB algorithm achieves the worst results. The NB algorithm assumes that each feature in the sample is independent of each other, and in the learning process, there are often correlations between different types of interaction behaviors of students, which are not completely independent. DNN algorithm has strong fitting ability, can fit any complex nonlinear relationship in theory, and can fully learn the relationship between features, so it achieves better prediction results. As an ensemble learning method, LightGBM integrates multiple decision tree classifiers, each of which is trained on the basis of the residual of the previous round of classifiers. During the training process, the bias is continuously reduced to improve the accuracy of the classifier. Compared with single algorithms, LightGBM achieves the best prediction performance.

4.3   Comparison of LightGBM with Other Classical Ensemble Learning Methods

In this experimental comparison, we use four commonly used ensemble learning algorithms to predict whether students can pass the course. These ensemble algorithms are all implemented based on decision trees. Among them, RF belongs to the extension of Bagging in the ensemble learning algorithm, and performs random feature selection on the basis of Bagging with decision tree as the base learner. AdaBoost, GBDT, and XGBoost all belong to Boost-type ensemble learning. The difference is that AdaBoost will process the samples from the previous training, increase the weight of wrongly classified samples and reduce the weight of correctly classified samples, and generate new training samples for the next classifier. Both GBDT and XGBoost train new classifiers through the residuals of the previous round of classifiers. XGBoost adds the complexity of the tree model to the regular term, so the generalization performance is better than GBDT. The prediction effects of these ensemble learning methods are shown in Table 2.

Table 2. Comparison with other ensemble learning algorithms

	Accuracy	Precision	Recall	F1-Score	AUC
RF	0.934	0.904	**0.983**	0.942	0.93
AdaBoost	0.929	0.909	0.966	0.936	0.925
GBDT	0.9356	0.912	0.976	0.943	0.932
XGBoost	0.937	0.919	0.97	0.944	0.934
Lightgbm	**0.941**	**0.924**	0.972	**0.947**	**0.938**

4.4 Predictive Performance of LightGBM at Different Stages of the Course

In order to better study the prediction performance of LightGBM and achieve the purpose of early prediction, we divide the courses into different course stages by time, such as 10%, 20%,…., 100%. Then, the prediction model based on LigthGBM is used to predict the performance of students under different course stages respectively.

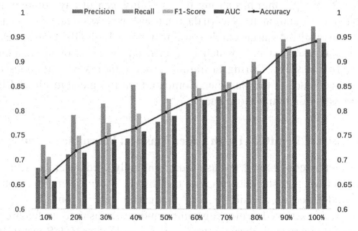

Fig. 1. Predictive performance of LightBDM at different course stages

From Fig. 1, we can easily find that as the course progresses, the accuracy of student predictions will gradually improve. As there is continuous development of the course, the data of students interacting with the online platform continues to increase, which helps the model to make more accurate predictions. Among them, when the course reaches 80% and above, we can make more accurate predictions for students.

4.5 Temporal Performance Evaluation of LightGBM

As opposed to the student performance prediction task in the traditional learning environment, the student performance prediction task in the online learning environment has the characteristics of big data, sparse and high dimensional features, which makes the model training time longer. Therefore, it is equally important to reduce the training speed of the model when ensuring the predictive performance of the model. We calculated the time of different models on the student performance prediction task, and the prediction performance of these models was similar to LightGBM. From Fig. 2, we find that LightGBM takes the shortest time on the student performance prediction task.

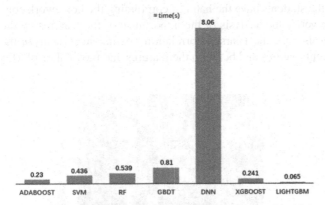

Fig. 2. Temporal performance of different prediction algorithms

4.6   Interaction Types Importance Analysis

While choosing a model that accurately predicts student performance is important, so is the interpret-ability of the model. Using LightGBM as a predictive method for student performance, it is possible to analyze the importance of different features to the prediction target. In the student performance prediction task, the analysis of feature importance not only provides guidance for teachers to help at-risk students, but also helps to optimize the design of online courses.

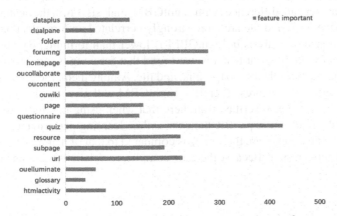

Fig. 3. Importance of features when predicting student performance

From Fig. 3, it can be seen that quiz is crucial for students to pass the course, because a lot of quiz interaction means that students will have a lot of quiz practice, which helps the students to pass the course. Forumng, homepage, and oucontent also plays a very important role. Among them, the visit to forumng means that students will conduct a lot of communication and discussion through the forum, the visit to homepage indicates that the students have a significant interest in the study of the course, the visit to the oucontent indicates that the students have the habit of completing the homework conscientiously.

In order to verify the analysis of the importance of the features by the LightGBM algorithm, we also use the Pearson correlation coefficient to analyze the correlation between different features and between the features and the final result (Fig. 4).

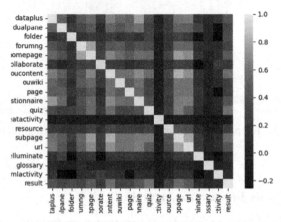

Fig. 4. A heatmap showing correlations between features and the final result.

On the heatmap of the correlation analysis, it increases as the color becomes lighter. We found that quiz and results were the lightest on the heatmap, reflecting that they had the highest correlation. Oucontent, homepage and results are also lighter in color on the heatmap, which means they are strongly correlated. However, through observation, we also found that there are differences with LightGBM analysis. From the heatmap, we can see that subpage, link, and file are more strongly correlated with results than forumng, but the importance of analysis in LightGBM is lower than forumng. By observing the correlations between different features, we found that forumng is more strongly correlated with other features than subpage, link, and file. Among them, file even has negative correlations with other features. Therefore LightGBM will give a higher importance to formng. Similarly, we also verified from here that when using the interaction between students and the platform to predict students' online learning performance, the prediction results of Naive Bayes are the worst, as compared to that of neural networks, which offered much better results. Because there are complex correlations between interactions.

5 Conclusions

In this paper, we provide a new perspective on student performance prediction in an online learning environment. In the online learning environment, the datasets used for student performance prediction have scalability problems, sparse and high dimensional features, as well as the time performance requirements for prediction models in practical applications. It is proposed to build a model using the LightGBM algorithm to predict students' ability to pass online learning courses, which is more suitable for predicting student performance in the online learning environment. Finally, six classic single machine learning algorithms and four other commonly used ensemble learning algorithms are compared to predict student performance. Experiments show that the prediction model using LightGBM algorithm not only has high accuracy, but also offers better time performance.

In addition, in order to study the impact of students' online learning interaction behavior on students' learning performance, the importance and correlation of different features were analyzed. We have found that taking more quizzes is essential for students to pass the course. At the same time, forum communication, maintaining interest in the course, and completing assignments can help students through the course. By analyzing the impact of different interaction behaviors on students' learning performance, it can help teachers to effectively guide students' learning, and help online learning courses to be reasonably and effectively designed.

Acknowledgements. This work was supported by the Natural Science Foundation of China (Nos.U1811264, 62066010), the Natural Science Foundation of Guangxi Province (No.2020GXNSFAA159055), Innovation Project of Guang Xi Graduate Education (No.YCBZ2021072), Guangxi Key Laboratory of Trusted Software (No.KX202058).

References

1. Chiu, Y.C., et al.: Predicting student performance in MOOCS using learning activity data. J. Inf. Sci. Eng. **34**(5), 1223–1235 (2018)
2. Hernández-Blanco, A., et al.: A systematic review of deep learning approaches to educational data mining. Complexity (2019)
3. Kew, S.N., Tasir, Z.: Identifying at-risk students in online learning by analysing learning behaviour: a systematic review. In: 2017 IEEE Conference on Big Data and Analytics (ICBDA). IEEE, pp. 118–123(2017)
4. Macfadyen, L.P., Dawson, S.: Mining LMS data to develop an "early warning system" for educators: a proof of concept. Comput. Educ. **54**(2), 588–599 (2010)
5. Asiah, M., Zulkarnaen, K.N., Safaai, D., et al.: A review on predictive modeling technique for student academic performance monitoring. MATEC Web Conf. EDP Sci. **255**, 03004 (2019)
6. Namoun, A., Alshanqiti, A.: Predicting student performance using data mining and learning analytics techniques: a systematic literature review. Appl. Sci. **11**(1), 237 (2021)
7. Tomasevic, N., Gvozdenovic, N., Vranes, S.: An overview and comparison of supervised data mining techniques for student exam performance prediction. Comput. Educ. **143**, 103676 (2020)

8. Zhang, W., Huang, X., Wang, S., et al.: Student performance prediction via online learning behavior analytics. In: 2017 International Symposium on Educational Technology (ISET). IEEE, pp. 153–157(2017)

9. Liu, W., Wu, J., Gao, X., et al.: An early warning model of student achievement based on decision trees algorithm. In: 2017 IEEE 6th International Conference on Teaching, Assessment, and Learning for Engineering (TALE). IEEE, pp. 517–222 (2017)

10. Wang, G.H., Zhang, J., Fu, G.S.: Predicting student behaviors and performance in online learning using decision tree. In: 2018 Seventh International Conference of Educational Innovation through Technology (EITT). IEEE, pp. 214–219 (2018)

11. Quan, W., Zhou, Q., Zhong, Y., et al.: Predicting at-risk students using campus meal consumption records. Int. J. Eng. Educ. **35**(2), 563–571 (2019)

12. Burman, I., Som, S.: Predicting students academic performance using support vector machine. In: 2019 Amity International Conference on Artificial Intelligence (AICAI). IEEE, pp. 756–759 (2019)

13. Al Mayahi, K., Al-Bahri, M.: Machine learning based predicting student academic success. In: 2020 12th International Congress on Ultra Modern Telecommunications and Control Systems and Workshops (ICUMT). IEEE, pp. 264–268 (2020)

14. Yang, Y., Hooshyar, D., Pedaste, M., Wang, M., Huang, Y.-M., Lim, H.: Predicting course achievement of university students based on their procrastination behaviour on Moodle. Soft Comput. **24**(24), 18777–18793 (2020). https://doi.org/10.1007/s00500-020-05110-4

15. Widyahastuti, F., Tjhin, V.U.: Predicting students performance in final examination using linear regression and multilayer perceptron. In: 2017 10th International Conference on Human System Interactions (HSI). IEEE, pp. 188–192 (2017)

16. Sandoval, I.P., Naranjo, D., Gilar, R., et al.: Neural network model for predicting student failure in the academic leveling course of Escuela Politécnica Nacional. Front. Psychol. **11**, 3383 (2020)

17. Karalar, H., Kapucu, C., Gürüler, H.: Predicting students at risk of academic failure using ensemble model during pandemic in a distance learning system. Int. J. Educ. Technol. Higher Educ. **18**(1), 1–18 (2021)

18. Breiman, L.: Random forests. Mach. Learn. **45**(1), 5–32 (2001)

19. Trakunphutthirak, R., Cheung, Y., Lee, V.C.S.: Detecting student at risk of failure: a case study of conceptualizing mining from internet access log files. In: 2018 IEEE International Conference on Data Mining Workshops (ICDMW). IEEE, pp. 365–371 (2018)

20. Hasan, R., Palaniappan, S., Mahmood, S., et al.: Predicting student performance in higher educational institutions using video learning analytics and data mining techniques. Appl. Sci. **10**(11), 3894 (2020)

21. Breiman, L.: Bagging predictors. Mach. Learn. **24**(2), 123–140 (1996)

22. Injadat, M., Moubayed, A., Nassif, A., Shami, A.: Multi-split optimized bagging ensemble model selection for multi-class educational data mining. Appl. Intell. **50**(12), 4506–4528 (2020). https://doi.org/10.1007/s10489-020-01776-3

23. Yan, L., Liu, Y.: An ensemble prediction model for potential student recommendation using machine learning. Symmetry **12**(5), 728 (2020)

24. Han, M., Tong, M., Chen, M., et al.: application of ensemble algorithm in students' performance prediction. In: 2017 6th IIAI International Congress on Advanced Applied Informatics (IIAI-AAI). IEEE, pp. 735–740(2017)

25. Ahmed, D.M., Abdulazeez, A.M., Zeebaree, D.Q., et al.: Predicting university's students performance based on machine learning techniques. In: 2021 IEEE International Conference on Automatic Control and Intelligent Systems (I2CACIS). IEEE, pp. 276–281 (2021)

26. Vultureanu-Albişi, A., Bădică, C.: Improving students' performance by interpretable explanations using ensemble tree-based approaches. In: 2021 IEEE 15th International Symposium on Applied Computational Intelligence and Informatics (SACI). IEEE, pp. 215–220 (2021)

27. Ke, G., Meng, Q., Finley, T., et al.: Lightgbm: a highly efficient gradient boosting decision tree. Adv. Neural Inf. Process. Syst. **30**, 3146–3154 (2017)
28. Kuzilek, J., Hlosta, M., Zdrahal, Z.: Open university learning analytics dataset. Sci. data **4**(1), 1–8 (2017)
29. Waheed, H., Hassan, S.U., Aljohani, N.R., et al.: Predicting academic performance of students from VLE big data using deep learning models. Comput. Human Behav. **104**, 106189 (2020)
30. Rivas, A., Gonzalez-Briones, A., Hernandez, G., et al.: Artificial neural network analysis of the academic performance of students in virtual learning environments. Neurocomputing **423**, 713–720 (2021)

Adapting on Road Traffic-Oriented Controlled Optimization of Phases to Heterogeneous Intersections

Ziyan Qiao[1], Rui Sun[1], Shiyao Chen[1], Dong Zi[1], Xingyu Wu[2], Qian Wang[2], Endong Tong[1], Wenjia Niu[1(✉)], and Jiqiang Liu[1]

[1] Beijing Key Laboratory of Security and Privacy in Intelligent Transportation, Beijing Jiaotong University, Beijing, China
{zyqiao,ruisun,chenshiyao,dzi,edtong,niuwj,jqliu}@bjtu.edu.cn
[2] School of Computer Science and Technology, Taiyuan University of Science and Technology, Taiyuan, China
{xuanyu,qianwang}@stu.tyust.edu.cn

Abstract. The optimization of traffic signal control has become a significant issue concerned by the whole society with the increasingly travel demands and the rise of vehicles on roadways. As one of the mature optimization, the Controlled Optimization of Phases (COP) plays an important role at traditional isolated intersections with 8 phases. In recent years, however, few previous studies have investigated the applicability of this algorithm at real heterogeneous intersections. In this paper, we propose an improved COP algorithm, in which we implement a Phase Processing method and embed an adaptor by reorganizing the workflow before the generation of signal timing plan. We are the first to extend the COP to support 4 phases of 3-direction intersection, aiming to push the development of COP, as a distributed and independently-deployed algorithm, towards more real but heterogeneous intersections. We respectively conduct the experiment at intersections with 4 phases and 8 phases and compare the detailed performance including average vehicle delay under different traffic flow. The results show the effectiveness and possibility of our method applying to heterogeneous intersections to some extent.

Keywords: Signal control optimization · Heterogeneous intersections · Adaptive control · Dynamic programming · Fixed-time control

1 Introduction

The development of transport is associated with our travel efficiency and quality with the increasingly travel demands and the rise of vehicles on roadways. It will cause traffic congestion even serious traffic accidents without an appropriate management. Intelligent Transport System (ITS) has developed in the early 19th century, which is a set of technologies and applications concerning the management road and vehicles including vehicles control, navigation systems [2],

© IFIP International Federation for Information Processing 2022
Published by Springer Nature Switzerland AG 2022
Z. Shi et al. (Eds.): IIP 2022, IFIP AICT 643, pp. 522–535, 2022.
https://doi.org/10.1007/978-3-031-03948-5_42

communication technologies [8], driver assistance [4], etc. Among those, signal control is a significant research for improving traffic situations with a valid signal management.

In order to reduce traffic congestion and improve travel efficiency and the experience of travelers, a multitude of methods has been proposed to optimize the signal control especially at intersections. It can be divided into three main methods, fixed-time control, driven control and adaptive control. In the set of fixed-time control, each signal controller has fixed time and same period. It has been certified to relieve traffic congestion in some simple situations, for example, an iterative method with delay-minimizing settings [1], a multi-objective genetic optimization algorithm [7], a cyclically time-expanded networks model (CTEN) [13]. However, it might cause undesired waiting time on the road when the traffic condition changed. Driven control partly solved this dilemma by change signal allocation flexibly utilizing collected data of vehicles (e.g. queue length or delay) that road detector captured. Successful methods including a signal control strategy from industry (SYLVIA) [6], an actuated signal control strategy to improve the operations of the CLL [17], etc. In recent years, in addition to above methods, adaptive control play a dominant role in the maintenance of road traffic at intersections. The real-time adaptive control, calculating and optimizing traffic performance objective functions using real-time data, has been proved to improve the traffic congestion. Using approximate dynamic programming and reinforcement learning to optimize traffic signal controllers could reduce vehicle delay [3]. An adaptive algorithm by solving a two-level optimization problem was testified that it would generate short queue length [5]. In the process of developing real-time adaptive control, there has been an increasing interest in the critical control algorithm, which is represented by the Controlled Optimization of Phases (COP) [11].

COP is a Dynamic Programming (DP) algorithm for optimal control. In recent years, Intelligent Traffic Signal System (I-SIG) has been deployed in California, Florida, and New York by the U.S. Department of Transportation (USDOT) [18], which is mainly based on COP algorithm with advanced technologies. It can significantly reduce waiting time, delay or queue length by updating the green time and phase sequence and achieved considerable performance in many researches. It usually applied in 2-stages signal plans or 5-stages signal plans.

A majority of previous studies for signal control addressed the phases optimization at traditional intersections with 8 phases by applying COP algorithm. Nevertheless, there is a complicated transport network consist of heterogeneous intersections in the real world including 4 phases, 10, phases, 12 phases, etc. The successful application of COP algorithm at traditional intersections cannot absolutely demonstrate it is applicable to all intersections with different phases. What is not yet clear is how to apply the COP algorithm to heterogeneous intersections and its application effect.

This paper proposes an extended signal control method based on the COP algorithm, in which we primarily improve the workflow and implement a Phase

Processing module consisting of an adapter for prejudging the feasible phases sequences to adapt heterogeneous intersections. In the simulated experiment, we evaluate its performance by comparing with traditional fixed-time signal control method at heterogeneous intersections. The empirical results suggest that our method can basically optimize signal control in different traffic flow.

This paper is organized as follows: In Sect. 2, we review DP algorithm and COP algorithm and the definition of heterogeneous intersections. Section 3 describes the framework implementation of improved signal control optimization at heterogeneous intersections. Experiment and results to test and compare the performance described in Sect. 4. Section 5 compares the related work. Finally, Sect. 6 concludes the main work of this paper and proposes the future research.

2   Preliminaries

Our approach is based on COP algorithm and DP algorithm at heterogeneous intersections. To understand the process of traffic signal control optimization, we briefly review related definitions and literature before describing our approach.

2.1   Heterogeneous Intersections and Its Phases

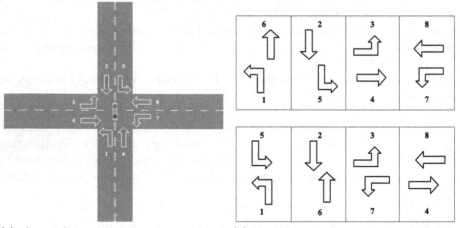

(a) A traditional intersection with 4 branches.

(b) Feasible sets of movements which has 4 phases.

Fig. 1. A schematic diagram of a traditional intersection with 4 branches.

Phases at Intersections. A set of movements which have no conflict in the same interval are referred as a phase. An Intersection has several phases according to specific environment. There are 2 movements in each branch, going straight and turning left [15] in Fig. 1(a) (For simplicity, we stipulate that turning right has a free right-of-way). As Fig. 1(b) showed, in some settings, there are 4 phases in a standard intersection with 4 branches [9]. In order to adjust phases sequences flexibly, each movement is marked with one phase in our method and experiment.

(a) An intersection with 3 branches at Santa Monica Blvd, Los Angeles, USA.

(b) An intersection with 5 branches at Emanuel Cleaver II Blvd, Kansas City, USA.

Fig. 2. Real-world heterogeneous intersections with different branches.

Heterogeneous Intersections. A heterogeneous intersection is an intersection with different branches and phases. In the real world, there are not always intersections with 4 branches and 8 phases, T-roads (3 branches) are also familiar. Figure 2 displays the factual intersections with 3 and 5 branches. Therefore, it is necessary to explore the feasibility of the signal control method based on COP algorithm at such heterogeneous intersections.

2.2 Controlled Optimization of Phases

COP algorithm is an effective method to optimize this plan based on DP algorithm. Without addressing the previous states and policies, the remain policies constitute an optimal strategy. This is referred as the principle of optimality. Dynamic Programming can be used to solve optimal control problems that satisfy the principle [14]. DP problems can be solved by following steps.

Step 1. Analyse the principle of optimality.
Step 2. Determine the state representation and state recursion equation, define the optimal value recursively.

Step 3. Determine the state transition sequence, calculate the optimal value from the bottom up.
Step 4. Construct the optimal solution.

The second step is the kernel of DP algorithm, it is the planning process for the optimal solution. $f(x_1, \ldots, x_k)$ is the state representation, where $x_1, \ldots, x_k$ is the list of parameters to describe the sub-problems, $f(\cdot)$ is the objective function.

COP is responsible for calculating a signal timing plan consisting of a phases sequence and correspondent duration [11]. As mentioned in Sect. 2.2, the key procedure to deploy the COP algorithm is determining appropriate state variable, decision variable and state transition equation. These essential definitions are as followed.

s_k: State variable, the total time steps when stage k completed.
u_k: Decision variable, denotes the green time steps allocated to stage k.
M_k: Performance function, measures the performance of the realized process.
V_k: Value function, accumulates the value of previous performance.
e: Effective clearance interval, the sum of yellow interval and the full red interval when all the phases meet red. In the full red interval, vehicles which passed stop lines can drive freely while other vehicles must wait for later green time.

3   Our Approach

3.1   Overview

As we referred previously, the signal control optimization deploying COP algorithm at a traditional intersection with 4 branches has successfully reduced traffic congestion. However, researchers have not treated heterogeneous intersections in much detail. In order to explore the availability of COP algorithm for heterogeneous intersections, we adjust the procedure of optimization based on an adaptive signal control method [5] with COP algorithm [11]. We consider an intersection with 3 branches. According to the explication in Sect. 2.1, there are 4 phases (Fig. 3).

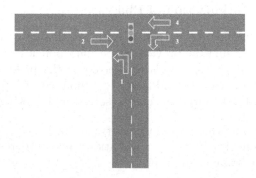

Fig. 3. Layout of an intersection with 3 branches and 4 phases in our method.

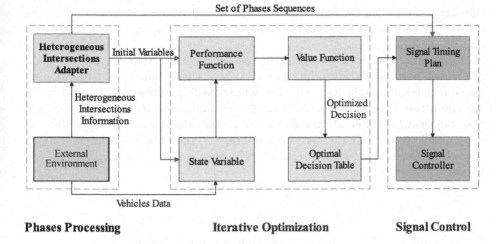

Fig. 4. Flowchart of traffic signal control.

Figure 4 presents the cardinal procedure of signal control optimization which is divided into three modules, Phases Processing module, Iterative Optimization module and Signal Control module. The heterogeneous intersections adapter firstly collects the phases information on heterogeneous intersections of external environment and generate a set of phases sequences for the final signal timing plan. Real-time vehicles data, the input of Iterative Optimization module, is used for calculation of the optimal decision and integrate into a decision table. A signal timing plan is continuing form by retrieving the table. Finally, the signal controller takes a corresponding adjustment.

3.2   Phase Processing and Iterative Calculation

Phase Processing module is responsible for generating a set of phases sequences and related variables for inputting the Iterative module. Distinguished from previous research with general intersections, we address the specific heterogeneous intersections in advance. On the one hand, there are different phases sequences at heterogeneous intersections. Additionally, some concurrent phases possibly produce conflict especially in complex intersections (e.g. turn left from North to West and go straight West to East). Therefore, a heterogeneous intersections adapter, the main component of this module, can analyse the phases information from the external environment and form a set of feasible phases sequences without phases conflict. This set plays an important role in selecting the optimal signal timing plan. On the other hand, some variables are initialized to satisfy later calculation according to the specific intersections and phases.

We specify present stage k, $k = 1, 2, ..., K$, where K is the maximal stage. Present phase is indexed by $p = 1, 2, ..., P$, where P is the total number of phases. $t = 1, 2, ..., T$ is the present time, where T is the total time steps allocated to the signal controller(We only consider the discrete time). Essential constants include the minimum and maximum green interval g_{min}, g_{max}, the maximum queue length Q_{max}, etc.

In Iterative Calculation module, the real-time vehicles data are collected and calculated periodically, including phase p_c and the estimated arrival time a_c which is indexed by vehicles c, etc. The whole feasible values of decision variable are enumerated, given s_k. If the sum of the minimum green interval and the effective clearance interval exceeds the total time steps allocated after stage k, s_k is unable to support the execution of stage k, then the green interval u_k at stage k sets to 0. Otherwise, it selects 0 or any integer between g_{min} and $s_k - e$, in which e is defined in Sect. 2.2.

$$U_k\left(s_k\right) = \begin{cases} 0, & s_k - g_{min} < e, \\ \{0, g_{min}, g_{min} + 1, \ldots, s_k - e\}, & s_k - g_{min} \geq e. \end{cases} \tag{1}$$

Subsequently, the state transition equation is expressed by Eq. 2.

$$s_{k-1} = \begin{cases} s_k, & u_k = 0 \\ s_k - u_k - e, & u_k \neq 0 \end{cases} \tag{2}$$

Given s_k and u_k, Eq. 3 describes the relationship between value function and performance function $M_k\left(s_k, u_k\right)$.

$$V_k\left(s_k, u_k\right) = M_k\left(s_k, u_k\right) + V_{k-1}\left(s_{k-1}, u_{k-1}\right) \tag{3}$$

By enumerating the decision variables in the Eq. 1, we discover the optimal value, that is, the optimal green interval allocated to stage k.

$$u_k^*\left(s_k\right) = \{u_k \in U_k\left(s_k\right) \mid \min V_k\left(s_k, u_k\right)\} \tag{4}$$

The above procedure is summarized by the Recursive algorithm.

Algorithm 1. Recursive algorithm

Input: T, P, K, e, g_{min}
Output: $u_k^*(s_k)$
 1: Initialize $V_0 = 0$;
 2: **for** $k = 1 : K$ **do**
 3:     **for** $s_k = e : T$ **do**
 4:         Generate decision variables u_k;
 5:         Generate state variables s_k;
 6:         Generate value function $V_k(s_k, u_k)$;
 7:         Store $u_k^*(s_k)$ in the optimal decision table;
 8:         **if** $V_k(s_k, u_k) == V_{k-j}$, for all $j < k$ **then**
 9:             STOP;
10:         **end if**
11:     **end for**
12: **end for**

After that, set $u_k^*(s_k)$ equals to T and retrieve $u_k^*(s_k)$ and s_k^* from the optimal decision table, which are used in calculating the concrete performance function. Average queue length and average vehicles delay are employed to be the performance measurement in our approach.

$Q_{p,k}(s_k, u_k)$, a function of s_k and u_k, denotes the queue length of phase p at stage k. It is calculated by Eq. 5.

$$Q_{p,k}(s_k, u_k) = \begin{cases} Q_{p,k-1}(s_{k-1}, u_{k-1}) + A_p(s_{k-1}, s_k), & \\ & p \neq Pr_k, \\ \max\{0, Q_{p,k-1}(s_{k-1}, u_{k-1}) + A_p(s_{k-1}, s_{k-1} + u_k) & \\ -N_{p_{\max}}\} + A_p(s_{k-1} + u_k, s_k), & p = Pr_k, \end{cases} \tag{5}$$

Where $N_{p_{max}}$ is the maximum number of vehicles at phase p that is discharged in the green interval, $A_p(s_{k-1}, s_k)$ denotes the number of vehicles arriving at phase p between s_{k-1} and s_k. $p = Pr_k$ signifies that phase p is in the green interval at stage k, when vehicles can through this phase until reaching the maximum emissions. Therefore, if the number of vehicles including queuing from stage $k-1$ and arriving during the green interval are completely discharged in the green interval, there is no vehicles up to present, then queue length is equals to the number of vehicles arriving in the effective clearance interval e. Otherwise, it is equaled to the number of vehicles including queuing from stage $k-1$ and arriving at phase p between s_{k-1} and s_k. The performance function of average queue length at stage k is given by Eq. 6, which is used in Eq. 3.

$$M_k(s_k, u_k) = \sum_p Q_{p,k}(s_k, u_k)/P \tag{6}$$

Vehicles delay is defined as a waiting interval of vehicles at phase from the estimated arrival time to its leaving time from stop line.

$$D_{p,k}(s_k, u_k) = \begin{cases} Q_{p,k-1}(s_{k-1}, u_{k-1}) \times (s_k - s_{k-1}) & \\ + \sum_{p, s_{k-1} \leq a_k \leq s_k} s_k - a_k, & p \neq Pr_k, \\ \min\{Q_{p,k-1}(s_{k-1}, u_{k-1}), N_{p_{\max}}\} \times u_k & \\ + \max\{0, Q_{p,k-1}(s_{k-1}, u_{k-1}) - N_{p_{\max}}\} \times (s_k - s_{k-1}) & \\ + \sum_{p, s_{k-1} + u_k \leq a_k \leq s_k} s_k - a_k, & \\ & p = Pr_k, \end{cases} \tag{7}$$

Where $\sum_{p, s_{k-1} \leq a_k \leq s_k}$ denotes a sum of vehicles waiting time arriving between stage $k-1$ and stage k. Similar to the calculation of queue length, vehicles delay also depends on the present phase p, phase p is in the green interval at stage k, it considers the maximum emissions $N_{p_{\max}}$ and the arrived vehicles after the green interval. Otherwise, it only considers the vehicles that have already queued or arrived between stage $k-1$ and stage k. The performance function of total vehicles delay at stage k is given by Eq. 6, which is used in Eq. 3.

$$M_k(s_k, u_k) = \sum_p D_{p,k}(s_k, u_k) \tag{8}$$

3.3 Signal Control and Workflow

In Signal Control module, signal timing plan is established by the optimal decision table and corresponding phase in the Iterative Optimization module. Meanwhile, it must check the set of phases sequences sent from the Phases Processing module to guarantee the feasibility of this plan. If the selected plan is nonexistent in the set of phases sequences, signal controller cannot adopt this plan and it must choose additional decisions which are discerned in the phases sequences set. Vehicles arriving at this intersection abide by the updated rule and produce new data as the input of next iteration. The complete workflow is shown in Algorithm 2 which includes above three modules. Finally, the access priorities of vehicles at the intersection are controlled by signal controller in the end of each stage.

4 Experiment

In order to validate the applicability of our extended method at heterogeneous intersections, we respectively apply the algorithm at two intersections with 4 phases and 8 phases. In Sect. 4.1, we introduce the experiment environment and initial setups. In Sect. 4.2, we demonstrate the comparison of average vehicles numbers and optimization rate of average vehicles delay. In Sect. 4.3, we analyse the results and evaluate our extended method.

Algorithm 2. Extended signal control algorithm

Input: Vehicles Data, Environment Data, Constants
Output: Signal Timing Plan
 1: Initialize Signal Controller, Heterogeneous Intersections Adapter;
 2: Collect heterogeneous intersections information;
 3: Analyse phases Composition;
 4: Generate feasible phases sequences $\mathbf{F}$ and related variables;
 5: **for** $k = 1 : K$ **do**
 6:    Apply Algorithm 1;
 7:    Generate optimal decision table;
 8:    Generate signal timing plan $\mathbf{M}$;
 9:    Check feasible phases sequences;
10:    **if** $\mathbf{M} \subseteq \mathbf{F}$ **then**
11:       Continue;
12:    **else**
13:       Select new decision from optimal decision table;
14:    **end if**
15:    Control vehicles following signal timing plan;
16: **end for**

4.1   General Setups

In order to validate the applicability of our extended method at heterogeneous intersections, we perform the experiment on the VISSIM simulation platform as shown in Fig. 5, which is a system modelling and dynamic simulation platform. The simulation and optimization program is established on the Visual Stdio and works on a PC. In our experiment, vehicles are generated at a Connected Vehicles (CV) environment with 70% penetration [10]. Therefore, we obtain vehicles information by Dedicated Short-Range Communications (DSRC) technology [12] while unequipped vehicles information is acquired by Estimation of Location and Speed (EVLS) algorithm [16]. We apply the extended method at the intersection with 4 phases and apply COP at the intersection with 8 phases. Synchronously run the fixed-time control as a benchmark. For each intersection, we run 10 periods. The simulation speed is 10 Sim.sec/s and the resolution is 5 time steps(s)/Sim.sec. The average vehicle speed is 13.889 m/s. In order to evaluate the performance of our extended method effectively, two traffic conditions are considered in each experiment, normal traffic flow and congested traffic flow. We respectively input 1000 vehicles and 2000 vehicles at the beginning of each period to simulate this two traffic conditions.

4.2   Comparison of Performance

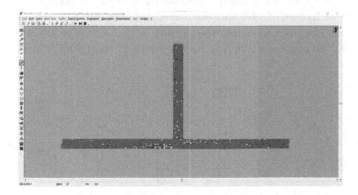

Fig. 5. Layout of an intersection with 3 branches and 4 phases in our method.

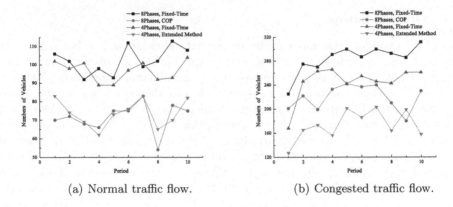

(a) Normal traffic flow.   (b) Congested traffic flow.

Fig. 6. Average numbers of vehicles in different traffic flow.

Average Numbers of Vehicles. The results of average vehicles numbers in each period and different traffic conditions are shown in Fig. 6. As Fig. 6(a) showed, the average vehicles numbers are almost equal between the fixed-time control in 8 and 4 phases when there is a normal traffic flow. Both of the average vehicles numbers reduced to a similar number when using COP in 8 phases and using our extended method in 4 phases. In Fig. 6(b), all the average vehicles numbers increased due to the set of congested traffic flow. Although the difference between two curves of using fixed-time control in 8 and 4 phases, the same gap and trend exist in both COP and our extended method. We can find that our extended method shows a comparable ability with COP algorithm in control of averaged vehicles numbers and it is independent of the traffic condition.

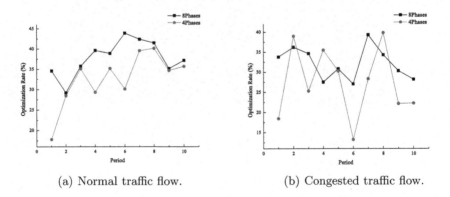

(a) Normal traffic flow.   (b) Congested traffic flow.

Fig. 7. Optimization rate of average vehicles delay in different traffic flow.

Average Vehicles Delay. Figure 7 illustrates the optimization rate of average delay compared with fixed-time control with 8 and 4 phases for each vehicle and every period. The positive optimization rate indicates that both COP and our extended method successfully decreased the vehicles delay than the fixed-time control. In Fig. 7(a), when the traffic condition is normal, despite the optimization rate of our extended method is sightly lower than COP, both the average optimization was maintained between 25% and 40% in addition to the first period. In Fig. 7(b), the optimization rate using our extended method in 4 phases in some periods is even higher than those using COP in 8 phases when there is a congested traffic flow. However, it did not perform better than COP in ten periods and produced large fluctuations during the whole periods when the traffic condition is congested.

4.3   Results and Discussions

Table 1. Comparison of the average delay optimization rate (%) in different traffic flow.

	Period	1	2	3	4	5	6	7	8	9	10	Average
Normal	8 phases	34.58	29.20	35.75	39.63	38.89	43.90	42.41	41.48	35.17	37.19	37.82
	4 phases	17.79	28.49	35.13	29.36	35.19	30.16	39.58	40.15	34.71	35.72	32.62
Congested	8 phases	33.81	36.24	34.63	27.54	30.85	27.07	39.33	34.32	30.36	28.23	32.24
	4 phases	18.46	39.00	25.30	35.19	30.28	13.26	28.39	39.87	22.2	22.32	27.46

The results suggest that the performance of our extended method applied to 4 phases extremely performs better than fixed-time control and it is basically comparable with COP algorithm. For the average vehicles numbers, it displays a significant advantage regardless of the traffic conditions. For the average vehicles delay, the performance of our extended method is related to the traffic conditions in some extent. As Table 1 showed, it even reaches approximately 40% at 8th period, while it is below 18% at 1st period in the congested traffic flow. Furthermore, The differences in the average optimization rate are less than 6% in both traffic flow. It might become to fluctuate with the increasing of vehicles. Therefore, we need to recognize the instability of our extended method applying to heterogeneous intersections. Overall, our extended method has achieved positive results for optimizing signal control in different traffic flow than using fixed-time control and it is comparable with traditional COP algorithm in different traffic flow.

5   Related work

The traditional COP algorithm proposed in 1997 [11] partially solved some problems in real-time adaptive signal control optimization. It is capable of improving traffic condition according to different performance criteria. However, it has rarely been generalized independently due to its simple configuration and limited exploration. Therefore, we extend the COP algorithm by adjusting its workflow and adding a Phase Processing module, which make it can be applied to signal control systems independently.

With the development of Internet of Vehicles, COP algorithm has been applied to optimization of real-time adaptive signal control combining with advanced technologies. Its effectiveness has been testified in many studies, while they mostly considered the traditional intersections with 8 phases. There are complex heterogeneous intersections in the real world(e.g. intersections with 4 phases or 12 phases). It is essential to explore the applicability of COP algorithm at heterogeneous intersections. Our extended method embeds a phases adapter, which is able to adapt different phases at heterogeneous intersections and empirical results shows that it successfully adapts the heterogeneous intersection with 4 phases.

6   Conclusion

The present study were designed to determine the effect of the Control Optimization of Phases applying to heterogeneous intersections. For this purpose, we extend the COP algorithm by adding a phases processing module and related variables and compare their performance at different intersections with 4 phases and traditional 8 phases. The findings in our experiment have shown that this method can successfully optimize the signal control than using fixed-time control and it is comparable with the COP algorithm. The results of this study indicate that our extended method can adapt heterogeneous intersections.

We would like to point out that the study has preliminarily tested our extended method at intersections with 4 phases or 8 phases. Despite its preliminary character, the research would seem to explore the applicability of the signal control optimization method at heterogeneous intersections. This research has thrown up many questions in need of further investigation. Considerably more work will need to be done to determine the performance of our extended method at complex intersections (e.g. 10 phases or 10 phases) and multiple heterogeneous intersections.

References

1. Allsop, R.E.: Delay-minimizing settings for fixed-time traffic signals at a single road junction. IMA J. Appl. Math. **8**(2), 164–185 (1971)
2. Atia, M.M., Karamat, T., Noureldin, A.: An enhanced 3D multi-sensor integrated navigation system for land-vehicles. J. Navig. **67**(4), 651–671 (2014)
3. Cai, C., Wong, C.K., Heydecker, B.G.: Adaptive traffic signal control using approximate dynamic programming. Transp. Res. Part C Emerg. Technol. **17**(5), 456–474 (2009)
4. Chiang, H.-H., Chen, Y.-L., Bing-Fei, W., Lee, T.-T.: Embedded driver-assistance system using multiple sensors for safe overtaking maneuver. IEEE Syst. J. **8**(3), 681–698 (2012)

5. Feng, Y., Head, K.L., Khoshmagham, S., Zamanipour, M.: A real-time adaptive signal control in a connected vehicle environment. Transp. Res. Part C Emerg. Technol. **55**, 460–473 (2015)
6. Grether, D., Bischoff, J., Nagel, K.: Traffic-actuated signal control: simulation of the user benefits in a big event real-world scenario. In: 2nd International Conference on Models and Technologies for ITS, Leuven, Belgium, pp. 11–12 (2011)
7. Hu, H., Gao, Y., Yang, X.: Multi-objective optimization method of fixed-time signal control of isolated intersections. In: 2010 International Conference on Computational and Information Sciences, pp. 1281–1284. IEEE (2010)
8. Inoue, H., Osawa, S., Yashiki, A., Makino, H.: Dedicated short-range communications (DSRC) for ahs services. In: IEEE Intelligent Vehicles Symposium, pp. 369–374 (2004)
9. Li, Z., Elefteriadou, L., Ranka, S.: Signal control optimization for automated vehicles at isolated signalized intersections. Transp. Res. Part C Emerg. Technol. **49**, 1–18 (2014)
10. Lu, N., Cheng, N., Zhang, N., Shen, X., Mark, J.W.: Connected vehicles: solutions and challenges. IEEE Internet Things J. **1**(4), 289–299 (2014)
11. Sen, S., Head, K.L.: Controlled optimization of phases at an intersection. Transp. Sci. **31**(1), 5–17 (1997)
12. Siegel, J.E., Erb, D.C., Sarma, S.E.: A survey of the connected vehicle landscape-architectures, enabling technologies, applications, and development areas. IEEE Trans. Intell. Transp. Syst. **19**(8), 2391–2406 (2017)
13. Thunig, T., Scheffler, R., Strehler, M., Nagel, K.: Optimization and simulation of fixed-time traffic signal control in real-world applications. Procedia Comput. Sci. **151**, 826–833 (2019)
14. Wang, F.-Y., Zhang, H., Liu, D.: Adaptive dynamic programming: an introduction. IEEE Comput. Intell. Mag. **4**(2), 39–47 (2009)
15. Wei, H., Zheng, G., Gayah, V., Li, Z.: A survey on traffic signal control methods. arXiv preprint arXiv:1904.08117 (2019)
16. Wong, W., Shen, S., Zhao, Y., Liu, H.X.: On the estimation of connected vehicle penetration rate based on single-source connected vehicle data. Transp. Res. Part B Methodol. **126**, 169–191 (2019)
17. Jiaming, W., Liu, P., Qin, X., Zhou, H., Yang, Z.: Developing an actuated signal control strategy to improve the operations of contraflow left-turn lane design at signalized intersections. Transp. Res. Part C Emerg. Technol. **104**, 53–65 (2019)
18. Xiang, Y., et al.: Congestion attack detection in intelligent traffic signal system: combining empirical and analytical methods. Secur. Commun. Netw. **2021** (2021). Hindawi

A Method of Garbage Quantity Prediction Based on Population Change

Qiumei Yu[1,2], Hongjie Wan[1,2], Junchen Ma[1,2], Huakang Li[3], and Guozi Sun[1,2(✉)]

[1] Key Laboratory of Urban Land Resources Monitoring and Simulation, MNR, Shenzhen, China
[2] School of Computer Science, NUPT, Nanjing, China
sun@njupt.edu.cn
[3] School of Artificial Intelligence and Advanced Computing, XJTLU, Suzhou, China

Abstract. Aiming at the problem that the amount of urban waste changes due to population changes and is difficult to predict, a method for predicting the amount of waste based on urban population changes is proposed. After analyzing the correlation between the urban population data of Shanghai and the annual output of garbage from 2000 to 2019, the correlation coefficient and strong correlation data items are calculated. On this basis, judge whether the original population data items meet the conditions of the grey prediction model, and determine whether it can be modeled according to the grey model. Based on the grey theory, this paper analyzes the basic situation of population changes and future population growth trend in Shanghai. Finally, the annual production of municipal solid waste in Shanghai from 2020 to 2025 is predicted based on multiple linear regression analysis. The results show that the waste production of Shanghai has shown a slow growth trend since 2019, and will not increase significantly in the natural state in recent years, which provides a reference basis for subsequent research and analysis.

Keywords: Population changes · Waste production · Correlation analysis · Grey prediction model · Multiple linear regression

1 Introduction

The research report issued by the Health and Family Planning Commission shows that during the 12th Five Year Plan period, the national migrant population will increase by about 8 million every year, and more than 253 million by the end of 2014. This large-scale population flow is bound to have a major impact on the population distribution and structure, national economic and industrial layout, economic, social and cultural environment of large and medium-sized cities in China, and even make great changes in the regional urban and rural population structure and sociology-economic layout [1]. As one of the key elements of urban productivity, with the high-speed flow of population between urban nodes across the country, it is bound to lead to the reconfiguration and integration of other elements, which may have a significant inactive influence on the entire urban network [4].

Published by Springer Nature Switzerland AG 2022
Z. Shi et al. (Eds.): IIP 2022, IFIP AICT 643, pp. 536–548, 2022.
https://doi.org/10.1007/978-3-031-03948-5_43

2 Background

2.1 A Subsection Sample

The report of the 19th CPC National Congress clearly pointed out that *"Promote Green Development and Strive To Solve Outstanding Environmental Problems"*, which further highlighted the importance of cooperation between green development and environmental protection [5]. Many researchers in China have also analyzed the impact causes and prediction results of waste production. It is generally believed that the impact of population on waste production accounts for the majority [6]. H. H. Huangfu used grey absolute correlation analysis and concluded that population index is one of the main factors affecting municipal solid waste [7]. W. Cao estimated and analyzed the per capita domestic waste production coefficient in Jinan in view of the large selection range and uncertainty of the per capita domestic waste production coefficient [9].

Some researchers have also investigated other reasons that can affect waste production. It still shows that the increase of urban domestic waste is related to the population. Z. Zeng [10] based on the statistical data of the total domestic waste removal and transportation in Anhui Province from 2009 to 2016, using the method of mathematical statistical analysis [11], analyzed the changes and influencing factors of the total domestic waste removal and transportation in Anhui Province. The conclusion is that the most direct reason for the change of the total amount of domestic waste treatment in Anhui Province is the change of the total urban population.

Therefore, understanding the distribution law of urban floating population and analyzing the relationship between population flow and domestic waste are of great significance to promote the construction of "landscape city, green city".

The goal of this paper is to predict the output of municipal solid waste by analyzing the population flow. Firstly, the correlation between population flow and waste production is analyzed [12], and then the development trend of population flow is predicted and analyzed through the grey prediction model. Finally, the output of urban domestic waste is predicted according to the population flow.

3 Model

In order to predict the annual output of municipal household waste more scientifically and rationally, the correlation between population data and waste yield needs to be analyzed and the data characteristics with strong correlation should be preserved before the model can be established. Then the annual output of garbage is predicted and analyzed using population data. The technical road-map for the experiment is shown in Fig. 1.

This section only describes urban population forecasting models and garbage yield forecasting models, and details such as correlation analysis will be covered in more detail in the next section.

3.1 Construct Urban Population Prediction Model

First of all, the method of grey theoretical system is used to analyze and calculate the population-related data, and then the grey prediction model is used for prediction analysis.

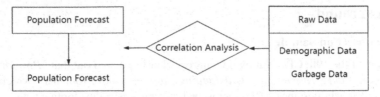

Fig. 1. The chart of experimental technology route.

Among them, the grey prediction model is to judge the similarity of the development trend between various factors in the system, process the original data with representative characteristics in the system accordingly, find the law of data change, and then predict the future development trend through differential equations.

In the grey prediction model, the GM (1, 1) model is a first-order model, which is more suitable for population growth models with stable growth rates.

1) The Class-Compare Verification
In order to make the grey prediction model more reliable in predicting urban population mobility, it is necessary to check the level ratio of the original data series before establishing the model to judge whether it meets the accuracy requirements of the grey model.

Assume $x^{(0)} = (X^{(0)}(1), X^{(0)}(2), \cdots, X^{(0)}(n))$ (n is the number of data) is the accumulated original data sequence and all are non-negative numbers.

Formula for calculating the level ratio of data series:

$$\rho(k) = \frac{x^{(0)}(k)}{x^{(0)}(k+1)} \tag{1}$$

Among, $\rho(k)$ is stepwise ratio, $x^{(0)}(k)$ and $x^{(0)}(k+1)$ are adjacent means.

If all $\rho(k)$ falls within the interval $\left(e^{\frac{-2}{n+1}}, e^{\frac{2}{n+2}} \right)$, the original data sequence can be modeled by GM(1, 1); On the contrary, the data sequence needs to be translated. Therefore, the class-compare verification can be used to verify whether the grey model is suitable for data prediction.

2) Grey Prediction Model
The grey prediction model generates a new number column by adding up, then establishes a first-order single-variable differential equation, and then predicts the data using the fitting function. The specific implementation steps are as follows:

a) The original data series for an element is known to be:

$$x^{(0)} = (X^{(0)}(1), X^{(0)}(2), \cdots, X^{(0)}(n)) \tag{2}$$

Accumulate $X^{(0)}$ once to generate a new sequence $X^{(1)}$:

$$x^{(1)} = (X^{(1)}(1), X^{(1)}(2), \cdots, X^{(1)}(n)) \tag{3}$$

Among,

$$x^{(1)}(k) = \sum_{i=1}^{k} x^{(0)}(i), k = 1, \cdots, n$$

Compared with the original sequence, the randomness of this new sequence is greatly and the stability is greatly increased.

b) Make $Z^{(1)}$ the nearest mean generation sequence of $X^{(1)}$:

$$Z^{(1)} = (z^{(1)}(2), z^{(1)}(3), \cdots, z^{(1)}(n)) \tag{4}$$

Among,

$$z^{(1)}(k) = \frac{1}{2}x^{(1)}(k) + \frac{1}{2}x^{(1)}(k-1)$$

c) The grey differential equation model for GM (1, 1) is:

$$u = X^{(0)}(k) + az^{(1)}(k) \tag{5}$$

Among, a is the development factor and u is the amount of ash.

d) By fitting the least squares to solve parameters a, u. The formula is calculated as follows:

$$\begin{bmatrix} a \\ u \end{bmatrix} = (B^T B)^{-1} B^T Y_n \tag{6}$$

Where B is the data matrix,

$$B = \begin{bmatrix} -z^{(1)}(2) & 1 \\ -z^{(1)}(3) & 1 \\ \vdots & \vdots \\ -z^{(1)}(n) & 1 \end{bmatrix}$$

Where Y_n is column vector,

$$Y_n = \left[x^0(2), x^0(3), x^0(4), \dots, x^0(n) \right]^T$$

e) The trend of change in the new series is approximately described by differential equations.

$$\frac{dx^{(1)}}{dt} + ax^{(1)} = u \tag{7}$$

The model's time response function is:

$$\hat{x}(t) = \left[x^{(1)}(0) - \frac{u}{a} \right] e^{-at} + \frac{u}{a} \tag{8}$$

The corresponding grey differential equation time response sequence is:

$$\hat{x}(k+1) = \left[x^{(1)}(0) - \frac{u}{a}\right]e^{-at} + \frac{u}{a}, \quad k = 1, \cdots, n \tag{9}$$

Assume $x^{(1)}(0) = x^{(0)}(1)$, so

$$\hat{x}(k+1) = \left[x^{(1)}(1) - \frac{u}{a}\right]e^{-at} + \frac{u}{a}, \quad k = 1, \cdots, n \tag{10}$$

Then do the tired and sub-tractable grey prediction equation:

$$\begin{aligned}\hat{x}^{(0)}(k+1) &= \hat{x}^{(1)}(k+1) - \hat{x}^{(1)}(k) \\ &= \left[x^{(0)}(1) - \frac{u}{a}\right]\left(1 - e^{-a}\right)e^{-ak} + \frac{u}{a} \\ &(k = 1, 2, \cdots, n-1)\end{aligned} \tag{11}$$

Finally, the model can be tested by residual test and correlation test.

3.2 Multiple Linear Regression Models

In this paper, the regression model is used to predict the output of urban household waste by analyzing the population flow. Linear Regression assumes that there is a linear relationship between the features and the results in the dataset, and thus the desired results are obtained. Its expression is:

$$Y = a_0 + a_1x_1 + a_2x_2 + \cdots a_nx_n + b \tag{12}$$

Where Y is the result set, x_i constitutes the feature set, a_i is the regression coefficient, b is the random error and follows the normal distribution $N(0, \sigma^2)$.

Assuming that α and β are the optimal solutions, the regression equation is $\alpha * X + \beta^T$. At this time, Y is obtained through the assumed optimal solution. There is a certain error between this and the actual results, which is optimized by the least square method.

The main idea of least squares optimization is to select unknown parameters to minimize the sum of residuals between theoretical values and observed values. The expression of objective function is:

$$\min f(x) = \sum_{i=1}^{n} l_i^2(x) = \sum_{i=1}^{n} [y_i - f(x_i, a_i)]^2 \tag{13}$$

Among, $l_i(x)(i = 1, 2, \cdots, n)$ is the residual function.

4   Analysis of Correlation

Before predicting the annual output of MSW, it is necessary to analyze the correction between urban population and MSW output.

4.1 The Source of Data

The statistical data of Shanghai were mainly obtained from The Shanghai Statistical Yearbook and the database of the National Bureau of Statistics. The data related to population flow in Shanghai from 1978 to 2018 and the original data of municipal solid waste production were obtained. Table 1 shows the data related to population mobility and the amount of urban domestic waste in Shanghai from 2015 to 2019.

Table 1. Relevant data 2015–2019.

X_0	2015	2016	2017	2018	2019
X_1	2415.27	2419.7	2418.33	2423.78	2428.14
X_2	3809	3816	3814	3823	3830
X_3	536.76	541.62	564.13	551.95	556.23
X_4	2.69	2.68	2.66	2.65	2.64
X_5	1442.97	1450	1455.13	1462.38	1469.3
X_6	10.59	13.07	11.77	9.84	9.14
X_7	12.42	12.35	12.64	12.57	12.52
X_8	11.61	11.2	11.85	13.75	13.69
X_9	5.32	4.64	4.17	3.92	3.41
Y	790	880	900	984	1038

In Table 1, the data are as follows:

$X0$: year
X_1: permanent resident population (10000 persons)
X_2: population density (person/km^2)
X_3: total households (10000 households)
X_4: population per household (person)
X_5: births (10000 persons)
X_6: deaths (10000 persons)
X_7: immigrant population (10000 persons)
X_8: emigration population (10000 persons)
Y: Domestic waste (10000 tons).

4.2 Data Analysis

The output of municipal solid waste is of great significance for waste treatment in the later stage. This paper mainly starts from the direction of population flow. On the analysis of influencing factors of waste production, in addition to selecting factors through theory and establishing model analysis, finally, on the basis of analysis conclusion, combined with the current objective conditions and policy factors, the future output of municipal solid waste in Shanghai is predicted.

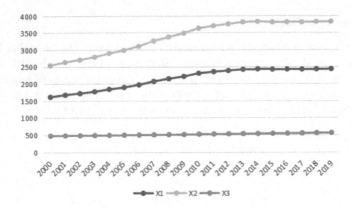

Fig. 2. X_1–X_3 related data change.

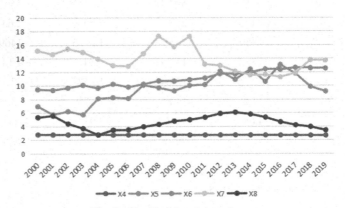

Fig. 3. X_4–X_9 related data change.

Figure 2 and Fig. 3 show a graph of changes in population-related data for 2000–2019.

Since 2000, the number of permanent residents in Shanghai has increased year by year, and the growth rate has increased significantly around 2010; The number of registered residence population and total number of households increased at the end of the year. The fluctuation of immigration and emigration rate also increased around 2010.

Figure 4 shows the curve of annual output of domestic waste in Shanghai from 2000 to 2019.

Comparing the quantity change curve of annual waste output in Fig. 2, the output increased sharply after 2010, and increased to 17 times the original in just four years by 2014.

The correlation between population mobility and the generation of waste must be positively correlated. When the population flow tends to be stable, coupled with the new methods of waste treatment, the waste output basically tends to be stable. Without special circumstances, the annual waste output should not increase significantly around 2010.

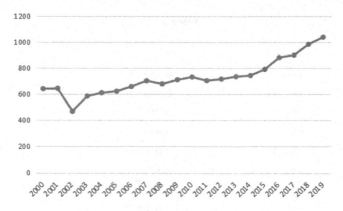

Fig. 4. Chart of annual output of garbage.

4.3 The Analysis of Correlation

The analysis of correlation refers to the analysis of more than two characteristic elements with correlation, so as to evaluate the degree of correlation between the two features. Correlation analysis can be carried out only when there is a certain connection or probability between the two features.

The commonly used Pearson product moment correlation coefficient is used to analyze the correlation between two continuous variables. It is a linear correlation coefficient, and the formula is:

$$r = \frac{\sum_{i=1}^{n}(x_i - \bar{x})(y_i - \bar{y})}{\sqrt{\sum_{i=1}^{n}(x_i - \bar{x})^2 \sum_{i=1}^{n}(y_i - \bar{y})^2}} \tag{14}$$

The value range of correlation coefficient r is $[-1, 1]$, when r is greater than 0, the correlation is positive. And when r is less than 0, the correlation is negative.

a) When r satisfies $|r| \geq 0.8$, the two variables are highly correlated.
b) When r satisfies $0.5 \leq |r| < 0.8$, there is a moderate correlation between the two variables.
c) When r satisfies $0.3 \leq |r| < 0.5$, there is a low correlation between the two variables.
d) The correlation is weak when it is less than 0.3.

Each data $(X_0 - X_8)$ in Fig. 2 and Fig. 3 were used as x variables respectively, and the data (Y) in Fig. 4 was used as y variables to conduct correlation analysis. The correlation analysis results are as follows:

It can be seen from Table 2 that X_4, X_7 and X_8 data features are negatively correlated with Y, while other data features are positively correlated.

The absolute value of correlation coefficient between X_5, X_7, X_8 and garbage yield Y is less than 0.85, so these three data are not used as reference for garbage yield prediction, and the final selection result is: X_0, X_1, X_2, X_3, X_4 and X_6 are closely related data items.

Table 2. .

(x, y)	r
(X_0, Y)	0.983
(X_1, Y)	0.953
(X_2, Y)	0.950
(X_3, Y)	0.947
(X_4, Y)	−0.870
(X_5, Y)	0.587
(X_6, Y)	0.852
(X_7, Y)	−0.382
(X_8, Y)	−0.322

5 Prediction of Urban Population Flow

In order to ensure the feasibility of the grey prediction model, this section first performs a hierarchical test on the distribution of the original data series $(X_0, X_1, X_2, X_3, X_4, X_6)$, and then establishes the model for population prediction, and objectively and effectively evaluates the accuracy of the model.

5.1 Check Data

The original data column (data are X_1, X_2, X_3, X_4, X_6, each item has 20 data from 2000 to 2019) is $X^{(0)}$, then $X^{(0)} = \{x^{(0)}(1), x^{(0)}(2), \cdots, x^{(0)}(20)\}$,

Table 3. Data level comparison result.

X	min $\rho(k)$	max $\rho(k)$
X_0	1.00	1.00
X_1	0.95	1.00
X_2	0.95	1.00
X_3	0.98	1.00
X_4	1.00	1.01
X_5	0.71	1.21
X_6	0.94	1.04
X_7	0.85	1.31
X_8	0.79	1.35

Calculate the stage ratio according to the formula:

$$\rho(k) = \frac{x^{(0)}(k)}{x^{(0)}(k+1)}, \quad k = 1, \cdots, n-1 \tag{15}$$

The calculation results of stage ratio inspection are spread in Table 3. According to the results in Table 3, it can be concluded that the level ratios of data series are all within the range $\left(e^{\frac{-2}{n+1}}, e^{\frac{2}{n+2}}\right)$.

All the levels are in $0.909 \leq \rho(k) \leq 1.095$, Therefore, the grey prediction conditions can be met and modeling can be carried out.

5.2 Forecast Urban Population Related Data

Table 4. Parameter calculation result.

X	a	u
X_1	−0.021	1735.853
X_2	−0.021	2737.710
X_3	−0.008	472.907
X_4	0.002	2.792
X_6	−0.018	9.125

1) Calculate the coefficient a, u according to the formula:

$$\begin{bmatrix} a \\ u \end{bmatrix} = (B^T B)^{-1} B^T Y_n \tag{16}$$

The results are shown in Table 4.

If a is positive, the development trend is decreasing. Otherwise, it increases.

2) According to the obtained parameters, determine the grey prediction model,

$$\hat{x}^{(0)}(k+1) = \left[x^{(0)}(1) - \frac{u}{a}\right](1 - e^{-a})e^{-ak} + \frac{u}{a} \tag{17}$$

The superscript ^ indicates the predicted value. Put $\hat{x}^{(0)}(k+1)$ into $X^{(0)}$, and delete $x^{(0)}(1)$, the first field of $X^{(0)}$. Then get a new sequence:

$$X_1^{(0)} = \{x^{(0)}(2), x^{(0)}(3) \cdots \cdots x^{(0)}(n), \hat{x}^{(0)}(k+1)\} \tag{18}$$

Construct the model of GM (1, 1) again, generate a new equation of prediction, etc. Until the completion of the prediction task and get a higher prediction result.

Table 5. Prediction result of GM (1,1).

X_0	2020	2021	2022	2023	2024	2025
X_1	2430.19	2435.11	2438.33	2441.83	2445.91	2449.29
X_2	3833.52	3841.54	3846.83	3852.62	3859.3	3864.86
X_3	561.50	566.66	571.55	576.87	582.01	587.22
X_4	2.63	2.62	2.60	2.59	2.58	2.57
X_6	12.63	12.57	12.6	12.62	12.61	12.64

3) Putting the coefficient a, u into the model, and predicting the urban population data of Shanghai from 2020 to 2025.

The results are shown in Table 5:

It can be seen from Table 5 that in the following years, the data of population flow in Shanghai do not change much, which was in line with the change trend described above.

6 Prediction of Municipal Solid Waste Output

According to what has been mentioned above, there is a close correlation between the output of municipal solid waste (MSW) and population flow, so it is feasible to make use of the development situation of urban population flow in Shanghai to forecast MSW.

In this section, the result set of the above predicted data items is used as the dependent variable x, and multiple linear regression is used to predict the output of MSW, and gradient improvement is used to reduce the error in the regression analysis.

6.1 Multiple Linear Regression

In regression analysis, if there are two or more independent variables, it is called multiple regression. Actually, a phenomenon is usually contacted with multiple factors. Using the optimal combination of multiple features to predict or evaluate dependent variables is more effective and practical than using only one feature.

Multiple linear regression calculation formula:

$$\hat{y} = w_1 * x_1 + w_2 * x_2 + \cdots + w_n * x_n + b \tag{19}$$

Among,

x: Influencing factors; w: Influencing weight;

n: the number of x; $\hat{y}$: the prediction output.

6.2 Experimental Results

Multiple linear regression was used to forecast and compare the waste yield. The results are shown in Table 6:

Table 6. Actual and predicted value of domestic waste in 2015–2019.

X_0	Actual value	Predicted value	Loss
2015	790	834.34	5.61
2016	880	879.38	0.07
2017	900	915.19	1.69
2018	984	959.42	2.50
2019	1038	1004.09	3.27%

Multiple regression analysis was conducted on the annual MSW output of Shanghai and the six factors of X_0, X_1, X_2, X_3, X_4 and X_6.

The model parameter is $b = -101254.17$, $w = [50.74, 0.56, -0.63, -0.12, 456.09, -19.95]$.

The accuracy of the above prediction model can reach 94.29%, and the annual output of municipal solid waste from 2020 to 2025 can be predicted by using this model. The results are shown in Table 7.

Table 7. Annual waste production forecast of Shanghai from 2020 to 2025.

X_0	2020	2021	2022	2023	2024	2025
Y	1046.37	1090. 80	1129.69	1173.13	1216.95	1260.28

The experimental results show that by 2025, the annual output of domestic garbage in Shanghai will be 12.6028 million tons, an increase of nearly 2.22 million tons compared with 2019, an increase of about 21.41%.

7 Conclusion

From the data correlation analysis, the average household population is negatively correlated with waste production. The grey prediction model is more applicable in population prediction and can be used to predict the short-term growth trend.

From the prediction results, the growth rate of waste production in Shanghai has decreased since 2019, but by 2025, the output is expected to reach 12.6028 million tons, an increase of about 21.41% compared with 2019. Waste treatment is still a major problem we have to face.

In the research of this paper, due to the periodic changes of the data, the prediction result may be the change result of a certain period. If it is necessary to predict more long-term data, these are far from enough and need to be further studied.

Acknowledgment. The authors would like to thank the anonymous reviewers for their elaborate reviews and feedback. This work is supported by the National Natural Science Foundation of

China (No. 61906099), the Open Fund of Key Laboratory of Urban Land Resources Monitoring and Simulation, Ministry of Natural Resources (No. KF-2019-04-065).

References

1. Wang, D., Zhu, W., Ye, H.: Equilibration effects of population migration on regional economic difference in china from 1985 to 2000. Popul. Econ. **6**, 1–9 (2002). (in Chinese)
2. Duan, P.Z., Liu, C.J.: The effect of population mobility on the regional disparity of economic growth. Chin. Soft Sci. Mag. **12**, 99–110 (2005). (in Chinese)
3. Liu, S.H., Hu, Z., Deng, Y., Wang, Y.J.: The regional types of China's floating population: identification methods and spatial patterns. J. Geog. Sci. **21**(1), 35–48 (2011). https://doi.org/10.1007/s11442-011-0827-8
4. Wang, G.X., Qin, Z.Q., Cheng, L.L.: Spatial distribution of population migration in China in the 1990s'. Scientia Geographica Sinica **32**(3), 273–281 (2012). (in Chinese)
5. Wang, S.W., Yang, L., Chang, M., Song, Y.Y.: Actively promote the accelerated development of the environmental protection industry. Chin. Dev. Obs. **22**, 55–57 (2017). (in Chinese)
6. Cao, S.S., Zong, C., Xia, S.Q., Chen, J.: Analysis of forecasting methods for future municipal waste production, vol. 48, no. 10, pp. 168–169 (2021). (in Chinese)
7. Yu, T., Huang, T., Pan, Y.X., Yang, L.H., Wang, L.: Comprehensive urban waste disposal forecasting mode based on the BP artificial neural network and grey relational degree. J. Saf. Environ. **4**, 94–97 (2013). (in Chinese)
8. Huangfu, H.H., Li, H.Y.: Analysis of the factors affecting the production of municipal solid waste. Sci. Technol. Manage. **20**(4), 44–49 (2018). (in Chinese)
9. Cao, W.: Analysis and prediction of domestic waste output per capita in Jinan. Environ. Sanitation Eng. **23**(4), 12–14 (2015). (in Chinese)
10. Zeng, C., Pan, C., Zhou, Z.K., Wu, K., Zhu, J.G.: Prediction of MSW output in Anhui province by least squares method and analysis of influence factors. Environ. Dev. **30**(9), 120–122, 124 (2018). (in Chinese)
11. Shilov, X., Zhu, M.: Least square method. Surveying and Mapping Press (1956). (in Chinese)
12. He, C.X., Long, W.J., Zhu, F.F.: Probability Theory and Mathematical Statistics. Higher Education Press (2012). (in Chinese)

Author Index

Printed in the United States
by Baker & Taylor Publisher Services